R. J. Mitchell

In memory of Leading Aircraftman
William Ewart Shelton

R. J. Mitchell
TO THE SPITFIRE

JOHN SHELTON

Fonthill Media Language Policy

Fonthill Media publishes in the international English language market. One language edition is published worldwide. As there are minor differences in spelling and presentation, especially with regard to American English and British English, a policy is necessary to define which form of English to use. The Fonthill Policy is to use the form of English native to the author. John Shelton was born and educated in the United Kingdom; therefore, British English has been adopted in this publication.

Fonthill Media Limited
Fonthill Media LLC
www.fonthillmedia.com
office@fonthillmedia.com

First published in the United Kingdom and the United States of America 2022

British Library Cataloguing in Publication Data:
A catalogue record for this book is available from the British Library

Copyright © John Shelton 2022

ISBN 978-1-78155-885-0

The right of John Shelton to be identified as the author of this work has been asserted by him in accordance with the Copyright, Designs and Patents Act 1988.

All rights reserved. No part of this publication may be reproduced, stored in a retrieval system or transmitted in any form or by any means, electronic, mechanical, photocopying, recording or otherwise, without prior permission in writing from Fonthill Media Limited

Typeset in Minion Pro 10pt on 13pt
Printed and bound in England

Foreword

Aviation historians have long been inspired by the Schneider trophy story and the genesis of the Spitfire. Even in a crowded field, John Shelton's work stands out for its technical mastery of R. J. Mitchell's achievement. In his most comprehensive narrative yet, we see more of Mitchell's complex character; the intensity of his work ethic, at considerable personal cost; his courage when facing cancer during his most vital project; and the role of chance and circumstance in the fulfilment of that project, just in the nick of time.

Dr Shelton doubts that the Spitfire would have been ready for the Battle of Britain without the risks run by the test pilots and members of the RAF High Speed Flight. Two of them lost their lives in Schneider trophy seaplanes, including Samuel Kinkead, killed at Calshot in 1928 attempting to beat 300 mph and set a new world record. Mitchell, who witnessed the accident, was greatly distressed. Yet, he knew—as did all 'his' pilots—that the prize they sought was national security against aerial attack and potential invasion, one day.

What emerges from this biography, is the versatility, ingenuity and single-mindedness of a design genius who knew that prestigious air races were by no means an end in themselves. In a rare public speech, Mitchell explained that more progress had been made in one year's preparation for a Schneider trophy contest than in three or four years of normal development. The work went on, and in 1931, Mitchell's Supermarine S.6B seaplane won the trophy outright and later raised the world speed record to 407 mph. This pace of advance had revolutionary consequences for fighter-plane development.

Almost 23,000 Spitfires were eventually produced: its longevity and adaptability meant that the Spitfire both 'saw in the era of the all-metal propeller driven fighter and saw it out' at the dawn of the jet age. Like all good biographers, Dr Shelton devotes time and attention, not only to his subject's successes, but also to the diversions, disappointments and sacrifices along the way. His clarity of prose and depth of technical expertise provide a degree of insight into R. J. Mitchell's personal and professional journey that will deservedly stand the test of time.

The Rt Hon. Julian Lewis, MP for New Forest East
Author of *Racing Ace: The Fights and Flights of 'Kink' Kinkead, DSO, DSC, DFC*

Preface

I have seen the future and it works.

Lincoln Steffens

R. J. Mitchell (right) with his S.6 Schneider Trophy winner.

Following the publication in 2008 of my *Schneider Trophy to Spitfire: The Design Career of R. J. Mitchell*, a much expanded and updated edition, entitled *R. J. Mitchell at Supermarine* was published in 2017. I have since been urged by Julian Mitchell, a great-nephew of the designer, to write more extensively on the life of his relative and have been most grateful to be given access to the family archive.

As a consequence, I have felt it best to bring together the various facets of the Mitchell story into one volume—more comprehensively than before, and sometimes for the first time: his beginnings, education and apprenticeship, hopes and disappointments, good fortunes and unhappy ones, family concerns, other personalities and rivalries, and his complicated personality—as well as the aircraft designs, the Schneider competitions, the importance of Napier and Rolls-Royce, and relevant political and economic considerations.

It is thus hoped that readers will now have access to a comprehensive account of the various aspects of the Mitchell story in one volume and thereby come fully to appreciate the complex of factors and the personal sacrifices of R. J. Mitchell, which contributed so much to the Second World War effort and, particularly, to the winning of the crucial Battle of Britain.

Dr John K. Shelton
Standon, July 2022

Acknowledgements

The excellent book, published by Putnam, *Supermarine Aircraft Since 1914*, is still the main reference source, but its scope was not concerned directly with Mitchell's development during his two decades as chief designer, which must be inferred from its survey of the company's aircraft, often arranged by type rather than chronologically. The fine *Spitfire Story* by Alfred Price is very informative about the genesis and development of Mitchell's fighter, but it is not concerned with his whole career. One thus turns to the work of his son, Gordon Mitchell, which does give considerable biographical information and a chronological survey of his father's whole design output, but quite a few aircraft are only briefly dealt with and there are no three-view drawings of the machines and no comprehensive set of photographs; the contributions to the book by Supermarine staff and pilots are often very informative.

The annual publications of *Jane's* have been important sources of information, as have the books by Barker, Mondey, James, Snaith, and Eves on the Schneider trophy contests. It is also hoped that the extracts from the reminiscences of various pilots (notably Biard, Orlebar, Schofield, Snaith, and Quill) will help restore memories of their achievements and contributions to British aviation between the two world wars. Additionally, the works of Penrose and Viscount Templewood have been valuable sources of information concerning the economic and political factors affecting British aircraft development (and therefore Mitchell) during this period; the recent works of Sinnot and McKinstry have also been very helpful in filling out this background to Mitchell's working life. In the particular context of Supermarine, contributions from employees and from colleagues of R.J., especially Buchanan, Griffiths, Shenstone, and Webb, have also been invaluable. It was also pleasing to come across the unpublished manuscript of Cozens, helpfully copied to me by Solent Sky and, more recently, the articles by Ackroyd, and the pdf publication, *Spitfire Mark by Mark, including the Seafire* by S. J. Lucas.

The general arrangement drawings are my own, based on those in Putnam and on photographic evidence.

I am particularly appreciative of the kind assistance I have received in the past from staff at the Royal Air Force Museum, Cambridge University Department of Manuscripts and Archives, the Royal Aeronautical Society, including the Yeovil and Southampton branches, and the staff at the Southampton Solent-Sky Museum, including Dave Whatley and the director,

Squadron Leader Alan Jones, whose early encouragement was much appreciated. More recently I have been grateful for the exchanges of information with Roland Machin and Tim Hillier-Graves (regarding Kerr Stuart apprenticeships), Dave Key (*The Supermariners*), and Julian Lewis (*Racing Ace*), who most kindly supplied a foreword to the present book. Apart from acknowledging the ever helpful and encyclopaedic advice on IT matters from my son, Rod, the final word should go to Julian Mitchell, a tireless local proponent of his great-uncle's memory and generous donor of fascinating material from his family archive.

Contents

Foreword   5
Preface   7
Acknowledgements   9
Introduction   13

1   No Ordinary Engineer   17
2   Normacot to Woolston (1885–1916)   35
3   Establishing Himself (1916–1919)   53
4   Early Military Designs and the Schneider Trophy (1919–1923)   77
5   Multitasking (1923–1924)   105
6   A Turning Point (1925)   131
7   Becoming 'R.J.'   155
8   Consolidation and International Successes (1926–1928)   167
9   Designer of the World's Fastest Plane (1927)   187
10   Taking a Chance with Rolls-Royce (1929)   207
11   The Air Yacht and the Giant (1930–1931)   235
12   Winning the Schneider Trophy Outright (1931)   253
13   His Last Flying Boats (1932–1934)   271
14   His First Spitfire (1934)   299
15   The Real Spitfire Emerges (1934–1936)   313
16   K5054   331
17   'It's All Over'   343

Afterword: After Mitchell	349
Appendix I: Mitchell Family Letters	377
Appendix II: Production Versions of the Spitfire	391
Appendix III: Notes on R. J. Mitchell's Wooden Hulls	417
Appendix IV: Jacques Schneider	421
Appendix V: Kinkead's S.5 Crash	423
Appendix VI: Lady Lucy Houston, DBE	429
Bibliography	435
Index	441

Introduction

Few people, except dedicated aviation buffs, are likely to be interested in the life stories of aircraft designers, but the continued appearance of the classic and distinctive shape of Reginald Mitchell's Spitfire, still to be seen flying at air shows and commemorative events over eighty years after the prototype's first flight in 1936, has called for an exception to the rule. Indeed, the appeal of the iconic Spitfire is such that in 2003, R. J. Mitchell was named the 'Greatest Midlander' in the BBC's online, TV, and radio vote.

Those who knew Mitchell agree that, despite the high reputation he earned as a designer, he was remarkably self-effacing, modest, and a man of few words. It was therefore not surprising that he did not consider recording the events of his relatively provincial life for posterity—such as meeting the popular prince of Wales, travelling to Venice on an aircraft carrier, or seeing the first large order for his Southampton flying boat or for the Spitfire. So we must look elsewhere to discover the man behind the various aircraft which resulted in his being considered one of the foremost designers in British aviation history.

A most important source of information is *R. J. Mitchell: School Days to Spitfire*, the biography by his son, Gordon: a work which also includes senior colleagues' accounts of working with R.J., although it must be kept in mind that these memories were largely in the nature of epitaphs to a respected colleague, that they concentrated on his workday activities, and that it has been noted that not all those who were approached actually contributed. There is one piece of oral history from a retired Supermarine worker, speaking of the Mitchell biography: 'It doesn't read like the same person as I knew. Because in work he was a bit of a grumpy old man, and used to lose his temper, you know'.

While some aspects of the son's biography do lean towards hagiography, he did nevertheless faithfully record his father's less sunny moments: how he had an 'extremely short temper' and 'could become unreasonably angry followed by a long period of moodiness when he would not say a word to anyone.' Certainly, the fierce work ethic and perfectionist drive that characterised his professional life resulted in a carapace of authority marked by silence rather than affability and a temperamental unwillingness to suffer fools gladly. Meanwhile, the RAF pilots who flew his Schneider trophy floatplanes have left only positive memories of 'Mitch'. It would seem that, when he was relaxed outside the office, one was more likely to experience what his secretary described as a 'very handsome man, with a lovely smile'.

Much of his make-up can be revealed by revisiting the whole history of the aircraft for which he was responsible and by his responses to design problems of the day: one can see that, as chief designer, his solutions show a mind distinguished from the ordinary by its ability to see to the essentials of a problem and that, as chief engineer, his company's products were the result of a strong will to continually refine the machinery and to see his wishes carried out.

Additionally, details of Mitchell's design activity provide an insight into the whole development of flying boats since his Commercial Amphibian of 1920 and can give a substantial perspective on contemporary hopes for this type of transport, which only ended in Britain with the demise of that heroic product of a rival company, the 1952 Saunders-Roe Princess. It is thus worth recording how, three years after his first main design of 1920, a small fleet of his Sea Eagle amphibians constituted the first British scheduled flying-boat service, operating between Southampton and the Channel Isles, and was joined in 1924 by his Swan, claimed by Supermarine to have been the world's first multi-engined amphibian passenger-carrying machine.

However, while a detailed account of his machines' development can be insightful, there are luckily not a few accounts by Mitchell's colleagues and by pilots that supply the more 'human' side of his career in the aviation industry, especially the lighter or poignant moments, the practical jokes, the rivalries, the hopes and the disappointments, the working conditions that had to be accepted, and the occasional injury or death.

Other material on Mitchell and his designs can inform our knowledge of the circumstances that led to the design of his famous fighter: in particular, his apprenticeship days, the precarious nature of the firm he first joined, his rise from draughtsman to chief designer and engineer, and the demands that his passion for design made upon his private life. In this last respect, the author is especially grateful for the assistance of R.J.'s great-nephew, Julian Mitchell, who has kindly made available press-cutting collections, photographs, and letters from the family archive.

As Mitchell began his professional career in locomotive engineering, and never had any formal education as an aircraft designer, it will be of equal interest to discover the story of how he learned his trade and how he solved the various aerodynamic problems that confronted him as his designs progressed. However, given that he had spent most of his first fifteen years at Supermarine creating slow-flying biplane flying boats, it only requires a little thought to appreciate that the dramatic appearance of his land-based Spitfire was not likely to have come from his drawing board by some magical conceptual leap. The most significant factor in this notable appearance of the Spitfire was the Schneider trophy series of competitions; accounts written at the time are not too easy to come by and so the events in which Mitchell was involved should benefit from being recounted.

From the account of his journey to the Spitfire, it will become obvious that R.J.'s design career was by no means planned or straightforward. Indeed, it owed quite a lot to luck as well as to exceptional ability, matched by a force of character and a drive for perfection, which often made life uncomfortable for those around him. The sunny side of his personality ran counter to his outbursts of temper, and accounts of his good rapport with colleagues could be at variance with the examples of his often taciturn and withdrawn nature. As there are similar accounts of his life at home, one cannot attribute his difficult moods just to certain managerial devices for establishing authority.

Given the evidence of colleagues and pilots and from the anecdotes that surface, modern readers with some acquaintance with Asperger's syndrome and or even cyclothymia, might be tempted to draw certain conclusions about the make-up of the man behind the aircraft; his marrying a woman eleven years older than himself and being, as his secretary said, 'rather nervous with female members of staff', also encourages amateur psychologising.

However, while it is not the purpose of this book to attempt any such study, readers might very well speculate on the psychological make-up of the man well known for both his irascibility and his kindliness—the man who produced, at virtually the same point in time, the slowest and the fastest aircraft in the RAF: the ungainly one that deserved its name 'Walrus' and the other, the sleek Spitfire, described by an Eagle squadron pilot as 'a thing of beauty to behold'. Being presented with the various personal details of working and living with Reginald Mitchell, readers should at least encounter a far more complex person than previously considered.

The observations that his colleagues have left were mainly written after Mitchell's death and have to be assessed in that light, but nevertheless, it is not too hard to come to an appreciation of the man behind the aircraft and the public image, and the sacrifices that he often had to make: in other words, the present book aims to avoid eulogy but to give, instead, a clear-eyed account of the circumstances of R. J. Mitchell's life and work, but which in no way denigrates his reputation.

Indeed, it is hoped that this more dispassionate picture of his life and work will actually increase his standing: his humility, the strain of meeting deadlines, and the family side of our designer, especially of his last years when faced with the illness which took his life at the early age of forty-two. These facts, taken in parallel with an account of his early years, the precarious finances of the company he joined, the design problems he had to confront, and Air Ministry requirements, should enhance an appreciation of his single-minded commitment to advancing the progress of aviation and to his vital contribution in the 1930s to the forthcoming battle for Britain.

Reginald Joseph Mitchell in his garden, 1931.

1

No Ordinary Engineer

> *I don't give a bugger whether it's elliptical or not, so long as it covers the guns.*
>
> R. J. Mitchell to Beverley Shenstone

A previously unknown letter, written by 'Flo' Mitchell reveals a chief designer who might not always have had the all-consuming passion for engineering that he is usually credited with. This letter was written to Reginald Mitchell's brothers, Eric and Billy, concerning the son, Gordon:

> Reg told Gordon this morning that the more he thought of it, the less inclined he was for Gordon to be an engineer and he asked him to consider it very carefully. He thinks it is highly probable that some other profession would be less strenuous and also he would like him to choose something that would enable him to spend considerable time outdoors.
>
> Mrs Florence Mitchell, 15 March 1937

Many colleagues of Reginald Mitchell have commented on his dedication, indeed on his perfectionism. His Schneider trophy winning racers and, of course, the Spitfire are evidence of a 'strenuous' work ethic. However, Florence Mitchell's letter gives a glimpse of a less familiar side of R. J. Mitchell than the stereotype of a man single-mindedly pursuing the career that culminated in the aircraft which contributed so much to winning the Battle of Britain.

Flo's letter was written late in her husband's short life, when he had every reason to have regrets about a life being cut short, but some earlier remarks by J. N. Boothman, the 1931 Schneider trophy winner, reported by Gordon Mitchell, have not been commented on:

> R.J. once said to me if he had his life again he would not have been an aeroplane designer but a surgeon—this was a long time before he was sick—and I remember about 1932 or 1933 an occasion when, having been out shooting with him early in the morning, there was a most gory procedure going on in the kitchen when he was explaining the inside of a rabbit to his son.

Here we have a fascinating glimpse of the family man, taking his parental duties seriously and (as an engineer, indeed) demonstrating to his son how an animal's organism 'works'. Perhaps, many readers today have to get used to the idea that Mitchell liked shooting animals. He had never been part of the farming community, where control of livestock was part of their way of life, and so one remembers the series of prestigious cars he owned later in life—perhaps enjoying the outdoors life that he wished for his son had the added attraction of shooting, which was a largely upper-class 'sport'.

He certainly enjoyed the material benefits of rising to become a director of the company for which he designed his aircraft, sending his son to an expensive boarding school, holidaying in expensive hotels on the south coast, and receiving the best medical attention and full-time nursing during his cancer treatment, convalescence, and decline. The fact that he graduated from coming to work on a motorcycle to driving there in a Rolls-Royce or the later Bentley might not be attributed to just taking an engineer's satisfaction in operating mechanically sophisticated machines; but, despite enjoying the pleasures that his status afforded, we shall see later that there is no direct evidence that he ever allowed his successes or status to radically change his generally unassuming demeanour.

As for his wish to have been a surgeon, no doubt everyone has visions of having a different career from time to time, but interestingly, Mitchell's alternative choice of a healing or life-saving career was mentioned at the height of his international success as a designer of the winning Schneider trophy aircraft: in a speech describing how 'racing machines of this sort are not safe to fly', he also made the revealing comment that the 'designing of such a machine involved considerable anxiety because everything had been sacrificed to speed [*see* also his *Sketch* article reproduced in Chapter 10]'. This comment was made in 1927, before the majority of Schneider trophy pilots were killed—one Frenchman, two Americans, five Italians, and two British (in his own aircraft). A colleague, Eric Lovell-Cooper, had felt the same about 'speeds that were suicidal then.' Thus, when we think about the man behind the career, it is easy to see a conflict between the patriotism of designing machines to win international trophies and having to make very serious compromises with pilot safety, especially as the British flyers of his aircraft spent evenings at his home during Schneider trophy contests.

Mitchell's anxiety about having to design racing aircraft that were likely to kill was surely intensified by the fact that most of his designing life was concerned with producing more sedate—and safe—passenger or reconnaissance aircraft. Writers have rightly commented on the impressive technical advances he made in high-speed design, but because of his very self-contained personality, less attention has been given to the various strains imposed on him by having to advance the reputation of Supermarine, by having to design potentially lethal machines, at the forefront of aviation technology, and with the added penalty of a usually almost impossibly tight schedule, with a fixed race date to meet.

Producing aircraft in time for Air Ministry trials or to meet production deadlines would always impose times of intense activity on the man who was both chief designer and also chief engineer at Supermarine. Such moments would seriously interfere with domestic life but this would be particularly so during the last international Schneider trophy competitions of 1929 and 1931; they would take place before a very expectant British press and public and would not allow the sort of relaxation that had been possible during sea voyages to the previous Trophy venues in Italy or America.

Nevertheless, in spite of his own experience of the demands of his industrial career, he did not think that a more academic career might suit his son better. On 10 February, 1937, he himself wrote to his son, who was at Clifton College boarding school that, instead of taking the advice of the school and aiming for Cambridge University, an apprenticeship at Rolls-Royce might be better: 'Cambridge … is probably OK for boys who wish to be highbrows on the academic side—schoolmasters and suchlike. I really think you are more suited to the practical side' (10 February 1937). It should be reported, however, that eleven days later, he was discussing accountancy as a possible career for his son.

The more popular image of our designer, dedicated to producing what his managing director called a 'killer fighter', has been shaped by the Second World War. In 1940, when the bombing of London began, the Hurricane fighter had been available in greater numbers than the Spitfire and accounted for more successes than the Supermarine product, yet the Hawker machine, unfairly, has never been the popular image of the Battle of Britain, even though it was, if possible, successfully employed not against protecting fighters but against the slower, less manoeuvrable bombers—the ones that obviously posed the real physical threat to the British people below.

Thus, when a film was made to boost morale, it featured the designer of the more 'glamorous' Spitfire, and as the 'few' Battle of Britain pilots who defended the 'many', were singled out in Churchill's memorable words, it is not surprising that a film about Mitchell was entitled *The First of the Few*. These pilots were, at least unconsciously, to be associated with King Arthur's knights in (camouflaged) armour, and the temptation to see the designer of the Spitfire in a similar light was not to be resisted—with his foreseeing the threat to his country, fighting against illness and approaching death in order to help save his homeland, while watching seagulls, envisaging a new shape for an aircraft to meet his country's hour of need.

The description of him in his son's biography, *Schooldays to Spitfire*, as having 'fair blond hair, the sort of colour seen on pictures of Plantaganet kings' is thus revealing. A press item, some years later, more prosaically, mentions his 'light reddish hair' (*see* p. 229) and the dispassionate historian also feels obliged to point out that the Spitfire's Merlin engine was not named after the wizard of Arthurian legend, according to the film, but followed a Rolls-Royce convention which adopted names of birds of prey for its engines (Eagle, Buzzard, Condor, etc.).

The First of the Few has been a strong influence on what popular views of R. J. Mitchell do exist but, as it was made in 1942 with its propagandist slant, it takes liberties with the facts as we know them. This is unfortunate as the film is still being shown and as it also gives an anodyne view of the designer. Screen dialogue was more decorous in those days, whereas those who worked with Mitchell often reported on his blunt, down-to-earth remarks. When his Type 300 design was named 'Spitfire', he made the well-known remark that 'It's the sort of bloody silly name they would give it', and there is his reported comment to his chief aerodynamicist, Beverley Shenstone, when the shape of the Spitfire wing was being discussed: 'I don't give a bugger whether it's elliptical or not, so long as it covers the guns'.

When the 1931 Schneider trophy engines began cutting out, due to excess sealant in the fuel piping being washed loose, he was equally blunt—'You'll just have to bloody-well fly them until all this stuff comes out'. Also, when the test pilot Jeffrey Quill had confessed to being over-awed by the Supermarine boffins with slide-rules sticking out of their pockets, Mitchell's advice was not for the polite circles of his day: 'If anybody ever tells you anything about aeroplanes which is so bloody complicated you can't understand it, take it from me it's all balls'.

These instances bear out Gordon Mitchell's report that his father's language in men's company 'was sometimes colourful', and it no doubt reflected his early apprenticeship at the Kerr Stuart locomotive works immediately after he left school. Yet film conventions of the time did not allow their heroes to offend with workplace language, and the scriptwriter was more at home with a portrait of Mitchell as more of an artist rather than as a practical, down-to-earth, engineer. The practical realities of Mitchell's aero-engineering career are mainly absent in the film and so it is no surprise that the picture of his gazing at seabirds for inspiration ignores the fact that the principles of flight had been established by observing birds gliding at the beginning of the nineteenth century by George Cayley.

While one suspects that Mitchell's expletives often belied the aesthetic considerations behind his designs, Quill supplied a necessary corrective when he wrote that Mitchell had better things to do than 'looking at bloody seagulls' and Lovell-Cooper, who eventually became chief draughtsman, was equally offended:

> People like to think of him watching the seagulls fly, well he probably did, everybody did. You couldn't help it down there—blooming seagulls all over the place. But one thing about it, we knew that seagulls couldn't ever be a satisfactory flying boat. Although they'd got the perfectly formed hull for the job, their wings were in the wrong place.

It is thus not surprising that the film also shows our designer refusing to retire due to ill-health and, instead, redoubling his efforts to design an aircraft to protect his country. In fact, this portrait does not fully do justice to him as his successful career at Supermarine was the result of a continual concern to turn out the best that current theories or materials would permit. His long-serving secretary, Vera Cross, makes the point that throughout her time with him, 'he was a great driving force and, once his mind was made up, he went all out to achieve his end'.

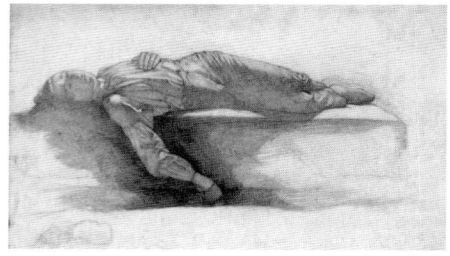

Sketch for *The Death of Chatterton* by Henry Wallis.

The film account has Mitchell die as the first prototype Spitfire takes to the skies, whereas, in fact, Mitchell died more than fifteen months after its first flight and letters actually testify to his frustration that he could not continue working on his later bomber design (*see* 'Afterword'). The suggestion that he could have saved or at least extended his life by not driving himself so hard has more to do with memories of the opera or the early death of poets like Keats or Chatterton from tuberculosis than the equally sad but more mundane reality of his rectal cancer.

However, especially at a time when any form of the disease was hardly spoken of, it did not

Leslie Howard playing R. J. Mitchell in the film *The First of the Few*.

accord well with the image portrayed in the film by a current matinee idol to mention the actual condition that was diagnosed in 1933 and eventually took his life four years later. Nevertheless, to discuss Mitchell's real medical condition does not diminish his image, especially his reaction to the result of his operation. Despite the potentially debilitating effects of the colostomy bag he had to wear for the rest of his life, he was determined to continue as before at the end of his convalescence. Sir Henry Royce, who had had to undergo the same procedure, also continued working but did so from his home.

Keeping his condition private and hoping that it might not deteriorate later, Mitchell returned to his office at the end of 1933; before the threat of Nazi Germany was inescapably obvious, he embarked on a work-rate even greater than before—assessed by Alan Clifton, who later became chief designer himself, as a pouring-out of new design proposals at an average rate of one per month. These designs also continued the wide range that was typical of the output that he oversaw—six proposals related to amphibians, eighteen to flying boats, three to fighters, and one to a bomber. Actually, if one includes the speculative sketches as well as the proposed variations of different types that he considered during this time, the number of possible projects as well as the completed aircraft (Scapa, Stranraer, and Spitfire), the number rises to forty-four from 1934 to 1936.

It might also be mentioned that, at that time, he became a pilot himself. On 22 December 1933, he had his first flying lesson and went solo on the first day of the following July. Having gained his pilot's licence (No. 7078), he would thereafter often fly himself on his visits to Rolls-Royce in Derby; this late activity raises interesting thoughts about his whole relationship with flight.

Flying clubs, assuming that he could have afforded membership in his early years, had not been developed, and so his boyhood passion for model aeroplanes was channelled into building, but not flying, the real thing. In his junior days with Supermarine, he had an early

Mitchell under instruction in a DH.60G Gipsy Moth, Hampshire Aeroplane Club, 1933.

thrill of flying when he was a passenger in one of the firm's Channel flying boats, taking the managing director to the 1919 Schneider trophy competition at Bournemouth, and he had many subsequent flights when Supermarine aircraft were being tested. Unfortunately, all the company's early two seaters had tandem seating and so it was not possible to have much (unofficial) instruction in a valuable company prototype.

The 1920s and '30s were the time when the flyer was something of a breed apart—as Stephen Spender wrote: 'He will watch the hawk with indifferent eye … this aristocrat, superb of all instinct.' Unfortunately, Reginald was too occupied with design, sport, and family life for the latent artist in him to respond to the dreamer's 'lonely impulse to delight', as Yeats put it. Significantly, and with the knowledge that his operation for the cancer might not eventually prove to be successful, it would seem that he now determined to grasp, before it might be too late, something of this aspiration that he had promised himself during his earlier hectic workdays.

He could now experience his own input to the sort of control surfaces he had spent the last fourteen years designing; he could now take full control of his own machine and its trajectory, watch the landscape tilt at his 'stick-and-rudder' command and, perhaps, despite his specialist knowledge, he could even still marvel how man could remain aloft without any apparent means of suspension. He was previously known to slip away from the office for the odd hour of golf or sailing; now, as a solo pilot, he could be even freer for a few brief hours from the more mundane demands of the design office or the boardroom.

Returning from Bristol, one day, he had to make an unscheduled landing at Middle Wallop. He telephoned his works to report the delay and asked that his wife be informed. Mrs Mitchell was not very reassured when she received the garbled message that 'he has come down wallop'. It is not known if any of his other landings were 'arrivals', but he was certainly not expected to do well in the 1936 Hampshire Aero Club spot-landing competition. However, well against the odds, he had backed himself and ended up by collecting the winner's prize money.

Mitchell continued flying until very close to his final illness in 1937, his last flight being a thirty-minute solo on 28 November 1936. Climbing into the cockpit of a 1930s biplane is none too straightforward at the best of times, and it throws further light on Mitchell's determination not to be defeated by his condition. He also determined to continue playing golf, winning a local competition in 1935; typically, he also designed an improved colostomy bag, which was reported in the medical press.

No doubt the exceptional work rate that Clifton had commented on was also driven by this need to defy his medical condition and, by 1935, to produce a better fighter than his first effort, the Type 224. As depicted in the film, he was seemingly driven to designing the Spitfire by having visited Germany and by seeing their aviation industry gearing up for war. The nearest Mitchell is believed to have come to visiting Germany was a skiing holiday in Austria with the managing director of Vickers, accompanied by their wives, *circa* 1934. However, he was obviously close enough to the aviation fraternity, who were well aware of the situation—in particular, his friend Major G. P. Bulman, the Air Ministry official responsible for the development of aero engines, who had toured German aviation establishments twice and had reported back his concerns about what he had learned.

Indeed, the Supermarine/Rolls-Royce initiative, the Spitfire, was not even a specific response to the rival Messerschmitt Bf 109, as is often stated. It is a fact that the German aircraft was chosen for squadron service immediately after it was known that the Spitfire was to be produced. Had Germany not felt the immediate pressure to get a rival machine into production, the developing Heinkel He 112 might have been chosen. Its elliptical wing submission might have had something of the same development potential (*see* Appendix II) for which the Spitfire became famous.

It has been necessary to correct earlier accounts of Mitchell as some sort of mild-mannered, consumptive artist, but it is even more important to be clear that this down-to-earth engineer could produce something that was startlingly new and aesthetically pleasing, when given a free hand.

The most striking example of this talent was the S.4 Schneider trophy floatplane of 1925. His previous trophy machines—the Sea Lions II and III—were based on an aircraft design that originated in 1918, before he joined the company, and he was prevented from any significant innovations by having to make use of this older type. Fortunately, government support for Britain's entry to the Schneider competition of 1925 allowed Mitchell the luxury (and challenge) of designing, without restrictions, an aircraft that would have to be a significant improvement on the present American racers and on his own past designs.

When the S.4 appeared from relative secrecy a few weeks before the contest, it is notable that Alan Clifton wrote of its 'breathtakingly clean lines, which caused a sensation when photos were released', and an entry in *Flight* accurately assessed its radically innovative appearance:

> It is little short of astonishing that he should have been able to break away from the types with which he had been connected, and not only abandon the flying-boat type in favour of a twin float arrangement, but actually change from braced biplane to the pure cantilever wing of the S.4.

In one 'bold' leap, and only three years later, he had broken away from the wire-braced flying-boat type of his 1922 winner (*see* photo p. 25)—to the entirely new lines of the S.4 cantilevered monoplane.

It ought to be recorded that, in 1924, the French air speed record holder, the Bernard V-2 landplane, had displayed some features (*see* Chapter 6) that might have prompted Mitchell's

Supermarine S.4 (1925).

design, but it might not be too biased to suggest that the S.4 lines the more strongly suggest the mind of an artist in tandem with that of an engineer: it is noticeable that Mitchell avoided the rather hump-backed rear fuselage of the French design and chose curving lines instead of angularity.

Produced in the same year as the S.4, his Southampton (*see* p. 26) was described as 'probably the most beautiful biplane flying boat that had ever been built' and—given the current lack of aerodynamic theory—Joe Smith was surely referring mainly to aesthetic considerations when he recorded the following description of Mitchell at the drawing board:

> He was an inveterate drawer on drawings, particularly general arrangements. He would modify the lines of an aircraft with the softest pencil he could find, and then remodify over the top with progressively thicker lines, until one would be faced with a new outline of lines about three sixteenths of an inch thick. But the results were always worthwhile, and the centre of the line was usually accepted when the thing was redrawn.

The various aircraft that came from this drawing board will be described in chronological order, as established by their first flights. Such a method is intended to give an accurate picture of the varied and contrasting design problems that Mitchell had to confront at any one particular time—in fact, this aspect of his design career was singled out by *Flight* magazine in his obituary: 'he frequently had to switch his mind from one problem to another of a totally different character.'

The preponderance of successful aircraft (there were certainly also some failures) indicate that the considerable output during his short working life was obviously not simply attributable to 'versatility' or talent. A capacity for hard, concentrated work was clearly involved. For example, between 1920 and 1922, the newly appointed chief designer, with only three previous years' experience in the aircraft industry, was responsible for the design of the Commercial Amphibian, a passenger-carrying prototype which required the innovation of a retracting undercarriage mechanism; the Seal, a fleet spotter with the added complexity of folding wings; the Scylla, a replacement for the large First World War Felixstowe coastal reconnaissance flying boat; and the Sea Lion II, a modification of an earlier company machine for the 1922 Schneider trophy contest.

It will also be seen that R. J. Mitchell's design career spans virtually the whole development of aviation since the pioneering days until just before the beginning of the jet era. During this time, the performances of aircraft and the expectations of those using them changed so rapidly that any designer, looking back over a career during these years, must have felt privileged to have been part of an industry at the most crucial part of its development. A simple illustration of this rapid advance might be a comparison of the technology and aerodynamic practice that Mitchell inherited, when he modified an aircraft for his first Schneider trophy winner in 1922, with that which had been developed for his winning design in 1931.

The first of these Schneider machines, the Sea Lion II had a wooden hull that was a fine example of the boat builder's craft. It had the usual biplane arrangement of the wings, separated by struts and braced by wires, as this approach was the almost universal way of achieving the necessary wing area for the lightest structure—the stressing considerations involved at that time being akin to those of the bridge builder. The flying surfaces were fabric-covered, again for lightness, and the power available to drive them through the air was 450 hp.

By contrast, Mitchell's S.6B of 1931 was of an all-metal, cantilever, monoplane structure with metal skinning to the flying surfaces whose design owed little directly to other industrial practices and was the result of exhaustive wind tunnel testing. The power available to this aircraft was now 2,350 hp and it gained the world absolute speed record at 407.3 mph. Over this very brief span of only nine years, the increase in maximum speed and power can be averaged out at 26 mph and 211 hp per year. The intensive wartime development of the Spitfire over a similar period was actually less—11 mph and 144 hp per year.

Sea Lion II.

Supermarine S.6B.

The Southampton Mk I.

Walrus prototype over Gibraltar.

Although a chronological account is necessary to show how the chief designer moved by no means in a straight line, from a dependency on the traditions of aircraft design and construction that he inherited to the originality of much of his later work, it will first be useful if the main types of his aircraft are distinguished. While the S.4 marked the beginning of one of Mitchell's main design types—the racing floatplane—1925 also saw the first flight of another of the designs of his early maturity, the Southampton; this machine represents the second main category of his aircraft: the larger flying boat. The third main type with which he was associated was the medium-sized amphibian. Here the particular requirements of the type did not require major departures from current practice and Mitchell obviously saw no reason to make changes for their own sake, as exemplified by the Walrus as late as 1936.

The following list of twenty distinct types of Supermarine aircraft that were completed and flew indicates the preponderance of these three types, as well as other different aircraft (including the Spitfire) that can be seen appearing from time to time:

Medium-sized flying boats	*Larger flying boats*	*Schneider trophy aircraft*	*Landplanes*
Commercial Amphibian	Swan	Sea Lion II/III	Sparrow I/II
Seal II	Southampton I–IV	S.4	Type 224
Sea King II	Nanok/Solent	S.5	Spitfire
Seagull II–IV	Air Yacht	S.6/6A/6B	
Scarab/Sheldrake	Scapa		
Seamew	Stranraer		
Seagull V/Walrus			

As Mitchell's main design work was concerned with passenger-carrying amphibians, naval reconnaissance flying boats, and ship-based fleet spotter planes, where speed was by no means the main criterion, the Schneider trophy machines were obviously a far more significant influence on the emergence of the Spitfire—as Quill said:

> At the time the Spitfire was designed, Mitchell's design team, because of its previous involvement with the S.4, S.5, S.6 and S.6B Schneider Trophy racing seaplanes … had more practical knowledge of high-speed aeronautics than any other design team in the world. They were mentally adjusted to, and dedicated to, the search for the ultimate in aerodynamic efficiency and the achievement of the highest possible speeds. They were not going to allow themselves to be constrained by convention or other extraneous considerations from achieving these aims. They were young and, I believe, very single-minded … Members of his team still retained the basic attitudes acquired from racing seaplane programmes throughout the life of the Spitfire.

It was from this experience that the otherwise unlikely development of a land-based fighter, the Spitfire, emerged from the drawing board of a designer whose only other non-marine aircraft (apart from the immediate precursor of the Spitfire, Type 224) had been a one-off response to an Air Ministry light plane competition ten years before. However, the link between Mitchell's specialised high-speed Schneider trophy designs and the Spitfire was not a direct one, as is sometimes stated or assumed, and so it is necessary to trace the history of the Schneider contests and their aircraft, in order to arrive at a more accurate assessment of the impact of these events upon Mitchell's career and its culmination in the Spitfire.

Also, the earlier list of aircraft for which Mitchell and his design team were responsible did not include a multitude of projects that never left the drawing board nor the three very large uncompleted projects that occupied a considerable amount of design time but which never flew: the Scylla, cancelled after the hull was completed; the Type 179 Giant, cancelled before the hull was completed; and the prototype Bomber, whose design was overseen by Mitchell and later abandoned after the two prototype fuselages were destroyed by enemy action. If these three uncompleted projects are added to the list of distinct types that actually flew, it is worth noting that, in the seventeen years that Mitchell was active as chief designer, he had had overall responsibility for twenty-three different types of aircraft.

It must be clear to even the casual observer that this considerable and varied output suggests that a capacity for concentrated work was one of Mitchell's main character traits. Alan Clifton, who knew Mitchell from when he joined him at Supermarine in 1923, has left an appreciation of Mitchell which attests to this aspect of the man; he recorded how Mitchell would visit the drawing office daily and study someone's detailed drawing, head on hands, thinking rather than speaking. In reply to questions, a small group would gradually gather round until some conclusion was reached; Mitchell would then move on to another board to repeat the process.

Ernest Mansbridge, who joined Clifton in 1924 to work on stressing, remembered Mitchell for a similar method of dealing with a problem by calling in the leaders of the relevant groups and getting them arguing among themselves. He would listen carefully, making sure that everyone had said what he wanted to, and then either make a decision or go home and sleep on it—although, in fact, Mansbridge expressed the suspicion that Mitchell's discussions were often a means of ensuring that he had not overlooked anything, having already reached a decision.

As he had also been appointed chief engineer, in 1920, his activities were not confined to the drawing office, and Arthur Black has given a glimpse of his daily inspection also of the manufacturing process, studying with complete concentration the developing shape of the aircraft being built: 'If he was satisfied, then he would pass on to the next job; but if he was not satisfied, then much of the design work and manufacture might well have to be done again.' Griffiths, who was Black's assistant, has also left the following anecdote from 1927 concerning attention to detail, which is also indicative of why Mitchell was respected in the firm:

> In the S.6 the fuel was carried in the floats and was pumped up through the struts to the engine. In level flight this would have been O K but during the race the aircraft was banked through 80 degrees in order to negotiate the sharp bends of the course and this created such high centrifugal force that the fuel supply would have been cut off. Thus a small header tank was located in front of the engine to hold a reserve of fuel sufficient to maintain a supply during turns, and the pumps were arranged to deliver an excess of fuel. This meant that on the straight part of the course some fuel had to be returned to the float tanks.
>
> A valve on the front of the header tank had two spring loaded ports which were supposed to split the overflow into equal parts for return to the floats, but inevitably it all went down one pipe resulting in a potential out of balance …
>
> We tried all sorts of combinations of spring-loaded valve flaps, differing pipe sizes and other devices to equalise the flow without success and the race was getting nearer every day.
>
> One Sunday morning [n.b.], near to exasperation, we were fitting yet another variation when Mitchell came along and stopped to have a look. At the top of the valve housing there was a small hole leading into the tank which was intended to allow air to escape as fuel went in.

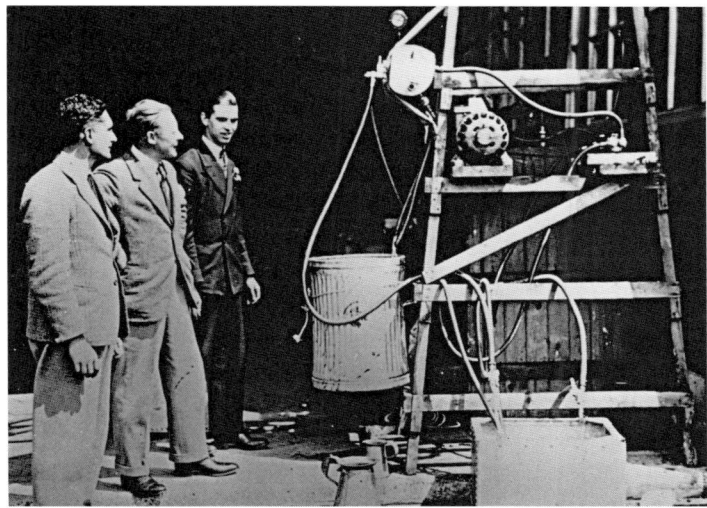

Mitchell (centre) with Arthur Black (chief metallurgist, right), with the typically improvised fuel system test rig mentioned in the text—the header tank is top centre, the dustbin simulated the engine and the square tanks the floats. It had been moved outside because of the fire risk—the motor, apparently, was not flameproof.

He pointed to the hole and asked, 'Why is that there?' and hearing that it was an air bleed was quiet for a few moments. He then said, 'Stuff it up.' I was sent to the stores to get an aluminium rivet of the right size and we hammered it in. We then reassemble the valve in its original form and switched on the pump for a test run.

Eureka—no matter what we did the fuel split into two equal parts!

Yet despite the dominant position he established at Supermarine, in those more authoritarian days, most accounts of Mitchell's personality agree on his ability to listen rather than parade his own opinions, on his basic shyness (he had a slight stammer), and on his lack of pomposity. One member of the 1931 RAF High Speed team, Flg Off. L. S. Snaith, has described Mitchell's demeanour when one of his racing seaplanes developed a nearly fatal rudder flutter, which resulted in buckled rear fuselage plates and raised serious doubts about the current Supermarine effort to compete safely in that year's Schneider trophy event. Practice flying had been stopped and all the experts called in; during the panic and hubbub that ensued, Mitchell sat in a corner hardly saying a word. Yet it was he who came up soon afterwards with the solution of adding balancing weights to the rudder (*see* p. 259).

Another member of the High Speed team, Flg Off. Atcherley, has also given a similar assessment of Mitchell: 'He was always keen to listen to pilots' opinions and never pressed his own views against theirs ... He set his sights deliberately high, for he had little use for "second-bests". Yet he was the most unpompous man I ever met.' A further example of his open-mindedness—which was to have very far-reaching results—was to be seen during the very early stages of the development of the Spitfire. At this time, when there was no formalised liaison between manufacturers and the air force, Mitchell got the Vickers chief test pilot, 'Mutt' Summers, to arrange a special visit to the Aeroplane and Armament Experimental Establishment at Martlesham Heath so that he could hear the views of the RAF test pilots on the merits and shortcomings of the current fighters in service.

This self-effacing willingness to listen to all points of view, however, was not matched by a readiness to bear fools gladly. Most accounts mention his shortness with those who did not get his message quickly enough. For example, Jack Davis, who joined as an apprentice in 1925, said that 'if someone made a suggestion which to him seemed inane, he would give the offender a killing glare'. Also, Joe Smith described how Mitchell occasionally 'let rip with us' when he was not satisfied with what had been done.

The following chapters will show how often his perfectionism resulted in either a new type of aircraft or a new piece of mechanism for an aircraft functioning satisfactorily virtually from the very start—by no means to be expected in these early days of aviation development. Perhaps the best examples of reliability would be the Schneider trophy racers, 1927 to 1931, where Mitchell was working under considerable time pressures and at the limits of technical knowledge, and yet he produced machines that, unlike most of the competition, were not seriously affected by malfunctions. Certainly, there were airframe failures, notably with the S.4 and, very likely, with Kinkead's S.5 (see Appendix V), but these were, essentially, attributable to the limitations of contemporary understanding rather than to any neglect of practical matters.

However wide-ranging and detailed Mitchell's own involvement in aircraft production was, the rapid development and complexity of aircraft necessitated an early expansion of design and technical staff; as he had begun with only a staff of seven, he was responsible for the appointment of virtually all of the teams which were built up between 1920 and 1935. The people that he had collected around him and his own hardworking and conscientious example were the most significant factors in producing the reliability of his aircraft. It is also a noteworthy fact of Mitchell's management style how many of these men rose 'through the ranks' to become the leaders of the various design and construction teams; clearly, they had measured up to Mitchell's standards.

At this point, Supermarine's long-serving test pilot, Capt. Henri C. Biard, ought also to be mentioned for, after all, he was the only man in the company who could tell Mitchell how his designs actually worked in the air. He had been a pilot in the First World War, became an instructor, and then first came to the notice of Supermarine as a pilot on their Channel services (see p. 60). Thus he had had a wide experience of different aircraft types, and Mitchell must have listened carefully to his comments about aircraft performance. There is some confirmation of the influence of Biard from a neighbour of his, G. A. Cozens. In the course of his observations on the early medium-sized amphibians, he wrote, 'Once more it was Captain Biard who put the Seal through its trials and [they were] his suggestions and advice that R. J. Mitchell carried out in establishing this aircraft as the first of the long line of Seagulls'. He continued test flying until the Vickers merger of 1928 but left soon thereafter.

Despite the overwhelming evidence of Mitchell's fierce work ethic, the growing need for an expanding team of experts, and his down-to-earth practicality, it is necessary to mention

Capt. Henri Biard.

Painting of first flight of Spitfire prototype by Jim Mitchell.

the more 'artistic' nature of our designer that, after all, produced the permanently appealing lines of the Spitfire. Gordon Mitchell, in his *Schooldays to Spitfire*, reproduces a hunting scene drawn by his father which was from the time before he joined the aircraft industry and was plunged into a very different, and challenging, world of engineering drawing. Unfortunately, the book does not contain any further information about this aspect of our designer, but it is also surely relevant that his brother Billy set up his own business designing patterns for the local pottery industry and that Jim Mitchell became an artist whose aviation prints of his uncle's Spitfires sold internationally.

While it must be admitted that denying that Mitchell was an ordinary engineer makes an assumption that there is such a type, the stereotype of the dreaming artist does, however, have some application to his life as, according to his son, practical matters such as money were left to his wife and she would hand out cash for his personal requirements and replace it when required. She also was accustomed to his talking at one moment and being miles away the next; indeed, she told a reporter later in life that 'he loved snooker, but even in the middle of a game he'd suddenly put down his cue and out would come an old envelope or a scrap of paper and, as he began to draw, he would give me a rapid explanation of the diagrams he was making'.

Mrs Mitchell soon learned to contact his personal secretary when preoccupation with some design problem led to the evening meal at home going cold. Soon after his 1927 appointment as director, it was decided that he needed an extra typist. Mitchell did not interview female staff but found that the nineteen-year-old who was selected, Vera Cross, soon became indispensable. As she grew into her job, she organised his non-too-systematic filing and relieved him of much of his correspondence, which he hated; she often consulted members of the design team when technical matters were involved, rather than distract her boss. She also learned how to prevent interruptions and often had to wait beyond office hours before letters were signed. After his death, Vera recalled:

He was a very handsome man, with a lovely smile, but he was rather nervous with female members of staff. He always dictated slowly, with only a slight hesitation in his speech … You soon got used to his moods and learnt to keep out of his way when he was concentrating on a problem … Normal working hours did not interest him, and if he was engaged on some important project he would work until quite late in the evenings and expect his staff to do the same.

It is no surprise, therefore, that Harry Griffiths, who joined Supermarine in 1923, has provided the following observation:

He had a small personal staff consisting of a clerk, two typists and an office boy—they were all loyal to him and understood his moods. When any unwanted visitor asked to see him, he would tell his staff, 'I'll see him in ten minutes' and they knew that this meant 'Get rid of him!'

Much of how he operated in his office can be put down to not wishing his concentration on a design problem to be interrupted. He was also well known for his silences when others were voluble and for his shyness amongst strangers, and so his office can be seen as a sanctuary necessary to his creativity. Leaving the office for a round of golf or for an hour of sailing was another necessity to his thinking. One imagines that Miss Cross learnt to cover for such absences if the managing director of Vickers telephoned, but Sir Robert McLean must have understood that Mitchell's inspirations were also dependent upon time away from the everyday world of the office and from even the necessary enquiries of his design colleagues—that the exacting concentration to achieve an adequate round of golf would rid his mind of everyday 'clutter', while tending his boat's sails required continual vigilance on the busy River Itchen and Southampton Water. His taking up flying in later years was an obvious extension of his escapism and was an even more effective way of gaining some necessary isolation from mundane distractions where 'human voices wake us, and we drown'.

Mitchell's Senior Design Team Before the Vickers Take-over in 1928
Arthur Shirvall joined as an apprentice in 1918 and was later attached to a qualified naval designer who had been seconded to help Supermarine with hull design; Mitchell greatly admired his drawing of hull lines ('Shirvall always makes things look very nice') and he was eventually put in charge of Hydrodynamic Hull Design and Tank Testing;

Harold Smith was taken on as an apprentice at about the same time and rose to become Chief Structural Engineer;

Jack Rice was apprenticed in 1922 and eventually became Head of Electrical Design;

Joe Smith, after an apprenticeship with Austin, joined in 1922 as a draughtsman; Mitchell made him Chief Draughtsman only five years later; after Mitchell's death he became Chief Designer and was responsible for the development of all the Spitfires after Mark I;

Alan Clifton had replied in 1922 to an advertisement for a "mathematician for strength calculations"; Mitchell, apparently, preferred to carry on doing all his own stress calculations rather than face the appointment procedure but he did see Clifton the following year, by which time he had a degree in engineering; he later became the Principal Assistant to Joe Smith, then Head of the Technical Office, and finally Chief Designer after Smith's death;

Eric Lovell-Cooper joined in 1924 as a draughtsman, coming from the Boulton Paul aviation company; he later became Chief Draughtsman;

Ernest Mansbridge also came in 1924, with an engineering degree; he worked with Clifton on stressing but later was directly responsible to Mitchell for aerodynamics, performance, weights and flight testing; his later duties were predominantly Flight-Testing and Performance Estimation;

Eric (Jack) Davis joined as apprentice in 1925 and later went for experience to the aircraft manufacturers Westland and Boulton Paul for two years; he later became Senior Design Draughtsman;

Arthur Black was appointed metallurgist in 1925; at this time much aircraft construction was changing from wood to metal and Supermarine was one of the first firms to employ such an expert; Black later became Chief Metallurgist.

Oliver Simmonds was another graduate, was appointed in 1924, but left four years later.

Mitchell reorganised the Design Department in 1926, putting Joe Smith at the head of the Drawing Office and *Frank Holroyd* as Assistant Chief Engineer at the head of the Technical Office. Holroyd was replaced after the take-over by Clifton.

[*Beverley Shenstone*, joined at the end of 1931; he was the first appointee to hold a degree in aeronautical engineering and came with experience of contemporary German aeronautics. He rose to the position of Chief Aerodynamicist.]

The Kerr Stuart machine shop and smithy as the apprentice Reg Mitchell would have known them.

2

Normacot to Woolston
(1885–1916)

In his early career, Mr Mitchell almost became an architect in the Surveyor's Department.

Lord Mayor of Stoke-on-Trent

Gordon Mitchell's book, when it first appeared in 1986, was the first work specifically concerned with the life, work, and reputation of R. J. Mitchell and is a praiseworthy effort of a son to commend his father to posterity. He records that Reginald was born on 20 May 1895 and at the age of eight went to the Queensberry Road Higher Elementary School in Normacot, Stoke-on-Trent, then to the Hanley High School. At the high school, he showed promise in mathematics, but it would appear that he was not a particularly studious boy; he was good at games and his practical, non-academic, side was plainly evident in his making a small-sized billiards table, as well as having developed a passion for making model aeroplanes.

It is worth recording that while our designer is best known for an aircraft he designed in the late 1930s, he began elementary school in 1903, the year that the Wright brothers made the first powered aircraft flight, lasting less than one minute in duration. Six years later, when he was in high school, Louis Blériot made a stir by flying the 22 miles across the Channel, and aerial activity came to Britain at about this time, with Alliot Verdon-Roe being credited with making the first flight by a British designed, built and powered aircraft on 8 June 1908—by which time Reginald had just turned thirteen.

The young Mitchell's interest in building model aircraft would have been informed by reports of early flying and by press photographs of the flying displays of the very earliest aircraft, particularly the successful machines by Farman, Blériot, and the Wright brothers. Versions of these machines were also seen in events organised in his area and would have inspired Reginald's models, but an account that they 'swooped and dipped' (which full-size machines seldom do outside of air shows) would seem at variance with the approach of a lad who, at the age of sixteen, made his own lathe and, later, a dynamo. More likely, his obsession would have been directed, in part, at least, towards trying to understanding the principles of aerodynamics, as exemplified by straight, level flight—a good preparation for the first Supermarine aircraft he designed in 1920, which had to satisfy the Air Ministry inspectors that it could 'fly itself' for at least three minutes (*see* Chapter 3).

Queensbury Road Higher Elementary School, 1903 (Reginald Mitchell, middle of second row).

Sydney Camm, designer of the future Hurricane, showing a similar interest in model flight.

While Reginald was not unusual in preferring sport to serious study, he did have the advantage of a good educational background. His father, Herbert Mitchell had left Holmfirth Valley and had moved to the Potteries to become a headmaster at the National School in Old Butt Lane, Kidsgrove. The son also had the advantage of a practical father as Herbert, the son of a millwright, had also been an installer of electrical lighting and telephones. He subsequently became a master printer at the firm of Wood, Mitchell and Company Limited, incorporated in December 1904. His increasing status permitted a move to a detached house, Victoria Cottage, No. 1 Meir Road in Normacot (*see* photo p. 160), where there were plenty of green fields nearby, over which his son could experiment with his flying models; there was also an unused coach house and stables at the rear of the house where his three sons were encouraged to work with tools—as long as they swept up after whatever they had been making.

Herbert Mitchell was a church warden at Normacot Church where he had a 'family pew' and the children attended church and Sunday school regularly; as those who later worked under him would attest, Reginald clearly inherited his parents' 'protestant ethic'—the belief that conscientious and worldly work was a duty that benefited both their souls and their society. Writers have alluded to the genius and aesthetics which culminated in the Spitfire, but credit must doubtless be given to the designer's parents for his steady dedication within the aviation industry, and to his determination to continue unflagging work after his surgery for cancer and the subsequent painful episodes that prefigured his early death.

It is not known if the father had anything to do with the young Reginald's deciding to read all the novels of Walter Scott, and perhaps time has exaggerated family lore, as a set of the Waverley novels available at the time ran to twenty-five volumes. Nevertheless, for a schoolboy to persevere to the bitter end of just one of these worthy novels (well before the impetus of GCE examinations) is praiseworthy enough and Herbert Mitchell would certainly have approved of Reginald's sticking to the task, given that he was known for demanding high standards of conduct and application as well as tidiness. Numerous accounts of the son's demands on his staff, when he had authority at Supermarine, suggest the adage: 'like father like son'.

Perseverance and application were certainly required when the son took his first major step towards his future career. He was apprenticed to the locomotive engineering firm of Kerr, Stuart and Co., in Fenton, one of the Potteries towns—although there is an interesting detail in a report of a luncheon, given after his aircraft had won the 1929 Schneider trophy competition. The lord mayor said:

> In his early career, Mr Mitchell almost became an architect in the Surveyor's department. There was no opening at the time and instead of pursuing a career in other channels, Mr Mitchell took up engineering and served his time with Messrs Kerr Stuart.

Sentinel, 27 September 29

Clearly, a white-collar job as an architect would very likely have suited Reginald as it could combine aesthetics and structures, but the father, who had, apparently, recognised his son's practical nature, had no hopes of his pursuing a strictly academic career. Shipbuilding, bridge building, or textiles might well have provided a good career in the world of industry at that time, and so it was fortunate that, apart from pottery or mining, there was also, locally, a locomotive maker of good standing to which the son could be apprenticed. Reginald was enrolled in 1911, aged sixteen, suddenly exchanging the high school world of satchel and cricket flannels for the universal 'snap' lunch box, tea can, and overalls that soon became covered in oil, grease, and dirt.

While motor transport was in its very infancy, the national railway network was then at the heart of the British economy, and the basic structure of mechanical engineering apprenticeships, such as Reginald's, were accordingly set out in a paper to the Institute of Locomotive Engineers in 1915 by Alfred Hill, who was the Great Eastern Railway's chief mechanical engineer. An apprentice would have to spend a minimum of three years out of five in the workshops, including a year on machines and lathes, a year in the fitting shop on bench work, and a year in the erecting shop. Some time in the smiths' shop, the boiler shop, pattern shop, foundry, and the running shed would also be considered useful.

Additionally, parents could purchase a 'premium apprenticeship', which also involved attending such evening science classes as the Locomotive Superintendent would consider necessary and whereby promotion from the shop floor to the drawing office would be conditional upon satisfactory progress. Thus, at the end of this instruction, premium apprentices would have a fair knowledge of mathematics, machine construction, drawing, applied mechanics, theoretical mechanics, and physics, and would thus have the prospect of a career away from the hard physical labour, which they had to endure in the early years of their apprenticeship—no longer having to wear the flat cap that was the hallmark of the manual worker (*see* photo of 'Reg' Mitchell, p. 54).

More specific details of Reginald's apprenticeship can be derived from Lionel Rolt's *Landscape with Machines*, where the author described how he also began a 'premium apprenticeship' with Kerr Stuart, a few years later, in 1928. His parents paid a premium of £100, to be returned at the end of the apprenticeship, if his work proved to be satisfactory. Meanwhile, he earned 10 shillings a week in the first year, 15 in the second, and £1 per week for the final year. Lionel was articled to the chief engineer of the company, whose duty was to ensure a full and in-depth knowledge of all aspects of railway engineering. Perhaps the two years he had already spent with an agricultural engineering company accounted for the shorter term of his apprenticeship which, nevertheless, involved periods in the boiler shop, the forge, and the machine shop, before progressing to the erecting shop.

Another premium apprentice with Kerr Stuart, Tom Coleman, has also recorded how, before Reginald, he spent a year in the erecting shop, followed by two years in the boiler shop, forge, and foundry. Finally, he progressed to the drawing office, 'gradually taking on some basic design tasks given to him by the qualified draughtsmen.' This apprentice was the son of Tom Coleman Sr, who was temporary head at Hanley High School when Reginald was there and possibly, therefore, had some influence on the family decision for Reginald to go to Kerr Stuart. Perhaps Tom Jr, who had joined North Staffordshire Railway in 1905, discussed the idea of Reginald's apprenticeship and possible future when he worked at the head offices in Stoke-on-Trent. There is certainly evidence that they kept in touch, as Tom received invitations from Supermarine to attend the Schneider trophy events in 1929 and 1931.

Whatever Reginald might have learned about his future training from the Colemans, his initiation into the railway workshops must have been a considerable culture shock to a lad brought up in a middle-class environment (including, as we have seen, the works of Walter Scott). He now had to take serious heed of the pottery firms' steam sirens, which each morning at eight o'clock 'would break into a frenzy of excited whoops to which Kerr Stuarts added a deep, mournful and slightly hoarse ground bass, like the voice of a liner lost in fog' and he would return each day, his overalls covered with the oil and grime of the engine sheds.

He was now also to experience at first hand the noise and heat of an industrial plant without, of course, the benefit of modern health and safety regulations. Here, in three bays of one large steel building, the wagon shop, the boiler shop, and the forge were 'indistinct in the shimmer of heat rising from the coke-fired riveting hearths of the boiler makers':

> Men seemed to be everywhere and their diverse and purposeful activity filled the whole building with a torrent of urgent sound. Pneumatic hammers closed stays and rivets with a deafening clamour like sudden bursts of machine-gun fire; tall steam hammers pounded and every now and again a heavy hot stamping press … hung poised for a moment, and then plummeted downwards with a crash that shook the ground.

The noise from 'Happy Sam'—a horseshoe shaped device with pneumatic hammers on opposite ends—could, it was claimed, be heard 2 miles away.

These graphic details also come from Rolt's book, and clearly, conditions would certainly not have been better in this Stygian world, into which the young Reginald Mitchell had been thrust, seven years earlier. It was a world of working men whose language was 'liberally salted with profanities and obscene four-letter words'. His shyness and slight stammer, which were mentioned in the reminiscences of later colleagues, would hardly have been improved by his first contact with these older men on the shop floor; but at least Gordon Mitchell describes one incident when he showed some of the determined spirit of his later years—his foreman had likened the tea that Reginald had made to urine (or blunter words to that effect) but was much better pleased with a second mug which Reginald had personally doctored accordingly.

Having completed his training in the workshops, he began, like Tom Coleman, attending the Wedgwood Memorial Institute, taking evening classes in technical drawing, mechanics and mathematics, and moved to the Kerr Stuart drawing offices. After his death, the *Evening Sentinel* (11 June 1937) wrote:

> In 1914, while attending classes at the Fenton Technical School, Mr Mitchell obtained the final certificate of the City and Guilds of London Institute, and in the following year, he gained second place in the examination of the Institute of Mechanical Engineers.

A *Birmingham Gazette* reporter wrote on 12 June 1937:

> His father once said of him: 'Twelve years ago, while his fellow students were enjoying themselves, he was studying hard and trying to get on. I have known him come home from a long day's work and snatch a hasty meal and leave home again without changing his grimy overalls to attend evening classes in science.'

The proud father's memories were perhaps slightly exaggerated, but this more cerebral work clearly matched Reginald's potential as he was awarded one of three special prizes presented by the Midland Counties Union. He was also awarded the second prize by the Union of Educational Institutions for his success in their examination in practical mathematics (advanced); for his prize, he selected *Applied Mathematics* by D. A. Low.

Reginald had obviously acknowledged that mathematics, rather than the novels of Walter Scott, was the basis of any career in engineering. Previously, training in an architect's department had been denied him but Alan Clifton has mentioned that, at this time, he 'also became an Associate Member of the Institute of Civil Engineers, an exacting qualification'. It would seem that Reginald was looking around for other fields of employment and it may be that the experiences of his apprenticeship had made the prospect of a career in the heavy engineering of the railway industry none too attractive. Although the embryo aviation world was a most unlikely career choice, with hindsight it might be observed that his youthful passion for flight might thereby be married to a less heavy form of engineering and, like architecture, would involve aesthetics as well as structures—for the future benefit of his country.

So, by the time he was twenty-one, he had successfully completed his apprenticeship and had set about establishing a firm theoretical foundation for some sort of career in construction. The First World War had been raging for two years and his wish to join the war effort, and certainly his interest in flight, were soon to become realised as he turned his back upon locomotive engineering and took the fateful decision to apply for the post of personal assistant to the managing director of the Pemberton Billing aviation works at Woolston, near Southampton.

After his apprenticeship, he had undertaken some part-time teaching at the Fenton Technical School. By this time, the Military Service Act had been passed, as conscription was now necessary to make good the horrendous losses in the battlefields of France and Belgium; from 2 March of that year, all men between the ages of eighteen and forty-one had to be considered for selection by local military service tribunals. As there were exemptions for those in such reserved occupations as farming, teaching, and industry, one can see that, as a qualified engineer and currently teaching, Reginald was not required for military service. The *Sentinel* (7 September 1929) supplied the particular detail that 'when he was old enough to join up and he was very anxious to serve in the Royal Flying Corps, the technical Department of the

A narrow-gauge loco built by Andrew Barclay & Co. Ltd, Kilmarnock, used for transporting RAF personnel at the Calshot RAF base. When Mitchell visited his aircraft there in the 1930s, he would no doubt have remembered, perhaps not entirely fondly, his apprenticeship days at Kerr, Stuart and Co. and their very similar Wren-type engines.

A poignant photo of a young British soldier of World War I—brother Eric, two years younger than Reginald, who served in Egypt—and survived the war.

Ministry of Munitions refused to release him.' At this time, the responsibility for the design of aircraft had been moved out of service hands and given to this Ministry. A letter of his, copied in Appendix I, also reveals his continued wish to fly for his country.

At this distance in time, one must make some assumptions about the young man's choice of employment. How did a twenty-one-year-old, who was trained by a railway firm, and who lived in Stoke-on-Trent—almost as far away from the sea as it was possible to be—come to begin work with a small marine aviation company on the (then) remote south coast? It is not known if Reginald had even seen the sea at this time, although his father might perhaps have found enough money to take his wife and the five children on holiday to one of the developing holiday resorts. A letter from Reginald to Eric, dated 9 September 1917, mentions a parents' later stay in Blackpool.

It is also unclear how he ended up being interviewed for a position with the Pemberton Billing aviation works at Woolston. A young man, keen to be involved with aircraft, might have visited his local library and looked at advertisements in *Flight* or *The Aeroplane*, which had just begun to appear. Here, he might have seen a vacancy for a trained draughtsman in the aircraft industry and perhaps learned something of the firm concerned, but as details of advertisers were subject to wartime censorship, it might have come as a surprise to the young applicant when he received an invitation for interview at what must have seemed a remote and little-known place on the south coast—Woolston had not yet been incorporated into the borough of Southampton.

It is not known if Mr Mitchell Sr argued against the move, on the grounds of far better prospects elsewhere in the railway world, nor if he was supported by his wife, who most probably would have liked to see her firstborn son living much closer to home. Yet a wise

Reginald's parents, Herbert and Eliza Jane.

father must acknowledge there comes a time when a son, now twenty-one, must strike out for himself and hope that his choice of employment might turn out, at least, to bring happiness. Herbert Mitchell had also to reckon with a young man of spirit; other later incidents would go to indicate that self-belief or stubbornness reinforced Reginald's somewhat idealistic decision to leave home and become part of an uncertain new form of transport just opening up.

Examples of this new aerial technology had already found their way into the Midlands and beyond. In 1910, Reginald would have been caught up in the local interest in flying when crowds flocked to aviation meetings at Wolverhampton and Burton-upon-Trent. Even nearer, a Wright brothers' machine was put on display at the Hanley (Stoke-on-Trent) Park Fête in the same year, and by the time the boy was just turning fifteen, Louis Paulhan, in a Farman biplane, passed no more than twelve miles west of the family home on the way to winning the *Daily Mail* London–Manchester competition. Two years later, another early aviator, Gustav Hamel, came to nearby Stafford and to Stone, to which special excursions were organised; for the Whitsuntide fete, he also came as near as Longton, a district within easy walking distance from Normacot, where the Mitchell family lived.

While his keeping of racing pigeons might not necessarily be considered to be an indication of his choice of a future career, the young Reginald's other more prophetic interest, in making model aeroplanes, must have been inspired by the newspaper articles and pictures of these various early aircraft when they came to these events near his home. Two of the most successful early shapes to be seen locally were the Blériot and the Farman types, and their box-girder fuselages would have inspired Reginald's home-built designs. It is worth noting however that

A Goupy biplane flown at the 1910 Burton-upon-Trent meet.

Louis Paulhan *en route* to winning the 1910 London–Manchester race in a Farman biplane.

while this basic structure became the norm in most aircraft until the late 1930s, Mitchell's first full-sized machines had boat-like hulls which led to the monocoque approach of most other aircraft designers much later. The fuselage of his S.4 of 1925 already showed the way to his Spitfire prototype in 1936.

Hamel's visit to Stafford would have created more of a stir than another event, which occurred on the continent in the same year, but was to have a profound effect on Reginald's future career. On 5 September 1912, at the Aéroclub de France, Jacques Schneider announced a trophy contest that was designed to develop aircraft that could also operate efficiently from water. As there was no airport infrastructure for landplanes but plenty of sheltered shipping ports with (flat) areas of water from which to operate, it would seem only sensible to consider developing seagoing aircraft for the new generation of transport vehicles.

Gustav Hamel at Lammascote Fields, Stafford, in a Blériot monoplane in 1912.

A small-scale replica of the Schneider Trophy presented to Mitchell after his designs won the three consecutive competitions, 1927, 1929, and 1931; small plaques on the sides of the replica record the various Supermarine wins and the pilots involved. This replica sold in 2010 for £27,000.

Thus the Schneider trophy, as it soon came to be known, was envisaged not as a speed event, but as a competition to find the best practical marine machines—hence the tests for flotation, navigability on water and taking-off and landing from water, which had to be successfully completed prior to the main flying event. The contest was to be held annually, to take place over open sea and over a distance of at least 150 nautical miles. Entries were to be limited to three aircraft selected by each country's aero club, with the winning club to organise the following contest; the country gaining three wins in five years became the outright holder of the trophy, and a substantial cash prize was offered to the winning pilot of each of the first three events. The trophy itself (now in the Science Museum, London, beside Mitchell's winning S.6B 1931 floatplane) was a large and handsome *art nouveau* creation in silver and bronze, measuring over 22 inches wide and mounted on a pedestal of dark veined marble.

Reginald might have heard of the first two events in 1913 and 1914, and perhaps seen pictures or drawings of the aircraft (especially after the 1914 victory of a British aircraft), but their waterborne performances were less than impressive; the first two competitions, with a total of thirteen entrants, produced only two aircraft to complete each event.

His offer to swim out to his test pilot in later years, if there were to be a crash, suggests he had learned to swim during his schooldays—several public baths had been opened locally by 1895—but his native Potteries were unlikely to have offered opportunities for much acquaintance with boats of any sort. Nevertheless, although the Pemberton Billing firm had diversified into landplanes as part of the war effort, our applicant was soon to be swept up in the owner's return to the original goal of producing 'boats which fly and not aeroplanes which float'; indeed, this original intention of the enterprise had been signified to Reginald by its telegraphic address 'Supermarine', and when Pemberton Billing was bought out by Scott-Paine, the new managing director chose this word for the company name—literally, the opposite of the more familiar 'submarine'—to indicate where his hopes for future aircraft also lay.

Of course, his apprenticeship with Kerr Stuart and Co. would hardly have prepared Reginald for the lightweight and fragile creations of the industry he was seeking to enter. However, as well as repairing and building other companies' machines (for which he had mainly needed skilled woodworkers), Noel Pemberton Billing was beginning to develop his own company designs. Thus the mathematics and engineering drawing courses that Reginald had attended would now be important recommendations. Scott-Paine had just appointed a chief designer, F. J. Hargreaves, and a head draughtsman, Cecil Richardson (of whom, *see* later). While a small firm, with no significant portfolio of company designs, was unlikely to have attracted a large field of well qualified applicants, the young Midlander must have shown some particular qualities or potential to be appointed to the post of personal assistant to the general manager. C. G. Grey, the editor of *Flight*, recorded that the young Mitchell 'had been discovered by Mr Pemberton Billing as a competent draughtsman' and so the interview must have occurred before 20 September 1916, when the company was sold to Hubert Scott-Paine.

Mitchell was thus not just applying for employment in a company not yet firmly established, but also engaged in a relatively esoteric form of engineering. One might say that this type of product was triply remote as 'hydro-aeroplanes', as they were then called, were less developed than the early landplanes; it was only on 28 March 1910 that Henri Fabre made the first take-off from water by a powered aircraft and in the January of the next year that Glenn Curtiss took off from water in San Diego with a more practical hydro-aeroplane. The first British aquatic events took place in November 1912 and involved an own-design machine on Lake Windermere and a converted Avro landplane at Barrow-in-Furness. An eyewitness account of the latter's first flight, on the 18th, was reported in *The Aeroplane*: 'The machine left the water several times, just rising clear, so that Commander Masterman saw daylight under the floats. He computes the distance travelled to be 50 or 60 yards in these skips.' The hydro-aeroplane then proceeded to capsize. It was repaired, however, and flown successfully with the newly formed Lake Flying Company of Windermere, which was contracted by the Royal Naval Air Service as the primary developer of seaplanes—much to the dismay of Beatrix Potter and Canon Rawnsley, founder of the National Trust.

No doubt Reginald's youthful idealism and his keenness to involve himself in this novel industry, far away from his native turf, overcame any misgivings he might have had when

PEMBERTON-BILLING LTD.

SUPERMARINE, P.B.—7. Span 57 ft. 6 ins. Overall Length, 34 ft. Weight, 3,000 lbs. Engine, 225 h.p. Speed, 45-70 m.p.h. Fuel capacity, 4 hours. Under stress of weather, at the will of the pilot, the aeronautical impedimenta, is instantly detachable, leaving an ordinary High-Speed motor craft, which contains the engine, pilot, passengers, petrol, instruments and gun.

Is equipped with water propeller and rudder, having a distance range of 200 miles and speed of 35 knots. Built under Pemberton-Billing's patents at his Southampton Works. Applications for licences to build under the French, German, Russian, Italian, Belgian, Norwegian, Australian, American, Japanese, and other Foreign and Colonial patents, are invited.

SOUTHAMPTON, ENGLAND.

Advertisement for a 1914 Pemberton-Billing project—a boat with detachable flying surfaces.

CONTRACTORS TO THE ADMIRALTY.

Telegrams: "SUPERMARINE."
'Phone: SOUTHAMPTON 1337.

The Supermarine Aviation Works Ltd.

ESTABLISHED 1912.

H. SCOTT-PAINE, GENERAL MANAGER

Designers & Constructors of Aircraft

Speed Boats and All Kinds of Racing Craft.

SEAPLANES & FLYING BOATS
PUSHER & TRACTOR SCOUTS
OBSERVATION AND PATROL
MACHINES. BATTLEPLANES

SPECIALITY: Rapid Production of Experimental Machines.

FLYING WATER & SLIPWAYS: **WOOLSTON.**

OFFICES & WORKS: **Southampton,** ENGLAND.

A 1917 advertisement for the Woolston factory, under new ownership and geared up for wartime orders.

he saw what a small-time operation the company was at that time, compared with the company of his apprenticeship: when Lesley Rolt had gone to Kerr Stuart, he mentioned how between 1894 and 1912 'a whole series of large new shops had been built to house the Erecting Shop (lofty as a cathedral), the Foundry, Heavy Forge, Boiler Shop, Wagon Shop, Joinery and Paint Shop' and how 'working at full pressure, this plant could employ over a thousand men'.

Comparable statistics were also reported on in *The Engineer*, 15 October 1909, which quoted a workforce of 850 when order books were buoyant, and the periodical noted that current orders included thirty-two engines for the South Indian Railway Co., 'several' for the Argentine Government Railway and 'an order for wagons for Columbia [*sic*.], in addition to track construction'. Quoted dimensions of the erecting shop, the foundry, and the wagon shop amounted to a total area of 1,790 sq. metres. With the new paint and patterns shops, the full expansion programme was expected to have been completed on the 15-acre site by 1911, the year when Reg Mitchell began his apprenticeship.

In contrast, the following extract from G. A. Cozens' manuscript, 'Concerning the Aircraft Industry in South Hampshire', describes the humble beginnings in 1912 of the firm at Oakbank Wharf, Woolston, which Reginald was to join four years later:

> Supermarine seems to have begun almost by accident and in the early stages the unpredictable nature of the firm's founder [Pemberton-Billing] and his equally colourful general manager [Scott-Paine] might have diverted the destiny of Supermarine in any one of several directions. The factory was in a part of Mr Kemp's boatyard just above the Floating Bridge on the Woolston side of the River Itchen, and a number of strange contrivances were built there. Mr Kemp often said that it was he who kept the little firm going, and indeed the works facilities like the sawmill were very useful and the workforce, who were largely the Kemp boatyard men at the start, were versatile and able to carry out some unusual projects.

G. A. Cozens lived close to the Supermarine works in the early days of the company and was a school friend of one of their workers as well as a neighbour of Biard, their test pilot. In his collection of information about the local aircraft industry, he has left some fascinating, often anecdotal, information concerning its formative years, particularly on the subject of Supermarine. This material reveals how important Supermarine was to this early development of what was a relatively esoteric branch of aviation, as well as how basic were design, building, and employment practices at about the time that R. J. Mitchell joined the firm. The author believes that this extract, and others following, while sometimes inaccurate, deserve to be more widely known. He is especially grateful to the Archive Section of Solent-Sky, Southampton, for making available a copy of this manuscript.

Gordon Mitchell also quotes from a November 1913 article in the *Southampton Times and Hampshire Express*, entitled (with misplaced participle) 'Flying Factory at Itchen Ferry':

> There is already on the site one large shed, once used as a coal wharf, which has been converted into an engine building. A second shed 200 feet by 60 feet is now being constructed. Cottages in Elm Road, facing the site, are to be altered into offices. The river frontage up to the Floating Bridge Company's premises has been secured for the building of 'Water Planes'.

In 1924, no less than eight years after Mitchell joined the firm, another new recruit, Eric Lovell-Cooper, was all for leaving, after he saw the 'offices'—which were sited in 'the cottages in Elm Road' immediately behind the workshops:

> Oh, gosh, it was awful! I thought, what have I let myself in for! It was row of derelict houses with a gateway. The house next door had an empty room full of derelict bicycles—that's what it looked like through the window. They weren't broken, they'd just been left there by the people at Supermarine's who rode to work. Above were the offices where all the girls worked. The bedrooms of the houses, you see.
>
> The drawing office was lit half by gas and half by electricity, and some of the gas was just jets, open fish-tail jets. Mitchell's office wasn't as big as this room; I thought, what the hell have I let myself in for? Is it worthwhile staying here?

In these modest premises, various prototypes had been produced by Pemberton Billing, but by 1914, development costs and a lack of orders had nearly bankrupted the fledgling business. Nevertheless, a year later, and thanks to the increasing demands of the war effort, the company had been able to continue by repairing other companies' aircraft and then to expand, having received a contract to build twelve Short S.38 seaplanes under licence, followed by a contract for thirty Norman Thompson NT.2B flying boats. Twenty-five of the latter were eventually built, and the Pemberton Billing firm was also given a production contract for twenty company-designed P.B.25 'scout' landplanes.

Additionally, Pemberton Billing's own P.B.29E Nighthawk had been created as a response to the 1915 bombing raids by German airships. In order to reach the heights attainable by these invaders and with sufficient firepower, an aircraft with a large wing area was required and this resulted in its quadruplane configuration. It crashed soon afterwards after delivery to naval pilots for handling trials, but by the time that Reginald arrived at Woolston, our builder of small model aeroplanes must at least have been excited to see its successor taking shape and to be involved in its completion: the new 60-foot span monster, the P.B.31E, stood nearly 18 feet high. It is often stated that Mitchell had arrived at Woolston in 1917; however, there are a number of drawings from July 1916 relating to the P.B.31E Nighthawk which were initialled 'R.J.M.'

Thus it was that Reginald began his unlikely start, many miles from home, with a fledgling company and a very small one, and far removed from a much more assured career in a well-established and thriving locomotive industry. However, in the year that he joined the company, the Air Ministry placed an order for twelve Short S.184 torpedo bomber floatplanes. This order, the P.B.25s being built, the optimism of youth, and a dream of taking part in the development of an industry of the future, must have helped to outweigh any homesickness and doubts about the viability of the company he had signed up to.

One can only imagine how Reginald must have had his provincial horizons suddenly widened. In the first place, the air was so different from that which shocked Lesley Rolt when he had gone as an apprentice to Kerr Stuart a few years after Reginald:

The nearly completed P.B.31, with Mitchell possibly fourth from the right.

> I felt oppressed by the all-pervading dirt and squalor of the endless cobbled streets lined by terrace houses of soot-blackened brick; by the smouldering waste tips, pit mounds and heaps of furnace slag … overlaid by a perpetual pall of smoke. The whole area was peppered with bottle ovens which when fired up belched dense black smoke.

In addition to cleaner air, there was the river which flowed wide and deep past the Pemberton Billing plant: compared with Stoke's modest river Trent and with James Brindley's narrow canal running alongside the Kerr Stuart locomotive works, the broad expanse of the River Itchen had to be crossed by a pontoon ferry which operated just downstream of the aircraft works; also below the works were the shipbuilders, John I. Thorneycroft and Co., who had recently finished their first Royal Navy ship, its 8-foot 6-inch draught presenting no flotation problems near to the aircraft works (*see* photograph, p. 79.)

The view from these works towards Southampton was hardly rural, but it was not impaired by smoke from the multitude of potters' kilns which burned 10 tons of coal per firing, and it benefited from being close to Southampton Water and the Solent. Also, as Cozens wrote, about six years after Reginald came to the area, it was, relatively, much more peaceful:

> I lived a mile from the Supermarine works and could hear an [aircraft] engine start, in those days a rare sound and quite distinct from the riveters at Thorneycroft or the rumble from the coaling wharf in the Docks.

Not far away, the Itchen flowed into Southampton Water, where the newly arrived Reginald could see impressive ocean liners being manoeuvred into Southampton docks and where

Hanley, Stoke-on-Trent, as late as 1930.

Supermarine Southamptons over Southampton docks (*Mauretania* in foreground) and about to overfly the River Itchen and the Supermarine factory at Woolston (far bank, centre right).

he would now have seen seagulls which (if not inspiring the shape of his aircraft designs, as implied by *The First of the Few*), at least symbolised the brave new world of aircraft transport of which he dreamed.

He had successfully survived his five years of apprenticeship in the world of men and he had just reached what was then the all-important age of majority. A developing self-reliance and the attractions of the new environment and its aeroplanes must have helped to overcome any fears of the 'foreign' world of the south and strangers or concerns about the status of the Woolston firm; on being offered the position of personal assistant to the general manager, Scott-Paine, it is reported that he straightway asked for his belongings to be sent down to him.

R. J. Mitchell at the time of his wedding, 22 July 1918.

3

Establishing Himself
(1916–1919)

At that time R.J. had a motorbike and sidecar, and I remember him driving into the yard on two wheels. He was very good looking and wore breeches and brown gaiters.

Authur Shirvall

When Reginald joined the Woolston company, it was some years after the early aviation pioneers had set up their firms: Shorts and Handley Page in 1909, Avro in 1910, Blackburn in 1911; they were now turning out large quantities aircraft for the war effort. It was thus fortunate for him—and for Britain in 1939—that a post of personal assistant had come up in a smaller firm that was only just beginning to have some success with its own designs.

Although our applicant had no obvious qualifications for work in aviation, there were, however, precedents in favour of his application: the pioneer aviator and designer, A. V. Roe, the superintendent of the Royal Aircraft Factory, H. Fowler, and S. T. A. 'Star' Richards, chief designer to Handley Page Aircraft, had also begun their careers as apprentices to railway companies; indeed, Richards had also been a personal assistant at Handley Page and Roy Chadwick, the designer of the Lancaster bomber, had begun as personal assistant to A. V. Roe. Reginald's City and Guilds and Institute of Mechanical Engineers qualifications, with the addition of his Midland Counties Mathematics Prize, would also have provided tangible support for his keenness to become part of the new and challenging world of aviation.

The photograph below shows that not all of his first months were spent in the drawing office familiarising himself with a very different form of engineering; it would appear that the small workforce meant that he had to literally roll up his sleeves and help out wherever necessary. In his own autobiography, the company's test pilot, Capt. Henri Biard, mentions that, at about this time, he was once introduced to a visitor while covered in dust from the coal he had been shovelling. Luckily, Reginald was no stranger to hard physical work. For example, Rolt has described how, at Kerr Stuart, steel plates 'an inch or more thick' were cut to shape, before flame cutting was available: Archdale machines drilled close spaces around the outline of the piece to be cut out, and then 'the metal between these holes was next cut through by hammer and chisel'. The photograph shows our new personal assistant being posed in a group photograph of fellow workers, although looking rather uncomfortable to be wearing a flat cap, reminiscent of his Kerr Stuart apprentice days, but at least he would have had no difficulty in satisfying any probationary period at Woolston and was quite familiar with what he would, in the future, come to ask of the company workers on the shop floor.

Supermarine workers, with tools of their trade, in front of a Norman Thompson NT.2B flying boat. Reginald Mitchell is standing, third from right.

Cozens on Supermarine Hull Construction and Workforce Conditions Current When Mitchell Joined the Company
In 1914 the firm built the small flying boat P.B.1 which was a credit to the workforce, and indeed it was judged to be the best example of aircraft construction at the 1914 Olympia Aero Show. This applied to the workmanship but unfortunately not to its performance.

The P.B.1 hull was of round construction, built by small boat methods with closely spaced wooden ribs of half inch square section like girl's hoops, joined by longitudinal stringers and covered by two layers of mahogany or cedarwood planking, laid so that the outside layer was sloping the opposite way to the inner layer, this was known as 'opposed diagonal planking'. There was a layer of doped fabric between the layers and the whole fastened by brass screws or copper nails and in some cases the nails were turned over and clinched or riveted over a small washer. This method produced a very strong but flexible wooden tube or cone and was the invention of the distinguished yacht designer Linton Hope, whose name was as well known in those days as Sir Barnes Wallis is known today …

The machine never flew and it is likely that the aerodynamics were wrong, the engine and propeller being at 15 degrees to the centre line of the hull so that it seemed the machine was intended to lift off as soon as the engine opened up. In any case the engine was not powerful enough to maintain flight.

An *Echo* 'Letterbox' contributor wrote to say that his father, who was working at Supermarine,

> was told to fetch an axe and Pemberton-Billing, after looking at the beautiful machine for a long while, broke it up.

> However, the Linton Hope hulls served Supermarine well for many years and was the chief reason for their success throughout the era of the wooden flying boats …
>
> When the Great War started the Supermarine factory [not yet so named] became involved in repairing damaged floatplanes from Calshot and no doubt the workforce gained experience from this, but the PB 9 was a typical Supermarine venture. It was almost certainly a copy of the successful Sopwith Tabloid which had won the first [second] Schneider Trophy at Monaco the year before but there is no doubt that the plans for the P.B.9 were little better than something on the back of an envelope, probably hastily drawn and given to a foreman, who was then told to do his best. However, the simplicity of the design and the construction did not detract from its performance and it handled well. Scott-Paine trusted his men to work well and he knew that they were the ultimate ones in whom he had to put his faith, it was long before the aircraft inspection board was established. The remarkable thing about the P.B.9 was that it only took seven days from the time the project was set in motion until it was finished, and a number of stories have been put forward as to how this was done, but the way Scott-Paine worked was always the same, and instead of locking the men in until they had finished, as one story said, he agreed with the foreman on a price for the job and left it to him. No doubt the men did work hard and long, but in their own way. They took into account the fact that there was inadequate lighting in the factory, and worked as much as possible during daylight, and they also had in mind the fact that the copal varnish had to dry and other practical things, so that, whatever the urgency was, the practical considerations were what counted. These thoughts are born out by the fact that the frame of the aircraft was constructed using ordinary carpenters' joints …
>
> The worst fear of craftsmen employed at Supermarine was that by some mischance his job could be lost for the most trivial accident, even breaking a thin twistdrill meant a walk to the storekeeper to ask for a new one and the payment of a fine. The problem was that the flying boat hulls were fastened by rows of small screws which meant drilling through two layers of cedar ply and into the rock elm ribs, which was hard on drills, but before long the men solved the trouble by making their own drills. They cut knitting needles or piano wire into lengths of about two inches and annealed one end, hammered the tip flat and hardened it like a spear. Each man had an Archimedes drill with a simple brass chuck which could be purchased as a part of a fretwork set and was suitable for drilling small holes at awkward angles because it was light and only needed a straight push and pull action.

The recent contract to build thirty Norman Thompson NT.2B trainer flying boats under licence would provide our ex-locomotive apprentice with early hands-on experience of contemporary aviation technology. Design experience of a more direct sort soon came Reginald's way when the firm received a contract to build fifteen Short S.184 floatplanes; firms licensed to manufacture Short's products were supplied with full sets of blueprints and had to send their staff to the parent company for instruction.

In a letter dated 1 October 1918, to his brother Eric, who was stationed with the British forces in Egypt, Reginald had written that he was very busy and with little spare time: 'We are building Short Seaplanes now, and are turning out about six a month. We have got to increase this to nine a month before Christmas.' It is unlikely that anyone outside the Air Ministry knew that the Supermarine contract for the Short 184 floatplanes was only a small part of the overall orders for 936 of these machines, but the industry was certainly experiencing just how good the war effort was for business. A small reflection of this vast war effort was that Reginald was able to report home that he had been promoted to assistant works manager, sharing the responsibility for overseeing the completion of the order for the Short seaplanes. In addition, the head draughtsman, Cecil Richardson, had left the company in the midsummer of that year, raising hopes of further promotion.

Also, the Pemberton Billing Company had taken on the building of two flying boats specified by another pioneer aviation group, the Admiralty design team. This group specialised in designing for the war effort and most of the early theoretical work, in particular, the seminal *Handbook of Stress Calculations*, came from this source. It was also fortunate for the new company and its new assistant works manager that some of this leading group were sent down to the works at Woolston to draft out details of the new naval machines.

The first two aircraft completed to Admiralty designs were accordingly known as AD Boats, and with the pusher biplane configuration of the firm's P.B.25 added to a new boat-like hull, there begins to appear the general flying boat formula that was, in the future, to inform Mitchell's Commercial Amphibian, Sea Eagle, and Sheldrake, and which eventually led to his well-known Walrus.

Of special importance, the particular details of flying-boat hull construction also came to the new company: F. Cowlin, the Technical Supervisor at the Royal Naval Air Station has recorded how he went down to the Woolston firm and 'learned a great deal about hull design from Linton Hope, who joined the section for a time while we were engaged on the AD Boats'. The lines and structure thus laid down by this well-known yacht designer became the basis of

An AD flying boat.

all the wooden flying-boat hulls that Mitchell subsequently utilised and were a considerable advance on the more universal box-girder structure employed by the current naval flying boat, the Felixstowe F.2. Penrose wrote:

> The Admiralty had found floatplanes too dependent on smooth water; they were interested in the far heavier flying-boat hull which in the Linton Hope approach consisted of a double skin of mahogany planking with fabric in between, with rock elm strips forming almost circular ribs, longitudinally stiffened by closely spaced stringers.

A second Admiralty design, the AD Navyplane, was another biplane pusher type of seaplane but this time it had twin floats instead of a flying-boat hull. Its detail design and construction were now entrusted to the Woolston firm and so there was work for Reginald to do, assisting in drawing up a specification for an improved version; yet as the war was almost at an end and as the Short 184 was performing adequately enough the duties for which the Navyplane was intended, nothing came of this effort. There was also a further requirement at this time—for a single-seat seaplane or flying-boat fighter—issued by the Air Department under specification N.1B. As the Supermarine design for this aircraft flew later than the other designs mentioned above, and as Mitchell's involvement with it was the greater, it will be described in the next chapter.

Meanwhile, Reginald's improved status and his firm's more secure position now enabled him to travel back to Stoke-on-Trent and to marry Florence Dayson, headmistress of Dresden Infants' School, at St Peters Church, Caverswall, on 22 July 1918. It is not known what understanding there had been between the two of them when Reginald left in 1916 or if absence from her was a decisive factor. In view of their joining the Woolston Tennis Club in 1923, one might speculate that Reginald first met his future wife via tennis and that, at the age of thirty-two, she would have good reason to be attracted to a fit young man, of 'stalwart build, with a fair skin which reddens in the sun, and light reddish hair'; he was not in danger of slaughter in France, and described as 'very good looking'. One might at least also imagine that the company of a mature professional woman would chime with his own mental make-up.

Speculation aside, 'Flo' was certainly eleven years older than he was and it might be inferred

that he was displaying at an early age a single-mindedness and determination to make what, particularly at that time, must have seemed an unusual match. Might his parents have even hoped he would have found someone of his own age when he departed to Southampton, given the shortage of eligible, uninjured young men not away fighting?

The above copy of the marriage certificate shows that Florence had resigned from her teaching post, that her father was a farmer, and that Reginald's father had also, by now, left teaching and was registered as a 'master printer'.

A previous letter to his brother, Eric, on 9 September, 1917, gave his bachelor address as Belgrave Villa, Chapel Street in the Woolston area, although he mentioned that he had previously changed his address twice, saying enigmatically, 'I rather like a change'. A letter of June 1918 gives another address: 87 Avenue Rd, Woolston. He now returned with a wife and they rented a house at 22 Bullar Road, a few miles north of his workplace, where Flo would have to allow for evenings with her new husband reading the *Handbook of Stress Calculations* and *H.B. 806* by the Technical Department of the Air Board, which contained a full account of the mathematical methods employed by the Department.

More theoretical information became available for Reginald to study in 1919, with the publication of *Aeroplane Structures* by A. J. Pippard and J. L. Pritchard and *Applied Aerodynamics* by L. Bairstow. The recent appointment of a professor of aerodynamics at Cambridge also marked the development of something approaching a systematic and scientific approach to the new technology, but how far the Woolston company was to become a significant part of it was by no means certain. The strong British presence at the 1919 Paris Air Show did not include any machines from Mitchell's firm.

At the time of the letter to Eric mentioning an increase in the production of Short seaplanes, Reginald was not to know that the Armistice would be signed a mere forty-one days later and

Supermarine workers, *c.* 1920, with an AD flying boat. The window to Mitchell's office and the drawing and technical accommodation are top right.

that all government contracts were about to be drastically curtailed. For the present, at least, he was hard at work again but now involved with a civilian project: the conversion of some of the now surplus naval AD Boats into passenger-carrying seaplanes.

Cozens' Account of the Earliest Flying-Boat Services and their Spartan Conditions
In the summer of 1919 they purchased some three seater flying boats which they had built and sold to the Air Ministry and which were now surplus when the war was over, and hastily made them ready to take joyriders from beaches along the South Coast while the summer lasted. The conversion from wartime use to peacetime was fairly basic and consisted of taking out the engine and fitting a more economical Beardmore 160 hp which caused the machines already prone to porpoising, to be even worse. The rest of the preparation was to paint out the RAF roundels, but not the red, white, and blue colours on the twin rudders, and SUPERMARINE was painted on each side of the bow.

When the pilot and his mechanic got to Bournemouth, or Brighton, or Bognor or elsewhere they planned to operate they anchored and relied on the local boatmen to ferry out the passengers and help with the refuelling. This enterprise started in July and continued through August and September. When the Air Registration Board was set up the three machines were painted blue, which was to be Supermarine's distinctive colour, and the letters G-EAEE, G-EAED and G-EAEK made them our first commercial flying boats.

Towards the end of September they were modified to carry three passengers and began flying to Le Havre and so became the world's first international flying boat service.

The experience gained in September and October 1919 by flying passengers across 114 miles to Le Havre led Supermarine to plan further efforts for 1920 and they built more machines with a higher bow to give the passengers more protection against wind and sea. They were known as Channel II's but the passengers still had an uncomfortable ride on many occasions and I remember seeing a Channel come up to a buoy just below the Floating Bridge [at Woolston] and although the three people were wearing flying coats and helmets they looked wet and miserable as they got into a boat that was rowed out to meet them.

It would appear that ten machines were registered as civilian Channel I's, G-EAED to G-EAM, but only G-EAWC and G-EAWP seem to be registered here as Channel II's. However, a number of Channel types were sold, especially to countries having offshore islands, and the skilful handling by the Supermarine test pilot Captain Henri Biard both on the water and in the air resulted in these being shipped out to New Zealand, Fiji, Japan, Bermuda, and at least one was used by Instone Airlines in the Bristol Channel and English Channel area.

Captain Biard was yet another of the colour[ful] personalities that Supermarine seemed to attract and he was an extremely good pilot, indeed he flew every kind of aircraft as it was produced, be it single or twin engine, light or heavy, on land or sea. One of the little known but important things he did was to train pilots for flying boats, something that even experienced land pilots found difficult, and it was a common sight to see a Channel taxiing up and down Southampton Water trying to take off, or landing with a series of bounces.

Some of the men who became popular Imperial Airways pilots on the Empire flying-boat routes with the 'C' class flying boats were trained on Supermarine Channels.

Initially, ten of these two-seaters, which had been in store, had been purchased back from the Admiralty with a view to offering trips from Southampton to various seaside resorts on the Isle of Wight, and drawings had to be prepared for the installation of passenger seating and a more economical engine. Naming the modified aircraft as 'Channels' indicates the very modest transport ambitions of the company and, in fact, the first of the passenger services were only between Southampton and Bournemouth. Nevertheless, Supermarine had the distinction of obtaining the first British Certificate of Air Worthiness for a British passenger-carrying flying boat in August 1919, and the flights were claimed to be the 'First Flying-Boat Passenger Service in the World'.

Reginald well might feel that he was at the threshold of a new system of transport when the service began on 28 September, but it gradually petered out with the onset of winter. Meanwhile, four of the converted AD Boats had gone to an embryo Norwegian air service and Reginald was also involved with the company's further purchase of another six AD Boats. He had to help convert them to a three-seat trainer version, and some were sold to the Norwegian government for use with their naval air services.

There then followed a Mark II conversion with a more powerful engine and three such aircraft went to the West Indies in 1920; two more had to be modified for photographic reconnaissance and were used for surveys of the Orinoco delta in Venezuela. Other Channels were also delivered to the New Zealand Flying School, the Royal Swedish Navy, and the Imperial Japanese Navy. The visiting Japanese officials were reported to have been particularly impressed by the handling of the Channel in strong winds and heavy seas by Henri Biard, who had now joined the company as test pilot in 1919.

A Channel II 'on the step'.

A completed Channel for Venezuela (note the anchor).

A total of eighteen machines were thus sold overseas, concluding with a sale to the Chilean Naval Air Service in 1922, and about this time, a separate Air Ministry had been created and the RAF staff college had been established at Cranfield. Thus, although Supermarine's order book was soon to be not so healthy, the newly married Reginald Mitchell, with the optimism of youth, could see here signs of a new system of transport being established and with government support; he could also look forward to his company taking a full part in these developments.

Compared with the previous group photograph, the one overleaf taken in 1922 now reveals Mr Mitchell, after he had absorbed a great deal of the aviation practice of other firms, with a more comfortable and assured stance, more at home amongst his design office staff with whom he had now begun to spend his productive years, His previous attire was no longer in evidence, to be replaced by a suit and a tie invariably held in place with a tie-clip. His highly polished shoes were the norm for office staff but a homburg hat was to become a Mitchell trademark, with a handkerchief in his breast pocket—the last perhaps being a contribution of his spouse.

Looking out over the River Itchen, down to Southampton Water and then, in his mind's eye, to the destinations of eighteen of the Channel flying boats—Europe, Japan, South America, or New Zealand—the industrial smog of the Potteries must have seemed a long way away, particularly as, in 1919, he had just been appointed chief designer, at the age of twenty-four. Other quite young designers must have had similar dreams: Chadwick at A. V. Roe was twenty-six and Pierson at Vickers was twenty-seven, Sopwith, Fairey, Handley Page, Folland and Blackburn were all in their early thirties, leaving Oswald Short at thirty-six and De Havilland at thirty-seven as the old men of the group.

The early Pemberton Billing, now Supermarine, interests had ranged from the very large Nighthawk landplane to a small 'scout', also a landplane, but Reginald Mitchell's early design experience now came to be closely involved with a fast seaplane type and its various transformations.

Reginald Mitchell (third from right) with his design staff, c. 1922.

The company's interest in this naval interceptor type had begun with an Air Ministry requirement, N.1B, for a fast manoeuvrable single-seat seaplane or flying boat fighter with a speed of 95 knots at 10,000 feet and a ceiling of at least 20,000 feet. This ambitious requirement arose particularly from the need to combat the German Brandenburg fighter seaplanes that had been operating over the North Sea. The resultant Baby had been designed by F. J. Hargreaves when he was in charge of the drawing and technical offices at Pemberton Billing at the time Reginald joined the company, and so it is entirely likely that he also had had some design input to the three N.1B airframes that were going through the works.

By the time of the Armistice, N59 had been completed and was being evaluated by the Navy and N60 was largely complete. The third, N61, was under construction and was most probably (in view of its extensive departures from the N59 design) the one retained by Scott-Paine for entry in the 1919 Schneider trophy competition—in the hope to gain some very useful publicity from an event to be staged by Great Britain.

The particular configuration of this aircraft, later named Sea Lion I, suggests that the modifications to the original Baby design were largely those of Hargreaves. The fin and rudder were enlarged in a shaping not followed later by Mitchell; likewise, the base of the latter was used as a water rudder, the interplane struts were splayed outwards, and the balanced ailerons on the top wing had an inverse taper. Also, the hull was decked to keep down spray and so the front of the fuselage was far less sleek than Mitchell's later Sea King II and Sea Lion II:

Establishing Himself (1916–1919)

The first N.1 Baby.

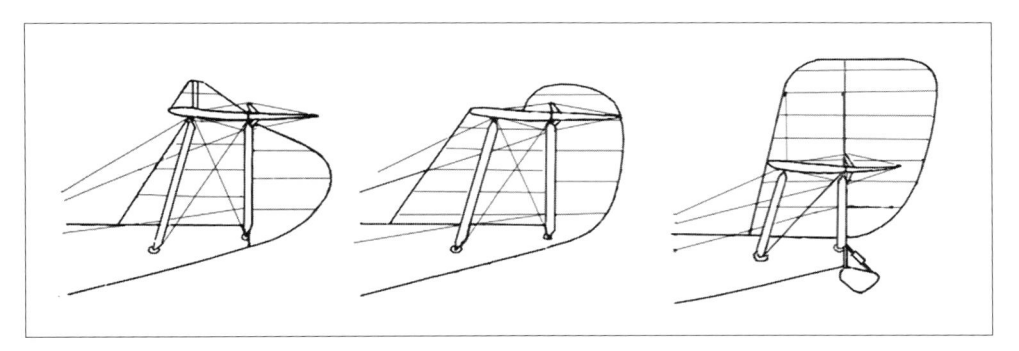

From left to right: N.1B Baby (1918); Sea Lion I (Hargreaves, 1919); Sea King II (Mitchell, 1921).

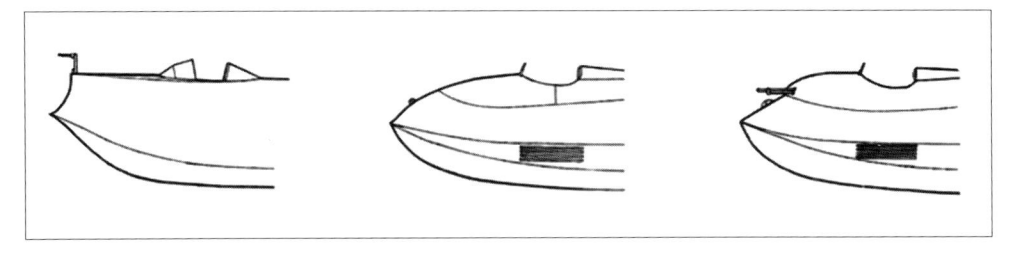

From left to right: Sea Lion I (Hargreaves, 1919); Sea Lion II (Mitchell, 1922); Sea King II (Mitchell, 1921).

The Sea Lion I and the 1919 Schneider Trophy Contest

Hargreaves' concern to advance the company's hopes of an Air Ministry order for a naval fighter via the Schneider contest was clear from his change from the 200 hp Hispano-Suiza engine of the N.1 Baby to the 450-hp Napier Lion, fast emerging as the outstanding British powerplant of the 1920s. The new engine resulted in the machine's new name, and it also produced a 24 per cent increase in its loaded weight. Consequently, an increase of the Sea Lion's wing area was provided. As, additionally, the hull was far from sleek, the overall design suggested that the man with responsibility for the Sea Lion seemed, nevertheless, to have favoured rugged seaworthiness at the expense of speed through the air.

Thus, when it came to selecting the three aircraft to represent Britain in the Schneider trophy competition, the Sea Lion was the Royal Aero Club's third choice over the slightly faster Avro 539A, possibly in order to hedge its bets because of the already proven seagoing qualities of Supermarine machines. Two modified landplanes—a Fairey IIIA and a Sopwith scout—were the other British entrants. However, by the actual time of the Schneider contest, Hargreaves had left Supermarine and it was Mitchell who now had responsibility for this third entrant. However, on the day of the competition, neither Mitchell nor anyone else was able to profit from the potential publicity of the contest—the reason was a combination of incompetent organisation and the British weather.

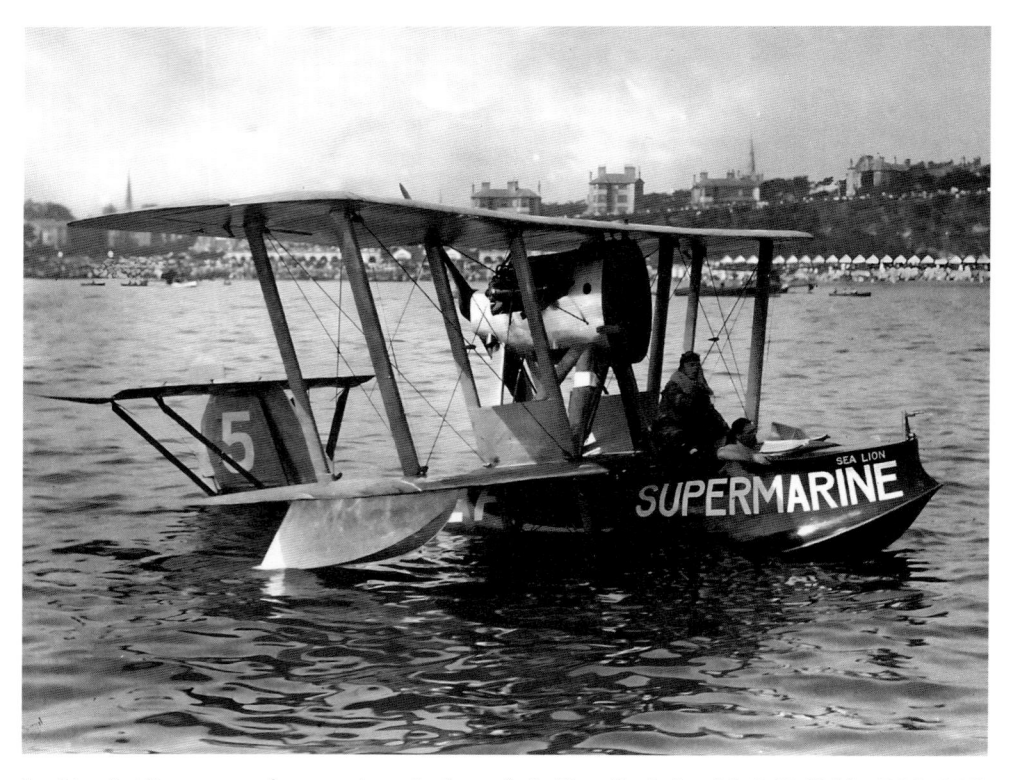

Sea Lion I at Bournemouth, an engineer in the cockpit. The pilot is Sqn Ldr B. D. Hobbs, DSO, DSC, and Bar, decorated after shooting down Zeppelin L.43 on 14 June 1917.

At about 11.30 a.m. on 10 September, a SPAD floatplane and a Savoia flying boat braved persistent fog and flew across from the competition base at Saunders Ltd on the Isle of Wight, the latter nearly hitting a rowing-boat and then being surrounded by a large and enthusiastic crowd which threatened its safety. The SPAD was towed in amidst bathers by the Supermarine motor launch and was later seen to have a leaking float, which was further impaired when hauled on to the beach by enthusiastic 'helpers'. By 2.30 p.m., a second French plane, a Nieuport, arrived, but the fog increased and a start time of 6 p.m. was announced. This time was later brought forward, to the consternation of the French who, it transpired, still had repairs to do and who, in the end, did not start the competition.

At 4.50 p.m., the Fairey IIIA got away, followed by the Supermarine Sea Lion; the Sopwith went next, and then the Savoia. However, the Fairey and the Sopwith aircraft soon returned, their pilots considering, rightly, that the poor visibility made flying too dangerous, particularly at the Swanage Bay turn. It was here that the pilot of the Sea Lion had to land in order to try to establish his position in relation to mist-shrouded cliffs, but the aircraft hit something in the water. The pilot took off nevertheless, but unfortunately, the earlier damage to the hull caused the plane to upend and threw the pilot into the sea.

Only Guido Janello in the Savoia S.13 completed the required ten laps, but then it was found that he had mistakenly rounded a boat anchored in a cove 2 miles short of the real marker. He was accordingly disqualified, although the Royal Aero Club did the decent thing and, at a meeting on 22 September, recommended that Italy be awarded the trophy. However, the *Fédération Aéronautique Internationale* (which oversaw the Schneider contests) ruled that the flight was invalid and it rather pointedly awarded the next venue to Italy.

The Sea King I

The next two Schneider trophy events took place in Italy but constructors from other countries apparently did not feel inclined to finance entries to what was not yet a major aeronautical event. Meanwhile, Mitchell was asked to persist with their fighter flying-boat concept.

Little is known about Mitchell's involvement in N60, the second of the N.1B Baby type mentioned above, which had also been bought back from the Air Ministry; it seems likely that it became the Sea King I, which appeared at the 1920 Olympia Aero Show—that is, after Mitchell's appointment as chief designer. But how long it had been in existence in its new guise before this date is unknown; certainly, a photograph from the show reveals a direct repetition of the earlier 1918 tail configuration and so it represents past practice rather than the future.

Perhaps its original specification with a Beardmore 160-hp engine was not expected to present directional problems, given that the N.1B Baby had flown with a 200-hp Hispano-Suiza engine, but Supermarine's proposed fitting of a 240-hp Siddeley Puma engine might have required some design responses from Mitchell, such as the fin and rudder of his later Mk II version (*see* drawings above). One speculates that at this time, the profitable modifications to the AD Boats had so preoccupied Supermarine that N60, unaltered by Mitchell, except perhaps in respect of its modified and raised cockpit fairing, was sent to the Olympia Aero Show essentially as a marker for the company's continuing interest in the naval fighter scout concept.

However, there is little information about the aircraft having been flown, although the following publicity for this aircraft would seem to imply that control, even with the original less powerful engine, had not been found to be quite adequate; it also reveals that the company was hoping to sell to the many private flyers that the First World War had produced, if military orders could not be achieved:

> The 'Sea King' is a small fast single-seater which for general purposes follows the structural methods of the 'Channel Type' boat. With its 160 hp Beardmore engine it puts up a speed of 96 knots, so that it is either a thoroughly sporting little vehicle for the single or unhappily married man, or is a useful small fast patrol machine for Naval work along troublesome coasts. Its chief difference in design from the 'Channel Type' lies in the fact that it only has a monoplane tail of the depressing kind and so takes rather more flying on the part of the pilot than does the bigger machine.

Had there been any sales, perhaps Mitchell would have wished to modify the tail surfaces but, unfortunately, neither the military nor the 'single or unhappily married man' came along to buy one and it had to await a Mk II, clearly modified by Mitchell, two years later.

C. G. Grey notes an interesting memory of the 1920 display of this aircraft:

> As one stepped onto the stand one had a feeling of confidence that here were people who really knew what they were at in the sea-flying game. Hubert [Scott-Paine] and his two brothers wore yachting caps and double-breasted reefer jackets and looked real sailor men. Their helpers wore jerseys ... and in each corner of the stand was a large coil of tarred rope flemished-down in workmanlike seafaring fashion.

Given what is known of his retiring nature, one imagines that Reginald was content to remain in his drawing office at these moments of showmanship and a commentator on Eric Lovell-Cooper's early days at Supermarine (*see* Chapter 2) would tend to bear this supposition out:

> When Eric arrived [1924], Supermarine's was managed by an eccentric businessman named Scott-Paine. He put the works on its feet and it became a name in the aircraft industry. He was a showman, that was all, but he was a jolly good one ... They used to write *another* Supermarine product! Big letters across. It could have been an empty crate—advertisement you see. His way of demonstrating the strength of a Supermarine product was to jump on it or try to put his fist through it.

No accounts have indicated that our young designer had first of all to ensure that the integrity of his structures should withstand an aviation equivalent of 'tyre kicking'; but while time may have exaggerated such a report, the important deduction is that Scott-Paine must have seen in his new recruit someone who had the potential to contribute a steadier, professionally trained input to the firm. It helps to account for his rapid rise to chief designer, with Scott-Paine soon coming to trust the more mundane but necessary details of aircraft production to him. Reginald as a novice designer was to prosper from that trust and he did so immediately with his next project.

The Commercial Amphibian: Mitchell's First Design

New orders for the services were likely to be scarce with the ending of the First World War—the flying boats that had been bought back by Supermarine for conversion were among some 5,000 serviceable airframes now surplus to requirements, including over 100 seaplanes. As Cozens reported: 'On the Marlands in the centre of Southampton there were hundreds of crates of surplus aeroplane engines and the common between Spring Road and Firgrove Road in Sholing was covered with aircraft frames.'

Meanwhile, the embryo commercial sector had been represented by the Supermarine Channel operations of 1919 mentioned earlier (on p. 60) and by the regular British commercial passenger and goods services between London and Paris, begun on 25 August of the same year by the Aircraft Transport and Travel Company. The formation of the Department of Civil Aviation at the Air Ministry, again in 1919, might also have been taken as a hopeful sign.

The first aircraft involved in this beginning of commercial flying after the end of the First World War were conversions of military machines like the Channels, which, as described by Cozens earlier, were by no means well-suited to their new roles. So, in March 1920, the new Department of Civil Aviation showed an important initiative by announcing two competitions for commercial designs 'of British Empire origin' to promote 'Safety, Comfort and Security' in air travel. With a view to developing international travel and bearing in mind the few airfields available, compared with large stretches of water worldwide, one of these competitions was specifically for amphibian seaplanes with a first prize of £10,000 and a second prize of £4,000.

It was not surprising that Mitchell was asked by Supermarine to design an entry for the seaplane competition, which was to commence on 1 September of that year. For the first time, Reginald had quite a free hand at this early stage in his career. Perhaps fortunately for him, the criteria that were laid down for the amphibian class could hardly be less modest—seating accommodation for a minimum of two persons exclusive of crew; a range of 350 nautical miles at 1,000 feet at a speed of not less than 80 mph; and a load capacity of 500 lb to include passengers and life belts but not including crew.

There was also a requirement of a flight of three minutes at 5,000 feet to check if the machine would fly itself and the entrants had to clear balloons at a height of 25 feet from a take-off run of no more than 400 yards. The amphibian competitors were required to take off from the experimental station at Felixstowe, pass as high as possible between marker boats 600 yards from the start buoy, and land at the experimental (land) station at Martlesham Heath. Taxiing on water had to include figures of eight, taking off and landing in rough weather, and mooring out for at least twenty-four hours in moderate weather. These marine trials were not unlike those which Schneider trophy racers had to complete before the actual flying contests and which reflected the same concern to develop aircraft that had practical seagoing features.

As Supermarine would obviously want to establish the firm as a serious contender in the new world of passenger transport, there would, clearly, be pressure on Reginald, the twenty-four-year-old, untried chief designer, to try to make his first design a winning one, even though he would expect to be measured against entries from other aviation companies which were better established and prosperous, thanks to the large wartime contracts that they had enjoyed.

In this respect, however, he had some good fortune. Shorts were notable manufacturers of large patrol flying boats during the First World War, with their F.3 and F.5 machines. When the war ended, some of these aircraft were still being built by the company, and in 1920,

Supermarine Commercial Amphibian (1920)

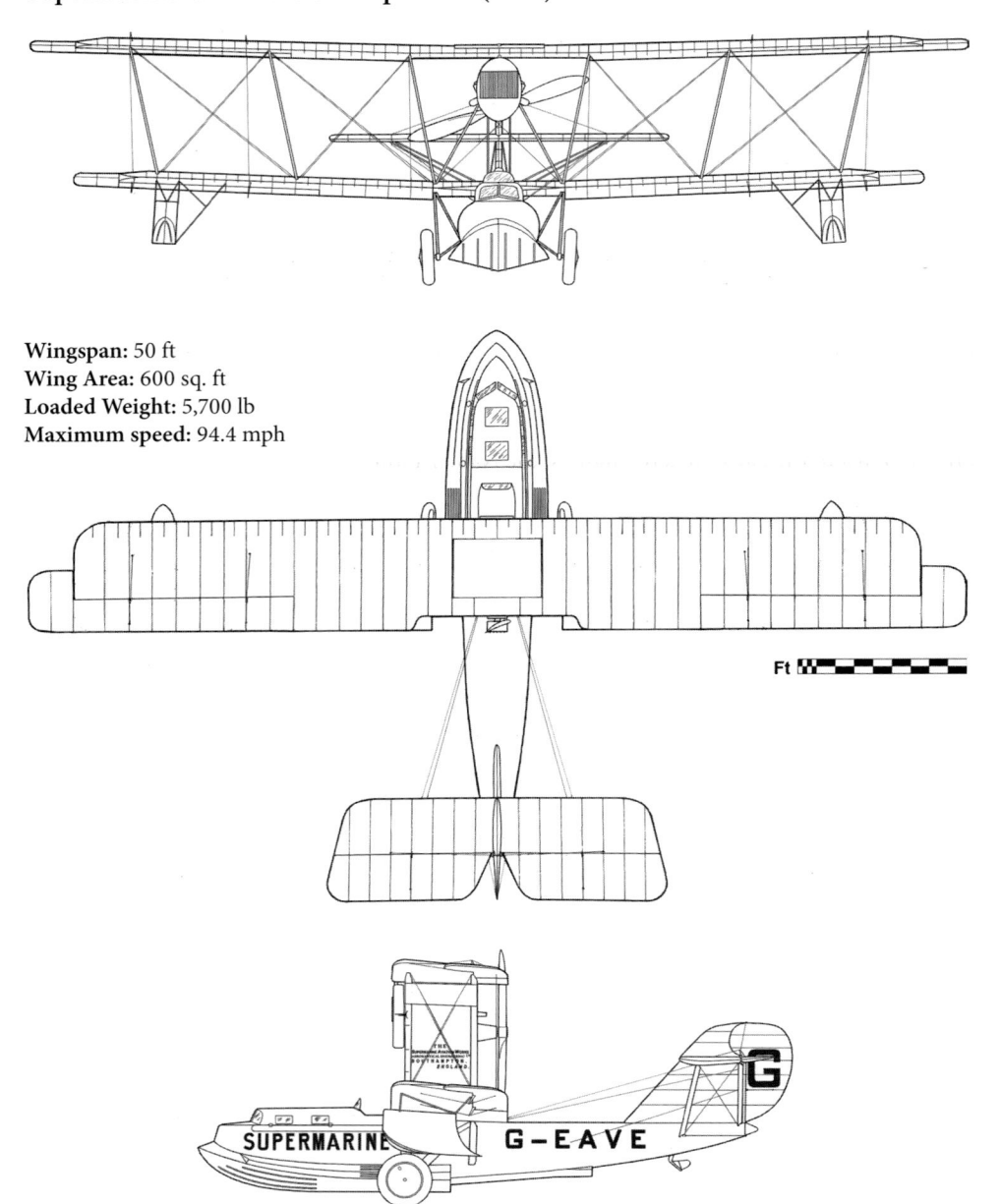

Wingspan: 50 ft
Wing Area: 600 sq. ft
Loaded Weight: 5,700 lb
Maximum speed: 94.4 mph

nine more had been ordered for the Imperial Japanese Navy; the company was also developing the Cromarty, an improved version of the F.5. It would seem that because of these commitments, they did not enter the new competition for passenger aircraft; as it turned out, another prominent aircraft producer, Fairey, merely entered an unadventurous version of their prolific Model III: a floatplane with added-on wheels. Saunders, on the other hand, had set about designing what might have been a formidable rival passenger amphibian with seating for seven, but it turned out later to be beset with various problems that could not be overcome in time for the competition.

Nevertheless, Reginald could expect strong opposition from the third entrant—the Viking III. The Vickers company had expanded into aircraft manufacture as early as 1911 and, while building a large number of Royal Aircraft Factory S.E.5s, it also produced its own heavy bomber, the Vimy, of which over 100 were eventually completed. Vickers' first amphibious aircraft type, the Viking, was begun in December 1918, and by the time of the competition, their amphibian had reached its third stage of development and the company could easily afford to install the latest in aero engines, the Napier Lion.

As the Supermarine response to the competition was the first major project our newly appointed designer was called upon to undertake, it surely deserves close attention. It is also surely very understandable that the end product would be a conservative one. Even had Reginald been an experienced aircraft engineer at this time, he would still, in all probability, have mainly followed previous best practice, in view of the little theoretical data that was available and as wind-tunnel experimentation or tank testing (for flying-boat hulls) was not available to his small firm. Also, there were only about twenty weeks separating the announcement date of the competition and that of the trials, leaving little time for innovative thinking to be tested out.

In the event, *Flight* reported:

> For the Martlesham amphibian trials the Supermarine Company designed and completed a flying boat in all respects in 10 weeks from the time when the first drawing was commenced to the time the aircraft was in the air; the actual building time being 4½ weeks.

Based on Channel flying surfaces, the Commercial Amphibian had a biplane layout in which similar dimensions of height and length were adopted and the sea rudder was similarly placed—vertically below the leading edge of the tailplane—but now converted to act also as a skid when taxiing over land. Between the Amphibian's struts, there were canvas stabilising screens, full length between the inner pairs and quarter length between the middle ones. These screens were relatively uncommon by this time but survived on several later Supermarine designs as well as on the Channel and Sea Lion, perhaps mainly to protect the engine and propeller from spray on take-off or landing. However, it was the present machine that was most extensively fitted with them; in this respect, it did not look particularly like an advanced design. The wing-tip floats were also of the Channel sort and the oval hull and general arrangement of its built-on planing surfaces employed the Linton-Hope/Channel principles of hull construction.

Not surprisingly, therefore, Supermarine described Mitchell's new design as 'practically a "Channel" type boat, with a wheeled undercarriage hinged on each side', although the new chief designer had incorporated features of a much smaller aircraft, the Sea Lion I. Its fin and

The Commercial Amphibian with ground handlers at Martlesham.

rudder outlines were similar, but a proportional increase in surface area above the tailplane allowed our designer to provide a more symmetrical appearance to the fin. Also, the Sea Lion's outwardly raked inter-plane struts were repeated in the new, and larger, machine. Thereafter, it would seem that Mitchell preferred the simplicity of equal span wings supported at right angles by the inter-plane struts. As many of the features from both the Channel and the Sea Lion I were thereafter abandoned by Mitchell, the present design can be regarded as something of a 'time capsule', a summing-up of earlier practices rather than a statement of the way forward.

Nevertheless, he also showed an early instance of boldness and originality by abandoning the biplane tailplane and twin rudders of the Channels in favour of a single fin and tailplane (the competition rival, the Vickers Viking III went through three more variants before the Mark VII, the Vanellus, appeared five years later with a more modern-looking single tailplane). Additionally, Reginald significantly remodelled the nose with a prominent boat-like entry to counter spray, a feature which was to prove successful in his future Sea Eagle, Scarab, and Seagull machines.

A further novel feature was his provision of a retracting undercarriage. At this time, an American landplane, the Dayton-Wright RB-1 Racer, featured the innovation of a fully-retracting landing gear, designed especially for the Gordon Bennett race of 1920, and a caption to a *Flight* photograph drew particular attention to the fact that 'the undercarriage and wheels are drawn up within the fuselage when in flight'. Understandably, Reginald's present concern was not with speed, but merely to lift the wheels out of the water, in order to facilitate take-off and alighting.

The first European design of this sort was the Sopwith Bat Boat of 1913, which, like the present rival Viking, had a mechanism which rotated the wheels upwards and forwards. Supermarine's concern for 'boats which fly' offered no previous experience of retractable undercarriages for Reginald to call upon and so it is noteworthy that, for his specially-designed mechanism, he chose a geometry which displaced the wheels outwards rather than forwards, thus avoiding any change of trim when the wheels were moved. He retained this sideways mode of retraction for all of his future amphibian undercarriages.

Flight reported one particular testing moment for the undercarriage:

> It is worthy to note that during the firm's trials at Southampton this aircraft landed in a ploughed field, with furrows of about 15 in., which not only pulled the amphibian up in a very short distance, but allowing for the heaviness of the ground, threw the boat forward on its nose, leaving the section of the hull on the earth for a distance of about 15 yards. The boat was dropped on its tail, which also speaks of the rigidity of tail construction, to put up with such treatment, and was flown off and landed at Eastleigh [the nearby airfield used by Supermarine].

One other feature of the Commercial Amphibian must also be mentioned: the enclosed passenger cabin for the two passengers, who were seated in tandem. The ministry's intention of ascertaining 'the best type of Float Seaplanes or Boat Seaplanes which will be safe, comfortable and economical' might have seemed to make an enclosure for seaplane passengers inevitable but perhaps it had been a typically sensible addition urged on Scott-Paine by our new chief designer. Certainly, the other two amphibian entries had open cockpits for their three passengers, one seated next to the pilot and the other two side-by-side behind. Open cockpits at this time were the norm and they saved weight, but they were far from ideal in seaplanes and in northern climates—one remembers Cozens' previous description of returning Channel passengers looking 'wet and miserable as they got into a boat that was rowed out to meet them'.

The concern of Supermarine that passengers in the open would not be very comfortable, and possibly a safety hazard, might very well have resulted from the experience of Supermarine's pilot, Biard, on Supermarine's Channel service to Le Havre on the 30 September 1919. He recorded that the weather on that day had developed into a gale with sleet and snow, but with a flask of rum donated by Scott-Paine for heating, a Belgian financier braved the open

A Commercial Amphibian's 'arrival'.

The Commercial Amphibian with cabin hatch open. Mitchell is centre, with Scott-Paine on the right.

cockpit of the Channel flying boat. The cold was such that Biard could hardly feel his feet and hands and then he was nearly blinded when the passenger, Capt. Alfred Loewenstein, tried to pass the flask to the rear cockpit but only succeeded in causing the rum to blow back into the pilot's eyes. Then the passenger tried to put up an umbrella, presumably hoping to keep the hail at bay without considering the effect of such a relatively fragile item being blown into the propeller that was directly behind the two of them. As it was impossible to converse in the conditions, even if there had been time, Biard had to resort to hitting the Belgian about the head, whereupon he disappeared into the well of the cockpit. (Loewenstein was to become a 'mystery of flying', on 4 July 1928, when he disappeared from a Fokker F.VII over the Channel.)

This glimpse into the pioneering days of aviation might seem amusing, though not to the pilot at the time, as was the arrival of the Supermarine crew for this 1920 competition dressed in heavy jerseys and sea boots—to become known by their competitors as 'the Supermen'. For their part, the Vickers people turned up in sailor's hats with 'Viking III' in gold on the hatbands, and *The Aeroplane* at the time noted that 'all the competitors treat the affair as a very good joke'. The same correspondent did however note that despite the apparently light-hearted or amateur approach to the event, the amphibian entrants hedged their bets by reserving their maritime tests until last 'as they wanted to complete land tests before chancing damage to their machines by awkwardly handled launches or a sudden squall'.

No serious adjustments or replacements to the Mitchell aircraft were required, despite its one-off design and the short notice of the competition, and the judges also noticed with approval an effective tiller arrangement for steering while taxiing on water, the equipment for sea use, and the way in which the shape of the forward part of the hull kept spray off the passengers' compartment. It might be expected that the company's marine experience would produce such comments; equally, it might not be too surprising that the very novel retracting undercarriage gave rise to criticism for being none too clean, from the mechanical and the maintenance points of view. The lateral control of the Commercial Amphibian was also considered not immediately responsive enough.

On the other hand, a comparison between the slab-sided, Consuta plywood-sheeted approach of the Vickers entry and the boat-like hull of the Supermarine entry showed that he had had the good fortune to have joined a firm that employed an effective flying-boat hull. It was inherently more streamlined than most landplane designs of the time and was to stand the firm and its chief designer in good stead for the rest of that decade.

In view of its performance in the competition as a whole and in view of the various features of the machine to receive favourable comment, the various criticisms might not have prevented Mitchell's aircraft taking first prize. Yet an increase of nearly 150 square feet of wing area compared with that of the Channel had been necessitated by the fitting of a more powerful but heavier Rolls-Royce Eagle engine in order to lift the additional weight of the landing gear and to address various other specifications of the competition. So the low power/weight ratio of the engine of the Commercial Amphibian, available cheaply to the company from war surplus supplies, produced a significant loss of certain competition points and resulted in its coming second to the Viking.

The final official report on 11 October stated that 'the results achieved for amphibians show that considerable advance has been attained … and the competing firms deserve congratulations on their enterprises.' They also recommended an increase in the second prize money as 'the proportion of the monetary awards does not adequately represent the relative merits of the first two machines'. The company's own assessment of the Amphibian was as follows:

The Commercial Amphibian being readied for launching from the Supermarine slipway, Woolston. Reginald Mitchell is standing nearest to the hull.

> The Supermarine Aviation Works … machine followed previous types of Supermarine in the general characteristics of structure and put up an extraordinarily good show in that competition. It completed all the tests satisfactorily, and was only beaten by competitors with engines of considerably greater power in the matter of speed and climb. It was awarded the second prize, and in view of the general excellence of the design and construction, the amount of this prize was increased from £4,000 to £8,000 by the Air Ministry.

In fact, there had only been two other entries, but the doubling of the prize money was noteworthy.

Particular reasons for the ministry's encouraging increase in the award might very well have been the more streamlined shape of the monocoque hull and the greater comfort of the enclosed cabin, which placed the passengers well ahead of a noisy engine. Frank Fredrickson, a Canadian in the Royal Flying Corps and later to win an Olympic gold medal for ice hockey, has recorded in his journal a positive reaction to the more attractive features of Mitchell's first design:

> Friday [28 September] we went to Martlesham Heath. It was intensely interesting. The Supermarine Amphibian appealed to me much more than the Vickers Viking or the Fairey machine, and I had the good fortune of flying in it from Martlesham Heath to Felixstowe Harbour.

One wonders if it was the relative comfort of the enclosed cabin which 'appealed' to Fredrickson rather than the appearance of this machine. For sure, it had shown early examples of boldness and practical imagination, but its stabilising screens between the wing struts certainly looked back to earlier designs, such as the biplanes which had visited the Stoke area when Reg Mitchell was still at school.

A Norman Thompson NT.2B flying boat with beaching gear.

As already mentioned, Reginald Mitchell was well acquainted with the Norman Thompson NT.2B and would have observed the Felixstowe F.5s being built by May Harden and May at Hythe on the opposite side of Southampton Water, but their hulls were, essentially, a continuation of the box-girder structures that he had seen earlier at Stone and Hanley, clad with plywood in view of their marine requirements. With the benefit of hindsight, one can see that the approach Reginald adopted led to the stressed skin engineering of modern aircraft (including the Spitfire), but in 1920, the relative sleekness to these hulls, thanks to the eye of the yacht designer, would have immediately appealed to the artist in our novice designer.

Also, the immediately essential practicality of the Linton-Hope approach was its flexibility; it was not 'stiffened' by plywood and could more easily absorb the jolts of sea take-offs and landings, where the shock-absorbing devices of landplane undercarriages, obviously, could not be employed. As C. G. Grey said of these hulls, 'they were almost basket-like in their flexibility, and so got through the water without that jarring shock which was common to most high-speed motor boats'—perhaps a feature that had also commended the Supermarine product to Fredrickson as he flew in it from a grass field at Martlesham to land on water at Felixstowe.

One can imagine how Mrs Mitchell must have felt at the promising start to her new husband's career, but she had other, more pressing, matters to attend to as their only child, Gordon, was born on 11 November of that year. The new father was now twenty-five and had been chief designer for one year; while it is not known exactly when he was also appointed to the position, it would seem likely that it followed from the 'extraordinary good show' of the Commercial Amphibian that year. The Mitchells now felt able to buy their own house, on Radstock Road, not far from the Supermarine works. Reginald had bought a motorcycle to travel from their first home to the works and Arthur Shirvall, who had joined as an apprentice in 1918, remembered the new father and successful designer: 'at that time R.J. had a motorbike and sidecar, and I remember him driving into the yard on two wheels. He was very good looking and wore breeches and brown gaiters.'

Sea Lion II, Reginald Mitchell (right) with test pilot Biard.

4

Early Military Designs and the Schneider Trophy (1919–1923)

> *In all essentials a standard type suitable for ordinary service duties, but was, nevertheless, able to defeat the specially designed racing machines with which it has to contend.*
>
> Supermarine publicity

Reginald Mitchell's success with the Commercial Amphibian, which was wrecked shortly after the Air Ministry competition by a bad landing, did not immediately further his civil transport imaginings, but it at least brought an order for a military development of this type as part of a ministry policy to assist the struggling aviation companies to stay in business.

This requirement represented a recognition that British air power needed the continued support of a healthy aviation industry especially as, by 1920, the RAF had been in action again with the new military tactic of 'control without occupation'—a very economical and swift-acting alternative to the employment of large army land forces in the policing of colonial and League of Nations mandated territories.

Actions had been required against the Bolsheviks in Russia, against the Afghans on the Indian frontier, and against tribesmen in Mesopotamia, Transjordania, the Sudan, and Somaliland. The Air Estimates of that year accordingly allocated £1,389,950 (compared with £54,282,064 in 1919) for the purchase of aeroplanes, engines, and spares, and recognised that contracts for new, experimental types would have to be spread around the various aviation firms in order to maintain the technical staffs that had been built up. Sopwith had already turned to making motorcycles, and Fairey, Gloster, Blackburn, Shorts, and Bristol were manufacturing bus or car components.

The Seal II: Mitchell's Second Design

In response to the new Air Ministry initiative—Specification 7/20 in particular—Reginald was now required to produce a three-seat amphibian for use as a fleet spotter, to be extremely seaworthy and to have the lowest possible landing speed with good control in order to land on aircraft carriers. His response was known as the Seal II, presumably with the Commercial

Supermarine Seal II (1921)

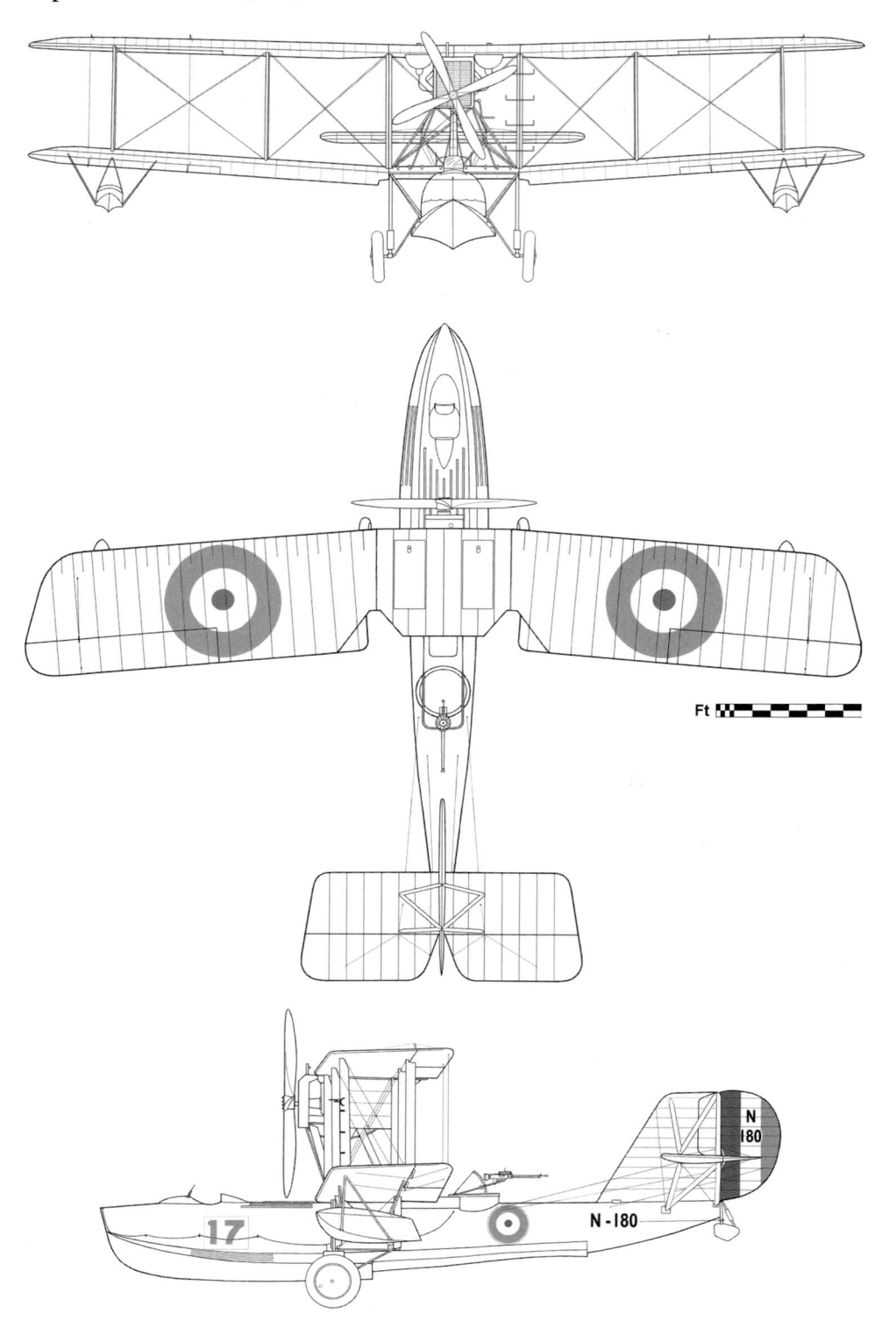

Amphibian being regarded as the Mark I predecessor, which had also been a three-seater, as well as being fitted with a retracting undercarriage.

Certain design changes show Supermarine's young designer eager to improve upon his previous effort and, in particular, its undercarriage geometry, which had attracted criticism. The earlier machine had a structure consisting of two steel tubes, hinged below the lower wing centre-section join with the lower main planes and the wheels were raised or lowered by sideways movements of a tube in the hull to the wheel axles; the new undercarriage now had a single strut, suspended from the lower wing and braced by two tubes hinged to positions on the hull. For retraction, the top of this main strut was moved inwards by means of a worm-and-bevel gear, thus reversing the previous method and siting the retracting mechanism further from the water; it was utilised on all future Supermarine amphibians up to and including the Sheldrake of 1927.

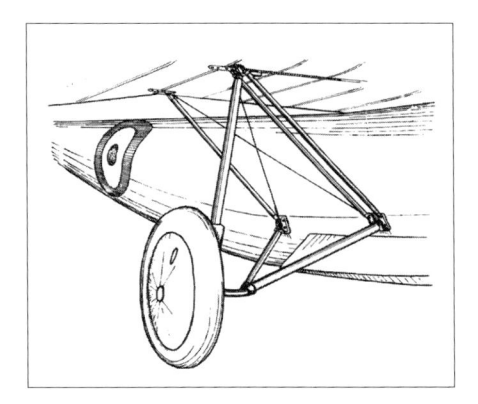

Sketch of Mitchell's improved retraction arrangement—used from the Seal to the Sheldrake.

Seal II at the Supermarine slipway, showing retracted undercarriage.

Reginald also improved on the previous aircraft by siting the tailskid/water rudder at the stern-post; this had the effect of increasing the wing incidence during taxiing and so improved the take-off performance from land or from a carrier deck. A *Flight* commentator noted what had been a further design consideration in the repositioning: 'it is much easier to provide the necessary strength and watertightness than it is with a rudder working in the trunk of the hull'. Also, the wing shape was new and this planform was retained by Mitchell for all his subsequent single-seat naval aircraft up to and including the Sheldrake. The wing-tip floats were less clumsy than before and, because of their decreased side area, were carried on struts to the waterline, thereby saving weight and perhaps decreasing frontal area drag.

The folding wing requirement for a shipboard aircraft had not been tackled by the Supermarine company since the Baby of 1918 and Reginald adopted a similar approach—one which he, again, persisted with in all his military aircraft until the Sheldrake. The forward wing strut at the joint between the wing centre section and the folding main plane was doubled so that one member carried the weight of the leading section of the wing when folded back. In order to keep storage space to a minimum, large cut-outs were made in the trailing edges of the wings so that they could fold close to the plane's centre-line; they were placed further forward than in the Commercial Amphibian in order not to project behind the trailing edges of the tail assembly when folded.

Supermarine Publicity

THE SUPERMARINE AMPHIBIAN 'SEAL MARK II'

The machine depicted in the accompanying illustrations is one of the most recent products of the Supermarine Aviation Works, Ltd, and has been built for the Royal Air Force as a deck landing amphibian for Fleet 'spotting' purposes.

The special requirements for a machine of this type are the lowest possible landing speed combined with a high degree of manoeuvrability at that speed, in order to permit landing on the deck of a seaplane carrier, combined with a very high degree of seaworthiness when used as a seaplane. The results of many tests with this particular machine demonstrate that these requirements and many others have been amply met by the 'Seal'.

Generally, the design of the machine follows standard Supermarine practice. The hull is of the well-known Supermarine circular construction, combining in a high degree the requisites of strength, lightness and resiliency. This hull is fitted with one cockpit right forward for the pilot, and a second, well aft the wings, accommodating in tandem observer and rear gunner, together with such equipment as is required for their use.

The upper wing is flat from end to end, the lower wing has an appreciable dihedral, and carries at its outer extremities a pair of wing-tip floats. Ailerons are fitted to both upper and lower wings.

At the rear end of the hull is mounted the tail unit. This consists of a monoplane tail, of the inverted wing section type, which is braced to the hull by steel tube stays running out to about one-third of the half span on each side. The tail is therefore largely overhung and there is little bracing to restrict the field of fire from the aft gun.

In addition there is a large fin and a balanced rudder, together with a small water-rudder beneath the hull.

> The wheeled undercarriage, which is based on the design used in the very successful Supermarine amphibian which did so well in the Air Ministry Competition, is arranged in such a manner that no landing loads are imposed on the hull structure when the wheels are in use. The loads on the wheels are transmitted through a nearly vertical telescopic strut furnished with shock-absorbers, to the lower wing centre section front spar, immediately under the centre section and engine mounting struts. The wheel axle is carried by a projecting triangular structure of steel tubes hinged to two points on each side of the hull. The nearly vertical strut is movable. When in its nearly vertical position, it maintains the wheels in position for landing. When the top end is withdrawn inboard, the wheels fold up round the hinges on the hull side and take up their position close under the wings and well clear of the water.
>
> The engine is the Napier of 450 hp. The engine mounting is unusual in that it is of the tractor type. This has been rendered possible by the fact that in this case the greater part of the useful load carried is aft of the wings in the tandem cockpits, and the success of the tractor mounting will allow this type of boat to be arranged either as a tractor in such a case as this or as a pusher in cases where the greatest useful load is concentrated forward.
>
> Very great attention has been paid in designing this engine installation to securing accessibility for inspection and adjustment of the engine and its accessories.

Thus, for centre of gravity considerations, and because the aircraft was not designed for passengers, the pilot was situated further forward and was now supplied with a machine gun in the nose that could be retracted and shielded during take-off and landing; the wireless operator was just aft of the wings and the rear gunner behind him, but with the fuel tanks separating the pilot and these other two crew members. As they were to be placed behind the wings, a tractor layout had to be chosen for the engine—also, to prevent the centre of gravity moving too far back. *Flight* believed this to be 'the first British flying boat to be designed as a tractor' and Supermarine's publicity for the Seal (*see* above), draws attention to this placement because of its relative novelty (at least in single-engined machines); after all, the usual pusher configuration kept the propeller as far back as possible, out of the spray generated at take-off or landing.

Supermarine also made the offer of a conventional pusher layout, presumably in the hope of civilian versions that would not, one might reasonably assume, need provision for a gunner and wireless operator behind the wings. Company publicity once more draws attention to its faith in the suitability of the Linton-Hope type of hull construction and its seaworthiness and to the manoeuvrability of the design. Our designer's own improved method of undercarriage retraction is amply described and attention is also drawn to another aspect of his typical concern with the practicality of his machines—in this case, the ease of access to the engine.

The Seal II, N146, first flew in May 1921 and was sent to the Marine and Armament Experimental Establishment (MAEE) on the Isle of Grain in June. Handling problems resulted in its return there in January 1922, when modifications to the tail were found to be more effective. One machine was sold to Japan, a nation keen to be kept abreast of Western technological developments, but no other orders were received. However, the Seal is important to our story as it is the one early Mitchell design that, basically, establishes the pattern for all his later military, medium-sized amphibians, up to and including the well-known Walrus.

Seal II with machine gun in nose.

The Sea King II

While it might be simpler, from a narrative point of view, to consider next the military development of the Seal, culminating in the well-known Walrus, and to have dealt with all the early civil amphibians in another, separate, section, the luxury of such an orderly development of a single type was not available to our new chief designer. Instead, he had found himself being required to produce three distinct types, each with novel requirements, and all conceived and built within the short space of one year. It is thus a more faithful reflection of the way in which Reginald had to respond to Supermarine's perception of the needs of the emerging aviation scene to describe next a third type of machine, the Sea King II.

At least he was on more familiar ground with this particular type as it represented the company's continuing faith in the naval 'scout' concept which had been first evidenced in the Pemberton Billing N.1B Baby. Reginald now produced an amphibian version, designed to meet an Air Ministry interest in a fighter design for shipboard use as company publicity proclaimed:

> A high performance fighting scout, specially adapted for getting off gun-turret platforms of capital ships, or getting off and landing on the decks of aircraft carriers. The strength and design of the hull are such that it can operate on and from the water under any weather conditions in which it would be possible to operate any other sea craft [boats] of equal size.

Supermarine Sea King II (1921)

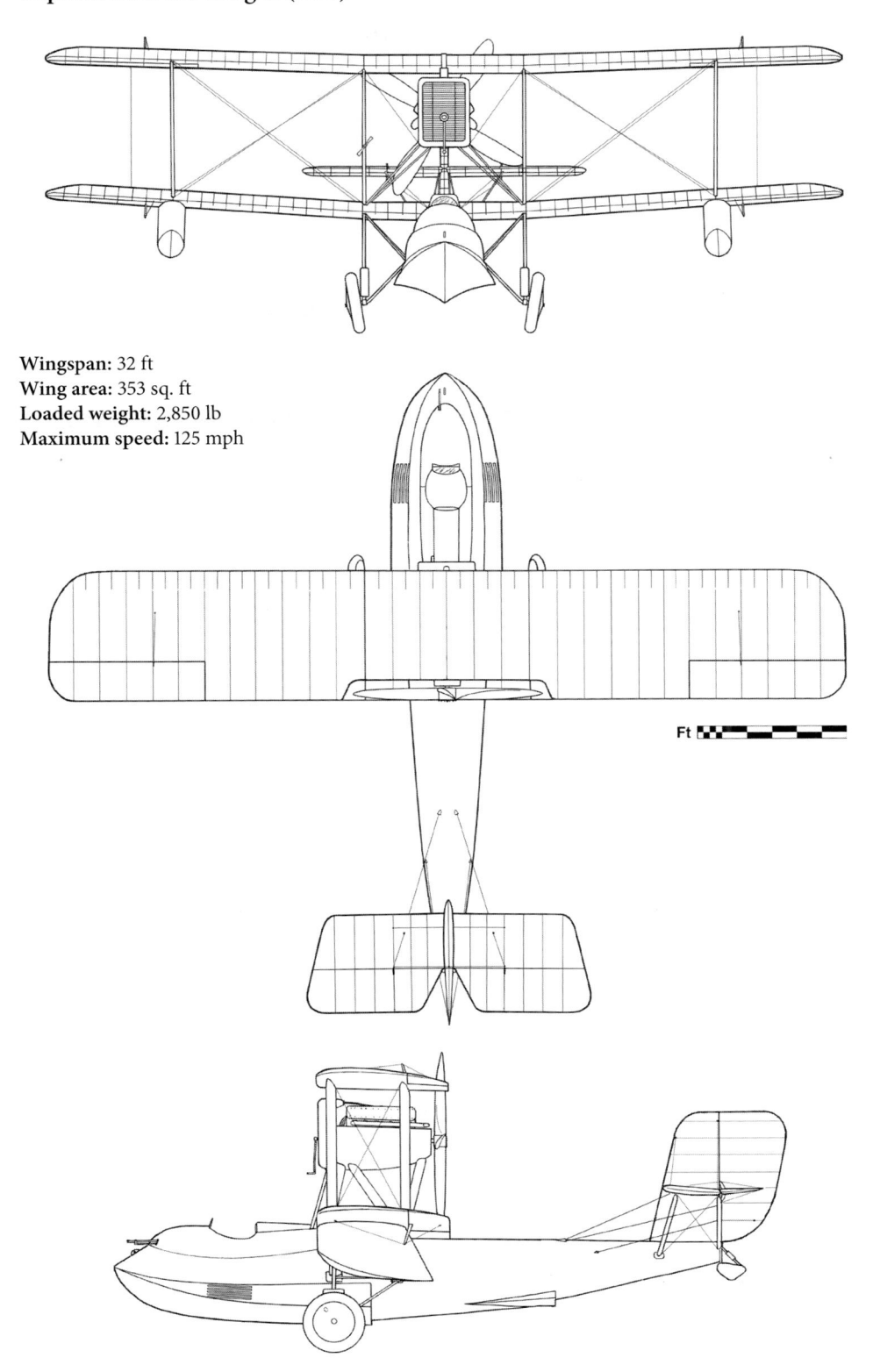

Wingspan: 32 ft
Wing area: 353 sq. ft
Loaded weight: 2,850 lb
Maximum speed: 125 mph

Sea King II, without registration letters, perhaps on taxiing trial.

The Sea King was produced at the end of 1921, after the Seal, but was much more of a direct modification of various earlier Pemberton Billing/Supermarine practices. Nevertheless, its modifications can be attributed entirely to Mitchell; indeed, it bore distinct evidence of his taking over the design department, however small, at Supermarine.

The most obvious revision of the earlier design was the more generous fin and rudder area than that handed down to Hargreaves by the Admiralty team, particularly as the 160-hp Beardmore engine of the Sea King I was now replaced by a much more powerful 300-hp Hispano-Suiza engine. It would appear from the Supermarine publicity quoted #opposite that this redesign had a noticeably beneficial effect.

As with his Seal, the tailplane was now placed almost midway up the fin, the retracting gear of the Seal was again utilised, and a Seal-type combined tailskid and sea rudder was also employed. The aerodynamically balanced ailerons and rudder of Hargreaves' Sea King I were again abandoned; at the same time, Reginald also devised a very simple method for the removal of the undercarriage system which enabled the company to offer the choice of flying boat or amphibian with minimum extra production costs.

Early Military Designs and the Schneider Trophy (1919–1923)

> **Supermarine Publicity**
>
> THE SUPERMARINE 'SEA KING' MARK II
>
> This single-seater amphibian flying boat has been designed as a high-performance fighting scout, specially adapted for getting off gun-turret platforms of capital ships, or getting off and landing on the decks of aircraft carriers.
>
> The strength and design of the hull are such that it can operate on and from the water under any weather conditions in which it would be possible to operate any other sea craft [boat] of equal size.
>
> The manoeuvrability of the 'Sea King' Mark II is one of its most important features. It can be looped, rolled, spun, and stunted in every possible way.
>
> Longitudinally, the machine is neutral, and flying at any speed throughout its entire range either with engine on, gliding, or climbing, no load is felt on the control stick. This balance has been obtained entirely on the stabilising surfaces, and no mechanical adjustment by the pilot is required.
>
> The hull is of circular construction with built-on steps, which can be replaced in case of damage. The steps are divided into watertight compartments, the top side being of single-skin planking, covered with fabric, treated with a tropical doping scheme.
>
> The engine, a 300 hp Hispano Suiza, is mounted in a streamlined nacelle, which contains oil tank, radiator and shutters, piping, controls, etc. The whole unit is very accessible and the engine can be replaced very easily.
>
> Interchangeability and ease of upkeep and repair have been carefully studied. The complete wing structure, including power unit, can be removed from the hull by withdrawing eight bolts. The wing structure consists of top and bottom centre sections, and top and bottom planes of equal span. One set of struts are carried on either side of the centre section. The top planes have a dihedral angle of 1° and the bottom planes one of 3°. The engine unit is carried on two sets of inwardly inclined N struts, and can be removed and replaced without interfering with any wing structure member.
>
> The petrol supply is by pressure, and every effort has been made to reduce the length of piping and eliminate as much as possible the carrying of piping into the hull.
>
> The amphibian undercarriage, which can be removed by the undoing of ten bolts in all, folds up under the wings, and when folded is well clear of the water. It is raised and lowered by a worm and bevel gear.
>
> The pilot's cockpit is in the nose of the boat and gives an almost unobstructed view in every direction. The equipment consists of a complete set of instruments, anchor and cable, bilge pump, towing fairleads and make-fast cleats, boathook, engine and cockpit covers, towing bridle and lifting slings, 'Pyrene' fire-extinguisher, Lewis gun and six double trays of ammunition.
>
> The tail-unit consists of fin and rudder of ample dimensions and a monoplane tail plane with reversed camber.
>
> The steerable tail skid is carried under the extreme end of the hull.

In other ways, the Sea King II continued previous Supermarine practice, particularly the Linton-Hope hull construction: 'with built-on steps, which can be replaced in case of damage … divided into watertight compartments, the top side being of single-skin planking, covered with fabric, treated with a tropical doping scheme'. The wing-tip floats, however, were the same full-depth type as employed on the Baby, Sea Lion I, and Sea King I, and the tailplane outline was similar to that of the Sea Lion I or the Seal II but with the lower position of the latter; its reversed camber continued the Baby method of counteracting nose-down tendencies at higher engine revolutions.

Once more, no orders for this type of aircraft were forthcoming, and with hindsight, it can be seen that the days of the flying-boat fighter were numbered. However, now that Channel aircraft sales were coming to an end, the managing director of Supermarine determined to continue with the fighter flying-boat proposition and sought publicity for it by deciding to enter a more powerful version of the aircraft in the forthcoming Schneider trophy contest.

The Sea Lion II: Mitchell's First Schneider Trophy Success

The previous two Schneider contests, in 1920 and 1921, had taken place in Italy and did not involve any country other than the sponsoring nation. It would appear that Supermarine were justified in not considering the expense of sending their Sea King II to compete in Italy, given their current Channel flying boat activity, as well as the rather precarious nature of these early competitions.

Yet according to the rules of the contest, Italy would win the Schneider trophy outright with a third victory. So, apart for the now more urgent need for publicity, a patriotic reason might have inspired Scott-Paine to consider an entry in 1922. As it turned out, the expected two French entries did not eventually present themselves for the competition and so a Supermarine entry was to become the only machine to try to stop an Italian triumph.

Meanwhile, one of the fortuitous events that influenced the progress of Mitchell's career was the French winning of the Gordon Bennett Cup for landplanes for the third consecutive time in 1920. As with the Schneider contest rules, this last win gave permanent possession to the winning country and, thus, despite the poor attendances in the fourth and fifth events, the Schneider trophy contest had ended up as the only international speed competition left. This would obviously suit Supermarine very well because of their concentration on seaplanes and, in particular, on flying boats because the recent contests had set the trend for entering this type of machine rather than any improvised landplane.

In addition, the rules had been changed in 1920 to encourage a more practical type of aircraft rather than an out-and-out racer: 300 kg of ballast had had to be carried and this favoured flying-boat designs; in fact, the winner that year had coped very well with appalling weather during the preliminary navigability trials. Although the ballast requirement was dropped in the following year, it was replaced by a watertightness test in which the aircraft had to remain afloat fully loaded for six hours after the navigability tests. Again, this rule tended to suggest the flying boat's suitability for the trophy contest, and it had no doubt been noted that the recent Italian designs to meet these requirements were, indeed, flying boats and that those which had failed had only done so because of over-ambitious power uprating.

Despite these favourable omens, any flying-boat entry from Supermarine was unlikely to have any financial backing from the British government, and the uncertain financial outlook of the Supermarine company at this time was such that, when its managing director did decide to enter an aircraft, he obtained the loan of a Lion engine from the manufacturers and a high-speed propeller, petrol, and oil from other companies; he had also negotiated a reduction in insurance rates.

Supermarine Sea Lion II (1922)

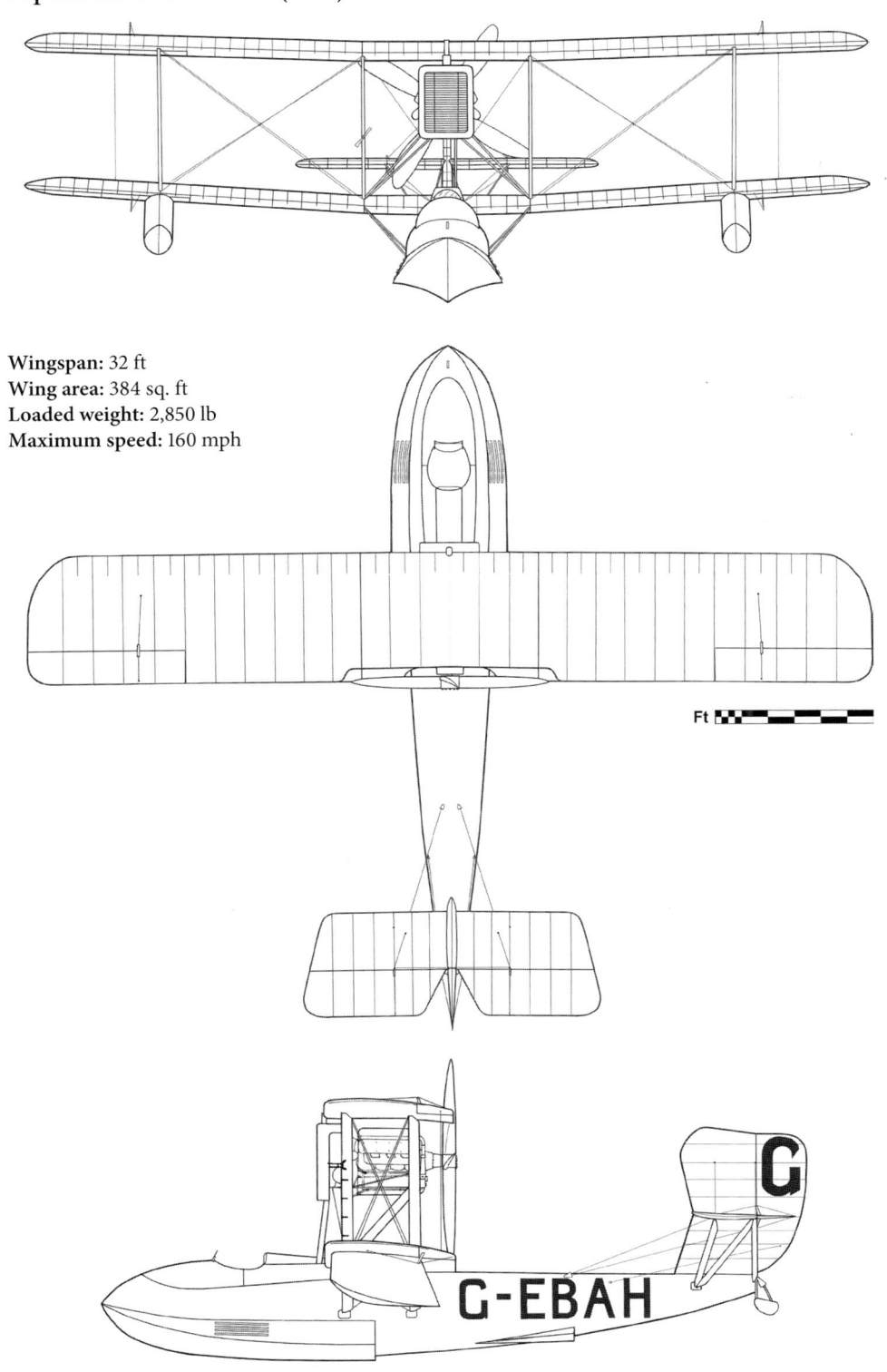

Wingspan: 32 ft
Wing area: 384 sq. ft
Loaded weight: 2,850 lb
Maximum speed: 160 mph

Scott-Paine also negotiated with the Royal Aero Club for the payment of the competition entry fee and, shortly afterwards, a payment of £100 towards the Company's costs. Nor was the company intending to incur the cost of designing and building an entirely new airframe. The fuselage of the salvaged Sea Lion I was with the Science Museum at South Kensington and so the fuselage of the Sea King II (which, in any case, was aerodynamically cleaner) was utilised.

Mitchell, no doubt having taken note of the sleek Savoia machine at the Bournemouth competition, aimed for increased speed by making the entry of the fuselage somewhat smoother (it was originally shaped to house a gun—*see* drawing p. 63), and his simplified method for the removal of the undercarriage system also enabled the hull to be easily stripped of the extra weight and drag of this item. Also, as the Napier replacement developed 150 hp more than the Hispano-Suiza engine originally fitted, he was able to decrease the area, and therefore the drag, of the wings by reducing their width.

However, it would appear that he revealed his inexperience of wooden structures, as Cozens reported:

> When the new racer was taken out on to the quay and the powerful Napier was run up, Captain Biard took one look at the vibrating tail and said he would never fly that aeroplane, but, with typical press-on spirit the riggers wrapped doped fabric round the fuselage and made the whole unit stiffer.

Sea Lion II fuselage with Napier Lion engine (Mitchell to right of Scott-Paine). For further photograph of the Sea Lion, *see* p. 25.

In response to the extra power of the engine, an additional increase in fin area was also called for. Reginald achieved this with least expenditure of time and money by merely modifying the vertical surfaces above the tailplane—the leading edge of the fin was given a pronounced forward curvature which proved to be effective but his pragmatism certainly won no prizes for elegance (*see* photo p. 25). It was also more cluttered with struts and wires than the Macchi M.7 which had not been a particularly impressive winner in the previous competition.

Although the finished machine was, in essence, Mitchell's Sea King, it was now named 'Sea Lion', in order to provide publicity for the loaned engine. It was also designated a Mark II, to distinguish it from Hargreaves' earlier design, but as a result, this misleadingly suggested that it was a direct development of it, contrary to its actual pedigree.

Due to bad weather and the date of the competition being put forward by fourteen days, there was little time to test out the result of Reginald's modifications. Indeed, there was a distinct possibility that the Sea Lion would not survive to compete at all, for Biard barely avoided crashing into a litter of ships when his engine stopped 200 feet above Southampton Docks on the take-off of his very first test flight.

Then Supermarine ran into difficulties over the delivery of the aircraft to the Naples venue; most fortunately, the General Steam Navigation Co., with whom Scott-Paine had business contacts, came to the rescue with SS *Philomel* which was diverted specially to Naples, with the aircraft and personnel, free of charge. Yet persistence with the challenge was justified as the test flying had shown that the machine was not only very manoeuvrable but was capable of coming close to the 160-mph target thought by Scott-Paine to be necessary for a win, given the indifferent showing of the Italians in the previous two competitions.

On arrival, Biard once more nearly came to grief when he flew the Sea Lion over Vesuvius, where the 'thermal' from the crater swept him upwards and left him several miles away before he could find his way back. He was a notorious practical joker but his undoubted professional skills were then well-exemplified in Naples. Putting sightseeing behind him, Biard gave the Italian opposition no clue as to the real capability of his aircraft by taking the corners of the competition circuit widely in practice whenever he thought he was being observed. He also kept his practice speeds close to that expected of the machine in Italian aviation circles—the estimated speed of the Sea King I with a Napier Lion engine had been 141 mph and that achieved by the Sea Lion I had been 147 mph.

The Sixth Schneider Trophy Contest, 12 August 1922 at Naples

The rules for 1922 were similar to those of the previous year with the navigability tests involving taxiing over the start/finish line, ascending and alighting, taxiing for half a mile twice at no less than 12 mph, flying round the circuit, and taxiing again over the line. These requirements were followed by the newly introduced six-hour flotation test and the course was new, consisting of thirteen laps instead of the previous sixteen. As the distance overall was to be 200 nautical miles, the longer straights, with only three corners, would obviously be good news for the faster machines—the Sea Lion's Napier engine was 150 hp more powerful than that of the rival Italian Savoia S.51 and 190 hp more than the engine of the Macchi M.7 and M.17.

After their previous experiences, the Italians had not opted for ambitious engine upratings but had put their faith in airframe innovations. All three Italian aircraft embodied the tried

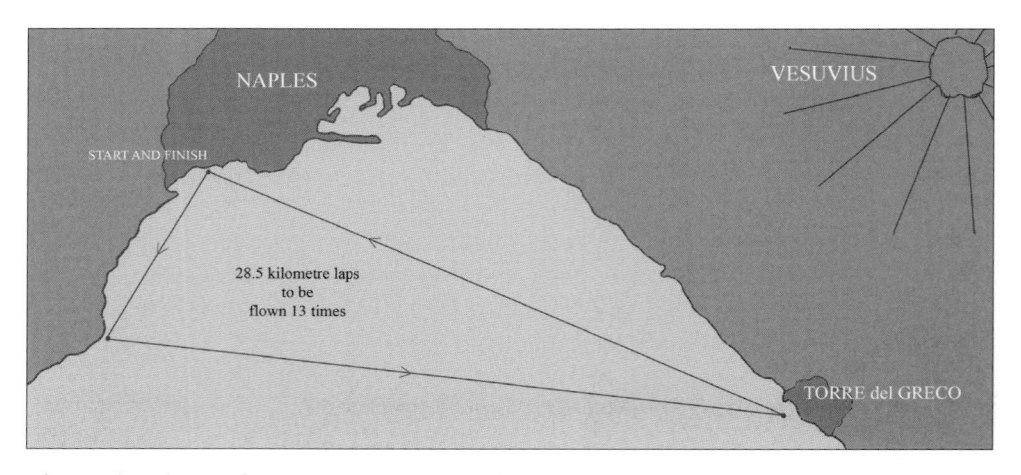

Above: Schneider Trophy contest course, 1922. *Below:* Savoia S.51.

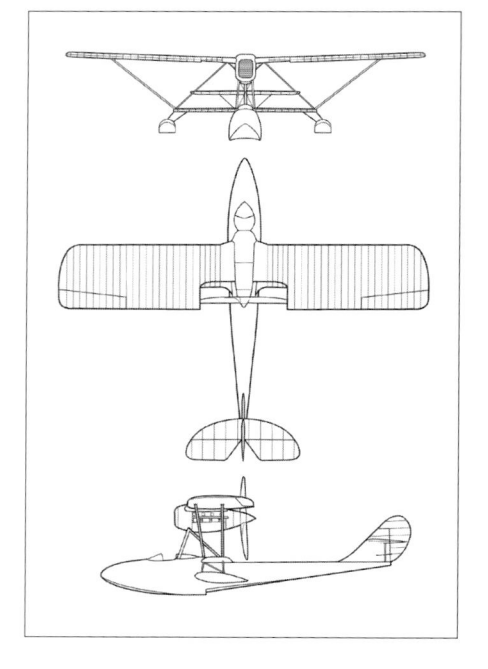

and tested approach of previous models but the hulls were even sleeker and the engine nacelles more streamlined. In addition, the S.51 also had a much smaller lower wing. This 'sesquiplane' arrangement was designed to reduce 'biplane interference' caused by lower pressure above the bottom wing affecting the higher pressure below the upper wing. A supporting lower wing, however, was still felt necessary to give structural integrity to the upper one but at least the new configuration allowed the removal of drag-inducing wire bracing.

Unfortunately, the short span of the lower wing, allied with the high-mounted engine and the small volume tip floats, resulted in the S.51 capsizing in a squall during the six-hour mooring-out test. Sportingly, Scott-Paine raised no objection to its being salvaged and returned to the contest, contrary to the actual rules of the competition. Due to the heat, the contest was delayed until 4 p.m. when Biard, in shirtsleeves and flannel trousers, took off; despite the time required by his take-off, Biard's first lap was calculated to have been flown at over 150 mph thanks to the Lion engine having just been re-tuned to suit the local conditions.

The Italians now realised that the Macchis could not compete if Biard kept going at that rate and so, according to various accounts, including Biard's 'ghosted' autobiography, they tried to prevent the Englishman from getting round them by flying close together in order to make overtaking difficult. The consistent claims by Supermarine for the exceptional manoeuvrability of their 'scout' flying boat type were then demonstrated when, as Biard narrated, he was able to close up, keep control in their prop wash, pull upwards, and dive

Sea Lion II rounding a course-marker balloon.

round and ahead of them at full throttle. Unfortunately, a more recent book records lap details that suggest his overtaking in this way was confined to Zanetti's M.17; another author notes that Biard passed Zanetti once and Corgnolino twice; in neither account did he encounter the Italians bunched together.

Whatever the truth of the matter, it is at least certain that Biard was able to ease back to avoid overtaxing his engine; as a result, his sixth lap was only six seconds better than that of Passaleva's S.51, then on its fourth lap. Yet its previous ducking had affected the bonding of the propeller's wooden laminations and so the Italian machine had to be flown with the engine throttled back to avoid excessive vibrations.

As Mitchell's upratings had produced a straight-line speed of about 160 mph—nearly 30 per cent faster than his Sea King II—he was thus able to taste the sweet pleasure of success with his design winning the Schneider trophy race for Britain at an average speed of 145.7 mph. Biard flew an additional two laps, gaining the following first FAI World Records for seaplanes:

(i.) Duration—1 hr 34 min. 51.6 sec.
(ii.) Distance flown—230 miles
(iii.) Fastest time for 100 km closed circuit—28 min. 41.4 sec. (130 mph)
(iv.) Fastest time for 200 km closed circuit—57 min. 37.4 sec. (129.4 mph).

On the victor's return to Southampton, Cozens described the reactions of the Supermarine workers who had run down to meet them:

They had taken the two swivel chairs from the office and fixed them to poles and they lifted Captain Biard and Scott-Paine in the chairs shoulder high and carried them round the works … Fireworks were let off and there was some horn blowing.

One suspects that Reginald's relatively recent arrival in the firm at the time as well as his temperamental self-effacingness account for there being no mention of him in the celebrations.

City dignitaries turned out in full ceremonial dress in recognition of Supermarine's international success. In their subsequent publicity, Supermarine tried to capitalise on their achievement by pointing out (rather disingenuously) that the aircraft was, basically, a standard machine:

> The machine is in general essentials of the same design as the 'Sea King' type already described, but is fitted with the Napier 'Lion' engine of 450 hp.
>
> The fact that the machine was in all essentials a standard type suitable for ordinary service duties, but was, nevertheless, able to defeat the specially designed racing machines with which it had to contend, is a very great tribute to the excellence of Supermarine design.

Nevertheless, our designer would have been only too aware that the Savoia S.51 should really have been the winner had it not been for the handicap of a damaged propeller, and this with an engine only two-thirds as powerful. One also wonders if Scott-Paine, bearing in mind his indebtedness to sponsors, would have been so sporting as to allow it to compete if he had known what the S.51 was really capable of. Later, on 22 December of that year, it captured the world speed record for seaplanes at 174.08 mph. No military orders resulted for the Sea Lion or for a development of the type, although all was not lost as the aircraft was purchased by the Air Ministry and used for research into high-speed seaplanes.

Nor were there any orders forthcoming for Reginald's Seal II fleet spotter, and the company had to come to terms with the post-war Anti-Waste League and the resultant work of the Geddes Committee Report which led to a slashing of all government expenditure. While, at the armistice, the RAF had been the largest air force in the world, the new secretary of state for air, Sir Samuel Hoare, reported that, by 1923, only 371 front-line aircraft remained, either in the British Isles or abroad, and assessed the current situation thus:

> Orders for military planes had almost come to an end and a demand for civil planes did not yet exist ... Only two thousand five hundred men and women were left in the industry and the few firms engaged on machines and engines were on the verge of closing down.

On the other hand, the actions mentioned earlier of 'control without occupation' had needed to be backed up by support for the ailing aircraft industry if there were to be an adequate response from the currently depleted provision abroad. At home, it had been accepted that over the next five years, thirty-four new squadrons should be formed, bringing the air defence of Great Britain up to fifty-two squadrons by 1928.

In the event, the home squadron numbers only rose to thirty-four by the date proposed but at least the 1923 Air Estimates of £10,783,000 had risen incrementally to £16,042,000 by this time. Also, five new aircraft carriers were being built or redeveloped from battlecruisers—HMS *Eagle*, *Hermes*, *Glorious*, *Courageous*, and *Furious*. Here at least was some slender encouragement to continue trading, even for Reginald's naval types.

The Seagull II

The first positive result of the new situation was felt by Supermarine when Commander James Bird, who had joined its board in 1919, approached Air Vice-Marshal Sir Geoffrey Salmond, then air member for supply and research at the Air Ministry. As a result, Bird received a formal reply that 'it might be inexpedient' to close down the works entirely as they were considering an order, 'the exact amount of which cannot yet be stated, but which might approach eighteen machines, spread over the period ending March 31st, 1924'.

Here was another piece of good fortune in Reginald Mitchell's journey towards the Spitfire, even though this Air Ministry lifeline came with the very cautious initial order for only two aircraft. These were completed by March 1922 and named Seagull II—the Seal II, confusingly, being its actual Mark I. The original fin had now been modified, as a result of the first aircraft's visit to the MAEE at Grain, and it was later again increased in area, in view of the more powerful Napier Lion II engine fitted, again in a tractor layout. After the two new aircraft—N158 and N159—were completed, the type was displayed in the same year at the third annual RAF Pageant, Hendon.

One particular improvement of the aircraft ought to be mentioned—Reginald had now moved the fuel tanks from the fuselage to positions under the centre section of the top wing, supplying petrol to the engine by gravity feed. During the First World War, the Felixstowe flying boats, which had fuel tanks conventionally placed in the fuselage, had suffered many forced landings from blocked pipes and fuel-pump failures; a later Supermarine comment on the Sea King II design acknowledged the problem and assured potential buyers that every effort had been made 'to reduce the length of piping and eliminate as much as possible the carrying of piping into the hull'. Had the First World War continued after 1918, such petrol feed problems would, no doubt, have been more speedily overcome by adopting gravity feed, but it is a reflection of the very slow pace of aircraft development after the Armistice that Supermarine drew particular attention to their adoption of gravity feed as late as 1922, with Reginald's latest design.

It is understandable that there would be stability considerations associated with placing large (and heavy) amounts of fuel under the top wing. For example, the Fairey Fawn (which had large tanks on its top wings) was described in 1923 by its Martlesham test pilot, H. F. V. Battle, as 'a shocker', being 'unstable fore and aft as well as laterally'. Reginald must have realised that Supermarine's suspended boat-like hulls made possible the new higher fuel arrangements without such stability problems, although there was the inconvenience of filling the tanks in the higher position, especially when a seaplane was not on a slipway.

Nevertheless, there was an additional important bonus—Supermarine was now able to announce that 'inter-communication between crew has been considered fully, and a through passage is arranged for this purpose'. Thus its chief designer was not only solving possible supply problems from petrol in lower positions but was also making an important step forward in the matter of crew communication. In passing, it should be noted that the constructional methods of the Linton-Hope hull had no structural bulkheads to be weakened or bracing wires to be forfeited by cutting through a passageway between the pilot and the other crew members.

A competitive test on the older HMS *Argus* between the Seagull and the Mark VII version of the Viking (whose predecessor had competed successfully with Mitchell's Commercial Amphibian in 1920) had found in favour of Mitchell's machine, and an RAF order for five

Supermarine Seagull II (1922)

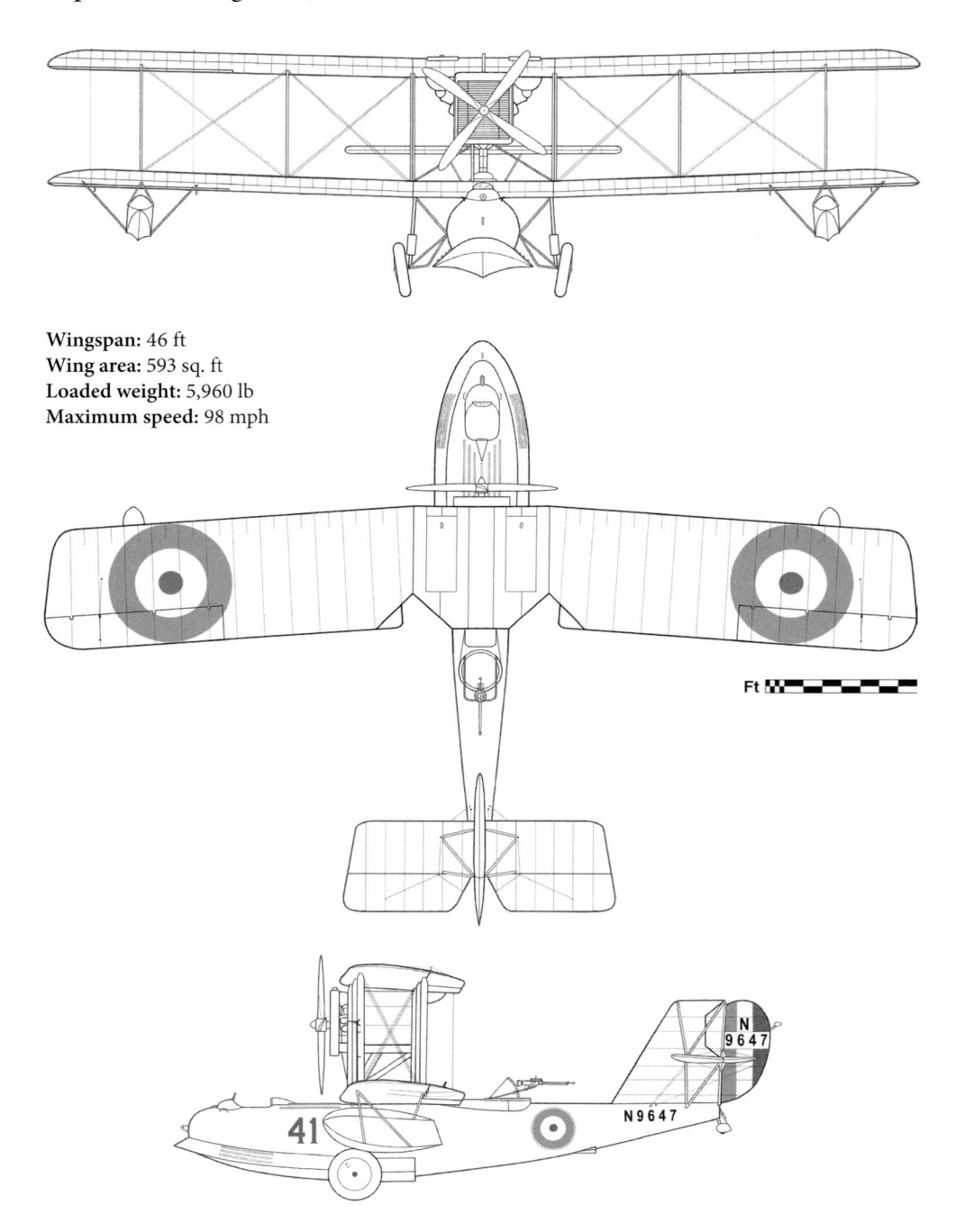

Wingspan: 46 ft
Wing area: 593 sq. ft
Loaded weight: 5,960 lb
Maximum speed: 98 mph

A Seagull II with Mitchell (left) and Biard.

Seagulls, N9562 to N9566, was received in September 1922. The under-secretary of state for air, the air vice-marshal, and the director of research visited the Supermarine works on 23 February 1923 to view the progress of the order. In the following year, a further order for five additional Seagulls (N9603 to 9607) was received; this was followed by a requirement for another thirteen (N9642 to N9654).

These aircraft equipped No. 440 (RAF) Fleet Reconnaissance Flight and some were placed aboard the recently commissioned aircraft carrier HMS *Eagle*. An additional machine was again sold to Japan. By this time, the wing-tip floats had been redesigned, the wings given a slight sweep back, the ailerons redesigned, and the fin area further enlarged.

The eventual sale of twenty-six of the machines was to be the largest of a company product since its designer had joined Supermarine and the transition from unproven beginner to winner of contracts and of an international competition must by now have begun to mark Mr Mitchell out as a man to watch, although his contribution to the next Schneider trophy contest was not to be auspicious.

The first Seagull II of the original order.

Seagull II of 440 Flight, off south coast of Malta. Note rungs on rear centre-section strut, for access to fuel tanks.

Sea Lion III: An Unhappy Return to the Schneider Competition

As the next Trophy contest was to be held in England, it was to be expected that Supermarine would be only too happy to capitalise on their 1922 publicity by competing, successfully it was hoped, without the cost of overseas travel and accommodation. Indeed, they could hardly have been better sited as the competition base was to be at the Saunders factory on the Isle of Wight, less than 20 miles from the Supermarine works at Woolston.

However, the company was now fully engaged in fulfilling the order for the first two batches of Seagulls and was not likely to be interested in designing and building a one-off specialist racer. As the top speed of the Sea Lion II was significantly less than that of the Italian record-breaking S.51, and as America was known to be preparing a formidable challenge, Scott-Paine did not immediately respond. Later, when he was persuaded to submit an entry, he confined himself to asking his chief designer to do his best with the previous year's Sea Lion II airframe.

Mitchell designed new wing-tip floats, which offered less frontal area, mounted them on streamlined struts, and added fairings around the main strut attachment points. As more power was to be available from a new engine, the rudder and fin were increased in area, with the resultant redesign looking somewhat like an extension of his early Sea King II outline and certainly less improvised than that of the Sea Lion II.

He fitted an uprated Napier Lion III engine and radiator into a more streamlined nacelle and the more powerful engine also allowed for a reduction in the wingspan by four feet; he also had fairings made behind the two hull steps, which might have inhibited the ability of the aircraft to take off, had it not been for the extra power now available. Nevertheless, his changes could hardly prevent the Supermarine entry from showing its, by now, venerable pedigree—as did the second British entry, the Blackburn Pellet, which was, like the Sea Lion, based on a hull built for the 1918 N.1B contract. A third entry from Hawker was to be a further uprated version of the Sopwith Schneider machine of 1919.

This impoverished showing prompted requests in parliament and in the press for government assistance with the building of new machines. However, no help was forthcoming, even though it was known that America, at least, was sending three government-sponsored aircraft which might show up the British entries in front of a large British crowd, likely to match the size of that which had turned out at Naples on the previous occasion.

It meanwhile became apparent that Italy would have had to rely solely on last year's S.51 because of economic and political problems; but, as C. G. Grey commented, 'there is no Italian entry due to the volcanic state of the Italian people'. Also, the Hawker aircraft was written off, following a dead-stick forced landing, and the Pellet sank in the tricky tidal waters of the Humber. It was salvaged and crated to Cowes but arrived without time for air-testing until the day before the navigation tests were to start; it was then found to be excessively nose-heavy and prone to engine overheating. While the trim problem was corrected without too much difficulty, the solution to the overheating required the bypassing of innovative wing radiators and the substitution of large draggy Lamblin radiators.

Stiffer opposition appeared to be coming from the French whose two state-supported Latham L.1 flying boats were each powered by two 400-hp engines mounted in tandem. They got as far as flying over to England for the contest, but one experienced loss of power in gale conditions and suffered such damage as to be eliminated; the second sheared a magneto drive

Supermarine Sea Lion III (1923)

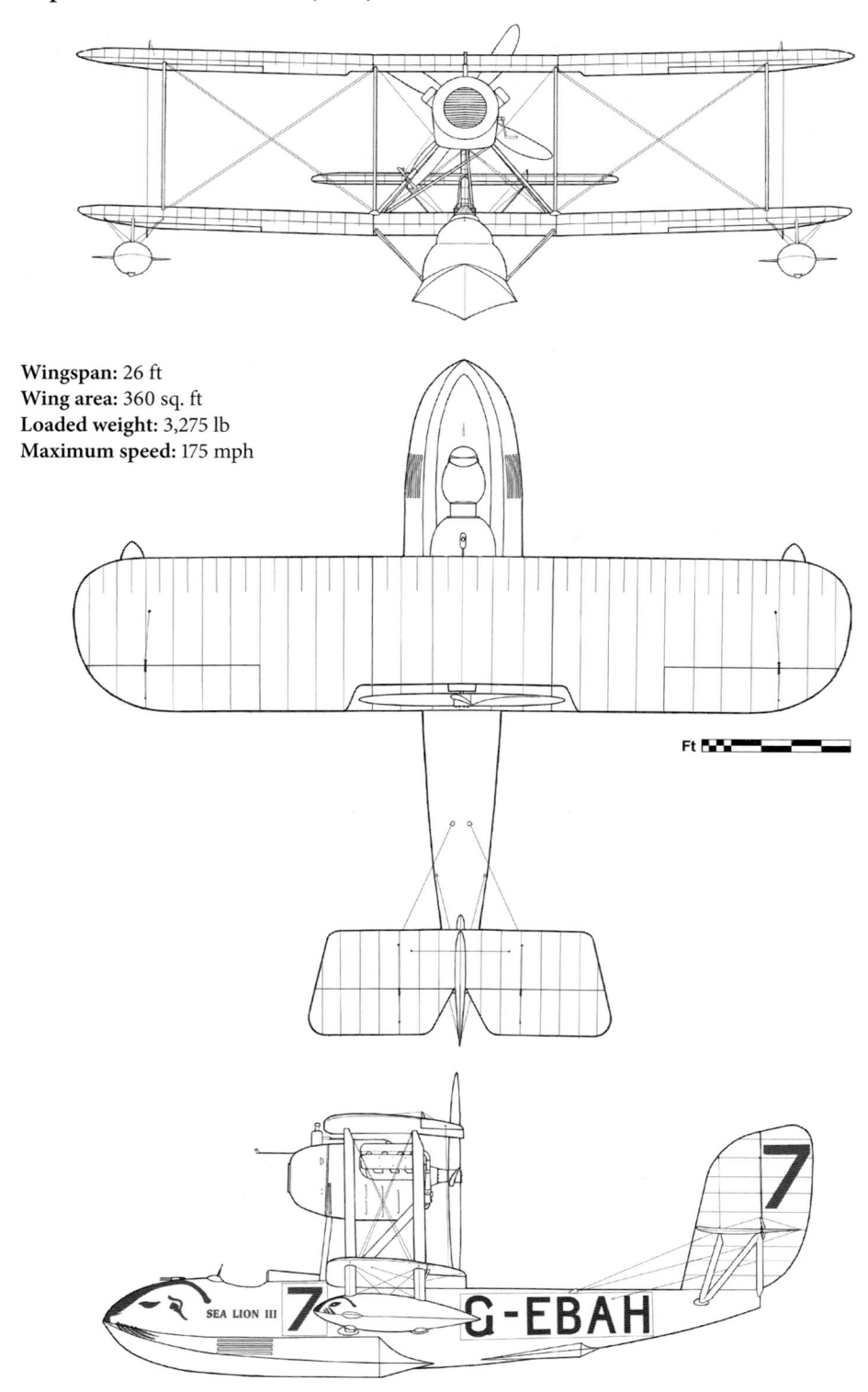

Wingspan: 26 ft
Wing area: 360 sq. ft
Loaded weight: 3,275 lb
Maximum speed: 175 mph

Supermarine Sea Lion III at Cowes, 1923. Biard is in the cockpit and fuselage 'all painted up to represent its name'.

at the outset of the contest and was also out of the competition. There were also two CAMS flying boats of traditional design, very similar to the Italian Savoias S.12 and 51 or the Macchi M.7, but their 360-hp engines were much less powerful than the now uprated 550-hp of the Sea Lion's Napier power plant.

As it turned out, one of the French machines, which had survived to compete, collided with a yacht and the damage to its hull put it out of the contest; also, the Blackburn Pellet sank after serious porpoising on take-off. Perhaps, therefore the Supermarine entry with an obsolescent aircraft might do better than expected, although one feels that the rather whimsical sea lion motif painted on the nose and floats was something of a self-deprecating gesture in the face of the expected serious opposition from America.

Prior to the 1923 contest, the Americans had not competed in the Schneider trophy competitions. In 1921, the US Navy contracted with the Curtiss Aeroplane and Motor Co. for the development of a pursuit (fighter) plane, the CR-1. It was soon to be tested in the newly established Pulitzer Trophy Race for landplanes and won at an average speed of 176.6 mph.

The US Army then took over the development of the Curtiss racers which were then fitted with of one of the great aero engines in aviation history, the Curtiss D-12, whose frontal area was about 50 per cent less than that of the rival Napier Lion; it was also delivering 465 hp with a power ratio of 1 lb per hp. The winning of the 1922 Pulitzer race with this engine was also due to the incorporation of radiators flush-mounted on the aircraft wings and to the use of metal propellers (the newer engines were producing airscrew tip speeds approaching the speed of sound, for which thicker, wooden blades were beginning to prove inadequate).

As racing brought about significant technical advances in aeronautical engineering and design, it was fortunate for Mitchell and the future Spitfire that the Pulitzer Trophy never established the same international following that the Schneider trophy did for seaplanes. Nevertheless, one effect of these races was immediately apparent—the American CR-3 entries also brought floatplane design back into the competition again. At the time, this reversion might not, in itself, have seemed a clear aerodynamic choice but rather the result of America capitalising on their landplane racing designs, which meant that landing wheels had, of necessity, to be replaced with floats.

The Seventh Schneider Trophy Contest, 28 September 1923 at Cowes

Perhaps the British government might have been persuaded to follow the French example and give some backing to Supermarine and other British aircraft firms had they known how the American challenge was to be conducted. Instead of leaving the competing to the various firms supplying the aircraft, the Americans gave the responsibility for

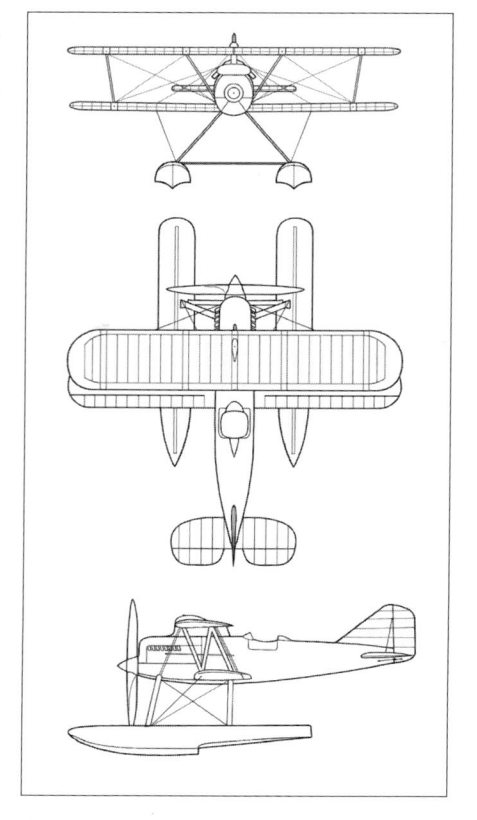

Curtiss CR-3.

the event to the US Navy, which, predictably, approached the contest as a military operation, bringing with them an impressive array of equipment and neatly uniformed support crews, several weeks in advance of the competition date; a large warship, the USS *Pittsburgh*, flagship of Naval Forces Europe, anchored off Cowes. At their disposal were four aircraft: a naval Aircraft Factory TR-3A (a carrier-based fighter), two of the specially designed Curtiss CR-3s, and a formidable Navy/Wright NW-2 racing design, with an engine reported to deliver 700 hp, which would have made it the highest-powered single-engined floatplane in the world. The American pilots were all navy fliers and had been practising since early July and thus gaining adequate familiarisation time with the new race aircraft.

Nevertheless, not all went smoothly for them. Four days before the contest, the powerful engine of the NW-2 blew up on a full-throttle test flight, and then, on 27 September, the day of the navigability tests, the American reserve machine, the TR-3A, had to be withdrawn due to a failure of its starting gear. The contestants who remained completed the navigability tests successfully and prepared for the flying contest. As the remaining two American aircraft had performed perfectly well in the calm conditions of the 27th, there was always the hope that poorer weather on the next day might not be so kind to their new, possibly more fragile, floatplanes. Yet there were good sea conditions on the next day and so the contest between the remaining two American and the single British and French aircraft would be decided by speed and reliability, not by the weather.

Early Military Designs and the Schneider Trophy (1919–1923)

From left to right: Curtiss CR-3, Sea Lion III, and CAMS 38 at the Saunders base, Cowes.

The Royal Aero Club had originally announced that, by lot, the flying order would be Italy, America, Britain, and France, with each team taking off as a group at fifteen-minute intervals. As the Italians had not shown, the first American took off at 11 a.m.; at 11.15, Biard, who was then manoeuvring for take-off, was astonished to see the Americans completing their first laps, indicating something like a 170-mph lap, including crossing the start line on the water.

The engine of the surviving CAMS machine failed on the second lap; of the three finishing machines, that of Lt David Rittenhouse came first, with an average speed of 177.3 mph, and the aircraft of Lt Rutledge Irvine was second with an average of 173.46 mph. Biard was thought to have become airborne before crossing the starting line and was disqualified. James Bird, a director of Supermarine, had forcefully protested and it was eventually ruled that Biard had only been making several bounces prior to the actual take-off. Nevertheless, the reinstatement was somewhat academic as, despite 75 more horsepower, Biard could only manage an average of 157.17 mph and so his Sea Lion had been well beaten into third place.

It must now have been very clear to Mitchell that an aircraft with a formidable in-line engine and propeller combination and cooled by flush-fitted wing radiators was going to be hard to beat; it must also have been clear to him that the European flying-boat approach with an engine mounted above the hull was no longer likely to be

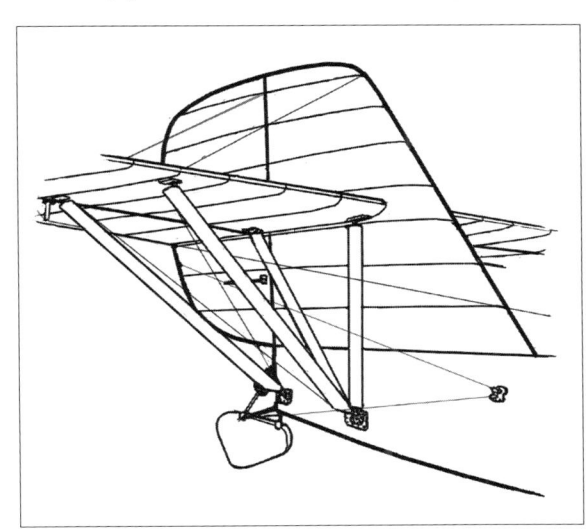

Sketch of typical Supermarine empennage from Sea Lion I (1919) to Scarab (1924).

competitive. The American configuration, despite the drag of floats, allowed for a less bulky fuselage and for an engine to be neatly cowled so as to merge into the streamlines of the fuselage. No doubt Mitchell had also noted that the Curtiss CR-3 designer, despite the necessity of float struts and bracings, had limited the number of certain drag-inducing items to sixteen struts, with twenty wires, whereas the Sea Lion tradition he had inherited had required thirty-three struts and forty-two wires.

At the end of the race, Biard made a consolatory gesture by pulling up to a considerable height and then descending in a series of tight spirals before alighting in front of the British crowd. In a speech afterwards, Scott-Paine praised the Napier engine 'that would have gone on for ever' and said that he felt the need 'to apologise to Capt. Biard because we did not give him a good enough machine'. Afterwards, Supermarine strove to keep up Air Ministry interests for a military version of their aircraft, drawing attention once again to the aircraft's strength, seaworthiness, manoeuvrability, and its essential military specification (the racing aircraft being still referred to as a 'fighting scout'):

> This single-seater amphibian flying boat has been designed as a high performance fighting scout, specially adapted for getting off gun platforms of capital ships, or getting off and landing on decks of aircraft carriers ... The fact that the machine was in all essentials a standard type suitable for ordinary service duties but was, nevertheless, able to defeat the specially designed racing machines with which it had to contend, is a very great tribute to the excellence of Supermarine design.
>
> The 'Sea Lion' Mark III was third in the Schneider Cup Race, 1923, and completed the triangular course at an average speed of 157 mph. For this race the machine was generally cleaned up in design, but was still a service type machine and by no means a specially designed racing machine. The maximum speed over a straight course is 175 mph.

Sea Lion III taking off and 'on the step'.

The Sea Lion, which had retained the Mark II registration G-EBAH, was returned as N170 to the MAEE at Grain with its undercarriage now restored, some of its hull fairings removed, and its whimsical markings painted out, but its career was short-lived, owing to its extremely lively take-off performance. When he first saw the aircraft, Biard had predicted that 'she was going to be a bit playful to get off the water' and so '"gave it the gun" from the start, took a phenomenally short run on the water and went straight into the air with speed enough to climb straight away'. As he reported, 'It was an interesting sensation; you switched on the engine, and before you could count 1, 2, 3, 4, fast—she was flying.'

Unfortunately, on 25 June the next year, an air force test pilot, Flg Off. E. E. Paull-Smith, did not appear to appreciate the lively character of the aircraft at take-off. As a result, he took off and fell back onto the water, rose to about 40 feet, stalled again, and dived into the sea. The pilot became the only fatality at the MAEE between the wars, and the machine was too extensively damaged to be considered worth restoring.

The Air Ministry placed no orders for a seaplane scout with Supermarine and this incident marked the end of Supermarine's attempts to interest the Air Ministry in such a concept. It also marked the beginning of Mitchell's portentous search for a worthy and dedicated Schneider trophy competitor.

HRH Edward, Prince of Wales with Reginald Mitchell and the Swan flying boat.

5

Multitasking
(1923–1924)

Seaplane travel will be one of the first methods of aerial locomotion.

Lord Apsley

While the military Seal II was being developed into the Seagull II and the Sea Lion II turned into the Sea Lion III, Supermarine had begun to see possibilities of again producing and selling civil aircraft. The Air Estimates now included an allocation for civil aviation, although it represented something less than 2.5 per cent of the total sum.

Mitchell's design team was also expanding. Arthur Shirvall, who had joined as an apprentice in 1918, was now entrusted with drawing up the ship lines for flying boat hulls; Joe Smith, later to become chief designer after Mitchell, had joined in 1922 as an additional draughtsman; and Alan Clifton was seen by Mitchell in the same year with a view to assisting with stress calculations. Mitchell decided to carry on this work without his help, but the developing work at Woolston saw him finally appointed the following year. He later succeeded Joe Smith as chief designer. Supermarine was thus able to contend successfully for an increased volume of work and Mitchell found himself even busier and, such was the still precarious nature of the aviation industry, having to apply himself to many different types of aircraft.

The first of these had been presented to him in the midst of his Sea Lion Schneider trophy activities when the Air Ministry gave approval for an air service between Southampton, Cherbourg and Le Havre. The route, with a subsequent extension to the Channel Isles, was to be operated by an air service named the British Marine Air Navigation Company and Hubert Scott-Paine and James Bird were to be its directors. Not surprisingly, the first Supermarine aircraft for this service was already being built when the Air Ministry granted the company a subsidy of £10,000 and agreed to pay £21,000 for aircraft and spares (later revised substantially downwards as the air miles generated were less than the Company had undertaken to fly).

The Sea Eagles

In so far as Mitchell had any control of what he was required to design for his company, he must have welcomed this new commercial amphibian project as being far more significant than his Schneider trophy work, successful or otherwise; designing aircraft for military purposes might keep him and his company in work, but developing civilian aerial transport was the real brave new world.

The aircraft for the new service was to be powered by the Rolls-Royce Eagle IX engine and thus Supermarine were able to continue the company's practice of finding maritime animal names beginning with 's' which, if possible, incorporated the name of the engine to be used. For the new 'Sea Eagle', Mitchell reverted to the customary pusher configuration for single-engined flying boats and went back to the more boat-like hull shape of the larger Channel and Commercial Amphibian designs. In fact, it would seem that he was so taken by developing the new form of transport that the fore section of the Sea Eagle resembled a cabin cruiser of the time, with its high, pointed prow, enclosed accommodation for passengers, large windows, and grab-rails running the length of the passenger compartment above the cabin and along the top of the hull. As the two planing steps were also joined by a continuous hard chine which ran three-quarters of the hull length, it embodied more than any other Mitchell design the original Pemberton Billing dream of 'boats which fly'.

As with the earlier, intermittent, service using Channel flying boats, the Air Navigation Company had to consider local hangarage for the aircraft and so wing folding was again adopted. It would seem that width rather than length was the important consideration because a forward-folding arrangement was again employed (which reduced the width of the Sea Eagle by 54 per cent while increasing the length by 15 per cent). There was also the structural advantage of hinging at the main spar, with no possibility of a wing folding backwards in flight, although this arrangement necessitated a cut-out in the leading edge of the wings, which did nothing for aerodynamic efficiency.

Mitchell continued the practice of gravity feed for the engine of this latest flying boat with apparently little qualms about stability problems as the fuel tank (and subsequently a second tank) was now attached to the top of the upper wing centre section. After its first flight in 1923, a *Flight* correspondent wrote that that 'this machine represents a great step forward in the development of the seaworthy [commercial] amphibian', having appreciated the 'most important innovation' that, in place of the usual tank in the hull, 'the main petrol tank has been mounted on top of the top plane, so that direct gravity feed, with its attendant simplicity and freedom from breakdown, can be used'. The writer also added:

> The fact that the engine is mounted high above and some distance aft of the cabin has resulted in reducing the noise audible in the cabin to a minimum, and as a matter of fact, in the 'Sea Eagle' it is possible for the passengers to converse in an ordinary tone of voice, without having to shout to one another.

(One remembers Biard's earlier 'communication problem' with Loewenstein in the Channel flying boat.) As the weight of the forward passenger cabin and its six passengers necessitated bringing the lift of the top wing well forward, Mitchell departed from all previous (and future) practice by the use of a pronounced stagger of the two wings. Again, one infers that Mitchell's normal preference was for the simplicity of biplanes with directly opposed wings.

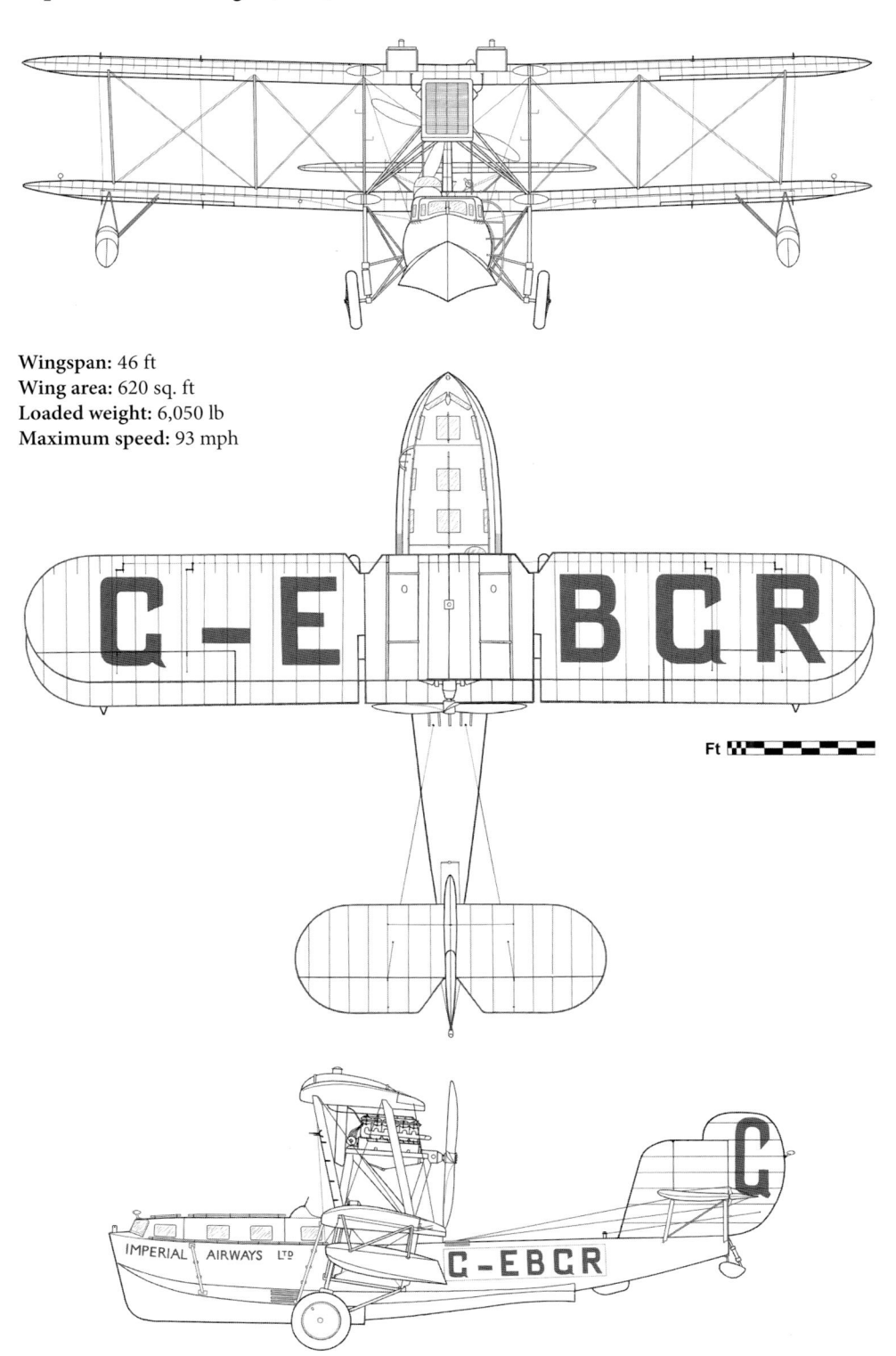

Supermarine Sea Eagle (1923)

Wingspan: 46 ft
Wing area: 620 sq. ft
Loaded weight: 6,050 lb
Maximum speed: 93 mph

A Sea Eagle with Biard aboard. Note the sea anchor below cockpit and original, single, fuel tank on top wing.

The first of the more 'passenger-friendly' Sea Eagles made its maiden flight in June 1923 and received its Certificate of Airworthiness on 11 July. Two days later, Supermarine entered the new aircraft in the King's Cup Air Race that had been initiated the year before by the Air Ministry, also to encourage aviation development. As it was a handicapped event, the entry of a commercial flying boat might not seem too strange but the carrying of four passengers must have had much to do with the Company being mindful of publicity generated by air races. Unfortunately, a burst tyre and its replacement led to a contravention of the race rules and the aircraft was disqualified.

On 5 August, Supermarine received a visit from Sir Sefton Brancker, the director of Civil Aviation, interested to see what Mitchell had designed for the service his ministry had approved. Nine days later, with five senior members of his department, he saw the Sea Eagle able to successfully taxi through lines of yachts now moored up for Cowes Week and took an hour-long flight which included circling the Royal Yacht and its guardship, HMS *Barham*. A short time later, Sir Sefton took a third flight to the Isle of Wight, with Lord Apsley, MP for the Southampton Itchen Division, who was prompted to prophesy afterwards in parliament that 'seaplane travel will be one of the first methods of aerial locomotion'. Some years later, Mitchell wrote that 'Our Empire is so widely spread that fast aerial transport is perhaps the most vital necessity to our existence.'

These demonstrations of the practicality of Mitchell's early contribution to the development of seaplane transport must have included an appreciation of the very sensible placing of the passenger compartment; in the following publicity, the company, not surprisingly, makes reference to the advantages of this arrangement:

A Sea Eagle on the Supermarine slipway prior to a demonstration flight for Sir Sefton Brancker. Note passenger access hatch at front.

> This machine was specially designed as a commercial amphibian or flying boat for passenger carrying work. It carries six passengers and pilot, with fuel for a distance of 230 miles. Extra tankage is fitted so that the range can be increased by reducing the number of passengers.
>
> The passengers are accommodated in a roomy cabin in the fore part of the hull. This cabin is very comfortably fitted out. Its position in front of the engine makes it very quiet and free from engine exhaust, gases, oil, etc.
>
> It is very efficiently heated and ventilated, and is fitted with sliding triplex windows along the two sides for use in the warm weather. The machine is very strongly built and very seaworthy, and has proved itself quite safe in the roughest of seas usually experienced in the Channel. It is fitted with either a Rolls-Royce 'Eagle IX' engine of 360 hp or a Napier 'Lion' of 450 hp.

Supermarine's experiences with the Channel service and with the Commercial Amphibian had obviously influenced Mitchell to give considerable thought to the enclosed cabin arrangement and heating, such that one passenger recorded descending into the Sea Eagle and finding 'a delightful little room' that the company had fitted with 'reposeful armchairs'.

Intermittent proving flights began in August with regular daily services between Southampton and Guernsey on 25 September 1923, so constituting the very first British scheduled flying-boat service. It was advertised to leave Woolston at 11.15 a.m. and return from St Peter Port at 3.30 p.m. The French section of the service did not materialise, but the Channel Isles service, often with breaks due to bad weather, continued with the Sea Eagles for the next five years, even though the single fare was not cheap for the 1920s at over £3 single and £7 return. Compared with boat transport, however, the normal flight of one and a half hours for the 112 miles was very attractive although, in adverse wind conditions, it might take well over two hours.

Cozens' Recollections of the Sea Eagle Service and Early Wireless Communication

The land planes flying from Croydon to the Continent carried wireless transmitters and receivers and had the benefit of a simple direction finding service, by which stations at Pulham in Norfolk and Lympne in Kent and Croydon could take bearings on an aircraft when its generator was running. Then Pulham and Lympne passed their bearings to Croydon, who would plot them, together with its own bearing, and so reach a 'fix' which would be passed to the aircraft pilot. The Sea Eagles ... operated outside the sector where the system could be applied, but they could speak to their bases at Woolston and Guernsey.

I lived a mile from the Supermarine works and could hear an engine start, in those days a rare sound and quite distinctive from the riveters at Thornycroft or the rumble from the coaling wharf in the Docks ... From the front gate I could watch the machine fly across the Dock Head and then go indoors and pick up the headphones of my crystal set. Soon I would hear 'leaving the coast at Beaulieu', and 'Passing the Needles', and about 90 minutes later and hoping the cat's whisker [fine wire detector] had not moved I would hear 'Passing the French coast at Ushant' and sometimes very faintly 'Approaching Guernsey and winding in'.

When the time came for the return trip I would hear the call in the reverse order ... Then I would cycle to the Floating Bridge in time to see the flying boat taxi up to its mooring ... 'Winding in' referred to the trailing aerial, a long wire with a weight on the end, which had to be wound on to a drum before the Sea Eagle could touch down ... By this time the Airline's operations were carried out from buildings along the side of the works and the staff were glad to have proper offices instead of the exposed Jopling's Wharf and along the side of the boatshop the words 'Woolston to Guernsey in 90 minutes' were painted in blue and white. The Sea Eagles were finished in copal varnish and white, and the windsock was an orange colour and the motor boat varnished, making the whole operation smart and attractive.

The third Sea Eagle being christened 'Sarnia' after its maiden flight to Guernsey, 13 October 1923.

The visit of HRH Edward, prince of Wales, 27 June 1924, accompanied by Imperial Airways directors, Hubert Scott-Paine and Col. Frank Searle (anxious that the royal visitor should not fall off the step ladder).

Nearly four years later, the fleet of three Sea Eagles was down to one: G-EBFK having crashed on 21 May (due to a bird strike, according to Cozens) and G-EBGS was rammed and sunk when moored at St Peter Port on 10 January 1927; a reward of £10 for the identity of the culprit was never claimed. At least, Mitchell's machines had not only operated the first British flying-boat service but they also had the distinction of forming part of the basic fleet of the organisation which eventually became British Airways.

On 31 March 1924, Imperial Airways Ltd was incorporated as the 'chosen instrument' of the British government for developing national commercial air transport on an economic basis, and the British Marine Air Navigation Co. was one of the four companies taken over for this purpose. Scott-Paine was a member of the Imperial board of directors and so was able to use his influence to keep the Solent area, and Southampton in particular, to the fore in British commercial flying-boat operations. The two Sea Eagles that were remaining by that time now had their fuselages painted with prominent 'Imperial Airways' lettering, and they continued their accustomed service to the Channel Isles under the control of the new national company from 1 May 1924.

In the following year it was reported in *The Aeroplane* that the Sea Eagles, 'during their hibernation have grown another 100 hp' and are 'now equipped with Napier "Lions"'. The last of the three Sea Eagles, G-EBGR, was finally retired in 1928, thus justifying Supermarine's claims that this type was 'very strongly built and very seaworthy'. A photograph from a correspondent to *The Aeroplane* showed a Sea Eagle hull at Heston Airport in 1954. At this time, the Imperial Airways marking had been painted out and the extant letters G-EBGS were now of a different character from those seen in photographs of the machines when in service. It has been stated that the hull in question was that of G-EBGR, the last survivor of

Sea Eagle in Imperial Airways livery. Note 'Airport' on roof behind—first use of the word?

the Eagle fleet, rather than that of G-EBGS, retrieved from Guernsey. Whatever the truth of the matter, a hull had been presented to BOAC and intended for restoration and display at the new London Airport, but nothing came of this proposal and this piece of industrial archaeology was burnt on 13 February 1954.

Supermarine remained in business in 1923, with the completing of the Seagull II orders and the small fleet of Sea Eagles. Mitchell could now relax a little and indulge in his love of sports—he and his wife had joined the Woolston Tennis Club and had the time to become sufficiently competent to have played a demonstration match against a couple, one of whom was Lord Apsley, safely returned from his public relations flight to the Isle of Wight.

In November 1923, James Bird resolved his increasing disagreements with Scott-Paine by buying him out for the not inconsiderable sum of £192,000 and the change in ownership also led to a change in Mitchell's status and terms of employment. Gordon Mitchell has recorded his father's new contract, safeguarded by home-town solicitors in Stoke. Acknowledgement of his contributions to Supermarine's developing military and commercial activities, and thus, his increasingly important position in the company is evidenced by the negotiation of an annual salary of £1,200, followed by £1,300 and no less than £1,400 in each of the remaining eight years. The value of £1,400 in 2000 might be estimated at about £84,000. There was also a generous endowment policy, an annual holiday of six weeks, and an undertaking that he would be awarded a technical directorship at the end of 1927.

Alan Clifton recalls being offered, the year before, a six-month contract at £3 10s per week—which would represent a mere £182 *per annum*. However, Mitchell's letter of appointment did add: 'to anyone really keen on his work, every opportunity will be given for advancement'. As Clifton rose to become head of the technical office and finally chief designer in 1956, it showed that Mitchell meant what he said, promoting men internally wherever possible if they justified their promise and shared his work ethic.

While developing single-engined flying boats, either medium-sized military or civil machines or the much smaller racing aircraft, Mitchell was now also setting about proving his worth with more ambitious designs. The first of these, was to have been a five-seat military seaplane and it had been ordered to Specification 14/21 in 1921 as part of the Air Ministry attempt to improve upon the Felixstowe F series flying boats.

The F.2A seaplanes of 1917 had been followed by the larger F.3; this machine had a wingspan of 101 feet but did not handle as well and there were again problems with leaking hulls, porpoising, and fuel supply. Nevertheless, such machines had been operated successfully in coastal-reconnaissance duties and so were replaced after the armistice by the F.5 from the same makers. The strengthened hull of the new machine made it considerably heavier than previously and test pilot D'Arcy Greig found it no better a performer on water than its predecessors:

> They were grossly underpowered by two Rolls-Royce Eagle VIII engines, and if there happened to be a flat calm at time of take-off, they frequently refused to unstick. On such occasions the pilot had to taxi frenziedly up and down the Solent and around in circles in order to disturb the surface of the water before trying again, but even then they sometimes failed to get airborne.

The Air Ministry was concerned to see if the Linton-Hope type of hull could be adopted on aircraft of the Felixstowe-Porte size, and so, in 1917, Specification N.4 had been issued for this purpose. However, established manufacturers of seaplanes were fully committed to the wartime production of standard service machines and the slow process of fulfilling this requirement lasted until well after the war, by which time Supermarine had come into contention. Contracts were issued to the company for a five-seat military flying boat and for a civil passenger amphibian.

N174—the military machine, named 'Scylla'—was drafted as a triplane with two main engines and a much smaller, auxiliary unit, sited in the hull to drive a water propeller for slow-speed taxiing. This last feature looked back to the earlier Pemberton Billing days of the company and, in particular, the P.B.7. The biplane stabilisers and the squarish fins also looked backwards—in this case, to the Nighthawk, to the AD Boat/Channel of those early days, and to a proposed Torpedo Carrier triplane of 1921.

Why only the hull of the Scylla was completed is unknown, as was its final fate. The primary purpose of the Scylla design was perhaps to investigate the manoeuvring of large seaplane hulls, as water rudders by themselves could be ineffective and asymmetric use of power with multi-engined flying boats often resulted in difficulties when taxiing through the water; this

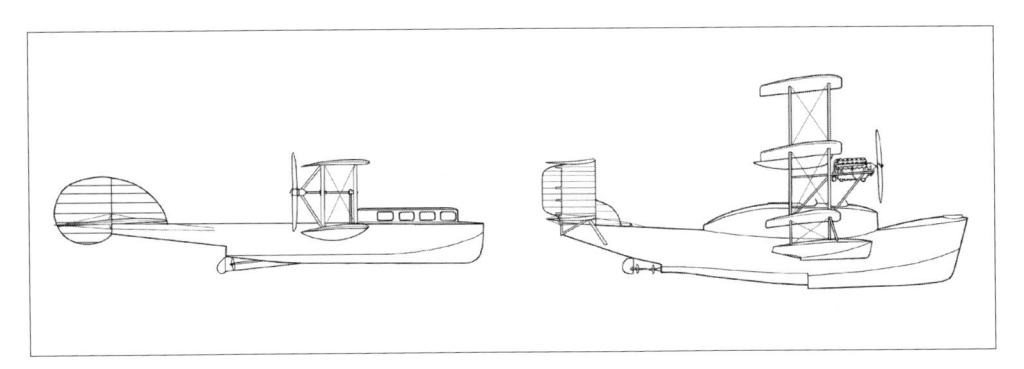

From left to right: P.B.7 and Scylla.

might account for the perfunctory drawing up of obsolescent flying surfaces. Whatever the truth of the matter, photographic evidence shows a completed hull, with a stub lower wing, balance floats, and twin engines; these were sited on a rather basic metal structure erected on the hull. There was also a sea rudder mounted behind a marine propeller. At this stage of construction, it was transported by road in March 1924 to the Marine Aircraft Experimental Establishment (MAEE), newly established at Felixstowe.

Six months later, it had been erected and taxiing tests begun, presumably to compare the efficacy of control by the main engines with that provided by the sea rudder and propeller. It would appear that these were discontinued by the following March and no attempt was made thereafter by Supermarine to make the structure into an airworthy military type, nor did the use of marine propellers become a feature of future flying boat design, at Supermarine or elsewhere.

The Swan

Mitchell's rapidly developing confidence as a designer, whose innovations are the main subject of the next chapter, would account for his being more attracted to a second specification: 21/22. This second project—N175, to be known as the Swan—represented a more promising progression from his successful Commercial Amphibian design and his Sea Eagle to a substantial twin-engined civil aircraft, carrying twelve passengers (twice as many as the latter). As it would come out at about the same size as the military Scylla, it could undoubtedly also be easily retrofitted for the military purposes specified for the Scylla, if need be.

The more forward-looking Swan first appeared in 1924 as an equal-span biplane and with folding wing arrangements like the Sea Eagle of the previous year. In some ways, the Swan might best be regarded as a scaled-up Sea Eagle, although Mitchell's more ambitious conception resulted in the necessity of accommodating the passengers in the main body of the hull rather than in the advantageous fore position provided in the earlier aircraft. Again, Sea Eagle practice was followed with fuel tanks situated high enough to provide gravity feed to the inter-plane engines, as well as to make the accommodation of the passengers roomy as well as fume-free. The fin and rudder outlines also resembled the smaller aircraft.

On the other hand, Mitchell's less complex use of dihedral only on the outer sections of the lower mainplane was an innovation, and the three vertical tail surfaces looked forward to his larger designs of the next decade. The single plane stabiliser was also new to larger Supermarine aircraft and was kept well clear of the water by the upward slope of the rear section of the hull—unusual for the time although not quite an innovation in flying-boat design (see the smaller French Tellier T3 or the Latham HB3), nor was it as graceful as the upward sweep of the future Southampton rear fuselage, but it did represent a new step in Mitchell hull design, without previous experimentation with smaller hulls.

The need to mount three fins had also led to a reversal of his earlier practice, from the Commercial Amphibian onwards, whereby the tailplane was supported by the fin and numerous struts (*see* drawing p. 101). Now, the fins rested on the tailplane and this new feature anticipated most of Mitchell's later seaplanes. On the other hand, the upturned prow (flared outwards at the top to counteract spray) and the raised cockpit superstructure were also very similar to that proposed for the Scylla and contributed significantly to the clumsiness of the hull profile. Cozens' comments are complementary, if not always complimentary:

Multitasking (1923–1924)   115

Supermarine Swan (1924)

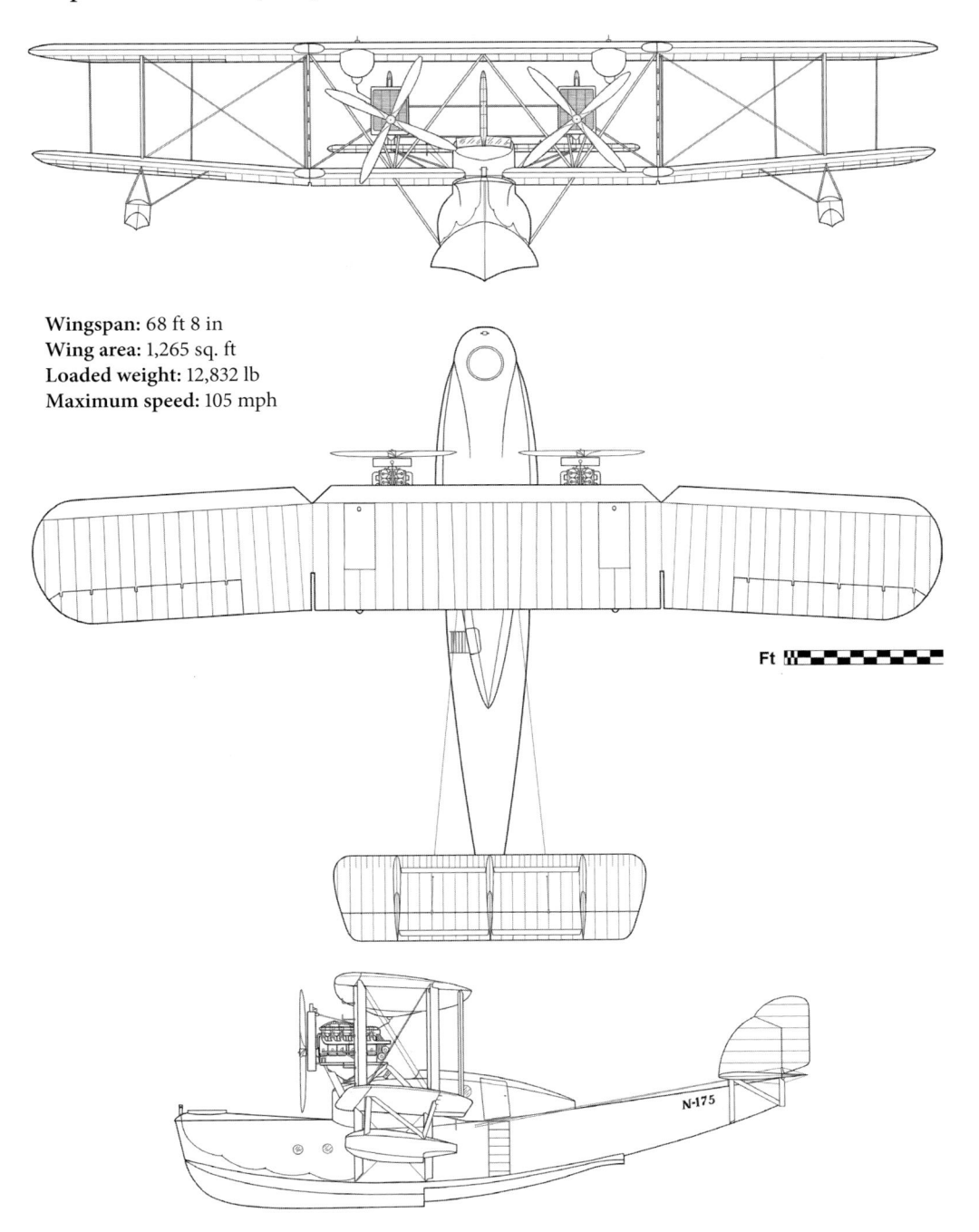

Wingspan: 68 ft 8 in
Wing area: 1,265 sq. ft
Loaded weight: 12,832 lb
Maximum speed: 105 mph

The Swan nearing completion.

The Swan had several features which showed improvements on previous designs, and no doubt these led to its success. The keel had an upward curve towards the tail that enabled it to take off more readily and this feature was noticeable in all later flying boat hulls built throughout the flying boat era, even to the Saunders-Roe Princess of the nineteen fifties, and it is very apparent if one compares the pictures of the Swan with that of the Channel I ... At any rate, Captain Biard was pleased and so was the Air Ministry, but no one could say that the Swan was a handsome machine with its rounded bow and strange-looking cabin and the pilot's cockpit at the top.

The 'strange-looking cabin', which housed a crew of two, had been sited on the top of the main fuselage so as to maximise the main hull space for passengers. When the Swan first flew on 25 March 1924, the proposed passenger windows had not yet been fitted; thus, the offending side-view was unrelieved.

While Supermarine had no doubt chosen its name to suit its proposed military role, it might seem to others that the name reflected its stark appearance—according to Ovid, the beautiful Scylla was turned into a thing of terror, and, in Homer, Odysseus manages to sail past the monster but not before she catches and devours six of his men. As Mitchell's new design was to have a more specific role, this second aircraft had been named 'Swan', although, despite its size, 'ugly duckling' comes more to mind.

When the new aircraft was first flown, it had triangular cut-outs in the leading edges of the wings to enable them to fold forwards. The Swan also had the retracting undercarriage arrangement of the sort Mitchell had designed for his single-engined amphibians but the vastly increased size and weight of this particular machine necessitated the novelty of some form of servo assistance. Biard described Mitchell's essentially simple solution as follows:

it would have been quite impossible to wind down the six-foot wheels and powerful landing-carriage, which had to stand the weight of several tons of aircraft and passengers! So a neat device was fitted to the machine to do the work quickly and efficiently for us. This consisted of a small propeller, which, when not in use, was set sideways to the direction in which we were flying. When we wanted to lower the landing-gear, this propeller was swung round to face the direction of our course, and the whirling propeller was connected by cogs to a handle which wound very rapidly round and lowered the wheels into place; by turning the propeller rearward the wheels were wound up out of our way under the wings, and the machine was then able to descend on water. This gear, after one or two adjustments following minor troubles during tests, when the Swan behaved neither like fish, flesh, nor fowl, proved remarkably efficient, and wound the heavy landing-gear into place in about half a minute or less.

Biard also describes the visit of the prince of Wales to Supermarine, and to the Swan in particular, on 27 June in the same year. (On being invited to climb the 10-foot steel ladder to the cabins, he declined, giving his dress sword as a reason.) His reported conversation was about England's need to possess efficient commercial aircraft and military aircraft to safeguard her colonial trade routes; Supermarine and Mitchell had an important part to play in both these developments.

This royal occasion coincided with the prince's opening of a very large floating dock in the port of Southampton, which was fully reported in the *Flight* issue of 3 July 1924:

Here [the royal party] were met by the Chairman of Supermarine, Mr Low, who presented Commander J. Bird, Managing Director, R. J. Mitchell and Captain Biard. The Prince also received the Chief of the Royal Spanish Naval Air Services, who was interested in the purchase of flying boats for his country. [*See* the Scarab below.]

The prince was then conducted on a tour of the Works. In No.1 Shop he inspected amphibian bombers under construction for the Spanish Government and he saw a completed aircraft of that kind moored in the Itchen ready for delivery.

In No. 2 Shed he watched sheet metal work, wing assembly and engine erection. Proceeding through the works, offices and stores, the Prince was shown a display of stainless steel fittings, a special feature of Supermarine.

In No. 3 Shop the building of the Seagull flying boat hulls were greatly admired by His Royal Highness.

He then spent some time in the hangar of Imperial Airways Ltd which adjoined the Supermarine premises. Here he was presented to Hubert Scott-Paine, the man who had helped found the Company.

His last visit was to the Swan, Mitchell's latest design for a large passenger-carrying aircraft. Before leaving to open the Floating Dock, he congratulated Supermarine on their splendid achievements.

The article did not prominently feature the man who was, after all, responsible for designing the three very different company types on display, but, nevertheless, the lad who had left his home town eight years before for an uncertain future was now, at twenty-nine, the company chief designer and engineer and had a photograph of himself, beside the prince and his very large creation, published in the Stoke *Sentinel* for all his family to see (*see* chapter frontispiece).

Swan after removal of folding wing arrangement, wing leading edge cut-outs, and undercarriage.

By the time of the prince's visit, plans for an RAF version of the Swan were also being actively pursued; this may also have had an influence on the decision to dispense with the amphibian undercarriage and the folding-wing arrangement. The Swan's Eagle engines were replaced by two Napier Lion IIBs, each developing 90 hp more than the Rolls-Royce units, which, with the removal of the undercarriage, increased the Swan's top speed by 13 mph. Its improved performance and the more forward-looking configuration throws additional light upon the decision to terminate the development of the military Scylla.

Meanwhile, the first of the 1917 N.4 specification aircraft, the Fairey-designed Atalanta, had made its maiden flight; while being regarded as an excellent machine in its own right, its 139-foot wingspan and four Rolls-Royce 650-hp Condor engines made it a less attractive proposition for the drastically reduced post-war services. In comparison, the Swan, with about half the wingspan, had only two 450-hp engines, but nevertheless was only 10 mph slower. Successful trials at the Marine Aircraft Experimental Establishment followed, and these were to have important results for the fortunes of Supermarine, as will be described in the next chapter.

When the Swan was returned to Supermarine, its fitting-out as a passenger-carrying aircraft was completed and the company was particularly concerned to stress the high standard of accommodation; their publicity also went on to make not only some serious claims for Supermarine's lead in seaplane development but also an assertion, at this stage in air transport development, for the superiority of this type of aircraft over landplane types:

This is a passenger-carrying flying boat or amphibian flying boat, fitted with either two Rolls-Royce 'Eagle IX' engines or two Napier 'Lion' engines. It carries twelve passengers, with luggage, together with a crew of two, complete navigation equipment and fuel for 300 miles. This is the first twin-engined amphibian flying boat to be built in the world and it may also be fairly claimed to be the first twin-engined commercial flying boat.

An important feature of this machine is that the whole of the hull is devoted to passenger accommodation. There are no internal obstructions of any kind, and the amount of room in the

Swan after conversion into the world's 'first twin-engined amphibian flying boat'.

saloon far exceeds that of any commercial landplane. The internal accommodation consists of one large passenger saloon, elaborately furnished and upholstered and with every comfort. Forward of the saloon is the luggage compartment, fitted with racks for the stowage of passenger baggage. Aft of the saloon is the buffet, with all necessary fittings to supply light refreshment during the journey. Still further aft are the lavatories, which are efficiently and fully equipped.

The pilot and the navigator are accommodated in a cabin specially built on top of the hull. In this position they are given an extremely good view in all directions, and are in a fine position for starting the engines, handling the machine on the water, and for operating the craft under all conditions.

The publicity mentions the originally planned twelve-passenger-carrying capability, although, in fact, the machine was finally fitted out with only ten seats. In this form, it was registered as G-EBJY and first flew on 9 June 1926, carrying a representative of Imperial Airways and eight excited female employees of Supermarine as passengers.

While the placing of the built-on crew compartment above the main hull had done nothing for the lines of the Swan's hull, its position, the Linton-Hope structure, and the slight reduction in passenger seating had allowed Supermarine to set new standards in passenger accommodation, which its test pilot, Henri Biard, fully confirmed:

The Swan, then the world's largest amphibian ... was a real cabin-liner of the air, with comfortable armchairs, big porthole windows, a commodious passage along the centre of the living accommodation, and all sorts of luxuries and refinements which were very new to aircraft at that time.

A more neutral observer from *The Aeroplane* agreed, saying that 'the appointments are exquisite' with 'a commodious passenger saloon padded luxuriously and in which there are ten cosy armchairs. An ample porthole is provided for each chair.'

Cozens describes a later, and more mundane, use for the passenger compartment in the course of his recollections of this aircraft:

Mitchell (right) in the Swan. Note the Linton-Hope fuselage structure of close-spaced hoops on longitudinal stringers.

> Both Rolls-Royce Eagles and Napier Lions were tried but the Lions were finally chosen. The writer recalls this machine when it was used in the colours of Imperial Airways as a freighter to bring bags of early potatoes and boxes of daffodils from the Channel Islands. The large mid-section made this possible and highly suitable for bulky cargoes. I remember seeing the horse drawn market carts down on the slipway being loaded from the Swan.

The unsold aircraft had been loaned by the Air Ministry to Imperial Airways in order to supplement the service of its remaining two smaller sisters, the Sea Eagles, on their Channel Isles service. It operated during 1926 and 1927, but as the *Guernsey Evening Press* reported, 'during the normal rigorous inspection prior to leaving Southampton on April 12, a structural defect was discovered which necessitated the stripping of the whole machine'. As a result, the Swan was scrapped, but Imperial Airways' next long-distance seaplane was not to be a replacement Swan, and so its main significance remained that of providing the prototype for the Royal Air Force's next standard maritime reconnaissance aircraft—the Supermarine Southampton of 1925.

Reginald Mitchell might have thought that he was well justifying his raised salary and the new terms of his employment with the production of this significantly larger flying boat. However, any hopes of developing larger passenger-carrying aircraft that he might now have had were tempered by the fact that the navy had found his Seagulls to have 'no potential naval use' because of their habit of porpoising on take-off and because they were difficult to land on the new aircraft carriers that were coming into service. These machines were then confined to coastal reconnaissance duties, but at least, the ministry retained faith in the company by placing an order for an improved version of the type.

The Sheldrake

This new aircraft featured flying surfaces that were virtually identical to those of the Seagull and would appear to have been a modification of the previous machine, built mainly to arrive at a hull shape, which was less prone to porpoising. In fact, it employed a boat-like hull very similar to that of the Sea Eagle, if the latter's passenger cabin were discounted.

However, although begun in 1924, about two years after the Seagull II, it only appeared in public in 1927 at a Hamble air pageant, having apparently spent much of the intervening time at the MAEE. As it still retained screens beside the engine, like its Seagull predecessor, it thus appeared particularly obsolescent, as Cozens observed:

> The writer especially remembers seeing a Sheldrake at the end of the line of aircraft on show at Hamble. This machine, N180, looked very much like an 'old gaffer' at Cowes in modern times, but it did have a certain dignity when it took off and was 'attacked' by three Gloster Gamecocks in their silver paint, black and white squares [No. 43 Squadron markings] and RAF roundels.

If the main purpose of the Sheldrake order had been to test better sea-going hulls, this would help explain its fleeting appearance in the succession of Supermarine aircraft. An additional factor was that the Air Ministry placed no further orders for this type of aircraft and the company's interests were extending in other directions: the first flights of the Sea Eagle and of the Sea Lion III, the larger Scylla and Swan being considered, the important activity around the twin-engined Southampton, and the new breed of Schneider trophy racers. Certainly, by 1927, no production orders were placed for this enigmatic machine. It was, however, important in respect of a Spanish order for twelve aircraft, named 'Scarab'.

King Alfonso of Spain was a regular visitor to the Hendon RAF pageants and must have had an early appreciation of the British 'control without occupation' tactics, in view of the war that was being fought in the early 1920s between Spain and the Berbers in Morocco. Accordingly, the Spanish Royal Naval Air Service asked Supermarine for an amphibian

The Sheldrake at the Hamble Air Pageant, 1927.

Supermarine Sheldrake (*c.* 1924)

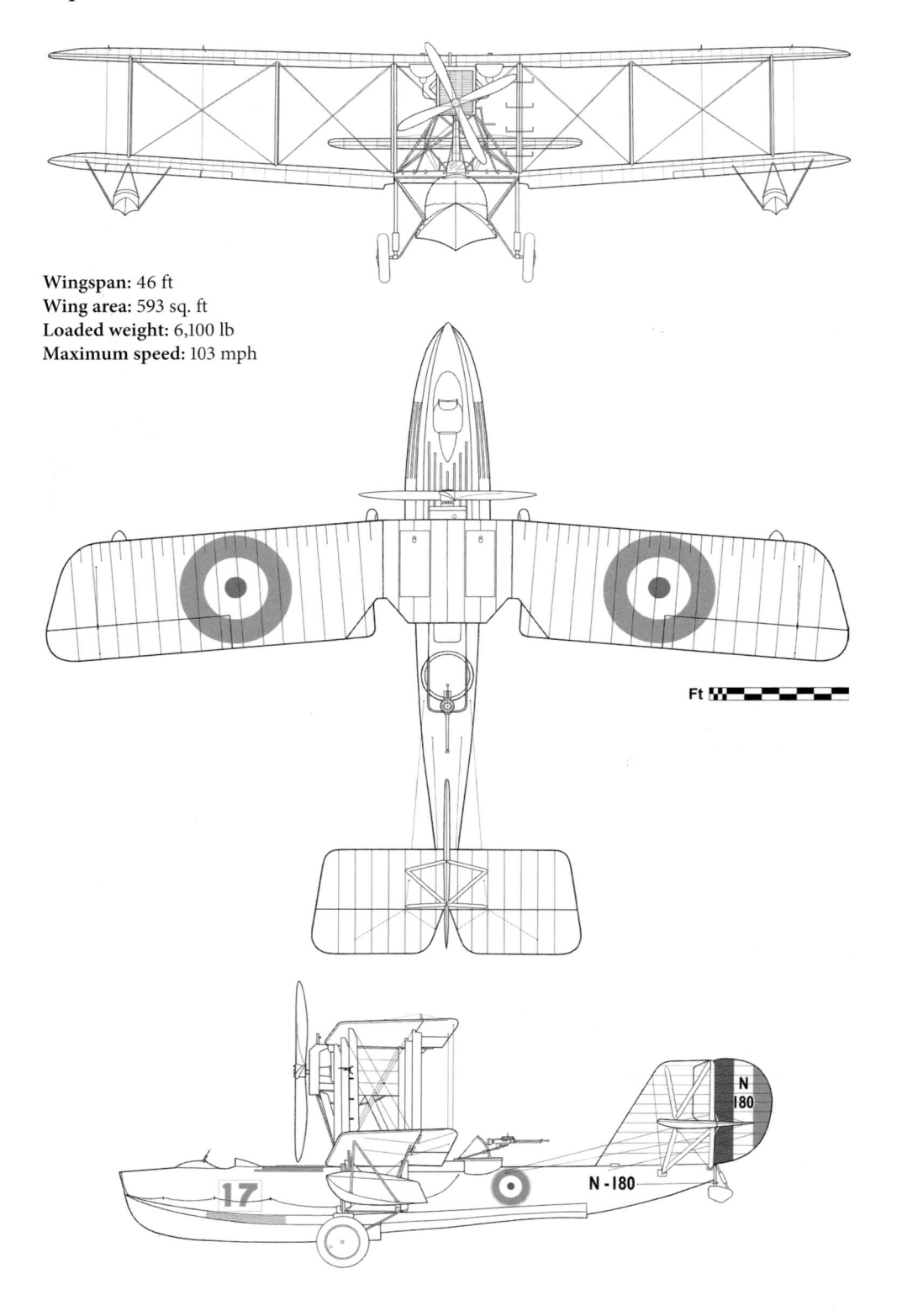

Wingspan: 46 ft
Wing area: 593 sq. ft
Loaded weight: 6,100 lb
Maximum speed: 103 mph

bomber to be produced, as the load-carrying capacity of the Sea Eagle promised a suitable basis for a design. Supermarine decided that the plans being drawn for their new Sheldrake would be a suitable model for the project, and doubtless, Mitchell was already envisaging improvements in respect of the Sheldrake.

The Scarab: An Amphibian Bomber

A year after the Sheldrake prototype was ordered, the second of our aircraft made its maiden flight. There was no prototype for this aircraft and, as it was in a great many respects similar to the Sheldrake, it seems obvious that the Air Ministry order for the earlier aircraft provided most of the design work for the Spanish order, at little extra cost to Supermarine.

When the new machine appeared, it could be seen that the Sheldrake upper wing fuel tanks, which had been similar to those of the Seagull II, were now replaced by larger ones situated on top of the centre section, following Sea Eagle practice. The engine was returned to the more familiar pusher configuration as the crew were all now, more conveniently, grouped together in front of the wings, with the navigator also having a cabin in the hull immediately behind and below his cockpit position. Dual controls could be fitted in the second cockpit, and the space not now required for fuselage petrol tanks was available for twelve 50-lb bombs, which could be dropped via a sealable aperture in the bottom of the hull. Four 100-lb bombs were also to be carried under the wings, and the total bomb load of 454 kg amounted to the equivalent of about six men; in addition to a crew of three, the machine would carry a machine gun, ammunition, and a considerable amount of fuel, thus making it an attractive single-engined proposition to its buyers, albeit an underpowered one.

Mitchell explaining features of the Scarab (possibly the novel bomb compartment) to HRH Edward, Prince of Wales, on his 1924 visit.

Supermarine Scarab (1924)

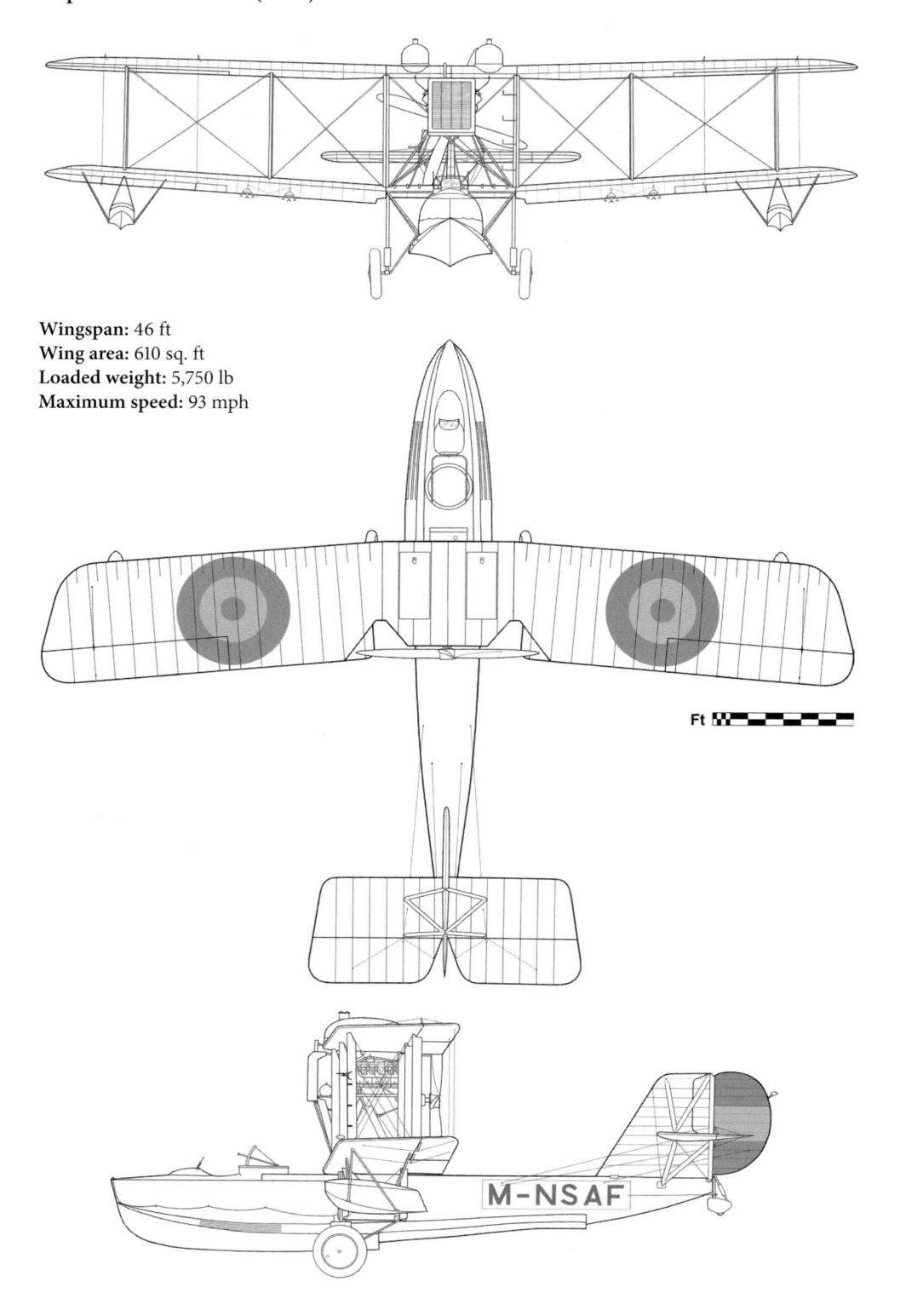

Wingspan: 46 ft
Wing area: 610 sq. ft
Loaded weight: 5,750 lb
Maximum speed: 93 mph

The first Scarab for the Spanish Royal Naval Air Service.

The first Scarab made its maiden flight on 21 May 1924, bearing the Spanish designation M-NSAA; it was assessed at Woolston on 27 September by an MAEE test pilot and granted its Certificate of Airworthiness. Whether all twelve of the Scarabs ordered by Spain actually saw service is unclear. One of the Scarabs was damaged on acceptance trials when its Spanish pilot hit the side of a Union-Castle liner when taking off; also, on transit to Spain, the machines had to survive a severe Bay of Biscay storm stowed under tarpaulins as deck cargo. Nevertheless, Scarabs were seen above Barcelona at the 1925 royal review of Spanish forces by King Alfonso and they equipped a seaplane carrier, the *Dédalo*. This vessel was a converted merchant vessel and lacked a landing deck; the aircraft were lowered into the water or raised from it by crane, like their Australian Seagull cousins (*see* Chapter 8).

Based at Cartagena and commanded by the king's nephew, the unit took part in actions against Riff and Jibala insurgents in the Spanish Moroccan campaign, including bombing raids in support of an amphibian landing at Al Hoceima. The Moroccan conflict ended soon afterwards in 1926, and Supermarine publicity, no doubt mindful of the new tactics of control without occupation, ran as follows:

THE SUPERMARINE 'SCARAB' BOMBER AMPHIBIAN FLYING BOAT

A recent development of the single-engined flying boat is the Supermarine 'Scarab', which has been specially designed for naval bombing and reconnaissance work. A large number of these machines have been bought by the Spanish Government, and these have been in operation for the past year in Morocco *with the most satisfactory results* [author's italics].

The hull is constructed on standard Supermarine lines and is very seaworthy. It is practically impossible to ship water over the cockpits. The machine handles very easily and effectively on the water by means of its water rudder and can be turned on a radius of one span. It tows very nicely under all conditions of wind and tide.

The whole of the crew are placed in front of the main planes, and thus intercommunication is excellent. The pilot is seated in the very bows of the machine, behind him is the gunner, and aft of the gunner is the navigator and wireless operator, who has both a cockpit in front of the main planes and a spacious wireless cabin in the hull immediately behind his cockpit.

The undercarriage is similar to that used on the Supermarine 'Seagull'.

The engine, to which is attached a pusher airscrew, is either a Rolls-Royce 'Eagle IX' or a Napier 'Lion'.

The fuel supply is by direct gravity feed from the petrol tanks situated on the top of the top centre section plane.

Provision is made for carrying a maximum bomb load of 1,000 lbs.

Only the Rolls-Royce engine was fitted to the Spanish Scarabs, and when the Sheldrake made its belated appearance, it was seen to be powered by a Lion engine. The Greek government had sent observers to the Scarab acceptance trials, but no other orders were forthcoming from abroad. Supermarine did not receive any British orders for the Scarab and the sole Sheldrake was not heard of again. It might, however, be noted in passing that the more successful hull planing configuration developed for the Sheldrake, and also employed on the Scarab, was an important influence upon the eventual Seagull V/Walrus design.

The early 1920s had thus seen Mitchell's gradual development of the medium-sized naval amphibian biplane and its diversion into the Sea Eagle passenger type. He had also had to turn his talents to the large Scylla and Swan and to the amphibian bomber for the Spanish Navy. In addition, and while the Swan and Scarab were being prepared for their first flights, the Air Ministry announced its competition for a two-seat, all-British light aircraft to take place at Lympne in September 1924.

The previous year, a similar competition had been sponsored by the duke of Sutherland, the under-secretary of state for air, and the *Daily Mail*, but it had not been of great interest to most of the larger aircraft companies as the various prizes had encouraged designs specifically for height or speed or for distance performances: the prize for the longest distance flown on one gallon of petrol, for example, had produced a succession of, essentially, gliders powered by adapted motorcycle engines.

As a result, the revised 1924 rules called for more all-round attainment whereby marks would be awarded for high-speed and low-speed performance, control, shortest take-off and landing runs, and dismantling and re-erecting (so the aircraft could be housed in modest hangarage). The engine size was raised from 750 cc to what was thought to be a more practicable 1,100 cc, and the total prize money had also been raised from £2,600 to £3,900, of which £2,000 would go to the winner. Later in the year, the enticing prospect was held out to prospective entrants that the Air Ministry would assist the development of ten light aeroplane clubs by providing an approved design selected from the competition entrants.

As specially designed small aero engines were now being developed and as the aircraft had to be dual control two-seaters, major British aircraft producers became interested in this more practical proposition and Mitchell now became engaged upon overseeing another 'first'—a very light machine and, exceptionally, a landplane as well.

The Sparrow I: Mitchell's First Landplane

Supermarine's publicity for their entry, the Sparrow, mentions a choice of two engines, but the only type used by Supermarine for the competition was the 35-hp Blackburne Thrush, whose name was perhaps its only endearing feature. Biard reported nineteen engine failures in the fortnight before the start of the competition, and matters were no better at Lympne. As a result, the Sparrow was not airborne enough to complete the preliminary flying tests and was eliminated.

This result could hardly have pleased the company as Supermarine had been joined by most of the other major manufacturers in producing an entry. Four of these were conventional single bay biplanes like the Swallow: the Vickers Vagabond, the Avro Avis, the Westland Woodpigeon, and the Hawker Cygnet. Of these, the last three had full span combined ailerons and flaps like the Mitchell machine—all designed, as the Supermarine publicity said, 'for reducing the landing speed and the runs to land and get off'. Hawkers had arrived at an even more similar formula to that of the Sparrow in that it was also a sesquiplane. In contrast to these entries, the Bristol Brownie, the Beardmore Wee Bee, and the Short Satellite represented the monoplane approach to the specification.

With so many companies addressing themselves to the same problems, with the same limit for power, seating, and other features, the prospect of seeing which designer came up with the best machine at the very same point in time was an intriguing one. This was particularly so because it would also have provided a comparison of the competing claims of the biplane and the monoplane approach to aircraft design, which was intensifying now that structural advances were making the latter type a much more practicable proposition. To those able to look back later from the perspective of the Supermarine Spitfire and the Hawker Hurricane days, it would have additionally been very interesting to have compared the design of Mitchell, who had now been a chief designer for just over four years, and that of Sydney Camm whose Cygnet was one of his first designs for Hawker.

An informed comparison was, unfortunately, not possible as there had not been enough time to match propellers to the various engines and their continual failures made matters worse. Of the nineteen entrants, only eight survived the eliminating trials and all but seven of the competitors had failed because of some sort of engine problem. Even a comparison between the six which finally competed for the prizes was not possible: the speed–range competition had to be preceded by ten trouble-free laps, and by the last day of competition, only the Beardmore and Bristol entries had done so, with engine throttled well back. The fact that the Beardmore and Bristol machines took first and second prizes, respectively, was not so much a vindication of the monoplane philosophy as a result of their particular engines holding out the best.

The Sparrow I at Lympne.

Supermarine Sparrow I (1924)

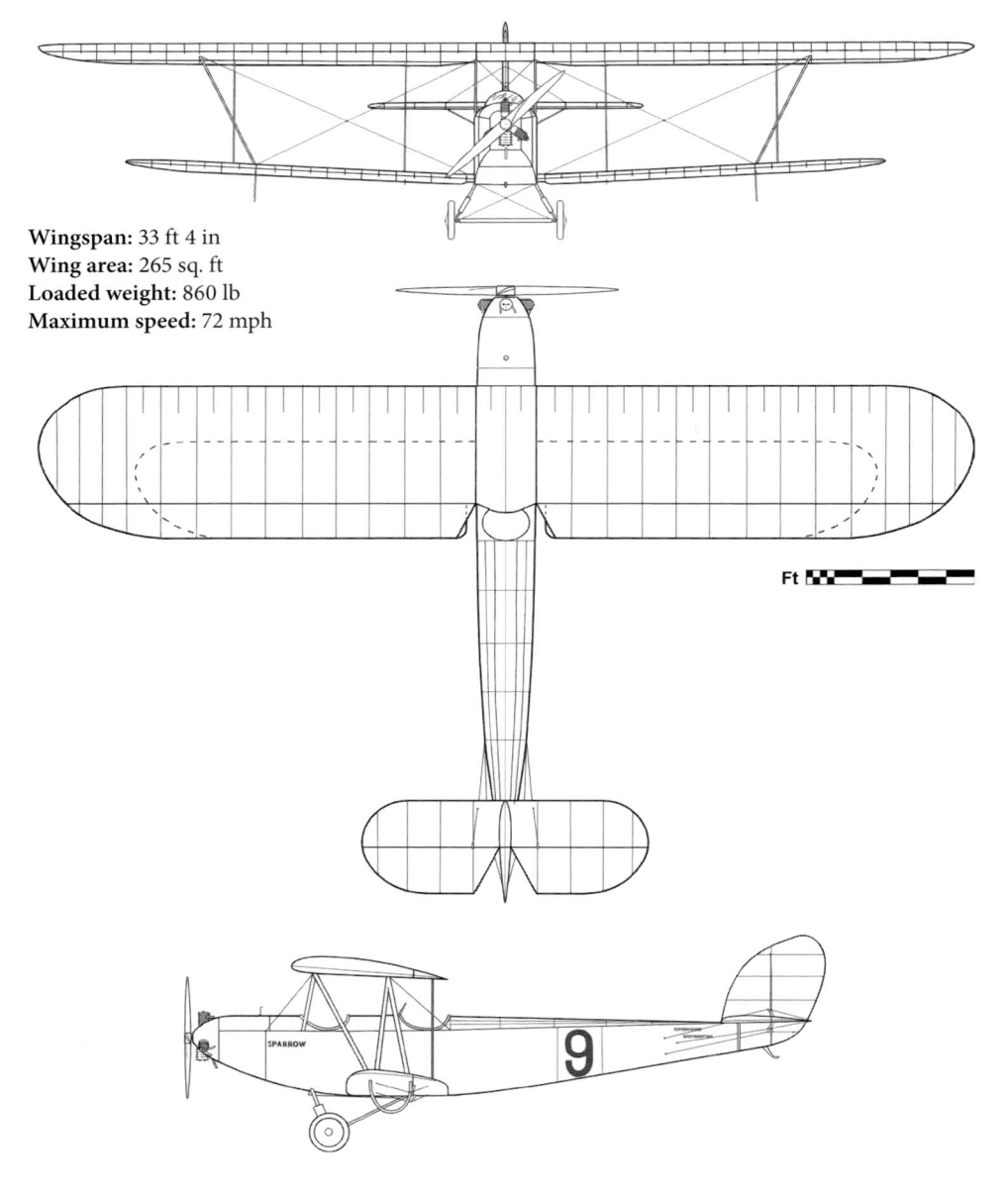

Wingspan: 33 ft 4 in
Wing area: 265 sq. ft
Loaded weight: 860 lb
Maximum speed: 72 mph

Official Air Ministry reports were made of all the entries, and despite having the lowest landing speed, the Sparrow was criticised for having the cockpits too far apart for good communication and for less than satisfactory vision from the front position; its exterior was also considered to be too cluttered with external control rods and cables (not an unfamiliar feature of Supermarine's flying boats of this time). H. F. V. Battle, test-flying for the Air Ministry, reported that 'these light planes caused us to have many forced landings', and it was also perceived that it would be necessary to think in terms of an engine that could develop more power than what was currently possible from the 1,100-cc limit imposed by the competition rules.

Thus, despite the good intentions of the Air Ministry, no orders were forthcoming for any of the machines. It had become only too obvious that it took much longer to produce a new and reliable power unit than to design and build an airframe. The next year, however, saw two very significant aircraft from the chief designer's drawing board: the S.4 racer and the Southampton reconnaissance flying boat.

Supermarine were free of Air Ministry guidelines for naming their landplane and the name 'Sparrow' which was chosen was appropriate enough, in view of its non-marine associations and size. Supermarine described it as follows

THE SUPERMARINE 'SPARROW'

A two-seater light aeroplane built for the Air Ministry Competition.

This—the first land machine built by the Supermarine works since the early days of the war—is a very neat biplane with a top wing of much greater chord, and appreciably larger span than those of the bottom. In addition, the wings are so staggered as to bring the trailing edge of the lower wing vertically below that of the upper wing. The two wings are also of different section, the upper wing being an American Sloane section, the lower known as A.D.1. Both these sections are of the low-resistance, high-speed type.

The fuselage is rectangular built with spruce longerons, spruce verticals and spruce diagonal members, and covered with three-ply.

The crew are seated one below the top centre-section and one behind the rear spar. The trailing edges of both wings are cut back from the fuselage, to give the passenger in the rear seat a view downwards.

The wings are built on spruce spars of channel section, with ribs of spruce and three-ply. Drag struts are box-form ribs and the leading edge nose is covered with three-ply. Outwardly raking interplane struts of 'N' type are fitted, one on each side. These are of steel tube with fairing. The usual streamlined wire flying and landing bracings are fitted.

The wings fold in the usual way about hinges on the inner ends of the rear spar, the wings flaps being folded right down when the wing is stowed.

The undercarriage is of the Vee type, with telescopic front legs, sprung on rubber rings. The tail unit is of normal form, comprising fixed tail plane, divided elevators, fin and rudder. The tail plane setting is adjustable on the ground.

The ailerons, which extend over the whole span of both planes, are also utilised as flaps for reducing the landing speed and the runs to land and get off. These features in performance have been given very careful consideration throughout the design, and as a result the landing speed of this machine has been reduced to a figure lower than that of any other two-seater aircraft.

Sensitivity and lightness of control are combined with marked efficiency in manoeuvrability, which render the machine not only highly suitable from the purely instructional point of view, but also remarkably safe.

The machine can be fitted either with a Blackburne 3-cylinder radial engine or a Bristol 'Cherub'. The aircraft is equally pleasant to fly from either seat, ballast being unnecessary during solo flights.

Mitchell and Biard with the S.4.

6

A Turning Point
(1925)

> *The firm has a very large Design Department, under the Chief Designer and Engineer,*
> *R. J. Mitchell, who has established himself as one of the leading flying-boat and amphibian*
> *designers in the country.*
>
> Supermarine publicity

It is surely no exaggeration to identify 1925 as the year when two of Mitchell's aircraft stood out dramatically from those that had preceded them. While he had had early successes, incrementally improving on conventional machines, this year marked his full emergence as a designer who was now striking out boldly into the future. After joining his firm at the age of twenty-one and assisting with the designs of others, he now produced—nine years later—the first standard naval reconnaissance aircraft since the end of the First World War and the racing floatplane that established the basic design configuration for all subsequent Schneider trophy machines.

While his 69-foot Swan and the diminutive Sparrow were being tested and flown, the company was fully engaged upon finishing the third production order for Seagulls and the Spanish Scarab contract. Thus, there was no great Supermarine interest in an entry for the proposed 1924 Schneider trophy contest, given the healthier state of the Supermarine production line and the lack of Air Ministry interest in the small fighter seaplane concept. Of much more potential interest was the fact that the improved performance of the modified Swan had been noted at the Marine Aircraft Experimental Establishment at Felixstowe, to which it had been sent in August 1924.

By this time, the question of a suitable replacement for the Felixstowe 'F' series of flying boats was becoming critical; the Air Ministry had issued specification N.4 in 1917 for the improvement of Porte's flying boats, but because of more immediate demands of the war effort, responses had been both disappointing and tardy. Thus, by the time that the various responses had been built and tested, they were hardly new designs, and because of the contraction of the air force following the end of the First World War and the number of Felixstowe F.3 and F.5 aircraft currently in service, there was little impetus for production orders for them. Also, these prototypes had wingspans of over 100 feet, with the Fairey Titania measuring 139 feet and powered by four 650-hp engines, and so were unlikely to attract serious funding in the straightened circumstances after 1918.

Whatever Mitchell's latent hopes might be for the development of aerial transport, Secretary of State for Air Sir Samuel Hoare recalled:

> In 1922, there were no aeroplanes capable of maintaining a long-distance service. The existing heavier-than-air machines were low-powered, very noisy and uncomfortable. Flying boats had almost ceased to exist and there was no plan for an Empire airline of any kind.

As an alternative approach to the situation, the Air Ministry authorised the building of six airships, the first two to inaugurate a service to Egypt in 1924. However, the many technical and logistical problems raised by bulky lighter-than-air machines brought about many embarrassing delays. Thus, the successful trials at Felixstowe of the more compact, twin-engined Swan had not gone unnoticed at the Air Ministry, whose officials had been very impressed by the standards set by the Sea Eagle in 1923; in comparison with the preceding prototypes, the Swan was a more economical proposition and it also embodied a Linton-Hope type of hull in which the Air Ministry was interested.

As a result of this appreciation of the standard in flying-boat performance that Mitchell had now established with the Swan, the Air Ministry took the unusual step of ordering a number of reconnaissance flying boats straight off the drawing board. It was fortunate all round that the Estimates of January had, at the expense of the army and the navy, provided for an increase of £2,500,000 for the RAF, and private relief in the ministry must have been more than matched by jubilation throughout the Supermarine works.

The Southampton I: The New RAF Standard Reconnaissance Flying Boat

By the time that Supermarine officially received Specification R.18/24 in August 1924 for a modified and slightly enlarged Swan-type flying boat, Mitchell was already having this aircraft's hull lines redrawn to improve the streamlining. The eventual modifications were such that a 'Swan Mark II' designation was less appropriate than a completely new name. Since the Swan was built as a civil aircraft, it was not subject to the 'Aircraft Nomenclature Committee', which allocated the names of water fowl for small multi-seat amphibians (e.g. Seagull, Sheldrake, and Seamew) and the names of 'seaboard British towns' for larger seaplanes. Thus 'Southampton' was chosen for the new air force machine—albeit an estuary port not a seaboard town, such as, say, the nearby Southsea. In negotiating this name, the company was now signifying Supermarine's increasing status where its factory was sited and whose dignitaries had welcomed home the successful Sea Lion II in 1922.

Supermarine Southampton (1925)

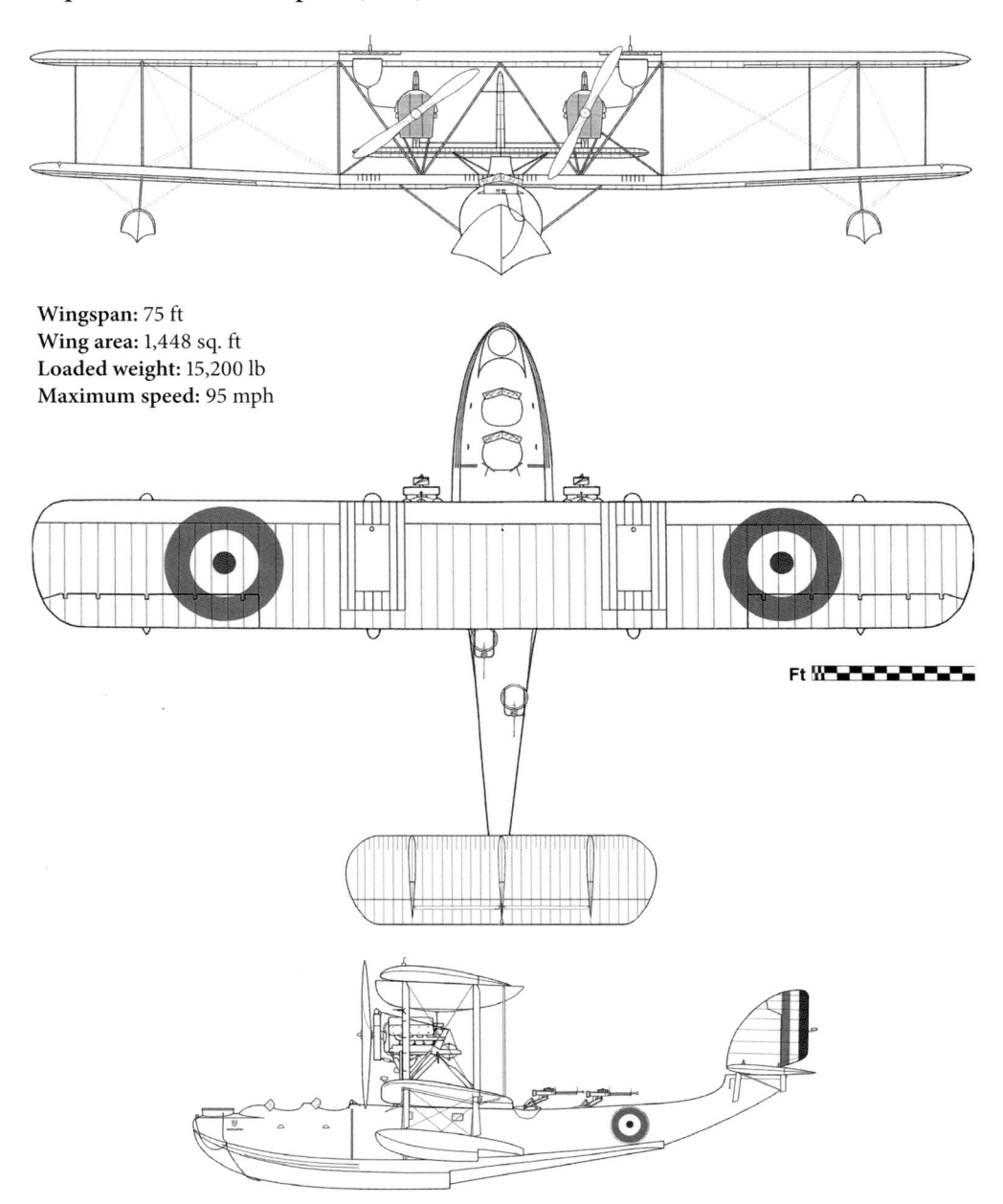

Wingspan: 75 ft
Wing area: 1,448 sq. ft
Loaded weight: 15,200 lb
Maximum speed: 95 mph

The first Southampton of the initial RAF order (with the originally designed floats).

> **Cozens Gives Some Interesting Information About the Construction of the Southampton Hull**
> Many considered the Southampton's wooden hull to be the ultimate in design and craftsmanship, in its shape and purpose Mitchell combined his experience in building with Captain Biard's reports on flying [Cozens mentions several times the importance of Biard's advice to Mitchell during these early years and this would have been especially important to Mitchell when there was little theory to guide designers; as Cozens was a neighbour of the test pilot, it would seem very likely that he heard of particular instances where advice was given—and no doubt listened to willingly.] and this was recognised by the people of Southampton who subscribed and had a silver shield with the Southampton coat of arms fixed to the bow of N9896.
>
> It was about this time that Scott-Paine and his co-director Commander Bird had a tremendous quarrel which ended with Scott-Paine leaving Supermarine with a fortune which he used to begin the British Power Boat Company at the old boat sheds at Hythe, where the May, Harden and May company built the Felixstowe flying boats of the Great War period.
>
> The late Mr Conrad Mann, who worked on the wooden Southamptons, told me they were built bottom side up so that the two steps and the curved keel, which had been a feature of the Swan, could be built. He said there were six men and two apprentices on each hull and the contract price agreed by them for each hull was £483. 19s. 4d. so that the money worked out as follows:
>
> | | | | |
> |---|---|---|---|
> | Contract price for 6 men to build 1 hull | £483 | 19s. | 4d. |
> | Wages for 6 men to build 1 hull | £357 | 19s. | 4d. |
> | Balance | £126 | 0s. | 0d. |
> | This was shared among the men giving each | £21 | 0s. | 0d. |
>
> The two apprentices were paid by the company.

> This arrangement seemed to work very well, giving both the management and the men every encouragement to build the machines as quickly as possible, and most of the men bought their bicycles with the lump sum bonus ...
>
> Extracts from letters about the Supermarine Southampton which appeared in the *Southern Evening Echo*:
>
> 'Southampton people had good cause to remember and honour that machine because it brought a good deal of prestige and a steady flow of work to the factory where it was built'.
>
> 'This was the time of the Depression and the General Strike, when a machine was finished there was an order for another one. With a steady wage and the prospect of another bonus, the workforce was fortunate and happy. This air of well-being, stimulated by the success of the Schneider Trophy Races, made the firm, and Woolston generally, a vigorous and active area.'
>
> 'About 20 [24 in fact] of the wooden flying boats were made and, as there was not enough floor space at Woolston, the main components were put on barges and ferried across to the boatsheds at Hythe for assembly. There were often three or four machines moored on the Hythe buoys, their varnished hulls and white wings making a picture that those who saw them would never forget.'
>
> This was brought to mind when a Group Captain who saw the picture of the wooden Southampton in the Echo remembered his early days on Flight 48[0], an RAF conversion flight stationed at Calshot to train pilots to fly Southamptons, looked in his logbook and found that he had flown that same machine in about 1928. He said that one day a second pilot wanted to change into the first pilot's seat and left his own seat and went to the one behind him, passing between the two propellers ... At the nearest point the two propellers were only nine inches apart!

The Cozens extract above contains the interesting information that a silver shield with the Southampton coat of arms was fixed to the bow of the first production aircraft (which is, indeed, visible in the photograph also above). The company could, with some confidence, thus mark its increasing importance in the manufacturing community of the area, as the Air Ministry order was substantial by the criteria of the day: it had called for six standard military aircraft (N9896–N9901) and for an experimental one, to be fitted with a metal hull. These aircraft were also the largest aircraft yet to come from a Supermarine production line—the Seagulls and Scarabs had a span of 46 feet, whereas the Southampton spanned 75 feet (6 feet 4 inches more than the 'prototype' Swan—no doubt a response to the MAEE report that the previous machine would have benefited from being 'lightened').

The new machine continued the planing configuration that Mitchell had been developing since 1923 with the Sea Eagle and the Sheldrake, but it was now a part of one of the most elegant hulls that Mitchell had ever been responsible for; indeed, the transformation of the lines of the Swan was striking. Taking advantage of the new, more utilitarian military requirements, he removed the *ad hoc*-looking, high-drag crew compartment above the Swan's lower wing and utilised the passenger baggage compartment area for the pilot and navigator, sitting in tandem in open cockpits. He also streamlined the Swan's nose and dramatically swept the rear of the hull upwards, terminating it in an integrated stub pylon to keep the empennage well clear of the water.

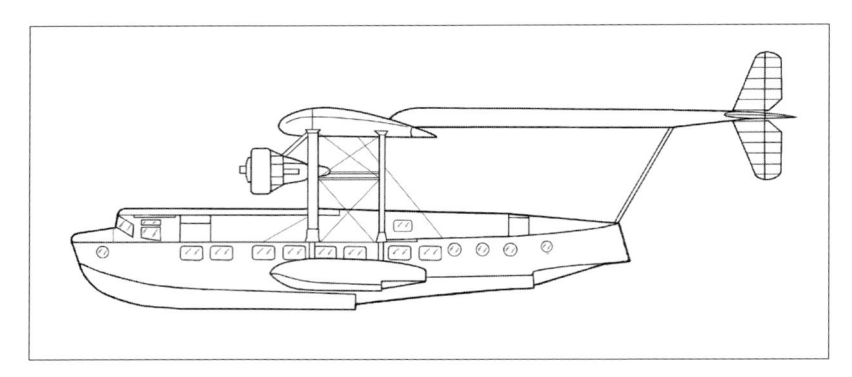

Sikorsky S-40.

While this last feature had been seen earlier (on both the small FBA and the Latham L-1 Schneider aircraft as well as on the First World War Grigorovich machines), its incorporation in the large Southampton hull was a novel and bold move, of which Mitchell must have been aware as a 1924 patent on behalf of himself and Supermarine draws explicit attention to the fact that 'the hull is curved upwardly and rearwardly'. Elsewhere, in larger hull designs, Curtiss and Sikorsky moved from the previous Felixstowe unswept approach to the employment of 'canoe'-type hulls with the empennage attached by booms subtended from the wings and supported by girders from the hull.

In contrast, the elegance of Mitchell's sweeping lines was emphasised and complemented by the redesign of the Swan fins, which were now swept back in a single curve, resulting in the new Southampton being regarded as 'probably the most beautiful biplane flying boat that had ever been built' and 'certainly the most beautiful hull ever built'. Fittingly, the control lines to the tail unit now ran within the hull rather than externally and untidily.

We can be sure, however, that the aeroplane's ability to maintain height on one engine as well as its maximum range of 500 miles weighed more strongly in Air Ministry minds than any aesthetic considerations. No doubt the Air Ministry advisers also appreciated the extreme practicality that was a feature of Mitchell's design: as with the Swan, Warren girders separated the centre section of the wings without the need for wire bracing and so enabled a change of engine or servicing to take place unimpeded and without interference to the airframe. This centre section was plywood-covered, again for ease of operation by mechanics, and the leading edges of the outer panels were also plywood-covered to ensure a smoother aerodynamic entry.

Notably, Mitchell did not incorporate the lower wing roots into the boat hull; instead, the wing superstructure had attachment points on the top of the hull (*see* photo, p. 420), braced by struts from the lower-wing centre-section spars to reinforced frames in the hull. In this way, Mitchell took advantage of the flexibility of the Linton-Hope-type hull and reduced the possibility of cracking around where the wings might have been fixed; he also created an unencumbered hull space with adequate headroom, setting new standards for crew communication.

Ahead of the pilot was a bow cockpit for a forward gunner, and a little further back from where the Swan crew had been located were two staggered cockpits for rear gunners, one on each side of the centre-line. Hammocks, basic cooking, and lavatory facilities were also provided, thus beginning the tradition of providing the RAF with maritime aircraft that could be reasonably self-sufficient for prolonged periods of time.

Supermarine publicity, which draws attention to the main technical features of the Southampton and its many up-to-date features likely to attract potential customers:

THE SUPERMARINE 'SOUTHAMPTON'

This machine, which appeared for the first time in the early part of 1925, is now the standard twin-engine reconnaissance flying-boat of the Royal Air Force, and has been ordered in large numbers for duty with the Naval Cooperation Squadrons.

Recently, a most instructive and successful cruise has been carried out around the British Isles by five of these machines, the total distance covered during the cruise being approximately 10,000 miles. Throughout, the weather was distinctly bad, yet the boats carried out the programme previously drawn up, and demonstrated that they can function successfully quite separately and independently of their land bases. Refuelling at sea was carried out on all occasions without a hitch.

This machine is fitted with two 470 hp Napier 'Lion' engines and is a biplane flying boat of very clean aerodynamic design. The empennage consists of a monoplane tail with three cantilever fins above it. This design of tail is one of the many novel features of the machine, and, in conjunction with the positioning of the rear guns, enables an unrestricted field of fire to be obtained. The design of armament on the 'Southampton' machine has proved that a flying boat can defend itself most efficiently, and has revolutionised all previous beliefs on this matter. The petrol is carried in the top planes, which not only permits a gravity feed, but also reduces the risk of fire to a minimum.

The machine is extremely seaworthy. It is capable of riding out the roughest of seas, and can be taken-off and landed with safety under these conditions. The hull is very roomy and efficiently fitted out for the crew. There is a through passage from bow to stern, and no petrol is carried in the hull. The standard arrangement of crew is as follows: In the bow is the gunner and bomb-operator. Behind him are the two pilots, in tandem, with complete dual control. The after pilot also has a complete navigating compartment. Aft of this is the W/T compartment, which opens out into two rear gun-ring positions behind the main planes. A crew of five is normally carried. The accommodation for the crew is very comfortable and efficiently planned, and is unusually free from noise and draught. Hammocks can be easily fitted, so that the crew can sleep on board and remain afloat for long periods.

The machine has been flown continually on one engine, and can be manoeuvred and turned against the pull of the one engine without difficulty.

The well-known qualities of the Napier 'Lion' engine have been used to the fullest extent by an efficient installation, with the result that not the slightest troubles have been experienced from the power units throughout the many thousands of hours of flying these machines have carried out.

The hull can be supplied either in wood or metal. The first duralumin hulls for the 'Southampton' have already seen considerable service and have proved themselves to be extremely robust and capable of standing up to heavy usage. They are 450 lbs (204 kgs) lighter than the wooden hulls, and this weight can be used either to increase range or military load.

Supermarine's publicity claimed:

Something of a record in design and construction was achieved with the first machine of this class, for it was designed and built in seven months, was flown for the first time one day and delivered by air from Southampton to the RAF at Felixstowe the next day.

In fact, the first flight was on 10 March 1925, and its delivery to the MAEE was five days later; nevertheless, officials must have been impressed by the efficiency with which the chief engineer had had the first Southampton delivered, and its cause could not have been harmed when, after being damaged there in a collision with a breakwater, it was taxied all the way back to Woolston for repairs. Pilots subsequently reported that it 'never gave the slightest trouble … and was a joy to fly', 'a great step forward, a delight to fly and operate'. Penrose reported for the year 1925 that 'it was the beautiful new Supermarine Southampton flying boat which was receiving unstinting approbation from RAF pilots', although it must be said that occupants of the rear cockpit were dangerously close to the propellers and had to avoid waving their arms about (*see* Cozens, p. 177); they also had to find some way to contend with over 90 dB of engine noise.

The combination of practicability, reliability, and range resulted in the RAF undertaking a series of long-range proving flights as soon as deliveries to 480 Coastal Reconnaissance Flight began. In the summer of 1925, four Southamptons flew a twenty-day cruise of 10,000 miles around the British Isles, including exercises with the Royal Navy in the Irish Sea, and a single Southampton—N9896, the first to be completed—made a three-day round trip from Felixstowe to Rosyth, followed by a fourteen-day exercise with the Isles of Scilly as base, and then by a week's cruise around coastal waters.

It can be no exaggeration, therefore, to say that the advent of the Southampton marked the real point at which Supermarine could finally anticipate economic stability and prosperity. In the Supermarine publicity (*see* above), confidence is expressed in features that should appeal to potential customers: ruggedness, manoeuvrability, and unrestricted (by contemporary standards) fields of fire. Mention is also made of the metal hull version of the Southampton that the company was contracted to build. In fact, the original order of six machines was eventually increased to a total of twenty-five, and this total was later increased to eighty-three,

The penultimate wooden hulled Southampton.

when the metal-hulled Marks II to IV were ordered and when sales were extended to Japan, Argentina, and Turkey. As a result, the company took out a lease on the Air Ministry's large flying-boat assembly units at Hythe on the opposite side of the Solent from Woolston, for final erection and testing of their new design.

Significantly, the Supermarine entry in *Jane's All the World's Aircraft* for 1925 records, for the first time, the identity of the company's chief designer:

> The firm has a very large Design Department continually employed on new designs, under the Chief Designer and Engineer, R. J. Mitchell, who has established himself as one of the leading flying boat and amphibian designers in the country.

A more independent view of Mitchell's achievement in the field of seaplane design came from the caption to a picture of a Southampton I flying boat at the beginning of *Jane's* for the same year: 'one of the most notable successes in post-war aircraft design'.

Mitchell had just passed his thirtieth birthday.

The S.4 and the 1925 Schneider Trophy Competition

Mitchell's last seaplanes kept his name in the minds of the Air Ministry and the aviation industry, but it was his singular contribution to the Schneider trophy competitions between 1927 and 1931 that was the more significant in the Spitfire story and by which he became known to the wider British public, however reluctantly. The efficiency of the Southampton and the elegance of its hull design could not have been clearer signs of the emergence of a designer in his own right, but nothing could have prepared the aviation world for his next Schneider trophy aircraft, the S.4, which also showed Mitchell moving ahead of other designers that were far more experienced in high-speed aircraft and beginning the establishment of his reputation in this field.

While the competition had continued to be organised by the national aviation clubs, the importance and costs of the meetings had produced, in 1923, the first appearance of an American government-subsidised team with military pilots and well-organised support staff. Fortunately for Mitchell, the British government had also begun to take these matters seriously, and orders for new machines were placed with Gloster and with Supermarine for 'technical purposes'—it being understood that if the machines proved to be suitable, they would be loaned to the manufacturers for the forthcoming contest. Flying was to be at the Air Ministry's risk, with insurance of personnel the responsibility of the firms involved.

For the first time, Mitchell had the possibility of producing a dedicated and competitive racing machine that was not dependent on straitened company resources and recycled airframes but, as we shall also see with the Spitfire, his initial response was not dramatically original; indeed, his proposed Sea Urchin still looked towards a flying boat approach, which was perhaps not surprising since almost all previous Supermarine design efforts had been directed into this type of seaplane.

In fact, the proposed Sea Urchin might well be regarded, essentially, as an improvement on the Savoia S.51 Schneider racer of 1922 as a similar sesquiplane arrangement was proposed, with a pusher propulsion unit. No slavish copying was to be seen, however, as Mitchell's hull

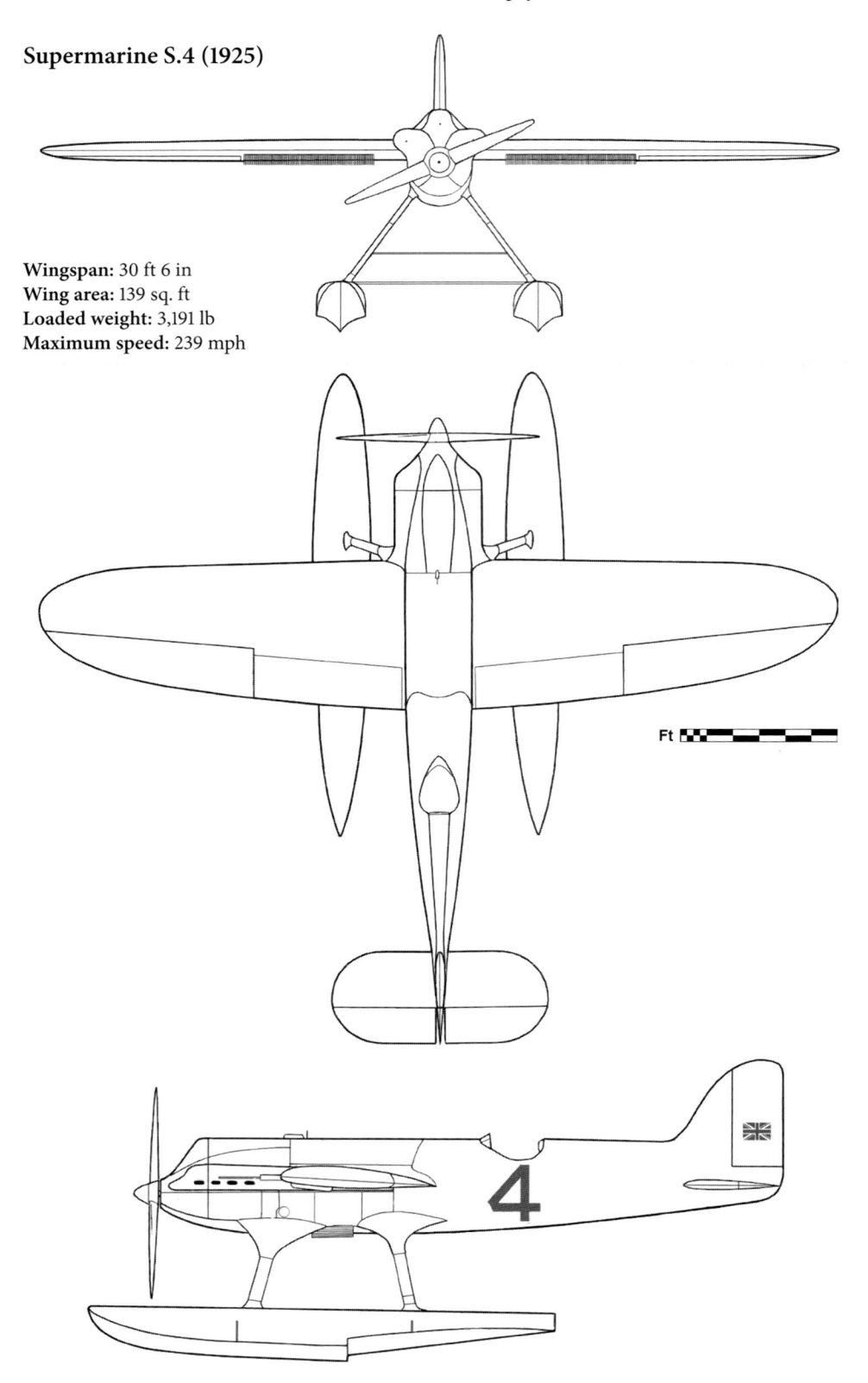

Supermarine S.4 (1925)

Wingspan: 30 ft 6 in
Wing area: 139 sq. ft
Loaded weight: 3,191 lb
Maximum speed: 239 mph

revealed an upswept rear fuselage similar to that being proposed for the Southampton and was to incorporate an integral fin and unbraced tailplane; additionally, the drag penalty of the high-mounted engine was to be reduced by situating the engine in the hull and driving the propeller through bevel-geared shafting—some response, at least, to the successful American in-line engined CR-3. Yet nothing eventually came of the Sea Urchin because, as Alan Clifton said, 'of doubts about the shaft drive'.

Meanwhile, the Gloster Aircraft Company, had produced the promising Gloster II floatplane, but it porpoised on landing after its first test flight and sank when one of the float struts collapsed. The Italians had purchased two of the American Curtiss D-12 engines for experimental purposes, but no plane from that country materialised in time for a 1924 contest either. So the American National Aerobatic Association, responsible for hosting the next event, declared it void and the Royal Aero Club cabled its 'warmest appreciation of this sporting action'. A second win, by a fly-over, would have put America in a strong position to win the Schneider trophy outright, on home ground, in 1925.

This unexpected turn of events gave the necessary breathing space for Mitchell to contemplate the necessity of a comprehensive move from the well-tried flying boat approach to a float monoplane, although the time available to construct this machine, with all the attendant problems of building such a novel aircraft, was not great—Supermarine only received official approval to begin building on 18 March 1925. The allocated Air Ministry serial number of the new machine was N197, although this was never carried; Supermarine referred to the new machine only as the S.4—'S' presumably referring to Schneider and '4' indicating that it was the successor of the Mark III Sea Lion.

The notable leap from this previous aircraft to the new design can be readily appreciated from the following side-views.

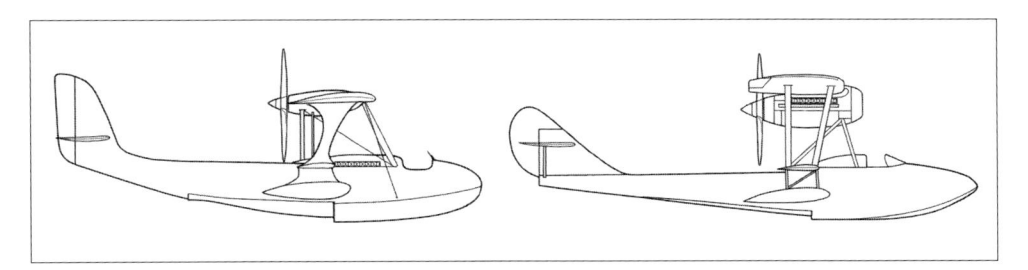

From left to right: Sea Urchin and Savoia S.51.

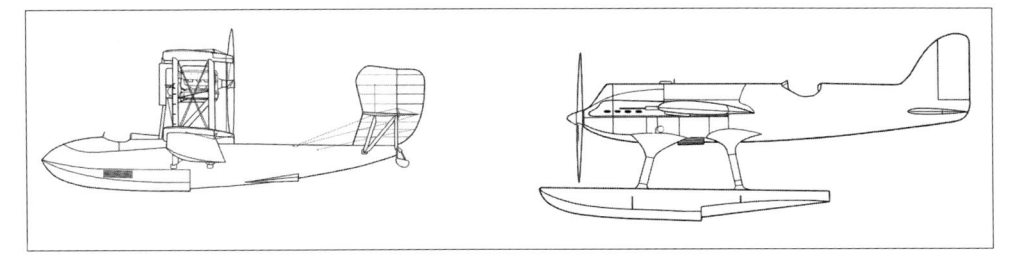

From left to right: Sea Lion II (1922) and S.4 (1925).

This dramatic emergence of the resultant S.4 was well recorded in the aviation press when finally invited to see the aircraft. The *Aeroplane* correspondent said that security had been such that the press visit on 17 September 'should be entitled "A Visit to Shush-ampton"' but he went on to report one's impression on seeing the machine for the first time:

> here at last Great Britain had produced a speed machine the designer of which, if not actually striking out on an absolutely new line of development, had at any rate tackled the problem of reducing head resistance in a way nobody in this country has hitherto attempted … When it is remembered that Mr Mitchell has hitherto almost exclusively devoted his attention to the flying-boat biplane, it is little short of astonishing that he should have been able so entirely to break away from the types which he has been so intimately connected for the past seven or eight years, and not only abandon the flying-boat type in favour of the twin-float arrangement, but actually change from the braced-biplane structure to the pure cantilever wing of the S.4.

Flight went further:

> Perhaps one may describe the Supermarine-Napier S.4 as having the appearance of having been designed in an inspired moment … and we think the greatest credit is due to Mr R. J. Mitchell, chief designer of the Supermarine Aviation Works, for his courage in breaking away from stereotyped methods and striking out on entirely novel lines.

Later, its special place in aviation history was recognised by an Italian rival designer—as E. Bazzocchi of Aeronautica Macchi said, 'the real revolution of 1925 was the appearance of the Supermarine; its very clean design set the pattern for all subsequent Schneider racers'. Mitchell could hardly fail to be pleased by his peers' recognition of his ground-breaking design and especially by a similar feature in his hometown newspaper, particularly as it again gave some publicity for the local firm, 'Wood, Mitchell and Co., printers, Hanley'. (*Sentinel*, 18 September 1925).

Mitchell's Spitfire, later, was preceded by another monoplane fighter and by the high-speed S.5/6 series of trophy racers; by comparison, the S.4 was far more dramatically original and unusual. On the other hand, it ought to be noted that nearly a year previously, the French speed record holder, the Bernard V-2 landplane, had displayed features that might have prompted Mitchell's design— its Hispano-Suiza engine's broad arrow design was similar to the S.4's Lion engine and was incorporated almost identically into the fuselage and wings; it also had cantilever flying surfaces and under-wing radiators.

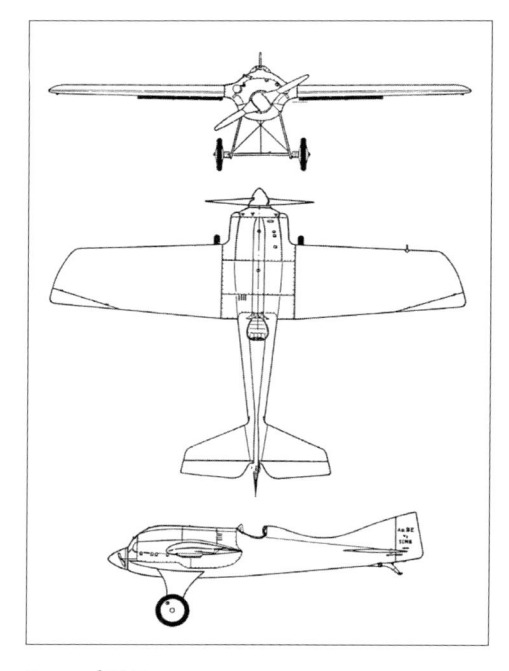

Bernard V-2.

The S.4 at Woolston prior to departure for America. The strut fairings are incomplete.

Nevertheless, when Harald Penrose of Westlands wrote of 'the startling novel and beautiful Supermarine S.4', he was at least reflecting the dramatic appearance of an entirely new floatplane design and was surely right in responding to its fine lines; it might not be unduly partisan to notice that Mitchell avoided the rather humpbacked rear fuselage of the French design and chose curving lines instead of angularity by way of semi-elliptical wings that were matched by a more rounded fin and tailplane.

Clifton also drew attention to the undoubtedly unique attachment of the floats: 'It was an exceptionally clean design, with a central skeleton of steel tubing which included daring cantilevered float struts.' This 'central skeleton' was, characteristic of Mitchell—a deceptively simple arrangement of two very strong 'A' frames that related directly to the three sections of the fuselage: the engine mounting was bolted to the front frame and the rear monocoque fuselage section to the rear one; between the two, the wing was fixed and the floats were attached to the feet of the frames. It was known in the works, less reverently, as 'the clothes horse'. The struts were carefully faired into the tops of the floats and into the fuselage, which, in its turn, was tailored to the contours of the engine cowlings.

The move from flying boat to floatplane brought the new requirement for floats and this led Supermarine prudently to order an alternative pair from Shorts who had recently installed their own testing tank designed specifically to simulate seaplane conditions. Some doubt has been expressed as to whether they were actually used instead of the wooden floats built by Supermarine but a comment by Oswald Short (*see* p. 195) would seem to suggest that it was the Short pair that was employed at the next competition.

The wing certainly represented a striking departure from earlier Supermarine structures, as Supermarine publicity was keen to point out:

In view of the extremely novel type of design and the large number of experimental features incorporated in this machine, this may be fairly considered a remarkable achievement.

The wing, which is of a new high-speed section, is built of wood and constructed as one unit. No fabric is used for covering; three-ply is used throughout, and in such a manner as to take its share of the load. The trailing portion of the wing can be used as a flap to reduce landing speed, and the ailerons are also geared in with the flap mechanism.

Newer Lamblin radiators were mounted on the underside of the wings and these, with their oil cooling fins, were the only significant protuberances exposed to the slipstream: coolant water was carried to and from the engine via troughs buried in the underside of the wings and the interconnected flaps and ailerons and the tail surfaces were activated also from within the structure via torque rods and tubes. The streamlining aluminium fairings from the engine section extended almost to a point level with the wing trailing edge, giving the wooden body protection from the searing heat from the Lion's stub exhausts.

> **The following reminiscence of Cozens reminds one that the S.4 was, despite its futuristic shape and polished metal cowlings, built with traditional woodworking techniques. Its sound, however, was something else—no doubt the result of its ungeared racing engine producing propeller tip speeds around the speed of sound (2,600 rpm turning an eight and a half foot airscrew—go figure):**
>
> After being beaten in 1923 by trying to make the best of an outdated machine, Mitchell went to the other extreme and produced something that was far ahead of its time. It was, of course, of wooden construction, not surprising as neither the designers nor the workforce were capable of building a sophisticated metal machine, and it exploited the Linton-Hope technique to the limit, and the cantilever wings and float struts were faired into the fuselage so that the whole was clean and the flying characteristics were bound to be a matter of some speculation. When considering it today, fifty six years later, one must concede that it was a daring gamble. It was built in great secrecy which gave rise to even more curiosity and expectancy than was usual for a Schneider Trophy, always a sensitive subject and it was guarded like a racehorse in a training stables.
>
> By raising the compression ratio the Napier's power was increased and the metal Fairey Reed propeller was quite new in design and construction, so that when it finally emerged and the engine was run-up a new sound came, something that the local people had never heard before, and indeed, very few people ever heard in all their life, a sort of high pitched scream of immense power.
>
> Radiator drag was reduced to a minimum by building it flush into the wings, and because it was made of thin copper plates soldered together it had to be very carefully formed and fitted ... Plainly, this aeroplane needed very skilful handling, more so because the mid-wing shape made visibility poor, and Captain Biard was the only man who could fly it, and an eyewitness said that even he made an airborne hop of a mile before he finally got off between Lee-on-Solent and Calshot.

Mitchell's design was built in five months and Biard first flew the machine on 24 August, 1925. According to Biard, Mitchell had put on a bathing costume, assuring his test pilot that 'if anything happens, I'll dive into the water and pull you out'. In fact, this offer was nearly taken up owing to the pilot's position. Centre of gravity considerations necessitated the cockpit being situated even further back behind the trailing edge of the wing than in the Bernard

The S.4 at Calshot.

machine and, with the high position of this wing, created a blind spot ahead when taking off and landing. Biard claimed to have nearly collided with the liner *Majestic* on take-off (having not seen it at all until the last minute), and when he came in to land, he nearly hit a dredger. However, the S.4 thereafter proceeded to gain the world speed record for seaplanes and the outright British speed record by registering 226.75 mph—nearly 40 mph more than the Curtiss CR-3 record.

In contrast to the Supermarine design, the new Gloster III, while also featuring an uprated Lion engine and a metal propeller, stayed with the current orthodoxy of the wire-braced biplane formula. The new Italian entry, the M.33, also retained many previous features—it was a flying boat that necessitated an engine mounted on struts above the fuselage and therefore unable to be effectively streamlined—but on the other hand, it now employed a cantilever wing, though less dramatically than the S.4 (*see* drawings p. 149). Nor were the Americans making bold advances, being restricted to developing the previous CR-3 by fairing the upper wing into the fuselage and installing an engine which was now developing 700 hp.

Owing to the short time between receiving Air Ministry backing for the building of the aircraft and the race itself, neither the S.4 nor the two Gloster IIIs had many suitable opportunities for test flights before planes and personnel had to be transported to America, along with a practice machine. On the other hand, they were the first to arrive at the proposed venue, Chesapeake Bay, near Baltimore, on 5 October—further evidence of Britain's new-found determination to compete seriously.

The actual base of operations was Bay Shore Park, a beach area 14 miles south-east of Baltimore, where tented accommodation for hangars and workshops was to be provided. This provision was found not to be ready, and it was only possible to begin erecting the aircraft on 12 October; even then, Mitchell and Folland, Gloster's designer, were appalled at the conditions that their ground crews had to work under. Several days elapsed before any

The British contingent en route to Baltimore: Mitchell, front row left; Folland, front row right; in between, team leader, Capt. Charles B. Wilson; Henri Biard behind.

flying was possible, the Gloster III going first, followed by the S.4 on 16 October. Then Biard went down with influenza and the weather worsened to gale conditions, causing the collapse of some of the tents. A heavy pole fell across the tail unit of the S.4, which necessitated hard work by four Supermarine rigger/engineers in order to get the aircraft ready in time for the navigation tests on the 23rd of the month.

By this time, Biard was up and about, although not his usual self, and the British team leader, Capt. Charles B. Wilson, suggested that the reserve pilot, Bert Hinkler, should take over the S.4. Biard resisted this, as only he had had experience of handling this advanced machine. Unfortunately, the S.4 story was not to have a *Boys' Own* ending as it crashed into the bay following a steep turn. This luckily occurred at low level and Biard survived. Mitchell, always concerned for the safety of his pilots, had set out to rescue him but his boat had engine failure and Biard was only picked up after some time in very cold water.

Flight had described how Biard took off and circled the tented area:

> [But] coming back over the pierhead ... at a height of about 800 ft he seemed to make a steeply banked turn, which at first led the spectators to believe he was stunting, but it was soon realised that the machine was in difficulty and not under proper control.

Aviation magazine reported:

> The machine appeared to stall and sideslip first one way and then the other from about 500 feet. After a half dozen of these right and left wing ups and downs, Captain Biard appeared to lose control completely and dropped about a hundred feet, pancaking into the bay.

The result was also described by one of the Schneider Committee:

> He decided to practise some sharp turns and completed one satisfactorily and then attempted another. It was noticed his aileron was hard down on the lower side. The machine seemed to get out of control and did a falling leaf descent, making a huge hole in the sea.

According to the *Baltimore Sun*, the S.4 'nosed into the water and … catapulted over on its back'.

These varying eyewitness accounts, however, did not record any structural failure, although the mention of a depressed aileron 'on the lower side' suggested an attempt to correct the effect of a wing twisting out of correct incidence. On the other hand, the *Times* correspondent at the contest said that the machine went out of control because the wings fluttered, which might have indicated that they were not torsionally strong enough, and the correspondent of the *Aeroplane* reported that 'Mr Biard after getting off made several sharp turns and put the machine on to vertical banks. After the last it seemed to develop wing flutter and get out of control'.

The S.4 taking off for the last time.

Later, in England, Biard was found to have two broken ribs and damage to some stomach muscles which later needed an operation. His own account of the crash was that, on coming out of a turn at speed and diving down for a straight run, the control column set up such violent side-to-side oscillations that he lost control. Wing flutter was being experienced at about this time with military aircraft. Penrose quotes a Flt Lt Linton Ragg of the Royal Aircraft Establishment at Farnborough as experiencing similar stick behaviour: 'wing flutter had caused trying [!] experiences, such as coming down with hand and knees badly bruised by the control column as it played hide-and-seek round the cockpit'.

It has also been suggested that Biard, probably still not sufficiently recovered from illness, had stalled through unfamiliarity with the effect of a very tight high-speed turn. In his report to the Royal Aeronautical Society given on 21 January 1926, Maj. J. S. Buchanan, the Air Ministry representative at Baltimore, merely stated that the S.4 stalled and crashed into the sea but, after his lecture, Biard made the rueful or joking rejoinder that 'I also note that Major Buchanan says, "High-speed diving is not necessary [during turns] in the Schneider race"—I will take this to heart but wish he had mentioned it before we went to America'.

However, while torsional weakness or a high-speed stall cannot be ruled out, 'flutter' might very well have been the most likely cause of the crash, especially as the landplane version which preceded the Gloster Schneider entry had had an emergency landing because of tail flutter and Biard had also reported a more minor tremor of the S.4 wings before going to America (as, it was revealed later, had the Italian M.33).

Certainly, as other aircraft caught up with the speed of the S.4, flutter and aileron reversal were soon to emerge as something needing to be understood and remedied: indeed, in 1926, the MAEE introduced 'terminal velocity' dive tests as standard. Biard's description of side-to-side movement of the control column, similar to that experienced by Ragg, points to aileron flutter and later remarks at Supermarine confirm this conclusion; Mitchell, concerned about the need to avoid overbalancing of the Spitfire ailerons in a dive, wrote somewhat enigmatically, 'I believe this is the cause of several accidents involving ailerons' and Ernest Mansbridge, explaining the thickness of the later Type 224 wing being due to caution, was more direct: 'We were still very concerned about possible flutter, having encountered that with the S.4 seaplane'—perhaps the definitive explanation.

After the crash of the S.4, the second Gloster III was hastily prepared as, unaccountably, the Royal Aero Club had only entered two machines, instead of the three permitted. They were handicapped by their protruding leading-edge radiators, which had had to be fitted when their wing surface radiators could not be readied in time. One of these aircraft was damaged during the preliminary tests, an Italian entry was unable to make the start line, and during the race proper, two of the three American R3C-2s had engine failure. As a result, of the eight aircraft that had come to Baltimore, only three finished, with America taking the trophy at an average speed of 232.562 mph, followed by the Gloster machine at an average of 199.167 mph, with the remaining Italian aircraft a disappointing third.

As the first two aircraft were floatplanes, it was now clearly evident that the flying-boat formula, still favoured by the Italians with their M.33, was now outdated and, in his report, Maj. Buchanan stressed the need for reducing fuselage drag, the need for wing surface radiators, and the need for ample time to test the efficiency of different propellers. He also called for the use of pilots trained for high-speed flight, as per the American Navy and Army teams of the last two contest wins.

A Turning Point (1925)

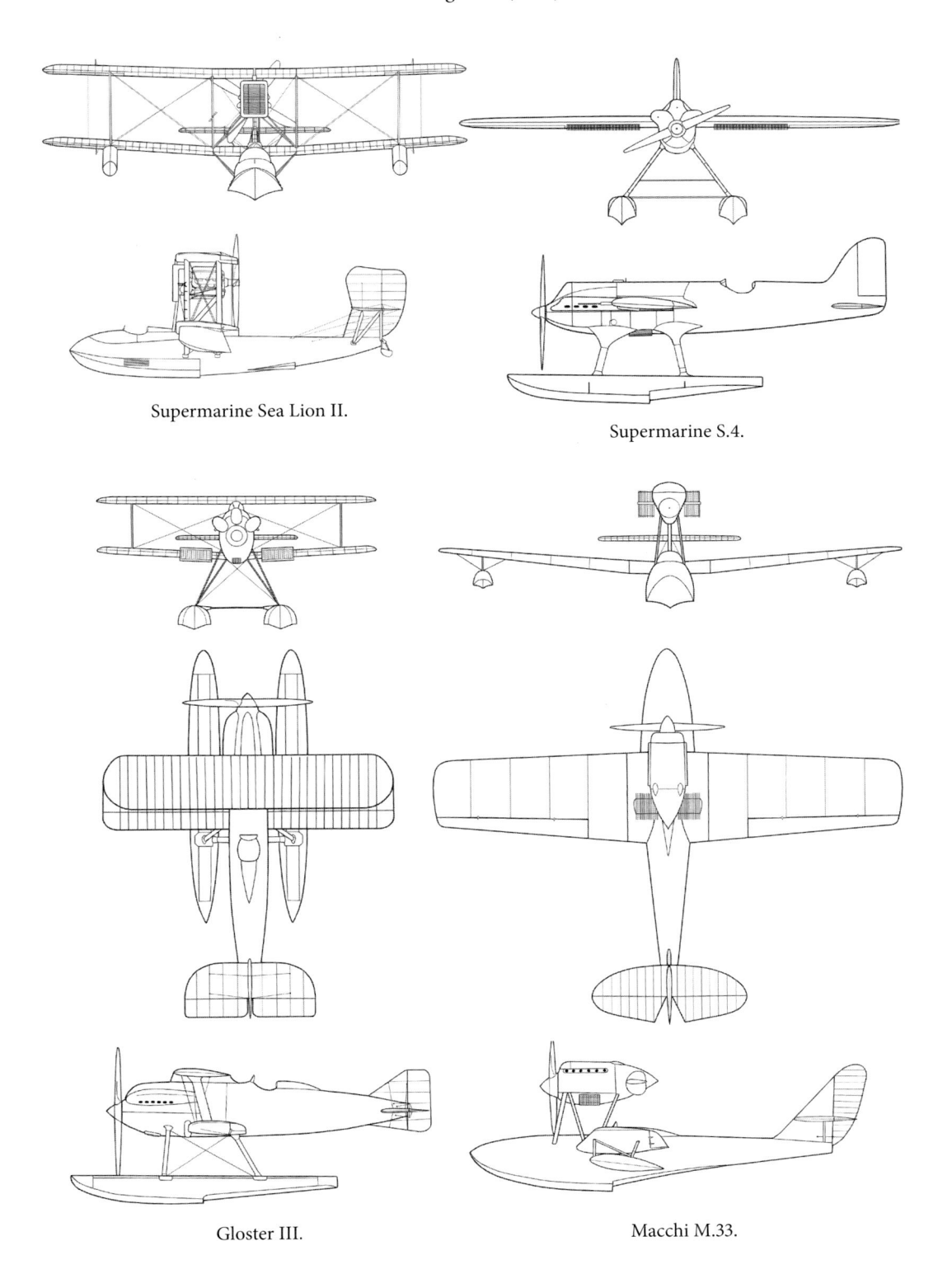

Supermarine Sea Lion II.

Supermarine S.4.

Gloster III.

Macchi M.33.

Despite civilian pilots' evident skill and willingness to take risks, it remained a fact that their usual flying experience was of much slower machines and that their comparatively isolated experiences of Schneider speeds was compounded by the very limited amount of practice time available—as we have seen, the Schneider events were characterised by late go-ahead decisions and, therefore, late delivery of new machines, not uncommonly coupled with curtailed flying at the race sites, either because of mechanical problems or because of weather unsuitable for specialist racing machines.

The case of Henri Biard was not untypical. Mitchell's S.4 was first flown by him on 25 August, and despite reporting slight wing tremors, he had to leave soon afterwards for the Schneider competition in America; influenza and damage to the floatplane resulted in his being only just ready for the Trophy navigability trials on the 23rd. It is to Biard's credit (or belief in his own immortality) that he was prepared to attempt to race in a somewhat suspect machine, with poor forward visibility for take-off and landing, and with little time to familiarise himself with what the other competitors had already surmised to be the fastest aircraft in the field. Not only had his experience on the revolutionary S.4 been very limited, but between his flying the Sea Lion III at a maximum speed of 175 mph in 1923, and achieving 239 mph in the new machine two years later, his day-to-day flying experience with Supermarine was with the Swan passenger amphibian, the Scarab reconnaissance amphibian, the Sparrow I light landplane, and the Southampton I flying boat, whose top speeds averaged out at something less than 100 mph.

Before the year of the eighth contest was over, it was announced that the next Schneider trophy was to be held in the following year in the week beginning 24 October. While the British Lion engine had been faultless in 1925 and was now developing almost 1 hp per lb—slightly better than the new Curtiss V-1400, which had been far less reliable—the perceived need for fundamental rethinking by British aircraft manufacturers and the need for a radical overhaul of the British effort prompted the Royal Aero Club to ask for a one-year postponement.

This time, the NAA refused. After all, they had now achieved two wins in a row and could very probably manage a third and final success without costly new designs, bearing in mind that the Americans had now set up a new world record for seaplanes at 245.71 mph in their existing R3C-2. Additionally, a delay might not be wise as American governmental priorities were hardening towards the development of air commerce and transport; barnstorming was not being encouraged as it was now more important to promote a public appreciation of safe commercial flying.

Fortunately for the future public standing of Mitchell and, arguably, for the later development of the Spitfire, events in Italy intervened. Mussolini had come to power in 1922 and, by now, felt it needful to demonstrate the success of his dictatorship—in particular, he decided that Italy must win the next Schneider trophy at (literally) all costs, despite the very obvious American lead in design. It was decreed that the state would provide all necessary financial and other assistance to create both a suitable airframe and a matching engine. Three aircraft were ordered, finished to contest standard, while another two were for training and practice flying, with an additional airframe for structural test work; an approach was also made to the United States for six of the Curtiss engines that had brought victory to the R3C-2 at Baltimore.

In the event, the Italian Air Ministry had been unable to obtain approval for the purchase of the American engines, but Fiat, having profited from the earlier study of the Curtis D-12 engine, were able to offer a twelve-cylinder 'V' that was capable of developing over 800 hp. The new AS.2 engine eventually produced 880 hp on the test bench, and by mid-August, the first competition aircraft was ready for testing. Yet engine heating and carburation problems soon began to emerge and one pilot was killed in training, so an application was made for a short delay, to which America sportingly agreed. The race date was put back to 11 November, and on 12 October, the Italian team set off for prohibition America with their new M.39s and with a plentiful supply of Chianti smuggled in their floats.

In reply, the Americans fielded an R3C-2 with the 1925 600-hp engine, another Curtiss floatplane with a 700-hp geared Packard engine (designated R3C-3), and also an R3C-4, which had a 700-hp Curtiss powerplant. There was also a Curtiss Hawk fighter equipped with floats for team practice and as a reserve. Against them, the Italians now revealed their M.39s, which looked to represent a formidable challenge and were known to have considerably more horsepower than the R3Cs.

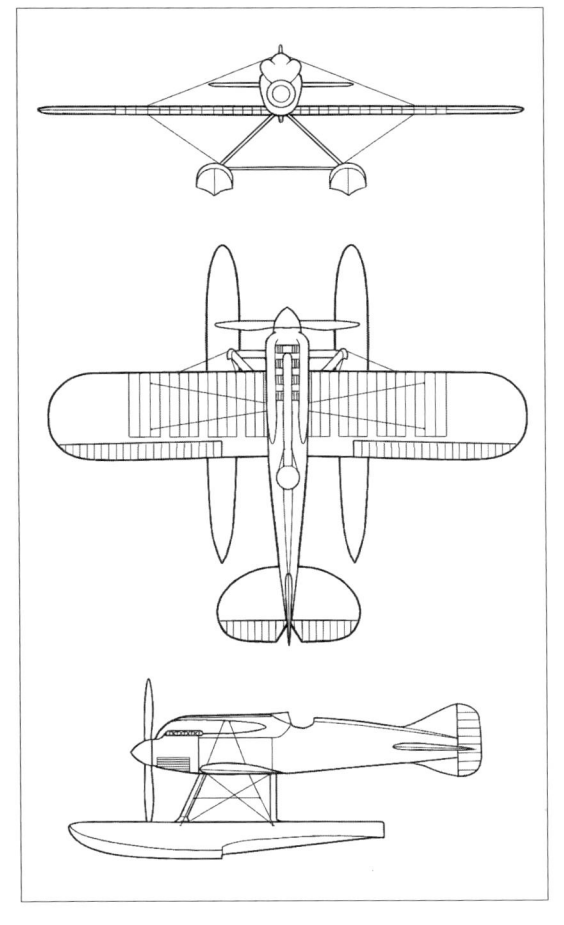

Macchi M.39.

Things did not go well for the Americans as the R3C-3 engine was not giving full power and the R3C-4 engine overheated during practice and was seriously damaged. Meanwhile, the Italians also had their engine problems: one M.39 had to be force-landed because of an engine fire and the engine of another had a connecting-rod failure; their carburation problems had also not been overcome. The earlier call for a year's postponement by both Italy and Britain began to seem rather sensible.

The flying competition of the ninth contest eventually took place on 13 November, without a British entry. One of the Italians dropped out of the competition on lap four as a result of a fractured oil pipe and then an American had to retire on the seventh lap with fuel supply problems; he landed safely but with a severely blistered hand from furiously operating a hand-pump for lifting fuel from the floats. Another of the Americans was hampered by a float-wing wire that had parted and was causing considerable flutter when approaching top speed.

Of the remaining four contestants, the Italian Maj. Mario de Bernardi came in first in one of the new Macchi M.39s at an average speed of 246.496 mph, followed by Lt C. F. Schilt in the ailing Curtiss R3C.2, returning a figure of 231.363 mph; Lt Adriano Bacula came in third, in the second M.39, having flown a circumspect 218.01 mph in order to ensure that he might do well if the two R3Cs dropped out, but beating as planned the slower Lt William G. Tomlinson in the reserve Curtiss F6C-1 Hawk, which could only achieve an average of 136.95 mph. De Bernardi duly sent a cable to Mussolini, stating: 'Your order to win at all costs has been obeyed.'

Thus the Italian victory had the important result of preventing a third American victory and the capturing of the Trophy outright, meaning that even though the American phase of the Schneider competitions had brought no success for Supermarine, Mitchell might yet have a further opportunity of improving on his unlucky Baltimore entry.

Meanwhile, and with the gift of hindsight, the American (mis)adventure can be seen as a most important milestone in Mitchell's career. His S.4 was to set the design pattern for all future Schneider trophy winners and its clean cantilever flying surfaces were to be echoed by similar silhouettes in the none-too-distant Second World War. Later, when Mitchell returned to the design of racing floatplanes, he turned from the wooden airframe of this 1925 aircraft to embrace the metal structures that were also to become a feature of the future generations of fighter aircraft.

We shall see the successful outcomes of the new technology when Mitchell's machines competed in the next three Schneider trophy competitions, and it is these that established his reputation beyond the aircraft industry; however, when one considers the quantum shift from the Sea Lion of 1922 to the S.4 of 1925, a special place should be reserved in British aviation history and in Mitchell's design career for the ill-fated but striking S.4. It was a failure but should not be underestimated as it marked out the emergence of a notably innovative designer dramatically pushing forward the frontiers of high-speed flight. Supermarine's publicity in 1926 (*see* below) draws particular attention to this and to the advanced design features which were employed; it also points out that the previously quoted top speed of over 226 mph was later increased to 239 mph and makes the claim that it was 'the fastest British aircraft of any type'.

Supermarine's publicity in 1926 draws particular attention to the fact that the S.4 was designed on the frontiers of aviation technology; one might not be too surprised that the company saw no reason to mention the loss of the machine:

The Supermarine-Napier S.4 is a twin-float cantilever monoplane of high performance. The machine was built as part of the Air Ministry's programme of high-speed development, and was loaned to the Supermarine Company for entry in last year's Schneider Trophy Race. Instructions to proceed with the construction of this aircraft were issued on March 18, 1925, and the first flight was carried out on August 25, 1925. In view of the extremely novel type of design and the large number of experimental features incorporated in this machine, this may be fairly considered a remarkable achievement.

The wing, which is of a new high-speed section, is built of wood and constructed as one unit. No fabric is used for covering; three-ply is used throughout, and in such a manner as to take its share of the load. The trailing portion of the wing can be used as a flap to reduce landing speed, and the ailerons are also geared in with the flap mechanism.

The chassis consists only of four high-tensile tubes, with two light horizontal bracing tubes. The main support tubes are braced together within the fuselage, and thus form a complete structure on which the remainder of the machine is erected. The engine bearers are built on forward, the wing is attached to the top, and the rear fuselage is bolted on to the aft end of this central section. It is well to note that this machine is not only based on excellent aerodynamic design, but the floats are admitted to represent a very great advance on anything previously achieved. A minimum of spray is caused when taking-off. It will be recalled that on September 13, 1925, this machine set up a World's Speed Record for Seaplanes, covering the 3-kilometre course at a speed of 226.6 mph Since this date the performance has been considerably improved by special tuning of the engine and fitting of a propeller of greater efficiency. At the same time, the S.4 achieved the distinction of being the fastest British aircraft of any type, achieving a maximum speed figure of 239 mph.

R.J. at his drawing board, circa 1931.

7

Becoming 'R.J.'

> *A mental picture which always springs to my mind when remembering him, is R.J. leaning over a drawing, chin in hand, thinking hard.*
>
> Joe Smith

Although the year 1925 had marked Mitchell's full emergence as a leading designer with his Southampton and especially with his S.4, his early successes and improvements on more traditional machines had already made some impression on the aviation industry. Edward Smithies has narrated how Eric Lovell-Cooper, who had begun work at Boulton & Paul Aviation, had learned of him at about this time:

> As a promising youngster he was advised to try for a job at Supermarine's. 'They were supposed to have a pretty bright chap there.' This was R. J. Mitchell …
>
> The first job he gave me to do [in 1924] was a radiator for the Southampton flying boat. He expanded a bit on what he wanted and I began to realise he broke all the cardinal rules of what I knew about aircraft design.

Mitchell was, in many ways, a cautious and gradual improver of tried designs but, at that point in time, he was also just about to be the creator of the racing floatplane that established the basic design configuration for all subsequent Schneider trophy machines, the future protagonist of the thin wing, and the man behind the Spitfire.

Joe Smith, who took over as chief designer after Mitchell's death, likewise identified his innovative capacity: 'Thinking back, I have realised that no other man of my experience has produced anything like the number of new and practical fundamental ideas that he did during his relatively short span of working.' Future chapters will describe such significant moments but, at this pivotal moment in his career, it would seem a good time to make some assessment of the nature of the man who was now departing from past practice—the man who by now had begun to contribute significantly to British flying boat development, who had thus had earned the respect of the company, and who had now become known (perhaps rather circumspectly) as 'R.J.'

Sir Robert McLean, the managing director of Vickers (Aviation), had identified Mitchell's main virtues as 'a curious mixture of dreams and common sense'—a combination of the practical and the aesthetic; and *Flight* magazine drew attention to another aspect of the make-up of the designer—what today would be called 'multitasking':

> His versatility will be appreciated when it is pointed out that his productions ranged from heavy, long-range flying boats to tiny single-seat landplane fighters and on more than one occasion he had two or three very different types of aircraft passing through the design stage at the same time, so that he frequently had to switch his mind from one problem to another of a totally different character.

This output earned the comment from Sir George Edwards (who rose from the ranks to become chief designer at Vickers in 1939) that Mitchell was 'the most versatile of all British designers'. Arthur Black, Mitchell's chief metallurgist, made a similar, retrospective, assessment:

> He designed an incredible number [of machines] ranging from large flying boats and amphibians to light aircraft and from racing planes and fighters to a four-engined bomber. This diversity of effort and its amount marks R. J. Mitchell for the genius he was.

If the enigmatic Scylla, the cancelled Giant, and the Bomber terminated by enemy action are added to the machines that flew, he had overall responsibility for twenty-three different types of aircraft in the seventeen years that he was active as chief designer—and it has been estimated that he had also considered nearly 100 other projected aircraft, modifications, or variants.

Clearly the capacity for hard work underlay his dreams of flight and resulted in the contemporary success of the Seagulls, the Sea Eagles, and the Southamptons—as well as the Scapas and the Stranraers that were to follow. Their reliability in service clearly indicate that, as chief designer and chief engineer, he was something of a perfectionist—doing his very best with the materials and theories available to him at the time.

With only seven drawing office staff when he became chief designer (and there were no more than double that number by 1923), the firm was small enough during the formative years of Supermarine that he could personally ensure that his own standards were applied at all stages of an aircraft's production. Alan Clifton, who knew Mitchell from when he joined him at Supermarine in 1923, has left an appreciation of Mitchell that attests to his attention to detail:

> he would visit the drawing office and study a drawing, head on hands and mostly thinking without speaking. Occasionally he would ask a question. The chap fetched to answer would stay, with the result that gradually a number of people were gathered. On rare occasions the whole drawing would be rejected, but normally a better alternative to some feature was described to the draughtsman, and Mitchell moved on to repeat the process.

This application to detail is confirmed by Joe Smith:

> When in the throes of a new design, the arrangement of which had been decided, he would spend almost all his time in the drawing office on the various boards. Here he would argue out the details with the draughtsmen concerned, and show a complete grasp of the whole aircraft ... Construction of the machine having begun, he would spend some time each day examining and assessing the

result. If he was not satisfied with the way something had turned out, he would go back to the drawing office and, having discussed the matter with the people concerned, either modify it or leave it, as the case might be. And always the practical aspects of the proposed alterations would be borne in mind in relation to the state of the aircraft, and the ability of the works to make the change.

This concern that nothing should be overlooked also explains the hours he spent alone in his office or abstracted while in company; reaching a decision was not to be hurried but the time spent did not imply indecision. Sir Henry Royce made the succinct remark: 'He is slow to decide and quick to act'. Harry Griffiths, Black's assistant, substantiated this view:

> When a problem was being discussed in the drawing office he would stand by the drawing-board listening to all the arguments as to what should be done—on these occasions he had the habit of rolling a pencil back and forth on his hand (it was always a very black pencil!)—and when he had heard enough he would push everyone aside, draw a few lines on top of the existing drawing saying, 'This is what you will do,' throw the pencil down and march back to his office.

As chief engineer, he would also regularly inspect the manufacturing process, again insisting on the same standards, as Black reported:

> I remember how R.J.'s well-built figure, medium height with fair colouring, could be seen in the workshop each morning, studying with complete concentration the developing shape of the aircraft being built. He would walk round it and study it from all angles, now and then examining a detail minutely. I sometimes wondered if he was aware how closely he was watched for some clue as to what his reactions were going to be. If he was satisfied, then he would pass on to the next job; but if he was not satisfied, then much of the design work and manufacture might well have to be done again. But his outlook was strictly practical and having discussed the matter with those concerned, a satisfactory compromise was usually arrived at.

Mansbridge, who joined in 1924 to work on stressing, remembered Mitchell for a similar method of dealing with overall design problems by calling in the leaders of the relevant groups and getting them arguing among themselves. He would listen carefully, making sure that everyone had said his piece, and then either make a decision or go home and sleep on it. Joe Smith put the matter in this way: 'his work was never far from his mind and I can remember many occasions when he arrived at the office with the complete solution of a particularly knotty problem which had baffled us all the night before'. In fact, Mansbridge suspected that, with many problems, Mitchell's discussions were essentially a means of ensuring that he had not overlooked anything and that, otherwise, he had already reached a decision beforehand.

This conscientiousness in the drawing office, in conference, and in the workshop resulted especially in the '108,000 machine miles, No Troubles' of the Far East Cruise of his Southamptons (*see* next chapter). Certainly, there was the crash of his S.4 and, later, of an S.5, but these were the only machines that he designed that, apparently, had serious structural failures. It is notable that both aircraft were produced to exceed contemporary air speed records and their problems could be largely attributed to the limitations of contemporary aerodynamic understanding rather than to any neglect of practical matters. Jack Davis, who joined in 1925 and became senior design draughtsman, observed that Mitchell strongly favoured the design and testing of 'a carefully graded structure', which bent more and more as the test load increased before finally failing; this was part and parcel of his preoccupation with design detail, dedicated to the reliability of his machines and their safety in the air.

When Clifton spoke of Mitchell's 'infinite capacity for taking pains', he also stressed that his 'innovative' contributions were 'pre-eminently practical' and Lovell-Cooper, from the start, identified both the pragmatism and the care as well as the innovation of his work:

> He knew how simple [the cardinal rules] were provided you did them the right way.... Mitchell wanted his designs to be the best of course, but not too much the best otherwise we wouldn't get the plane produced in time. He'd got the right idea about aircraft.

It is not surprising, therefore, that the chief designer's son spoke of 'the great importance he attached to the exercise of common sense, attention to detail, and hard work as recipes for success; but he always put special emphasis on the first of these attributes. This was drummed into me many times.'

Arthur Shirvall described the father as 'a down-to-earth engineer who did things in the simplest possible way', and Sir Robert McLean expanded on his remark about dreams and common sense when he said that Mitchell's mind embraced no idea 'too daring or adventurous to be considered, never from the academic point of view, but always from that of practical application.' The fact that Mitchell's feet were firmly on the ground must, in the early years, have established his position amongst the men who had to turn his ideas into reliable machinery.

Joe Smith, although eulogising somewhat from the distance of seventeen years since his predecessor's death, spoke warmly of this quality of leadership, which was additional to his work ethic, his conscientiousness, and his common sense:

> He never shirked full responsibility, and his technical integrity was unquestioned. He won the complete respect and the confidence of his staff, in whom he created a continuous sense of achievement. He placed himself firmly at the helm, and having made decisions, expected and obtained full cooperation of all concerned.

Again speaking after Mitchell's death, he continued by describing another aspect of his leadership:

> But, in spite of being the unquestioned leader, he was always ready to listen to and to consider another point of view, or to modify his ideas to meet any technical criticism which he thought justified ... The effect of this attitude on the team of young and keen engineers which he collected around him can well be imagined.

As the workplace in Mitchell's time was more authoritarian than today, his consulting and considering the views of those subordinate to him was something to be appreciated by them, and the end result was observed by the record-breaking pilot, Alex Henshaw; he gave the following brief account of his first impressions of Supermarine when he joined them shortly after Mitchell's death:

> To start with, it was on a smaller scale and less affluent and ostentatious in its general mode of work and most of the operatives were ordinary people who had been in amphibious aviation for a long time and were dedicated to their work.... A small but dedicated group accustomed to working under pressure with limited resources, to turn out a finished job in which all would take pride.

This passion of Reginald Mitchell and his team for engineering detail and their ability, particularly, to get their very fast racing aircraft into the air on time was very obvious when the two Supermarine entries were the only aircraft to finish in the 1927 Venice Schneider trophy competition. No doubt, Vickers were also well aware of previous successful Supermarine products when looking for expansion in the aviation field and so it was significant that, when they took over the seaplane firm, Mitchell's contract to remain with Supermarine until 1933 was retained. With few exceptions, his design team was kept on in the new organisation as a separate entity, and its products were advertised separately under the title 'The Supermarine Aviation Works (Vickers) Ltd'—a clear acknowledgment of what had been built up by Mitchell at the Woolston works.

There had been, however, a Vickers man sent down at the take-over to be Mitchell's chief assistant, and a clash of different design philosophies has been suggested—Barnes Wallis' championing geodetic structures *v.* Mitchell's development of a stressed skin approach. However, the transfer of Wallis occurred well before the 1934 advent of the Vickers Type 253 biplane that exemplified his approach; thus, when Wallis began to interview the various members of the design staff in order to form an assessment of those he would be dealing with, it was obvious that Mitchell's resentment was essentially motivated by the implied criticism of the abilities of his team, not by a difference in design philosophies.

In any case, there was little chance of an exchange of views between the two men, as Wallis' stay at Woolston was short-lived: Mitchell disappeared for about ten days, having reportedly suggested to his staff not to make Wallis too comfortable. Lovell-Cooper has left his version of the episode:

> Wallis'd just done the R100, the big airship, and come back with flying colours, the wonder man of the air! He turned up immediately after the Christmas holidays, took over Mitchell's office and went and sat in his chair ...
> Mitchell came to me and said, 'You might put a desk up in the loft for Wallis!' There was a V-shaped roof over our place and you reached it by a sloping gangway. It was a most precarious thing to walk up—sheer drop of about forty feet down below with no railing! If you got near the edge and suffered from vertigo I should think you'd have had it.
> 'Oh,' said Mitchell, 'you can put a desk and a chair up there for Mr Wallis but don't make him too comfortable!'
> To cut the story short, Barnes Wallis realised the game was up. That was the last we saw of him! He went back to Vickers. Mitchell said, 'It's either him or me!' I heard him say that. 'You can make your own choice!'

Mitchell's reappearance, after the Vickers board recalled Wallis to their Weybridge factory, might tell us something about the *prima-donna* nature of chief designers; it certainly indicates the status of Mitchell in the expanded company set-up and his faith in the integrity of the design team which he had built up and shaped over the previous nine years. An interesting side-line to the Wallis interlude was reported by Shenstone in his diary: when asked by Mitchell, about three years later, to obtain from Wallis some information about strength testing that had just been carried out on a Vickers aircraft, the answer was a blunt 'No'.

It has already been noted how Mitchell promoted internally, but new technologies required new men, and so there had been some recent appointments to the design team, including Alan Clifton, Ernest Mansbridge, and Arthur Black. In addition, specialist recruits could be afforded after the Vickers takeover, such as William Munro (hydrodynamicist) and Beverley Shenstone (aerodynamicist). The addition of new men meant that Mitchell's detailed work at the drawing board could now be more completely delegated, and his daily work was now very much a matter of checking, approving drawings or initiatives of his deputies, and making the case for Supermarine proposals to the Vickers board. Thus the discussions with colleagues described above were now even more crucial, while not inhibiting the continuation of his own innovative ideas.

However, it has not been recorded how, as a young man, Mitchell comported himself during his early years in authority, when it might have been tempting for a young man to compensate for insecurity by being over assertive. A member of the 1929 Schneider trophy team, Flg Off. L. R. L. Atcherley, supplied an assessment that might therefore be relevant when he said that Mitchell 'was the most unpompous man I ever met'. Of course, his engineering and draughting background and, especially, his knowledge of the 'dark arts' of mathematics, now beginning to be applied more systematically to aero design, would have marked him out for respect, but his lack of 'side', and the very practical knowledge gained in his apprentice days, must have been very important in not alienating those older men, on whom he must have relied for guidance when having to leave behind his locomotive knowhow for the unfamiliar world of boatbuilding and lightweight wooden structures.

On the other hand, he had to be firm in establishing his high standards of workmanship—as Griffiths said: 'he was somewhat retiring yet he was decisive and when necessary could be very firm.' Thus, despite his willingness to listen to others, to lead by example, and to associate with the workforce outside working hours, his family background must also have played a vital role in his success.

The Mitchells had moved up in the world from the terraced house at 115 Congleton Road, Kidsgrove, and then at 87 Chaplin Road, Normacot, to No. 1 Meir Road, a detached house, although in this same district. His father had been a headmaster and thus an authority figure

115 Congleton Road.

87 Chapel Road.

Victoria Cottage, No. 1 Meir Road.

(in those days, at least); having taught printing classes in his spare time, he gave up teaching, becoming managing director of his own printing firm, and rising to a prominent position in the local Freemason fraternity. In addition, his mother had also been a teacher at Kidsgrove before having to spend her time looking after a growing family. Although the Mitchells never moved into the most affluent neighbourhoods, it is very likely that their protestant ethics and professional backgrounds resulted in their son not finding it too unnatural or too difficult to give orders, aided by an independent trait in his make-up: doctoring his foreman's tea was an early example of assertiveness, as was leaving the close-knit community of Normacot for the south of England. This move to Woolston must have taken some courage and self-belief, not to mention his marrying a much older woman.

Mitchell's technical knowledge and his taking full responsibility for the company's products were obviously prime factors in establishing the dominant position he came to occupy at Supermarine. He was called 'Mitch' by the breezy RAF High Speed Flight Schneider trophy pilots; however, in the works, 'R.J.' became the limit of familiarity, a compromise between acknowledging 'Mr Mitchell', as the boss, and the 'Reg' or 'Reggie' among family and close friends.

Accounts of his lack of pomposity, his ability to listen rather than parade his own opinions, his basic shyness, and his slight stammer are not the most usual qualities of a leader but, in Mitchell's case, they resulted in a habitual reserve that established authority. The need to prove himself, particularly with his first designs, had clearly led to his close attention to all aspects of his designs, and to what Smith called 'his habitual expression of concentration'—perhaps signified by the clicking of his thumb and fingers, by which his secretary always knew of his return to his office.

On the other hand, when Flg Off. Atcherley first met Mitchell in 1929, he was 'struck by his young and carefree looks', and Quill spoke of getting to know him better 'in the relaxed atmosphere of the airfield', away from the office. Flg Off. Snaith, one of the 1931 Schneider trophy pilots, said that there was 'rarely a day when he failed to visit us. Sometimes in the evening he came to the Mess and after dinner joined us in games, and there we discovered his guilty secret—he was lousy at shove-ha'penny'. It would seem that Mitchell must have been much less intense when away from the demands of authority, as well as being drawn to the company of these exceptional pilots, out of respect for their skills.

At the works, a more forbidding conscientiousness was clearly evident, but it resulted in either a new type of aircraft or a new piece of mechanism for an aircraft functioning satisfactorily virtually from the very start—by no means to be expected in these early days of aviation development. Perhaps the best examples of reliability would be the Schneider trophy racers, 1927 to 1931, where he was

Biard and Mitchell relaxing on board ship to Baltimore for the 1925 Schneider Trophy competition.

working under very considerable time pressures and at the limits of technical knowledge; yet the company produced machines that were not seriously affected by malfunctions, unlike those of most of the competition.

To this end, he also 'spent hours alone in his office', as Jack Davis noted, imagining new structures or anticipating problems or possible mechanical failures; Smith also recounts how it was necessary to take care not to disturb him:

> A mental picture which always springs to my mind when remembering him, is R.J. leaning over a drawing, chin in hand, thinking hard. A great deal of his working life was spent in this attitude, and the results of this thinking made his reputation. His genius undoubtedly lay in his ability not only to appreciate clearly the ideal solution to a given problem, but also the difficulties and, by careful consideration, to arrive at an efficient compromise.
>
> One result of his habit of deep concentration was that he naturally objected to having his train of thought interrupted. His staff soon learned that life became easier if they avoided such interruption … If you went into his office and found that you could only see R.J.'s back bending over a drawing, you took a hasty look at the back of his neck. If this was normal, you waited for him to speak, but if it rapidly became red, you beat a hasty retreat!

However self-effacing he might have been and however willing to listen to all points of view—when his train of thought was not interrupted—his perfectionism meant that he was not noted for a readiness to bear fools gladly. It has been previously noted how he would give a 'killing glare' to anyone whom he considered to have made an inane remark, and his son also mentions his shortness with those who did not understand his instructions quickly enough:

> My father had an extremely short temper, could become unreasonably angry, followed by a long period of moodiness when he would not say a word to anyone. He had no time at all for anyone he considered a fool and could be very rude if the individual concerned did not quickly get the message.

Mitchell's condition after his operation for bowel cancer in 1933 exacerbated this testiness, which was unfortunate for those working with him: 'none of us knew at the time', Webb reported and Lovell-Cooper recorded that 'he used to have terrible tempers as you can imagine. He was in shocking distress a lot of the time'. Yet even before then, it was not unknown for him to contemptuously flick aside a drawing that did not satisfy him and even to tear it into shreds if it particularly displeased him; his secretary, Miss Vera Cross, reported that he had no time for those who did not measure up to his standards.

Joe Smith, his longest and trusted colleague, also said that R.J. 'occasionally let rip with us when he was dissatisfied with our work' but on the other hand, he added the qualification that he 'was an essentially friendly person, and normally even-tempered'. Thus, while the mantle of authority was obviously most in evidence at work, Joe Smith remembered that he could also be charming with 'an engaging smile which often transformed his serious demeanour', and Harry Griffiths said that 'he could be moody but in general he had a pleasant personality'. Webb recalled that, when still a very junior apprentice, he found that the great man 'was friendly and pleasant' and that he put him completely at ease.

Something of this apparently contradictory character of martinet and concerned colleague was captured by Harry Griffiths:

I've already said that his office was immediately over the laboratory and occasionally he would come downstairs to see Arthur [Black] and would always stop and ask how I was getting on. Sometimes these visits would be to ask the boss if he fancied a game of golf and off they would go for the afternoon. On another occasion he came and played merry hell because the office was untidy, although in fact it was no worse than usual.

His being in a position of authority in the workplace and his somewhat volcanic moments carried over into his domestic life. The son remembers that his father was 'damned difficult to live with' and that there were occasionally 'some pretty awful rows.… He had a short fuse and would very easily explode if he thought something was not as it ought to be.… He was a very affectionate father but very strict—he kept you on your toes.' Hence a revealing anecdote: once, having been shown round his father's workplace, Gordon was asked how he had got on; to the reply that he had enjoyed it, the father rejoined, 'I don't care a damn whether you enjoyed it, I want to know what you learnt'. Was the father replicating his own father?

His son's accounts of the sterner or more difficult domestic moments were balanced by examples of 'a wicked sense of fun', and this less well-known side to his personality can be glimpsed in the quiet humour to be found in his speeches. Sir George Edwards, who eventually rose to become managing director after McLean, alluded to the fact when he wrote that Mitchell was able to 'get the best out of his team … with an authority based on his own great technical skill and the ability to unite this with a warm humanity and a willingness at the right time to join in the fun and games'. No examples of board room horseplay have come to light, but Webb has a clear recollection of earlier times:

> They were a very high-spirited crowd and given to rather boyish pranks but after all they were youngish and very hard working and so played hard as well. The advent of the [Vickers'] takeover sobered them up a bit—alas—or were they just getting older? Marsh-Hume [the business manager] was a bit pompous and so he was the inevitable target for the other bright young men in the form of Wilf Elliot [works manager], Henri Biard, Charles Grey [secretary] and R. J. Mitchell, who had been known on more than one occasion to congregate outside Hume's bungalow and serenade him in the early hours in a raucous and unmelodious manner to the discomfort and embarrassment of Hume and his missus and the fury of Hume's neighbours.

One notices that Webb did not say that the 'pranks' disappeared entirely, and there are various later accounts of practical jokes, including R.J.'s dismantling of a colleague's bed when staying at a hotel and his setting fire to another's notes during his speech.

There is also the following anecdote from Major G. P. Bulman, just two years before 'Reg' visited Buckingham Palace to receive his CBE:

> We happened to run into each other at the Paris [Aero] Salon, in 1930, probably, and together spent the evening by visiting the famous Folies-Bergère (as all good Englishmen do). Having a drink in the bar during the interval Reg (a most shy man) was confronted by a would-be alluring damsel whose attentions he repelled with a note taken from his pocket, begging her to resume her promenade. At the end of the show we went to the cloakroom to regain our overcoats.… 'My God!', he suddenly exclaimed, 'I must have given my cloakroom ticket to that ruddy girl in the interval instead of the cash I thought I had.' He then spotted the coat still on

HRH the prince of Wales in front of the Swan, 27 June 1924. On the prince's left is James Bird, director, and next to him is R.J. Henri Biard is behind him; on far left is Charles Grey, secretary, and next to him in front, is Wilf Elliot, works manager—the 'singers' mentioned #above.

its peg with huge relief, but the French attendant with typical Gallic logic replied, 'No ticket, no coat' and was adamant … After a word between us I started to assail the vigilant Frenchman with a torrent of terrible French and worked him in his gathering fury towards the far end of the counter away from the precious coat…. Mitch leapt over the counter, grabbed his coat and took to his heels. I followed with all speed, the two of us tearing round a corner outside, choking with laughter—one of the world's most famous aircraft designers and a British Government representative [then assistant director (engines) in the Joint Directorate of Scientific Research and Technical Development, Air Ministry].

This incident, and other accounts of R.J.'s practical joking, must be added to the perceived mixture of irascibility and friendliness that characterised his strictly professional, but often brooding, demeanour; one also remembers Sir Robert McLean's succinct assessment of his personality as a 'mixture of dreams and common sense'. Thus, a final assessment must be that, beneath his habitual reserve was a complexity not easily shared with others but that from this complexity, his combination of caution and daring, hopes and disappointments, came the steadfast mind that balanced up the goal and its practical attainment, which, as we shall see, was most evidenced in the designing of the Spitfire.

In the last resort, one's possibly prurient human interest in a man's private life must yield to an appreciation of the qualities that produced the present interest in the life of a working engineer. McLean wrote:

> The impression left on the mind of one who had been in the closest contact with Mitchell for many years, in his plans for the future and in his views on these new problems that arise from day to day in the evolution of flying, was that of a critical mind, not prepared to jump to conclusions or take decisions except of grounds of whose soundness he had satisfied himself. At the same time, no idea was too daring or adventurous to be considered, never from the academic point of view, but always from that of practical application.

Supermarine publicity for the Far East Flight.

8

Consolidation and International Successes (1926–1928)

> *A number of the metal-hulled 'Southamptons' are now being completed to equip the RAF Far East Flight. These machines will be flown out to India, via the Mediterranean, and then on to Singapore and along the Dutch East Indies to Australia.*
>
> *Jane's All the World's Aircraft*

A previous chapter showed how R.J., in 1925, had set a new standard in reconnaissance flying-boat design and had produced a revolutionary floatplane racing machine; both had shown the emergence of a creator of elegant shapes and a designer who had fully transcended the design precedents of his company.

Yet however far in advance of contemporary practice such products might be, they only formed part of a busy designer's overall responsibilities. It is instructive therefore to note that, as late as 1926, Supermarine was still advertising the 1919 Channel flying boat in its four-seat passenger-carrying and dual-control trainer versions—with a photograph of the last one sold, to Chile in 1922. It is clear from the accompanying text that the company was still hoping for civil contracts:

> A machine of this type was used to demonstrate to representatives of the Port of London Authority, the Trinity Brethren, and Scotland Yard that a flying boat could be handled in a busy waterway, and that it was possible to use the Thames as an air port.

Note that the now familiar 'airport' was not yet in common use.

In the years that followed, R.J.'s varied work pattern intensified as the company began to prosper. Apart from overseeing the first orders for twenty-four Southampton Is (by far the most significant requirement that Supermarine had so far received), there was the need to improve upon the performance of this aircraft, there were specifications for larger flying boats to meet, it was necessary to start meeting the exacting demands for improved Schneider trophy floatplanes, and there was now the important move from mainly wood construction to metal.

The Sparrow II

A good example of the diversity of the Supermarine output (and of the fundamental insecurity of the aero industry) was that the small Sparrow landplane still continued to occupy the time of the company. In September 1926, a second light aircraft competition was organised, again at Lympne, over a series of courses totalling about 2,000 miles, and with a similar engine size restriction. This time, the Supermarine machine was fitted with a version of the engine that had powered the two most successful aircraft of the 1924 Competition—a Bristol Cherub III of 32 hp.

Given the previous criticisms of pilot view, R.J. also replaced the previous biplane structure with a parasol high-wing monoplane configuration; the resulting aircraft was now designated Sparrow II. The one-piece wing was smaller in total area than the biplane surfaces of Sparrow I, but its thick aerofoil section gave it what Biard described as 'an exceptionally low landing and starting speed, which would have been most useful in a machine meant for small aerodromes'. He also recalled how, when Sir Sefton Brancker, then director of Civil Aviation, was a passenger in the Sparrow, he had become more than a little interested when their groundspeed dropped to 20 mph during a landing into a strong headwind. It was perhaps fortunate for the company's reputation that he was not aboard a few days later:

> We went up in fine style, circled round, dived and so on, and then I came down, vaguely aware that there had been some sort of commotion among the Directors who were watching below. Mr Mitchell came running up as I climbed out of the cockpit. 'Didn't you see the wings? Couldn't you see the wings?' he asked in a very agitated voice. It happened that I couldn't properly see them from the cockpit, because they were away up above my head. But he told me the whole time I was flying the wings had been trying to swing round, first one way and then the other.

Suitably stiffened up, the machine was duly entered in the 1926 *Daily Mail* two-seater light aeroplane competition, but when Biard took off on 12 September, the first day of flying, the weather had worsened and after less than 30 miles outward bound for Brighton, he decided that battling the strong headwind would not allow him sufficient petrol to complete the circuit. He returned to base at Lympne and, hopeful of better conditions, refuelled and set off again. This time, when he had reached Beachy Head, his passenger, one of the Supermarine mechanics, pointed out that one of the pins holding the wing struts in place had nearly worked itself out. To avoid the 'very annoying' prospect of the wings again coming off, Biard hastily landed on the Head, where the aircraft was promptly blown on its side.

By the time that it had been righted, it was too dark to attempt the return flight to Lympne, and so an uncomfortable night was spent beside the machine. The next morning, the engine had to be run flat out while Biard and his mechanic guided the Sparrow several hundred yards up the slope of Beachy Head; then, leaving behind his passenger who insisted on his responsibility for the lead ballast that the competition handicappers had required, Biard turned downhill, made a successful take-off in the lightened plane, and finally returned to base.

Unfortunately, the rules of the contest required that each of the six circuits had to be completed in the day allotted and thus the Sparrow II was eliminated on the first day of the competition (eventually won by Sydney Camm's Cygnet). Supermarine entered the Sparrow five days later for the Steward's Prize for the eliminated aircraft and in the Grosvenor Cup Race on the same day. It was unplaced in both.

Supermarine Sparrow II (1926)

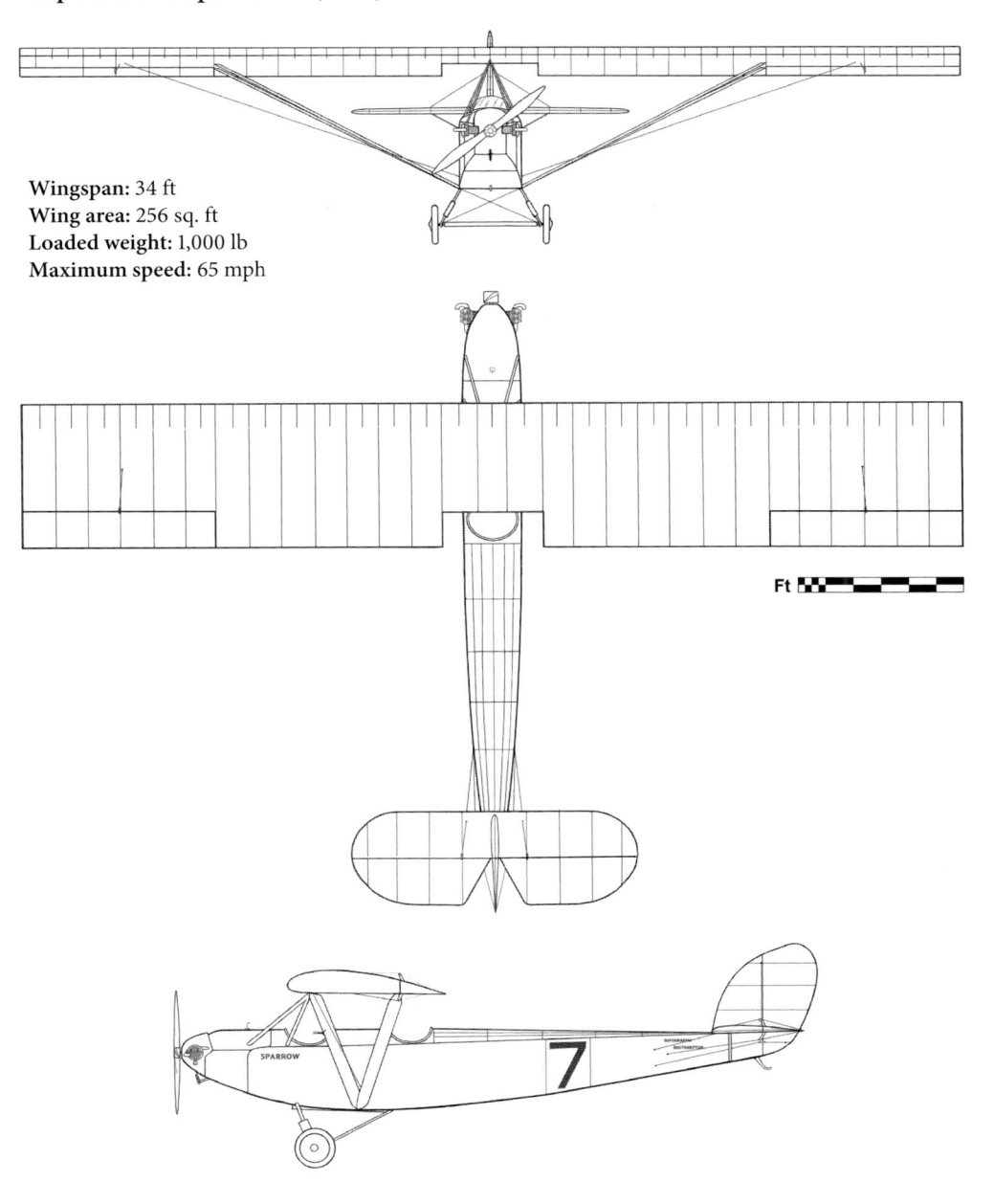

Wingspan: 34 ft
Wing area: 256 sq. ft
Loaded weight: 1,000 lb
Maximum speed: 65 mph

Sparrow II.

While no orders for flying club aircraft materialised, the new configuration of the Sparrow II had no doubt been encouraged by the expectation of an Air Ministry contract for flight comparison trials of identical area wings with different aerofoils, with the parasol wing layout reducing interference effects of the fuselage to a minimum. An SA 12 aerofoil proved to be the best, giving the machine an excellent balance and making it easy to fly 'hands off'. It also gave the shortest climb time to the 5,000-foot test height and, as a result, was used on the Nanok/Solent machine (described below). Thereafter, the Sparrow II was stored in a shed at Hythe until May 1929, when it was given to the Halton Aero Club and registered G-EBJP. It may have survived until as late as 1933, but there is little evidence of its being flown by members.

There were to be no further excursions by Supermarine into the light aeroplane field as the de Havilland DH.60 Moth aircraft, sensibly powered by a more powerful engine incidentally, was accepted by the Air Ministry in 1925 as the basis for Britain's first five civil flying clubs (and thus it was in a DH.60G Gipsy Moth that Mitchell gained his pilot's certificate in 1934). By 1939, there were sixty-six clubs in Great Britain, and so Supermarine and all the other light aircraft competitors had not been wrong in putting in their bids.

The Seagull III and IV

Meanwhile, as the last batch of Seagull IIs and the Scarab order were approaching completion, a tropicalised version of the former was commissioned by the Australian government. It had been decided that their air force should assist in the hydrographic survey of the Great Barrier Reef, and so No. 101 (Fleet Cooperation) Flight was formed on 1 July 1925; six Supermarine Seagull III amphibians were ordered (A9-1 to A9-6). These machines were essentially Mk IIs, but fitted with larger radiators, and the first of these was ready by February 1926.

By this time, six of the RAF aircraft had served a tour of duty with HMS *Eagle* and the type had then been pronounced as having 'no potential naval use', particularly because of their habit of porpoising on take-off and needing a protracted take-off run. They were confined to coastal, non-carrier, reconnaissance duties, and so the type did not come into contention

A Seagull III returning to the Supermarine works after a launching ceremony performed by Lady Cook, wife of the Australian high commissioner.

as a future replacement for the long-serving Fairey III series, although it was given a place in the popular final set piece of the fifth RAF Pageant where it summoned Flycatchers, followed by Blackburn Darts, to destroy two large replica warships.

In sharp contrast, the Australian Seagulls were used more thoroughly, as their survey work extended into 1927 and continued on northwards to include some 10,000 square miles of New Guinea and with one staged flight of 13,000 miles. Referred to by the natives as 'the canoe that goes for up', it was also pronounced a 'delightful' aircraft to fly by one pilot, Commander F. J. Crowther, although he did note that, in these tropical regions, it took more than an hour to reach 8,000 feet. Yet a Vickers Victoria transport, at about the same time and also in a hot climate, took nearly two hours to reach 10,000 feet.

Traditional Supermarine ruggedness was also evident after the survey work was completed, as the Seagulls were assigned to the seaplane tender HMAS *Albatross*, commissioned in 1929, and they continued in carrier use until 1933 when this vessel was placed in reserve. The Seagulls were then transferred to RAN cruisers, lowered, and hoisted aboard, like the Spanish Scarabs before them. Three RAF Seagulls, no longer required and engineless, were also acquired at the scrap price of £100 each. They were initially intended to be used for spares but were found to be in such excellent condition that they were restored to full-service use.

Due to its habit of porpoising on take-off, the type continued to occupy the minds of R.J.'s design team even until 1928; fitting hydro-vanes was considered and various permutations of the hull step position were tried out on N9565 and N9606. One aircraft, N9605, was fitted with Handley Page wing slots and a new tail unit with twin fins and rudders. This aircraft was converted to take passengers in 1929, as the Supermarine company was looking forward to a small fleet of this later model resuming the 1923 Southampton–Channel Islands routes. A pilot service was begun in July by the prototype five-passenger conversion (G-AAIZ) but most of August was void owing to serious damage caused by it hitting a submerged rock. Then, on 2 September, the short-lived business ceased when the aircraft ran into engine trouble.

A Seagull III at Hobart, 1930.

Two other Seagulls, N9653 and N9654, were converted for civilian use. Registered as G-EBXH and G-EBXI respectively, they were used by Coastal Flying Boat Services based at Shoreham-by-Sea but this also failed, owing to inadequate public response. However, two other modifications of the Seagull were of significance to R.J.'s team. One was concerned with equipping a Seagull to initiate the testing of catapults for launching aircraft and the second was the exchanging of the usual water-cooled Napier Lion engine for an air-cooled radial engine in a pusher configuration. As we shall see later, when the ubiquitous Seagull V/Walrus appeared, it was as an aircraft engined in this way and stressed for catapult launching.

Another influence upon the eventual Seagull V/Walrus design was the more successful hull planing arrangement that, it is assumed, had been tested out with the Sheldrake. The other design activities of the time, notably the Southampton and Schneider trophy aircraft development programmes and the intermittent work on the Sparrow and Seagull types, must have contributed to its ultimate neglect—as with another machine of this time, the unimpressive Seamew.

The Seamew

The pressing need for better types to serve the Royal Navy was such that, even while the orders for the Blackburn R.1 Blackburn and Avro 555 Bison three-seat gunnery spotters were being fulfilled, Specification 37/22 was issued for a replacement. However, the efforts of Hawker, Blackburn, and Fairey all came to nothing when this last requirement was cancelled because of the poor performance of the contenders when ready by 1925. Thus, Supermarine clearly had motivation, as well as previous experience, to produce a successful contender when Specification 29/24 was issued.

Consolidation and International Successes (1926–1928) 173

Supermarine Seamew (1928)

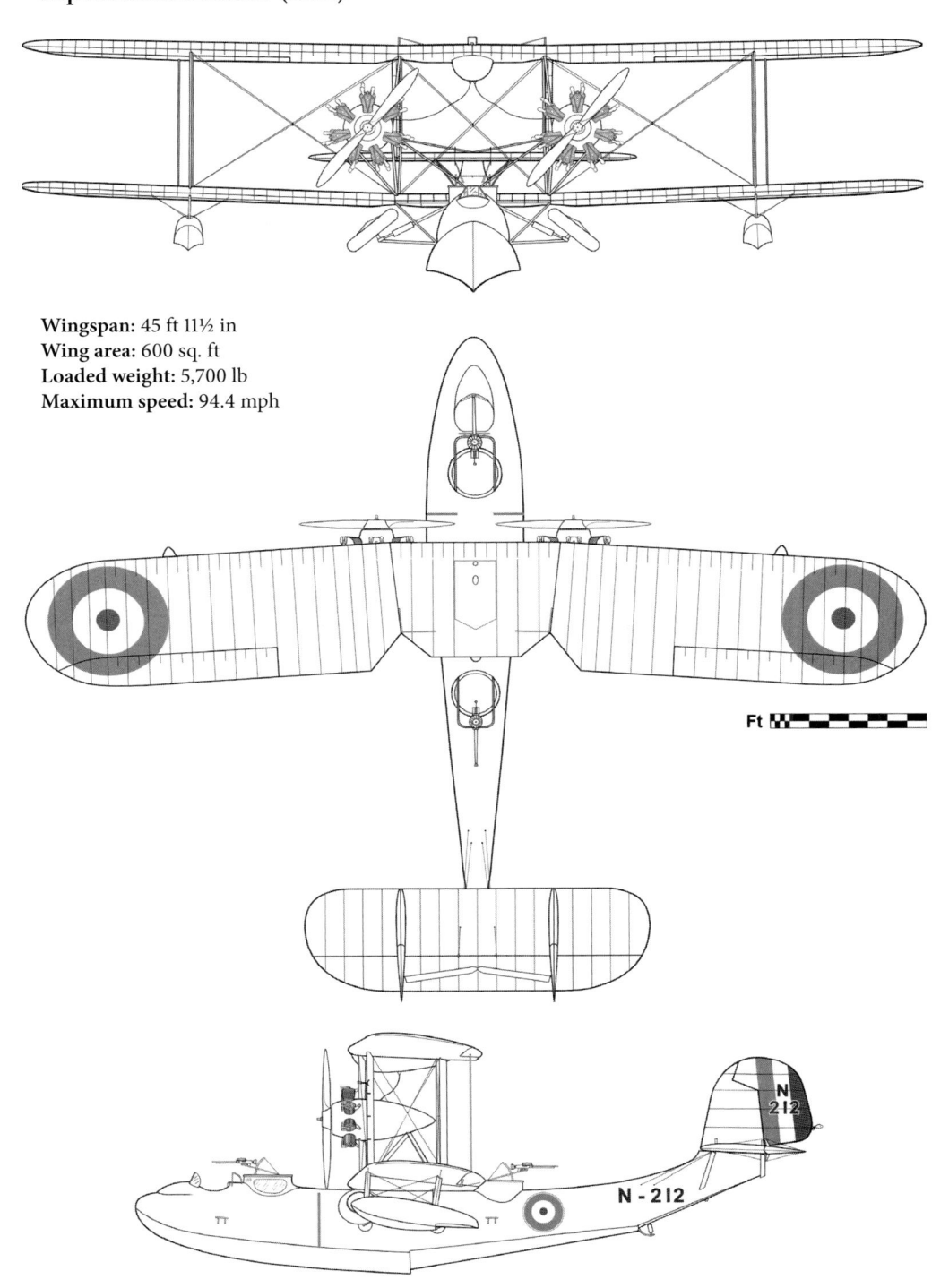

Wingspan: 45 ft 11½ in
Wing area: 600 sq. ft
Loaded weight: 5,700 lb
Maximum speed: 94.4 mph

In response, the relatively small, shipborne Seamew was drawn up by R.J. in order to carry the requisite three crewmen, the additional weight of gun positions both fore and aft, retracting undercarriage, and folding wing mechanisms. It was to be powered by two 238-hp Armstrong Siddley Lynx engines—no doubt having regard to the underpowered Scarab predecessor of identical wing area. Also, in view of the Ministry's concern with slow landing speeds for its deck-landing types, it is no surprise that R.J. was now proposing thick, high-lift aerofoils for the wings as the design of arrester mechanisms at this time was none too advanced for coping with fast 'arrivals'.

Thinking was sufficiently advanced by the next year for the Ministry to issue Supermarine with a contract for two machines of this type. With R.J. having to supervise the Southampton developments, especially in respect of new metal hulls and metal wing fittings, the urgent requirement to complete the S.4 and then the S.5 Schneider trophy racer programmes, the Australian Seagull orders, the Sheldrake and Sparrow testing, and the Seagull IV activity, it is perhaps not surprising that the Seamew was slow to materialise.

No doubt because of its early gestation, it was still, like the early Mk I Southamptons, of wooden construction, although the wing structures made far more extensive use of stainless-steel fittings—a special interest of Supermarine. Unfortunately, when the type finally made its first flight on 9 January 1928, the Seamew was found to be one of the relatively few aircraft designed by R.J., which did not live up to its design projections. The first to fly, N212, was found to be nose-heavy and the forward-facing propellers had only a very short life, due to water impact during the take-off run. N213 was therefore fitted with smaller diameter four-blade propellers, to try to overcome the problem of water ingestion, but this expedient then affected the amphibian's rate of climb and speed. By 1930, balanced rudders had been fitted and the tailplane had been given more negative incidence to counteract the nose-heaviness problems.

Additionally, it was now found that the stainless-steel fittings of one of the mainplanes were in need of replacing, owing to the inferior quality of the materials supplied. Similar problems had appeared on operational Southamptons, but the more extensive use of this metal in the Seamew suggested the need for a more radical rebuilding of the airframe than

Seamew N212 and Mitchell.

The Seamew, fitted with balanced rudders.

simply replacement of parts. However, such a course of action was not justified by the overall performance of the aircraft and so the type was not proceeded with. The problem of spray affecting the forward-facing propellers of the smaller type of flying boat must have convinced R.J. of the advantage of a single, more powerful, pusher engine configuration, further protected by the forward chines of a relatively wide hull—another factor in the eventual design of the Seagull V/Walrus.

There were various Air Ministry specifications from 1923 onwards for naval torpedo, fleet-spotter, or interceptor aircraft and for aircraft having interchangeable wheel and float undercarriages (with the Fairey IIIF emerging as a very successful contender in most of these roles). The Southampton firm, by now, had had experience of the float-equipped S.4, as well as previous interests in torpedo or deck-landing machines; also, as we know, they had for a long time cherished notions of a small manoeuvrable fighter flying boat. Nevertheless, the Seamew represented the last small- or medium-sized Supermarine aircraft built specifically for British naval requirements. As we shall see in Chapter 13, the original requirement for the later Walrus came from Australia.

Southampton Development

While the Seamew was proving a disappointment, the Southampton I had fulfilled the expectations of the RAF in the cruises around the British Isles; these were followed, in 1926, by a flight of two Southamptons from Plymouth to Egypt, via Bordeaux, Naples, Malta, Benghazi, and Sollum to Aboukir, and calling at Athens and Corfu on the return flight. Supermarine had emerged after 1918 as the main British firm specialising in flying boats and so it is not surprising, therefore, that the order for the first batch of Southamptons was not the last.

The Southamptons first equipped No. 480 (Coastal Reconnaissance) Flight at Calshot—which later became No. 201 Squadron—and afterwards four other squadrons were also supplied with Southamptons: No. 204 Squadron at Plymouth, No. 210 Squadron at Felixstowe and Pembroke Dock, No. 203 Squadron in Iraq and No. 205 Squadron at Singapore. And during this time there was also continuous detailed development of this flying boat. In view of the effect of this work on the Southampton upon other Supermarine projects, it is worthwhile giving a resumé of the various Southampton orders and developments undertaken from 1926 (*see* grey box below; the development details also remind us of R.J.'s day-to-day concerns between the highlights of new design first flights or Schneider contests.

Details of Southampton Design Activity
- increased incidence to wingtip floats (they tended to dig in) and later redesign of them;
- N9896 experimentally fitted with alternative fuel tanks to replace the normal external underwing tanks; later fitted with a fore and an aft gun turret on the centre-line of the top wing—the Mark III;
- N9900, from the original order, modified to carry torpedoes; formed the basis for the Danish Nanok order (see below);
- N218 with an experimental metal hull, also from the original order; later used as a test-bed for the Bristol Jupiter IX engine; also fitted with Handley Page leading-edge slots;
- twelve aircraft (S1036–1045 and S1058–1059) built in 1926; S1059 fitted with a canopy over the two pilots' cockpits. All the Southamptons supplied for No. 203 Squadron in Iraq were so modified—known as the 'Persian Gulf' type;
- eight aircraft (S1121–1128) ordered in 1926 with instructions that the last two should be fitted with metal hulls. These last two became the first Southampton Mark IIs; S1122 fitted with Kestrel engines;
- four (S1149–1152) built for the Far East Flight (see below) with modified fuel tanks of increased capacity and with increased radiator surface areas;
- five (S1158–1162) built during 1927; S1159 went to Australia;
- nine more (S1228–1236) built in 1927;
- eight (HB1–HB8)—for the Argentine Naval Air Force, fitted with Lorraine 12E engines, 1929;
- three experimental airframes ordered in 1928: N251 to be fitted with a special hull built by S. O. Sanders Ltd.; N252 to be converted to take three Jupiter XFBM engines—the Southampton X (see later); N253—the fitting of Kestrel IV engines to S1149 and the fitting of an all metal airframe with Frise balanced ailerons;
- three batches of five each ordered: (S1298–1302), (S1419–1423), and (S1643–1647); additionally S1464 ordered;
- S1648 ordered in 1931 as an 'Improved Southampton Mark IV'—renamed Scapa (see next);
- two aircraft (K2964–2965) ordered;
- six (N3–8) fitted with Hispano-Suiza 12Nbr engines—which produced vibration necessitating the strengthening of the rear part of the hull and tail surfaces. These were delivered to Turkey in 1934.

> **Cozens Again Provides Information and Anecdote about the Southampton**
> Metal frames were becoming common on aircraft but it took a long time before there was an attempt to use metal for the skin, especially if there was the risk of contact with salt water and the danger of corrosion ... Some wooden Southamptons were fitted with stainless steel bottoms and some were built with stainless steel bottoms and duralumin hulls, and of course the expected corrosion did appear, and like other companies building flying boats, Supermarine set up a metallurgical section to try to overcome it. [*See* appointment of Arthur Black, p. 33.] ... the men on the workshop floor had to change to metalworking, but they were practical men and times were difficult, the General Strike was hardly over, and most of them stayed, in any case woodworkers were still needed for building wings and control surfaces ...
>
> Mr S. F. Tilman, who was concerned with Southamptons while in the RAF, wrote in the *Southern Evening Echo* 'Letterbox':
>
> 'I think the City of Southampton should be proud of the Supermarine Southampton flying boats. The "Swampton" as we affectionately called it, was the mainstay of Coastal Command for at least twelve years, and saw service in Hong Kong, Singapore, Iraq, Gibraltar, Egypt, and Pembroke Dock, Mount Batten, Calshot and Felixstowe ...
>
> 'Southamptons made many other memorable flights including escorting the Prince of Wales on a tour of the Baltic and Scandinavia. This particular flight was made by 201 Squadron from Calshot, and the only thing that went wrong was when the C.O. of the Squadron, in spite of his own explicit orders that it should not be done, signalled with his arms from the centre cockpit and had his thumb chopped off by one of the propellers.'

Harry Griffiths recorded an incident involving one of the Southampton developments, which gives an insight into the sort of unanticipated problems that would arise after a design had left R.J.'s drawing office:

The firm received an order from the Turkish government for a number of Southampton flying boats, but it was specified that they were to be fitted with Hispano-Suiza engines instead of the Napier Lions which were standard.

In fact the installation looked very much neater but on test flights the pilots reported heavy vibration on the control column during take-off and climb to cruising height.

Arthur [Black, chief metallurgist] obtained a Vibrograph which produced traces on a celluloid strip—a cumbersome device. Being rather small I could get into the rear of the hull so I was deputed to use it during ground engine runs and subsequently on a test flight. I had to kneel on the cockpit floor and hold it against the control column during take-off, and then crawl down to the rear and get a number of readings on the way back.

After that the theory was that I could go back to the rear gunner's position and enjoy the rest of the flight.

I got the readings and then was horribly airsick all down the outside of the hull—fortunately the spray on landing cleaned everything up, but after we had come ashore I went to first aid who gave me a dose of Sal Volatile which made me feel worse. What's more, not having a flying helmet, I was deafened for several hours afterwards from the engine and propeller noise.

We projected the traces onto a screen and measured frequencies and amplitudes but they really told us nothing except that the aircraft was shaking like mad under certain conditions.

So there had to be another approach, and Oscar [in charge of structure testing] came up with the idea that if he sat in the cockpit and held the control column while I thumped on various parts of the tailplane we might find out where the trouble came from.

I was on top of a trestle thumping away when I heard a voice below. It was Trevor Westbrook, the works superintendent, who called up: 'Griffiths, if you are trying to smash that bloody aeroplane go to the stores and get a sledgehammer, don't use your fist, you might hurt yourself!'

Well you didn't shout back to the works superintendent from the top of a trestle so I climbed down to explain when, to steady myself, I caught hold of a strut which ran from the hull to the mid span of the tail.

Oscar stood up in the cockpit all excited and shouted, 'That's it! What did you do?' So I stayed halfway down the trestle and gave the strut a series of hard thumps, just by way of confirmation, before going down to the ground and explaining.

The drawing office stiffened up the strut and everybody was happy, including the works superintendent.

After 1918, good quality timber was at a premium, and this was another good reason to encourage the use of metal. A Mark II version of the Southampton, with a metal hull, was ordered, and after the shortage of workers with the appropriate skills was overcome, a total of seventy-nine production machines were eventually completed between 1925 and 1934. Separate metal hulls were also manufactured for replacement of damaged hulls as well as for the retrofitting of all Mark I Southamptons. The fact that R.J. had designed the Southampton so that the entire wing structure could be removed as a single unit was an important factor in the decision to upgrade the Mark Is with the new hulls.

The early establishment of a metallurgy department, headed by Arthur Black, marked the end of the traditional Supermarine wooden hull of which the company had been justifiably proud. However, replacing the double-bottomed wooden hull with the single-skinned duralumin hull of the Mark II Southampton, provided even more internal space and a saving of 300 lb in weight; a further 400 lb, caused by gradual water soakage into the earlier wooden hull, was also eliminated. These weight reductions, together with a change from the Napier Lion V engine to the more powerful Lion Va, increased the Southampton's range by 200 miles. Increased-load testing was carried out at the MAEE at Felixstowe in 1927, and it was found that, at any weight up to 18,000 lb, control, manoeuvrability and take-off were unaffected.

At this time, the only earlier long-distance flight by standard RAF machines that had exceeded the two Southamptons' 7,000-mile Mediterranean cruise was across the land mass of Africa, from Cairo to Cape Town, using relatively small DH.9s. The lack of prepared landing strips for larger aeroplanes and the short range of aircraft at this time had not encouraged long-distance military or commercial flying; now, the advent of the efficient and reliable Southampton—able to use the widespread landing areas provided by lakes, large rivers, and the sea—gave increased confidence to the political consideration of the possibility of opening up air routes to the far-flung outposts of the British Empire.

A metal-hulled Southampton II moored on River Itchen, in front of a wooden-hulled Mk I.

> The Supermarine publicity giving a relatively comprehensive account of the physical features of the Southampton as a practical proposition and as a fighting machine—including the torpedo version—and offers wooden or metal hull and wing (some other nations might prefer to work with the older technology):
>
> TYPE—Twin-engined, five-seat reconnaissance flying boat.
>
> WINGS—Equal-winged, unstaggered biplane. Top and bottom centre-sections of equal span, interconnected by vertical struts at their extremities, and four sets of struts in the form of a 'W' when viewed from the front, in between which are mounted the engines. One set of vertical interplane struts to each outer wing section. Normal structure of wood covered with fabric. A set of metal wings has been produced. The metal wings are approximately 200 lbs (90 kg) lighter than the wooden ones, with which they are interchangeable. Ailerons fitted to all four planes.
>
> HULL—Can be supplied in either wood or metal. The metal hull is 300 lbs (136 kg) lighter than the wooden hull. Wooden hull of normal Supermarine circular-section, flexible construction, with two built-on steps. Metal hull of same form, built entirely of duralumin, with stainless steel fittings.
>
> TAIL UNIT—Monoplane type, with three fins and balanced rudders mounted above. Tailplane of cantilever type and is adjustable. One-piece unbalanced elevator.
>
> POWER PLANT—Two 470-hp Napier 'Lion' engines, on separate removable mountings, carried above the bottom centre-section. Each engine unit is self-contained and includes radiator, oil tanks and cooler, and all instruments, and may be removed without disturbing the main wing structure. Main fuel tanks (2) under top centre-section, giving gravity feed to engines. The 'Southampton' has been fitted with two Bristol 'Jupiter VIII' geared radial air-cooled engines. With these engines the useful load was increased by 500 lbs (227 kg).
> The 'Southampton' flying boats supplied to the Argentine Navy are fitted with 450 hp Lorraine-Dietrich water-cooled engines. The Rolls-Royce F type engines can also be fitted.
>
> ACCOMMODATION—In nose is cockpit for gunner and bomber. Provided with Lewis gun, on Scarff mounting. Behind are two pilot's cockpits, in tandem, with dual control. The after-pilot also has complete navigating equipment. Below wings is the wireless compartment, which opens out into two staggered cockpits, aft of the wings, each equipped with Scarff gun-mountings.

> A crew of five is normally carried. Inside of hull, which is free from obstructions, may be equipped with hammocks and cooking apparatus, so that crew may sleep on board and remain afloat for long periods. Can be arranged to carry two 18 in. torpedoes, one on each side of hull. Winches for lifting torpedoes into position are carried under bottom centre-section.

The Royal Air Force Far East Flight

It may be recalled that one of the topics of conversation between the prince of Wales and Henri Biard during the 1924 royal visit to Supermarine concerned the development of Imperial air routes. One further advantage of the new metal hull of the Southampton was thus significant: its greater ability to withstand the rapid encrustation by barnacles and other marine growths encountered in tropical waters.

So the new Mark II machine duly encouraged the Air Ministry to order, in 1926, four new Southamptons specifically to initiate a proving cruise to the far reaches of the empire—as the secretary of state for air put it: 'to show the Air Force, as the Navy showed the Fleet, in the distant parts of the Empire'. For this flight, R.J. provided larger fuel and oil tanks, along with radiators providing 50 per cent more cooling area.

Confidence in his metal-hulled machine is evident from the fact that the proposed cruise, by a flight of basically standard RAF machines, was to incorporate overflights of countries only previously visited by the pioneering Cobham and to go as far as Australia—which had only been visited, singly, by four previous aeroplanes. Additionally, it was to circumnavigate that continent—a feat that had been achieved only once to that date, by a Fairey IIID between 6 and 18 May 1924. Knowledgeable readers of the 1927 issue of *Jane's All the World's Aircraft* would therefore have been well aware of the ambition, and confidence, of Supermarine when the company announced:

N218, the prototype Southampton Mark II.

A number of the metal-hulled 'Southamptons' are now being completed to equip the RAF Far East Flight. These Southamptons will be flown out to India, via the Mediterranean, and then on to Singapore and along the Dutch East Indies to Australia, where an extended flight round the Australian seaboard, in conjunction with the Royal Australian Air Force, is contemplated.

The leader of the Southampton's earlier Mediterranean cruise, Squadron Leader Livock, was again chosen, as well as Flight Lieutenant H. G. Sawyer, who, as a very junior officer, had been entrusted to take part in some of the early British Isles proving flights of the Southampton I. Yet on the occasion of this much more extensive and important Far East Flight, a group captain was put in command—H. M. Cave-Brown-Cave (who, on arrival in Australia, became known as 'Home-Sweet-Home'). His orders were 'to open the air route to Australia and the East, to select landing sites, to see how far flying boats and their crews were capable of operating away from fixed bases and under widely varying climatic conditions, and to show the flag'.

Thus, while there was a clear imperialist motive behind the proposed flight, the other main concern was to prove the feasibility of reliable transport—with scheduled stops organised for servicing and for inspections to see how the aircraft were standing up to the very testing itinerary. The main cruise began from Plymouth on 17 October 1927 and finished at Seletar, Singapore, on 28 February 1928. The engines were replaced on arrival at Singapore and one of the aircraft, as prearranged, was dismantled and sent back to England for detailed inspection. A relief machine, which had been shipped to Singapore, joined the remaining three planes, and from 21 May, they then proceeded to circumnavigate Australia and fly around the China Sea to Hong Kong, arriving back at Singapore on 11 December 1928. During the whole cruise, the Southamptons only fell behind schedule three times—twice because of bad weather and once with engine trouble; one machine, additionally, was delayed by a cracked airscrew boss.

The first flight to Australia, by a lone Vickers Vimy, had taken place nine years earlier, and two American Douglas DCWs, out of an initial flight of four aircraft, had previously flown around the world, in pre-arranged, well supported stages (by the placing of extra sets of pontoons, engines, and enough replacement airframe parts for two more aircraft at specified waypoints along the route). While in no way denigrating this latter achievement, a comparison with the Southamptons' Far East Cruise is instructive: the entire Supermarine formation flew 27,000 miles, in formation, without any elaborate backup arrangements. There were breaks in the itinerary for crew relief and public relations activities, but the important fact was that all the four aircraft flew consistently at an average speed of 80 mph and in sixty-two timetabled stages of about 400 miles at a time. As might be expected, minor running repairs and maintenances had to be carried out, but as Supermarine proclaimed, the entire flight gave 'no trouble of any consequence' during the whole cruise.

R.J.'s attention to the soundness of his aircraft was thus convincingly demonstrated as was the potentiality of the seaplane for civil transport, even though his livelihood had to depend mainly on designing military aircraft. Other nations made more publicised formation flights in following years, yet the Southamptons' Far East Cruise must be regarded as directly instrumental in the establishment of the Imperial Airways Empire routes of the 1930s and as one of the milestones in aviation history. The *Daily Mail* was in no doubt: 'As a demonstration of reliability, the flight will rank as one of the greatest feats in the history of aviation'.

Another extended formation flight carried out by R.J.'s aircraft, the Baltic flight of 1930, took in the cities of Esbjerg, Copenhagen, Stockholm, Helsinki, Tallin, Riga, and Memel—again,

Southamptons of 201 Squadron during 1930 Baltic flight.

without mishap. Squadron Leader Livock, who was second in command of the Far East flight and leader of this formation flight, gives a full account of these events in his autobiography, *To the Ends of the Air*, well worth reading for its accounts of the difficulties and frustrations encountered when pioneering air routes in areas where, understandably, there was little comprehension of aviators' special needs.

These cruises had taken place at the time when Supermarine was winning successive Schneider trophy contests, and so R.J. and his designs were becoming more widely known outside the British aviation community. The prestige of these Schneider wins reinforced the reputation of the Southampton and led to sales in Argentina, Japan, Turkey, Australia, and Denmark. The US government, usually a staunch supporter of its own native industry, also made enquiries that, perhaps because of the worsening economic situation there, did not materialise into orders.

The Nanok/Solent: R.J.'s First Air Yacht

Following the widespread recognition of the Southampton's qualities, Denmark requested a version of the type to carry torpedoes in a similar manner to that devised for N9900, one of the Southampton developments outlined earlier and alluded to in their publicity. Called '*Nanok*', Inuit for polar bear, a Southampton was uprated to carry the heavier armament by having a slightly larger, thicker wing and a third engine, with weight being saved by the provision for only a single rear gunner.

The engines selected were Armstrong-Siddeley Jaguar IVAs. They first carried the Nanok into the air on 21 June 1927, whereupon it was found that the additional power caused the machine to become distinctly nose-heavy. Mitchells' expedient was to have an auxiliary elevator fitted, higher up and between the three fins. However, the extra drag of this unit lowered the flying speed some mph below that contracted for and the rate of climb was disappointing. Biard also records that the engines had a tendency to cut out and that the vibration experienced with the differently engined Turkish batch of Southamptons (mentioned above) also occurred with the Nanok.

In view of later developments, Supermarine publicity in *Jane's*, 1927 is interesting as, under the heading of the 'Solent', it actually describes the torpedo-carrying 'Nanok':

> The first machine of this type was completed in June, 1927 and was built specially to the order of the Royal Danish Naval Air Service, who have renamed it 'Nanok'. The hull of the machine is very similar to that of the Supermarine 'Southampton' but the superstructure is entirely different. The three Armstrong-Siddeley 'Jaguar' engines are mounted as tractors about midway in between the top and bottom planes. A new thick wing section, which has been designed by the Supermarine Aviation Works, Ltd, has been used and has shown itself to have excellent all-round properties. Two 1,500 lb torpedoes can be carried, one on each side of the hull, suspended from the bottom centre section, which is fitted with all necessary accessories, including winches for lifting the torpedoes on to the carriers.

In fact, the main change to the engine arrangement was not the position of the thrust lines but rather the change from Warren interplane girders to more conventional struts in order to accommodate the third engine; the aerofoil section mentioned was the SA12, which had been tested out on the Sparrow II. However, the positioning of the torpedoes, one on each side of the aircraft, added to the other various difficulties associated with this machine: Biard reported control problems which he experienced by the sudden change of trim when only dropping one torpedo, it being suspended fairly well out from the centre-line of the flying boat. Such lurches, necessarily at low level, could hardly have induced confidence in pilots assessing the Nanok, and in the end, the Royal Danish Navy took delivery of a standard Southampton fitted with Jaguar VI engines.

The RAF did not warm to the idea of a Southampton torpedo variant either and so Supermarine were now left with a modified but unwanted flying boat. Although a Southampton was loaned to Imperial Airways between November 1929 and February 1930, and a Japanese-owned Southampton was converted for passenger carrying in 1930, the only Southampton-type flying boat actually used for civil purposes at about this time was its prototype, the Swan. The Supermarine description of the now envisaged 'civil Southampton' is uncannily similar to that of the early aircraft:

> The passengers are accommodated in a roomy and comfortable saloon. It is fitted with spacious wicker chairs with deep and well-sprung cushions, carpets, hinged triplex glass portholes which can be opened by the passengers, cupboards and lockers, racks for lifebelts, etc. The whole saloon is beautifully finished and upholstered. There is no petrol inside the hull and the passengers may smoke without least danger. Being situated well clear of the engines, the saloon is free of engine exhaust gases, oil, vibration, etc., and is very quiet, thus enabling the passengers to converse quite

normally. There is a through passageway from stem to stern of the hull. Adjacent to the saloon is the luggage compartment, which is fitted with racks for the stowage of passengers' luggage and freight, and is separated from the saloon by a partition. Access to the luggage compartment is by means of a door in the partition and a hatch in the deck can also be provided. This hatch enables the freight to be easily and quickly removed, and could be used as an emergency exit if required. Lavatory accommodation is fitted as desired.

Nanok with torpedo under port wing.

Nanok with torpedo under starboard wing. Note the auxiliary elevator.

The passenger comforts to which attention is drawn gives, by implication, an interesting insight into the more spartan conditions normally experienced by air travellers of the late 1920s. It also reminds one that, at this time, the relative bulk of a flying boat hull made flying boat transport a likely leader in the early development of commercial aviation; the young and confident Mitchell must have felt he was on the cusp of a new era of British transport and, indeed, leading the way.

Unfortunately, hopes for the civil version of the Southampton never materialised, but at least, the Hon. A. E. Guinness was subsequently convinced of the potential of a flying boat for comfortable travel. As well as owning *Fantôme*, the largest and most spectacular barque-rigged yacht in the British registry, the Nanok variant was sold to him as an 'air yacht' with comfortable cabins to carry up to twelve passengers in the luxury envisioned above. Now registered G-AAAB, it soon became a familiar sight, flying for the next two years from the Hythe seaplane base on Southampton Water to Dún Laoghaire harbour, County Dublin, and thence to Lough Corrib, County Galway, close to Ashford Castle, its owner's Irish home. The advantages of a seaplane for commuting were no doubt obvious to the new owner, given the terrain of the remote parts of Ireland where, as Biard recorded, 'even a train was a novelty there, and many of the peasants had never even heard of anything mechanical that could fly, for many of the older people could not read'.

Another air yacht was to follow in 1930, again a cancelled military prototype, but with a much briefer and more chequered career (*see* Chapter 11).

The Solent Air Yacht.

Mitchell apparently satisfied with an S.5 engine test.

9

Designer of the World's Fastest Plane (1927)

The praise of everyone intimately connected with the technical side of the achievement was also bestowed upon Mr Mitchell as he stood with his wife to see the result posted on the board.

Southern Daily Echo

While the Southampton and Seagull development and the Sparrow II and Seamew testing were taking place, R.J. again became involved with the Schneider trophy contests that were soon to result in the Supermarine chief designer's becoming known outside the aeronautical community for his outstanding contribution to high-speed flight. The shy young man from Stoke-on-Trent who joined his firm as the personal assistant to the general manager in 1916 was soon to be honoured at Buckingham Palace, to give a talk on the BBC, and to be elected a fellow of the Royal Aeronautical Society. His solid, everyday work on the various amphibians and flying boats that were sold to Imperial Airways, to the Royal Air Force, to the Royal Australian Air Force and elsewhere had resulted in his becoming one of the directors of Vickers (Aviation) in 1928, but it was unlikely to have placed his name in front of the general public. This recognition, never very welcomed by him, was essentially due to his Schneider trophy aircraft of 1927, 1929, and 1931.

Full Government Support

By now, R.J. had gathered a group of men around him who must share the credit for the later designs; he was also very fortunate to be well served by British aero-engine manufacturers. Also, as we have seen, events themselves had conspired to present him with the platform for his more public successes: the damage to an Italian propeller in 1922, the sporting American cancellation of the 1924 contest, the demise of international landplane contests, and the intervention of Mussolini in 1926 had all contributed to the Schneider trophy remaining still to be competed for in 1927 as the most significant international aviation contest. Government backing for a British entry had already been in evidence in 1925 but was now so wholehearted that it had prompted *Flight* to comment that 'Never in the history of British aviation have we tackled an International speed race in so thorough a manner'.

The trophy was always intended as an international competition by Jacques Schneider. It began in 1913 as a contest between the aero clubs of various nations, most of whose members were enthusiastic amateurs, as were their pilots. Yet while the Schneider trophy continued to be organised by the clubs, the character and costs of the meetings had now begun to produce confrontations of government-subsidised teams with outstanding military pilots and support staff.

Clearly, if the Schneider competitions were held on a bi-annual basis, a government would be able to spread its considerable costs; America, in a reversal of the previous year's vote, now opted for a two-yearly event. However, Italy, currently holding the world seaplane record at 258.87 mph and contemplating further development of the winning Fiat engine and M.39 airframe, voted for a competition in 1927. So did Britain, mainly thanks to Air Vice-Marshal W. G. H. Salmond, the air member for supply and research at the Air Ministry, and the secretary for state for air, Sir Samuel Hoare. Britain's preliminary efforts were already dedicated to achieving a win in 1927, and it was now appreciated how the Schneider competition could develop the country's own aircraft designs and military capability.

Great secrecy was now maintained by the rival camps, as the machines were now funded by their governments—Supermarine publicity photographs now show R.J.'s new trophy racers guarded by soldiers with fixed bayonets:

> Armed guards are watching night and day over the secret super-planes that will represent Great Britain.... Remarkable precautions have been taken to prevent any leakage of the details of their design or performance. This is not because they are military machines, but because it is not desired that either Italy or America should become aware of the bid which Britain intends to make for the trophy.... No one is allowed to approach near the sheds without an official permit and an official escort. Even those who are working on the machines have been sworn to secrecy.
>
> *Air Force Gazette*, 4 August 1927

However, this was at a time when preparations for the next year's competition were becoming more newsworthy—if only because the popular press was raising doubts about the ability of the human frame to withstand the unprecedented speeds that were being predicted for the machines now being designed. As a consequence, the press was hungry for information and for photographs of the intrepid pilots and even of the designers of what were often referred to in the popular press as 'flying bullets'.

Once more, R.J.'s efforts were recognised in his hometown press, again with the obligatory publicity for the local family firm:

> [The Schneider Competition] will also have particular local interest, since the Supermarine-Napier S.5 monoplane, on which very great hopes are placed, has been designed by Mr Reginald J. Mitchell, son of Herbert Mitchell, of Messrs Wood, Mitchell and Co., Hanley.
>
> *Sentinel*, 11 August 1927

It is easy to understand that R.J., because of his dislike of being in the limelight, did not welcome the 'very great hopes' of the press and his reticence was reinforced by the government's concern for him to be tight-lipped about his design and its speeds.

Photographs of him now began to appear, typically unsmiling, compared with those taken at informal moments among his staff or the RAF pilots of his racers.

A press or a company PR camera always seemed to produce a rather defensive posture from our chief designer, and the scant details that appeared in the press about R.J.'s education and apprenticeship with Kerr Stuart meanwhile told the general public nothing about the thorough preparations that were necessary for the development of an aircraft that had to extend the boundaries of current technologies and aerodynamics.

In fact, funds from the existing Air Ministry development budget were utilised in advance of any Treasury decision about the costs thereof; specifications for new racing engines and aircraft had already been drawn up as early as March 1926. Work was soon under way, involving careful appraisal by wind tunnel and tank testing of ¼ scale models, with particular attention paid to floats, flush wing radiators, and airscrews: Gloster, Supermarine and Shorts had been asked to design machines capable of speeds not less than 265 mph at 1,000 feet. On 1 October, a high-speed flight was formed, consisting of exceptional air force personnel, to test the new racing machines.

The British effort was still to be spearheaded by the existing Napier Lion engine and faith in this reliable engine was justified as it was now made to deliver 900 hp in the ungeared model and 875 hp in a geared version. Just as metal propellers were found to be superior to wooden ones as tip speeds increased, so it was predicted that any extra weight and loss of rpm because of reduction gearing would be more than compensated for by greater propeller efficiency. R.J. later wrote: 'The Fairey Reed propeller used on the S.5 was only working at about nine percent efficiency [at 100 mph], whereas it reached the extremely high figure of eighty percent at 300 mph.'

The trophy competition would be a means of testing this development in aircraft engineering, but the Air Ministry were not following the previous American and current Italian concentration of effort on one aircraft type only. The British were clearly hedging their bets by supporting Supermarine and Gloster entries, with both geared and ungeared engines; there was also to be a Short seaplane powered by a more standard air-cooled radial engine. This last was a considerable departure from the water-cooled, in-line type of engines, which had resulted in the sleek, streamlined winners of the last three contests, but as previous and current post-war RAF fighters were all powered by radial engines, there was a good reason for seeing what sort of performance the trophy competition might produce with the Crusader. Its Bristol Mercury I radial air-cooled engine had individual 'helmets' fitted to the nine protruding cylinders—a compromise between streamlining and cooling. (In passing, it ought to be noticed that this Air Ministry order for seven machines was the largest ever given for British Schneider trophy entrance and was only matched by Italy in the following year.)

As we shall see, R.J.'s forthcoming design, the S.5, was to stay with his S.4 monoplane formula of 1925 and was followed in this respect by the Short Crusader. In contrast, the Gloster IV proposal was to favour the more traditional biplane approach, although for the new contest, the Gloster wing layout approached that of a sesquiplane. The resultant decrease in wing area was possible because of the extra power that the Napier Lion engine was now actually producing and its accompanying reduction in frontal area permitted an even sleeker model for the forthcoming contest. Streamlining was furthered by the removal of the top-wing pylon mounting in favour of careful fairing into the top of the fuselage, as had been the case with the Curtiss machines from 1925 onwards. In this way, an increase of 70 mph was achieved while adhering to the biplane formula; the shorter wingspan coupled with wire bracing was, at least, expected to produce a robust airframe that would be less susceptible to the problem of flutter that had been emerging since the 1925 contest.

Meanwhile, the Macchi opposition was to be equipped with an even more attractive development of the M.39. This, the M.52, also had reduced area flying surfaces because of the promise of more power being available; uprating of the previous year's Fiat A.S.2 engine was expected to produce 1,000 hp, compared with the previous 800 hp. The engine was also to be lighter and so the floats were reduced in length and volume; the wings were more swept back to accommodate the backward movement of the centre of gravity. The Fiat engine also allowed a smaller frontal area to be designed in, but its reliability was still to prove a problem, mainly owing to the new use of alloys, coupled with a higher compression ratio and higher rpm; it was reported that six out of twelve engines ordered for the development programme had been damaged beyond repair during tests.

The S.5

For the new Supermarine machine, R.J.'s continuation of the newer monoplane approach was hardly unexpected and he was also content to use the reliable Napier Lion engine: in the discussion which followed the 1925 Buchanan lecture, he had remarked that 'At one time I thought that the "Lion" engine was at a disadvantage with the American engines, but I have changed my views rather, and certainly consider the "Lion" is capable of winning the Schneider Cup'. Indeed, he (and Folland for Glosters) consulted with Napiers and the new Lion was designed whereby the engine's frontal area was reduced by repositioning the magnetos; additionally, the cam covers of the three-cylinder engine banks were even contoured to mate with the fuselage streamlining fairings without the need for any cowling.

R.J. then continued these lines without reference to a theoretically ideal aerodynamic shape—the S.4 had widened to maximum thickness at about 30 per cent of the fuselage length, whereas the new body tapered as soon as feasible, resulting in the slimmest fuselage of all the current and subsequent contenders. There was no room for a conventional seat and the pilots sat on a cushion on the floor of the machine, their legs almost horizontal and their shoulders coming up to and pressing against the underside of the cockpit coaming.

One can thus begin to appreciate our designer's anxiety, mentioned earlier, about having to produce, to say the least, 'pilot-unfriendly' machines. Oliver Simmonds, who was with Supermarine from 1924 to 1928, some years later described how the fuselage diameter of the S.5 had been determined; he had asked one of the team to put a piece of plywood up against a wall

Designer of the World's Fastest Plane (1927) 191

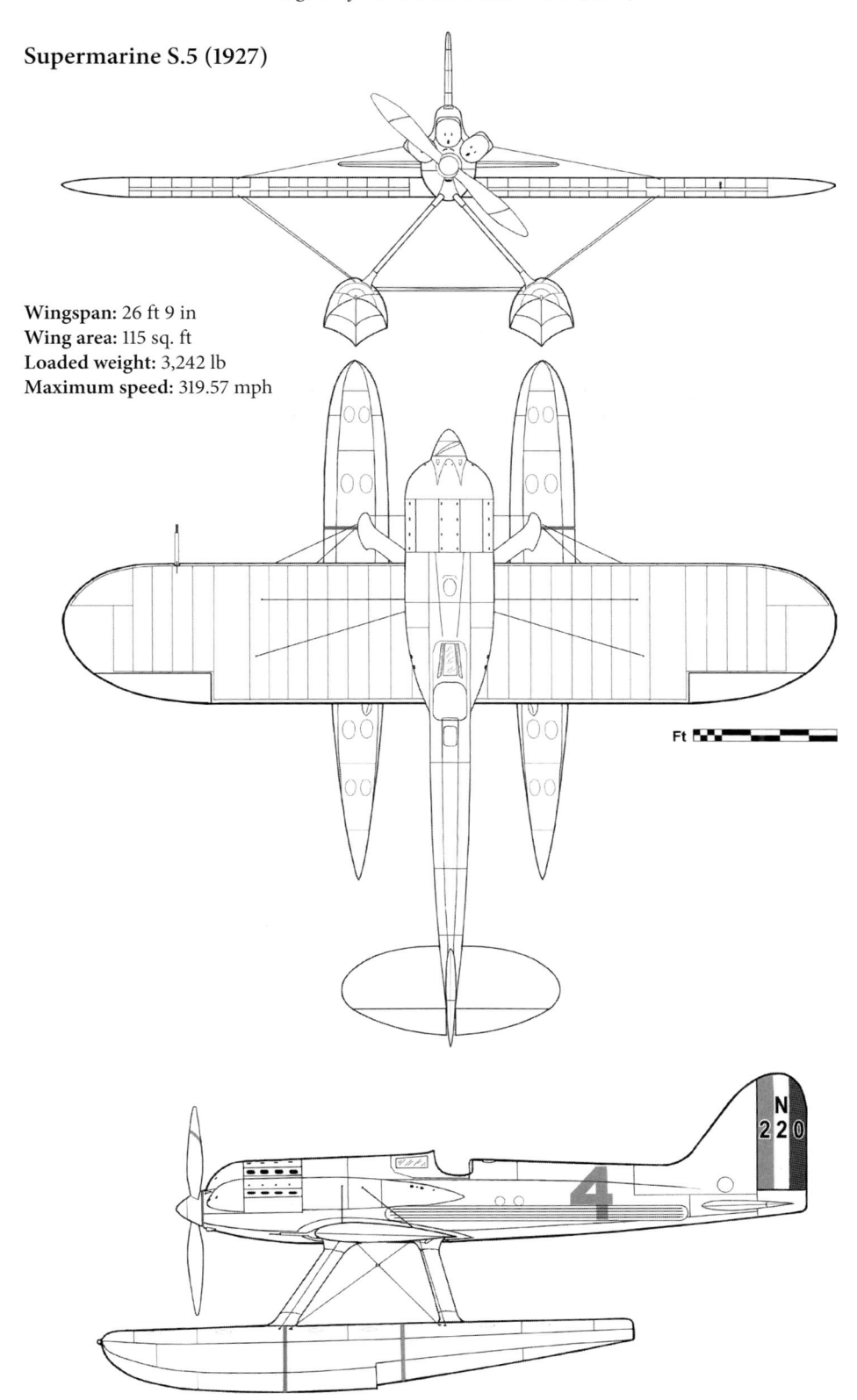

Supermarine S.5 (1927)

Wingspan: 26 ft 9 in
Wing area: 115 sq. ft
Loaded weight: 3,242 lb
Maximum speed: 319.57 mph

A Supermarine S.5 awaiting cowlings for the Napier Lion engine. Note the forward-hinged coaming for cockpit access.

and then sat on the floor with his back to the plywood, while a colleague drew a line around his torso; this produced the fuselage cross section. Flt Lt H. M. Schofield, one of the pilots of the newly formed RAF High Speed Flight, described their visit to Supermarine 'for a fitting':

> The method of reaching the seat was to squeeze in sideways and down as far as possible so that the shoulders were below the top fairing, then turn to face the front, and in my case it needed no ordinary effort to get my shoulders home. There were many sighs of relief from the watching design staff when the last man had been 'tried-in', for it had been a near thing and it did look as though it was not going to be enough at times.

In his speech to the Royal Aeronautical Society reproduced below, Mitchell said: 'On several occasions during the construction of the fuselage the pilots were fitted, and much trouble was experienced through their being of varying dimensions.'

As there was now insufficient room for the fuel tank in the fuselage, the starboard float was used. This expedient allowed R.J. at least to improve pilot view by moving the cockpit further forward, as well as giving the aircraft more stability in the air by lowering its centre of gravity. More importantly, it would also help towards counteracting the torque of the engine, which, during take-off, was expected to cause the opposing float to dig in and swing the aircraft off line before it gained sufficient airspeed to be effectively governed by the control surfaces. He also offset the fuel-loaded starboard float an extra 6 inches from the centre-line as an additional response to this expected problem.

However, the most telling improvement, apart from a more powerful engine, was the estimated increase of about 24 mph by the proposed change from the Lamblin-type underwing radiators of the S.4 to a system akin to that had been adopted by the Curtiss racers and, subsequently, in the Macchi M.39. The new radiators were to be made out of copper sheets, 8.5 inches wide, with corrugations on the inner surfaces to form channels for the coolant, which was taken along troughs behind the rear wing spar to these radiators, back along the leading edge of the wing and then pumped to a header-tank behind the engine block. These radiator panels were formed to the contours of the wing surfaces and attached, top and bottom. They thus offered virtually no additional drag. Attention was even paid to the effect of different paints on the effectiveness of the radiators. The lubricating oil was also cooled via surface radiators, consisting of corrugations that ran along the outsides of the fuselage and up to a header tank behind the cockpit.

In terms of structure, the Supermarine contender continued the move away from its S.4 predecessor. In line with the company's other developments at the time, the new machine was of mixed metal and wood construction; the flying surfaces were, like those of the S.4, of wooden construction and ply-covered but the all-metal fuselage was a stressed-skin structure (which looked forward to that of the Spitfire). As Arthur Black had been recruited by R.J. in 1926, as one of the first metallurgists to the aircraft industry, R.J. took the decision to have new floats, as well as the fuselage also made in metal.

Extract from Mitchell's speech to the Royal Aeronautical Society in 1927; the importance which he attached to reducing frontal drag and which was of particular importance when he came to the Spitfire, is very evident:

(a) The primary object in lowering the wing on the fuselage was to improve the view of the pilot, which was never very good on the S.4 The higher position of the wing no doubt gave a lower resistance due to fairing in the outside engine blocks and thus saving a certain amount of frontal area. A loss in speed of about 3 miles per hour is estimated from this alteration. This loss is more than balanced, however, by the importance of the improved view.

(b) The system of wire bracing of the wings to the fuselage and floats was adopted for a number of reasons. The unbraced wings and chassis of the S.4 were very high in structure weight, and it was found very difficult to construct an unbraced wing sufficiently strong and rigid without making it very thick at the root, and thus increasing its resistance. The adoption of bracing was largely responsible for a reduction in structure weight of 45 per cent for the S.4 to 36 per cent for the S.5, with its corresponding reduction in resistance; also for the elimination of the two struts between the floats, and for the reduction in frontal area of the four main chassis struts. Against these must be set the addition of fourteen wires. It is not easy to estimate the final effect of a number of alterations of this nature, but from the analysis of the resistance of the two machines it is given on fairly good grounds that the overall effect was an appreciable saving in resistance, amounting to an increase in speed of approximately five miles an hour.

(c) The cross-sectional area of the fuselage has been reduced by about 35 per cent. This very large reduction was obtained through the redesign of the engine and the very closely fitting fuselage. This almost amounted to a duralumin skin in order to ensure that the very smallest amount of cross-sectional area was added. On several occasions during the construction of the

> fuselage the pilots were fitted, and much trouble was experienced through their being of varying dimensions ... The reduction in body resistance was responsible for an increase in speed of approximately 11 mph.
>
> The floats were also reduced in frontal area by about 14 per cent. This was accomplished by using a much lower reserve buoyancy. The reserve buoyancy was 55 per cent for the 'S.4' floats and 40 per cent. for the starboard float of the 'S.5' [now being used for fuel tankage]. This figure is extremely low and called for very efficient lines.
>
> The estimated increase in speed due to reduction in float resistance is 4 mph. These reductions in resistance of fuselage and floats are due to lower cross-sectional areas and not to improvements in form.
>
> (d) Wing surface radiators were first fitted to the American machines in the 1925 race, and gave these machines a very big advantage in speed. The radiators added a certain amount of resistance to the machine due to their external corrugations increasing the area of exposed surface. As about 70 per cent. of the resistance of a high-speed wing is skin friction, and the corrugations almost double the area of surface, it is reasonable to suppose that an increase of at least 30 per cent. of resistance is added to the wing. It is evident that a saving in resistance would result if radiators could be made with a flat outer surface, and that they would give no direct resistance to the machine. After much experimental work, radiators with a flat outer surface were produced. The chief difficulty experienced was in sufficiently strengthening and supporting the outer skin to enable it to stand the heavy air loads without making the radiators unduly heavy. The estimated increase of speed due to their use in place of Lamblin radiators used on the 'S.4' is 24 mph.

The new machine was designated 'S.5' as it represented a complete redesign of the previous monoplane, incorporating the new information gained from meticulous work at the National Physical Laboratory test facilities, sponsored by the Air Ministry. R.J. had sent down three models for wind tunnel testing: one was a shoulder-wing design with wing roots cranked downwards and supported by streamlined struts from the floats; a second model had a low wing, similarly braced by struts; and the third was also a low wing design but with bracing wires.

Biard's problems with forward vision during landing and take-off in the S.4 were no doubt an influence on these considerations. Eventually, the low wing position was chosen, particularly as it had been found that wires offered less resistance than struts. The new bracing between the floats and, from them, to the bottom of the wings also allowed a wire 'cage' to be completed as the wires from the upper fuselage to the top of the wings were fixed immediately above the float-bracing attachment points. R.J. was clearly guarding against any wing flexing that might have contributed to the S.4 crash.

Whatever his private thoughts were about the need to step back from the dramatically revolutionary, 'clean', cantilevered S.4, the pragmatic reversion to wire bracing also brought a further reduction in the weight and drag of the very sturdy float struts of the S.4. The balancing out of advantages and disadvantages attendant upon the wish to reduce frontal area and weight against the need to ensure adequate strength and pilot view was set out after the race in his speech to the Royal Aeronautical Society in 1927. In this, he described how he had predicted that his design changes alone would achieve an extra 40 mph, irrespective of the increases that a more powerful engine would bring (*see* grey box above) and Schofield mentioned that, with the second S.5 (which was to come first in the forthcoming contest) 'the hundreds of tiny rivets all over the skin were now flush with the surface instead of projecting like a mass of wee knobs as they had done' in the first S.5 (*see* a similar concern with the Spitfire, mentioned on p. 392).

The result of all these design considerations culminated in a design which, when it went to Venice to compete in the 1927 Schneider trophy competition, was seen by the Italians as a direct copy of the Macchi M.39 which had won the previous year. Penrose quotes an opposite view by Oswald Short:

> In 1926 I was invited to visit two Italian firms interested in my particular form of metal aircraft, and I was shown the M.39 undergoing its first engine test. I remarked that I could have sworn the floats had been made in our own shops. [Shorts had supplied floats to the 1925 British Schneider machines.] One of the Macchi staff replied, 'Yes, when Mr Macchi Junior was in America for the 1925 Schneider, no doubt he kept his eyes wide open'. Undoubtedly Mr Macchi observed the clean lines of the Supermarine and noticed that the attempt to produce a comparatively thin wing in pure cantilever led to trouble; he also saw the American float strut system was the cleanest. These facts no doubt led to the M.39 design and to avoid trouble the wing was braced to the floats and the top of the fuselage and this requirement alone, apart from the good view, would suggest dropping the wing to obtain reasonable angles on the bracing wires [as, of course, did Mitchell when he reverted to wire bracing]. The M.39 of 1926 was therefore a combination of the good points of the 1925 British and American machines and no one begrudges Messrs Macchi the credit of their achievement.

The *Engineering Times* appeared to have been prompted to a similar defence:

> It is not too much to say that the modern history of the race has been profoundly influenced by the genius of a young British designer, Mr R. J. Mitchell … Italy, in the following year, produced a monoplane seaplane, which one hopes it is not unfair to describe as a legitimate and clever development of the original British design.

While R.J., like other engineers, was perfectly willing to profit from the successful design solutions of others (*see* particularly his Dornier-inspired air yacht in Chapter 11), the Italian criticism had not taken into account Mitchell's trendsetting S.4 of 1925, how long Mitchell had been contemplating his latest design, or how the wind tunnel tests had influenced his more pragmatic choice of this layout.

Supermarine's description of the new racer includes details of the genesis of the S.5 machine and its increasing use of metal structures:

The S.5 is naturally a development of the S.4 and it may be interesting, therefore, to indicate the manner in which progress has been made. The shapes of all parasite parts, such as body and floats, have been arrived at as a result of lengthy wind-tunnel tests, and the cross-sectional areas of these components have been reduced to a minimum. In place of the cantilever float struts on the S.4, a peripheral system of wire-bracing has been adopted. The new Supermarine high-speed wing radiators completely eliminate radiator drag, as their surface is entirely coincident with the normal surface of the wings.

WINGS—Low-wing, braced monoplane. Bi-convex wing section, of medium thickness. Wing structure of wood, consisting of two spars and normal ribs, except for wider flanges necessary to secure the fixings for the wing radiators. Wing covered with ¼ in. plywood, over which are placed the wing radiators. Wings braced with streamline wires to top of fuselage and to floats.

FUSELAGE—Oval section, of metal monocoque construction. Built up of a number of closely-spaced transverse formers, covered with sheet duralumin, reinforced with longitudinal stringers. Front portion of fuselage acts as an engine-bearer, the two main bearers, of box-section, being secured direct to sides of fuselage and supported by reinforced cradles. The fuselage frames, to which wings and floats are attached, are strengthened and the skin in this region, as well as below engine, is laminated.

TAIL UNIT—Monoplane type. Fin built integral with fuselage. All controls internal.

FLOATS—Twin, long, single-step, streamline floats, of duralumin construction. Built up of one central longitudinal bulkhead, to which are attached transverse frames, which are interconnected by light longitudinal members, the whole being covered with duralumin sheet. The centre-section of the starboard float is built in the form of a petrol tank of steel, and to balance the machine laterally the whole chassis is slightly offset, relative to centre-line of body. Floats attached to fuselage by four struts, each pair meeting at a point under the centre-line of the fuselage.

POWER PLANT—One special Napier 'Lion' racing engine, completely cowled-in. Either geared or direct drive engines may be fitted without alteration. Wing radiators header tank in centre cylinder-block fairing. Main petrol tank in starboard float, with auxiliary gravity tank in fairing of starboard cylinder-block. Total fuel capacity 55 galls (250 litres). Oil-coolers set along sides of fuselage.

ACCOMMODATION—Pilot's cockpit situated over trailing-edge of wing.

The S.5 at Calshot after release of first photographs.

There was also to have been an American private entry to this year's Schneider competition, which deserves a mention, as it shows the determination of the British at this time to press for a victory. Due to problems with the American machine, a request for a thirty-day delay was made at the end of July—after all, the Americans had agreed to an eighteen-day postponement in 1926—but Britain would not accede to the new request. The cost of rearranging travel and accommodation arrangements would have been an obvious reason for Britain's refusal, but her comparative preparedness for the event on the due date was surely the main factor. The word 'comparative' is used advisedly because the Short Crusader and the first of the two Gloster IVs were only delivered in May, with the first S.5 being ready in early June. However, the 14th had seen the first flight of the S.5 and 284 mph had been achieved.

Later, on 3 August, the Gloster machine put up 277 mph. Because of the straight-line development from the 1921 Mark I, the new Gloster was unproblematic; early nose-heaviness in the S.5 was quickly corrected by an adjustment of the tailplane setting—the log of high-speed pilot Webster recorded 'very very, nice. No snags'. Only the Crusader appeared not to be justifying faith in the British entries as it proved to be markedly slower and was afflicted by sudden engine cut-outs—'with a whip that nearly took it out of the machine'. This was sometimes followed by the engine cutting back in just as unexpectedly, which was not only alarming but also very uncomfortable for the pilot—as Schofield also said, 'the backrest gave me a kick in the back that I shall remember for a long time. I literally felt quite silly'. The high-speed pilots were perhaps being even a little kind when they named the machine 'Curious Ada'.

The Tenth Schneider Trophy Contest, 26 September 1927, at Venice

Notwithstanding the disappointments with the Crusader, it had been decided to take this machine to Venice, along with the Supermarine and Gloster aircraft. Despite all the well-laid plans, there had been, as usual, little time for practice and certain necessary modifications before shipment but, at least, the travel arrangements had been designed to allow adequate practice time at the contest venue.

One S.5, a Gloster, and the Crusader left for Italy on 17 August on SS *Eworth*, and ten days later, Flo Mitchell had the thrill of accompanying her husband, along with the remaining racers. After a sea voyage on SS *Egyptian Prince* to the Grand Harbour, Malta, they transferred to the aircraft carrier HMS *Eagle*, accompanied by four destroyers, to the 'floating city' of Venice. As the competition did not start until 26 September, Mrs Mitchell—ex-headmistress, after all—could make good use of the latest Baedeker guide: *The Mediterranean; Seaports and Sea Routes*.

Unfortunately, at the competition site, things did not start well. Bad weather prevented test flying until 10 September, only thirteen days before the navigation tests were due; then,

HMS *Eagle*.

on the following day, the Crusader crashed. On take-off, a roll to starboard was seen to go past the vertical and the machine crashed into the water but, luckily, the machine had not reached any great height, although the speed would have reached over 150 mph. Even more fortunately, the pilot, Schofield, did not pay the ultimate penalty for not, apparently, paying attention to pre-flight checks—it was found that the crash had been due to crossed aileron control cables on re-rigging in Venice.

The second batch of British planes arrived the next day but bad weather again prevented test flying until the 21st, when it was found that a previous problem of fumes in the cockpit still needed attention. As a result, Flt Lt S. M. Kinkead was confined to his room all the next day. His machine also required attention as part of his spinner had come adrift, causing severe vibration.

An Italian pilot was not as lucky as Schofield and was killed during practice. The new Italian engines were also proving unreliable, and when their pilots arrived on the 19th, they appeared not to want to fly flat out. This reticence had the effect of supplying no pre-race information to the British, except that the Italians still favoured their climbing turn technique at the pylons; as a result, the British team could devise no special tactics.

The three competing entries were finalised as Flt Lt S. N. Webster in the Supermarine N220, Flt Lt O. E. Worsley in the Supermarine N219, and Kinkead in the better of the two Glosters. It was decided that N220, and the Gloster, N223, with the unproven geared engines, were to fly flat out, with the expectation that Worsley, in the ungeared S.5, would be likely to finish if, for any reason, the engines in the other two, more complex, machines failed. They had also decided to continue with their technique of level flight with the turns as tight as possible.

The navigation and watertightness tests were held on Friday 23 September, as arranged, and all duly completed them without trouble, with the exception of Webster, who had to make a second attempt as he was judged to have crossed the start line incorrectly. This he made good on the next morning, in time for the contest proper on Sunday the 25th. Italy also had had the time to replace a suspect geared engine with a direct drive A.S.2 engine from the previous year.

Large crowds began to gather, and not just locals who were strongly supporting the 'local boy', Capt. Arturo Ferrarin; Maj. Mario de Bernardi was also a national favourite, having won the previous year, and he was therefore well-supported by those brought in by the Italian State Railway on special half-fare excursions. Unfortunately, a strong wind and a heavy swell made conditions too problematic for the sensitive floatplanes. Slower, more seaworthy, flying boats would have coped with rougher seas and would have vindicated Jacques Schneider's aim to develop practical, as well as fast, seaplanes, but by now, the trophy competition had developed a breed of specialist floatplanes of a very different sort, with almost marginal buoyancy from the floats. Jacques Schneider, whatever his views on how his competition had developed, was not able to attend the event as he was recovering from an operation.

The crowds had to return on 26 September, when conditions had improved, and it was possible to commence the contest at 2.30 p.m. when Kinkead took off in the Gloster, followed by Webster and then de Bernardi. The new member of the Italian team, Capt. Frederico Guazzetti, was next, then Worsley and, finally, Ferrarin. A new contest rule was that the start line should now be crossed airborne; this allowed an immediate assessment of likely performance over all the seven laps. British timekeepers made de Bernardi fifteen seconds better than Kinkead in the Gloster, with Webster equal to the Italian. These calculations were rendered academic when Ferrarin disappointed his local supporters by turning off the course on the first lap with two pistons burnt through, followed by de Bernardi on lap two, suffering from a connecting rod failure.

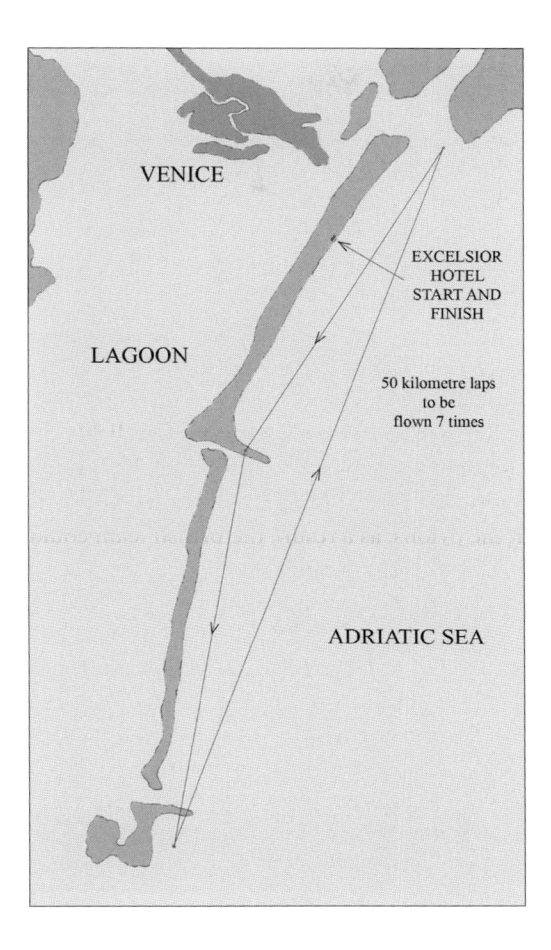

Schneider Trophy course, 1927.

The third Macchi, with the older replacement engine, proved no match for the British with their new uprated Lions, but then Kinkead retired at the beginning of the sixth lap when violent vibrations made it seem prudent to do so. This turned out to have been a wise decision as the previous vibrations were found to have caused a shear line to develop about three-quarters around the circumference of the propeller shaft.

Then, on the penultimate lap and in sight of being placed, the last Italian, Guazzetti, pulled out in spectacular fashion. Schofield (now able to walk with the aid of sticks) witnessed his 'hair-raising dashes in all directions when he was blinded by the bursting of a petrol pipe'. Luckily, he managed to get down safely although not before giving some of the spectators a scare, as Rodwell (later Air Commodore) Banks reported:

> I went to Venice, to see Webster of the RAF High Speed Flight team win; and, with others, including the Crown Prince of Italy, was nearly knocked off the top of the Excelsior Hotel on the Lido when … the pilot of one of the Macchis had engine trouble. He managed to turn his machine off the course but appeared to fly directly at us. However, he 'leapfrogged' the Hotel to land in the lagoon at the other side.

An S.5 over the Lido, with HMS *Eagle* in background.

The S.5 flown by Flt Lt Worsley and the Gloster IVB, flown at lower altitude by Flt Lt Kinkead (in order to improve his peripheral view of the course).

Webster meanwhile had safely completed the required seven laps but carried on flying; his lap counter was a board with holes covered with paper, and after punching out the seventh, he found that he had been airborne for only forty-six minutes instead of the expected fifty-plus. Thinking that he might have miscounted somehow, he managed to complete an extra lap without having to force-land for lack of fuel. Watched by Mussolini, he thus led a British whitewash with an average speed for the actual distance of the contest of 281.65 mph—a new record for seaplanes and bettering by 3 mph the world speed record for landplanes. Worsley came second at 273.01 mph in the second, ungeared, S.5; as Webster said afterwards, 'I was pretty sure it was in the bag. I knew I had the legs on Worsley'.

The skill of these specially selected pilots is demonstrated by the fact that the RAF front-line fighter at this time—the Armstrong-Whitworth Siskin IIIA—had a top speed of only 186 mph and that, despite light rain and haze towards the end of the competition, both men, while having to negotiate two sharp turns per lap, had averaged about 87 per cent of the maximum speed available to them. As Schofield said: 'It must be remembered that we were the first Service team, that our work ... carried with it an increase of speed of a proportion unheard of before.'

It might be that Schofield's account of the Venice event was slightly coloured by an over-compensation for his unfortunate part in it, but it is undeniable that the unprecedented leap in speeds took place in racing aircraft where concerns to reduce drag had now resulted in extremely limited, almost non-existent forward views. While the S.5 was slightly better, the Gloster contender had been introduced to Schofield as 'the blind wonder', and this did not just refer to the fact that 'it was impossible to see a thing anywhere over the top plane or indeed anything useful ahead at all, when sitting on the water' (or with the nose raised for landings). Only when Schofield saw some reasonable height on the altimeter could he put the nose down a little and see the horizon ahead: 'a spot more height, and it was possible to get a generally helpful impression on either side, but it was still disconcertingly blind in most important points'. He said of Kinkead, who flew the Gloster in the actual competition, that 'he flew his deadly accurate course almost blind'.

Meanwhile, the *Southern Daily Echo* of 26 September managed to extract some 'human interest' regarding the Mitchells:

> A man of just over 30 years of age, whose engineering capabilities were so great that he was not allowed to join any of the fighting services when he was 20, is the silent hero of Britain's Schneider trophy victory yesterday at the Lido. He is Mr R. J. Mitchell, the designer of the Supermarine Napier machine, the fastest in the world.
>
> He witnessed the victory of his creation from the shores of the Lido, and while the plaudits of the crowd were handed out to the pilot, the praise of everyone intimately connected with the technical side of the achievement was also bestowed upon Mr Mitchell as he stood with his wife to see the result posted on the board.

After the victory, the participants returned more rapidly than when they had set out for Venice. The winner, Flt Lt Webster, flew into Croydon Aerodrome, escorted by six RAF fighters, and was met by the under-secretary of state for air and a military band. The *Dispatch* for 2 October reported a rather different return by train for the Supermarine team:

SILENT HERO OF AIR TRIUMPH
DESIGNER OF WORLD'S FASTEST 'PLANE

Three hours after the tumult and the shouting at Croydon had died, seven men without whom the Schneider Cup could never have been won, slipped quietly into London, unhonoured and unsung. They were the mechanics of the British team, with Mr R. J. Mitchell, who designed the winning 'plane. No one at Victoria, when the Dover-Calais Continental boat express drew in just after six o'clock, recognised these seven stalwarts dressed in mufti. Before the train arrived they had modestly torn down the notice on the window of the Pullman which proclaimed their identity.

Back in England, any celebration by the Mitchells was cut short by a telegram from Stoke-on-Trent, where their son Gordon had been staying for the duration of the contest with his uncle Eric. A car accident had left the boy with severe concussion but, fortunately, they found that there had been no permanent damage. Nevertheless, Gordon had had to spend three weeks in a darkened room and he remembers his father keeping him company for many hours, trying to cheer him up; he later quoted from a letter from his father to a Mrs Frost, who knew Reginald from his Stoke days: 'Please excuse me for not replying before but since returning from Italy I have been away from Southampton and have not been able to attend to my correspondence.' Perhaps R.J.'s dislike of wearing his heart on his sleeve rather than his dislike of writing letters accounted for his not elaborating on the cause of his absence from home.

On returning to Southampton, R.J. was then forced into the limelight. At an official reception given by the corporation of Southampton, he made a short speech, in which he typically praised the Supermarine team who went to Venice with him:

> I think our victory will raise the Union Jack a little higher. We have all worked very hard to win, and I am sorry that the mechanics are not present to share in this reception because they worked harder than anybody. Four hours before the Schneider race, a leak was discovered in a wing radiator but everyone got down to work and it was repaired just in time.

There followed further calls for our chief designer to practice his speech-making. On 7 October at a Southampton Rotary Club meeting, a much longer speech was reported by the *Southern Daily Echo*:

A MODEST REPLY

Mr Mitchell said that he would hate anyone to think that it had been an individual triumph, as he had been so considerably helped by a very large number of people—his personal assistants and draughtsmen, as well as those engaged on the constructional side. The machine itself has been a source of considerable anxiety to him right from the start, and he was very pleased that at the moment it was safely in a box.

The designing of such a machine involved considerable anxiety because everything was sacrificed to speed. Such things as floats were made just large enough to support the machine on the water, and the wings were cut down to a size that was considered just sufficient to ensure a safe landing.

The engine itself was developed to such an extent that its life was only of about five hours' duration. After having done five hours' running it had to be removed and changed. The sparking plugs had to be removed and changed after each flight, and everything was so cut down it really became dangerous to fly.

>It was no use giving the impression that racing machines of this kind were safe to fly, because they were not, and many a time he had felt thankful that it was only a single seater. Therefore he paid a very high tribute to the pilots—they were real heroes and deserved the fullest measure of credit for their work.

In the new year, more speechmaking was necessary—the Staffordshire Society held its twenty-second annual banquet at the Midland Grand Hotel, St Pancras, on 15 February, and the *Sentinel* reported back to R.J.'s home town that he had praised the pilots who 'had to go into special training for nearly a year during which time they did experimental flying and carried out dangerous trials with the aircraft. Many a time he had been glad that the machines were only single-seaters.' It is noteworthy that here, in the preceding speech, and in a following speech, R.J. alluded to the danger of flying his racing designs.

Twelve days later, he was the principal guest at the annual dinner of the Stoke-on-Trent Association of Engineers, held at the North Stafford Hotel, accompanied by his father, with whom he had been staying for several days. The *Sentinel* reported a polished speech (perhaps after consultation with the company's press officer?) in which he paid tribute to the education and training he had been given in his hometown but then went on, one suspects, to prepare the ground for the financing of a new aircraft for the next competition (after all, he had just recently been appointed a director of his company):

>Referring to the winning of the Schneider Trophy, Mr Mitchell said: 'I have heard the question asked, "How is it that so much money and energy are spent in producing a machine with the object of driving an airman through the air faster than he wishes to go?" In the first place, it is a good thing for England to be kept to the forefront in international trials, even of a sporting nature.
>
>'But apart from the sporting side, I speak from experience when I say that a great deal of knowledge is gained from the designing and construction of such craft, and this knowledge is applicable to the improvement of other types of aircraft such as are used in the Royal Air Force. The design of these Service craft, in fact, has been very much improved as a result of these contests. For this reason alone these sporting contests are worth continuing. Furthermore, it is not only the aircraft industry which is helped. The research work that is entailed helps other branches of engineering and in various ways, such as the development of sparking plugs and magnetos and the working of new alloys. As an example, I may quote the new Ethyl fuel. The first real trial of this spirit was in the Schneider Trophy machines last year, and it is largely due to its success therein that it is now put on the market as a commercial commodity.'

Not long after the British victory in Venice, on 4 November, Mario de Bernardi showed what his M.52 aircraft was capable of when its engine was running properly by setting up a new world speed record of 297.817 mph. Despite R.J.'s wish to keep his S.5 'safely in a box', the Air Ministry had the third S.5, not used in Venice, prepared for an attempt to recapture the record.

In his speech at Stoke-on-Trent, R.J. had made the revealing remark that air racing had 'the object of driving an airman through the air faster than he wishes to go', and more than once prior to this, he had said that he was glad that his machines 'were only single-seaters'. Unfortunately, the fear that his pared-down racers might result in deaths was now realised.

This new speed record attempt was to be flown by Flt Lt Kinkead, who had had to retire from the Schneider trophy race in the Gloster machine. He was a First World War pilot, particularly active afterwards in 'control without occupation', with a DSC and Bar, a DFC and Bar, and a DSO. Unfortunately, the attempt was to end in tragedy. Poor weather had delayed the speed record attempt for ten days but, on the morning of 11 March 1928, a test run in windy conditions suggested that a significant advance on the existing record might be achieved when the weather was calmer. On the next day, an oil leak had to be put right and then a snowstorm made low-level, high-speed, flying impossible. Yet shortly after 4 p.m., conditions changed dramatically to calm and sunny although accompanied by a sea mist.

Perhaps owing to the frustration of the postponed flights on previous days, Kinkead decided to make the attempt. At 5 p.m., he took off and, in accordance with the regulations, alighted as required—to prove the seaworthiness of the aircraft. In fact, two landings were required; the previous day's test run was counted as providing the first. In order that speed should not be built up in a dive, it was then necessary to descend to 150 feet, which had to be achieved 500 m before the start of the timed 3-km course.

Precisely what happened then will never be fully established as the S.5 was barely visible to the witnesses on the land who, according to a *Flight* report, included several foreign air attachés, Biard, and Mitchell. Some believed that Kinkead had decided to abandon the attempt because of the conditions and stalled on the landing approach; others maintained that with the poor visibility, he never levelled out and flew straight into the sea while still intent on the speed record. Sun glare, coupled with an obscured horizon and a waveless sea, would have given precious little information to confirm altitude or flying attitude. A sudden dive into the sea was the opinion of many.

In these conditions, Kinkead had displayed his skill as a pilot by having just previously made a successful landing; he had also previously overcome similar conditions when he had practiced on the S.5 before setting off for Venice. Schofield remembered his previous flying when he wrote:

> One of his very first flights was on such a day as that on which he crashed. Sky and sea blended together so ethereally that is was impossible to tell where one finished and the other started.... Yet Kink insisted that he knew exactly what he was doing, and put up his usual faultless show. For the greater part of the time he cannot have known in what direction he was flying, and his 'landing' must have been accompanied by no small quantity of Faith and Hope.
>
> It was on a similar day a few short weeks afterwards, whilst completing what looked like being a record speed run over the same waters, that he suddenly turned down and vanished for ever.

Structural failure cannot be ruled out as Kinkead was flying the aircraft that had not been tried out in Venice and, with a light fuel load and sprint tuned engine, would have been travelling faster than the other S.5s the year before. Certainly, the inquest verdict of a stall while landing, is the least convincing of the explanations (*see* Appendix V). Biard, who was standing next to the chief designer at the time of the accident, is quoted as being quite certain that the crash was a result of structural failure, and his likely reaction at the time might well have contributed to the designer's distress.

R.J. was always known to be tense and difficult to live with before and during high-speed and test flights. He had established a good rapport with the pilots—to whom he was 'Mitch'—and so he would usually stand apart from the other company watchers at these times, unsmiling and anxious. As Arthur Black had observed: 'when early test flights of a new aircraft were in progress, his concern was so great that it paid not to attempt polite conversation'; his son remembered how his frequent moments of testiness, even at home, were especially evident before a test flight:

> You could sense that at home. He had a short fuse and would very easily explode if he thought something was not as it ought to be. But people just accepted that's the way he was. They knew the best thing was not to try to make pleasant conversation—they just left him quietly to get on with it.
>
> Interview with *Southern Daily Echo*, April 23, 2005

The death of Kinkead left Mitchell brooding for some time, despite the assurances of his colleagues that there was no reason why he personally should feel in any way responsible. It is not known whether his distress had thus been increased by a private suspicion that the design had had a fatal weakness when pushed beyond speeds previously experienced, but his concern must have been added to later by the fact that Kinkead's death turned out to have been in vain. Flt Lt D'Arcy Greig, had taken over the High Speed Flight, re-formed for the next Schneider trophy contest, and N220 had been readied for an attempt to beat the Italian record speed, which had now been raised to 318.57 mph. However, the slightly higher speed achieved by Supermarine did not give a margin sufficient to justify a claim to the FAI.

The S.5s were thereafter to be relegated to practice machines for the eleventh competition although, in the event, N219 was returned to Supermarine in July 1929 for a complete overhaul and the fitting of a new geared Lion engine. On the strength of this, it made up the number in the competition of that year and came third, with a speed only 2 mph slower than the substitute Macchi M.52, with an engine developing over 100 hp more thrust.

'Mitch' with Sqn Ldr A. H. Orlebar in front of the S.6.

10

Taking a Chance with Rolls-Royce (1929)

> *The Rolls-Royce engineers had discussed separately with Reggie Mitchell, the Supermarine designer, and myself, the possibilities latent in this engine....*
> *To me it meant a desperate gamble to back something virtually untried.*
>
> Maj. J. P. Bulman

Once the excitement of the 1927 Schneider competition win had subsided, the design and cost implications of competing for the next Schneider trophy were now even more clear to all potential entrants, especially as only two of the six competing aircraft had finished the course this last time. Thus it was that the Royal Aero Club, which would organise the next competition, now supported the change to biannual competitions, starting in 1929; the FIA, at its January meeting in 1928, concurred. The rules of the competition were amended to the effect that a permanent holder of the trophy would have had to gain three victories, not within five years as before, but in the course of successive contests.

Britain would certainly welcome a longer lead time in order to improve upon the performance of the S.5, in time for the defence of the trophy, which would take place in front of a home crowd. The failure of Greig's S.5 to significantly improve upon the world speed record of the Macchi M.52 allowed for no complacency and suggested that the present Supermarine machines or engines might not be capable of much further direct development. Yet for a redesign, further government support would be vital—as R.J. himself had said in his 1927 lecture to the Royal Aeronautical Society:

> After the failure of the British team to win the race in America in 1925, it was brought home to all interested that our machines were a long way inferior to the American machines and that if we wished to hold our own again in this important field of aviation we should have to treat the matter much more seriously. Furthermore, it became obvious to all that machines could no longer be entered for these races by private enterprise. It is true that the Air Ministry had loaned machines for the race but very little opportunity had been given for research and experimental work and the engine designers had been working independently.

Perhaps his words reflected a fear that the Treasury would not support the cost of another competition entry as word had probably got around that Churchill, then chancellor of the exchequer, had taken some persuading to agree funds in 1927 and that Sir Hugh Trenchard, the chief of the air staff, was not at all keen on his RAF getting mixed up with air racing.

Once again events favoured R.J. as Churchill, no doubt because of the resounding success over Mussolini's aircraft in Venice, gave the new project his full blessing, asking Sir Samuel Hoare how much money he needed. Trenchard then not only accepted the inevitable but took a personal interest in the arrangements and in selecting the next high-speed team.

With this backing, the Air Ministry's support was extended in the direction wished for: allowing more time for the design of special airframes, racing engines, and fuel, and for the mating of the engines to the propellers and to the shape of the airframe or *vice versa*.

One particular development in the competition, at least as far as British designers were concerned, was the emergence of a Rolls-Royce racing engine. Britain and Mitchell had been fortunate that their winning Napier engine of 1927 had not been a new and, therefore, possibly unreliable design but had been in continuous development since before its use in his 1922 Schneider trophy winner; it had been producing 450 hp in 1919 and this had actually been increased to 900 hp by 1927. It is also noteworthy that, during this time, no Schneider aircraft powered by these Napier Lions failed to complete the course because of engine problems. Nevertheless, the question had to be asked whether this remarkable engine was now reaching the end of its development potential, especially as Napier had not developed a supercharger.

Meanwhile, in 1924, Rolls-Royce had begun to make an engine to rival the Curtiss D-12, which had powered the 1923 and 1925 Schneider trophy winners. The resultant Kestrel then went on to power a whole range of classic RAF Hawker biplanes: the Hart, Fury, Audax, Hind, *et al*. It was significant that, in 1921, Arthur Rowledge, who had been responsible for the Lion engine, had moved to Rolls-Royce and had been influential in recruiting James Ellor from the Royal Aircraft Establishment to work on supercharging the Kestrel. His current concern was the proposed Buzzard; it was larger than the Kestrel and developing 825 hp, but it had a tendency to crack its cylinder head after only a short run.

R.J.'s only direct experience of this company's engines at this time was in connection with their Eagle in his earlier slow-flying aircraft and he apparently asked Major G. P. Bulman, the Air Ministry official responsible for the development of aero engines, for his views. He later described how he had found that R.J., something of a 'chancer' as we have seen, was willing to invest his company's time and effort and his own future reputation in high-speed flight—with a gamble on an untried engine from a different maker, however well thought of in other respects:

> The Rolls-Royce engineers had discussed separately with Reggie Mitchell, the Supermarine designer, and myself, the possibilities latent in this engine, given intensive effort for a short life, and were enthusiastic in their hopes. To Mitchell it would mean a considerable rehash of his S.5 to accommodate the bigger and heavier engine, with its extra cooling and heavier fuel load. To me it meant a desperate gamble to back something virtually untried, entirely contrary to my habit, and to commit the Air Ministry and the nation to a gigantic bet, instead of playing safe by putting all one's money on the well-tried faithful Lion.
>
> Mitchell and I met together alone three times over a short period to resolve the problem

Commander James Bird of Supermarine and Bulman accordingly called on Henry Royce, then living in semi-retirement at his West Wittering home on the Sussex coast. They pressed on him the matter of national prestige as well as the eventual benefit to the British aircraft industry and Royce agreed that the company should take up the challenge of developing a special racing engine; it was also agreed that, as it was already October 1928, the partially developed 36.7-litre Buzzard engine would have to be the basis for the project.

According to Rodwell Banks, Rowledge, Ernest Hives (the head of the Experimental Shop), and A. C. Lovesey (his assistant) then went down to West Wittering:

> It was a bright autumn morning and Royce suggested a stroll along the beach; as they walked he pointed out the local places of interest. But Royce, who walked with a stick, was a semi-invalid and he soon tired.
>
> 'Let's find a sheltered spot,' he said, 'and have a talk.' Seated on the sand dunes against a groyne, Royce sketched the rough outline of a racing engine in the sand with his stick. Each man was asked his opinion in turn, the sand was raked over and adjustments made.

The new engine was to be separately designated the 'R' engine, with a hoped-for output of 1,800 hp.

There followed an 'interesting' example of how Mitchell's career was at times influenced by events outside his control. Bulman had reported back to his chief, Sir John Higgins, the air member for supply and research, who immediately asked the managing director of Rolls-Royce to call and agree to undertake the project. Bulman then gave a colourful account of a meeting that seemed to dash hopes of a formidable powerplant for Mitchell's next design:

> Claude Johnson, who had built up the Firm's worldwide reputation on Royce's technical brilliance and vision, a man of striking personality, had died in 1926, and his successor [his brother, Basil] it was who came to see Josh and myself, alone. To our utter amazement he begged to be excused from our commission. Racing and all its aspects were things, he said, strictly to be avoided by his firm. Its reputation for sheer quality and perfection must not be smirched by sordid competition of this sort. To participate unwillingly, and quite possibly fail, would be a calamity for the firm with the loss of its prestige. And so on, in dreary defeatism.

Bulman then described how, knowing that the firm's engineers were only too keen to take up the challenge, came out with 'a single word, unprintable in polite context and essentially masculine'. Luckily, Sir John was well aware of the desire of 'his masters' to fend off attempts by rival countries to win the next Schneider trophy competition:

> Higgins turned and looked at me for a long second, and then in a steely voice of real Air Marshal calibre said to our guest, 'I order your firm to take on this job. We have complete faith in your technical team. The necessary arrangement will be made between our respective staffs. Good afternoon.' As our disconsolate and vanquished visitor closed the door behind him Josh said to me, 'Thank you for summing up the discussion so succinctly,' and gave a huge chuckle as I shot out of his office to telephone the glad tidings to Rowledge in Derby.

Nevertheless, Bulman was right to call the project something of a 'desperate gamble to back something virtually untried' as it would involve building a different crankcase to conform to

R.J.'s first limousine.

the sort of shape that Mitchell was likely to develop out of the S.5 configuration and designing a supercharger to give boost at very low level. Of course, R.J. was also gambling his future reputation in high-speed flight: as Bulman said, it was 'mutually agreed that we should back the Rolls project, largely—and for my part wholly—on the faith that I had in the Derby team'.

R.J. now signalled his own appreciation of the Derby brand and his own increased status by becoming the owner of his first Rolls-Royce car—an all-black 20 hp soft-topped limousine. His son informs us that it became known as 'The Hearse' and how his father disliked stopping during their drives up to his hometown. It would seem, however, that sitting behind a steering wheel for several hours at a time, 'doing nothing' as it were, at least shortened the, perhaps obligatory, journey. There is no evidence of strained relations between the home-based family and the successful son living in some style on the south coast—and he was very pleased to receive regular parcels of the oatcakes for which the Potteries were known—but the annual Christmas visits sometimes appeared, even to his young son, to be 'rather hard going' as far as the father was concerned.

One can only speculate about the family dynamics when the eldest son arrived back home at Meir Road in an expensive limousine, especially as even smaller private cars were by no means numerous. While the Mitchell and the Dayson parents had been presented, quite early on, with their grandchild, Gordon, old family ties had to contend with the effect of more than ten years of separation. Reginald was now in firm charge of a large drawing office and construction staff; he had been to America and, on an aircraft carrier to Venice, had met the future king of Great Britain and been featured in the national press. His mind must have often longed to be back at his drawing board, eager to solve some new challenge, in the company of his circle of assistants.

Meanwhile, it had become clear that Italy was intent on winning the trophy next time and why it had supported the move to biannual contests—taking note of the previous determined and thorough British campaign that had led to their 1927 success, the government ordered engines from Isotta-Fraschini and Fiat and new machines from Macchi, Fiat, Piaggio, and Savoia-Marchetti.

The Fiat C.29 proved to have a layout similar to the Macchi but with a mere 22-foot wingspan as it was to be powered by the lightest engine for its power in the world—the 1,000-hp Fiat AS.5; the Macchi M.67 emerged as a further development of the M.39 and M.52—after all, the latter had set the new world record, which Supermarine had been unable to better and was now to rely on an Isotta-Fraschini engine with three banks of six cylinders, expected to deliver 1,800 hp.

The five Mitchell children—Eric, Doris, Reg, Hilda, and Billy, *c.* 1929.

Meir Road, No. 1 on left (*see also* p. 160).

The other two Italian designs were very different from the layouts now coming to be expected for the Schneider trophy contest. The Savoia-Marchetti S.65 was, admittedly, a floatplane, but it had twin booms supporting the tail unit, thus allowing for two engines to be mounted in a central nacelle. The pilot was placed in between the tandem arrangement and the tractor/propeller combination of two 1,000-hp Isotta-Fraschini engines promised formidable power. It would also present no torque complications on take-off, something that, before the advent of variable pitch propellers, was becoming ever more of a problem. On the other hand, the Piaggio Pc.7 represented a quite revolutionary departure from all other Schneider trophy designs as it had neither floats nor any conventional flying-boat hull. Instead, it had a watertight fuselage with a marine propeller to get it up on hydrofoils, at which point a conventional airscrew was to be engaged for take-off. It also had a cantilever, elliptical wing (which closely foreshadowed that of the Spitfire—*see* p. 322).

A German, an American, and two French entries were projected but none of these materialised, leaving the contest again between the Italians and the British. This time, British entries were ordered only from Supermarine and Gloster. The design of the latter company, designated Mark VI, now finally embodied the monoplane approach. This change of philosophy was particularly influenced by the fact that the pilot's less than satisfactory forward view in the Mark IV would have been even worse if a top wing had had to be placed sufficiently far forward to support a new and heavier engine. In fact, this engine showed that Napier was still not done and their now supercharged Lion was developing 1,320 hp. It also gave some insurance against the possible failure of the brand-new Rolls-Royce engine to be employed by Supermarine. The wings were an interesting shape; like the Short Crusader of 1927, the new Gloster had wings that could not be exactly described as elliptical but which had a thin, high-speed, section at the roots, widening out to a thicker section towards the tips for low-speed lateral control (*see* also drawing p. 322).

The S.6 and Squadron Leader Orlebar

R.J. was content to rely on the rightness of his previous design to handle the significantly more powerful engine and so his main design effort was now directed towards the realisation of an all-metal aircraft larger than the S.5 in order to accommodate the projected bigger and heavier engine: the 930 lb of the 1927 Lion was to be replaced by an engine weighing 1,530 lb. First configuration drawings of the 'R' engine were sent to him on 3 July 1928, and so he was able to influence the shape of the cam covers so that, as with the S.5, they would conform to the streamlines he was developing for his new machine—as Bulman reported: 'the cylinder blocks and valve gear casing were trimmed down and externally reshaped to come within the frontal area and line of the new Supermarine S.6 designed by Mitchell'.

Rolls-Royce achieved an eventual 1,900 hp by August—a power increase of 211 per cent over the previous Lion engine. R.J. was reported to have said: 'Go steady with your horsepower', alluding no doubt to accommodating such a massive power increase as well as the cooling problems that would be encountered in what turned out to be a loaded aircraft weight increase of 78 per cent. R.J. had to consider the airframe implications of the change from the Lion engine with a 24-litre capacity to the proposed Rolls-Royce 'R' of 36.7 litres, not to mention the dangerous challenges that his designs might present to the pilots.

Mitchell and Henry Royce.

The most obvious change from the S.5 shape was the different cowling necessitated by the 'V' shape of the new engine. Its extra weight also involved placing the cockpit further back and its increased fuel consumption meant that both floats had to be used for the tanks—the new engine was going to consume nearly 2.5 gallons per minute. As the empty weight of the S.6, at 4,471 lb, was 1,791 lb heavier than that of the S.5, the wingspan was slightly increased, giving an additional area of 30 sq. feet, and the front float struts had to be attached further forward on the fuselage to support the combined effects of a longer and heavier engine.

Supermarine drew attention to an advantage of this change of position: 'In place of the cantilever engine mounting used on the S.5, the front float struts have been moved forward to provide a substantial saving in weight'. Likewise, flaps were still not employed to achieve a slower landing speed: whatever R.J.'s concerns for pilot safety, performance was the first priority, given the exceptional skills of the specially selected High Speed Flight airmen and the fact that floatplanes had access to relatively unlimited landing areas.

Solving the constructional and loading problems in itself had justified the new 'S.6' designation, but these matters were relatively straightforward compared with contending with the heat generated by the new engine. The extra plumbing for the fuel transfer from two floats (see the incident narrated on p. 28) was as nothing compared with that required for cooling the engine oil. The channels for oil cooling running along the sides of the S.5 were now increased in length and new ones added to the underside of the fuselage as well, with the collection point now being the void inside the fin. Their efficiency had additionally to be increased by devising some method of ensuring maximum contact of the oil with the outer surfaces of the system which was exposed to the slipstream.

Supermarine publicity described the new 'oil tank' and the method employed to enhance the cooling of the oil:

> By a new form of internal construction, the oil-coolers have an increased efficiency of about 40 per cent ... A large number of sloping gutters are arranged along the sides of the fin, so that the oil, after being sprayed from the pipe at the top of the fin, is made to trickle down the gutters and over the internal structure, thereby ensuring that the greatest possible amount of oil is in contact with the metal all the time.
>
> A similar purpose is served by the oil-coolers along the sides and belly of the fuselage. Those along the sides take the oil to the fin and those along the belly return it to the engine. These coolers are shallow channels of tinned steel attached to the sides of the fuselage. They owe much of their efficiency to a number of tongues of copper foil athwart the flow of oil. These are soldered to the sides of the cooler and project at right angles into the stream of oil. They are staggered in such a way that the flow of the oil is not seriously impeded.

Nevertheless, Greig found that the position of the oil pipes, running along the outside of a very narrow fuselage, 'turned the inside of the cockpit into something approaching an extremely hot Turkish bath' with the oil temperature gauge reading 'around 136 degrees centigrade'.

Other aspects of the design reflected constructional changes beginning to take place in the aircraft industry, and Supermarine were thus anxious to point out that their move to metal construction was not just with respect to the framework of their machine but that it placed them in the forefront of the use of load-bearing external skinning. Instead of being plywood-covered with the radiator panels externally attached, as with the S.5, the wing structure was now sheeted with the panels alone. Supermarine publicity drew attention to both this stressed skinning and to the use of new materials:

> Unlike the S.5, which had wooden wings covered with plywood, over which were placed the wing radiators, the S.6 has metal wings, and the radiators, which [now] consist of two thicknesses of duralumin with water spaces between, are made as a wing covering to take torsional loads ... This method saves a considerable amount of weight over previous practice. The fuselage is all of metal and the skin takes practically all the stresses. The front portion of the fuselage acts as an engine-bearer and the [laminated] skin in this region takes all the engine loads.

The experience gained by this comprehensive use of stressed skinning was obviously extremely important when it came to the design of the Spitfire.

However, while his fighter and other designs usually revealed some concession to aesthetics, it would seem that the inputs from wind tunnel data, the substitution of the larger V engine and its enormous demands, had somehow now given the S.6 an unusually stark appearance—compared with the rival Gloster VI, described by one newspaper as 'more the conception of an artist ... than the work of a designer who is bound by the principles of engineering and the comparative inelasticity of metal and timber'.

Despite the gap of two years between competitions that had now been agreed on, the scheduled start of the eleventh competition was less than six weeks away before R.J.'s uncompromising and complex airframes could be tested in the air; even then, flying time was limited. The main reason for this delay was to be found at Rolls-Royce. The new engine had been first sketched out in the previous October, and by May, it was delivering 1,545 hp; after about quarter of an hour of high-speed running, parts began to fail. Finally, on 27 July, the new engine passed the magic one-hour mark at full throttle and supercharger boost. The competition was scheduled to begin on 6 September.

A few days later, with the blending of a special fuel by Rodwell Banks, the company was able to achieve an engine run of 100 minutes and 1,850 hp. The end of testing was much to the relief of the good citizens of Derby, as the tests had also required the simultaneous running of three 600-hp Kestrel aero engines that drove fans to cool the crankcase of the 'R' engine, to disperse fumes in the test house, and to simulate 400 mph airflow conditions in flight.

These were the days before modern health and safety regulations and Banks, describing the din of a total of four aero-engines within the test sheds, wrote that 'reverberation from walls and roof is such that at certain engine speeds one cannot keep still: the whole body seems in a state of high frequency vibration. One shouts at the top of one's voice but cannot even feel the vibration of the vocal chords.' People living up to 15 miles away, on the outskirts of Nottingham, reported still being able to hear the engine runs and the ears of the Rolls-Royce workers were plugged with cotton wool. They were also well supplied with milk to counteract the notoriously laxative effect of breathing in the Castrol engine oil, ejected out of the open exhaust ports of the 'R' engine and deposited on the walls of the test cell. *Flight* reported that one early run was consuming oil at the rate of 112 gallons per hour and that the state of the test shed inside was 'a wonder to behold'.

Meanwhile, a new High Speed Flight had been formed in February 1928. Greig, who had been posted in after the death of Kinkead, had recommended members of his Hendon aerobatic team: Flt Lt G. H. Stainforth and Flg Offs R. D. H. Waghorn and R. L. R. Atcherley—the last being long remembered for his aerobatic display in a Gloster Gamecock at the 1926 RAF Display at Hendon. He also recommended Flt Lt J. N. Bootham, of whom we shall hear later, but he was on an overseas posting. Greig then prepared to hand over command to a squadron leader, A. H. Orlebar, with the new title: 'officer commanding the High Speed Flight'.

Orlebar was also to command the flight for the following contest and it was to prove a wise choice. Bulman later said:

> He was the inspiration and father of the whole outfit, yet always modest, approachable and self-effacing. He himself flew each aircraft before he would allow any of his team to take over, and personally tried out every modification and adjustment made.

Here was another example of good fortune aiding a Mitchell design, and the considerable similarity in the characters of the two men was surely an extra bonus. The mutual respect that developed between the two men was confirmed by R.J. being addressed as 'Mitch', but only by the uninhibited RAF pilots.

As before, none of these airmen had been trained as maritime pilots and so time was needed to convert onto seaplanes that stood a good chance of being the fastest in the world. Webster, the 1927 winner, narrated:

> I was test flying at Martlesham Heath when I was sent off to Felixstowe, which wasn't far away, to join the High Speed Flight. I had never flown a seaplane but took to it like a duck to water! We were flying everything at Martlesham—the Inflexible, the Vixen, a Gamecock, the Hinaidi and

The S.6 airframe receiving the new Rolls-Royce 'R' engine.

Mitchell at the 'R' engine installation.

a Sidestrand—so we tended to take everything in our stride. I had over one hundred and twenty types in my logbook. We had a Flycatcher on floats for practice flying and my first flight in that was on 17 February; then we moved on to the old Bamel and the Gloster IIIs. I did quite a lot of flying in the Bamel. We used to pop back to Martlesham to do normal testing between practice flights. I also had three flights in the Crusader at Felixstowe.

In the following year, Waghorn's experience was similar:

We started with the Fairey III.D, and Flycatcher, and then worked through to the Gloster IV, the Gloster IV.A, and Gloster IV.B. I don't think any of us found any jump from a land plane to the ordinary seaplane as from the handling point of view; they are remarkably similar. However, our first flight in the Gloster IV saw a decided jump. The whine of the fast revving engine, the seemingly endless take-off with its attendant jolts and jars magnified in some extraordinary way; the difficulty of knowing what speed you are travelling at and the apparent magnification of any inaccuracy in flying, all helped in giving me, at any rate, a very vivid impression of my first flight in a high-speed seaplane.

Waghorn also described how they put their time to good use in the practice machines by concentrating on devising the best technique for cornering: to achieve a turn at a constant height, as was the previous practice, it was necessary to apply rudder to correct the tendency of the banking aircraft to yaw upward; this, in turn, increased resistance during the turn. It was decided, therefore, that any tendency to climb at the pylons would not be corrected too strongly. Additionally, two scientists from the Royal Aircraft Establishment were attached to the High Speed Flight, and they installed instruments in the aircraft to monitor speed, acceleration, and climb in order to evolve the most efficient turning circle—a compromise between tight, high g sharp turns and loss of speed and wider sweeps, which incurred less drag.

N247, the first of the two S.6s.

With the increased speed in the turns, pilots had now to get used to the threat of blacking out—as Atcherley recalled:

> I went 'out' halfway round a turn at Calshot Castle, the sharpest of the four turns, and flew completely unconscious at about 500 feet halfway back to Cowes before regaining my senses [*see* map on p. 224.] Even then, there was a very frightening lapse of seconds when one realised that one was flying and had been 'out' but still could not see or move one's hands.

Not surprisingly, he admitted that 'it made me brood a bit'.

These preparations received a serious setback when the actual contest aircraft finally arrived as it was found that the effects of the greatly increased torque from the new engine had not been fully anticipated. The S.6 revealed an exaggerated tendency to dig in the left float and describe circles in the water. Orlebar reported that the gyrations 'had rather shaken' Mitchell. Waghorn described the situation as follows:

> With the arrival of the S.6 our hopes had risen considerably only to be immediately lowered to the depths when Squadron Leader Orlebar started his initial tests in Southampton Water. The S.5 in her take-off had been so straightforward that we had assumed that her elder brother would also prove himself equally docile while being broken in. [The floats were no longer rigged asymmetrically.] We were therefore very surprised to see the behaviour of the S.6 on her first test. The S.6 behaved much as a horse refusing a fence. She sat on her tail and it seemed as if no amount of coaxing would get her forward. Furthermore, she dug her left wing into the water and not content with so much mischief started a gigantic porpoising. Time and again the Squadron Leader tried and, although he had overcome the porpoising, she still continued to dig her left wing in and to swing viciously to the left. To the rest of us in the Seacar [the Supermarine speed boat] alongside, it was a heart-rending although impressive sight. From the Seacar we had a close-up of the whole proceedings and a very good view it was, not that one could see much of the pilot and fuselage, as most of the time they were enclosed in a whirl of spray. After about half an hour of this we returned to Calshot in a rather dejected frame of mind, as it certainly had not been a good beginning.

One can easily, therefore, imagine the chief designer's feelings, seeing his aircraft quite unwilling to fly; when Orlebar pointed out to Mitchell that the first machine's number—247—added up to thirteen, 'the poor chap replied with feeling that he had not designed that', so the commanding officer kept the matter to himself.

D'Arcy Greig also tried to take off without success, but later in the day when a little wind had got up, Orlebar finally succeeded. A solution to the torque problem at take-off would be found with the arrival of variable-pitch propellers, but in the meantime, a special technique was worked out whereby it was necessary to keep the stick well back, contrary to all basic flying instruction, in order to maximise lift at the extreme low end of the aircraft's airspeed. Additionally, the take-off had to begin with any breeze kept on the left quarter; this allowed for a nice judgement of acceleration while being pulled by the propeller torque to face directly into wind by the time that lift-off speed was attained.

> **Waghorn's Description of the Solution to the S.6 Take-off Problem**
> The main trouble was the wing digging business and due, without doubt to the enormous torque effect of the slow revving engine and propeller. Mitchell's first move was, therefore, to shift nearly all the petrol into the starboard float and put in hand the immediate construction of a new and larger petrol tank for this float. The result of this was in the end satisfactory enough though there were a good many anxious trials before she got safely into the air. To start with, it was a peculiarly delicate task for Squadron Leader Orlebar. He was swinging, he knew, and his left wing wasn't very far from the water and still he couldn't tell how much owing to the mass of spray enveloping the fuselage. He found out subsequently that a lot of the initial resistance to any acceleration was in part due to the very smooth, almost oily state of the water on which the first taxiing trials took place …
>
> The difference in behaviour in the S.6 when she passed from an oily to a rippled patch was most interesting … I was once watching Atcherley trying to take her off. The sea was oily and the machine obstinate. She never looked like getting on the step. Atcherley shouted to me that he was packing up. We had, however, noticed a patch of rippled water in the distance, and got him to try once more over on that particular bit. The result was magical, and he got off on the first attempt. The torque effect is greatest at slow revs. and the trouble was that being at the peak of the power drag curve, the drag of the floats was just about counterbalancing the thrust. The nose of the machine coming out very high and the tail of the floats digging right into the water, set up a very high resistance. We had, therefore, to fit a faster revving propeller, with more power for the take-off. This also gave more power for the top speed; but we already had more power than specified and therefore more heat to dissipate than the original radiators were designed for. Hence it was going to be necessary to throttle down to keep the water cool. That very slight increase in wind, by about 4 mph, made the difference; whether it was chiefly the increased control given to the rudder or chiefly the surface of the water affecting the floats, I am not prepared to say—perhaps a combination of both. But certain it was that provided you kept the machine into, or slightly to the right of the wind, you could get her on to the step. If she once got to the left of the wind it was hopeless … Whilst discussing these difficulties it is perhaps easy to assume that the S.6 had a bad take-off. Actually, this was not the case; provided one got her into the wind and on her step she accelerated like the proverbial gun.

Once in the air, Orlebar was extremely impressed with the accuracy of Mitch's forecast of the new machine's behaviour: 'He had told me about the possibility of the wing dropping when she first got in the air, and that is why I was prepared for it and shut the throttle momentarily'. He then found that the wing came up easily and, having touched down, was then able to climb away for the new machine's first air test: 'Mitch had said he hoped for a speed of something up to 340 mph, and I achieved an indicated 345.'

The looming deadline of the trophy start date meant that necessary modifications and adjustments could not proceed at a normal company pace; these included overcoming aileron stiffness, re-rigging to counteract a tendency to fly left-wing low, and the fitting of an elastic bungee to the control stick to save the pilot from having continually to counteract tail-heaviness. Additionally, the cooling system was now found to be inadequate and so extra radiator piping had to be created along the sides of the floats; small wing-tip scoops were also fitted, supplying an extra flow of ram air over the inner surface of the radiators—an unforeseen bonus, at least, for using the radiators as load-bearing skinning for the wing.

The *Sentinel* had managed to glean some information—perhaps from one of the High Speed Flight members—when it informed its readers about the local son's continued attention to detail on 7 September 1929:

> He stands a little apart from the crowd, for he is a modest, unassuming man.... He watches with a certain measure of anxiety.... He does not talk a great deal, but when he does his remarks are to the point. If slight adjustments are needed in a machine which he has designed, he does not seek to gloss over the fact. He just proceeds to correct the error.

Unsurprisingly a local 'special representative' noted: 'I had a letter this morning from Mr R. J. Mitchell, the Schneider Trophy 'plane designer, and, by his own account, he is one of the busiest men in the British base at Calshot these days' (*Southern Daily Echo*, 23 August 1929).

The previous victory had sharpened this public interest in him and his aircraft; it thus placed a further burden on his shoulders at a time when he could hardly have needed popular national newspapers to remind him of his responsibilities:

> The coming air contest for the Schneider Trophy overshadows all other sporting events. To win the Trophy is the greatest of all stimulants to promote the 'air-sense' of the nation and so high do the nations of the world place its value that the entry of the teams is the immediate interest and concern of the various Governments of all the contestants. It is up to us as the greatest of all maritime nations to win.
>
> *Express*, 25 August 1929

But, at least the S.6s were now coming up to expectations and testing could thereafter be mainly confined to assessing the efficiency of different propellers, fuel consumption, and perfecting flying techniques in the very short time that was now left before the competition was due to start.

The Italians also had had to wait until August for their new machines and it was soon found that the Piaggio Pc.7 was a non-starter as it was impossible to achieve transition from taxiing to flight. Also, one of the Fiat C.29s caught fire on its second flight, was repaired, and then stalled after a third attempt at a take-off and sank. Meanwhile, the first of the Macchi M67s was looking decidedly promising, reaching 362 mph, but then it too crashed at low level. This time, the pilot, Giuseppe Motta, was killed. Visibility had been similar to that when Kinkead had died; additionally, the Italian's windscreen might have been fogged by exhaust fumes. As the second C.29 and the other two M.67s were not then ready for the competition, Italy requested a one-month postponement on 22 August, but by this time, the costs and logistics of rearranging the event were such that the Royal Aero Club felt obliged to stick to the rules and refused the next day.

It is interesting that when this request was turned down, only one of the new British contenders had flown: Orlebar's first successful take-off was on 10 August, and the Gloster VI and the second S.6 were not first tested until 25 August, by which time the first S.6 had gone back to Supermarine for the fitting of extra radiation. Nor could adequate practice time on the new aircraft be certain—the engines could only be guaranteed for a high-speed run of one hour and they were required to be taken back to Derby for overhaul after every five hours' running.

The delays caused by the removal of time-expired engines and the fitting of overhauled power plants were compounded by the British weather. These highly specialised Schneider machines required good visibility, gentle winds, and short, choppy water without 'white horses'. Too much of a swell would cause the noses of the floats to dig in and set up an eventually uncontrollable porpoising; on the other hand, flat calms would prevent 'unsticking' as well as producing a mirror-like surface that would make it both difficult and dangerous to judge the aircraft's height above the water—the long, flat landing approach of over 100 mph without the aid of flaps that had had to be carefully judged for the S.5 had not diminished.

As it turned out, the Gloster VIs were soon to be withdrawn as their engines could not be made to run properly. So the British had been taking something of a gamble by not agreeing to a postponement, although the first S.6 was proving an unproblematic machine in the air, when the overriding requirements of High Speed Flight might well have created a machine that was difficult to fly. Indeed, the flying qualities were better that those of Mitchell's previous, smaller, machine, even though, or perhaps because, the wing loading had risen from 28 to 40 lb/sq. feet. Waghorn testified:

> While flying, she gave me the feeling of great stability, and when not flying low, the slow revs of the engine gave me the impression that I remember I got when I flew a Horsley [bomber] after having just left the seat of a Gamecock [fighter]. On turns she was delightful. Perhaps she was a little heavier laterally than the S.5 and the Glosters, but then she was a much bigger and heavier machine. There was no noticeable torque effect against a left-hand turn which had been so tiring in the S.5, and, generally speaking, gave me a feeling of great trust and confidence, and I never had cause to change my opinion …
>
> The S.6 appeared to stall about 3 mph slower than the S.5, but airspeed indicators are not infallible at such a speed. However, it can be taken that she stalled in the region of 95 and was certainly no faster than the S.5. She was extraordinarily stable at the stall. The S.5 would quiver at the stall and flick over either side at the slightest provocation. The S.6 showed no tendency to drop either wing, but would sink on an even keel. On one such occasion, while testing the stalling speed, I found the machine on an even keel sinking at about 87 mph. When one considers the behaviour of her elder brother at a similar speed it is all the more interesting, especially when you realise the extra top speed of the S.6.

The Eleventh Schneider Trophy Contest, 7 September 1929, at Calshot

To avoid Britain winning by a fly-over, Italy had decided not to withdraw and sent over their (as yet) untested aircraft—the second Fiat C.29, the Savoia-Marchetti S.65, and the two Macchi M.67s, as well as the older Macchi M.52R world speed record holder and an M.52 practice machine. By this time, both the Supermarine aircraft were ready and, because Gloster's problems had not been solved, it was decided to call up one of the 1927 S.5 machines—Worsley's N219, but now fitted with a geared Lion engine.

Despite a lack of flight testing, especially on the Italian side, the navigation tests on 6 September went well, and all the aircraft were moored out for the watertightness test. Some hours later, Mitchell had to be aroused from sleep in the Officers' Mess, after being up late superintending final preparations: it was discovered that one of the new planes, Atcherley's

N248, was listing, with over two hours to go of the required six-hour flotation test. Mitchell decided that it would hold out for about three hours and went back to rest. By the due time, the machine had a very pronounced list but was able to be beached and a leak repaired.

Meanwhile, a further problem was also discovered, this time with Waghorn's N247, when traces of white metal were found on a spark plug during the routine plug change; internal damage was strongly suspected and thus a change of the offending parts would be necessary. The Schneider trophy rules did not allow changing 'any major component' at this stage in the competition, but luckily, a substitution of parts was permissible. While major overhauls would normally be carried out at Rolls-Royce with the engine having been removed from the aircraft at Calshot, it was now necessary to devise some means of offering the intact machine up to the replacement block; as Orlebar later reported, 'poor Mitch was hauled out again' to supervise the operation. Luckily, a number of Rolls-Royce mechanics had come down by coach to see the competition, and they were rounded up by policemen from various hotels around Southampton.

By working through the early hours of the morning, under the supervision of Lovesey (one of the men who had originally discussed the engine with Royce), they were able to make the change, especially assisted by a left-handed fitter who was able to reach and knock out one particular gudgeon pin. It was also fortunate that thanks to Rolls-Royce craftsmanship, the spare block fitted in all particulars, as all the 'R' engine parts were handmade.

The mechanics had thus managed to avoid manoeuvring the aircraft for the change but the rest of the effort had been entirely necessary. It was found that one piston head had almost melted through and its cylinder lining was badly scored—an engine failure, at the very least, would have been inevitable, on the next run. The damage was attributed to unmixed fuel being drawn into the engine from the supercharger during slow running before take-off, thus washing lubricant from the cylinder walls. As a precautionary measure, thereafter, it was decided that no engine was to have long periods of slow running prior to the beginning of the contest.

When Orlebar arrived in the morning for the contest, he was not a little surprised to see a group of unknown and tired mechanics on site but he thought it best not to distract Waghorn by telling him what he learned of the work, which had only been finished by 6 a.m.

Among the spectators of the competition was the prince of Wales, who had been flown around the course in a Southampton flying boat, and Lady Astor, who was seen by the chief of the air staff, Sir Hugh Trenchard, talking to Lawrence of Arabia. (Lawrence, having enlisted as Aircraftsman T. E. Shaw, had worked with Scott-Paine on air-sea rescue boats and was currently acting as secretary to the wing commander in charge of race organisation. 'Keep your eye on that damned fellow,' Trenchard told D'Arcy Greig. Lawrence had embarrassed the RAF, still a relatively fledgling service, by joining the 'other ranks' after his earlier charismatic desert operations.)

The new Labour prime minister, Ramsay MacDonald, and the prince of Wales watched the race from aboard the aircraft carrier HMS *Argus*; other notable spectators were Mitchell's parents, brothers, and sisters. This was the first Schneider competition to be held in England since his early days with Supermarine and so he ensured that his family were also given VIP treatment.

Schneider trophy rules still restricted entries to three aircraft per country, and it was announced that they were to fly in the following order: Waghorn in the S.6, Warrant Officer Dal Molin in the M.52, Greig in the S.5, Lieutenant Remo Cadringher in one of the new M.67s,

An S.6 on its launching pontoon prior to the 1929 contest. The air scoops mentioned earlier can be seen projecting under the starboard wing tip.

Crowds on Southsea beach for the 1929 Competition.

Atcherley in the second S.6, and Lieutenant Geovanni Monti in the second M.67. There was to be a gap of fifteen minutes between the take-off times of each competitor—the Schneider event was never organised as a race but as a competition to determine which of the aircraft had the best performance.

The British tactics for the new competition resulted from the fact that the new Gloster machine had had to be withdrawn and the older S.5 substituted and because the unknown M.67s were due to set off after the first British machine. Consideration had also to be paid to the compromise that had had to be worked out with reference to the fuel consumption and engine temperature of the British entries: cooling was so critical that a temperature of 95 degrees had not to be exceeded although this throttling back did allow a nicely judged decrease in the weight of fuel carried. Thus it was decided that Waghorn would fly as fast as possible, consistent with keeping to a safe engine temperature; that Atcherley, in the second S.6 would risk a higher temperature if the performances of the two preceding Italians made it necessary to go faster than Waghorn; and that Greig, in the slower S.5, would provide additional backup.

The Italians' new engines had been refusing to run smoothly at full throttle so it had been decided to leave the new M.67s to the last in the hope that the first two British pilots would overstrain their new engines or run out of fuel for fear of being overtaken, thus allowing the Italians to avoid pushing their own relatively untried engines unnecessarily. In response, Orlebar arranged for Atcherley to delay his start for almost all of the fifteen-minute gap allowed between competitors so that, if Cadringher went off on time, the British would have nearly half an hour in which to assess the speed of the first M.67 and to adjust the performance of his aircraft accordingly.

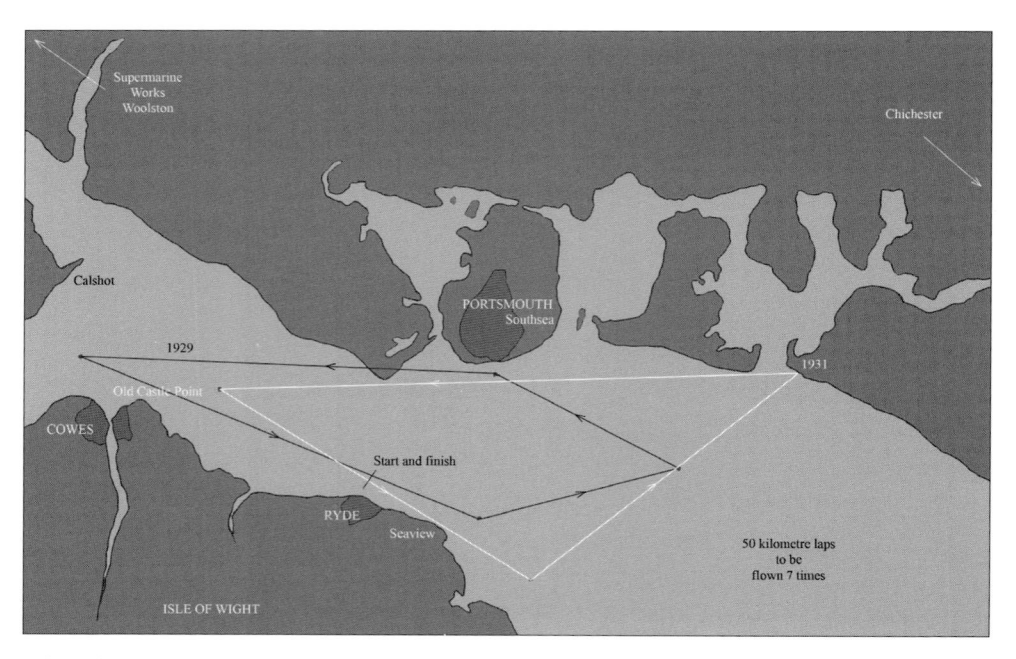

Schneider Trophy course, Calshot, 1929 and 1931.

Yet things did not work out as planned, especially for the Italians. Waghorn began with a disappointing first lap of 324 mph owing to a somewhat erratic flight path as shipping had made it hard for him to pick up a sight of the pylon marking the second turn point. It was, nevertheless, no surprise that he was seen to be to be faster than Dal Molin, who was timed at 286 mph; this was at least 2 mph faster than Greig whose S.5, surprisingly, was not being overtaken by Cadringher in the first of the new M.67s. Then, the Italian (on only his second flight in the machine) retired on lap two as it transpired that he had been nearly blinded by fumes from his exhaust on the windscreen and half suffocated. The course was a left-hand circuit and the exhaust ports of his central bank of cylinders were on the left-hand side. It was now necessary for Atcherley to fly faster than Waghorn to be sure of seeing off the last M.67, but he too had a visual problem:

> I thought she was never going to 'unstick', and if it had not so obviously been an occasion of 'now or never' I would have throttled back in an effort to damp the vicious porpoising that had begun … I believe my take-off took one minute forty seconds … and I became literally soaked to the waist as she careered blindly through the water in a cloud of spray … my goggles became opaque with brine from the spray and I found I could no longer wipe them clean with my left glove. I knocked them up from my eyes but the slipstream took charge and snapped them from the strap behind my helmet. Although I carried a spare pair round my neck, I found I could not get these up to my eyes with only one hand to spare.

Flying at over 300 mph and without goggles, he had to tuck down as far as possible behind the windscreen and press on. As a result, he came near to killing not only himself but also Commander Alan Goodfellow, the observer at the first turn. He and an Italian official had climbed to the top of the 30-foot pylon, which was mounted on an old destroyer between Seaview and Chichester Harbour; he reported that 'as he came rapidly nearer we realised that he was heading straight for the top of the pylon … At the very last moment he saw us and swerved sharply, passing not more than a wingspan inside the pylon.' The moment the incident was over, Goodfellow described how the Italian observer 'danced an excited jig on top of our somewhat perilous perch and shouted down to his fellow Italian observer on the deck, "*Eliminato, eliminato.*" He probably doesn't know to this day how near he came to getting my foot in his backside.'

Atcherley carried on and in the process established the fastest lap of the contest at 332 mph. This speed was far better than that of the last Italian, Monti; he was also suffering from fumes in the cockpit and then his misery was added to by a serious leak in the cooling system, which sprayed back steam and nearly boiling water. Fortunately, he managed to get down safely, also on his second lap. Waghorn, meanwhile, ran out of fuel within sight of the finishing line but, like Webster before him in 1927, he had miscalculated the number of laps and had, in fact, come down on an extra one.

So, despite the expenditure by both nations on eleven new machines, the 1929 Schneider trophy was won by one of the only two to complete the course. Waghorn, in the new S.6, was first with an average speed of 328.63 mph—20 mph more than the current (straight line) absolute world speed record held by a Macchi 52bis; Dal Molin, now using a flatter parabolic cornering technique, was second in the 1927 M.52, at an average speed of 284.2 mph; and Greig, also in an aircraft from the previous contest, averaged 282.11 mph. Atcherley, in the second new S.6 had flown at an average speed of 325.44 mph, but his disqualification denied

Scoreboard showing the race results before the disqualification of Atcherley (No. 8 on the board).

Mitchell the satisfaction of having both of his two new aircraft designs coming first and second as well as being the only machines designed in 1929 to complete the course. On the other hand, such were the vicissitudes of the Schneider trophy that the contest might have been won by Italy if it were not for the fortuitous presence of the Rolls-Royce engineers who had worked overnight to get Waghorn's engine ready.

> **As a final comment on the 1929 Contest, a continuation of Waghorn's account of flying the new S.6 gives a fascinating insight into the problems of negotiating the course made unfamiliar by the sudden assemblage of spectators' boats and into the very limited view from low down behind the engine:**
>
> The day was unique, a deep blue sky of a type rarely seen in this country coupled with an amazingly good visibility. At the time it was blowing 10 miles an hour, and all was bustle on the tarmac … At about seven minutes to two my engine was started by Lovesey, the Rolls expert, and was run by him for barely two minutes [to avoid another piston problem—*see* p. 222]. I then climbed in and made myself as comfortable as possible. At two minutes to two I was lowered into the water and started to take-off immediately.
>
> … once off the water I made my way towards Old Castle Point, and then turned left and dived over the starting line at about 350 miles an hour. The pylons were mounted on destroyers and stood out quite well, provided they were not anchored against a background of shipping. One could not get a view directly ahead and I had to pick up the correct line largely while turning

the previous pylon. On the long legs we picked our course mainly by landmarks or shipping we had passed over. As an example, the Seaview turn was anchored, say, half a mile from the shore. By plotting our radius of turn on the chart, and from previous practice, we knew that we should have to have the coast, say, five hundred yards on our right. By aiming to do this we would arrive in approximately the correct position; when within about 200 yards off the pylon we could see it, so the actual turn itself was gauged with the pylon in view.

The first lap was naturally the most difficult, because we were not used to the various groups of shipping, which afterwards helped so much on our course keeping. As an example, while passing the Seaview turn on my first lap, I looked for the Chichester turn ship and picked out the only isolated vessel in that area. I made for it, and while still some little way from it, saw the pylon away on my left. I had been quite unable to see it as it had had a background of shipping immediately behind it. The ship which I had mistaken for the turn ship was, in fact, an oil tanker, and should not have been allowed to stray where it had. Atcherley actually turned round it. My own detour cost me six miles an hour, and this is the reason my first lap speed was only 324. From the Chichester turn I could see the Southsea pylon while still turning and had no difficulty at all in passing it, the esplanade on my right being also a great help. Next I came to what was the most difficult leg of the course—that from Southsea to Cowes—as there was no land and practically no shipping to guide one on approaching the turn. To make matters more interesting for the competitors, someone had conveniently parked a Flotilla of Destroyers immediately behind the pylons; hence the amazing turns of some of the Italians embracing all the Destroyers … Once round the Cowes turn the course was plain sailing again, there being plenty of shipping and the shore of the Isle of Wight to help one.

I had completed several laps, everything was going beautifully—never a miss from the engine, and the machine handling perfectly—when I noticed the Italian Macchi diving towards the starting line just as I was coming up to the Cowes turn; at the Seaview turn I couldn't see him at all; at the Chichester turn I saw him a speck in front, and at the Southsea turn I saw him disappearing over Alverstoke. This time much nearer, and I was obviously overtaking him rapidly, the question was—could I overtake him on the straight before the Cowes turn, or just after? I hoped for the latter, for if I should catch him before the turn I should not be able to see him.

However, it planned out as I hoped, for on rounding the Cowes pylon I saw him just coming out of his turn a few hundred yards in front. I decided to pass him on the inside and swung about a hundred yards to the left to clear him. I passed him about half way down the straight.

By now I had completed five laps and everything was going just as it should. The air in the cockpit was very hot, but owing to a stream of fresh air from a ventilating pipe over my face I wasn't too uncomfortable. An attempt to rest my knees on the sides of the fuselage was abruptly stopped when I discovered that they were, to all intents and purposes, 'red-hot', a slight exaggeration, perhaps, but that is what it felt like, and through my slacks, too! I was flying at about 150 to 200 feet, as I found at that height I got the best view of the course, and it was sufficiently low to be able to keep level. I had been running all the time somewhat below full throttle, as owing to the unexpected increase in power and consequent petrol consumption of the engine, she would not last the course with the petrol we were able to safely carry. The rate that petrol can be poured out of a two-gallon tin will give some idea of the rate the engine was consuming its petrol during the race. I had therefore been told on no account to use full throttle as I shouldn't finish the course; imagine, then my feelings when the engine momentarily cut right out and started missing badly just after I had finished what I imagined was my sixth lap. Would the Rolls engineers ever believe that I hadn't given full throttle? I began to gain height and continued round the course with the engine spluttering and

> only taking about half throttle. I climbed as much as possible in the hope that should she run right out, I could perhaps glide the remaining distance over the line. I was incidentally getting a very fine 'bird's eye view' of the entire course, but under the circumstances was not impressed. I got to the Cowes turn, and while banking, the engine cut out completely, and I was forced to land off Old Castle Point—only a few miles short of the finish. I leave my feelings to your imagination.
>
> It was twenty minutes later that I learnt I had done an extra lap, and I also realised how deadly accurate had been Lovesay's estimation of the petrol consumption [the amount had been reduced when it had been decided to run slightly throttled back].

Mitchell had the satisfaction of having his family, as well as the large crowds of patriotic spectators, see all three of the aircraft he had designed complete the course, and while Atcherley had subsequently been disqualified, he had achieved the world closed circuit speed records for 50 km and 100 km at 332.49 and 331.75 mph, respectively, on his sixth and seventh laps. Three days later, a new world absolute air speed record was established, fittingly, by Orlebar, with a speed of 355.8 mph. The existing Italian record of 318.62 mph was further exceeded two days later, on 12 September, when the commanding officer reached 357.7 mph. An *Empire News Bulletin* newsreel supplied a caption which spoke of his 'travelling faster than any human being has ever travelled since the world began'—the truism nevertheless indicating something of the awe that Schneider trophy speeds generated in the thirties.

Not surprisingly, therefore, Mitchell now came in for even more unwelcome press attention but at least his press photographs were more in keeping with another newspaper description of him as 'a visionary of speed'. Locally, the *Sentinel* (17 September 1929) detailed a congratulatory

Two more formal portraits of R.J. that appeared in the press from 1929 onwards, possibly showing the influence of Supermarine public relations.

telegram to him from Sir Francis Joseph, president of the North Staffordshire Chamber of Commerce, and also one from the Stoke-on-Trent Rotary Club, and went on to headline 'Britain's Day of Glory' followed by the comment: 'No man has done more for Britain's credit in the great trial of engineering science. Our heartiest congratulations to him and to his proud father, Mr Herbert Mitchell'.

In the national press, the RAF pilots were rightly praised, but the *Manchester Guardian* correspondent, Maj. F. A. de Vere Robertson, a former Air Ministry press officer and regular aviation writer, not only singled out the contribution of Supermarine's chief designer and engineer, but also gave a glimpse of his appearance and demeanour:

> Apart from the pilots, there is one man who stands out ... above all others during the last month at Calshot. He is Mr R. J. Mitchell, chief designer of the Supermarine Aviation Works, Ltd ... Of medium height and stalwart build, with a fair skin which reddens in the sun, and light reddish hair, Mr Mitchell looks an embodiment of calmness and sangfroid. I said to him chaffingly a few days before the race that I did not believe he possessed a nervous system. He replied, in his quiet, convincing manner, for he is a man of few words, that he was always on tenterhooks when his machines were in the air.

The Times added a comment, which had now become almost a press cliché, when it paid tribute to 'the genius of the brilliant young designer of the Supermarine Aviation Works, Mr R. J. Mitchell'. The *Southern Daily Echo*, of the same date, recorded the approval of royalty:

PRINCE'S CONGRATULATIONS

On Saturday after the race, the modest and unassuming Mr Mitchell had the honour of being personally congratulated by the Prince of Wales. The Prince said he regarded the British victory as a magnificent performance. Nothing had given him greater pleasure. He also discussed with Mr Mitchell the planes and various details of their construction as well as their flying qualities and speeds. Amongst other things, the Prince asked was what speed Mr Mitchell expected the S6 to attain in the attempt on the world's speed record. The designer confided to him his opinion and the Prince was deeply interested and impressed.

HRH the prince of Wales with the High Speed Flight and Mitchell (far right).

R. J. Mitchell's article in *Sketch* (5 September 1929)
This gives a 'plain man's guide' to the design considerations behind the S.6, prior to the eleventh Schneider Trophy contest, embodies his well-known 'fetish' for reducing frontal area and his concern for the pilots (note the words 'anxiety' and 'ordeal'). Another version of this article appeared two days later in the *Morning Post* and the main differences are given in square brackets.

Machines built to compete in the Schneider Trophy race are the outcome of many months of intensive research and an expenditure of large sums of money.

The first stage is the selection of the engine, a less difficult matter than might be supposed, since there is a very limited number of firms in any one country which build racing engines reaching the superlative standard of excellence demanded.

Having made his selection, the designer draws up provisional plans based, as a rule, on the successful machines of the previous race, although it sometimes happens that for some reason he finds it necessary to make fundamental changes. Right from the commencement, the engine and machine are developed together. The aeroplane designer's task may be summed up as being to get every possible ounce of speed with the power at his disposal.

His chief problems concern head-resistance and weight.

The size must obviously be cut down to an absolute minimum, so as to offer the least possible resistance to the terrific air pressure encountered at over 300 mph.

There is a point below which it is impossible to reduce the frontal area of the engine but the designer makes it exactly fit the fuselage [and this calls for very accurate design and construction].

Compact as is the modern racing engine, it is correct to say that, from a front view, the shape and size of the engine are those of the whole fuselage. This enormously increases the difficulties of construction since in an ordinary machine there is usually a foot or two occupied by engine-mounting supports while it is essential that strength shall not be sacrificed [there is usually a foot or two to spare around the engine, taken up by engine-mounting supports, making the construction a much simpler matter. The importance of keeping this frontal area of the fuselage down to the absolute minimum is illustrated by the fact that if the S.5's fuselage had been increased by 10 per cent, the speed of the machine would have been about 7 mph less.

Many special devices are employed in design in order to reduce weight and head resistance. Here is an example of that careful search which we must always conduct for some slight saving in size and weight. The 1927 winning seaplane had a brass radiator which fitted over the wing covering. There would appear little room for improvement in this direction, but this year we have done even better by using a duralumin radiator which itself forms the wing covering and resists torsional stresses induced in the wing].

The weight impacts directly on the frontal area of the machine, for each decrease in weight brings a corresponding decrease in the size of the wings which will keep it in the air, and if wings and fuselage are lighter, smaller floats will support it on the water. All this means so much less air-resistance and a higher maximum speed.

But reductions in size and weight are not enough. Every part of the machine which meets the wind, and in particular floats and fuselage, must be streamlined so as still further to bring down air-resistance.

Landing and getting-off speeds at present approach 100 mph, so that the floats and their supports must be tremendously strong.

But in addition to this and the need for little wind-resistance, they must have sufficient buoyancy to support the weight of the machine on the water with a fairly large factor of safety, and must be so designed that during the take-off they offer the least resistance to the water. [They must skim over the water with as little resistance as possible so as to reach the necessary velocity with the least possible loss of power. Otherwise, the pilot will find it impossible to attain the required speed to get his machine into the air, for the airscrew, at the relatively low speed of the take-off (about 100 mph), can only work at a very low efficiency. The Fairey Reed propeller used on the S.5 was only working at about nine per cent efficiency at this speed, whereas it reached the extremely high figure of eighty per cent at 300 mph.

In the wind tunnels of the National Physical Laboratory, Teddington, and the Royal Aircraft Establishment, Farnborough … many models of fuselages and floats are made and tested and the forms giving lowest air resistance finally evolved. The great importance of this work can be easily understood when it is realised that a very small alteration to the form of one of these bodies may double its air resistance and thus greatly reduce speed].

On no account must the designer forget the pilot.

When speeds become really high, it was found that a machine which had adequate control for the get-off was so sensitive at its top speed that the pilot had the greatest difficulty in maintaining steady flight, as much smaller movements of the 'stick' are necessary at high speed. [If sufficient control is given at the taking-off speed, they become ten times more effective at the maximum flying speed.]

This trouble has now been overcome by arranging that the initial movement of the stick produces less effect on the controls than the further movements.

Another point to be considered is the provision of the best possible view [especially for the dangerous business of landing] which becomes very dangerous if the pilot is 'blind' when he nears the water. In this respect the low wing monoplane, to which type all this year's British competitors belong, has certain obvious advantages.

Exhaust fumes must be excluded from the cockpit, but a good supply of cool air has to be admitted, while in some machines this year there is a supply of oxygen in case of emergency.

The dashboard is not cumbered with a single unnecessary instrument. Thermometers show the temperature of the water as it enters and leaves the engine. Another pair of thermometers indicate oil temperatures, and there is an oil-pressure gauge, together with an air-speed indicator and a 'rev-counter' to show the speed of the engine. [and a 'cross-level' which indicates if the angle of banking is correct. This, as any pilot knows, is a comparatively simple set of instruments.] Not one of these could be safely dispensed with.

Even when the machine is completed the designer still has plenty to do correcting those slight faults, inseparable from a new design. [As soon as the race is over he must digest the lessons learnt, sort them out, and store them away in his mind against the time when he will be called upon to go through the same ordeal once more and still greater speeds will be expected.]

Of all the hundreds and thousands who will witness the race on Saturday, it may be taken for granted that very few will ever know the anxiety of the little group of men who created the machines and engines which will flash round the course at speeds no human ever previously attained.

Nearly three weeks later, Mitchell and his wife were back in Stoke-on-Trent for a luncheon given in his honour by the North Staffordshire Chamber of Commerce. Apart from some gracious references to his hosts and to his hometown, he also gave full appreciation of the efforts of all those who tended to be forgotten by the headline makers. The *Sentinel* of 27 September 1929 recorded the long speech, which showed how his speech-making had progressed or been assisted by his company, even though his reticence must have been tested to the full:

> I consider that designing aeroplanes is a very easy matter in comparison with making a speech, especially when I have been preceded by such eloquent speakers as Sir Francis [Joseph, chairman of the Chamber of Commerce] and the Lord Mayor. I should feel very much happier if I were possessed with half their ability in that direction, and on this account I must crave your very kind indulgence.
>
> My wife and I are overwhelmed by the reception you have given us. Although we have been away from North Staffordshire for a number of years we are proud to look upon Stoke-on-Trent as our home, and it gives us very great pleasure to know we have so many friends in North Staffordshire.
>
> I do not forget that I received my education and my early engineering training in this district, and for this reason it gives me very great pleasure to have had the opportunity of doing something that merits your approval.

As the Schneider trophy events had been 'very ably reported', he went on to describe the preparations necessary for the event:

> The designing and construction of one of these machines entails at least a year of really hard work for hundreds of people and the carrying out of very intensive research work. It means the exercising of great genius, skill and hard work on the part of the persons and firms who design and construct the engines.
>
> The trying of large numbers of models of bodies, wings, floats, etc., in the wind tunnels, the trying out of new methods of construction, new materials, new ideas of fuel systems, propellers, and hundreds other items—all to gain a little more speed and score over our rivals.
>
> As the machine nears completion, I must admit that this becomes a very anxious time for the designer, as by one short flight all his work is to be proved good or bad. If his work is bad, he knows that the first flight is fraught with danger to the pilot.
>
> The completion of the first flight brings a feeling of intense relief. After this, all efforts are concentrated on making the machine suitable for the race. The pilot must be adequately protected from the wind, he must be supplied with fresh air and must be entirely free from exhaust fumes. The machine must control well in a sharp turn without throttling down. Consumption trials, propeller trials, all have to be carried out. Everything done has some little object in view.
>
> Finally, we concentrate on obtaining the very last mile of speed out of the machine. I well remember at this stage how I envied one of two of the reporters of our daily Press, who, in a few flashing words and in a single night, could increase the speed of our machine by 20 miles an hour.
>
> I also remember how I was encouraged by the great interest taken in the event in North Staffordshire and how the position was so ably summed up by our own local paper, the *Sentinel*, a copy of which I received daily at the air station at Calshot.

He then combined a compliment to the best-known local product with a clear justification for government support for another Supermarine design for the next Schneider trophy competition:

> Just as this county, through the medium of North Staffordshire, has established itself as the producer of the finest china in the world, so the British aircraft industry is striving, finally to establish supremacy.
>
> We feel that our latest victory has had a big effect in that direction. Success in one industry helps towards success in other industries. We are endeavouring to uphold British prestige whether

it be in the production of the finest china or the production of the fastest aircraft. It all has a big effect on our foreign trade.

Although the design and production of machines for this race entailed fairly considerable expense, it was easily the most economical and most efficient form of aircraft development. A great amount of knowledge and experience was gained which was used for the improvement of our service aircraft and for the development of civil aviation, from the light aeroplane to the large commercial machines used in our Empire routes.

I think it is safe to say that more genuine progress is made in this branch of aviation in one year by the designing and construction of these high-speed machines than would be made in three or four years by the normal processes of development.

Without, obviously, being aware of how his future designs would be bound up with the Rolls-Royce company and the Spitfire, he concluded with a 'wholehearted tribute' to the company that had just 'established itself as the finest designers of aero engines in the world.'

Sentinel photograph at the time of R.J.'s speech, showing Herbert Mitchell senior far left, R.J. middle back row and Flo Mitchell seated left of the mayoress.

Supermarine publicity montage for the Southampton X.

11

The Air Yacht and the Giant
(1930–1931)

> *My impression was that R.J. who had always been more of a practical engineer than a technician had allowed himself to be lured by some of his bright boys into following other people's ideas instead of his own.*
>
> Denis le P. Webb

Although the last two consecutive Schneider wins had made the standing of Supermarine in the aviation world an enviable one, success in the world of the larger military and civil flying boats was no more secure and far more subject to the direction (or misdirection) of the Air Ministry. It was hardly likely that Supermarine were unaware of the situation, but as Lovell-Cooper mentioned, their new Vickers chairman made it very clear what would be expected of them:

> I remember him telling Mitchell, 'The Schneider Trophy things bring a lot of credit to the firm but they don't fill the coffers! We've got to produce some aeroplanes that pay their way and fill up the money-bags!'

Unfortunately, the eventual outcome was that, despite the Far East Cruise of the Southampton IIs, the excellent squadron service of this type, and its continuous development, Supermarine was not able to capitalise on these successes in the civil aviation field. In the flying boat operations of the developing Imperial Airways Empire routes, Shorts were to sweep the board, and other companies began to provide rival aircraft.

Shorts' intervention had commenced with the Cromarty, begun in 1918 and finally completed in 1921. The aircraft did not secure a government contract but the Air Ministry had had more than enough experience of water soakage problems with wooden hulls at the MAEE, and accordingly, they contracted Shorts to make a metal hull for a Felixstowe 5 superstructure at the very time that the first orders for the wooden Supermarine Southampton I were being contemplated. The resultant Short S.2 first flew in 1924 but was soon written off when it stalled into rough water from about 30 feet. At least the strength of its hull was demonstrated by the fact that it was virtually undamaged and remained watertight.

There then followed a ministry order for a metal-hulled Short S.5 Singapore I. Again, Shorts did not get a production order but it was this particular aircraft which was loaned to Cobham by the Air Council for what must rank as one of the great early aerial survey flights; it went clockwise via Malta, the Nile, and the Great Lakes, round the coastline via Durban and Cape Town, and returned along the western seaboard between 17 November 1927 and 31 May 1928.

Just before this, on 12 August 1927, the Singapore had joined a Southampton in a 9,400-mile Baltic cruise, accompanied by aircraft from two other companies, which had by now entered the flying boat field. One machine was the Saunders A.3 Valkyrie, which, like the Short Singapore, had a wingspan about 20 feet greater than the Supermarine aircraft. However, its all-wooden construction, completed at the time of the change to metal-hulled Southamptons, was an important factor in no production orders being issued for this aircraft.

Yet it did mark the employment of three engines, as did the other participant in the Baltic trip—the 95-foot wingspan, metal-hulled Blackburn Iris II. This aircraft was faster than the Southampton II, could carry a heavier load, and had a tail gunner's position—not standard in flying boats before 1930, and only appearing in a production Supermarine machine with the Stranraer of 1934. Ominously for Mitchell's company, it was chosen as the flagship of the Baltic cruise and accordingly carried Sir Samuel Hoare, in his second term as secretary of state for air, on his visit to an aero exhibition in Copenhagen.

Thus it was that after the production and development of R.J.'s own metal-hulled Southampton IIs had peaked by 1928, there was a significant falling-off in Supermarine flying-boat building until the appearance of the Scapa in 1932 (*see* Chapter 13). During this time, Shorts developed a civil version of the Singapore, the Calcutta, and later, the Kent, which supplied the flying-boat components of the Imperial Airways fleet and, in the military field, their Rangoon gave way to their Singapore III, of which thirty-three were built. A limited number of the Blackburn Iris machines were ordered for long-range reconnaissance duties.

The Solent/Nanok design had been an early Supermarine response to the rival three-engined types beginning to appear, but no orders were forthcoming for the type. Thereafter the Air Ministry had initiated a search for an improved and more powerful type to replace the standard Southampton equipment; the result was the Saunders-Roe A.14 and the Southampton X, but as it turned out, neither progressed beyond the prototype stage.

The first of these orders, N251, was to be an aircraft that mated a Southampton superstructure to an experimental hull, which Saunders wanted to develop as a successor to the wooden Valkyrie machine. The new metal hull used corrugated panels for the outer skin to supplant the usual stringer structure and was assembled at the Cowes factory, now owned by Saunders-Roe Ltd. N251 was given the newly formed company's type number A.14 and features no more in the Supermarine story, except perhaps for its leading to the Saunders-Roe A.27 London, which later competed successfully for orders against R.J.'s Stranraer in 1934.

The second order, N252, produced an aircraft that, despite being designated a Southampton Mark X, was quite unlike the earlier versions. In fact, it was far more similar in appearance to the next Saunders-Roe flying boat, the A.7: both were sesquiplanes and had three engines and twin fins. For the first time with Supermarine, the Mark X had straight sides and utilised the external horizontal corrugations of the A.14 hull, in response to Vickers' cost-conscious avoidance of complex curvatures, which were time-consuming to produce, however attractive they had looked to R.J. and Supermarine. It had stainless steel sheeting below the waterline and also a position for a rear gunner in the tail—a first for Supermarine although it did not become a production machine. Other departures from the Southampton II were the shapes of the tail surfaces and of the floats, which were larger, in order to accommodate extra fuel—something learned from the Schneider trophy machines, no doubt. The superstructure was also a departure, literally, in that its construction was undertaken by the new parent firm, Vickers, at Weybridge.

Flight testing began in March 1930 by Capt. J. 'Mutt' Summers, Vickers' chief test pilot—no longer by the long-serving Biard, an early consequence of the Vickers takeover. As the Mark X turned out at over 300 lb above its estimated weight of 10,090 lb empty, it unsurprisingly performed below expectations: its estimated 15,000 feet ceiling was found to have been extremely optimistic, and its maximum speed to be 15 mph below estimate. Its original Armstrong-Siddeley Jaguar VIC engines were then exchanged for other engine combinations and, with Bristol Jupiter XFBMs, attained a ceiling of 11,800 feet and a top speed within 5 mph of its specification.

There were also changes to the strutting, the engines were given Townend drag-reducing ring cowlings, smaller floats were employed, and the flight deck was enclosed. At 130 mph, it was now faster than the three-engined Saunders-Roe A.7 Severn, the Short Rangoon, and the Blackburn Iris III. Yet signs were not good for Supermarine: the Short S.15, built for the Japanese government in the same year could achieve 136 mph and it was a Saunders A.7 Severn which was sent, also in 1930, on a 6,530-mile proving flight to the Middle East and back. It accompanied the faster and more powerful Short Singapore II whose four engines gave it a top speed of 140 mph.

Perhaps because both the Supermarine and the Vickers contributions to the Southampton X came out overweight and in view of earlier tensions in the Supermarine design office mentioned in Chapter 11, no further joint projects were initiated between the two design teams; Alan Clifton's report that Supermarine's next, individual, attempt to improve on the Southampton, the Scapa, came out 'bang on the weight target' might therefore be seen to contain a certain amount of self-satisfaction. Also, Webb was no doubt reflecting general company morale at the time when he noted that 'since Vickers took over in 1928 the only successful aircraft produced by us had been the S.6 Schneider seaplanes'; he also wrote

> We naturally considered that we built rather better aircraft than Vickers and the idea of being bossed about by them did not appeal to us at all. A rather crude joke went round the workshops in the form of a question: 'Why are we like a bunch of choirboys? Because we're being buggered by Vickers!'

By the end of 1929, Supermarine had several flying-boat projects under consideration: a Southampton replacement, a civil version called the Sea Hawk, and an Air Yacht—all with three engines; a four-engined civil project, and the six-engined 'Giant'. Of these, only the Southampton replacement and the Air Yacht were completed.

The Air Yacht: The Dornier Influence

The aircraft, which later became known as the Air Yacht, began as Air Ministry Specification 4/27, calling for an armed reconnaissance flying boat, larger than the Seamew. The response was originally drawn up, between the 1927 and 1929 Schneider trophy activities, as a biplane and as an alternative monoplane, the latter showing an interest in Dornier-like sponsons, instead of wing-tip floats.

Southampton fuselage features were still in evidence but, after the Vickers takeover, the general arrangement that emerged showed a monoplane of utilitarian appearance although with an engineering structure of considerable aerodynamic cleanness for its time. The sesquiplane compromise between the monoplane and biplane formulae, which the Southampton X represented, was gone, and instead, there appeared an all metal monoplane with a wingspan of 92 feet and powered by three engines, which were now faired into the wings—as with all Mitchell's later multi-engined flying boats. In the present case, their thrust lines were above the top surface of the wing to maximise water clearance for the propellers.

The aircraft was, in many ways, more reminiscent of the earlier Sparrow II as it had a plank-shaped parasol wing with sloping V struts supporting the wing about two-thirds out from the centre-line, but the hull, on the other hand, was of the corrugated flat-sided type like the contemporary Southampton X and Saunders-Roe A.14. Southampton triple fins were retained but, in keeping with the other lines of the machine, they were extremely angular. The cabane of struts supporting the wing was laterally braced with elegance, having a minimalist pair of struts extending from the right-hand side of the fuselage to the strut positions under the left wing.

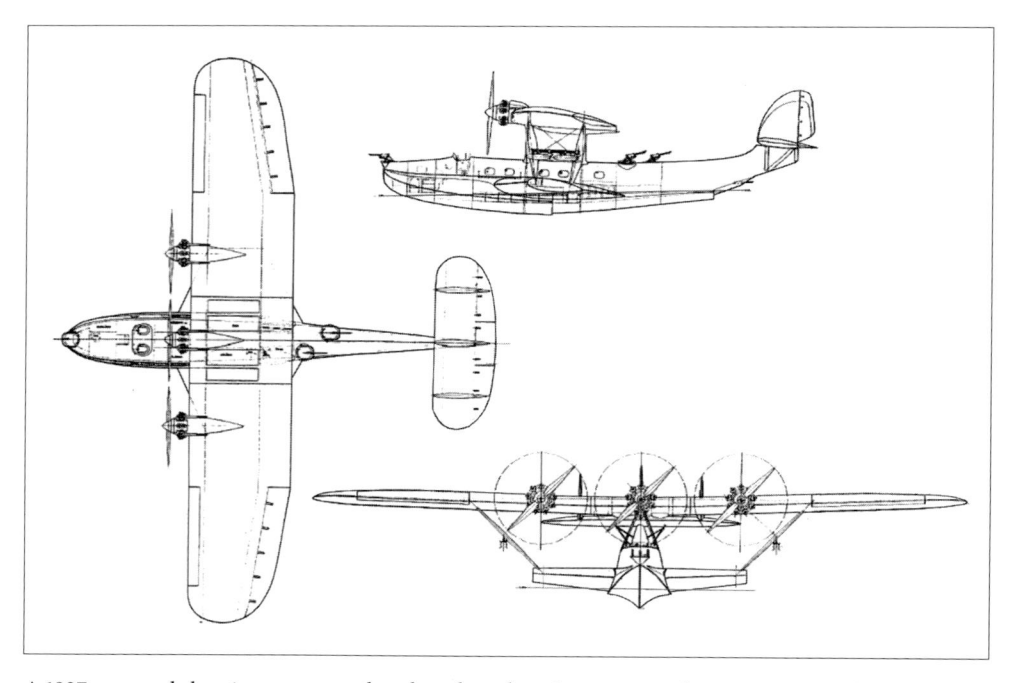

A 1927 proposal showing sponsons, bomb rack under wing struts, and gun position under tail.

Supermarine Air Yacht (1930)

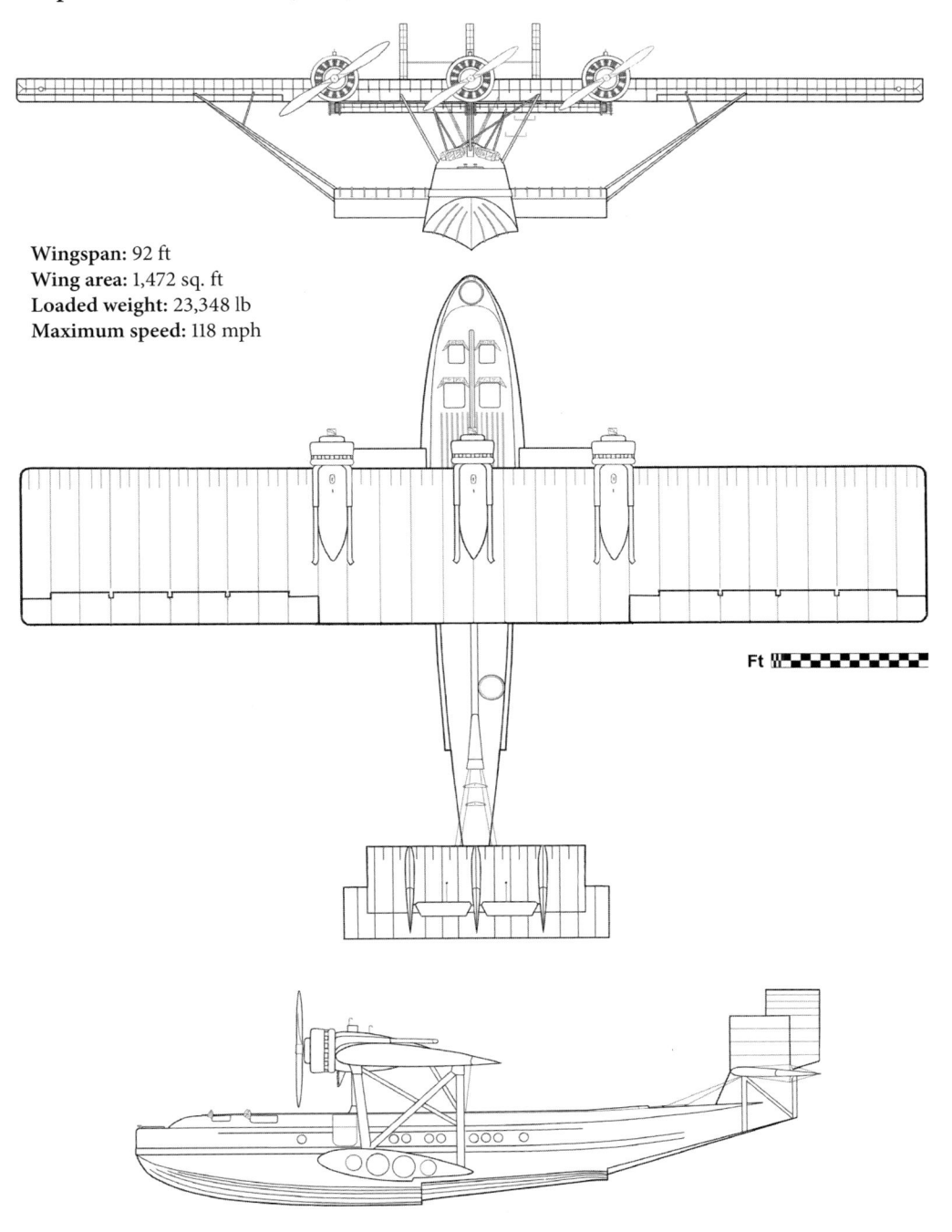

Wingspan: 92 ft
Wing area: 1,472 sq. ft
Loaded weight: 23,348 lb
Maximum speed: 118 mph

Dornier Wal.

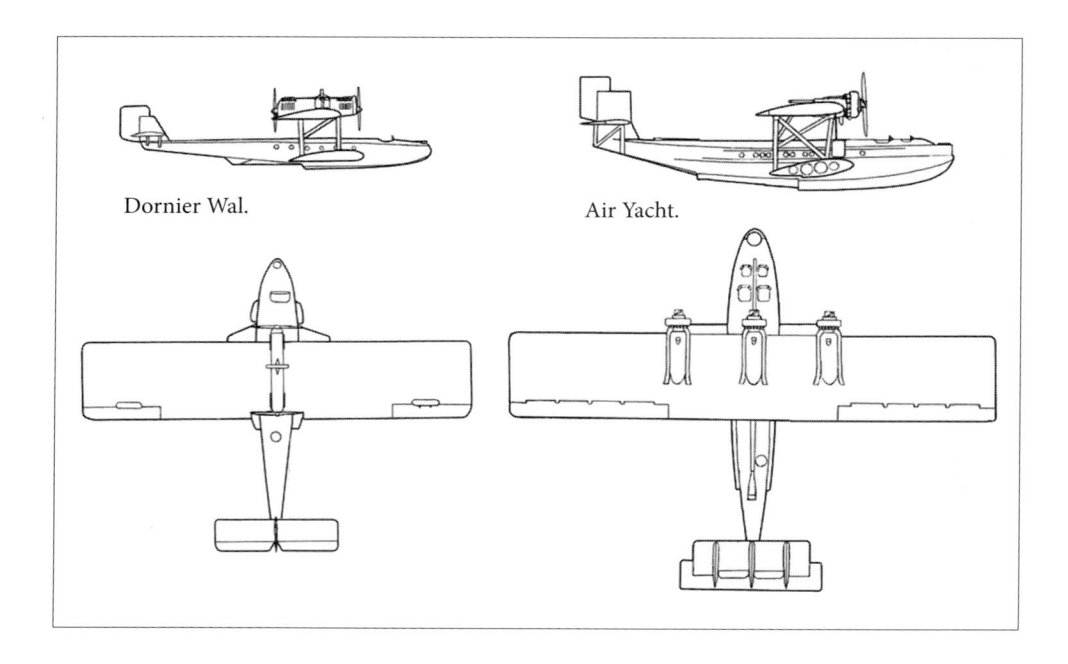

Air Yacht.

Supermarine's move to all-metal aircraft with stainless steel fittings was by now well established but, like most of contemporary British flying boats, the new design still had fabric-covered flying surfaces. It had, however, one feature that made it stand out from all other Supermarine aircraft and its contemporaries; this was the employment of sponsons attached to the lower sides of the hull instead of the customary wing-tip floats. The final result was a completely different design from that of all previous and future Supermarine flying boats, and had it not been for the different mounting of the engines, the similarity with the Dornier Wal series of flying boats would have been, to say the least, uncanny.

While it was the later Mk X version of the Wal that made a great impression in British aviation circles, R.J.'s new design made its first flight on 30 February before the Mk X flying boat visited Britain and it was being designed only slightly later than was the German machine. Yet one of the earlier Wal machines had been tested at Calshot and so one must look towards the earlier Wal series, developed before the mid-1930s, as the main inspiration of the British aircraft.

These earlier Wals had two engines and carried up to ten passengers; their development, the Super Wal, had four engines and could carry nineteen passengers at a cruising speed of 115 mph. Mitchell's aircraft was expected to have had a performance somewhat similar to the later machine. For the early flights, it was powered by Armstrong-Siddeley-geared Jaguar VIs with Townend drag-reducing cowling rings; these engines delivered 490 hp each, and Biard regarded the resultant top speed as 'quite fast' (he was still testing for Supermarine as the aircraft flew a month before the Southampton X with Mutt Summers, although being designed later).

On 8 May 1931, Supermarine's flying boat was flown to the Marine Aircraft Establishment at Felixstowe, but there was no evidence of any urgency in the testing programme; it was reported to have only flown nine times by the end of July and to have spent 570 hours at its moorings. Perhaps the Air Ministry was influenced by the government's 1928 planning assumption that no

The Air Yacht, in its original form.

Another view of the Air Yacht with original 'V' struts and Armstrong Siddeley Jaguar VI engines.

major war seemed likely for the foreseeable future. However tardily, its general flying qualities were found to be good but that, with one of the three engines throttled back, it could not maintain height and that it was unstable with one engine out (*see* details of its crash, p. 244).

Nevertheless, the Air Ministry supported the Supermarine design by paying for repairs when the starboard sponson failed in fairly rough seas and when the other one showed signs of similar structural problems, perhaps giving the lie to a commonly held view that the powers that be were generally hostile to the monoplane concept. Nevertheless, it has to be admitted that the aircraft did not give a dramatic argument for going over to monoplanes—its maximum speed was well below the 130 mph that the contemporary biplane, the Southampton X, eventually achieved with only slightly more powerful engines.

The Supermarine aircraft was accordingly re-engined with 525-hp Armstrong-Siddeley Panthers and was then found to be capable of 117 mph; however, it was still not possible to maintain height with any significant payload with one engine throttled back. Penrose, while reporting design problems, did compare its design favourably against two more traditionally-built flying boats: 'unfortunately the sponsons suffered battering by waves and even on calm water gave inferior take-off compared with the usual chined British hull'. He added that there were problems with aileron snatch. But then, he went on to say that 'assessed as an engineering structure of considerable aerodynamic cleanness', the machine was 'a big step forward compared with the established three-engined Iris biplane, of which four were in the course of delivering to the RAF, or the Calcutta-derived Short Rangoon prototype due to fly in the summer.'

By 1931, Supermarine had replaced the original V struts from the sponsons by a firmer bracing of N struts and were having to consider a non-military role for the machine, fulfilling a conditional order from the Hon. A. E. Guinness for a replacement for his 'Solent' Air Yacht, which he had found to have insufficient headroom for his liking. Registered G-AASE and now known as the Air Yacht, the boxy hull now provided very suitable dimensions for the passenger cabin, which Supermarine quoted as a generous 35 feet in length, 6 feet 6 inches in height, and 8 feet in width. It was luxuriously appointed with an owner's cabin complete with bed, bath and toilet, a galley with full cooking facilities, and additional wash basins, toilet, and comfortable lounge with settees and sideboards in a separate cabin for five other passengers.

There was rather more basic accommodation for the crew below their open cockpits in the nose, with seats for two on either side of a gangway and with a folding seat in between for a mechanic; the rear cockpit was available for the use of up to four passengers. Electric lighting was fitted throughout the interior, which Biard described as 'one of the most luxurious that anyone had then seen' and 'fitted out in glass and silver, with deep-pile rugs underfoot ... the chairs were deeply sprung, the cabins softly lighted ... The interior was roomy, with plenty of height and elbow-room' and the temperature could even be regulated by a blown air system.

G-AASE 'on the step'.

By June 1931, the total cost of the Air Yacht had risen into the region of £52,000, but in the event, it was never sold to Guinness, who bought a Saunders-Roe aircraft instead. Webb probably reflected company gossip at the time when he gave the following downbeat assessment of this episode in Supermarine's history:

> At this time we were having trouble with the Air Yacht which was well down on performance and so we fitted Panther engines of 525 hp in place of the Jaguar VI engines of 490 hp. I think this increase of hp was to a large extent negatived by the addition of several large struts between the sponsons and mainplanes … Henri Biard and, later, Tommy Rose, were about the only pilots who could do anything with it …
>
> My impression was that R.J. who had always been more of a practical engineer than a technician had allowed himself to be lured by some of his bright boys into following other people's ideas instead of his own.

Another Supermarine employee, Harry Griffiths, also gave a negative report:

> It had a very long take-off run and there was always doubts as to whether it would leave the water at all with a full load of passengers, stores and fuel.
>
> Refuelling in those days was done with hand pumps from barrels taken out on a barge. There is a story (unconfirmed but, knowing the man, possibly true) that Biard, the test pilot, refused to attempt a full load take-off and 'went through the motions' of filling with fuel by pumping from a number of barrels, some of which were empty.

As with his other parasol-winged design, the Sparrow II, the unwanted Air Yacht was taken for storage to the Hythe flying-boat hangar until rescue came in the formidable form of the American, Mrs June Jewell James, as reported in *Flight*:

> On October 1932 the Air Yacht was bought by a Mrs J. J. James, of Kenya Park, Rownhams (Southampton)—a keen motor-boat and flying enthusiast … On October 11, the *Windward III*, as the air yacht is called, piloted by Capt. H. C. Biard, and with Mrs James on board, left Southampton on a cruise 'somewhere around the Mediterranean and North Africa'.

Mrs James had been shown over the aircraft at the Hythe base and, as a result, negotiated the purchase of the Air Yacht from Supermarine. She then became so impatient to have the use of her new purchase that she insisted on starting some days before a prearranged departure date and Biard, who had been seconded to her by Supermarine, has supplied a description of the frantic preparations and the one-and-only cruise attempted in the aircraft as well as the problems of accommodating a very rich and self-willed owner.

Despite some exaggerations, his (ghosted?) account is of interest to social historians as well as to those interested in the ability of another Mitchell design to withstand what were, clearly, extremely unfriendly conditions. After the near-drowning of the owner and her companions during a severe storm in Cherbourg Harbour, Biard then flew the Air Yacht down to Naples, whence Mrs James proceeded to obtain audiences with both the pope and Mussolini. Having flown to France to collect Mrs James, who had then gone on to Paris, Biard had to hand over the Air Yacht to a relief pilot as his stomach muscles, which had been torn in the S.4 crash, needed surgery. Unfortunately, this pilot, Tommy Rose, although a very experienced pilot (as Webb had indicated, above), lost the power of one engine on take-off and stalled into the sea off Positano on 25 January 1933. The owner suffered a broken leg but there were otherwise no serious injuries sustained; the aircraft was too badly damaged to be worth salvaging.

> **Biard's Account of the Cherbourg Episode**
>
> At the time, the air-yacht was high and dry on the mud, having her engines given a final thorough overhaul preparatory to the trip; she had very little petrol aboard; one of the engines was actually more or less in pieces for cleaning, and one of the rudder control-wires was being renewed. These explanations made no difference to the owner. She wanted to start. She was told that the machine weighed thirteen tons, and that it naturally could not start till the tide had come in under its floats [sponsons]. She wanted to know why it could not be carried down to the water at once. In America, as she quite rightly said, they would have got that aircraft into the water somehow; why was England so slow and hopeless? Well, in the end the machine had to wait till the tide came in. The adjustments were completed, however, and everything made good so that we could start late that same afternoon; an extremely unusual concession, as anyone who has had much to do with flying contracts will readily understand. Extra mechanics were drafted on to the job; the disassembled engine grew while one watched; the afternoon rang and echoed with the sound of hammers and spanners and the growl of engines being tested. Finally, about teatime, we were all aboard, the whistle sounded to clear the passage ahead of us, and the air-yacht made a stately ascent and headed away towards the distant coast of France.
>
> I put the machine down according to orders in Cherbourg harbour, and took a look at the weather. The clouds were gathering blackly over the Atlantic … I had a hard look at the barometer, and it had fallen a good deal even in the couple of hours we had taken to cover the 150 miles from Southampton. Cherbourg harbour gives very little protection, and I strongly advised the owner to let us go on to a more sheltered spot, but she had had enough of English assistance that afternoon (she was still sore about having been made to wait to start the trip), and she said we would stay where we were. Moreover, she said that the party would sleep on board the air-yacht.
>
> There were seven people aboard, and I felt a good deal of responsibility at the time. Judging by the look of the sky and the sea, which was getting dirtier every minute, there was going to be something really unusual in the way of a gale before morning; and a monoplane with an enormous wingspan is about the nastiest thing in the world to try to keep peaceful at moorings in a real storm. About ten o'clock that evening, while I was watching the barometer falling perceptibly minute by minute, a smart motor-launch came chuffing alongside and hailed us. It bore a message from the Admiral of the Port—a message that sounded uncommonly like a command—saying that our position was very dangerous, that there was going to be a devil of a storm, and that no responsibility whatever could be taken for us unless the passengers came instantly ashore. Our owner sent back a message saying that she had no intention whatever of quitting the air-yacht …
>
> The storm seemed years in coming, and when it did come, it just arrived without the slightest warning. One moment we were rocking gently in the long swell; next, a cyclone had struck us like a giant fist, and the air-yacht was leaping, squealing at her cables, throbbing as if stricken unto death, bouncing from wave-crest to wave-crest, and every second trying to dip first one and then the other wing-tip under the waves, which had become mountains high all in a moment.

> I kept her nose into the wind, to lessen the strain, and I sat at my controls doing what I could—attempting to keep the wings more or less level and the nose from swinging round. Within two minutes from the time the first squall struck us, all the passengers were clamouring in the passage and in my control-cabin ... The wind yelled, the waves thudded on the hull like gigantic hammers, and presently the gale became so bad that the wind under the wings made the air-yacht try to fly, and actually did lift her time after time, two or three yards off the water and into the air, until her mooring ropes jerked her down again with a dreadful wallop on to the rearing waves ...
>
> I managed to get some distress rockets out, and sent them whizzing and hissing up in the air, sending clouds of sparks down-wind. I hoped that the lighthouse would see them and help us, for I felt sure the machine could not live through the night, and some of the passengers were now in a dreadful state of sickness, bruises, and general helplessness. In fact, I was not much better myself.
>
> It was nearly three hours after the first squall struck us—three of the longest, most horrible hours I have ever spent in any aircraft—that the pilot-tug suddenly loomed up alongside us in the screaming wind, and lowered a lifeboat to take us aboard. Our machine was still frantically bumping up into the air and down again on to the sea, and we were all more or less dead of bruises and exposure. But even then the owner was undaunted. She had a favourite little dog aboard with her, and she wanted a lifebelt to tie to him before she transferred him to the lifeboat ...
>
> The time was not one for niceties of behaviour, and we had no lifebelt to spare, so I lifted the owner into the boat when a suitable moment came, flung the dog in as well, hurled in the rest of the passengers one after the other without a single casualty or miss, and finally jumped myself. I certainly expected, when I went down next morning to look, to find the harbour swept clear of all signs of our air-yacht. But, to my surprise, she was still there, practically undamaged ... We stayed a day or two in the town, and ... one afternoon our owner wanted to go suddenly aboard the air-yacht. The only boat available was a little French naval launch, which was puffing busily out from the shore on some affair of its own. Without a second thought, my employer waved to it and called for it to come and take her aboard her aircraft.
>
> Some sort of misunderstanding occurred. Probably the lady spoke in English, whereas the young lieutenant in charge of the launch knew nothing but French. In any case, he seems to have explained, perhaps abruptly, that Navy launches were not ferry-boats plying for hire, and incontinently headed out into the Bay again.
>
> The tone of his reply seriously annoyed our owner. Impulsively she turned straight back again towards the town, and sent what was probably the longest telegram in the history of the French Republic straight to the President himself! She explained the whole affair, and demanded an apology for the way in which she had been spoken to by the lieutenant. What is more, she got it.

Thus ended the Air Yacht. By this time, any hopes of a military role for it were well past, yet this unique Supermarine aircraft did look forward to the Saunders-Roe A.33, eight years later. This aircraft, also a 90-foot parasol monoplane with similar 'N' struts from sponsons, was built in 1938 to the same specification as the Short Sunderland, but the old porpoising problem caused structural failure of the mainplane on the first high-speed taxiing test and it was not proceeded with.

Had R.J. lived long enough, and had the Air Ministry generally shown a more single-minded faith in the future of monoplane flying boats, one wonders what would have transpired if his last flying boat had been developed from the monoplane Air Yacht—if it would have shared some of the duties of the Sunderland or been a Supermarine equivalent of the American Catalina, which equipped twenty-one RAF and RCAF squadrons during the Second World War. Incidentally, the predecessor of the Catalina was the Consolidated Commodore, with a parasol, fabric-covered, wing like the Air Yacht and with about the same span; it appeared in the same year as R.J.'s machine but was far less clean, aerodynamically, with well over thirty supporting struts.

Due to the design activity around the Air Yacht, the Southampton X, and the S.6, as well as all the later Southampton II developments, it is not surprising that in the hiatus between the company's Seagull III of 1926 and the Seagull V of 1933, Saunders-Roe were able to successfully enter the smaller flying-boat field, which had been the almost exclusive province of Supermarine ever since 1918. The company's first product, the A.17 Cutty Sark of 1929, was a metal-hulled amphibian that employed a semi-retracting undercarriage similar to the well-tried Supermarine type; it was in one of these aircraft that the prince of Wales arrived to witness Supermarine's triumph in the 1929 Schneider trophy competition.

A scaled-up version, the A.19 Cloud, followed a year later; seventeen were ordered by the Air Ministry for RAF pilot and navigator training. Ironically, it was an aircraft of this type that was sold to Guinness instead of the Supermarine Air Yacht. A Cutty Sark also offered a Channel Isles service during the summer of 1929 and later appeared on the first Isle of Man aerial service (piloted by the aforementioned Tommy Rose).

The Type 179: 'Giant'

It might be recalled how Biard had been impressed by the standard of the Supermarine accommodation in the Swan and the Solent; even greater luxury was available a decade later when Short's C class flying boats operated the Imperial Airways routes. Yet during this period, the Dornier company had also been developing their series of monoplane flying boats, with an ever-increasing payload of passengers, baggage, and facilities. At the time that their Mark X arrived at Calshot in November 1930 for a two week stay, this version was powered by twelve 610-hp engines, with a crew of ten. It was capable of carrying seventy passengers in seven luxurious and roomy cabins; the Westland test pilot, Harald Penrose, described it as 'a humbling sight'.

He narrated how, like every other designer and pilot, he tried to find an excuse for inspecting the aircraft and Biard, indeed, managed an invitation to handle the controls, as did the master of Sempill, who left an account of what was obviously a very memorable experience of the 157-foot span, twelve-engined aircraft:

> Just aft of the control room is the entrance to the main spars [of the wings] and passageway to the engines so that the mechanics can make adjustments if necessary. Throughout the flight an inspector is able to check every mechanism and fuel connection from stem to stern and tip to tip. By the time you have explored the whole ship, climbing up and down ladders and watching what is going on, you are glad to have a rest in the luxurious seats of the huge multi-partitioned cabin, and there you will find that the well-equipped galley is by no means an ornament.

Not entirely to be outdone, on 18 May 1929, the Air Ministry sent Specification R.20/28 to Supermarine for a forty-seat civil flying boat. Mitchell's response, Type 179, turned out to be a striking departure from the usual large British biplane flying boats mentioned above

Artist's drawing of Type 179 as originally proposed.

as it was first projected as a high-winged monoplane, with three fins, a relatively flat-sided fuselage, and with bulbous floats attached to the underside of each wing root. Six engines were to be mounted in tandem on pylons above the wing, Dornier-X fashion and, notably, it had provision for passenger seating in the leading edge of the very thick wing. While the new design was essentially a development from the Air Yacht, the former plank-shaped wing was now to be replaced by the first appearance of Mitchell elliptical flying surfaces; its proposed torsion-resisting nose section also looked forward to the wing structure of the Spitfire, as did the use of a single spar—although in this case, it was to be 6 feet in depth.

Had R.J.'s design been completed, its size would certainly have put his company ahead of other large flying-boat contenders: it was to have a wingspan 65 feet more than the contemporary six-engined Short Sarafand and nearly 3 feet more than that of the imposing Dornier X. About this time, there was another very large, seven-engined aircraft—the Russian K-7 designed by Constantin Kalinin, which, interestingly, also featured an early example of the elliptical wing. It should, however, be pointed out that while this plane has always attracted the attention of air historians because of its size (and because it flew), Mitchell's projected machine would have had a wingspan greater by 10 feet. It should also be noted that the K-7 did not precede the Supermarine design, its construction beginning in 1931.

With a span of 185 feet, Supermarine's name 'Giant' was therefore appropriate and it would have been a considerable challenge to the fifteen-seat Short Kent, which had just been ordered

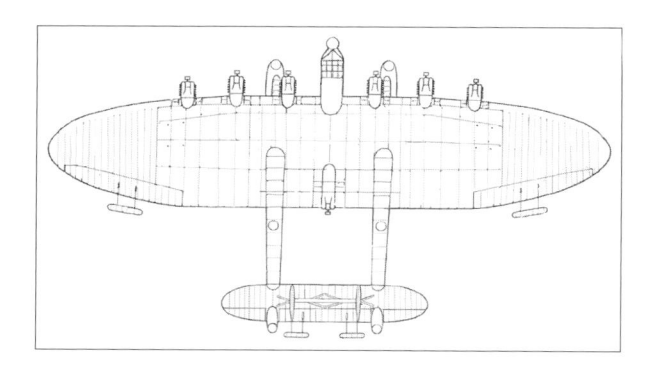

Kalinin K-7.

for the Mediterranean section of the Imperial Airways UK-to-India route; the Air Ministry *Report on the Progress of Civil Aviation 1930*, referring to Type 179, speaks of a 'Mediterranean Flying Boat' being built: 'with the idea of increasing length of flight stages on routes such as through the Mediterranean. Luxurious accommodation will be provided for forty passengers, while detachable bunks are being fitted in order that sleeping accommodation may be available for half that number'.

Almost twelve months after the issue of the original specification, a contract was drawn up for one aircraft, costed out at the remarkably precise figure of £86,585. By then, a replacement of the rather untidy arrangement of three rows of forward-facing Bristol Jupiter radial engines was being considered. The choice of Rolls-Royce steam-cooled engines was also the occasion for a neater mounting arrangement, still above the wing, whereby two inner nacelles housed two engines apiece, driving fore and aft propellers, and two outer nacelles had a single engine each, driving a tractor propeller. Shenstone commented later that 'the NACA work on optimum engine position had not been completed and many thought that engines in the leading edge would be bad'.

Feasibility studies were also made for using the leading edge of the wing as a condenser for the steam-cooling system, a variation on the wing surface radiator system of the S.5/6s. Thus by the time that the keel of the Giant was laid down, most of the Dornier influence had disappeared.

The design was registered as G-ABLE, and by the end of 1931, other changes had been decided upon. An auxiliary tailplane was to be mounted above the main unit and the three rudders were to be replaced by a single one with a Flettner-type servo unit carried on outriggers, as with most of the contemporary Short flying boats. The passenger positions in the leading edges of the wings had been eliminated in order to accommodate the evaporative cooling system (*see* Chapter 14), and the wing was reduced in thickness; it was now to have an easier-to-produce tapered wing, and R.J. had decided upon the wisdom of returning to conventional wing-tip floats, which were smaller and placed further outboard.

When one considers the Supermarine predecessors, the angular Air Yacht, or the traditional Seamew, the original sketches of the Giant showed a tentative move forward whereas the model of it shown opposite reveals a very considerable advance in design; the upswept tail section, the nicely streamlined engine nacelles and the fore part of the hull, reveal R.J.'s thinking to be in advance of forthcoming larger American flying boats. For example, the Sikorsky S-40, of the same year that the keel of the Giant was laid down, represents a traditional approach

Supermarine model of proposed Type 179 Giant showing revised hull, wing, engine mountings, and floats.

The Sikorsky S-42 at Supermarine.

of struts and wires; also, the 'canoe' hull and the necessary twin booms for the tail section, which no doubt achieved a good weight/strength ratio, did not represent the way forward for future flying-boat designs (*see* drawing on p. 136).

The later Sikorsky S-42 had a tail unit integral with the main fuselage and had lost most of its predecessor's struts and wires; coming a few years later than the proposed Giant, it had its engines neatly faired into the wing. It did, however, still retain wing and tailplane struts—compared with Mitchell's projected cantilever structures—and this in a machine that was to have a wingspan of 118 feet, compared with the proposed 185-foot span of Mitchell's design.

By 1931, Supermarine felt able to outline something of their chief designer's progressive thinking:

The wing is constructed in metal, with the exception of the covering of the trailing portion, which is of fabric. The main spar structure is of stainless steel throughout, including the nose covering, which provides the torsional rigidity essential in a monoplane wing.

The hull is built in stainless steel, thus limiting entirely the well-known corrosion troubles experienced with duralumin hulls, especially when operating in tropical waters. For the same reason, there is a very great saving on maintenance costs for this component.

Alas, early in the following year, the project was cancelled in view of the continued economic problems that faced the country; the Air Estimates for that year, £19,702,700, were the lowest since the nadir of 1925. Joe Smith, the chief draughtsman, was left with the unpleasant task of laying off twenty of his drawing office staff. Consternation was not limited to Supermarine as questions were asked in parliament, where the under-secretary for air justified the government's decision, claiming that over 70 per cent of the estimated cost would be saved by cancellation.

Two years later, when R.J. was invited to write something for the *Daily Mirror* about the Macpherson Robertson England–Australia Air Race, he was still feeling raw about the Giant cancellation and the dashing of his ambitions to lead in the design of future civil flying boats. He was unusually forthright:

As far as technique is concerned, British aviation is well to the front. Our Empire is so widely spread that fast aerial transport is perhaps the most vital necessity to our existence. Why are we so slow in the development of our big airliners?

Another view of the Giant model, illustrating graphically what was lost to British aviation at the time (the Southampton in the background, left, makes the point).

A considerable amount of the Giant hull had been completed, and extensive design work at the frontiers of current technology had been spread over nearly three years. Not surprisingly, the editor of the *Aeroplane*, C. G. Grey, saw this decision as nothing but short-termism and exclaimed:

> If this be the new Government's idea of economy, then God help England. A Chancellor who understood the difference between false economy and efficient expenditure and had sufficient intellect to keep in touch with the great developments of the day, of which air transport is perhaps the most important to the welfare of the Empire, would have realised that cancellation of the Supermarine [Giant] is the falsest of false economy. To stop important experimental engineering, costing only a few tens of thousands, which when finished would show the way towards earning millions, is economy going mad.

Had the Giant been built, perhaps R.J.'s bomber might have been designed earlier and might even have been in the air when the critical need arose for such a weapon; on the other hand, it might be recorded in the government's defence that the Germans had not felt justified in putting their huge Do X into quantity production. One British aircraft of a somewhat similar type did actually fly. This was the Blackburn Sydney, which in 1930 represented the first British flying boat in the heavyweight class; this monoplane with a metal-skinned wing, albeit braced and of only 100-foot span, could also have spearheaded the movement away from the traditional British fabric-covered biplane with an aircraft not dissimilar to the Air Yacht. The Air Ministry, however, did not place a production order. Shenstone later commented, in sorrow if not anger:

> One of the objects of the big six-engined flying boats was to compare biplane with monoplane. Shorts got the order for the biplane, which was not cancelled. This, the Short Sarafand, was completed, but nobody learned anything about monoplanes thereby. Even if the monoplane had been a failure when completed, it would have helped everyone's future designs, whereas the biplane was close to its end and in the view of some, had already outlived itself.

It was thus fated that Mitchell would not be remembered, as might otherwise have been predicted, for his contribution to the future of passenger flying boats, to the main flowering of the Imperial Airways routes, or for the creation of equivalents of the well-known wartime monoplanes—the Sunderland and the Catalina.

S.6B Propeller.

12

Winning the Schneider Trophy Outright (1931)

One of the most brilliant designers in the world ... his genius has made possible the production of machines which are a triumph of intellectual brilliance.

Evening Sentinel

By March 1930, the Air Ministry was aware that government backing was being proposed for French and Italian entries for the next Schneider trophy contest in 1931. With the possibility of a third win, and therefore the outright capture of the trophy in front of a home crowd, Supermarine and Rolls-Royce began discussions. In March 1930, they wrote to the Air Ministry, predicting an increase of 25 mph on the Schneider course, assuming that the S.6s would be loaned back for up-rating and that they would be piloted by High Speed Flight pilots.

At the victory ceremony on the evening of the 1929 win, the prime minister had said that Britain would accept any challenge for 1931 that might be forthcoming. However, a cooler appraisal of the cost of a fresh competition, given the pressing problems of the country's worsening economic situation, resulted in an official statement shortly afterwards in which it was announced that the original aims of Jacques Schneider were no longer being fulfilled and that sufficient data about High Speed Flight had been accumulated from the previous competitions. It did not, however, wish to discourage participation in future events 'on the basis of private enterprise'.

The United States had come to such a decision in 1926, and the failure of so many of the specially designed aircraft in the 1929 competition could have done little to help the pro-Schneider lobby. It had been, indeed, fortunate for Mitchell's career that this international seaplane contest had continued thus far, but when the government had just placed an order for the Hawker Fury as the RAF front-line interceptor, it might be forgiven for questioning whether esoteric floatplanes and their competitions were the most obvious or economic path for the development of the nation's military aircraft.

On the other hand, as *Flight* said, 'The importance of the spur which a fixed definite date of such a contest provides cannot easily be overrated' and Mitchell, obviously with a more vested interest in competition work, joined in. In a 1929 article, 'Racing Seaplanes and their Influence on Design', he wrote:

During the last ten years there has been an almost constant increase in speed of our racing types. To maintain this steady increase very definite progress has been essential year by year. It has been necessary to increase the aerodynamic efficiency and the power-to-weight ratios of our machines; to reduce the consumption and the frontal areas of our engines; to devise new methods of construction; and to develop the use of new materials.

In particular, he put his finger on the essence of the matter (and, as it turned out, on the importance of the Schneider events to the Battle of Britain) when referring to engine design:

It is quite safe to say that the engine used in this year's winning S.6 machine ... would have taken at least three times as long to produce under normal processes of development had it not been for the spur of international competition. There is little doubt that this intensive engine development will have a very pronounced effect on our aircraft during the next few years.

More immediately, the winning of the Schneider trophy outright was tantalisingly close and R.J. was beginning to look towards a top speed of 400 mph for his next Schneider machine. Such hopes were dashed by the further announcement on 15 January 1931 that 'no assistance can be given by His Majesty's Government either direct or indirect, whether by the loan of pilots or material, the organisation of the race, or the policing of the course, or in any other way'. It would be hard to imagine a more comprehensive rejection, covering, as it did, all past ways in which the government had helped as well as 'any other' that could be imagined.

The response—especially in aviation circles—was outrage. The Society of British Aircraft Constructors sent a circular letter to every member of parliament saying that 'the British victories in the last two contests have given to British aviation and technique, both in aircraft and engines, a prestige in the minds of foreign buyers of aircraft that probably could not have been attained in any other way'. The prominent aviation writer, C. G. Grey, made the typically waspish response that 'a Government that will give £80,000 to subsidise a lot of squalling foreigners at Covent Garden and will refuse £80,000 to win the world's greatest advertisement for British aircraft is unworthy of the Nation'.

Also, the *Daily Mail* discovered that the under-secretary of state for air, Fred Montague, was a member of the Magicians' Circle and claimed that 'the disappearance of the Schneider Trophy appears to be one of his most amazing feats'. The Stoke-on-Trent *Evening Sentinel* quoted an interview with Mitchell which reflected the general unhappiness within the aircraft industry, and, particularly, within Supermarine: 'British aircraft today are unquestionably superior to any other aircraft in the world ... But if we drop our research work now and allow things to drift, in a year or two's time we may have lost that position'. Even Sir Samuel Hoare, by now the secretary of state for India, wrote to *The Times* (as one did) saying:

Now when every other industry is passing through a period of unprecedented depression, the export of our aircraft to foreign countries, already to be valued in many millions, is steadily rising. This change I mainly assign to the reputation that we have won for ourselves in foreign markets, and that we should not have won to the same degree without the resounding victories in the Schneider Trophy.

The government then made a slight concession by undertaking to help with the provision of service pilots and facilities if 'a definite undertaking is given immediately that the necessary funds will be made available from private sources'.

Enter Lady Houston

While the Royal Aero Club had received promises of financial support totalling £22,000, it was clearly unlikely to underwrite the £100,000 they had estimated to be the cost of financing the production of two new and improved machines and the necessary engines to propel them. Fortunately, at this point, another formidable and extremely wealthy lady steps onto the stage—Lady Lucy Houston. It would appear that a prominent flier of the time and president of the Royal Aeronautical Society since 1927, Colonel the Master of Sempill, who knew Lady Houston well and was one of her favourite Britons, had much to do with engaging her well-known championship of matters British. In the event, 'to prevent the Socialist Government being spoilsports', she promised £100,000 (about £5 million in 2000) to sponsor Britain's entry—and, incidentally, to try to embarrass the Labour prime minister, as her jingoistic press release clearly revealed:

> I am utterly weary of the lie-down-and-kick-me attitude of the Socialist Government. To plead poverty as a reason for objecting to England entering a race against teams supplied by nations much less wealthy than our own is a very poor excuse. To down anything that extols and glorifies the wonderful spirit that even a Labour Government cannot knock out of we British seems their chief aim. It is down with the Navy, down with the Army, down with the Air Force, down with our supremacy in India—but up with Ghandi, up with strikes which every honest workman detests, the ultimate aim of which is to bring about revolution and ruin and beggary of all in the kingdom. Everyone will soon have to prostrate before every foreigner and cry 'Forgive me for living'. That is why I have guaranteed the money necessary to give England the chance of winning and retaining for ever the Schneider Trophy. I live for England and want to see England always on top.

Lady Houston subsequently felt it necessary to cable the Press Association:

> I have received a telegram saying the Government has insisted on a banker's guarantee being given for the £100,000 promised. This is the sort of insult only a Labour Government could be guilty of, but I am instructing my bankers to do this.

It was unfortunate for the government that the former small part actress (*see* Appendix VI) was now in a position to embarrass them so effectively, and Air Marshal Geoffrey Salmond, soon to become chief of the air staff, kept her in touch with the preparations for the contest. Despite the eccentricity of her receiving him recumbent beneath a Union flag, it was thanks to her that Supermarine and Rolls-Royce were guaranteed the chance for Mitchell to crown his high-speed designs with a third consecutive winning machine—perhaps the new aircraft should have had a similar union flag image on its fin, as did the S.4.

As there was, by now, little more than a year left for all the work required in time for the competition in the September, Mitchell might have been less than totally overjoyed at this further stroke of luck; he was, among other things, in the midst of creating the Giant, by far the biggest project in the company's history and liable to attract even wider attention than the next Schneider racer when completed.

He now had to live up to his elevated press reputation: in view of his previous two competition victories and his comparative youthfulness, the *Evening Sentinel* (22 August 1931) showed little reticence in proclaiming that 'as well as being one of the most brilliant designers in the world, Mr R. J. Mitchell, of Stoke-on-Trent … is one of the youngest, for his age is only 36' and that his 'genius has made possible the production of machines which are a triumph of intellectual brilliance' (10 September 1931); the *Sunday Express* (23 August 1931) described him as 'a visionary of speed'.

However much he might be able to ignore or deprecate such descriptions, it was imperative not to let down Lady Houston—or Rolls-Royce, especially in view of that firm's recent contribution to Sir Henry Segrave's new water-speed record in *Miss England III*. As well as the reputation of Vickers-Supermarine being at stake, there had also been some more silent funding: Major Bulman had allocated (as he confessed much later) a further £52,000 from his Air Ministry engine vote, under the guise of 'general development work' for the service.

As time and money were distinctly limited, Mitchell had to restrict himself to adapting last year's design to handle the much greater power that a new Rolls-Royce engine promised; as a result, the aircraft was designated S.6B and two machines from the previous competition were also to be called up and to be fitted with the new engine.

The S.6B: Schneider Trophy Outright Winner

His new airframes would be expected to approach an unprecedented 400 mph, while contending with the stresses of repeated sharp cornering, and there was his constant concern to avoid another death in a Schneider machine of his making. Additionally, the whole contest was now scheduled to be held on one day, with the competition aircraft now required to take off and land immediately prior to the start of the race proper, instead of their navigability and seaworthiness tests being carried out with minimal fuel the day before. Thus the floats and their supports would now have to withstand landings with the oil and fuel used for these preliminary requirements, plus the full load needed for the actual circuit flying (also increased, due the even greedier new Rolls-Royce engine being developed).

Meanwhile, Derby had once more to put up with the noise of engine testing, accompanied by the three Kestrel engines driving fans. The mayor had to make appeals to the patriotism of its citizens as the tests ran from 1 April to 12 August before the uprated engine could run for a full hour at 3,200 revolutions per minute and full power—exactly one month before the scheduled contest date. The contribution of Rolls-Royce to the winning of the Schneider trophy can be encapsulated in some statistics: the Buzzard engine, from which the Schneider trophy 'R' engine was developed, produced 825 hp, and this was increased to 1,900 hp for the 1929 contest engine (and then to 2,350 hp two years later), but while the power had now increased by 24 per cent, the weight had only risen by 7 per cent.

In the course of this development the consumption of oil had again risen—to a rate of 50 gallons per hour—but this was subsequently brought down to a more manageable 14 gallons per hour. Mitchell could accommodate the requisite amount of oil within his still slender fuselage/fin but the increase in power by 450 hp at an additional 300 rpm presented him with even more heat to dissipate and an expected increase in the tendency of the aircraft to swing to the left as the greater torque of the engine pushed the opposing float even further down on that side.

Thus new floats were provided, and with additional radiator surfaces right down to their chines, so that now no less than 470 sq. feet of the 948 sq. feet of the aircraft's available surface area (49.6 per cent) was being used for cooling purposes; additionally, experimentation was undertaken to improve the efficiency of the wing-tip air scoops that had been used on the S.6 to cool the inside surfaces of the wing radiators. There were now what Supermarine estimated at 'something like 40,000 btu' to be dissipated every minute (the equivalent of 234 modern fan heaters running at full power), and so it is understandable why Mitchell, in a radio broadcast after the competition, described the S.6B as a 'flying radiator'.

Supermarine Publicity Gave Particularly Detailed and Interesting Accounts of Some of the Design and Structural Considerations

The problem of supplying enough cooling surface water and oil was one that presented the greatest difficulty.

In the 1929 Schneider Trophy Contest the two S.6s were flown with the engine slightly throttled down, because there was not enough radiator surface on the machine to cool the engine when running at full throttle. In that Contest the Rolls-Royce R engine gave an output of 1,900 hp, and for this year's Contest the power output of the new R engine was increased to 2,350.

In the S.6B the entire upper and lower surfaces of the wings and the upper surfaces of the floats constitute water radiators.

Some idea of the difficulties confronted by the designers can be gained if one realises that to keep the engine running at normal temperatures something like 40,000 B.T. units of heat must be dissipated each minute from the water and oil cooling surfaces, which is equivalent to approximately 1,000 hp in heat loss from these surfaces.

The new floats have greatly increased aero and hydro-dynamic qualities, and the starboard float carries considerably more fuel than the port float, the differences in load balancing the tremendous turning moment of the engine, particularly during the take-off. Full engine torque has the effect of transferring a load of approximately 500 lbs from one float to the other.

The construction of the new floats was complicated by the necessity for fitting water-cooling surfaces on the whole of the upper surfaces. When filled with water from the engine at a temperature near boiling point, the radiators expand nearly half an inch, and to prevent buckling of the outer skin, the designer had to incorporate an ingenious elastic framework to take up this expansion. It was also found essential to insulate the fuel tanks from the water-cooling surface to prevent evaporation of the petrol.

Like the floats of the S.6, they carry all the petrol in steel tanks which are built as part of the floats. The fuel is forced by engine-driven pumps to a small pressure-tank in the fuselage which feeds direct to the engine. On steeply-banked turns the sudden application of centrifugal loads, equal to 5 or 6 G, prevents the pumps from working, and the small pressure tank carries just enough fuel to keep the engine running during each turn. Immediately the turn is concluded the pumps begin to operate again and the pressure-tank is replenished.

258 R. J. Mitchell: To the Spitfire

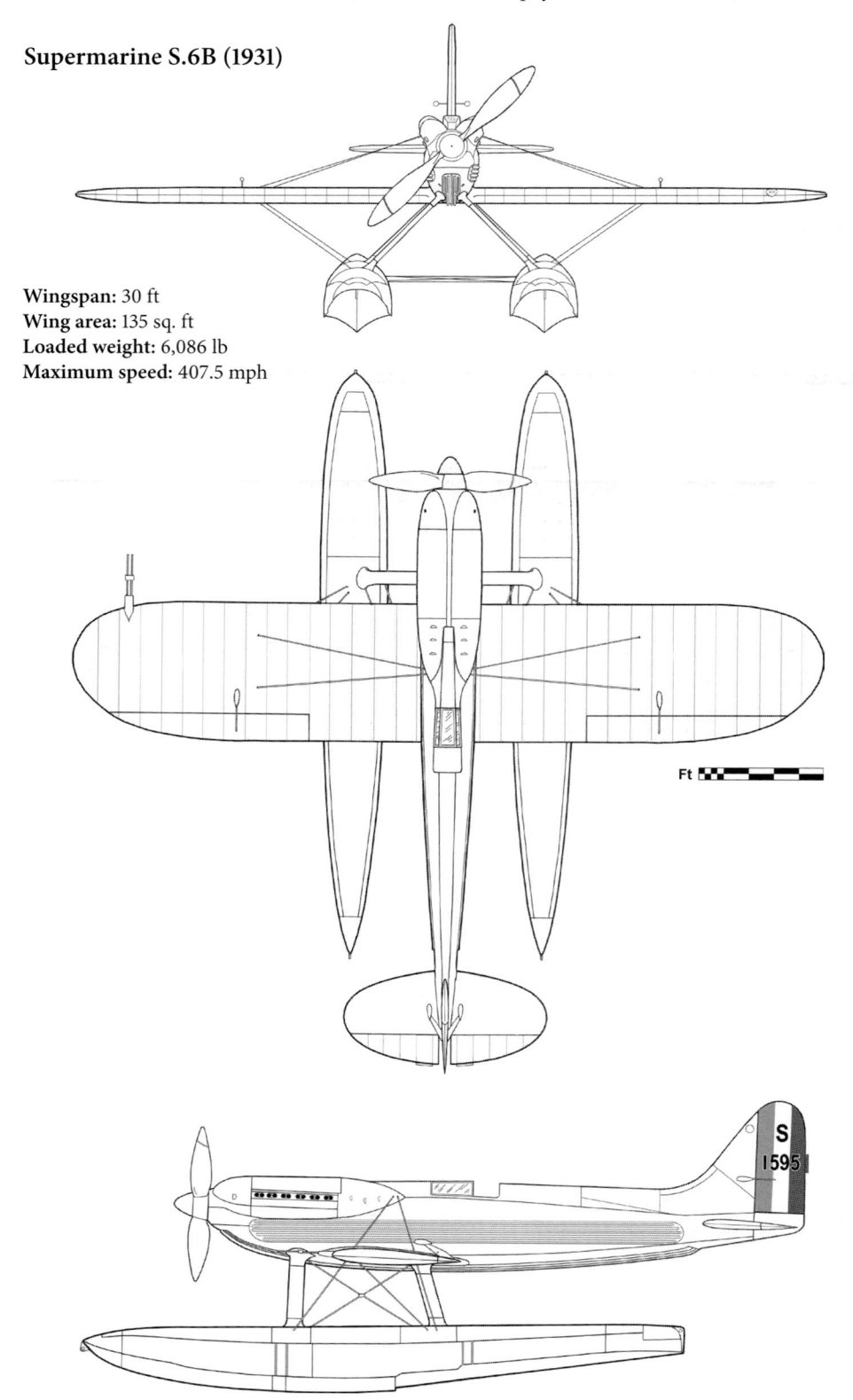

Supermarine S.6B (1931)

Wingspan: 30 ft
Wing area: 135 sq. ft
Loaded weight: 6,086 lb
Maximum speed: 407.5 mph

The first of the S.6Bs at Calshot.

The need to enlarge the cooling area was at least facilitated by the otherwise unwelcome increase in the size of the floats required to accommodate more fuel, as mentioned earlier. Extensive wind tunnel testing at the National Physical Laboratory and tank testing at Vickers, nevertheless, led to a narrower float design, albeit of increased length, which reduced drag significantly as well as giving increased fore-and-aft stability on the water. An additional, typically Mitchell, small detail was the extension of the side plating ¾ inches below the chines and as far as the step to improve the running of the floats and to decrease spray.

The two S.6Bs built with these various features were given the serials S1595 and S1596 and the two uprated 1929 machines, N247 and N248, were redesignated S.6As. In anticipation of there being four Supermarine racers available, Flying Officer L. S. Snaith was added to the High Speed Flight, which had now consisted of Flight Lieutenants J. N. Bootham, E. J. L. Hope, F. W. Long, and G. H. Stainforth (Atcherley, Greig, and Waghorn had by now been posted away).

Flying with the new machines began when the first of the S.6As, N247, arrived on 20 May, and almost at once, more alterations to the basic S.6 design were found to be necessary—an alarming oscillation of the rudder during an early high-speed run had caused the buckling of rear fuselage plates, stress cracks around some of the rivet holes and stretched control wires. (For Mitchell's reaction, *see* Chapter 1, p. 29.) As there was little time available for fundamental investigation or possible redesign before the contest was due to take place, the last bay of the fuselage was strengthened and Mitchell placed streamlined bob weights on the forward-projecting control horns attached to the sides of the rudder and, for good measure, to the ailerons.

All the aircraft were so modified, and Orlebar explained the theory behind Mitch's solution as follows:

Flt Lt Long returning from a test run. Bob weights visible.

The weight of the movable control surfaces was all behind the hinge, and they, therefore, had a tendency to lag behind any movement, caused by vibration, of the fixed surfaces. Having lagged, they would want to flick over, and this tended to increase the whole movement, so causing the serious flapping which develops into flutter. This accentuating of the movement is avoided if the whole dead weight of the control is equally in front and behind the hinge, when the control only tends to conform to any movement of the fixed surface. Therefore, since the hinge position could not be altered [in the time available], it was necessary to fit horns on to the rudder and ailerons carrying heavy streamlined lead weights well forward of the hinge in order to adjust the balance.

Weights were also needed in response to pilots' reports of some instability on take-off and during turns. Mitchell decided that this problem was due to the centre of gravity being too far back and so he had about 25 lb of lead placed in the nose of each float and reduced the amount of oil, which was, again, being carried all the way back to the fin. Orlebar had also reported nose-heaviness during level flight, but the proposal to add some backward pressure on the stick by fitting a bungee cord was not favoured by the pilots. He then described how Mitchell 'produced a splendid gadget to cure the trouble'—he had metal strips, 9 inches long and 1 inch wide, fitted to the trailing edge of the elevators. They were bent downwards by about 1 degree, thereby utilising the slipstream at high speed to deflect the elevator upwards slightly and to prevent any load on the stick.

This principle of trimming had been established by Anton Flettner during the First World War and was evident in the servo rudders on the DH.10 and the Short Singapore I in 1926 but Orlebar might not have come across any examples of the trim tab approach—being regarded as an advanced feature with the Boeing 247, which first flew two years later in 1933, and proposed by Mitchell for his uncompleted Giant in 1929. The CO was certainly impressed by the immediate effect of Mitch's modification: 'I was able to take my hand and feet off the

S1595, moored off the Woolston slipway, after the fitting of bob weights.

controls at about 330 mph and the machine carried on straight ahead perfectly happily. It was an extraordinarily good shot to get her so exactly right the first time.'

A third problem to emerge was more worrying—when the first new S.6B arrived, it would not get into the air at all as it gyrated in 'a very good imitation of a kitten chasing its tail', as Orlebar said. During the course of trying to overcome these rotations, S1595 damaged a wing radiator by fouling a barge and had to go back from Calshot to Supermarine for repair. In the meantime, its smaller 8-foot 8-inch diameter propeller was fitted to N247, which then also obliged by simply gyrating on (and in) the water, thus pointing to the problem—the slipstream from this sized propeller would appear to be creating a side pressure that the rudder was unable to counteract. A wider 'thrust cylinder' from a larger propeller might therefore take some of this pressure off the fin and rudder and so a 1929 propeller, which was 9 feet 6 inches in diameter, was fitted to S1595 when it was returned. The new machine then took off with no more difficulty than was usual with these racers.

Three of the six airscrews ordered from Fairey Reed for the S.6B had been finished to the smaller size and had therefore to be abandoned but, as an expedient, it was possible to beat out the small extra pieces at the ends of the remaining blanks to produce 9-foot 1½-inch diameter propellers while the 1929 ones were also reused. With the S.6, a reduction in the pitch of the propeller had assisted take-offs; now, an increase in propeller diameter had the desired effect, but again, the result was an increase in fuel consumption and a higher engine temperature. Once more, Mitchell had to accept a slightly lower airspeed than his design was capable of.

Meanwhile, the uprated competition engines were prone to cutting out because of choked fuel filters. This was found to be the result of the fuel mixture (25 per cent benzole, 74.78 per cent aviation petrol, and 0.22 per cent tetraethyl lead) causing the excess compound used to seal the joints in the fuel system to come adrift. As mentioned earlier, Mitch's response was both practical and blunt: 'You'll just have to bloody-well fly them until all this stuff comes out'.

While trim problems had now been overcome, propellers matched to engines, and fuel lines being cleared of excess sealant, take-offs were still far from being, literally, a 'racing certainty'. The problem had been described by Waghorn in 1929:

> Owing to the slow revs of engine and propeller, coupled with the great power and consequent torque effect, the first thing that happened on opening up the engine was that the left wing tried to dig itself into the water. This almost submerged the left float, and the drag so produced swung the machine rapidly to the left, making her quite uncontrollable; the more the machine swung to the left of the wind the more rapid did the swing become, until centrifugal force became greater than the drag of the left float, and she would suddenly throw her right wing down rather violently making it essential to shut off the engine. With a fairly fresh wind and full load it is advisable to take-off directly into wind, and with that end in view we found it essential to point the machine about 70 degrees to the right of the wind and to have right rudder on from the start. The machine then runs along with its left wing a few inches from the water across wind, but not swinging. Having got her therefore running across the wind at 40–50 mph, one is now confronted with what is really the trickiest part of the proceedings, and that is to get her into the wind without letting her swing right round, which she will want to do; once left rudder is applied the machine will accelerate rapidly; provided you have not put on too much rudder she should reach her hump speed by the time she is directly into the wind. At this point she assumes a new position on the water—very much lower in front—and accelerates rapidly up to taking-off speed. She seems to leave the water at about 100 miles an hour.

With the much-increased power of the new engines, this problem now called for even greater vigilance and judgement. There was also a tendency still for the noses of the floats to dig in, causing the aircraft then to porpoise; this had to be resisted by holding the control column right back, contrary to all the training pilots are given for normal take-offs. Snaith described how these procedures would cause the S.6 to quite suddenly 'leap off the water and into the air at a pronounced angle and in a partially stalled condition, virtually hanging on its propeller … The whole manoeuvre was complicated because many a time we had to take off blind, our goggles being misted up or covered with water'.

Setting aside any speculations about these pilots' belief in their own immortality, one must undoubtedly admire their skill and 'press on' attitude, sitting now behind a 2,350-hp engine, and keeping the head well down to shield the goggles from the worst of the spray, in order to make the nice calculation of aiming to the right of the wind in order to be pulled by the propeller torque straight into wind by the time take-off speed was reached.

Blacking-out at very low altitudes during the high-speed turns had also to be contended with and, at the other end of a flight, there was the problem of landing with a long flat approach, touching down on the heels of the floats, with the nose of the aircraft increasingly impeding forward vision as the angle of attack was increased to maintain lift as the airspeed dropped. Is it adequately appreciated that the British success in the Battle of Britain and later owes much to the highly skilful but dangerous developmental work undertaken by the high-speed pilots on these racers? One thinks particularly of the first group of high-speed pilots who had experienced the initial dramatic leap in the performance of these aircraft and the flying skills needed to control them. Schofield had previously reported how he had had to learn to land the Gloster racer at over 130 mph—only about 20 mph slower than the top speed of current RAF fighters—and feel his way on to the surface 'without seeing it at all'. He had soon

S1596 taking off amidst the usual spray.

discovered that it was not possible to help matters by looking down the side of the machine because of the 'searing wave of flame' coming back from the exhausts.

While Schofield seems to have made more of the new landing problems than, for instance, Greig, it is notable that the British team had now begun to have its accidents. Mitchell had been required to produce the fastest aircraft in the world but he had also to watch them fly virtually at sea level, often in hazy conditions, and taking off and landing without the aid of flaps or variable pitch propellers, amongst busy shipping lanes.

After Kinkead's death in 1928, Flight Lieutenant Hope had virtually written off one of the modified S.6A machines. A piece of the cowling from N248 worked loose in flight, and as he was managing a successful emergency landing, the wash from a passing ship caused the sensitive machine to cartwheel and sink in fifty feet of water. The pilot survived but was withdrawn from the team because of a punctured eardrum. He was the son of the influential hull designer mentioned in Chapter 3; as Group Captain E. J. Linton Hope, AFC, he was killed in action in August 1941.

He was replaced by Lieutenant G. L. Brinton. On 18 August, on his first take-off in N247, the second backup machine, he, like the pilot of the Sea Lion III seven years before him, apparently seemed not to get the take-off technique right. At a height of about 10 feet, it would appear that he had pushed the stick forward and the machine hit the water, bounced back at a sharper angle of attack, hit the water again, and then, from about 30 feet, dived in. D'Arcy Greig explained the circumstance as follows:

> if the machine developed fore and aft pitching motions, known as porpoising, during any stage of take-off, there was only one sure remedy—close the throttle, slow down and taxi back for another attempt. Any other form of remedial action or an attempt to carry on, was only courting disaster, for in these circumstances the amplitude of the pitching invariably increased until the machine was eventually thrown into the air without flying speed. If this happened, a crash was almost a certainty.

'Mitch' with (*left to right*) Flt Lts Snaith, Stainforth and Hope and Lt Brinton.

Brinton's crash was described by Penrose—the machine 'bounced, dropped back, bounced again, stalled its starboard wing, tilted steeply and struck the water hard. The floats were torn off ... and young Brinton was jammed in the fuselage and drowned'. *Time* magazine reported:

> A young lieutenant last week climbed into the cockpit of the Supermarine S.6, which won the Schneider Cup two years ago. He was Lt Gerald Lewis Brinton, 26, youngest member of the British Schneider Cup team. It was his first flight in the S.6. The plane slid along the surface of the Solent until it was going about 200 mph. It cleared the water for a second and then dropped back to it. A tower of spray shot up. The S.6 bounced 40 feet in the air and then plunged down into the Solent, nose first. When Lt Brinton's fellow officers reached the ship in a speedboat, it had risen again, upside down, with wings and tail torn off. The wreckage was towed ashore and the dead body of Lt Brinton removed from the tail of the fuselage, where the shock had wedged it.

The writer of this slightly dramatised account did not elaborate on the fate of Brinton's body; it was first assumed to have been lost at sea and only later was it found jammed into the rear of the fuselage. It is not recorded how the actual discovery of the body was received by Mitchell, but in view of his well-known concern for the pilots of his machines, an explanation of the need to cut into the damaged machine for its recovery must have required considerable tact.

At about the same time, a French and an Italian pilot were killed while practising with their teams. The French entries were to be, essentially, uprated versions of the 1927 machines that did not compete that year and were suffering from control problems because their wing areas had now been reduced in order to increase their competitiveness. One machine was considerably damaged in a landing accident, and on 30 July, another was completely destroyed, killing its pilot. Prior to this, on 18 January, the Italians had responded to the disappointment of the last competition with an attempt on the world speed record. Unfortunately, their Savoia S.65 plunged into Lake Garda, killing its pilot, Dal Molin, who had come second in 1929. It was suspected that he had been overcome by fumes.

Meanwhile, Macchi were developing their M.67 layout into a new machine that was also to kill one of its pilots. The main feature of the new Macchi was, like that of the S.6B, the incorporation of a more powerful power plant into a relatively unchanged airframe, but the Italian design also featured the then advanced engineering of contra-rotating propellers. This bold approach to the elimination of torque problems on take-off was to be achieved by, essentially, bolting two Fiat engines in tandem and by driving separate propellers via individual reduction gearing to coaxial shafts. Extra speed would also be gained by not having to rig the wings slightly out of true and by not needing such large floats to counteract torque.

Since the demise of the S.65, Italy had to pin all its hopes on this new Macchi M.C.72, which, with 2,500 hp now available, was looking extremely competitive. The surface-cooling arrangements were very similar to those of the S.6s, except that the float struts had a very broad chord, which was also utilised for heat dissipation. Not surprisingly, its revolutionary engine was plagued with problems, especially carburation, and during a fly-past to demonstrate its erratic behaviour to those on the ground, Giovanni Monti, another 1927 contest pilot, crashed and died in unsolved circumstances. This accident took place on 2 August, at which time the French planes were still not ready and the remaining pilots were also in considerable need of experience of High Speed Flight in contest machines.

As a result of such accidents and other setbacks to the French and Italian teams, a joint request for a postponement of at least six months was received on 3 September by the Royal Aero Club; this presented a difficult decision. By this time, it was felt that all the significant problems with the S.6Bs had been solved and Hope's S.6A had been salvaged and was well on the way to being restored to flying condition (it flew again on 6 September). On the other hand, bad weather had prevented any practice in the competition machines since 26 August and so the risk of being barely prepared to compete on the due date of 12 September had to be weighed against the hope of winning by a fly-over, which would immediately ensure permanent possession of the Schneider trophy for Britain. It had also to be borne in mind that finance for future contests was extremely uncertain.

These considerations were all evident in the response of Harold Perrin, the Royal Aero Club secretary:

> My Committee has decided with regret that it is impossible to accede to your request. We took into consideration that only nine days remain before the appointed date, that the elaborate preparations are virtually complete, and that very large expenditure has been incurred by all concerned, including many local authorities and private interests [i.e. Lady Houston, whose £100,000 had, obviously, now been spent].

The Air Ministry was then informed on 5 September that neither France nor Italy would be able to compete, although Italy attempted to upstage what looked like an inevitable win for Britain by going for a new world speed record in the M.C.72, which, when it functioned properly, promised to approach the magic 400-mph mark. However, after a few successful runs, it was opened up again and then flew into rising ground on far side of Lake Garda, killing yet another pilot, Stanislao Bellini. A study of the remains later suggested that the engine had exploded.

The Final Schneider Trophy Contest, 13 September 1931, at Calshot

On the day that had been set for the competition, the weather was squally and the sea was running with an unpromising lop and so there was little prospect of racing that day. The clerk of the course was not for postponing, but Bulman has described how Orlebar gave him 'a terrific wink' as they climbed into a Fairey floatplane for a fly-round and he guessed his intent: 'They came back twenty minutes later. The rotund and normally rather pompous Clerk looked grey and was very wet. "Quite impossible," he said. "Out of the question. Race postponed."' Orlebar had presumably flown so as to produce spray over the cockpit and no doubt had also exaggerated the bumpy flying conditions.

In contrast, the following day was almost perfect with visibility of over 10 miles. In view of the fly-over situation, it was decided that the first S.6B, S1595, was to complete the course without putting undue strain on the airframe or on the engine—Mitch's valiant efforts to prevent engine overheating once again could not quite cope with prolonged full throttle flying. If this attempt were to fail, then the repaired S.6A, N248, would aim to finish the course and therefore win the trophy outright; with less radiator area on its shorter floats, it also had to be flown circumspectly, to avoid engine overheating, but it still ought to win the trophy at a very respectable speed, if called upon. The second S.6B, S1596, would be available to make trebly sure of a win, but it was hoped that it could be retained instead to give the crowds the additional thrill of seeing the setting of a new world speed record. Orlebar gave the senior pilot, Stainforth, first choice and he opted for the proposed attempt on the speed record; the next most senior man, Boothman, then opted to fly first in the competition itself and, hopefully, to have the honour of winning the trophy.

So, just before 1 p.m. on 13 September, Boothman taxied out in S1595, the machine never having been flown in practice for longer than twenty-seven minutes, nor had it been considered wise to practice the landing, with all the necessary fuel for the 350 km of the competition course and for the required preliminary landing, as the new rules required. Nevertheless, he took off without any apparent difficulty, landed at about 160 mph without mishap, and then took off again after a period of less than two minutes; he then flew the prescribed seven laps, all within about 4 mph of each other.

Lady Houston had come over in her steam yacht, *Liberty*, to watch her machines flying and two days later gave a celebratory lunch on board, which was attended by Mitchell and his wife and the High Speed Flight. Cozens' information about the S.5 and S.6 series repeats information that has been given in other accounts, but the following anecdote relating to Lady Houston and the 1931 Schneider Cup win is worth recording:

Lady Houston's yacht, SY *Liberty*.

Winning the Schneider Trophy Outright (1931)

Lady Houston with the RAF High Speed Flight on her yacht. Mitch, standing, far right.

> She was afforded the rare privilege of mooring her yacht on the RAF buoys inside Calshot … In the evenings the *Liberty* had a string of electric lights from her bowsprit to the mastheads and down to the stern, and this seemed to add just the right touch to the celebration of victory.

(Miles Macnaie, her recent biographer, has discovered a file in the Treasury papers at the National Archives, Kew, noting that she 'regards the Schneider trophy aircraft and engines as her own property'; on 10 February, the minister for air advised that no prior conditions attached to her donation and that therefore there was no 'contract of ownership'.)

The Air Ministry then set about disbanding the High Speed Flight and restoring the Calshot base to its normal flying-boat duties (the resident flying-boat squadron having been relocated to Stranraer). However, Rolls-Royce particularly wanted to have produced the first aero engine to exceed the new magic mark of 400 mph. Mitchell had somewhat diffidently indicated the same in an interview with the Southampton *Daily Echo*, after the competition, when he said that 'with a specially tuned up engine, I am very hopeful we may get very near to an average speed of 400 mph, which is our ambition'.

This crowning success of his S.6B was achieved after the intercession of Sir Henry Royce (knighted in 1930 for his services to the aircraft industry). For this special sprint machine, Mitchell had the wing-tip air scoops removed and a specially prepared engine was to be supplied—with a new fuel mixture of 30 per cent benzole, 60 per cent methanol, and 10 per cent acetone plus a 5cc/gallon

Houston commemorative plaque at Calshot.

tetraethyl-lead solution, which required the wearing of goggles when filling up the fuel tanks. To absorb the increased power of the new engine, a 9-foot 6-inch propeller was fitted, but on 16 September, during a test flight, Flt Lt Stainforth lost control of S1596 when the heel of his shoe jammed under the rudder bar during the landing and so another S.6 went under the waves—the fourth of the seven S.5/6 aircraft, of which two, Kinkead's and Hope's, were salvaged.

After delays caused by bad weather, Stainforth squeezed into the cockpit of S1595, fitted with the special sprint engine that had fortunately not yet been installed in the other machine, and the required four runs were photographically measured. There was some concern that bad light and a low evening sun might prevent confirmation and that a rerun, which would necessitate the engine first going back to Derby for inspection, might not be allowed in view of the continued disruption of normal RAF duties at Calshot. It was now thirteen days since Stainforth's ducking, but eventually, at 4 a.m., the results were telephoned through and Mitchell was informed; he was 'too sleepy to be more than mildly enthusiastic' that the world absolute speed record had just been raised by nearly 30 mph to 407.5 mph. (From February to September 1932, the outright land, water, and air speed records were all held by Rolls-Royce 'R' powered machines.)

The resultant appearance of Reginald Mitchell in the 1932 New Year's Day honours list was also a matter of mixed feelings as the award involved our retiring designer undergoing some particularly unwanted ostentation, including having to wear: 'breeches of plain black of evening dress material or stockinet, with three small black cloth or silk buttons, and black buckles at the knee. Black silk hose, plain Court shoes with bows and no buckles'.

Unsurprisingly, he was all for having nothing to do with the ceremony, but his son remembers his being talked round by Mrs Mitchell, who was, no doubt, far less daunted by having to buy a new outfit for the occasion, as well as being insistent that he would have to go through the pomp and ceremony for the sake of his family and the firm. In view of Supermarine's current lack of success in supplying aircraft to Imperial Airways, Mitchell might have been permitted a wry smile on reading the official honours list letter from King George V, who was entitled 'of the British Dominions beyond the Seas, Emperor of India and Sovereign of the Most Excellent Order of the British Empire', but he nevertheless 'did the thing which should be done'.

He then had to give a talk—broadcast by the BBC on 23 February 1932—where in a typically self-effacing manner he explained in layman's terms the broad design problems that 'the designer' had had to overcome and expressed his admiration for 'the great courage and great skill' of the pilots of the High Speed Flight. His son reported that because of his slight stammer, he had spent a good deal of time rehearsing his speech and only had one slight pause in the ordeal, which must have seemed much longer than its actual six minutes.

R. J. Mitchell on the occasion of his receiving the CBE in the 1932 New Year's Honours List.

Despite the award giving considerable private self-satisfaction, the lasting acknowledgement of his work was from Rolls-Royce and the RAF. As we shall see in the following chapters, the Air Ministry not only accepted a Mitchell proposal for a Rolls-Royce-backed land-based fighter (from a firm specialising in maritime reconnaissance aircraft, after all) but also kept faith with the company during the Spitfire's future production problems.

By way of a postscript to Mitchell's trophy successes, a review of the top speeds and different records of Mitchell's Schneider trophy racers indicates the rate of aircraft and engine development spearheaded by Mitchell in one formative decade:

1922 Sea Lion II	129.66 mph (1st World Record for Maritime Aircraft)
1923 Sea Lion III	157.17 mph
1925 S.4	226.75 mph (World Speed Record for Seaplanes)
1928 S.5	319.57 mph
1929 S.6	337.7 mph (World Absolute Air Speed Record)
1931 S.6B	407.5 mph (World Absolute Air Speed Record)

It is worth recording that three years later, in 1934, the French Caudron C.460 gained the landplane record at the much lower speed of 314 mph.

In an article in the Aeronautical Supplement to *The Aeroplane*, Mitchell gave a remarkable set of figures that showed how his engineering skill and attention to the detail of cooling his Schneider racers contributed to their success:

Radiator type	corrugated brass	flat brass	flat dural	dural with 12% internal cooling
aircraft	Curtiss CR-3	S.5	S.6	S.6B
radiator weight per hp dissipated	300	410	75	67
hp dissipated per unit area of cooling surface	50	66	81	92
resistance per hp dissipated	15	0	0	0

These entries can also be seen to chart Mitchell's gradual rise to public notice—the performances of the S.4 and S.5 revealed that the Sea Lion II win was not just a flash in the pan, and being elected a fellow of the Royal Aeronautical Society in 1929 was an acknowledgement by his fellow professionals of his contributions to advanced aviation technology. However, as Mitchell always gave full credit to others in his speeches, he would not would begrudge, in this chapter concerning his notable Schneider trophy successes, a final word about the pilots concerned.

Instances of these pilots' skill and courage are noted in the preceding pages, including flying and alighting at unprecedented speeds, in machines with extremely limited vision at altitudes that gave little margin for error and little possibility of survival if things went badly wrong. Undoubtedly, other pilots would have accepted the challenges of flying beyond the boundaries of previous experience but it was those mentioned above to whom credit must go; if these pilots had not successfully flown their, frankly, dangerous aircraft, the Spitfire might not have been ready in time for the Battle of Britain. One notes D'Arcy Greig's dedication in *My Golden Flying Years*: 'to all those involved with the Schneider trophy races that helped so much in the development of the Spitfire in later years'.

The Supermarine Stranraer prototype.

13

His Last Flying Boats
(1932–1934)

The biplane was close to its end and, in the view of some, had already outlived itself.

Beverley Shenstone

The chief factor that was to alter the fortunes of the aviation industry, and the fate of R.J.'s last designs in particular, was the eventual collapse of the International Disarmament Conference and the final realisation that Germany's ambitions required an adequate response. A significant stage in the change was identified by *The Aeroplane*:

> The Air Debate of 8th March marked a turning point in the history of the RAF, for the House of Commons showed for the first time a proper appreciation of air power. No Debate on any Service Estimates has been so largely attended for many years.

This year, 1932, marked the first time that these estimates had gone over the £20,000,000 mark, and there was also a proposal for a dramatic increase in the number of squadrons. The existing seventy-five units were to increase to 116, with a threefold expansion of the number of home-based aircraft—the 1923 proposed increase in the number of home defence squadrons to fifty-two had never been fully implemented.

Unfortunately, drift and indecision, influenced by strong pacifist sentiments and the depressed economic situation, were also characteristic features of this period of government, despite Hitler's ominous withdrawal of Germany from the League of Nations and from the Geneva Disarmament Conference in 1933. The view of the prime minister, Stanley Baldwin, that 'the bomber will always get through' did not encourage a strenuous policy of fighter development nor, on the other hand, did it result in the creation of a retaliatory, modern bomber force that might deter enemy aggression.

In this climate of uncertainty, if not timidity, R.J. was, however, encouraged to design two more traditional flying boats, which, despite the obsolescence of their configuration, were ordered in some numbers and which both saw military action; he also designed the Walrus, which was eventually ordered in large numbers and featured in innumerable wartime activities. The last of these came as a straight-line development from the early Supermarine pusher amphibian type, while the other two, the Scapa and the Stranraer, were in the tradition of the larger Southampton twin-engined biplane.

The Scapa

The first of the new designs owed its origin to the last of the three experimental Southamptons, N253; it was ordered in 1928, to be fitted with a metal superstructure and with the new Rolls-Royce Kestrel engines. While the experimental N251 design work had been largely to the benefit of the Saunders company and N252 had been the unsuccessful pairing with Vickers, this third order was to prove far more significant than just marking Supermarine's move to all-metal structures.

The proposed new Kestrel powerplant was the response of Rolls-Royce to the Curtiss engine, which had created a stir in aviation circles when it was fitted to the new Fairey Fox bomber. It is not surprising that, in view of the Schneider trophy performance of the Curtiss powerplant, the new sleek Kestrel engines gave the N253 Southampton 10 mph more top speed and it took fourteen minutes less to reach 5,000 feet than the standard 500-hp Napier Lion-powered Southamptons, whose combined power had been 20 hp more than that of the new Kestrels.

There was thus considerable attraction to the possibility of equipping the new design with the newly developed Kestrel III of 525 hp and also of staying with the two-engine formula. In the still relatively depressed economic situation and with Shorts' lead in three-engined flying boats, a more aerodynamically efficient version of the Southampton II, with the cheapness of using only two of the new and more efficient engines, was considered very likely to gain approval at the Air Ministry. Supermarine offered the last contracted Southampton, S1648, as the proposed Southampton IV prototype, at no extra cost—one of several initiatives by McLean at that time to win new orders.

Accordingly, the new machine—to be known as the Scapa—has been regarded as, essentially, an 'improved Southampton', particularly as its hull planing geometry was closely based on that of the earlier aircraft. This similarity was very much a compliment to the intuitively designed Southampton hull of 1925, as the now available use of tank testing did not suggest any real need to depart from the basic shape of its predecessor. Indeed, a wider beam behind the step, to discourage water striking the tail surfaces, was replaced by the older Southampton after-portion when actual take-offs revealed an unpleasant pitching when the newer rear step made contact with the water.

Nevertheless, the eventual Scapa was, effectively, a new design. The need to stretch the Southampton design resulted in a lengthened bow with a deepened forefoot, which, with a flatter top-decking, gave more useable space within, as well as effectively altering the overall appearance of the previous Southampton hull. The new decking also allowed the now enclosed cockpit to merge better with the sides than had been possible with the 'Persian Gulf' Southamptons of No. 203 Squadron and the flatter coamings of the two midship gunners' cockpits could now offer less resistance to the airflow. The Air Yacht tradition of flat plates and rectangular sections was still evident, although corrugated plating had given way to construction methods employed in the Southampton II, and the upswept tail section and other curvatures restored something of the elegance of the earlier machine.

Supermarine Scapa (1932)

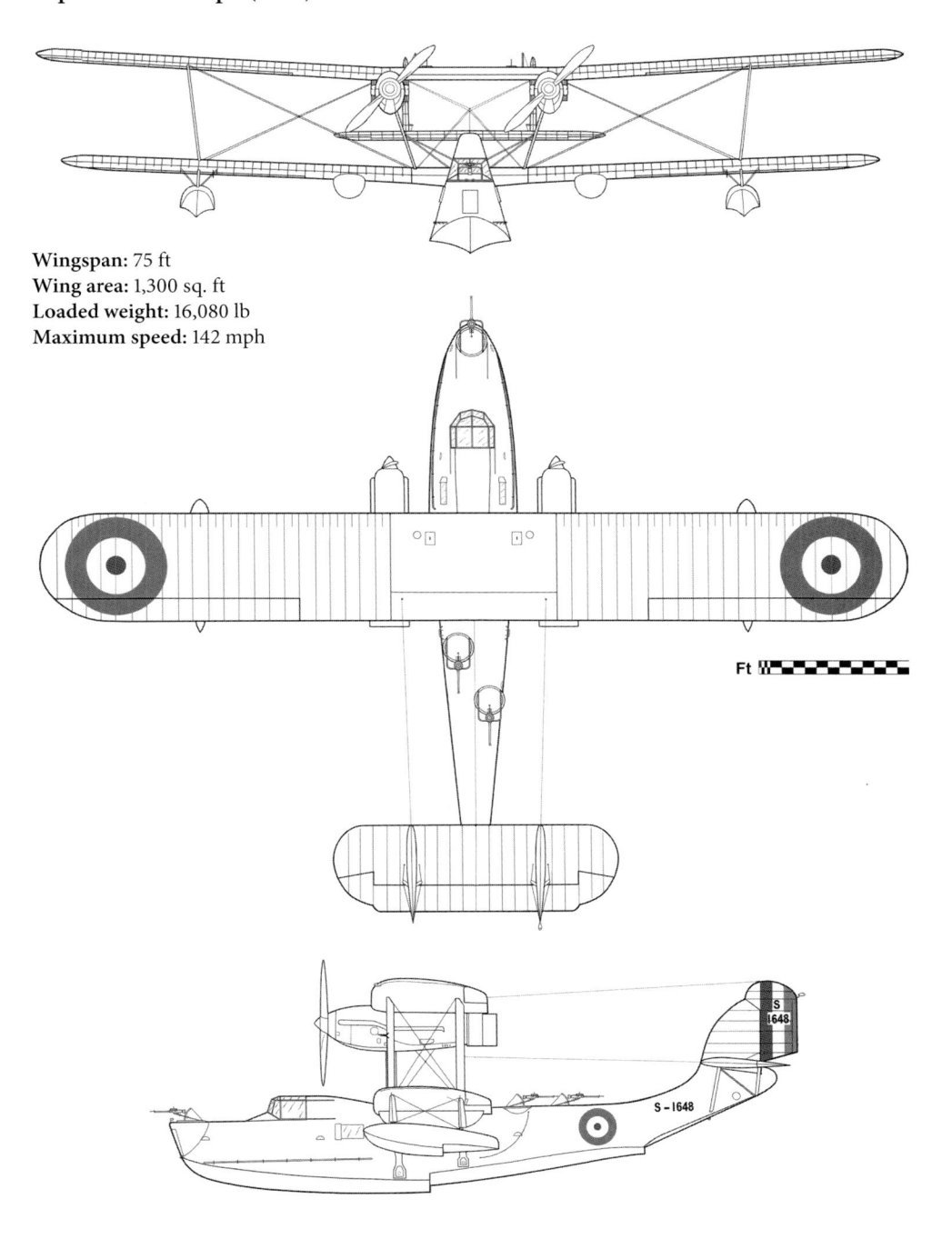

Wingspan: 75 ft
Wing area: 1,300 sq. ft
Loaded weight: 16,080 lb
Maximum speed: 142 mph

Supermarine publicity draws attention to its service testing, no doubt because actual performance data was now being withheld—an early indication of troubled times ahead; nevertheless, the information about structure, accommodation and equipment is, at least, quite full:

The 'Scapa' is the latest twin-engined reconnaissance flying boat, and was designed to replace the 'Southampton', which has been the standard R.A.F. reconnaissance flying-boat for nearly eight years. The 'Scapa' has been subjected to very severe and thorough testing both by the firm's personnel and by the R.A.F., at the Marine Aircraft Experimental Establishment, at Felixstowe. In these tests, the prototype maintained height with normal load and with one engine switched off. The 'Scapa' also showed that its top speed and ceiling are higher, the range greater and the take-off quicker than any other British flying-boat with one, two, three or four engines [an oblique reference to the rival Blackburn, Saunders-Roe and Short aircraft].

    WINGS. Unequal span three-bay biplane. Upper wing in three sections. Lower wing in four. Upper and lower centre-sections interconnected by two pairs of struts and form middle bay. Outer wing sections have one pair of parallel interplane struts each. Structure entirely of metal, with fabric covering. Spars and ribs of anodically-treated aluminium alloy, with stainless steel fittings. Leading-edge covered with duralumin sheet. Ailerons on all four wings.

    HULL. Characteristic Supermarine two-stepped hull of anodically-treated aluminium alloy. Internal structure consists of a number of transverse frames with longitudinal stringers and flat sheet outer plating. Wing-tip floats of similar construction as hull.

    TAIL UNIT. Monoplane type. Tail-plane mounted on up-turned end of hull and braced with 'N' struts on either side. Two cantilever fins and rudders mounted above tail-plane. Balanced rudders. Aluminium alloy framework, with fabric covering.

    POWER PLANT. Two Rolls-Royce 'Kestrel' III M.S. twelve cylinder Vee water-cooled engines, in monocoque nacelles, mounted directly to the under surface of the upper centre-section. Nacelles have quickly detachable cowling and folding working platforms. Large manholes give access to back of engines. Radiators at rear ends of nacelles. Fuel tanks (two) with total capacity of 460 Imp. gallons in centre-section. feed by engine pumps, but in event of pump failure, fuel supply maintained by gravity. Tanks have jettison valves. Oil tanks form leading edge of centre-section. Compressed air starter and alternate hand-turning gear.

    ACCOMMODATION. Cockpit in nose for gunner observer. Scarff ring may be slid clear back to cockpit for mooring operations. All marine gear, bomb-sights and releases also located in this cockpit. Then follows enclosed cockpit for two side-by-side, with dual controls. Second pilot's controls detachable. Between pilot's cockpit and front spar frame is navigator's and engineer's compartment. Between spar frames on port side is wireless compartment. Aft of main planes are two staggered gunner's cockpits, with Scarff rings. Behind rear cockpit is a lavatory and stowage for collapsible dinghy, engine-ladder, maintenance platform and spare airscrew. Provision made in body of hull for cruising equipment, including cooking-stove, ice-chest, water-tanks, etc. Drogue stowed in trailing-edge of lower wing, near hull.

    ARMAMENT. Three Scarff ring mountings and three Lewis guns. Five 97-round drums of ammunition for each gun. Provision made for 1,000 lbs of bombs.

S1648, the Scapa prototype.

The superstructure offered even more evidence that the new prototype was very much more than a Mark IV version of its predecessor. The redesign meant that it was no longer necessary to sweep back the outer sections of the mainplanes as had been necessary with the changing service loads of later Southamptons. In fact, the outlines of all the flying surfaces differed significantly, with the tailplane being reminiscent of the Seamew and the fins looking not unlike those of the Southampton X or even the Swan. Two fins now replaced the triple-fin arrangement of the Air Yacht or standard Southampton and were well within the slipstreams of the engines, now positioned directly under the top wing.

This upward re-siting of the engines was probably influenced by the water ingestion problems experienced by the Seamew and by the current concern for cleaning up drag-inducing features. The new arrangement allowed R.J. to dispense with the engine support struttage of his previous inter-wing-engined designs and the large Warren bracing of the Southampton superstructure. His decision to return to wire bracing with the S.5 and S.6 must have been a factor here and also led to a single bay structure, even though the new machine's wingspan was to be 75 feet.

Another aspect of the aerodynamic clean-up was the attaching of the lower wings directly to the fuselage via an elegant, slightly gull-wing, centre section. Shenstone considered the resulting aircraft 'perhaps the cleanest biplane flying boat ever built, with minimum struttage and clean nacelles faired into the wing'. He did not mention the very 'boxy' radiators which projected on either side to the rear of these nacelles, although their positioning least compromised the overall lines of the design.

In view of all the new design features of this prototype Southampton IV, a new name for the type was justified, although no new name had materialised when 'Mutt' Summers took S1648 up for its first flight on 8 July 1932. After numerous tests, mainly concerned with the rear step modification, it was delivered on 29 October to the MAEE for further trials, which included a maximum duration flight of ten hours over the North Sea.

Scapas under construction at the Woolston works. Foreground, right, shows an engine nacelle with radiator already attached to rear.

In the following May, the prototype was flown to the Kalafrana flying-boat base, Malta, for overseas acceptance trials with No. 202 Squadron (the pilot was Flt Lt George Pickering who was later recruited as a Supermarine test pilot by R.J. His logbook entries show 'Mr Mitchell' as P2 in several of his later flights). These trials involved a long-distance flight to Gibraltar and back and a cruise to Port Sudan via Sollum, Aboukir, and Lake Timsah. On its return, the Scapa took part in the 1934 flypast of 'the competition' at the Hendon RAF Display with, as Penrose reported, 'the clean Supermarine twin-engined Scapa leading, followed by the four-engined Short Singapore, triple-engined Blackburn Perth, the distinctive gull-winged Short Knuckleduster, the Saro R24/31 London and the three Saro Cloud trainers'.

The Air Ministry ordered twelve of the new Scapas (K4191 to K4202); and three replacements (K7304 to K7306) were ordered later. Fittingly, the first batch went to No. 202 Squadron, whose pilots must have been particularly impressed by its performance during the acceptance trials, having been equipped since 1929 with Fairey III floatplanes. The squadron soon undertook the almost traditional long-distance cruise with their new type: a notable 9,000-mile return flight with two machines to Calabar, Nigeria, via Algiers, Gibraltar, and the Gambia. Additionally, the old No. 204 Squadron Southamptons were replaced by their Supermarine successors. After this, in 1937, No. 240 Squadron was re-formed at Calshot from the Seaplane Training Squadron C Flight and took over some of the No. 202 Squadron Scapas; they then were sent to Egypt during the Italy–Abyssinia conflict. Scapas of No. 202 Squadron took part in anti-submarine patrols during the Spanish Civil War to protect neutral shipping. One Scapa was attached to No. 228 Squadron where it was involved with early radar experiments.

Scapa prototype over Southampton Water.

The penultimate Scapa of the fifteen built.

During this time, the Royal Australian Air Force had been operating their older Supermarine Seagulls more thoroughly than the British, including a race between the machines at the annual regatta in Hervey Bay, north of Brisbane. And by now, British warships were being modified for catapult-assisted take-offs; in fact, as early as 1925, a Seagull II had been used at the Royal Aircraft Establishment to test the first British catapult for launching aeroplanes.

Thus Supermarine might reasonably hope that the poor deck landing characteristics of the early Seagulls might not be considered relevant to the ordering of an improved catapult version for capital ships at some time in the future. Also the Australian navy was more proactive in these matters and they were again to require naval aircraft after 1924, when the government began a five-year programme of obtaining new ships from Britain, including a seaplane carrier, the *Albatross*. However, as their chief of air staff, Air Marshal Sir Richard Williams, has narrated, procurement of suitable aircraft, again from Supermarine, was by no means straightforward:

> The only aircraft we had which could be used in the carrier … were the Seagulls. If they were used we would be in the proud position of having a new carrier equipped with aircraft declared obsolete by the RAF before the carrier contract was to let. To avoid such a farcical situation, new aircraft would have to be purchased.

Accordingly, he had a requirement issued in 1930 for a new machine which would be of metal construction and carry a crew of three—pilot, observer, and wireless operator—located close to one another. The wings had to fold and there had to be a catapult-launching capability with a full military load of up to 7,500 lb. The new machine should be a pusher, have a maximum speed of 135 miles per hour, and be able to operate in open seas with 6-foot waves. As metal hulls were by no means the norm at that time and as the current Australian Seagull III was limited to a loaded weight of 5,691 lb and had a maximum speed of 82 mph, C. G. Grey's comment that the Australians wanted everything except 'a little … boy to do the cooking' was understandable.

While substantial improvements on current amphibian design would be needed, Williams was nevertheless taken aback by the response he received to the enquiry he circulated among the British aircraft firms, particularly the one from Vickers:

> Most British manufacturers ignored our correspondence, some said they had nothing that would meet out specification. Vickers's aviation representative in London, an RAF officer, wrote to say that they did not have a boat amphibian but they had a very good landplane that had recently put up a record for long distance flying, and he was sure that it would meet our needs. It had fixed wings but they could make them to fold and they could fit it to be picked up by a crane. Although it was landplane they could fit a float undercarriage with wheels in the floats (although they had never made such an undercarriage). It was now fitted for a crew of two who were about six feet apart with a petrol tank between them that filled the fuselage and made it necessary for pilot and observer to communicate with one another by means of a note attached to an endless string running between the two cockpits. They were sure they could put a wireless operator into the rear cockpit with the observer and arrange for the aircraft to be catapulted. It was, of course, a tractor but they were sure that we would find it satisfactory for our work.

Vickers had taken over Supermarine in 1928, and it would seem that the 'Vickers aviation representative in London', apart from his condescension, was merely reflecting his company's landplane speciality without reference to the extensive experience of their newly acquired subsidiary in flying boat, amphibian and folding-wing naval reconnaissance aircraft and, indeed, with the required three crew members. Such experience was evident as early as the Supermarine Seagull II of 1923; indeed, the re-siting of petrol tanks in order to facilitate crew communication had been an important feature of this design, and it might also be noted that one of these aircraft was experimentally fitted with a pusher engine and one was used for catapult launching trials in May 1926.

Also, the Supermarine Scarab, which first flew in 1924, had conformed to the main Australian configuration requirements, including a pusher engine, although—like the Seagulls—it did not have a metal hull. However, the metal-hulled Southampton II had begun appearing from 1925 and so it would have been surely feasible to offer to develop one of their smaller aircraft with such a hull for the RAAF. Then, in the following year a new interest was reported in *Flypast; A Record of Aviation in Australia*: 'an offer from Supermarine Aviation Works (Vickers) Ltd, for two boat amphibians (£9375 each) fitted with Armstrong Siddeley Panthers (£1900 each)'. This offer might possibly refer to two aircraft with two engines each—as a reconnaissance aircraft of carrier size currently in the Supermarine portfolio was their twin-engined Seamew, projected as a ship-borne spotter amphibian in 1924 and first flown in January 1928. Thus it had the required folding wings and a retractable undercarriage—as well as being designed for a crew of three. Interestingly, exactly two of these machines had been built and were not attracting any orders nearer to home, and fitting with Panther engines had been considered.

If these proposed purchases were indeed the Seamews, they had already proved to be a disappointment to Supermarine, as well as beginning to look decidedly dated. The apparently un-energetic response from Supermarine was also evident in a second Supermarine project, also never built—Type 178 02, dating from 1931—which might also have been a projected Seagull III replacement.

At this time, a sluggish response from Supermarine might not have been too unexpected, especially as the main interest of the company was now moving from their traditional medium-sized spotter planes to large, multi-engined metal flying boats. In addition, the design team was heavily involved with the development and testing of their racing monoplanes for the 1927 to 1931 Schneider trophy competitions and another distraction must have been the number of modifications needed to the Southampton X and the Air Yacht, whose designs represented a completely new approach to hull design.

There were also proposals to extend the life of the Southampton II, still under consideration in 1930, as well as Type 178 to 183 projects, with numerous variants—mainly passenger flying boats, but also mail carriers and two land plane fighters. Numerous consultations with Roll-Royce in connection with that company's new evaporative cooling system, were also occupying the company's time—with the Scapa, which first flew in 1932, and particularly with the Giant, whose design was under continual revision until 1932.

Meanwhile the Australian economic situation had deteriorated, and funds for new naval aircraft were not approved; the obsolescent Supermarine Seagull IIIs had to be taken aboard the newly commissioned HMAS *Albatross* on 25 February 1929. Nevertheless, it was to be expected that money would eventually have to be found not only to equip *Albatross* but also

HMAS *Albatross* with one of its Seagull IIIs on crane.

her companion cruisers and battleships under construction. So, a private venture replacement for the Australian Seagull III was also authorised by Supermarine.

The Seagull V

By the end of 1931, Supermarine had begun the design and construction of a prototype, Type 223, identified as Seagull V, with perhaps a projected Type 178 or 181 regarded as its Mark IV. Air Marshal Williams also supplies a fuller account of how Supermarine/Vickers finally got round to producing an eventual Seagull replacement and how catapult testing of the prototype did not go smoothly:

> We did not get much information on progress with this aircraft and consequently it was the first thing I inquired about on reaching London. Vickers's aviation representative at this time was W. B. Caddell.... When I contacted him regarding the prototype being produced by Supermarine and now being referred to as Seagull V, he could not tell me what the position was and suggested we might go to Southampton to see for ourselves.
> We found that the metal boat fuselage and the wooden wing frames had been almost completed but the receipt of a large contract from the Air Ministry for another aircraft [12 Scapas] had caused these components to be pushed to the back of the workshop and work had ceased on them. I informed Caddell of our need for this aircraft and he undertook to have the prototype completed.

Supermarine Walrus/Seagull V (1933)

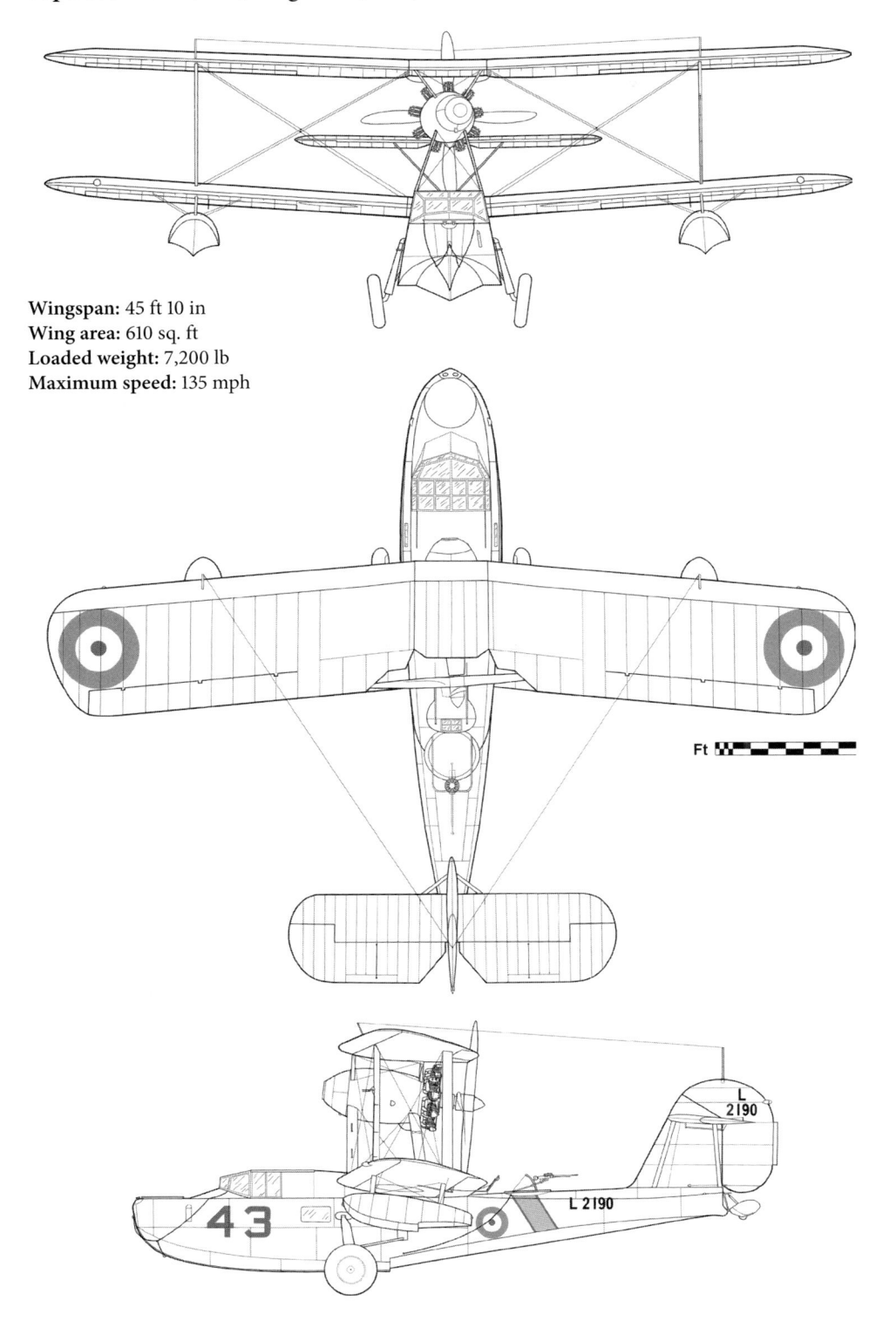

Wingspan: 45 ft 10 in
Wing area: 610 sq. ft
Loaded weight: 7,200 lb
Maximum speed: 135 mph

Seagull V prototype being readied for a catapult trial.

Not too long afterwards, Caddell rang to report that the Seagull V prototype had completed its flying trials satisfactorily and asked about an order:

> I drew his attention to the fact that it had yet to be catapult tested. His reply was that he did not think that necessary: provision had been made for it in the design and lugs to take the catapulting mechanism had been incorporated. He finished by saying, 'After all, old man, we've been in this aircraft business for a long time you know'. I said I was aware of that fact but that I really did want it catapulted and that I was not prepared to recommend the placing of an order until this had been done.
>
> A day or two later Caddell rang to say that he had been unable to get the use of a catapult for this test, that the only one available seemed to be one owned by the Air Ministry at Farnborough, and if that were to be used I had better make the necessary arrangements; no doubt Farnborough would charge Vickers for its use.
>
> I went to the Air Ministry and saw the Director of Technical Development, Group Captain Henry Cave-Brown-Cave, who had led a formation of four flying boats from Singapore to Australia in 1928. He told me that the catapult had not been used for some time and would have to be overhauled before use. 'Anyway', he said, 'who's to pay for this? The RAF is not interested in an aircraft of this type, nor so far as I know is the Navy.' I told him that I had no money but after a little discussion he suggested that I leave the matter with him and he would see if he could provide the funds from his experimental or developmental vote. The next day he advised me that he was having the catapult overhauled.

In due course this work was completed and Seagull V went to Farnborough for catapulting. I could not attend the trials but expected Caddell to ring me soon after their completion and again raise the question 'What about an order?' He did not do so and I rang him on the following day to learn that when catapulted the aircraft had buckled on both sides at the point of the catapult lugs and that the wireless operator's seat had collapsed. I thought perhaps it would not improve our relations if I reminded him of what he had told me about Vickers having been in the aviation business for a long time, but he was rather embarrassed when I saw him next. The necessary strengthening modifications were carried out and the catapulting was completed satisfactorily.

The question of an order now did arise but I had no authority to place one. I visualised Australia being in the foolish position of having a seaplane carrier with no seaplanes if there was much further delay in getting new aircraft, so I signed a contract for 24, picturing some of the Treasury boys going off into a deep coma if they had known what I was doing. I was banking on the Minister giving covering approval, which he did subsequently.

In view of the limitations of the Seagull II/III, the Seagull V had had to be a complete redesign for reasons other than obsolescence (the earliest version of the type, the Seal, was first flown in 1921). In fact, it might be fairly accurate to say that the only influence of the older type on the Seagull V was the basic layout of the last experimental Seagull II, N9644, a biplane that had reverted to a pusher air-cooled power unit. This 'parentage' was plain to be seen in the

The Seagull V prototype on Southampton Water, originally numbered N-1 and later purchased by the Air Ministry as K4797.

basic configuration of the new design but, otherwise, the move to metal structures, slab-sided fuselages, and the experience of the intervening years produced a quite distinct type within an older formula.

One important example of the redesign was the employment of a fully retracting undercarriage. Due to the specific requirements of the amphibian types that they specialised in, Supermarine had had to devise mechanisms that raised the wheels out of the water to facilitate waterborne taxiing but not necessarily out of the aircraft slipstream for flight; now, at last, the Seagull V hydraulics—modified later for the Spitfire—equipped a British military aircraft with drag-reducing full retracts for the first time. Alan Clifton has recalled that he persuaded R.J. to retract the wheels into the wing, saying 'We shall have to do it eventually, why not now?'

A more obvious aspect of the redesign of the Seagull II/III predecessor was the hull. It shared the more aggressive, slab-sided features of the Scapa (and the later Stranraer) but had no upward sweep to the tail unit, as did the Seamew and these other two types. The result of this particular return to the Seagull and Scarab configuration was a more utilitarian appearance to the hull, accentuated by a one-step planing surface. The hull was further simplified by a Saunders-derived arrangement whereby the complex curves of the typical flying-boat hull bottom were replaced by a flat surfaced 'V' below a horizontal 'bench' which terminated at the chines.

> **The combination of traditional and new features was continued in the mixture of metal and wood construction employed in the Seagull V. This composite structure is well documented in the following company publicity whilst, again, performance details are withheld:**
>
> The 'Seagull V' is the latest single-engined amphibian designed by the Supermarine Company specially for fleet-spotting work from aircraft carriers. The boat is therefore very compactly built and has folding wings.
> The addition of detachable dual-controls widens the scope of the machine and the enclosed accommodation, in conjunction with the pusher engine, makes the cabin very quiet and comfortable for fleet-spotting, photography, wireless communication, etc. Catapulting points are provided.
> TYPE. Single-engined fleet-spotter amphibian.
> WINGS. Equal span single-bay biplane. Small centre-section carried on engine-mounting struts. Outer wings fold round rear spar hinges on centre-section and hull. One pair of parallel interplane struts on either side. Wing structure consists of two stainless steel spars, with tubular flanges and corrugated webs, and a subsidiary structure of spruce and three-ply. Plywood leading-edge and fabric covering. Inset ailerons on all four wings.
> HULL. Flat-sided single-step hull, of anodically-treated aluminium alloy. Normal Supermarine system of construction. Wing-tip floats of similar construction.
> TAIL UNIT. Monoplane type. Tailplane carried on top of fin built integral with hull. Tailplane and elevators built of steel spars and wooden ribs, with fabric covering. Rudder of wood, with fabric covering.
> UNDERCARRIAGE. Retractable type. Each unit consists of an oleo leg and radius-rod hinged to the side of the hull. In raised position, wheels are housed in recesses in underside of lower wings. Lifting gear partly compensated and operated manually by hydraulic mechanism. Wheel brakes

Another view of the prototype—with wheels now fully retracted.

A Walrus aboard ship, showing the simplified hull configuration.

> POWER PLANT. One Bristol 'Pegasus' II L2P nine-cylinder radial air-cooled engine, driving pusher airscrew. Monococque nacelle, with manhole to give access to back of engine. Two fuel tanks (each 75 gallons) in upper wings, with gravity feed to engine. Oil tank in nose of nacelle. Hand inertia starter.
> ACCOMMODATION. Bow cockpit, with Scarff ring and stowage for marine gear. Enclosed cockpit, with pilot on left side. Detachable controls to right seat. Between pilots' seats and front spar frame is navigator's compartment. Between spar frames wireless compartment. Aft of wings is aft-gunner's cockpit, with special gun mounting.
> DIMENSIONS, WEIGHTS AND PERFORMANCE. No data available.

The necessary move to metal hulls also led to the direct attachment of the lower wings to the hull; in this respect, the new design was similar to the Scapa and the Stranraer, although in this case there was no elegant lower centre section, but then, speed was not a requisite in a ship's aircraft where spotting would be one of its main functions. Also, the upper centre section had a less than tidy trailing edge, as it had to be cut back for clearance of the pusher propeller and also cut into for the folding-wing arrangement. However, the lower wing had lost the large cut-outs of earlier designs as a result of the neater device of hinging the inner portion of the wing behind the rear spar; the inner sections of the wing could thus be folded away in order to clear the hull sides when the wings were stowed.

The wings were supported by single bay struts similar to the recent Seamew and Scapa designs but the single-engine nacelle had the more traditional Supermarine position between the wings. This nacelle also contributed to the 'minimalist' appearance of the Seagull V by a visible offset of a few degrees to counteract the corkscrew pressure of the propeller slipstream on one side of the fin. The propeller was simply two two-bladers bolted together at right angles.

By June 1933, the prototype Seagull was complete and could be seen to be no beauty. Its functional appearance (to say the least), allied with its very traditional configuration, appeared to have won it no friends when seen by the Air Ministry's director of technical development. Those at Supermarine with long memories of the inability of the company to win orders for their naval amphibian fighter could hardly have been encouraged by his comment to Clifton: 'Very interesting; but of course we have no requirement for anything like this'.

Perhaps this reaction had some bearing on the test pilot's performance at the second Society of British Aircraft Constructors (SBAC) Show at Hendon. The *Aeroplane* nicely described the event:

> This boat made its maiden flight on 21 June, five days before its first public appearance, but Mr Summers proved its qualities by throwing it about in a most carefree manner. Of its performance little is known but there can be little doubt about its amiability and general handiness in the air and on the ground. One must be prepared to see all sorts of aeroplanes looping and rolling with abandon nowadays, but somehow one has, up to now, looked to the flying boat to preserve that Victorian dignity which one associates with crinolines, side whiskers, bell-bottom trousers and metal hulls. The Seagull V destroyed all one's illusions.

Henry Knowler, chief designer at Saunders-Roe, who was watching the display in the company of Mitchell, reported R.J.'s understandable surprise and anxiety at the low-level antics of the five-day old prototype. 'He looped the bloody thing,' R.J. kept repeating to everyone he met.

He had obviously not heard that a disgruntled American pilot had once done the same over Killingholme in a 95-foot Felixstowe flying boat, nor did he live to see Pickering's testing of production Walruses (the later British Seagull V), as described by Peter Weston, a Supermarine apprentice, in 1938:

> At the finish of the test he would fly very low over the river, by low I mean about 300 feet or so, in front of the flight shed and loop the Walrus to signal that it had passed the test; if not, he would just land and return up the slip and it would be worked upon. If you haven't seen a Walrus looped, you haven't lived.

It was at this time that R.J. consulted his doctor just before taking a holiday in August 1933. His moments of irascibility that were well known to his staff were, rightly, attributed to his make-up and to maintaining the high standards he set, but there was also another explanation that was not known to them. He had not been feeling well for some time and cancer of the bowel was diagnosed. An operation was performed almost immediately and Mitchell then went to Bournemouth to convalesce.

During the chief designer's absence from work, the Air Ministry had issued another specification that was unlikely to be matched by a simple development of the Scapa, now being prepared for service with the navy. This latest requirement, R.24/31, was for another general-purpose coastal patrol flying boat, of robust and simple construction with low maintenance costs, yet capable of carrying a 1,000-lb greater load for the same 1,000-mile range of the Scapa and being able to maintain height on one engine with 60 per cent of fuel on board. Thus, an enlarged and substantially altered version of the Scapa had to be projected and this was submitted, alongside one from Saunders-Roe, their A.27. Only the latter was accepted and, known as the London, was later ordered to replace the Southamptons and Scapas of Nos 201 and 202 Squadron respectively.

To further increase Supermarine's uncertainties, the Short Singapore III with a maximum speed of 145 mph was being ordered to replace other Scapas with Nos 204 and 240 Squadrons. However, the Short machines had about the same speed as that estimated for the new Supermarine aircraft and were powered by twice as many engines. The Singapore was, admittedly, larger than the Scapa and, therefore, needed more power for the same speed; also, the even larger Short Sarafand was only a few mph faster with six engines. Thus, given an economic situation in which orders for these larger flying boats were likely to be kept to the minimum, it seemed a distinct possibility that a performance from R.J.'s smaller, twin-engined R.24/31 project, if significantly better than that of the Saunders-Roe London, might still stand a chance of winning Air Ministry contracts, given the growing calls for British rearmament.

Another reason for anticipating orders for the proposed new design was not simply based on the good performance figures that the Scapa had returned but because R.J., now returned after his operation, had come to believe a significant improvement could be achieved by employing a thin wing—for other than Schneider trophy racers—and contrary to the generally perceived wisdom of the day.

The Stranraer

The engines chosen initially to pull the new machine's thinner aerofoil through the air and to give it the required one-engine performance required by the Air Ministry specification were 820-hp Bristol Pegasus IIIMs, providing a combined 590 hp more than the Kestrels of the Scapa. The two engines were to be mounted with the same thrust line as the Kestrels and in streamlined fairings but, being air-cooled radials, did not incur the extra weight and drag penalties of the Scapa radiators, which had been fixed to the sides of the engine nacelles; long-chord Townend drag-reducing rings surrounded the cylinder heads and their oil coolers formed part of the top centre-section leading edge. Against these improvements, however, there was the additional 12 per cent increase in wing area of the new machine; this extra drag and weight was added to by the two-bay strut arrangement required to support the extra 10 feet of wingspan that was needed to meet the new load-carrying requirements of the R.24/31 specification.

Extra depth to the hull allowed the top of the enclosed cockpit to form a continuous line with the single midships gunner's cockpit, which was now placed in the centre of the hull top. Now, for the first time, Supermarine had built a larger service aircraft which made it possible to install the second rear gunner, more sensibly, in a faired-in cockpit in the tail. This had been proposed for the unsuccessful Vickers/Southampton X prototype, with its wingspan of 79 feet, and so presented little difficulty for the new 85-footer.

This repositioning of a crew member and his armament, coupled with the shorter length of the radial engines in front of the centre of gravity resulted, from the outset, in the need for a sharper sweepback for the wings than was common in Mitchell designs. The leading edges of the fins were now straight, but they matched the swept-back wings and the somewhat angular appearance of the hull; they were, typically, a pleasing continuation of the line of the upswept tail pylon.

Supermarine Stranraer (1934)

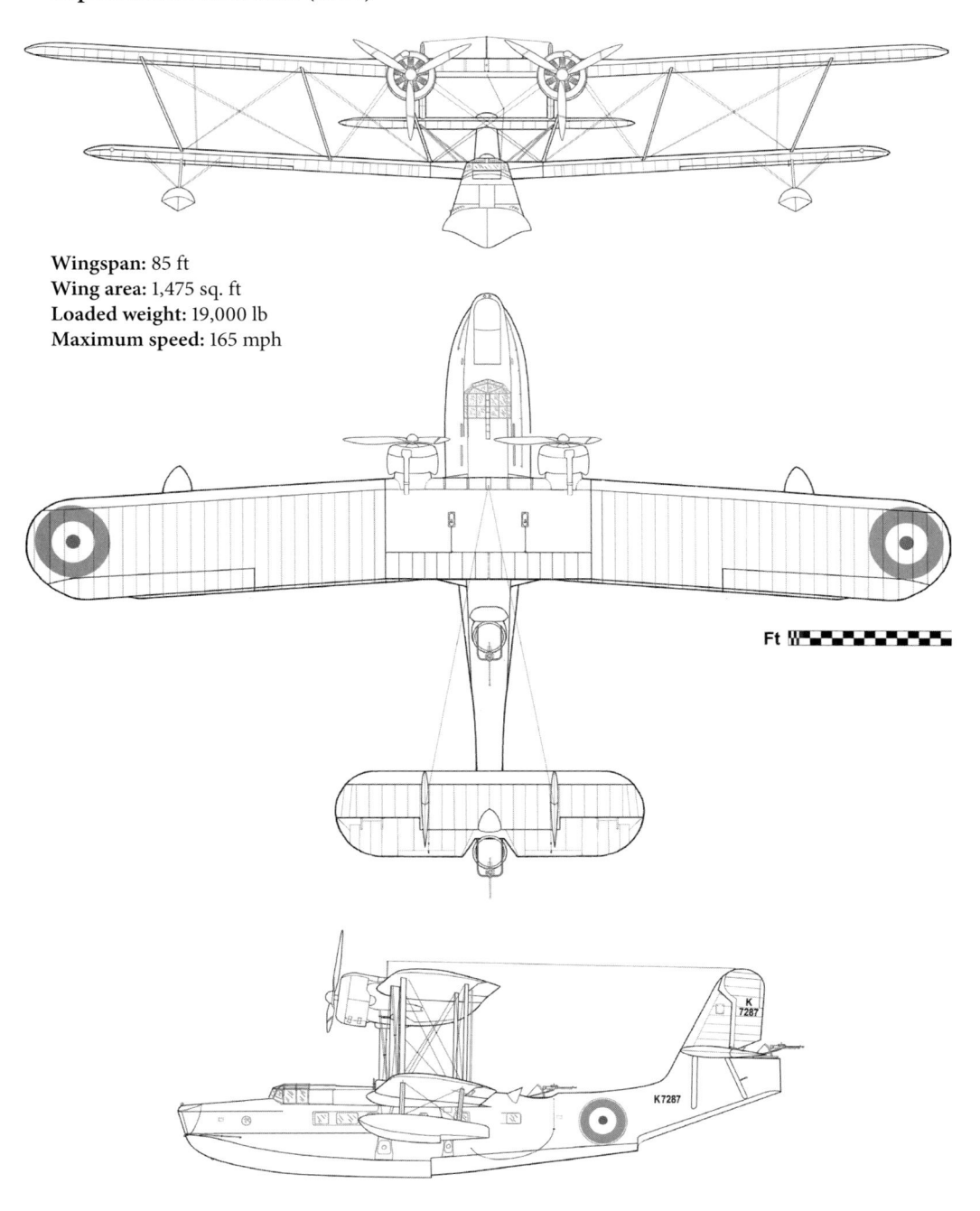

Wingspan: 85 ft
Wing area: 1,475 sq. ft
Loaded weight: 19,000 lb
Maximum speed: 165 mph

Another view of K3973, the prototype Stranraer.

The Stranraer prototype on its beaching gear.

> **The Supermarine Publicity Concentrated Particularly on the Metallurgy of the Stranraer**
> TYPE. Twin-engined long-distance reconnaissance and bombing flying boat.
>   WINGS. Unequal span biplane. Upper centre-section carried above hull by splayed-out struts supporting engine nacelles, lower ends of which are attached to lower wing-stubs. Each outer wing bay has two sets of slightly splayed-out parallel interplane struts. Wing structure of 'Alclad' with important fittings made of stainless steel, the whole being covered with fabric. Ailerons on all four wings.
>   HULL. Typical Supermarine two-step hull, made entirely of 'Alclad', except for the principal fittings, which are of stainless steel. Structure consists of transverse frames and internal longitudinals, the whole covered with smooth 'Alclad' plating.
>   TAIL UNIT. Monoplane type, with twin fins and rudders. 'Alclad' framework with fabric covering. All movable surfaces balanced. Trimming-tabs in rudders and elevators.
>   POWER PLANT. Two Bristol 'Pegasus X' nine-cylinder radial air-cooled engines, mounted in 'Alclad' monocoque nacelles immediately below the upper centre-section. Townend rings. Openings in nacelles give access to all parts of engine requiring periodical inspection. Large manholes give access to rear of engines. Two 'Alclad' fuel tanks (250 Imp. gallons = 1,136.7 litres each) in upper centre-section, with pump-assisted gravity feed. Jettison valves fitted. Two oil tanks (26 Imp. gallons = 118.2 litres each) form leading-edge of centre-section. Oil coolers incorporated with the tanks. Hand and electric starting.
>   ACCOMMODATION. In the bow is a bombing and gunnery station. A hinged watertight door is provided in the nose for bomb-sighting. The gun-mounting is arranged to slide aft, clear of the cockpit, for mooring operations. The marine equipment is stowed in a compartment adjacent to the cockpit. Behind this is the pilot's enclosed compartment, with side-by-side seating for two, with dual controls. Immediately aft of the pilot's cockpit and forward of the front spar frame is the accommodation for the navigator, and between the spar-frames is the wireless operator's and engineer's position. Aft of the wings is the midships gun position and a further gun position is located in the extreme tail. A lavatory is provided in the rear portion of the hull. For cruising, provision is made for sleeping quarters, food and water storage, cooking, etc. Special equipment includes a collapsible dinghy, engine-changing derrick, engine ladder, maintenance platform, spare airscrew, etc. Folding drogues are stowed aft of the midship gun position. Provision can be made for the transport of a torpedo or a spare engine on the lower centre-section.

The Air Ministry requirement for a flying boat 'of robust and simple construction with low maintenance costs' resulted in its stainless-steel fittings being given anodic treatment to inhibit corrosion and in the extensive use of Alclad, a new composite duralumin plate coated with pure aluminium on each side, again to counter corrosion. Its 'general purpose' character was evidenced by the fitting of carriers below the inner sections of the lower wings for up to four 250-lb bombs or extra fuel tanks; also, the flatter fuselage section between the lower wing roots was even more convenient than that of the Scapa for transporting supplies, such as a spare engine.

At the time that the designing and constructing of the new prototype were well under way, the Australian Seagull V order had not yet been concluded and the Scapa flying boat contract was still being fulfilled. Nevertheless, the new prototype, K3973, was ready to be test

K7287, the first production Stranraer.

flown by Summers on 27 July 1934 and delivered in very short time to MAEE, Felixstowe, for service assessment. The performance of the aircraft was such that an order for seventeen aircraft (K7287 to K7303) was placed with Supermarine by the following year; it was now named 'Stranraer'.

The standard service machine was fitted with the more powerful 920-hp Pegasus X engines and had a maximum speed of 165 mph, making it the fastest biplane flying boat to enter RAF service, yet it had a stalling speed of only 51 mph. Its maximum ceiling was 20,000 feet and it could climb to the first 10,000 feet at 1,000 feet per minute. As it was necessary to withhold these performance details because of the developing international situation, the company had to be content with the by-no-means despairing comment that the aircraft 'passed all its tests brilliantly' and went on to claim:

> The outstanding feature of this flying boat is that the performance obtained during a series of extended service trials, whether in respect of speed, climb, ceiling or take-off, is unequalled by any other British flying boat. All the specification requirements were exceeded by large margins.

It must have been gratifying, consequently, for Supermarine to see the Saunders-Roe London flying boat replaced by their new aircraft with Nos 201 and 240 Squadrons and to see another rival company's aircraft, the Singapore III, superseded by the Stranraer with No. 209 Squadron. Other machines replaced the Scapas with No. 228 Squadron, and so the total of Stranraers ordered from Supermarine, including the prototype, came to eighteen.

The Walrus

While the Stranraer was being built, the Seagull V was undergoing modifications and trials. The rigidity of the undercarriage and the lack of steering capacity on the ground had been noted and these deficiencies had had to be put right; by this time, it had been discovered that another make of aircraft had been allocated its N-1 number, so the prototype now became N-2 and went to the MAEE on 29 July, just over six weeks after its maiden flight.

Evaluation tests then lasted until the end of October, after which the Seagull went to the Royal Aircraft Establishment at Farnborough for the catapulting trials required by the Australian government, as described earlier. By this time, the empty weight of the aircraft had gone up to 5,016 lb, and R.J. ordered an aerodynamic clean-up as parasitic drag had appreciably reduced the performance of the heavier machine.

Despite the lengthy testing, no British order was expected; Webb, now in the business manager's department, relates how serving officers at the nearby flying-boat base at Calshot could also see no use for it: one of them asked, 'What are you people doing wasting our time on a machine like that—it will be shot out of the skies by the fighters?' So Webb pointed out that there would be no fighters with enough range to shoot anything down in mid-ocean and that, catapulted from a cruiser or battleship (and before the advent of naval radar), it would be the eyes of the fleet.

The prototype was then taken back to home waters for the continuation of trials at Sheerness and in the Solent until May when it was returned to Supermarine for the fitting of redesigned wing-tip floats for improved buoyancy and for an improved layout of the observer's compartment. Further fleet operation trials continued, including 'sea state' landings in 30-knot winds and 6-foot waves off the Kyles of Bute, and underway recovery onto a warship making up to 13 knots through rough water. As a result, their government finally ordered twenty-four production Seagull Vs (A2-1 to A2-24).

In these trials, the Royal Navy had been evaluating the aircraft for the Australians and thus it would appear that the future of R.J.'s design might rest solely with the Australian government's requirement. Yet movements were afoot nearer to home:

> To the late Rear Admiral Maitland W. S. Boucher, DSO, Royal Navy [at that time serving in the Naval Air Division], goes the initiative for the introduction to the Fleet Air Arm of this somewhat improbable looking, yet highly successful flying machine.
>
> He said to me one day in late 1933, 'I've just been to Supermarines. I've seen a small amphibian. It looks handy, tough and versatile … something the Navy needs. I want you to put it through its service trials. Off you go.' With a Supermarine Southampton flying boat course at Calshot and some tests at Felixstowe intervening, off I went to Woolston to collect Seagull V N-2 early in 1934.

Caspar John, son of the artist Augustus John and later admiral of the fleet, then narrated how he took the prototype to Gibraltar for rough weather take-offs and landings and for fleet cooperation exercises, after which it was described as 'the complete answer to our prayers'.

Thereafter, N-2 was purchased by the Air Ministry, renumbered K4797, and on New Year's Day, 1935, it was handed over to the Fleet Air Arm for a short series of official acceptance trials. As the prototype had first flown in June, 1933, it is clear that the Admiralty had needed some time to be convinced that operation from their capital ships would work smoothly on

The second production Seagull V on HMAS *Sidney*.

A2-2, being catapulted from HMAS *Sidney*.

the open sea. No doubt the Australian initiative helped to overcome any doubters and an initial British order was now placed on 18 May for twelve aircraft. The first machine of the 1934 Australian order flew on 25 June 1935, and after a further eleven had been completed, the Air Ministry took delivery of their own first batch. The rest of the Australian order was then completed, along with a second batch of eight for the Air Ministry, and the developing international situation then contributed to a much larger British order for twenty-eight more.

A name was now to be chosen for the British machine, unlike its Australian predecessor, which retained the Seagull V appellation. In the past, Supermarine amphibians had been favoured mainly with anodyne seabird names: Sea Eagle, Seagull, Sheldrake, Seamew, and so on, while the name Sea Lion was a nod in the direction of the engine used. It is thus an interesting comment on this latest amphibian's 'somewhat improbable' appearance that the far less glamorous name 'Walrus' was now chosen.

Nevertheless, it was not only the first British aircraft to be catapulted with a full military load but it was also the first British-designed military aircraft with a retracting undercarriage. (Thus it was that Admiral Sir Roger Backhouse received a ducking when the prototype Walrus, being used as his 'barge', was landed at sea with the undercarriage still down and turned turtle. After that, the Walrus was fitted with a horn to warn pilots of what was then a novel feature.) The original batches of forty-eight aircraft ordered for the navy was increased dramatically in 1936 with the requirement for another 168 machines. Despite its initially very doubtful future and its backward-looking appearance, the Walrus then became the last and the most successful of all Mitchell's reconnaissance amphibians and the navy's standard wartime fleet spotter.

Alex Henshaw, better known for high-speed flying and for testing the production Spitfires built at Castle Bromwich, has left the following (mainly) affectionate memory of flying the Walrus:

> Most pilots looked upon the Walrus as an ugly duckling and I may have thought the same. There was, however, something endearing about it. I am not sure if it was the incongruity amidst the sleek fighters and that I felt sorry for it, or that it operated in an environment which appealed to me and that when the going got rough it did its job like a professional. Certainly it was one of the noisiest, coldest and most uncomfortable machines I have ever flown and I never seemed to be able to climb in or out of the cramped cockpit without leaving a piece of skin behind. Strong it certainly was, and it could be landed on grass with the wheels up without much damage. I never tried this but George [Pickering], on our first flight together, said, 'The Walrus is not for the absent-minded.' He then went on to tell me of pilots who had landed it on water with the wheels down, or landed on the tarmac wheels up—both with spectacular results. I always felt you could land it on a postage stamp or in a puddle of water when you got used to its rather strange ungainly ways. At first it reminded me of a large iron dustbin filled with empty soup tins: in rough water it seemed to float in about the same manner and with as much noise. Operating in calm weather was pleasant, orthodox and easy. In really rough seas, however, I can only describe the experience as a wrestling match blindfolded. The noise of the waves pounding over the foredeck, the hull hammering until it must surely cave in and the surging wind and the water cascading over the cockpit was all rather frightening. As you peered through a constant stream of water over the screen and opened the throttle the first bout of wrestling was on. If a sudden huge wave hit you before you were ready, you throttled back, took another breath and waited your opportunity to plunge in again. The trick was to judge your wave roll accurately and to watch out for the heavy

foaming tops that sometimes accompanied them. Although I was nearly always cold when I started this exercise, by the time I had kicked the rudder hard to port and starboard a few dozen times, twisted, pushed and pulled the control column into my stomach, plunged through waves I felt sure would take us down to the ocean bed and then finally hung on to the prop. as I literally lifted this clattering tin can into the air with the tail still clipping those furious waves below, I was in a bath of perspiration.

As this book has included a number of accounts of flying Mitchell's aircraft, one cannot resist a contribution from Ann Welch, a wartime ferry pilot:

Further to my comment on sometimes being a bit vague as to what aircraft one was actually flying, because of the continuous chopping and changing of types—such as looking at the small print on the airspeed indicator to see if it was a Spitfire or a Seafire [i.e. calibrations in mph or knots]; one soon learnt little reminders, like if the rudder bar was under water you were in a Walrus. Not too much imagination is required here. Late one evening we had a Walrus for on-ferrying from Hamble to Lee. It had about 150 gallons of water sloshing about inside it, and the poor girl took off and sort of phugoided away into the dusk.

The eventual orders for the Walrus (746 Mk Is and IIs) do not conceal the poorer showing of Supermarine's other staple product, the large flying boat; the Air Yacht did not live up to its original expectations and the cancellation of the Giant was a major blow to R.J.'s likely chances of becoming a leader in large civil seaplane design. While the Stranraer had the best

A Walrus being retrieved by a warship. One crew member is outboard on the wing, presumably to assist prevention of the aircraft from swinging into the ship; the other is preparing to attach the hook from the ship's crane.

range and endurance performance of all British Coastal Command aircraft until the advent of the Short Sunderland, it was the last of the biplane type.

Lack of urgent Air Ministry thinking about the needs of naval flying is evidenced by the fact that Short's Sunderland flying boat, the Stranraer's successor, was the result of an order for a civil aircraft from Imperial Airways. The establishment in 1936 of Coastal Command might have been seen as a significant step in the right direction but, as the title of Andrew Hendrie's history of the service indicates, it was the 'Cinderella Service'—rearmament was concentrated upon developing aircraft for Bomber Command and for Fighter Command while naval thinking was mainly concerned with its warship fleet—although this, at least, benefited the Walrus orders.

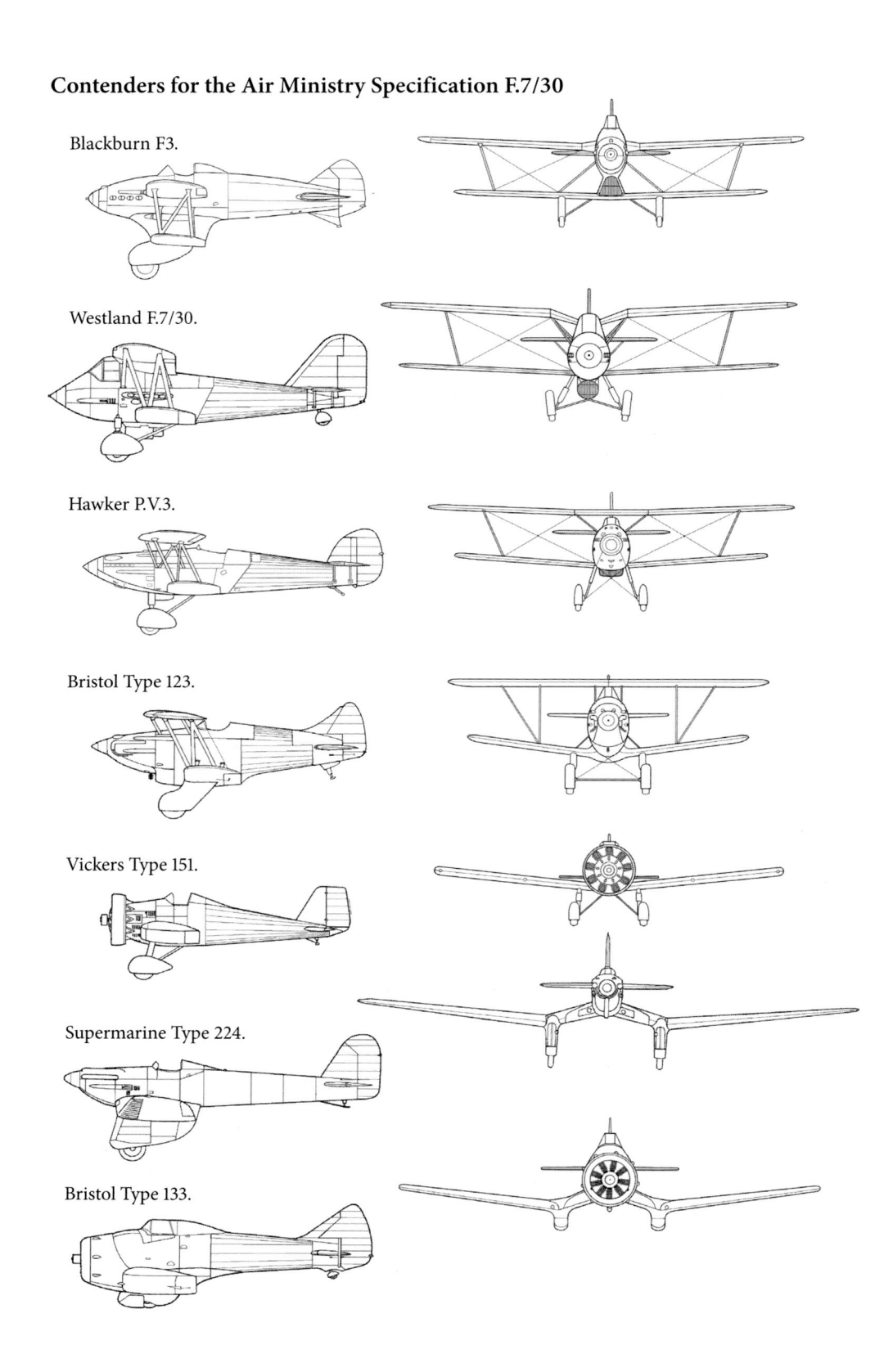

Contenders for the Air Ministry Specification F.7/30

Blackburn F3.

Westland F.7/30.

Hawker P.V.3.

Bristol Type 123.

Vickers Type 151.

Supermarine Type 224.

Bristol Type 133.

14

His First Spitfire
(1934)

Mitchell was uneasy about his first venture into military aircraft.

Alan Clifton

The comprehensive winning of the Schneider trophy in 1931 with a fly-over might have been regarded by other nations as opportunist, but it was the result of both Rolls-Royce and Supermarine being able to deliver, on the due date, new machinery that was perfectly reliable while being at the forefront of aviation technology. Indeed, of the twenty-one aircraft that completed their event, one-third were Supermarine machines. Only one—the S.4—failed.

Due to the pre-eminent position of the 'S' series in high-speed design and reliability in the preceding years, it was not surprising that Rolls-Royce and Supermarine were encouraged by the Air Ministry to proceed with the design of a land-based fighter—and as we shall see, it was fortunate for Britain's impending rearmament activity that Mitchell and Rolls-Royce had had the unimpeded freedom to experiment with high-speed design for the Schneider trophy competitions.

R.J.'s acquaintance with the land-based fighter concept, in fact, began almost at the same time as the last of his Schneider trophy racers, when the Air Ministry issued Specification F.7/30. This required a day and night fighter with a top speed of at least 195 mph at 15,000 feet, with the highest possible rate of climb, and armed with four machine guns—either all in the fuselage or two in the wings outside the propeller arc.

From this date, leading aircraft firms became engaged in a contract race to produce the required fighter, but none found it easy to meet the requirements; in fact, the first Supermarine fighter design turned out to be more significant for prompting the company to enter the bidding rather than for actually providing a successful formula for winning a contract. As we shall see, much of its underperformance was not entirely of R.J.'s making, but it, at least, gives the lie to the still popular assumption that the legendary Spitfire emerged directly from the Schneider trophy machines or rose as some single conceptual leap after its designer returned to work at the end of 1933—any culturally biased view of Mitchell as a doe-eyed consumptive, gaining inspiration by looking at seabirds could not be further from the truth.

In the first place, he had to turn his mind to a military aspect of aviation he had only briefly been engaged upon with the Sea King II fighter of 1921, and that aircraft was a flying boat, albeit a fast and manoeuvrable one. Additionally, armament on his slower reconnaissance flying boats was provided via gunners in cockpits not via guns that would now probably need to be buried in the wings. There exist some general arrangement drawings of a 'Proposed Single Seater Fleet Fighter' in response to Spec. 21/26 but nothing came of this and Alan Clifton, who joined Mitchell's design team in 1922, presumably had no knowledge of this project as he later recalled that R.J. was uneasy about 'his first venture into military aircraft', recognising that he was 'no expert in the field'. After all, his racing machines had virtually no forward view, were designed purely for short spells of very high speed, and required an extremely long landing and taking-off run, only feasible on large stretches of water. Thus, with typical pragmatism, R.J. asked 'Mutt' Summers, Vickers' chief test pilot, to arrange a visit to the Martlesham test centre to find out what the RAF pilots considered to be most important in a fighting machine.

The Extracts Below are from the Specification Generally Considered to be the Most Influential Requirement in the Years Before the Second World War

SPECIFICATION No F.7/30
1st October, 1931

1. General Requirements
(a) The aircraft is to fulfil the duties of 'Single Seater Fighter' for day and night flying. A satisfactory fighting view is essential and designers should consider the advantages offered in this respect by low wing monoplane or pusher*.
The main requirements for the aircraft are:
  (i) Highest possible rate of climb
  (ii) Highest possible speed at 15,000 feet
  (iii) Fighting view
  (iv) Manoeuvrability
  (iv) Capability of easy and rapid production in quantity
  (vi) Ease of maintenance ...
(b) The aircraft must have a good degree of positive stability about all axes in flight and trimming gear must be fitted so that the tail incidence can be adjusted in flight to ensure that the aircraft will fly horizontally at all speeds within the flying range, without requiring attention from the pilot ...
(d) The aircraft must have a high degree of manoeuvrability. It must answer all controls quickly and must not be tiring to fly. The control must be adequate to stop an incipient spin when the aircraft is stalled.
   An approved type of slot control, or other means which will ensure adequate lateral control and stability, at and below stalling speed, is to be embodied ...
2. Power Unit
(a) Any approved British engine may be used ...
(f) The airscrews preferably to be of metal construction, and is to be designed in accordance with the required performance of the aircraft as specified in paragraph 4 of this Specification ...

> 4. Contract Performance
> The performance of the aircraft, as ascertained during the official type trials when carrying the total load specified in paragraph 3 [660 lb] and with an airscrew satisfying the requirements of paragraph 2 shall be:
> Horizontal speed at 15,000 ft not less than 195 mph†
> Alighting speed not to exceed 60 mph
> Service ceiling not less than 28,000 ft
> Time to 15,000 ft not more than 8½ mins
> The specified alighting speed must not be exceeded, but may be obtained by variable camber or equivalent devices provided that control and manoeuvrability are not adversely affected …
> 7. Disposition of Crew. Armament and Equipment
> (a) the Pilot's view is to conform as closely as possible to that obtained in 'pusher' aircraft. The following requirements indicate the ideal view which is considered to be necessary, and the aircraft should be designed to conform as closely to them as possible in practice.
> The pilot must have a clear view forward and upward for formation work and manoeuvring, and particular care is needed to prevent his view of hostile aircraft being blanked out by top planes and centre sections …
> 8. Arrangements for alighting and taking off …
> (b) The aircraft is to be suitable for operation from small, rough-surfaced and enclosed aerodromes.
>
> [* The implied alternative to a 'pusher' would be the more conventional 'tractor' configuration. Presumably, the specification assumed that, with a pusher arrangement, the pilot would be well ahead of the wing(s) and propeller.]
> † Some accounts of F.7/30 erroneously give a specific speed to be aimed at.
> The full text can be found in Alfred Price, The Spitfire Story.]

The F.7/30 requirements that were issued for the replacement of the contemporary front-line fighter, the Bristol Bulldog, also represented something of a quantum shift for the more established landplane designers. However, while the Air Ministry strategists correctly forecast that the main role of a British fighter force would be to intercept enemy bombers at an engagement height of over 15,000 feet and at speeds of over 200 mph, their F.7/30 requirements for both a day and a night capability, with low landing speeds, were to conflict with these height and speed considerations. Had these issues been successfully addressed at this time, the panic to produce effective fighters in the late 1930s could very well have been avoided. In order to fully understand this situation and the significance of F.7/30, a brief survey of British fighters of the 1920s and 30s is first required.

Specification F.7/30 and Contemporary British Fighters

Following the end of the First World War, the huge surplus of military aircraft had done nothing to encourage the development of new British state-of-the-art fighters, especially as the general mood of the country was for putting militarism to the back of the mind. Britain's current pursuit of her interests and commitments in the empire and the Middle East led to new military actions, but the unopposed employment of existing First World War machines against tribal uprisings militated against the urgent development of new aircraft types. There was also the government's 'ten-year rule' assumption that no major war was likely to break out in the near future, thus giving time to speed up military development if and when danger was perceived.

In such a situation, it is not surprising that aircraft procurement procedures would be leisurely. After an Air Ministry specification for a new type was issued, a design competition between interested manufacturers began; this was followed by an order for a prototype for one or more of the most promising proposals, which could lead to an order for a whole squadron of the most successful type; after squadron evaluation, a larger order might then be forthcoming. C. G. Grey's estimation was that 'the time from issue of the specification till as many as three squadrons were equipped with the winning type was generally seven years'.

Meanwhile, the Air Ministry staff obviously had to justify their existence by requiring a modicum of new types, but the RAF had no recent combat experience for requiring anything more than straightforward improvements on existing models. Also, the aircraft firms were reluctant to spend much research and development time on bold innovations: as the Air Ministry usually ordered only one prototype at a time from a firm, there was a distinct company tendency to play safe, gradually developing well-tried designs that were less likely to fail than machines with too many innovative features.

Thus the British fighters of the next two decades continued a tradition of fixed-undercarriage, wire-braced biplanes with radial, air-cooled engines that, because of their lightness and compact shape, were, at least, exceptionally manoeuvrable. Yet the drag penalty of this type of machine, with its attendant struts and wires, began to have an increasingly inhibiting effect on performance: with aircraft of similar configurations, speed does not increase in direct proportion to an increase in power.

At least, R.J. had a sharpened awareness of the problem, thanks to his Schneider trophy activities, as he indicated in a newspaper article quoted earlier:

> If the S.5's fuselage had been increased by ten percent, the speed of the machine would have been about 7 mph less … a very small alteration to the form of one of these bodies may double its air resistance and thus greatly reduce speed.

The top speed improvement of the 1929 Bristol Bulldog (440 hp/175 mph) over that of the similarly configured 1918 Sopwith Snipe (230 hp/121 mph) was about 45 per cent for a power increase of 90 per cent. As the Bulldog's increase in speed—54 mph—was reached after eleven years of fighter development, then to replace this machine about three years later, with an F.7/30 design, a designer might be predicted to produce an aircraft with a top speed of around 190 mph, assuming a similarly configured machine. It can thus be seen that the F.7/30 requirement for a top speed of 'not less than 195 mph', while carrying twice the number of machine guns, whose extra weight would inhibit the projected airspeed, was a significant challenge (although tempered by realism) to an unadventurous aircraft industry.

The RAF had begun large-scale air exercises from 1927, and as a result, it was appreciated how the biplane formula also limited the fighter pilot's view of 'invading' bombers. In this respect, the F.7/30 requirement was quite specific: 'the pilot must have a clear view forward and upward' and 'particular care is needed to prevent his view of hostile aircraft being blanked out by top planes and centre sections'. One suspects, thereby, a strong hint that monoplane prototypes might be welcome but it is a reflection of the 1930 design scene that all except three of the eight aircraft presented for consideration were biplanes. Mitchell's entry was, unsurprisingly, a monoplane but the only aircraft that was submitted with a retracting undercarriage was not his.

By way of comparison, it should be noted that, also in 1930, the Boeing 200 had appeared—a cantilever monoplane (with semi-retractable undercarriage); it was followed a year later by the Lockheed Orion—also a cantilever monoplane with a fully retractable undercarriage. This situation had not gone unnoticed outside the Air Ministry as in the 1934 MacRobertson Trophy England–Australia Air Race, second and third places were taken by American airliners—the Douglas DC-2 and the Boeing 247-D. The *London Post* commented: 'It has been realised with astonishment that America now has, in hundreds, standard commercial aeroplanes with a higher top speed than the fastest aeroplane in regular service in any squadron in the whole of the Royal Air Force'.

With the performance requirements of F.7/30 given above, it is evident that the Air Ministry was feeling its way towards responding to the new standards—and fortunately so as by 1935, other leading aviation nations were beginning to produce or design monoplane fighters: the Russian Polikarpov II, the Japanese Mitsubishi A5M, the French Morane-Saulnier MS405, the American Curtiss P-36, and the Messerchmitt Bf 109. Some of these were to have retractable undercarriages and so it was a pity that F.7/30 did not contain a specific requirement in this respect.

Also, the Hawker Hornet, which had appeared in 1929, had already shown the advantage of a low-drag in-line power unit, but the new Air Ministry specification gave no specific steer towards any particular engine configuration—contrary to the impression given by the employment of the in-line Rolls-Royce Goshawk engine in five of the competing designs, including R.J.'s. It was thus unfortunate for those fitted with this more streamlined engine that its novel evaporative cooling system proved troublesome, to say the least.

The steam condensers of the Westland entry could not cope with varying flight and atmospheric conditions, and the Blackburn machine exceeded maximum temperatures within a few minutes. Additionally, the latter had ground-handling problems, caused by its high centre of gravity. Repeated taxiing tests caused cracks and dents in the metal fuselage skin to the extent that the Air Ministry withdrew its support for the project; it never flew, thus justifying the opinion of its test pilot, 'Dasher' Blake, that 'the little beast has no future'. The performance of the Westland entry had been diagnosed as 'woeful' as its top speed was disappointing and it took nearly nineteen minutes to reach 20,000 feet. Two other prototypes, also powered by the Goshawk engine (the Hawker P.V.3 and the Bristol Type 123) fared little better. Type 123 was laterally unstable and was withdrawn; the Hawker entry (essentially, a re-engined Fury) paid only a brief visit to Martlesham owing to its unsatisfactory cooling system (but at least, the company's decision to rethink its response led to the Battle of Britain Hurricane).

Two of the above four aircraft, the Blackburn and the Westland, appeared also to have been unduly influenced by the Ministry concern for a good pilot position and were also conventional biplanes with fixed undercarriages. Of the two monoplane rivals to R.J.'s Type 224 entry, the Vickers Type 151 Jockey was 10 mph slower, having begun some years earlier as a rival to the Hawker Fury for Spec. 20/27. It used the Wibault-Vickers corrugated metal skinned method that had too high a drag penalty at the speeds now being demanded. The intention to power the Jockey with a supercharged Mercury engine was never realised after the sole prototype was lost to a flat spin in June 1932.

Yet at least the other monoplane contender might very well have represented a more than adequate response to the new specification—Bristol decided to improve upon its Type 123 entry with its forward-looking cantilever monoplane, Type 133, the first prototype RAF fighter with retractable wheels and with its stressed-skin construction employing the recently invented Alclad sheeting. Its test pilot, Cyril Uwins, was very impressed by its performance and its top speed of 260 mph, but when the aircraft was almost ready to go for competitive tests at Martlesham Heath, it also entered into a flat spin that was irrecoverable and the test pilot had to abandon another one-and-only prototype.

Meanwhile, the F.7/30 competition had one late entry—the Gloster S.S.37—of a proven, fabric-covered, biplane configuration. Its obsolescent airframe included a fixed undercarriage and was powered by an air-cooled radial engine, both likely to induce significant drag penalties, yet it still attained the requirements of F.7/30. When fitted with a Bristol Mercury IX engine, developing 830 hp, it achieved with a top speed of 253 mph, and thereby went on to gain an Air Ministry contract for the aircraft that was to become known as the Gladiator.

The Type 224: The First Spitfire

By October 1931, when the F.7/30 specification had finally been officially issued, R.J. had already begun to design his response. As Type 224, it was to be an all-metal structure and to be powered by the Rolls-Royce Goshawk evaporatively-cooled engine. The Air Ministry's only requirement of the type of power plant for the new fighter projects was that it should be an 'approved British engine' and, along with Bristol (Type 123), Hawker, Westland, and Blackburn, Supermarine chose this engine, which was predicted to produce 660 hp (compared with the 450 hp of the Bristol Jupiter VII radial engine of the current fighter, the Bristol Bulldog). As the Goshawk was an in-line engine, its low drag profile might also be expected to contribute to an impressive performance, comparable to that which had been achieved by the Fairey Fox with the Curtiss D-12 engine.

Additionally, the new engine was designed to work with a new cooling system, the so-called evaporative method, which was expected to bring with it significant reductions in drag by not requiring conventional radiators to keep the engine coolant below boiling point. In the new system, the water in the engine was kept under pressure, allowing it to heat to 150 degrees Celsius, and then the superheated water was released as steam into a suitable container, with sides exposed to the airflow, where it would condense on cooling and be returned to the engine. The greater efficiency of this cooling method would require an aircraft to carry less water and could operate via, and under, the skin of the aircraft, resulting in a zero-drag cooling system.

R.J. might have been permitted a wry smile at a return to something akin to his early experience as an apprentice at the Fenton locomotive works and Supermarine would have felt particularly confident about this aspect of the F.7/30 project, as their Type 179 large passenger-carrying aircraft was to have employed steam-cooled engines, using the leading edge of the wing for the condensers—in its turn, a development of the low-drag surface radiators used by the S.5 and S.6. The company submission to the Air Ministry made specific reference to their experiments in connection with the earlier Type 179 wing structure and cooling system in order to strengthen their case. In the Type 224 proposal, however, the leading-edge

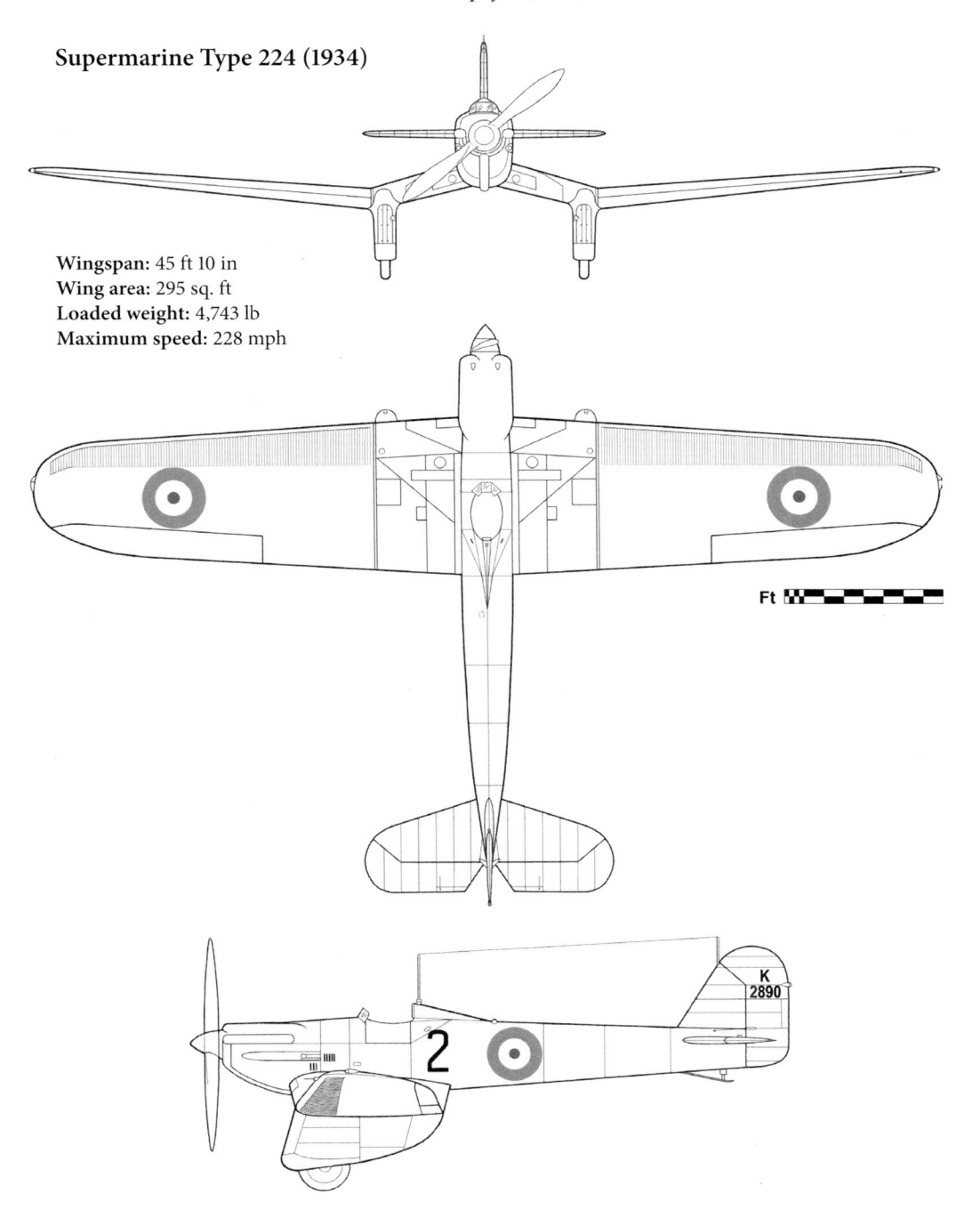

Supermarine Type 224 (1934)

Wingspan: 45 ft 10 in
Wing area: 295 sq. ft
Loaded weight: 4,743 lb
Maximum speed: 228 mph

condensers were to be made more thermally efficient for their size by having fore-and-aft corrugations exposed to the airflow, although this resulted in some drag penalty—an obvious design compromise, given the fact that Mitchell had not employed the radiator corrugations of the American Curtis CR-3 racers in 1927.

The Supermarine submission also made reference to information gained from the Vickers wind tunnel even though, by now, R.J. was becoming sceptical of the value of small-scale test models as predictors of how the full-scale versions would perform. Although straight wings and a retractable undercarriage had been considered, an eventual inverted gull-wing, fixed-undercarriage configuration was arrived at by comparative wind tunnel tests. As Supermarine had been devising undercarriages that could be raised ever since the Commercial Amphibian of 1920, it might have been expected that a fully retractable, drag-reducing arrangement would have been incorporated in their Type 224 entry of the early 1930s. However, the cranked wing that had been decided upon meant that a fixed undercarriage would be reasonably short and light and would be advantageous for certain other new considerations.

One advantage was that a gun could be housed in each undercarriage fairing without attempting to bury the armaments in the wings (whose leading edges were to be used for evaporative engine cooling) or without incurring any extra drag by more external wing mountings. In addition, tanks for the condensed water coolant could also be situated in the fairings and, in conjunction with the inverted gull-wing wing configuration, produced two very convenient low points where the coolant could collect.

Supermarine's submission also drew attention to how the cranked wing would allow a short, low drag undercarriage and, additionally, pointed out how it would provide a wide track for easy taxiing, would give a low centre of gravity, and present 'exceptional' visibility for the pilot 'for fighting, formation work, or landing' (*pace* F.7/30). The wind tunnel was additionally used on the wing configuration to find the best combination of anhedral for the inner wing

Type 224 under construction.

panels and dihedral for the outer ones, in order to achieve lateral stability; rather unusually, a full-scale mock-up of the open cockpit section was used to test the effect of variously shaped windscreens upon cockpit draught—evidence that R.J. was also paying due attention to the F.7/30 requirement that 'the cockpit is to be adequately screened from the wind' (although, by this time, the use of covered canopies was becoming more widespread as speeds increased).

With the fuselage generally, the company was on more familiar ground, using Schneider-type constructional techniques, including flush riveted panels, in order to provide 'a rigid mounting for the tail unit and for the prevention of tail flutter' (*pace* also the S.6B incident). Their submission to the Air Ministry additionally drew attention to the cantilever tail unit (which had been a feature of the S.5 and S.6 racers) and to the use of mass balances in the control surfaces (a neater solution than the *ad hoc* application of bob weights to the S.6 machines). By this time, flutter had become an increasing preoccupation as speeds had increased and Supermarine were obviously at pains to assure their potential customer that they also knew what they were doing in this respect.

In view of the ministry's slow landing speed requirement, R.J.'s Schneider experience was not much help as the wing loading of the S.6B had been 42 lb per sq. ft. A large air brake was now employed, and this could be lowered from the underside of the fuselage but the Air Ministry was, nevertheless, concerned that the projected wing loading of only 15 lb/sq. ft was too high; their requirement was not just for a day fighter but also for a night fighter that would have to land with very limited assistance from the ground. As a result, the wingspan was eventually fixed at a generous 45 feet 10 inches and, in combination with a fuselage about the same length as the 30-foot span S.6, Type 224 looked somewhat out of proportion. Appearance aside, the Air Ministry requirement that aircraft submitted must 'be suitable for operation from small, rough-surfaced and enclosed aerodromes' had an inhibiting effect upon designing a top-speed machine, especially where increased streamlining was leading to flatter and longer gliding approaches.

Disappointment

Before R.J.'s operation in 1933, Supermarine had received the official instructions to proceed with the Type 224 as detailed above and the aircraft was ready for testing early in 1934. On 19 February, 'Mutt' Summers took it up for its first flight, and it duly appeared at the RAF Display at Hendon on 30 June. However, its performance had proved a disappointment.

The much larger wingspan of Type 224 made for somewhat lethargic handling, although this fact might not have been too critical in view of the main ministry requirements of a fast zone defence aircraft—speed and climb. At that time, it was not expected that the enemy bombers would be protected by fighters as they were stationed too far away, but Mitchell's aircraft was still not competitive. The best performance figures of the Supermarine prototype were a maximum speed of 228 mph and a climb to 15,000 feet in nine and a half minutes; indeed, the Gauntlet II, which was about to enter squadron service, had a maximum speed of 230 mph and could climb to 20,000 feet in nine minutes.

However, the real difficulty was with the cooling system as a whole. It had been arranged for the water, which had condensed in the leading edge and had collected in the tanks in the undercarriage fairings, to be pumped up to a header tank behind the engine; however, at the

Type 224 with 'New Type' No. 2, Hendon, 1934.

low-pressure side of the pump, the water would often turn into steam again, creating vapour locks and causing the pump to cease to operate. (R.J.'s early apprenticeship to a locomotive manufacturer did not include high-altitude problems.)

These cooling difficulties occurred particularly during rapid climbs and this meant having to level off until the system was working normally again; one can appreciate why Mitchell was not happy with his prototype, designed for the fastest possible climb in order to intercept enemy bombers. Mansbridge said:

> We always knew when he got to 15,000 ft because a couple of bursts of steam would emerge from the wing tips. The climb was made at full power and relatively low airspeed, and when it reached that altitude the condenser was full and steam would start to trail back from the relief valves in the wing tips. Once that happened the pilot had to level off to give the engine time to cool down a little, before resuming the climb.

Jeffrey Quill, who had by now joined Vickers as a test pilot, has recorded how he did not exactly please the chief designer when he commented on these problems:

> The evaporative cooling system was a real pain in the backside, with the red [warning] lights flashing on all the time. I once made a jocular remark to Mitchell about the system. I said that with the red lights flashing on all over the place, one had to be a plumber to understand what was going on. [Characteristically] He didn't say anything, he just looked very sour. He was rather sensitive about the aeroplane and obviously I had trodden on his toes.

Junkers Ju 87 Stuka.

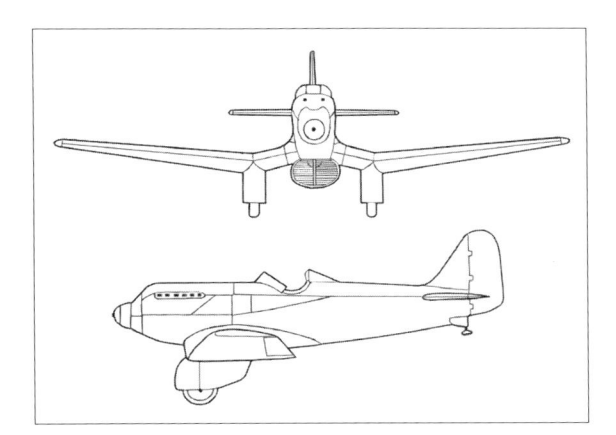

Kawasaki Ki-5.

On the other hand, it ought to be pointed out that from an aerodynamic point of view, R.J.'s approach to F.7/30 had stood out from all those of his rivals except the Bristol Type 133 and its distinctive configuration was by no means eccentric. Junkers were producing an aircraft that was similarly configured to the Type 224—the Ju 87 Stuka, which notably featured an inverted cranked wing and fixed undercarriage and, in the case of early models, the wheels were similarly encased.

It first flew after Type 224, on 17 September 1935, and a year later, Blohm und Voss produced their Ha 137, a fighter type which also had a cranked wing and a 'trousered' undercarriage. These features can also be seen in the Kawasaki Ki-5—not surprisingly as it came from the same designer. Like the Type 224, it first flew in February 1934, thus showing that there had been nothing derivative or eccentric about Mitchell's basic approach. The Japanese fighter had a span about 11 feet less and, with over 200 hp more, could reach 240 mph—about 10 mph better than the Supermarine prototype. Despite R.J.'s disappointment with his fighter, it can thus be seen that its top speed of 228 mph was actually quite creditable for its 600-hp engine power, despite the imposed penalty of the much larger wingspan.

Type 224 with tufts fixed to observe airflow with experimental wing fillets.

However, the performance was not promising enough and, almost immediately, R.J. made some alterations to improve the performance of Type 224; in particular (and in respect of the future Spitfire), he instigated experiments with various sorts of wing root fillets. None of the Schneider racing machines had had any such fairings, even though such an improvement had been evident as early as 1930 with the American Northrop Alpha. This aircraft was further developed two years later into a fast transport, the Northrop Gamma, which also featured a fully enclosed cockpit. Both these features, which were lacking in R.J.'s original 1931 design of Type 224, were also evident in two other designs for entry in the MacRobertson Trophy England–Australia race of 1934. The sleek winning de Haviland DH.88, was one and another was the Bellanca 'Irish Swoop', whose wing fillets Mitchell inspected closely when it was flown to Southampton for the fitting of its cowling.

More radical ideas for improving Type 224 were detailed on 26 July 1934 (*see* Supermarine Specification Number 425a—p. 315). These included a retractable undercarriage, the removal of the corrugations in the leading edge of the wing and elimination of its cranked configuration. The proposed modifications were expected to improve the maximum speed of Type 224 by 30 mph but, three years after the issue of the F.7/30 specification, it was understandable that the Air Ministry were now looking towards aircraft with which Type 224 would not be able to compete.

Thus it was that R.J.'s Type 224 design was to remain part of the history of unsuccessful experimental aircraft, despite the company's early hopes for it. It was to have been called 'Spitfire'—as Supermarine indicated via a brief announcement in 1934:

> The 'Spitfire' is a single-seat day and night fighter monoplane built to the Air Ministry specification. It is a low-wing cantilever monoplane with the inner sections sloping down to the undercarriage enclosures. It has a Rolls-Royce 'Goshawk' steam-cooled engine with condensers built into the wing surfaces. Armament consists of four machine guns. No further details are available for publication.

Thus, had Mitchell only lived to 1935, he would have been known for designing the first RAF standard coastal flying boat after the end of the First World War, the standard Second World War fleet spotter amphibian, and the Schneider trophy winning and World Air Speed breaking floatplanes between these two wars. The name Spitfire might very well have been allocated only to Type 224 and to a footnote in aviation history.

Supermarine Spitfire prototype (as at March 1936)

Wingspan: 36 ft 10 in
Wing area: 242 sq. ft
Loaded weight: 5,359 lb
Maximum speed: 367 mph (Mk.1)

15

The Real Spitfire Emerges
(1934–1936)

Mitchell took advantage of everything he could which would improve the aircraft.

Alan Clifton

The Japanese invasion of Manchuria in 1931 and the failure of the League of Nations to respond effectively led to the end of the 'ten-year' rule, and by 1933, Germany had begun to emerge as a distinct threat to peace. The reaction of the British Government, however, had not immediately given rise to vigorous fighter rearmament, reflecting the view expressed by the prime minister, Stanley Baldwin, that 'I think it is as well for the man in the street to realise that there is no power on earth that can save him from being bombed. Whatever people may tell him, the bomber will always get through. The only defence is offence'. However, it was only to be expected that the nation would be happier in the knowledge that there could be a defence against the bomber, and it was thus to the credit of Neville Chamberlain, then chancellor of the exchequer, that he was advocating the need for effective—that is, fighter—defences.

Personnel had also been changing in the Air Ministry. The chief of the air staff, Sir Hugh Trenchard, who had favoured the bomber approach, had retired; his successor, Sir John Salmond, was more sceptical of this approach. He and his deputy, Sir Charles Burnett, were actively supported by Hugh Dowding, who had joined the Air Staff in 1930 as air member for research and supply; as he later became the commanding officer of RAF Fighter Command, it is not surprising that he held the view that 'the best defence of the country is fear of the fighter'. In addition, from 1934, an Operational Requirements Committee was formed for the purpose of bringing together the views of the Air Staff, the revised Research and Development Committee, and the operational commands of the RAF.

Later pages will describe the way in which the eventual Spitfire came into being and the support that was required when doubts began to arise about its practical viability. It was thus fortunate for Mitchell that the Air Ministry and its departments were now populated with RAF officers who had by now come to the conclusion that fighter development had to be significantly stepped up. While their F.7/30 can be seen as the milestone specification which brought our seaplane designer into the reckoning, the future support of some Air Ministry officials in certain difficult days ahead for the Spitfire-to-be had much to do with the close and mutually respectful relations between Supermarine and the RAF that had been established since the Southampton and S.5/6 days. It might be noted that two particular ministry men were active at this time: Group Captain Cave-Brown-Cave, the director of technical development from 1931 to 1935, who had led the Far East Flight in one of Mitchell's very reliable Southamptons, and Major Buchanan who had been the Air Ministry representative at the 1925 Schneider Competition and vocal afterwards in his support for effective British participation in these events.

It would seem that R.J. was also reinvigorated. After his operation, he had been warned that the cancer might return in two or three years, with fatal consequences, and he had to contend with the potentially debilitating effects of the colostomy bag he had to wear for the rest of his life. Obviously, his tennis and cricketing days with the works teams were over but, typically, he designed an improved colostomy bag, continued to play golf, and also began to take up flying lessons. This defiance of his condition was even more marked at work, where his work rate became even greater than before (as described in Chapter 1).

Incidentally, this work rate was not driven by visiting Germany and seeing their aviation industry gearing up for war—as depicted in the wartime film, *The First of the Few*. It is fairly certain that he never visited that country, but he was obviously close enough to the aviation fraternity who were well aware of the situation—in particular, his friend Bulman, who had toured German aviation establishments twice and reported back his concerns over what he had learned. R.J. would most probably have been aware of Churchill's warnings about Germany's developing air power; armed with secret information, his message could hardly have been clearer when, on 28 November 1934, in the House of Commons, he asserted that, by the end of 1935, Germany's air forces would be at least as strong as Britain's, that by the end of 1936, they would be nearly 50 per cent stronger, and that 'Germany has between 200 and 300 machines with a speed of 220 to 230 mph, now carrying mails and passengers but convertible into long distance bombers in a few hours'.

While, in these circumstances, R.J.'s Type 224 'Spitfire' was failing to impress in the F.7/30 exercise, the other entry of a forward-looking design, the Bristol Type 133, might very well have attracted favourable Ministry support and brought a halt to the design work which was to result in the Spitfire.

This rival prototype was another monoplane and was also the first British fighter design with both retractable wheels and stressed-skin construction. It additionally had a relatively streamlined sliding cockpit canopy and the wing roots were aerodynamically faired into the fuselage with fillets (which R.J. had only experimented with during the latter days of Type 224). However, as mentioned previously, this one-and-only prototype crashed and so time and opportunity were available for R.J. to try to improve upon the Supermarine proposal—although, in view of the other disappointing responses to F.7/30, there was even talk in the Ministry of purchasing Poland's all-metal monoplane, the PZL P.24. This machine had attracted considerable interest at the 1934 Paris Air Show and was faster than any of the British prototypes, besides being equipped with the more impressive firepower of two cannons as well as two machine guns.

Also, in view of the greater urgency now being given to fighter development and even before trials of the F.7/30 prototypes had been concluded, Specification F.5/34 was issued, making very clear the unsatisfactory situation as regards the current fighter proposals and representing even more stringent demands on the aircraft designers. It was specified that 'the maximum speed at an altitude of 15,000 feet shall not be less than 275 mph' and 'the time taken to reach 20,000 feet is not to exceed 7½ minutes'. While an enclosed cockpit was only specified as 'admissible' and evaporative cooling was not ruled out, a retractable undercarriage, on the other hand, was 'required', as were eight machine guns.

This new specification had actually been drawn up to provide a replacement for the Hawker Fury, Britain's 'interceptor' fighter (designed for very rapid response once an intruder was detected) but it surely reflected the serious disappointment with the F.7/30 examples currently testing at Martlesham, which were to be 'zone' fighters, designed for patrolling specified areas, day or night. While there might still be a need for both types of fighter in the minds of the Air Ministry, R.J.'s 425a resubmission no longer looked very promising—a revised Type 224 was only predicted to have a top speed of 265 mph and no significant increase in the rate of climb—8¼ minutes to 15,000 ft. It is not surprising, therefore, that R.J. went back to the drawing board in earnest and to Type 300.

The Following Proposals for Considerable Modifications to Type 224 Show that Progress Towards the Eventual Spitfire Was by no Means Direct or Immediate

SUPERMARINE SPECIFICATION No.425a
26th July 1934.

Supermarine Day and Night Fighter to Air Ministry
Specification F.7/30
Proposed Modifications

Arrangement
It is proposed to modify the existing aeroplane by building a new pair of wings incorporating a retracting chassis. The new wings are of reduced area, the present inner sections of negative dihedral being dispensed with. Split trailing-edge flaps are provided to increase the lift and thus retain the same landing speed. The existing aircraft is shown on Drawing No 22400, Sheet 1 and the proposed arrangement on Drawing No 300000, Sheet 2*.

Construction
Construction is greatly simplified by making each wing in one piece. Other features which simplify construction are the substitution of lattice for a plate web, enabling the riveting of the nose to be more easily carried out, and the provision of smooth in place of corrugated covering.

Pilot's View
As a result of eliminating the downward-sloping wing roots, the view for a pilot is not quite so good close in to the fuselage, but is improved further out by the reduction of span.

Main Particulars and Dimensions

	Existing Machine	Modified Machine
Span	45 ft 10 ins	39 ft 4 ins
Length Overall	29 ft 10 ins	29 ft 4 ins
Wing Area (gross)	295 sq.ft	255 sq.ft
Wing Loading	16.8 lb/sq.ft	18.4 lb/sq.ft
Power Loading	8.25 lb/bhp	7.85 lb/bhp

Weight and Performance

It is estimated that the proposed modifications will result in a saving of 250 pounds weight, and an improvement in top speed of 30 mph, the climb remaining practically unaltered. The following features giving the comparisons between the existing and the modified aeroplanes, are estimated. Performance tests so far carried out are incomplete, but present indications are that the estimates are reasonably correct.

	Existing Machine	Modified Machine
Weight	4,950 pounds	4,700 pounds
Max. Speed	235 mph	265 mph
Climb to 15,000 ft	8 mins	8¼ mins

[*discussed on p. 318).]

Type 300: Towards the Real Spitfire

As the extensive modifications to Type 224 that had been proposed were deemed too late to qualify for re-entry into the F.7/30 exercise, the Air Ministry, in their concern to improve the fighter breed, encouraged Supermarine to proceed independently with a new design, Type 300. When a special specification, F.37/34, was drawn up (*see* p. 320) for this 'experimental fighter', it stated that 'the aircraft shall conform to all the requirements stated in Specification F.7/30', thus permitting Mitchell to continue developing his four-gun aircraft, but without other firms being invited to tender in the usual way. The word 'experimental' might be seen to reflect decreasing confidence in Supermarine among some Air Ministry officials after the experience of Type 224 or else to indicate that the successive Schneider trophy wins by the Rolls-Royce/Supermarine combination had not been forgotten by some of the new Air Ministry officials and was included to deflect criticism that the normal method of aircraft procurement was being bypassed.

Whatever the support there might be for a new Supermarine project, it was not lost on the company that Hawker had also been encouraged to substantially modify their F.7/30 entry with a rival 'experimental' offering. Only three months after the new Supermarine F.37/34 Specification had been formulated, the Air Ministry had additionally issued F.10/35, calling for an aircraft with a top speed of more than 310 mph at 15,000 feet and at least six, and preferably eight, guns to 'produce the maximum hitting power possible in the short time available for one attack'.

REQUIREMENTS FOR SINGLE-ENGINE SINGLE-SEATER DAY AND NIGHT FIGHTER (F.10/35)
April 1935

1. General

The Air Staff require a single-engine single-seater day and night fighter which can fulfil the following conditions:
(a) Have a speed in excess of the contemporary bomber of at least 40 mph at 15,000 ft.
(b) Have a number of forward firing machine guns that can produce the maximum hitting power possible in the short space of time available for one attack. To attain this object it is proposed to mount as many guns as possible and it is considered that eight guns should be provided.

The requirements are given in more detail below.

2. Performance
(a) Speed. the maximum possible and not less than 310 mph at 15,000 ft at maximum power with the highest possible speed between 5,000 and 15,000 ft.
(b) Climb. The best possible to 20,000 ft but secondary to speed and hitting power.
(c) Service Ceiling. Not less than 30,000 ft is desirable.
(d) Endurance. ¼ hour at maximum power at sea level plus 1 hour at maximum power at which engine can be run continuously at 15,000 ft. This should provide ½ hour at maximum power at which engine can be run continuously (for climb etc.), plus 1 hour at most economic speed at 15,000 ft (for patrol), plus ¼ hour at maximum power at 15,000 ft. (for attack). To allow for possible increase in engine power during the life of this aircraft, tankage is to be provided to cover ¼ hour at maximum power at sea level plus ¼ hours at maximum power at which engine can be run continuously at 15,000 ft.
(e) Take off and landing. The aircraft to be capable of taking off and landing over a 50 ft barrier in a distance of 500 yards.

3. Armament

Not less than 6 guns, but 8 guns are desirable. These should be located outside the airscrew disc …

5. View
(a) The upper hemisphere must be, so far as possible, unobstructed to the view of the pilot to facilitate search and attack. A good view for formation flying is required, both for formation leader and flank aircraft and for night landing …

6. Handling
(a) A high degree of manoeuvrability at high speeds is not required but good control at low speeds is essential
(b) A minimum alteration of tail trim with variations of throttle settings is required.
(c) The aircraft must be a steady firing platform …

[For the full text, again, *see* Alfred Price, *The Spitfire Story*; above are the paragraphs considered most relevant to the present narrative.]

Clearly, with these other specifications looming, R.J.'s determination to improve upon his fighter design would have to be redoubled and the most obvious change first embodied in Type 300 was a result of freedom from the previous Air Ministry insistence on a large wingspan; as stated in Specification 425a, the Type 224 span was to have been reduced by 6 feet 6 inches and the gross wing area by 40 sq. feet—resulting in a more pronounced taper to the Type 224 wing planform. While it was still to be designed around the troublesome evaporatively cooled Goshawk engine, it had now proposed an enclosed cockpit and a retractable undercarriage.

It is often claimed that the need to accommodate this last feature, plus the required armament buried in the wings, resulted in the famous Spitfire wing, but it should be noted that the early drawings for Type 300 show that the housing of these components had been allowed for without any need for a broad, elliptically shaped wing. Indeed, one might say that the projection, Sheet 2, referred to in the Supermarine Specification 425a as the 'proposed arrangement' of the Type 224 replacement, had not immediately shown any spectacular movement in the direction of the eventual Spitfire.

While it was proposed that the earlier fixed undercarriage and the cranked wing would now be removed, the tailplane and fin had a familiar look, the cockpit enclosure was straightforwardly placed over the retained pilot position, and two of the guns were still mounted in the fuselage and firing through the propeller arc. One might perhaps forgive the rather unadventurous character of this first revision, bearing in mind that its chief designer, however motivated to produce an effective fighter, must also have been very concerned about his health some time before and after his colostomy in the summer of 1933, besides having to recuperate from the operation and having to come to terms with its consequences. Nor would it ever be far from his private thoughts that the cancer might recur, fatally—given the limited state of medical knowledge or procedures at that time.

A further preoccupation was the design and production of the Stranraer, whose first flight had just taken place on 27 July 1934, but the later Sheet 11 drawing of September 1934 nevertheless shows a significant advance in thinking, with a proposed thinner wing and with all the required four guns situated in the wings, outboard of the propeller arc, and also now outboard of the wheel wells. As an adequate wing thickness had now to be retained

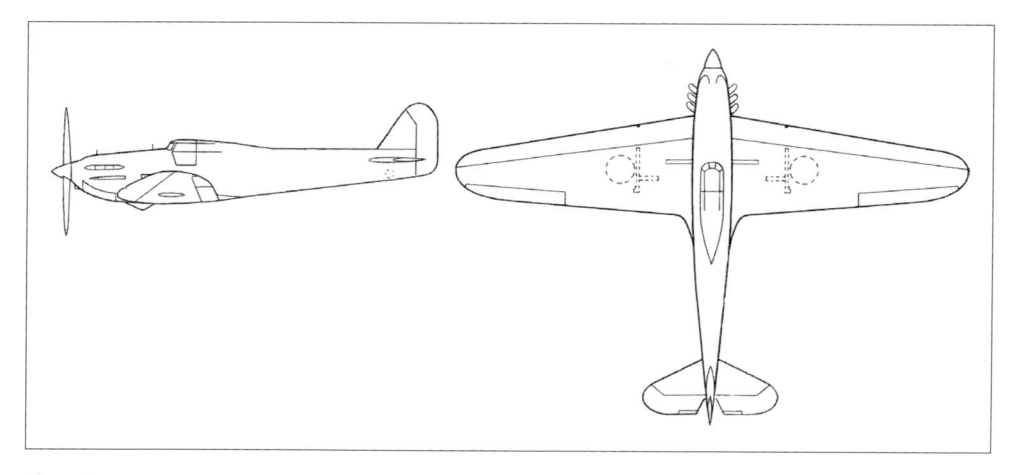

Sheet 2.

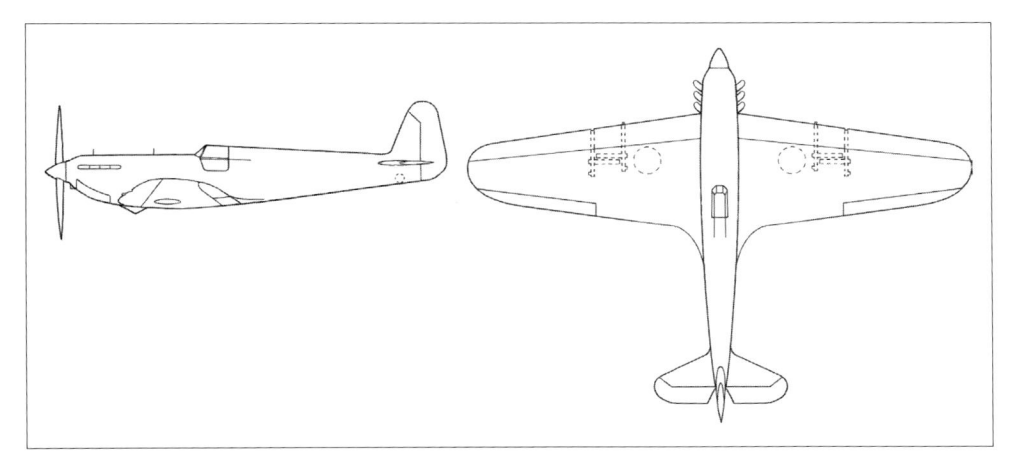

Sheet 11.

considerably further outboard to accommodate all the guns in their new position, a move to a broader (but not elliptical) shape can now be seen. There was now no room for fuel tanks in the wings and their relocation in the fuselage resulted in a more rearward placement of the cockpit position. This latter was now better integrated into a narrower fuselage shape, somewhat reminiscent of the S.5/6 configuration. With the broader wing, spanning 5 feet less, and the more 'purposeful-looking' fuselage, Sheet 11 shows a more determined movement towards the eventual Spitfire. It also increases our regard for R.J.'s fortitude in the face of his personal worries.

It was perhaps at this stage of thinking that the chairman, Robert McLean, claimed to have taken the decision that the Supermarine team should produce a 'real killer fighter' in advance of any Air Ministry specification and that 'in no circumstances would any technical member of the Air Ministry be consulted or allowed to interfere with the designer'. This statement was made some years later and would appear to have overdramatised the situation more than somewhat, but it did, at least, reflect the disappointment with Type 224, adversely affected as it was by Air Ministry requirements, and it was also an acknowledgement of R.J.'s redoubled thoughts for his new fighter.

In the whole saga of the Spitfire's eventual emergence, it ought also to be mentioned that McLean had not been entirely unwavering in this support for R.J.'s new proposals. The alternative machine, which might also have ended Mitchell's hopes of producing the 'killer fighter', was the parent company's Venom, designed to meet the more recent F.5/34 specification, and a development of the promising but ill-fated F.7/30 entry, the Type 151 Jockey, which had succumbed to a flat spin. Indeed, Beverley Shenstone, R.J.'s chief aerodynamicist, later said that, in his opinion, the Spitfire would not have been born 'if Mitchell had not been willing to stand up to McLean, particularly in the era when McLean clearly preferred the Venom concept to the Spitfire concept because it was cheaper and lighter'.

Like the future Spitfire, the Venom had a stressed-skin cantilever wing, retractable undercarriage, and a metal monocoque fuselage. In fact, when it did fly, three months after the Spitfire prototype, it attained a top speed only 37 mph lower than the Supermarine prototype, and with a less powerful, radial, engine. As a director and a member of the Vickers-Supermarine joint design committee that had been set up in 1931, R.J. would have been well aware that this machine might come to be ordered for squadron service rather than his Type 300. Yet as Sheet 11 had embodied a smoother contour to the fuselage and a thinner wing, R.J. would have been able to point out that his latest proposals would promise a higher speed: the Stranraer's first flight of that year had just proved the effectiveness of R.J.'s employing wings thinner than was normally expected. The thickness/chord ratio of his biplane reconnaissance flying boat was 9 per cent—even lower than the 9.8 per cent of his 1929 monoplane racing machine. There was also a more powerful inline engine from Rolls-Royce in the offing.

Whatever tensions there might have been in the Vickers boardroom, the prospect of a Vickers/Supermarine/Rolls-Royce/Mitchell new design had stirred up the new blood within the Air Ministry for events moved very quickly. On 1 December, £10,000 was allocated for Supermarine to build a prototype and, when a full design conference was called at the Air Ministry on the 5th of the same month, it was headed by Air Marshal Hugh Dowding. The whole contract situation regarding Type 300 was finally regularised in Mitchell's favour when Specification F.37/34 was officially signed on 3 January 1935. By this time, it was formally stated that 'the engine to be installed shall be the Rolls-Royce P.V. XII'.

SPECIFICATION F.37/34
3rd January 1935

Experimental High-Speed Single Seat Fighter
(Supermarine Aviation Works)

1. General
This specification is intended to cover the design and construction of an experimental high-speed single seat fighter substantially as described in the Supermarine Specification No 425a and drawing No 300000 Sheet 13, except that an improvement in the pilot's view is desirable. The aircraft shall conform to all the requirements stated in Specification F.7/30 and all corrigenda thereto, except as stated hereunder.

2. Power Unit
(a) The engine to be installed shall be the Rolls Royce P.V.XII ...
(d) A cooling system is to be of the evaporative cooling type using wing condensation in association with an auxiliary radiator ...

[For the full text, again, *see* Alfred Price, *The Spitfire Story*; above are the paragraphs considered most relevant to the present narrative.]

The Rolls-Royce PV-12 and the Skewed Elliptical Wing

Rolls-Royce had decided that their current engines were not capable of being developed into the sort of power plant needed for the next generation of military aircraft. Something between their 21-litre Kestrel and Goshawk engines and their 37-litre Schneider trophy 'R' engine was thought to be more appropriate and so the company had begun design work on a further 12-cylinder Vee engine, initially expected to deliver 1,000 hp. While this proposal was to become the famous Merlin, it was first known by its initials, which stood for 'private venture' and clearly indicated the engine company's own appreciation of the need for Britain to develop new aircraft. Once Supermarine learned that this new engine was coming up to expectations, it had been decided that their new fighter should be powered by it, and it was this decision that led to the famous elliptical wing of the eventual Spitfire.

In July 1934, the new Rolls-Royce engine had passed its 100-hour test and Supermarine's adoption of the PV-12 was seen to be significant:

> The larger PV-12 engine weighed about one-third more than the Goshawk. So, to compensate for the forward shift of the centre of gravity, the sweep-back of the leading edge of the wing [of the first Type 300 proposals] was reduced. From there it was a short step to embody the elliptical wing (Ackroyd).

This statement appears to state that the elliptical shape was arrived at after the decision to move the centre of lift forward, although it might be that the writer was assuming that the two decisions occurred virtually simultaneously; it also begs the interesting question as to who 'embodied' the elliptical wing.

At least, certain facts are well documented—the developed shape of the Spitfire wing and the various technical considerations involved are well covered by a member's summing up at the Southampton RAeS branch *Mitchell Memorial Symposium: 'Forty Years of the Spitfire'*:

> The main spar, previously swept back, was set normal to the fuselage axis. The span, wing area and thickness to chord ratio were reduced. The straight tapered wing gave place to the elliptical form of lower aspect ratio. Thus the greater and more constant chord in the inner regions of the wing gave more space for the landing flap, undercarriage, radiator and gun installation, and provided sufficient thickness for a good structure. For optimum bending strength the spar should have been placed at 30% chord but, as this would have encroached on installation space, the 25% chord position was a better choice. This must have been intentional as it was also the aerodynamic datum for the varying incidence which was progressively reduced from root to tip. From the unswept spar at 25% chord the familiar asymmetric ellipse naturally followed.

Nevertheless, it must be borne in mind that Mitchell had been involved with elliptical wings five years earlier, in January 1929, when the first sketches for the Giant had shown what appears to be a perfectly elliptical wing and tailplane. Before that, in 1925, he had also produced something approaching a skewed elliptical wing shape with his S.4 Schneider trophy floatplane; had he not been preoccupied with the novel wing radiator panels in his S.5 and S.6 machines (1927–1931), he might also have chosen an elliptical wing at that time—certainly, the wing tips featured an elliptical shaping and the tailplanes were almost perfectly elliptical.

Parallel chord, or even straight tapered wings, required less man-hours in the drawing office and in the works, but Mitchell, earlier than 1930, was familiar with the generous expenditure on Schneider trophy racers which produced more complex, efficient, but expensive wing planforms, including the intriguing elliptical-winged Piaggio P.7:

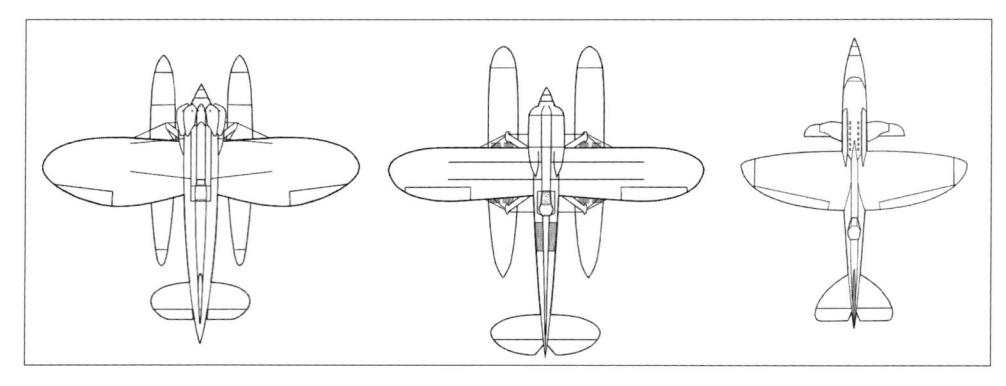

From left to right: Gloster IV, Short Crusader, and Piaggio P.7.

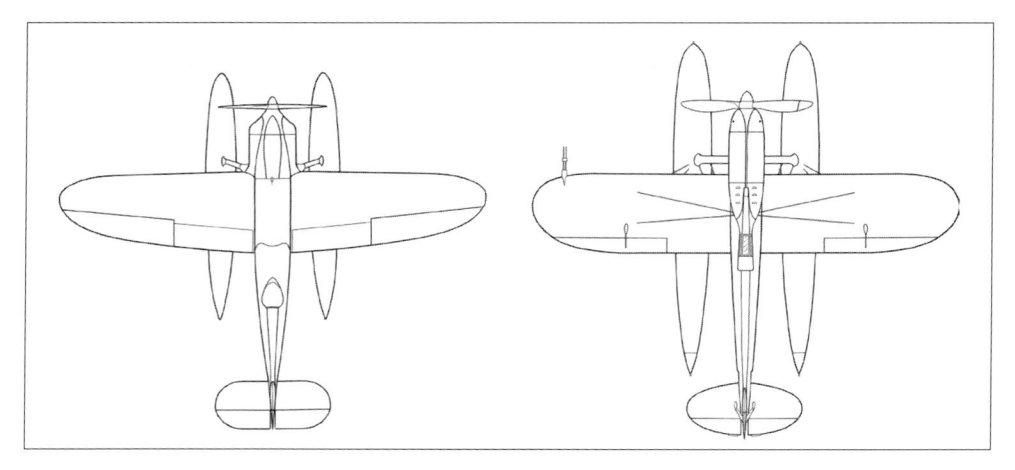

From left to right: S.4 and S.6.

So, before and when the decisions were taken about the wing shape for the future Spitfire, Mitchell's mind would have been perfectly tuned to the need to go for a more costly, unprecedentedly thin, complex, possibly elliptical wing, if that were needed.

The question remains as to whether the eventual shape of this wing was a result of Mitchell's previous designing or of current pressure from his design staff. His willingness, throughout his designing career, to listen to the views of his team and to modify his own ideas has been well documented, and we have seen a specific example from 1933 when Clifton recalled persuading his boss that the Seagull V/Walrus wheels should be fully retractable into the wing. However, when we come to the Spitfire design, there is no similar record of anyone saying directly: 'R.J., what about an elliptical wing?' or, more accurately, 'R.J., how about a skewed elliptical wing?' (i.e. skewed forward, leading to a leading edge ellipse shallower than the trailing edge ellipse).

The first result of employing the considerably heavier PV-12 was, surely, that the backward-sloping leading edge, as evident in Sheets 2 and 11, would have to be projected further forward. If such an arrangement placed the spar at right angles to the aircraft's fore-and-aft axis, it would reduce torsional loads and allow an improvement in weight/strength considerations; it also would have the added advantage of a more straightforward construction, particularly as the washout to be built into the wing (a retained feature of the Type 224 design) would be much more easily manufactured if the wing ribs were to be set at right angles to the main spar.

That these practical considerations might resolve specifically into an elliptical sort of shape would certainly have had the wholehearted approval of the aerodynamicist, Shenstone, who had said:

> The elliptical wing was decided upon quite early on. Aerodynamically it was the best for our purpose because the induced drag, that caused in producing lift, was lowest when this shape was used; the ellipse was an ideal shape, theoretically a perfection. There were other advantages, so far as we were concerned. To reduce drag we wanted the lowest possible wing thickness-to-chord ratio, consistent with the necessary strength. But near the root the wing had to be thick enough to accommodate the retracted undercarriage and the guns; so to achieve a good thickness-to-chord ratio we wanted the wing to have a wide chord near the root. A straight-tapered wing starts to reduce in chord from the moment it leaves the root; an elliptic wing, on the other hand, tapers only very slowly at first then progressively more rapidly towards the tip. Mitchell was an intensely practical man and he liked practical solutions to problems.

However, this does not help in discovering exactly when, and by whom, the elliptical character of the wing was arrived at; Shenstone merely says (not very helpfully!) that the elliptical shape of the Type 300 wing 'was decided upon quite early on' (note the passive tense).

Provenance

Opinion about the subsequent origin of this elliptical wing might be divided essentially between those who wish to see it as the latest example of the intuitive genius of R. J. Mitchell or those who regard it as the composite wisdom of his design team, led by the chief aerodynamicist, Beverley Shenstone. David Faddy, in an article on his father, Alfred Faddy, a senior member of R.J.'s team, suggests that it was Alfred who had persuaded Mitchell to take seriously a suggestion by Shenstone to adopt an elliptical approach to the shape of the Spitfire wing. Yet at the *Symposium* mentioned above, a member reported the following 'agnostic' assessment: 'During the discussion, Mr Clifton [by then chief designer at Supermarine and in the presence of Shenstone] was asked the origin of the elliptical wing form. No authoritative reason was put forward.'

As Sheet 11 (issued in September 1934) showed a broader wing already accepting all four guns and a retracting undercarriage, an even broader (and elliptical?) wing must have been specifically arrived at later when considering accommodating these guns in a wing that was to be even thinner. In this connection, Clifton's later comments on R.J.'s doubts about information derived from model testing are very relevant:

> I think that Mitchell decided to make the wing as thin as he did, and I wouldn't like to be positive about this, but my recollection was that it was against some advice from the National Physical Laboratory in that case where wind tunnel tests, I believe, showed that there was no advantage in going below a thickness chord ratio of 15%, whereas, the [Spitfire] wing was 13% at the root and 6% at the tip. I believe that this was due to the fact that at that time the question of the transition

from laminar to turbulent flow in relation to the difference between model and full scale wasn't understood and subsequently it was found that when you made proper allowance for that, there was an advantage, as the testing could be shown to prove, in going thinner.

At about that time, Hawkers had been advised by the National Physical Laboratory that their new wind tunnel results had shown no drag penalty with the thicker Hurricane wing; however, the laboratory scientists later found this advice to be incorrect—they attributed their earlier views to high wind tunnel turbulence, not appreciated at that time. Clifton here appears in no doubt that the decision to go thinner was R.J.'s and Harry Griffiths, writing retrospectively in 1992, put the matter thus:

> He had one strong fetish, namely that for maximum performance the frontal area of an aircraft had to be as small as possible, hence … his insistence on the thin wing on the Spitfire against the advice of the experts at Farnborough.

If lack of rigidity in the cantilever wing had been the reason for the crash of the S.4, R.J. would have to do better this time, and with a wing of unprecedentedly thin cross section. Credit for enabling this outcome should rightly go to R.J.'s design team, as Shenstone said: 'Joe Smith, in charge of structural design, deserves all credit for producing a wing that was both strong enough and stiff enough within the severe volumetric constraints.' Its chosen thickness/chord ratio of 13 per cent at the root and only 6 per cent near the tip, comparing very favourably with the Messerschmitt Bf 109 and the later Typhoon, which were 14 per cent and 9 per cent, and 14.5 per cent and 10 per cent, respectively, at the same positions.

The essence of the solution that Joe Smith proposed was a spring-leaf sort of arrangement of the main spar which contributed significantly to the strength/weight ratio of the thin wing and which, at the same time, was a novel approach to progressively lightening the spar as it approached the wing tip. The two booms that made up the spar began as a concentric arrangement of square tubes, each longer than the next as they increased in cross section, and with the outer laminations changing to channel section nearer the tip, with a final termination in angle section:

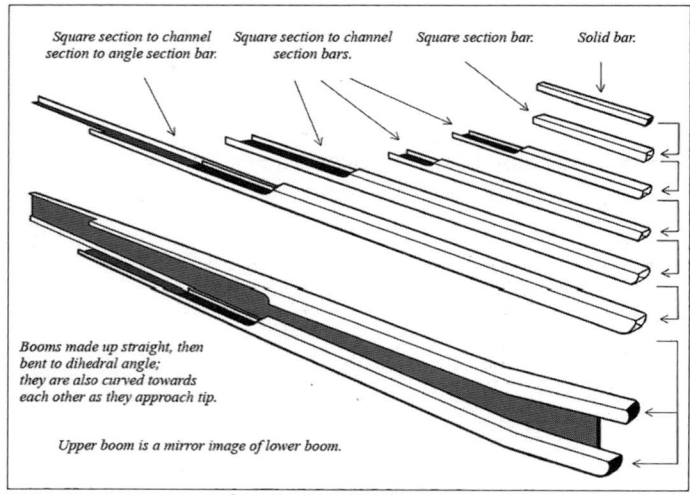

Schematic view of Spitfire wing spar.

One notices that Shenstone, while giving credit to Smith, had spoken of 'our purpose' and of 'we' wanting the thinnest wing possible, but before the aerodynamicist had joined Supermarine, R.J. had been given some earlier information by C. G. Grey:

> An interesting point about those Curtiss biplane racers [of 1923–26] was that the wings came almost to a knife-edge in front [producing an extremely low thickness/chord ratio of 6%]. One of the American technical people told me at the time that they had come to the conclusion that, at the speed which these machines reached, the air was compressed so much in the front of the leading edge that it paid to cut it. I passed the information on to R. J. Mitchell of Supermarine's who went into the idea quite deeply, and though he could not quite put a cutting edge on his Schneider Trophy monoplanes of 1927–9 and 1931, he used the thinnest possible wings, and won every time.

It would seem most likely, therefore, that after Mitchell had fully recovered from his operation and come to terms with its consequences, he became more than ever determined to produce once more the fastest aircraft in the world, and that an unprecedentedly thin wing, however difficult to design and produce, would have been the prime consideration passed down to his design staff.

Certainly, he was aiming at a much higher speed than that originally specified ('not less than 195 mph') because, at the time that the Spitfire prototype first flew, he was known to be initially very disappointed in its top speed. As mentioned earlier, the Air Ministry had issued their F.5/34 and F.10/35 specifications, calling for minimum speeds of 275 mph and 310 mph respectively and so R.J.'s prototype was only sent for service evaluation when it reached 349 mph.

While no effort had been spared to ensure that his wing would give Supermarine the edge over any possible rival, it would seem reasonable to assume that R.J. was also becoming concerned that his four-gun fighter would not provide the firepower that was now being looked for by the Air Ministry in these other two specifications—eight, or at least six, guns. Thus one speculates that the breadth of his wing as finally proposed had the added attraction of being capable of taking additional guns, especially as he would have known that the in-house rival, the Venom, was currently building with a specified armament of eight guns in response to F.5/34.

Speculation aside, the outcome is well established. Squadron Leader Ralph Sorley, at that time in charge of the operational requirements section at the Air Ministry, recalled that towards the end of April 1935, 'I was soon busy convincing Camm [Hurricane] and Mitchell of the vital necessity of building the eight-gun concept into their designs, and, from that moment, I had their willing and enthusiastic cooperation.' He reported back that 'Mitchell … is naturally desirous of bringing the aircraft now building into line with this specification [F.10/35]. He says he can include 4 additional guns without trouble or delay.'

Sorley also mentioned that at that visit to Supermarine, he saw the 'mock-up of a fighter which they are building to Specification F.37/34', and so it could very well be that R.J., a man of few words, did not mention that he had already anticipated such a request in the final version of the wing that was now being built, although, as reported by Price, the actual detail of the modifications would require some detailed working out:

Jack Davis, working in the Supermarine drawing office, was given the task of redesigning the wing to take the extra four guns. He recalled: 'It did not take me long to work out where the guns had to go. The rib positions had all been decided so it was just a question of fitting the guns in between them. But as one went further out the wing became thinner and the ammunition boxes had to be longer to accommodate the 300 rounds required for each gun. That meant the outer guns had to be quite a long way out. In fact, to get them into the wing, I had to design very shallow blisters to fit around them. The aerodynamics people did not like the idea but they accepted it: there was no alternative if we were to get the eight guns in without redesigning the entire wing.'

Leadership

It might seem purely academic to have asked what was the actual order in which the main factors governing the eventual broad elliptical shape of the Spitfire wing were arrived at. Discussions about centre of lift, area, span, thickness, or number of guns would have taken place formally and informally within R.J.'s design team but, without compelling evidence to the contrary, Mitchell's usual overall direction should surely not be in doubt.

Comments made by R.J.'s design colleagues are worth recalling. It was reported earlier that Mansbridge described how he dealt with overall design problems by calling in the leaders of the relevant groups and getting them arguing among themselves; it also might be remembered that Joe Smith had agreed that 'he was always ready to listen to and to consider another point of view, or to modify his ideas to meet any technical criticism which he thought justified'—but he also spoke of 'the many occasions when he arrived at the office with the complete solution of a particularly knotty problem which had baffled us all the night before'. In fact, Mansbridge expressed the suspicion that Mitchell's discussions were often a means of ensuring that he had not overlooked anything and that, otherwise, 'he had already reached a decision beforehand'.

It is thus noticeable how such memories of R.J.'s staff can be seen to express dependence on him for a lead or how he 'orchestrated' their advice but, many other times, he was shut away in his office, not welcoming visitors or requiring any discussion—as Smith said: 'he naturally objected to having his train of thought interrupted' and it is worth repeating his observation that 'he was an inveterate drawer on drawings, particularly general arrangements'.

There is no reason to suppose that Mitchell's methods were any different when the Type 300 general arrangement drawings were made, and indeed, there is evidence of 'the inveterate drawer on drawings': on Sheet 2, the planform of the Type 224 tailplane is clearly continued but its leading edge is more prominently swept back—in sympathy with the new wing shape; on Sheet 11, the tailplane outline is again modified—in relation to the larger wing root/fuselage fairing; and, with the Spitfire, the general approach of the horn-balanced tailplane is continued, but now, it is modified with a more elliptical character, resembling the new wing shape.

Similar alterations can be seen in earlier designs: the change from the Swan fin and rudder to their aesthetically pleasing single curve in keeping with the general configuration of the Southampton or the reversion to the rectangular fins of the 'boxy' Air Yacht. In this context, therefore, it is interesting to compare the more unified Spitfire planform with that of the prototype Heinkel He 112, mentioned in Chapter 1, whose tailplane is in no way matched to its elliptical wing shape.

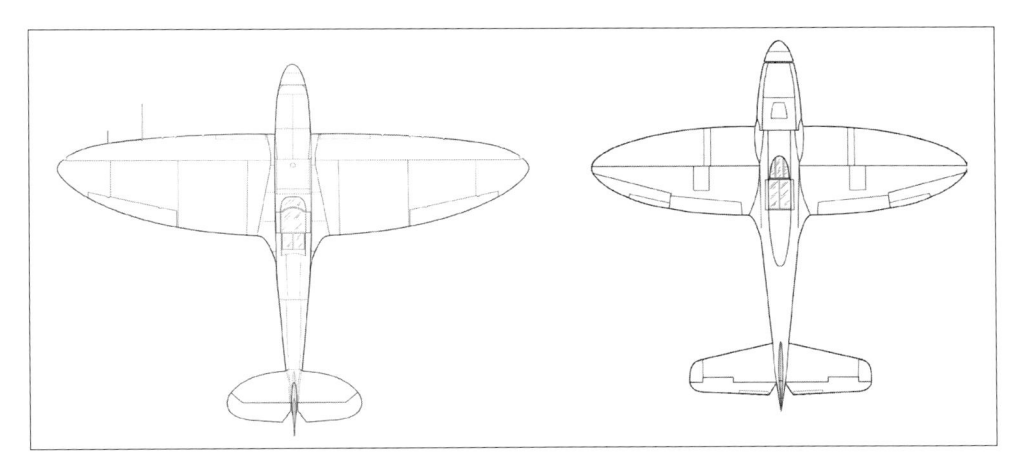

From left to right: Spitfire prototype and Heinkel He 112.

Considering the limited extent of precise aerodynamic data in those days, it is hard to resist the conclusion that all the Type 300 planforms, especially the final elliptical shape, came to his draughtsmen at least partially from R.J.'s initial sense of 'what looked right'—that the very practical considerations of span, depth, and width did not, strictly speaking, require the curvaceous planform of the elliptical wing for the speeds and altitudes contemplated in 1936 but, as Shenstone said, 'it looked nice'. Thus Joe Smith was surely referring in no small measure to aesthetic considerations when he described R.J. at the drawing board:

> He would modify the lines of an aircraft with the softest pencil he could find, and then remodify over the top with progressively thicker lines, until one would be faced with a new outline of lines about three sixteenths of an inch thick.

As mentioned, no 'eureka moment' has ever been claimed for the actual appearance of the Spitfire's distinctively modified elliptical wing shape but one suspects that intuition had quite a lot to do with the finally developed outcome. In an earlier chapter, it had already been said that R.J.'s expletives often belied the aesthetic considerations behind his designs: one cannot be sure of the context in which R.J. said to Shenstone that he did not 'give a bugger whether it's elliptical or not, so long as it covers the guns', but the remark at least complements his managing director's description of him (and his wing) as 'a mixture of dreams and common sense'.

Very substantial (and, it would appear, largely unsupported) claims have been made in a recent book for Shenstone's influence upon the shape of the Spitfire wing. One must certainly expect that the advice of this brilliant young man would not have been ignored and one might thus speculate that R.J. felt confident to pursue the very thin wing, against the technical advice mentioned above, having been supported by detailed and persuasive theoretical submissions from Shenstone.

The very final shape of the Spitfire wing, particularly the straightened leading-edge component, the shape of the trailing edge, and the aerofoil selection might indeed owe a great deal to the younger man's views, who had had direct experience of German and American aerodynamic theory, and it would fit with R.J.'s habitual management style that he recognised that the new man might well help Supermarine to progress beyond their already acknowledged lead in high-speed design. We should thus readily give the chief designer credit for not being so flushed by his earlier Schneider trophy successes that he did not seek out what the younger man, Shenstone, might contribute.

Nevertheless, in the following detail, quoted in Acroyd, R. J. Fenner of the design office unquestionably accepts that it was Mitchell who was the originator of the basic design concepts which governed the developing shape of its wing:

> When we came to the final version with the Merlin engine [i.e. the PV-12, January 1935] RJM had fixed the smaller wing area, lower thickness/chord ratio and the optimum single spar position and I had the job of producing the lay-out to meet his proposals.... The planform of the wing was, originally, perfectly elliptical and then bent forward along its major axis until the optimum spar position was straight. I remember clearly making several drawings of alternative planforms and RJM, in his rounds of the drawing boards, selecting the scheme as described except for minor changes to the wing tips.

In view of the earlier discussion of the possible sequence of design decisions, it is particularly interesting that Fenner recalls a 'perfectly elliptical' wing shape which was then projected forward; in the present context, it is significant that he gives R.J. the credit for establishing the essential wing parameters of area, thickness and spar position. And he also describes his making the rounds of the drawing office and supplying follow-up inputs, as has been his custom since 1920.

Later, we find a report of an exchange at the RAeS *Symposium*, which followed a question about the possible (but unlikely) influence of the Heinkel He 70 on the Spitfire wing shape:

> Clifton: I can't tell you what was in Mitchell's mind and it would be just speculation, but he was a very open-minded chap. He looked at everything and listened to everybody and made his mind up.... Mr Beverley Shenston is here and he might be able to tell you something about this because he was our Aerodynamicist at the time. He is in the audience ...
>
> Shenstone: I don't think R.J. cared at all what the Germans were doing but he did care about the shape of the wings, but he didn't copy anything. I think all of us at the time realised that the thinnest wing can often be the best, whereas earlier, people were afraid of very thin wings in case they broke off.

While thus deferring to Mitchell, Shenstone continued by making the point that it was the chief designer who 'took advantage of everything he could which would improve his aircraft' and Clifton echoed Shenstone: 'Mitchell was trying to put the thing together to get the maximum possible result'.

In a speech at Stoke-on-Trent in 1927, R.J. had said of his S.5: 'Everything done has some little object in view.... We concentrate on obtaining the very last mile of speed out of the machine.' At that time, performance was more important than avoiding any complexity of manufacture but the same can be seen to be true of his later fighter, even though intended for large scale production. The Spitfire tailplane is illustrative: Quill spoke of the 'unusually thin tailplane of 9% thickness/chord ratio', for which R.J. had to devise a special method for attaching the skin to the ribs as it had proved impossible to use conventional riveting methods.

One might add a further point—previous chapters have given instances where R.J. took gambles and so his concern to minimise frontal area was such that the cockpit design might hardly satisfy the Air Ministry's requirement that 'the pilot's view is to conform as closely as possible to that in "pusher" aircraft'. Indeed, his personal assistant, Harold Payn, sent him a memorandum in March 1935 that questioned the proposed pilot view in Type 300. (The more humpbacked appearance of the Hawker rival showed a more faithful attention to this F.7/30 guideline.) R.J.'s response to Payn illustrates his overriding concern for performance and the simplicity of genius:

> It is agreed that the view can be improved, but only with the sacrifice of performance by increasing the size of the body. In the design of this aircraft the performance has been considered of paramount importance, and various sacrifices of other requirements have been made to obtain this object. It is considered desirable not to depart from this policy. If at a later date it is thought necessary to improve the view at the nose, this is best done by merely raising the pilot, and can easily be done at a later date if considered necessary.

Thus it was surely R.J. who eventually decided to chance it by calling for complex and sophisticated flying surfaces, whatever production problems might meet opposition from the Air Ministry thereafter. The views of his design team he listened to and incorporated into his final structures, but what set him apart was his ability to grasp from the outset the essentials of a proposal and then, while accepting sensible modifications, to have them carried out—his secretary, Vera Cross, had observed that 'he was a great driving force and, once his mind was made up, he went all out to achieve his end'. Thus it should be noted that tenacity and, indeed, obstinacy were almost as important as intuition, aesthetics, and long practical experience, particularly where the forging of a revolutionary new wing was concerned.

So it might not be too fanciful for one to accept a description of Mitchell's Spitfire, especially its elliptical wing, as a 'visionary' piece of aerodynamic sculpturing or, in respect of the cliché that a camel was a horse designed by a committee, for one ultimately being disposed to see the elegant Spitfire as a thoroughbred 'sired' by the head trainer of the Supermarine racing stable.

K5054, the prototype Spitfire showing off its classic lines (as well at the arrangement of the retractable undercarriage and the access panels to the machine guns outboard of the wheels).

16

K5054

If the fighter boys could cope with a machine like this, it was going to be an ace.

H. J. Penrose

Perhaps the last words on the overall design of the fighter might be a quotation from the normally factual account in *Supermarine Aircraft since 1914*, which aptly, even poetically, sums up the design history of the Spitfire: 'It is a matter of history that there emerged from the ungainly angular Supermarine Type 224, like a butterfly from its chrysalis, one of the most beautiful aeroplanes ever designed'.

The prototype Spitfire, K5054, finally emerged from the works (if not from the chrysalis) at the beginning of February 1936. It had been built in a corner of the Woolston workshops behind a tarpaulin screen for security—in particular, because Lufthansa seaplane pilots used the Supermarine slipway for refuelling and for having their mail checked by British customs. Webb also remembered:

> The first engine run was carried out at night for security reasons, with the tail skid lashed to a holding-down ring on the quay normally used for tethering down flying boats. [The foreman, Gerry] Scrubby, recalling the occasion, said that the flames from the exhaust were spectacular, as was the noise.

The new machine now had a ducted under-wing radiator of the type recently devised by F. Meredith of the Royal Aircraft Establishment, Farnborough. This new radiator not only made little difference to the basic lines of the machine but actually used the heat exchange of the radiator to produce some thrust at high speed. The new system used ethylene glycol, which had a much higher boiling point than water, making the proposed evaporative cooling system redundant. Apart from the problems mentioned earlier, water loss during inverted flight in Type 224 had never been entirely solved and, with hindsight, one wonders about the wisdom of the Air Ministry's accepting the design of fighter prototypes having considerable areas of condenser exposed to enemy fire.

The tail configuration of the original design had also been altered. These changes to the tail were a consequence of wind tunnel testing for spinning characteristics. While R.J., by

K5054, before its first flight, unpainted and without wheel covers.

now, had sufficient faith in his experience and intuitions to dispense with most of such time-consuming testing, spin had been the cause of too many accidents in the history of aviation—recently, with the Bristol and Vickers low-wing fighter prototypes; perhaps the Vickers board had insisted that any possibly useful information should not be ignored. As a result of these tests, the fuselage length had been increased by 9 inches and the tailplane had been raised: an increase in height of 12 inches had been recommended but a compromise of 7 inches was reached with its designer. Perhaps aesthetics was a factor in the final outcome; certainly, this relatively small change and the lengthening of the fuselage had little effect upon the overall visual appeal of his general arrangement.

After initial engine runs had been completed, the airscrew and wings were removed and all the components taken by lorry to Eastleigh aerodrome for re-erection in the Supermarine hangar (where one of the S.6 aircraft, less engine, was still stored). The maiden flight of K5054 was on 5 March 1936, with the undercarriage locked down—according to Webb, there was some trouble with the 'up' locks. Jeffrey Quill reported:

> the aeroplane was airborne after a very short run and climbed away comfortably. Mutt [Summers] did not retract the undercarriage on this first flight—deliberately, of course—but cruised fairly gently around for some minutes, checked the lowering of the flaps and the slow flying and stalling characteristics, and then brought K5054 in to land. Although he had less room than he would probably have liked [because the wind was across the airfield], he put the aeroplane down on three points without much 'float', in which he was certainly aided by the fine-pitch setting of the propeller ... When Mutt shut down the engine and everybody crowded round the cockpit, with R. J. foremost, Mutt pulled off his helmet and said firmly, 'I don't want anything touched'.

Clifton's version of the event was recorded at the Symposium: 'After a typical sideslip landing he said "Don't alter anything"'.

As it was by no means unknown for prototypes to have to undergo costly modifications immediately after their flight characteristics were first discovered, this comment must have been a matter of great satisfaction for R.J. and his design team; it meant that there were no major mechanical, control or stability problems calling for urgent attention and that the aircraft could next be tested without any alterations.

The aircraft was flown again on March 10, with the undercarriage operating normally; after further test flights, Summers reported that 'the handling qualities of this machine are remarkably good'—the first of a procession of such comments from a multitude of Spitfire pilots. Incidentally, in the test pilot's log, the aircraft was described as the Spitfire II.

The prototype before the undercarriage bottom fairing doors were discarded.

The prototype, with flaps lowered (at original, shallower, angle).

By the end of March, Jeffrey Quill made his first two flights after a briefing from Summers:

> He stressed the need to make a careful approach during the landing. The flaps could be lowered only to 57 degrees on the prototype. With the wooden prop ticking over there was very little drag during the landing approach and she came in very flat. If one approached too fast, one could use up all of the airfield in no time at all.
>
> Then it was my turn, and off I went. Of course, at that time I had no idea of the eventual significance of the aeroplane. To me it was just the firm's latest product, running in competition with Hawkers and a highly important venture. And if I bent it I would probably be out on my neck!
>
> I made my first flight, getting the feel of the aircraft, and landed normally. Then I decided to taxi back to the take-off point and do another take-off. That second time did not feel quite right, and only when I was airborne did I realise I had left the flaps down. I retracted the flaps, flew around a bit, then went back and landed. Of course, everyone had noticed my faux pas. But Mitchell was very kind about it. He just grinned and said, 'Well, now we know she will take off with the flaps down'.

Quill also recollected the significantly higher cruising speed and the outstanding stall performance, which was another feature of the aircraft's characteristics so often commented upon later:

> The aircraft began to skip along as if on skates with the speed mounting up steadily and an immediate impression of effortless performance was accentuated by the low revs of the propeller at that low altitude. The aeroplane just seemed to chunter along at an outstandingly higher cruising speed than I had ever experienced before … it wasn't until after the touch-down that the mild buffeting associated with the stalling of the wing became apparent. 'Here,' I thought to myself, 'is a real lady.'

Nevertheless, it was discovered quite early that the rudder horn balance was too large and resulted in directional instability at high speed. More seriously, R.J. confessed to being very disappointed that the top speed was 'a lot slower than I had hoped for'. Quill stated: 'unless the Spitfire offered some very substantial speed advantage over the Hurricane, it was unlikely to be put into production. Thus the disappointing speed performance of our prototype at that early stage was something of a crisis and R.J. was a very worried man'—by this time, F.10/35 was calling for a maximum speed of 'not less than 310 mph at 15,000 ft'.

The prototype was taken into the works for modification and a special paint job; by 9 May 1936, it re-emerged with a revised rudder balance and a very smooth light blue-grey finish, thanks to automobile paint supplied by Rolls-Royce. In the afternoon, it was flown by Summers and Quill took R.J. up in the company's Miles Falcon, along with a photographer for *Flight* magazine, to observe his creation from the air. Despite the smooth new finish, the speed of K5054 was still less than hoped for as its top speed, now 335 mph, was still too close to that of the Hurricane, rumoured to be achieving 330 mph.

Notwithstanding the need to respond urgently to German rearmament, little information was still shared between aircraft constructors, as Shenstone described:

> There was absolutely zero intercommunication between designers in different firms, not even very much between Mitchell and the Pierson-Wallis combination at Vickers Weybridge. We never knew our opposite numbers in other firms. Gouge [Shorts] never discussed with Mitchell, nor Mitchell with Camm [Hawkers].

The Spitfire prototype, painted and with revised rudder.

Believed to have been taken during Mitchell's last airborne viewing of his fighter.

Thus it was that Mitchell first saw the prototype Hurricane only after its maiden flight, and Quill reported:

> He did not see it close up but only at a distance. He came back to Itchen very worried, and walked into the erection shed and looked at the first incomplete Spitfire. He said, 'Camm's got a tiny little machine. Ours looks far too big'.

In fact, the Hurricane had 3 feet more span than the Spitfire but one can understand R.J.'s sensitivity to size after the failure of the Type 224 fighter project; also the supposedly narrow margin between the top speeds of the two new aircraft might very well have resulted in a contract going exclusively to the company that had already supplied the RAF with the Hart, Demon, and Fury fighters and which had recently absorbed the company that had just supplied the latest front-line fighter, the Gladiator. Luckily, the fitting of a new propeller (Quill recalled the previous flight testing of 'some 15 to 20 different designs') on 15 May produced a dramatic increase to 349 mph.

This improvement is even more dramatic when viewed against the fighter development figures given earlier. The Gladiator's increase in power had produced a 12 per cent advance in speed whereas a similar increase in power eventually gave the Supermarine aircraft the very impressive leap of more than 100 mph:

Type	Power	Power Increase	Top Speed	Increase over previous type
Gladiator I	830 hp	30%	253 mph	12%
Spitfire 1	1079 hp	30%	362 mph	43%

It is worth noting that as early as 1933, the German *Reichluftministerium* had called for a new breed of fighter, capable of at least 250 mph at 19,690 feet, whereas the earlier British F.7/30 and F.37/34, which resulted in the eventual Spitfire, had only required a top speed of at least 195 mph at 15,000 feet. Thus the 362-mph figure finally achieved by the Spitfire prototype reveals how far in advance of initial requirements was Mitchell's fighter, thanks mainly to its thin, elliptical wing.

Penrose's memory of his first flight in the Spitfire admirably illustrates the startlingly new advance in its performance:

> So swiftly were we climbing that I was surprised to find the altimeter already showed 5,000 ft. I levelled off and felt the controls grow firmer with increasing speed; tried a gentle turn, and then steeper. Nothing in it! ... Suddenly a Gladiator appeared 1,000 ft above me, offering opportunity of a mock dog-fight with this latest contemporary biplane fighter of the RAF. I drew the stick back in manner long accustomed, unprepared for the lightness of response A vice clamped my temples, face and muscles sagged, and all was blackness. My pull on the stick relaxed instantly yet returning vision found the Spitfire poised almost vertically and the Gladiator 2,000 ft below. Ah! If the fighter boys could cope with a machine like this it was going to be an ace.

Naming the Spitfire

When did R. J. Mitchell say that 'Spitfire' was 'a bloody silly name' for his fighter? It is reported that Vickers' chairman had instructed W. B. Caddell, his personal assistant, to contact the Air Ministry, and on 20 December 1933 he requested that the name 'Spitfire' be reserved for Type 224—'our day and night fighter being built at Southampton'. H. Grinstead, for the Air Ministry, replied that 'Until accepted for supply to the RAF, it is requested that you will continue to refer to this aircraft by the title Supermarine F.7/30'. However, Price noted that in the logbook of test pilot George Pickering, the earlier Type 224 was known as the Spitfire some time before July 1935 and Summers had later referred to Type 300 as 'Spitfire II'; so Mitchell's reported remark might have been made about this time or earlier—when this fighter was so designated, in the brief announcement by Supermarine in 1934 (*see* p. 310).

Thereafter, the revised project, following the disappointment of Type 224, was usually referred to in the works as 'the fighter'—after all, his most beautiful racer was only ever known as the 'S.4'. Gordon Mitchell's book copies a Supermarine document of 29 February

1936, in which the soon-to-fly aircraft was referred to merely as the 'Modified Single-seater Fighter K5054' and he also noted that his father, on occasions, erroneously referred in his diary to his machine as F.37/35.

When Mitchell made the well-known comment, it was, perhaps, because he was voicing his general dislike of PR names for his machinery or because he did not want reminding of the disappointment of Type 224, his first Spitfire. Whatever the views of its designer, Supermarine publicity for 1936 read:

THE SUPERMARINE 'SPITFIRE I.'

The 'Spitfire' is a single-seat day and night fighter monoplane in which much of the pioneer work done by the Supermarine Company in the design and construction of high-speed seaplanes for the Schneider Trophy Contests has been incorporated. [The company is silent about Type 224.] The latest technique developed by the Company in flush-rivetted stressed-skin construction has been used, giving exceptional cleanliness and stiffness to wings and fuselage for a structure weight never before attained in this class of aircraft. The 'Spitfire' is fitted with a Rolls-Royce 'Merlin' engine, retractable undercarriage and split trailing-edge flaps. It is claimed to be the fastest military aeroplane in the world.

No further details of the machine are available for publication.

It is interesting to note how, for the very first time when announcing an entirely new Supermarine design, the aircraft had been designated a Mark One. It might be that the company was merely wanting to avoid any further references to Type 224, and thus to draw a line under that less than successful machine but, in view of the many variants to be produced in the next nine years, one likes to think that the designation was prophetic.

Vickers' suggested name for the new fighter was, in all probability, inspired by Ann McLean, the chairman's daughter, who had habitually been referred to as 'a right Spitfire'. As well as the comment: 'It's the sort of bloody silly name they would give it', Mitchell was also reported as saying that it could be called 'Spit-Blood' for all he cared. Mansbridge's daughter has recorded that 'Shrew', 'Shrike', and even 'Scarab' had also been considered, and it is a matter of speculation as to whether our chief designer would have preferred any of these. Yet by this time, the Aircraft Nomenclature Committee was no more and names were now selected, in discussion with the manufacturer, by the Air Member for Supply: for fighters, especially, words indicating speed and aggression were now being chosen (for example, 'Fury', 'Gladiator', 'Gauntlet', 'Whirlwind', and 'Hurricane') and 'Spitfire' more or less fell into this general category.

However, the Supermarine name also had a 'British' pedigree as well—it had been applied in previous times to cannons emitting fire, to angry cats, and to anyone displaying irascibility or a hot temper, especially women—as evidenced in 1762 when Lord Amherst is quoted as saying to his mistress: 'Not so fast, I beg of you, my dear little spitfire'; Shakespeare echoed the general sentiment when King Lear defies the elements: 'Rumble thy bellyful! Spit fire! spout rain!' In 1778, a Royal Navy vessel was named *Spitfire*—a euphemistic version of *Cacafuego*, a Spanish treasure galleon captured by Sir Francis Drake; thereafter, the navy used the name nine other times up to 1912. It was also to be seen in the titles of several pre-war films and thus at that time was not a relatively obscure word in the English vocabulary; yet by today, it would probably have become obsolete had it not been for the Battle of Britain, and many wartime actions thereafter, involving Mitchell's fighter.

RAF Acceptance

Now that the newly christened Spitfire had achieved its better performance figures, the company considered that it was safe to send their machine to the Aircraft and Armament Experimental Establishment at Martlesham Heath for evaluation and service testing (and, as it turned out, an inspection by King Edward VIII in R.J.'s presence).

It had been mentioned earlier how the prototype Walrus was landed in the sea with the undercarriage still down and turned turtle. Thus the Spitfire prototype had also been fitted with an audible warning to prevent similar sorts of accidents on land. This precautionary measure nearly failed to prevent costly delays to the testing programme when it was flown by an A&AEE pilot for the first time. Flt Lt (later Air Marshal Sir) Humphrey Edwardes-Jones' account to Price of this first flight also indicates something of the impact of Mitchell's new design upon the test centre:

> Usually the first flight of a new aircraft did not mean a thing at Martlesham, they were happening all the time. But on this occasion the buzz got around that the Spitfire was something special and everybody turned out to watch—I can remember seeing the cooks in their white hats lining the road. I took off, retracted the undercarriage and flew around for about 20 minutes. I found that she handled very well. Then I went back to the airfield.
>
> There was no air traffic control in those days and I had no radio. As I made my approach I could make out a Super Fury some way in front of me doing S turns to lose height before it landed. I thought it was going to get in my way but then I saw it swing out to one side and land, so I knew I was all right. But it had distracted my attention at a very important time. As I was coming in to land I had a funny feeling that something was wrong. Then it suddenly occurred to me: I had forgotten to lower the undercarriage! The klaxon horn, which had come on when I throttled back with the wheels still up, was barely audible with the hood open and the engine running. I lowered the undercarriage and it came down and locked with a reassuring 'clunk'. Then I continued down and landed. Afterwards people said to me, 'You've got a nerve, leaving it so late before you put the wheels down'. But I just grinned and shrugged my shoulders. In the months that followed I would go quite cold just thinking about it: supposing I had landed the first Spitfire wheels-up! I kept the story to myself for many years afterwards.

With hindsight, one wonders how a crash-landing of the one-and-only, unknown, and untried prototype would have affected its future. The concern of Edwardes-Jones and of Quill before him that they should not damage a new prototype was foremost a matter of the professional test pilot's self-esteem, but the usual Air Ministry practice of only ordering one prototype from a firm was hardly wise—for the German contract exercise, equivalent to the British F.7/30 one, four firms had each been authorised to build three prototypes.

Events in Europe were certainly beginning to create an even more urgent need to find an adequate replacement for the standard RAF fighters of the day and thus it was that this first flight at the A&AEE took place as soon as the aircraft had been delivered by Summers and he had briefed the service pilot. The usual preliminaries were dispensed with and Edwardes-Jones was instructed to telephone the Air Ministry as soon as he got down:

Normally, a firm's test pilot would bring in a prototype aircraft for service testing, and it would be first handed over to the boffins who would weigh it very carefully and check that the structure was as it should be. It was usually about 10 days before it came out for its first flight with us. With the Spitfire prototype, it was quite different. Mutt Summers brought her over, and orders came from the Air Ministry that I was to fly the aircraft that same day and report my impressions …

Once down I rang the number at the Air Ministry I had been given, as ordered. The officer at the other end [Air Vice Marshal Wilfred Freeman, Air Member for Research and Development] said … 'All I want to know is whether you think the young pilot officers and others we are getting in the Air Force will be able to cope with the aircraft'. I took a deep breath—I was supposed to be the expert, having jolly nearly landed with the undercarriage up! Then I realised that it was just a silly mistake on my part and I told him that if there were proper indications of the undercarriage position in the cockpit, there should be no difficulty. On the strength of that brief conversation the Air Ministry signed a contract for the first 310 Spitfires on 3 June, eight days later.

This extract provides an interesting subtext to the conclusion of the Martlesham report on the handling trials of K5054:

The aeroplane is simple and easy to fly and has no vices. All controls are entirely satisfactory for this type and no modification to them is required, except that the elevator control might be improved by reducing the gear ratio between the control column and elevator. The controls are well harmonised and appear to give an excellent compromise between manoeuvrability and steadiness for shooting. Take-off and landing are straightforward and easy.

The aeroplane has rather a flat glide, even when the undercarriage and flaps are down and has a considerable float if the approach is made a little too fast. This defect could be remedied by fitting higher drag flaps.

In general the handling of this aeroplane is such that it can be flown by the average fully trained service fighter pilot, but there can be no doubt that it would be improved by having flaps giving a higher drag.

The extract also reflects the report by McKinstry that the aforementioned Sorley had recommended the aircraft was ordered 'without the delay of prototype testing' and also the view of the director of technical development, Commodore R. H. Verney, that as soon as the aircraft had flown, that 'would be the time for a production gamble'. Thus after K5054 had been sent to Martlesham in mid-May, the order for 310 Spitfires was placed in June—well before the formal A&AEE report, dated 'September 1936', had been received.

At last, the Air Ministry could now envisage the possibility of supplying their fighter squadrons with a trendsetting new fighter capable of a maximum speed some 120 mph faster than its namesake two years earlier. However, the acquisition of this new aircraft was not to be without its production problems, compared with the Mark I Hawker Hurricane rival, with its traditional structure and fabric covering, which went into mass production with little difficulty.

The very large initial order for the Spitfire had gone to a company with a limited number of skilled metalworkers and so required different sections of the machine, which embodied advanced structural features, to be subcontracted out to inexperienced firms. The problems were, not surprisingly, most acute in respect of the wings although an incident recalled by Quill revealed the general novelty of the advanced technology of the design. After an unscheduled stop at an RAF airfield in December 1936, Quill was disconcerted to hear tapping noises coming from the rear of the aircraft:

> I checked I had shut everything down but the tapping sound continued. Then as I climbed out I saw the reason. Several mechanics were standing around the rear fuselage, tapping it with their knuckles disbelievingly. 'My God,' one of them exclaimed, it's made of tin!'

So, after the lean years of the early 1930s, Supermarine was suddenly engulfed with work. The Australian order for twenty-four Seagull Vs in 1934 had been followed by one for seventeen Stranraers and an initial order for forty-eight Walruses in 1935. The unprecedentedly huge requirement of 310 Spitfires in June of the next year was followed a month later with an order for 168 more Walruses. A visibly impressive demonstration of the previous five years' work by R.J. and his design team was at the Vickers Press Day on 18 June, also in 1936, when the parent company's prototype Wellington and Wellesley bomber on display were joined by Mitchell's Scapa, his Stranraer, his Walrus, and the Spitfire prototype. As Alan Clifton later commented, not entirely jokingly: 'One might have thought the Air Power of Britain was intended to consist almost entirely of Supermarine aircraft'.

It is a nice illustration of R.J.'s especial pride in his fighter creation that, when an oil leak was discovered, he took the view of the test pilot that there was enough oil in the machine to risk a five-minute flight for the large gathering of pressmen. Against the (predictable) advice of the expert from Rolls-Royce, he had agonised for a few minutes and then said to Quill, 'Get in and fly it'. Almost as soon as the pilot was airborne, an oil pipe finally fractured and only some very skilful airmanship saved the one

R.J.'s last car: a 1936 3.5-litre Bentley.

and only prototype once again. Of all the aircraft at the press day, R.J. followed the progress of the Spitfire the most closely, as Quill recalled: 'Whenever the new fighter was flying Mitchell would get into his car and drive from his office to Eastleigh. As I was coming in to land I would see his yellow Rolls-Royce parked and know he was there. He kept a close eye on things.' On 7 April 1936, he also visited Martlesham with his son, Gordon, to see how the service testing of the Spitfire was going.

On the 27th of the same month, it was put on public display at the Royal Air Force Pageant at Hendon and two days later was demonstrated at the SBAC display at Hatfield with slow and fast runs, finished off by a display of fast aerobatics. The *Flight* report on this last display aptly summed up the sort of machine that Mitchell had been working towards:

> It is claimed—and the claim seems indisputable—that the Spitfire is the fastest military aeroplane in the world. It is surprisingly small and light for a machine of its calibre (the structural weight is said to have been brought down to a level never before attained in the single-seat fighter class), and its speed and manoeuvrability are something to marvel at.

By the time that the Martlesham verdict on the Spitfire prototype was received in September 1936, the company was fully engaged in preparations for the production of the Mark I version for squadron service. Meanwhile, the prototype Spitfire was extensively modified to bring it in line with the forthcoming production standard, including the fitting of the 1,030-hp Merlin II, and its high gloss finish was replaced by the Air Ministry dark green and earth day fighter camouflage scheme.

The prototype, having fulfilled its main purpose, was then subject to a series of accidents: a wheels-up landing on 22 March 1938 due to g-induced oil pressure failure; brake failure on 15 May, resulting in its nose in gorse beyond the airfield; and a ground loop nine days later, due to the undercarriage collapsing. It was finally written off after a fatal landing accident on 4 September, just one day after England had declared war with Germany.

The first production Mark I Spitfire made its maiden flight on 14 May 1938, and the first service machine, K9789, was delivered to No. 19 Squadron on 4 August that year—just over a year after Reginald Mitchell had died.

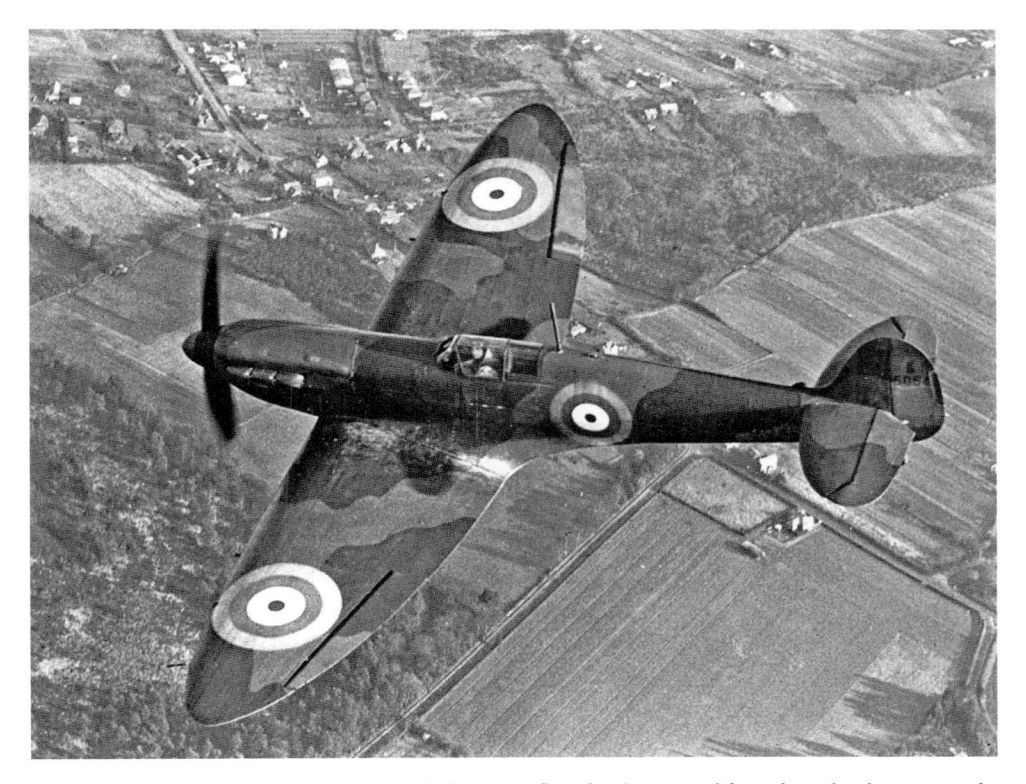

Jeffrey Quill flying the Spitfire prototype with the camouflage finish it carried for its later development trials.

R. J. Mitchell with his son, Gordon, 1937.

17

'It's All Over'

O you who turn the wheel and look to windward,
Consider Phlebas, who was once handsome and tall as you.

T. S. Eliot

It is clear that Mitchell was quietly very proud of his new fighter to the extent, as we have seen, of risking a flight with suspect oil pressure at the Vickers Press Day on 18 June 1936. Previously he had shown the still secret prototype to his son, Gordon, and on 7 April 1936, he also visited Martlesham with him to see how the service testing of the Spitfire was going. Unlike his son, he was not interested in photography, but he posed for a photograph, standing beside his new creation, and then he returned the compliment:

Once it was seen that the performance of the Spitfire had outstripped other rival efforts to supply Britain with the much-needed high-performance fighter, it was again clear to his employers and to the Air Ministry that he was living up to his public image of 1931 as 'the brilliant young designer of the Supermarine Aviation Works'. It might thus be reasonably wondered if all this public success, usually not expected by a mere designer, had altered him, but we do have the evidence of Webb that 'It was quite obvious that R.J.'s successes had not gone to his head and never did. Later, if he saw me footslogging over to Southampton and he was making his stately way in his Rolls-Royce, he would not be above offering me a lift'. As late as 1937, the *Bournemouth Daily Echo* wrote that he 'combined with his great gifts a very charming personality and a modesty concerning his achievements which almost amounted to humility.'

This last comment, like many accounts of the man, was written after Mitchell's death and its writer was unlikely to dwell on his irascible moments or his failure to produce successful machines for the long-distance requirements of Imperial Airways. Perhaps the earlier disappointments of his Seamew, the Air Yacht, and the Southampton X (all using air-cooled radial engines) had led him to offer later designs employing water-cooled engines when customers were showing a preference for the alternative type. In this respect at least, it might be held that his successes had led him to place too much confidence in his own judgement—it is certainly a fact that from 1927 to 1933, there had been no significant orders for Supermarine's staple productions of maritime aircraft.

Gordon Mitchell, photographed by his father in front of the prototype Spitfire, 1937.

Nevertheless, Mitchell could have felt justly proud of his contribution to the success of his company. The number of his aircraft, including prototypes and uncompleted airframes, ordered or built from 1920 to 1933 was 155—an average of about one per month; this figure for these essentially hand-built machines rose to an average of about twelve per month in each of his last three years at Woolston. The increasing prosperity of his firm, backed by the parent company, Vickers, is plain to see from a comparison of the two photographs on the opposite page of the Supermarine works, taken twenty years apart.

Unfortunately for Supermarine, Imperial Airways announced in 1935 the placing of their order with Shorts for twenty-eight flying boats in the long-distance category. Perhaps it was significant that Supermarine's current poor showing coincided with the time that Mitchell had consulted his doctor just before taking a holiday in August 1933 and, after his operation for bowel cancer, being told that there was always the possibility that the cancer would return, with fatal consequences.

It is perhaps unnecessary to dwell on the embarrassments of having to live permanently with the colostomy bag that was necessary, and it is not surprising that such a very private man would keep his medical condition private. Clifton who, after all, had been in the design office since 1923 and, by now, was a senior colleague, only knew of the nature and the effect of Mitchell's operation when told by the son many years later.

There would also be the continual awareness that the next four years would determine his fate. The son mentioned a brief entry in his father's diary on 31 December 1935, which seemed to indicate a worry that symptoms might have recurred and there was another on 15 August 1936, where he noted '3 years on'. Unhappily, he now began to experience bouts of pain, and in February of the following year, he was back in hospital, where tests revealed that the cancer had returned and that he had probably three or four months left to live.

The Supermarine works, 1920.

The Supermarine works, 1940.

Whatever they might have come to suspect, his colleagues now had to recognise the seriousness of his condition. He continued to go in to work whenever possible but his deterioration was such that on 29 April 1937, he went, in a specially chartered flight, with his wife and a nurse to the Cancer Clinic in Vienna. Unhappily, they returned on 25 May with no further hope in sight.

Harry Griffiths described how he received the news of Mitchell's death, seventeen days later:

On the day he died Arthur [Black] and I were standing at the bench discussing a problem when Vera Cross, R.J.'s faithful secretary over many years, came in and just said, 'It's all over.' Arthur looked at me and shook his head, then he turned away and was silent for a long time.

Significantly, this recollection prompted Griffiths' memory of Mitchell's relationship with his colleagues:

> At the annual dinner that year we stood in silence in his memory and then drank a toast: 'To a very gallant gentleman.'
>
> The Christmas before his untimely death he arrived late for the annual design staff dinner, and in spite of a place having been kept for him at the head of the table he insisted on sitting at the other end with us lads and sharing a joke and some wine.

Thus, as he invariably gave full credit to his design staff in his speeches, it was fitting that he requested they be given first place in his funeral cortège.

It is noteworthy too that, on his death, he was still well remembered outside Southampton and Stoke-on-Trent, six years after his last Schneider trophy win (and a decade before the full significance of his Spitfire design was widely appreciated). His death was reported in the local *Southern Daily Echo* and as far away as *The Scotsman* that he had been suffering for a long time from 'an internal illness', and a contemporary scrapbook of agency-supplied cuttings, kindly made available by the Mitchell family, instances reports or obituaries in seven local papers (Southampton, Isle of Wight, Bournemouth, Portsmouth, Stoke-on-Trent, Newcastle, and Stafford) and in twenty-eight national publications (for example, the *Times*, *Daily Telegraph*, *Daily Express*, *Daily Mail*, *Morning Post*, *Daily Mirror*, *News of the World*, *Tatler*, *Illustrated London News*, and *Evening Standard*), in twenty-four other local papers (including Birmingham, Manchester, Edinburgh, Liverpool, Leeds, Sheffield, Glasgow, Bristol, Aberdeen, Greenock, Cardiff, Grimsby, Yeovil, Dundee, and Belfast), and in six New York publications. Only the editor of *The Aeroplane*, the forthright C. G. Grey, mentioned the word 'cancer'.

The Southern Daily Echo for Friday, 11 June 1937, printed a long obituary recording the whole of his design career, and gave the time of death on that day as 2 p.m.:

> FOUR YEARS' FIGHT AGAINST ILLNESS
>
> Last April Mr Mitchell flew from Southampton to Vienna in a specially chartered plane to see a specialist. He remained in a sanatorium there for a month but the illness was too far advanced for the treatment to be effective. So he flew home again and resigned himself to awaiting the end, which, he knew, was very near.
>
> Last Sunday [6 June] he sat in his garden for the last time

On the 15th of the month, the paper recorded the funeral service, which was attended by a very large congregation:

> The Supermarine Aviation Works (Vickers), Ltd of which Mr Mitchell was a director and chief designer, was represented not only by directors and heads of department, but over 100 members of the staff followed the cortège from Mr Mitchell's residence, in Russell Place, to Highfield Church where the funeral service was held....
>
> Evidence of the great sympathy evoked by Mr Mitchell's death was shown not only by the large attendance at the church, but by the great number of wreaths sent. Four motor-cars laden with flowers preceded the hearse.

Late photograph of R. J. Mitchell in his garden with his Irish setter, Bondy.

At the funeral were representatives of Southampton Corporation, the Air Council, three Air Ministry departments, the RAF Establishment, Farnborough, RAF Coastal Command, the RAF Station Calshot, the Royal Aeronautical Society, the Royal Aero Club, and included the following, familiar to these pages: Wing Commander W. T. Cave-Brown-Cave, Wing Commander A. H. Orlebar, Maj. G. P. Bulman, Sir Robert McLean, Commander James Bird, Joe Smith, Arthur Black, Alan Clifton, Trevor Westbrook, Jeffrey Quill, George Pickering, and Arthur Shirval; the aeronautical companies represented were: Rolls-Royce, the Bristol Aeroplane Company, Short Brothers, Handley Page, Fairey Aviation, Sauders-Roe, and Airspeed. Also represented were seventeen local organisations and clubs, including the Masonic Lodge of Concorde, No. 4910, of which Mitchell had been a member. Among the 150 wreaths were those from Henry Folland, Henri Biard, Vera Cross, and 'the Schneider Boys'.

The funeral service was followed by a cremation at South Stoneham and, as the service ended, 'three RAF 'planes, flying in formation, roared low over the crematorium, dipping in a final salute.'

The presiding vicar said that, during the last few months, 'increasingly he found comfort in his Bible and his prayers, and I was overjoyed that on Easter Day [28 March] he felt well enough to come to this church to receive Holy Communion.' It must be said that there appears to have been no mention of churchgoing since his schooldays, and he often played a round of golf with his wife on Sunday mornings, but he did say to brother Eric on his last visit, 'My work was important but there are other things as well that are important in life.' The wife of his test pilot, George Pickering, said:

Mrs Florence Mitchell, 1938. She moved to Reading in 1940 when her son went to university there; she drove for Vickers during the war and also did a considerable amount of work in connection with the National Savings Campaign in that district. After a year-long illness, she died on 3 January 1946.

> There are more important things in the world than flying ... There is so much beauty all around us. I wish I had spent more time appreciating beauty. It is too late now but tell George that there are more important things in life than speed. Tell him to look at beautiful things while he has time.

It would seem that, looking back, the artist in him had not been sufficiently fulfilled, that the satisfaction of work well done was not quite enough. No doubt he regretted not having spent more time playing tennis or golf with his wife, or being able to watch his son becoming a man and a father. Typically, he had determined to work to the end, to defy as long as possible his affliction; so, when he came to fully appreciate the preciousness of the simple and beautiful things around him, it was too late.

Meanwhile, the conscientiousness, which had been evident throughout his working life and which had produced such an absorbing professional career, was evident in his concern for the future of his small family: the obituary in the *Southern Daily Echo* mentioned that 'Mr Mitchell quietly set about arranging his affairs and the future of his wife and son, Gordon, down to the smallest detail.' The editor was unaware that, while he was in Vienna, he had written to his managing director (by then Sir Charles Craven) concerning his wife and son and, while there, had received news of a generous settlement from the company.

Those who have been curious to discover the man behind the machine will have found evidence that he could be irascible and harsh; he was kind and considerate; he became a pilot; he shot small animals; he liked billiards, golf, tennis, cricket, and sailing; he too often sacrificed his private life for designing aircraft of high quality; he deliberated carefully before acting; he could be a chancer; he could be a martinet at work and at home; he was noted for humility and listening to others; he kept in touch with his family back home; he was shy and often withdrawn; he had a temper; and he enjoyed the status of a quite large house and garden in a prosperous suburb and a succession of luxurious cars. In other words, he was singularly human and fallible—but because of his equally singular work ethic, Shenstone summed up his professionalism in a sentence that should be an epitaph to how he tried to lead his life in general: Mitchell always did the thing which should be done.

Afterword: After Mitchell

The last Spitfire to be built flew over the grave of the man who gave this country the greatest fighter plane in history.

B. Simpson, RAF fitter

Our chief designer never actually saw his Spitfire go into squadron service before the start of the Second World War as he died on 11 June 1937—the very day that his first Spitfire, Type 224, was finally retired, to eventually become a ground target at the gunnery range at Orfordness.

Before his death, Mitchell had had the satisfaction of attending the Vickers Press Day where his Scapa, Walrus, Spitfire, and Stranraer were all on display together. With the last three, he had produced, respectively, the slowest and the fastest aircraft for the RAF and the fastest biplane flying boat. After the orders for the fifteen production Scapas and seventeen Stranraers, he then saw his company receive initial orders for a total of 217 Walruses and 310 Spitfires.

Besides his world speed breaking Schneider trophy racers, here was no mean an epitaph for a designer even though he did not live to see how future wartime requirements resulted in the extraordinary development and the huge orders for the Spitfire. Nevertheless, he had created a team that could carry on from where he had had to leave off and so a description of just how they did so with his initial concepts will be a necessary afterword on his design career.

The B.12/36 Bomber and the Bombing

By the early part of 1937, Mitchell was to be seen less and less at Supermarine as it had become clear that the cancer operation of 1933 had not been a successful procedure. Yet in the last full year of his life and even when he was supervising the finishing touches to the Spitfire design, another major innovative project for a bomber had been occupying his mind. This was in response to Air Ministry Specification B.12/36 for a high-speed, four-engined bomber with a range of 3,000 miles, capable of carrying a 14,000-lb bomb load or twenty-four soldiers.

It also had to be capable of being broken down into component parts for transport by the existing railway system and of lifting off from a 500-foot runway, clearing a height of

50 feet at the end; there was also a requirement for a catapult take-off capability, in order to extend the bomber's potential range and load capacity. At the same time, the wingspan was to be limited to no more than 100 feet, in respect of transport considerations and perhaps to discourage the design of very large, over-expensive aircraft rather than because of the size of existing hangars. It also had to have a retractable ventral turret as well as nose and tail guns and to be capable of staying afloat for several hours in the event of being forced down in the North Sea or Channel, as might be expected if the international situation did not improve.

It is interesting that Shorts and Supermarine were each awarded contracts for two prototypes rather than, for example, the Handley-Page or Vickers firms, which had extensive experience of the larger sort of land-based machines. The response received from Supermarine must have confirmed the officials' regard for Mitchell's importance to the aviation industry—his tender for the bomber had a proposed wingspan of 97 feet but was to make use of a single-spar wing supported by torsion-resistant leading-edge boxes on a similar principle to that developed for the much smaller Spitfire; unusually for its time, fuel was to be carried in these leading edges, even outboard of the engines, thereby saving weight, and with the tanks adding to the rigidity of the wing.

Behind this spar component, the structure allowed sufficient room for the main stowage of bombs, thus avoiding the need for conventional tiered bomb stowage in the fuselage which would have substantially increased its cross-section and its drag component—further evidence of paying, instinctively as it were, particular attention to the reduction of frontal area. The Polish PZL P.37 medium bomber had made use of bomb bays in the wing between the engines and the fuselage, but Mitchell's more extensive proposal was not adopted in any of the other front-line bombers of the Second World War. As a result, Bomber Command officers, when they inspected the Supermarine mock-up in October 1937, after Mitchell's

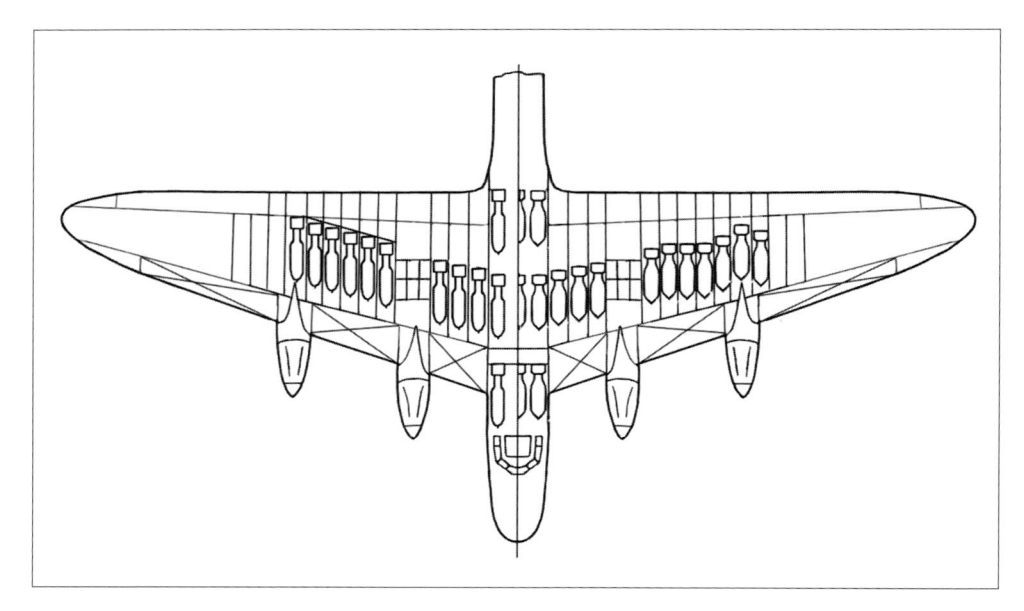

From Supermarine Drawing 31600 Sheets 5/6 showing alternative stowage of 29 × 250-lb bombs (right) and of 27 × 500-lb bombs (left). Leading edge fuel tanks also shown.

Supermarine model of Type 317.

death, were concerned about the restricted headroom throughout the fuselage; however for Mitchell, performance usually took precedence over comfort.

A further refinement was the proposal to place the required armament well below the eye-line of the gunners, not only giving them an improved view but also enabling a reduction in the cross-section of the turret and a more rapid traverse of the guns.

Mitchell had overseen a first proposal, Type 317, which had a single fin and a wing with a swept-back leading edge; it was to be powered by Bristol Hercules engines providing an estimated top speed of 390 mph. Revisions followed at the beginning of 1937, by which time the chief designer's condition had meant that his Personal Assistant, Maj. H. J. Payn, had taken over the design department. New proposals were embodied in Type 317 in which wing leading and trailing edges tapering almost equally, with slightly skewed-elliptical outer sections; the fuselage was lengthened and slimmed down at the rear and the redesigned tailpane had fins and rudder at the tips.

In November 1938, Mitchell's team had been able to submit a lighter and smaller design than their rivals and produced a set of estimated performance figures which make an intriguing comparison with published results for the earliest marks of the other British four-engined bombers of comparable size:

Aircraft	Power Rating	Range	Bomb Load	Max. Speed
Supermarine	1,330 hp	3,680 miles	8,000 lb	330 mph (estimate)
Stirling I	1,590 hp	1,930 miles	5,000 lb	260 mph
Halifax BI	1,145 hp	1,860 miles	5,800 lb	265 mph
Lancaster I	1,390 hp	2,530 miles	7,000 lb	287 mph

More often than not, Supermarine estimates were actually achieved when their designs flew (one remembers Orlebar's comments about the correct estimate on the S.6B or the Spitfire performance when the right propeller was found), and so it will always be a matter of conjecture as to whether the extraordinarily competitive figures for Supermarine's proposed bomber would have been attained, and at what saving of life when war did begin. After all, it was conceived at the same time as the Stirling and Halifax but with an estimated speed close to that of the new fighters; its estimated range and bomb load were also impressive. It might, however, be maintained that with the need for volume production—probably using standard gun turrets and being forced to add a dorsal one too—the Supermarine figures might have turned out to be closer to those actually achieved by the other firms' products.

Unfortunately, the project had only reached the stage of two prototype fuselages when they were destroyed by enemy bombing. The first attack upon Supermarine took place on 15 September 1940, mainly causing civilian casualties in surrounding houses and with only very minor damage to Supermarine; this was followed by another attempt nine days later when even more unfortunate civilians were killed and the aircraft factory was again left mostly intact. The three light anti-aircraft batteries positioned near the factory had now been supplemented by barrage balloons, but two days later, on 26 September, two successive waves of German bombers delivered an estimated 36 tons of bombs more accurately. This time, many Supermarine workers were killed or seriously injured and damage to the factory was extensive. Although thirteen Spitfire fuselages were destroyed or badly damaged, most of the machinery and jigs were still useable but, as the two half-completed bomber fuselages were badly damaged, it was decided that Supermarine should concentrate upon its other current products, especially the Spitfire.

One of the bomber fuselages before their destruction by enemy action.

Author's painting of proposed bomber, based upon Supermarine Drawing 316000 Sheet 2 and Supermarine models.

The Sea Otter and Seagull ASR.I

While Mitchell could not have guessed at the very wide use of his Walrus in later years, he had been aware of a requirement for an improved version and had met the Air Ministry's director of technical development as late in his life as February 1936 to discuss this project. On 17 April, the company received instructions to proceed with a heavier machine which was to have a longer range and a dive-bombing capability. A greater load capability was also a requirement, which would prove to be justified as its predecessor, the Walrus, had, on occasion, to taxi rather than fly back to base because of the number of survivors rescued.

The hull of the new design, in particular, showed a marked similarity to the Walrus, although it was slightly more rounded at the front; this less angular feature was carried through more thoroughly in respect of the flying surfaces. However, the most noticeable change was a reversion to a tractor-engined configuration with the nacelle raised to occupy most of the centre section of the top wing. This neater engine mounting also permitted a tidier trailing-edge for the folding wing arrangement, and the previous offsetting of the engine was avoided by giving the fin an aerofoil section.

Due to the other pressing demands at the time, the design and the construction of the prototype aircraft was not completed until September 1938, and thus Mitchell never saw this eventual development of his Walrus. Named 'Sea Otter', 292 were eventually built, of which all except the two prototypes were subcontracted to Saunders-Roe; it represented the last biplane flying boat from the long line of Supermarine aircraft to have come from Mitchell's drawing board.

There was one further seaplane, a monoplane this time, also required for air-sea rescue, which deserves a mention. As it appeared as late as 1948, it might more than most of those mentioned above be called a posthumous Mitchell machine. It had a cantilever, variable-incidence wing with full-span flaps and leading-edge slats, mounted on a central pylon, which also supported a Rolls-Royce Griffon engine with contra-rotating propellers.

The prototype Sea Otter.

The first Seagull ASR.I.

These features, and the butterfly tail with end-plate fins, revealed how far thinking had outstripped the old amphibians that Mitchell knew, but its single-step planing surfaces and aggressive nose still embodied the basic Walrus seagoing formula. Only three prototypes were built, which, in the context of the story of Mitchell's designs at least, was a pity in that a production order for this ASR.I would have prolonged a venerable Supermarine name—it was designated 'Seagull'. Also in the Supermarine tradition, it set up a 100-km closed-circuit record in 1950 for amphibians with a speed of 241.9 mph.

The Sea Otter only came into service use at the end of the war, and the only other Mitchell aircraft that saw Second World War service were the Spitfire, Stranraer, and Walrus.

The Walrus in Wartime

The initially perceived need of the Walrus for fleet spotting and maritime reconnaissance generally was supplemented by the anticipated need to rescue 'ditched' aircrews and also by the need for a Mk II training version. As a result, the first 217 ordered eventually rose to a grand total of 746, and by January 1940, the Mark I aircraft formed the major part of the equipment of No. 700 Squadron, which embodied all the catapult units aboard British warships; the Walrus also served on most capital ships of the Australian and New Zealand Royal Navies.

At the same time, new Spitfire orders were coming in so that, by the end of 1939, the Walrus production had to be transferred to the company's old rivals, Saunders-Roe, including the Mark IIs, which were built with wooden hulls. This apparently backward step was a means of saving on priority light alloys for this training version; it could also be produced and repaired by workers who were in less demand than those who worked in metal.

In addition to fleet spotting and naval reconnaissance duties, the standard Walrus was also used for photoreconnaissance, artillery spotting, anti-submarine convoy patrol, and communication work. Mitchell had produced an aircraft that was to operate in most theatres of war from the African deserts to the Pacific Ocean; it also carried secret agents and landed on jungle airstrips and ice floes and was variously fitted with bombs, depth-charges, air-sea

A demonstration of air-sea rescue by Walrus.

rescue containers, and the later air-to-surface vessel radar for reconnaissance. After the war, one Walrus made an unlikely appearance as the winner of the 1946 Folkestone Trophy Race at Lympne, and another was used for spotting unfortunate whales from SS *Balaena* in the Antarctic during 1947.

The varied wartime duties of the Walrus said as much about the exigencies of war as they did about the suitability of the machine for these varied roles, but its low speed was a bonus in most of these circumstances. Its varied employment was also a testimony to the basic integrity of the structure created by Mitchell and his team and to its culmination of a succession of very sturdy smaller flying-boat designs from his company.

The Stranraer in Wartime

The other Mitchell flying-boat category, the larger long-range patrol seaplane, did not have any successors after the Stranraer. It served with No. 228 Squadron when it was needed to patrol the North Sea, and some of the Stranraers of this unit were transferred to No. 209 Squadron and, in particular, assisted in patrols between Scotland and Norway. Fitted with extra fuel tankage under one wing and bombs under the other, they conducted patrols against enemy shipping until replaced in April 1941 by the ubiquitous Short Sunderland. No. 240 Squadron was also equipped with the Stranraer and made the last operational patrol of the type on 17 March 1941, after which it was replaced by the Catalina.

In addition to the 17 production Stranraers for the RAF, the RCAF also adopted the type and 40 were built by Canadian Vickers. These saw a great deal more service than their British counterparts, in the battle against the U-boats in the Atlantic, and they operated with bomber reconnaissance squadrons, Nos 4, 5, 6, 7, 9, 117, and 120. They were finally replaced on active service by the Canadian Catalina, the Canso, in March 1941.

In view of their original low-maintenance specification and their associated anti-corrosion features, it is worth recording that the last RCAF Stranraer was retired as late as 20 January 1946 and that fourteen of the aircraft were sold to the civil sector, especially to private airline companies in Canada, where the lakes of the Northern Territory provided ready-made runways—just as in the pioneering flying-boat days. The last one of these Stranraers served in these spartan regions until 1958.

A Stranraer of No. 240 Squadron touching down.

First of the Canadian-built Stranraers, with bombs under wing.

The longevity of the Stranraer does not conceal the fact that, in this larger flying-boat category, the influence of Mitchell was relatively short-lived. The early and single-minded approach of Shorts to all-metal aircraft had paid dividends and led to the military development of the Sunderland, which dominated the wartime long-range sea patrol effort. In addition to its military counterpart, Short's clean, streamlined civilian version had monopolised the flying-boat provision on the Imperial Airways routes just prior to the outbreak of the war and represented a major step forward in flying-boat design without any convincing rival proposals from Supermarine. Mitchell's death at least spared his learning that 749 Sunderlands (the military version of the Imperial Airways design) were eventually built and that Hargreaves, who had left Supermarine and had made way for Mitchell to become chief designer, was awarded an MBE for overseeing their production.

Thus it came about that the most enduring memorial to Mitchell's career as chief engineer and chief designer was to be not a development of his many large flying boats but the landplane Spitfire; it continued in service in front-line fighting situations long after any of Mitchell's other aircraft and was still being improved upon long after the Stranraer, Walrus, or Sea Otter had ceased to be regarded as having any further potential.

Joe Smith Takes Over

After the death of Mitchell, his personal assistant, Maj. H. J. Payn, had taken over the design department but had to leave when it was decided that his wife's German connections posed too great a security risk. He was replaced by Joe Smith, who was finally appointed chief designer in 1941, and the credit for fully realising the potential of Mitchell's fighter design must go to him and his team.

Joe Smith had faith in the development potential of Mitchell's design, saying that it would 'see us through the war'. His Schneider trophy experience with Mitchell of developing the 900-hp S.5 into the similar, but somewhat larger, 1,900-hp S.6 and then into the 2,350-hp S.6B must surely have pointed the way. Quill also suggests one other particular event that might very well have been of considerable influence on Smith's faith in the long-term potential of Mitchell's design. This event was also associated with a speed competition—in this case, Supermarine's planned attempt upon the world land speed record then held by the Howard Hughes H-I racer.

Joe Smith.

A specially prepared 'Speed Spitfire' airframe with a Merlin engine developing 2,000 hp promised a top speed of 425 mph at sea level but, in the end, the venture was abandoned after Germany put up the record to 469 mph with the Messerschmitt Me 209. Unable to compete with this one-off propaganda aircraft spanning 7 feet less than the company's Bf 109 fighter,

Smith must nevertheless have appreciated that his development of the basic Spitfire airframe clearly revealed the future potential of the Mitchell design, given the current Mark I aircraft's 367 mph with a Merlin II rated at 990 hp. J. D. Scott wrote in his history of Vickers, 'By 1940 Joe Smith ... had reached the conclusion that the Spitfire design was capable of the most extensive, and indeed of almost infinite, development'. The various marks of Spitfire that were produced demonstrated this was the case, to the extent that Rolls-Royce, when designing the Griffon engine to succeed the Merlin, tailored the new engine to fit the existing fighter's airframe.

Nearly thirty main variants of the Spitfire followed Mitchell's prototype, and it is a measure of the contribution of Smith and the design team to the war effort that an average of about four distinct marks of Spitfire per year were developed. Whether Mitchell would have pursued a similar course, would have come up with some ingenious stroke of lateral thinking, or would have been permitted to go for a completely new design, must always remain a matter of speculation. Certainly, the pressures of war would not encourage the tooling-up necessary for a new type as long as modifications of existing aircraft could conceivably meet the changing wartime requirements—as Smith said, justifying his continuous modifications to the Spitfire type, 'the hard school of war leaves no room for sentimental attachments and the efficiency of the machine as a fighter weapon is the only criterion'. However, as we shall see, the realisation of Mitchell's prototype was by no means straightforward.

Spitfire Production Problems

Full-scale production of the sophisticated all-metal machine presented many challenges and, unfortunately, many delays. As a result, Air Ministry frustrations with the first stuttering supply of the Spitfire might very well have resulted in an early termination of the type. Lack of frankness on the part of the chairman of Vickers, Sir Robert McLean, and mismanagement at Lord Nuffield's huge Castle Bromwich aircraft factory, caused growing concern at the Air Ministry and, thereafter, in the government.

At Supermarine, the order for 310 Spitfires just eight days after the Martlesham test of the prototype presented immediate problems, not only because Supermarine lacked sufficient capacity and skilled local labour for the initial order but also because virtually a whole new set of drawings was needed—in-house arrangements sufficient for the production of a 'one-off' prototype would not do for the firms to whom work would have to be subcontracted. Some of these companies had no previous experience of aircraft manufacture and so the parent firm was further burdened with a high level of supervision and with replying to a multitude of queries.

The dismay at the Air Ministry over the non-appearance of the fighter, contrary to the chairman's assurances, was such that the secretary of state for air, Lord Swinton, was considering requiring the Air Council to see the whole Vickers board in order to 'put an end to what can only be described as an intolerable situation'. The replacement of Sir Robert McLean by Sir Charles Craven as managing director of Vickers Aviation was eventually to achieve the required results, but a turn-around in production figures could not be achieved overnight. It thus emerged that the first Spitfire would not be delivered by December 1937, as promised, and was not likely to appear before the following February. By the end of 1937, just six fuselages had been completed and were awaiting the delivery of wings from subcontractors. Craven therefore had to revoke McLean's unrealistic production estimates and could only promise fourteen aircraft in the first quarter of 1938.

Yet even this modest response to the original order for 310 Spitfires was not met. The first production aircraft first flew on 14 May 1938, and it was two months before the second was ready. Meanwhile, the concern over German militarisation produced a *Times* editorial on 18 July that stated that 'the delay in the production of the Spitfire has been one of the most disappointing features in the progress of the air programme'.

Despite this situation, Chamberlain's cabinet on 7 November decided that bomber production should only be such that jobs would not be lost, whereas it set an ambitious target of 3,700 fighters. Credit is not often given to Chamberlain for his foresight and it should be noted that victory in the Battle of Britain was particularly assisted by replacement aircraft being more readily available to the RAF than was the case with the Luftwaffe.

It is clear that, at this time, Mitchell's Spitfire had been regarded as the vital element in Britain's defences but serious problems with the special Castle Bromwich factory soon began to erode this view. While it was only to be expected that extensive work would be required for the new production lines to be put in place, it had been discovered that by the end of 1939, the aircraft plant still looked like a construction site and that Lord Nuffield appeared to be no longer up to the job; he seemed often vague and unable to grasp detail yet his autocratic manner made him unwilling to accept Ministry 'interference'—that is, their extreme concern that none of the promised sixty Spitfires per week from April 1940 had appeared. It was thus fortunate that on 14 May during a telephone exchange, Lord Beaverbrook, the new minister of aircraft production, engineered his resignation, as referenced on the *Supermariners* blog:

> In an almost legendary telephone conversation Lord Beaverbrook berated Lord Nuffield over his failures. Beaverbrook's criticism so enraged Lord Nuffield that he sarcastically suggested that Lord Beaverbrook 'should see if he could do any better' to which Lord Beaverbrook curtly responded by saying that he accepted Lord Nuffield's offer.

Vickers were tasked with reorganising the West Bromwich facility. A recent account by Leo McKinstry of the company's findings showed a lack of organisation of the building work and fitting out (even by 1942 building work was still going on), poor record keeping of supplies, and, more seriously, a management that had not effectively tackled poor timekeeping and frequent petty labour disputes by the work force. It was not good for general morale or propaganda purposes for this situation to become widely known, especially the labour disputes, but many dismissals followed; production gradually improved thereafter with nearly 200 aircraft being produced by the end of October 1940, rising to over six hundred by the following February.

By 4 August 1938, No. 19 Squadron had received its first operational Spitfire from Supermarine, and by September 1939, Supermarine had produced almost all the original order of 310 machines. Yet thirty-six were lost in accidents; then, when the number produced had risen to over 500 by March 1940, ninety-eight had been written off in accidents or were being repaired. As the Spitfire was still regarded as the best machine to oppose the Messerschmitt Bf 109, the need to conserve stocks was such that Air Vice-Marshal Dowding persuaded Churchill not to send any of these aircraft abroad to assist in the defence of France.

Nevertheless, during the actions above the troops being evacuated at Dunkirk in May and June 1940, 386 Hurricanes were lost while the much smaller number of Spitfires available was depleted by seventy-six. This engagement left a mere 331 Spitfires and Hurricanes available, but at least, Supermarine was working well and delivered its 1,000th fighter in August 1940. Thus, while more Spitfires would have been very welcome when war began in earnest in this year, a sufficient number was available to begin the development of the image of Mitchell's fighter in the public imagination.

The Rise of the Spitfire Legend

A large number of these early fighters was paid for by the emergence of a scheme that played a significant part in placing the Spitfire in the forefront of the popular imagination. After the mining millionaire, Sir Harry Oakes, gave £5,000 to fund one of these aircraft, other individuals took up the idea of buying a Spitfire with enthusiasm, including the National Federation of Hosiery Manufacturers and a lady called Dorothy who collected funds from others with the same Christian name. Towns and cities also organised the funding of aircraft, including two from Mitchell's home town. Thus, by the spring of 1940 when the fund closed, £13,000,000 had been raised, financing over 2,500 aircraft. The owner of the Vienna Cancer Clinic, to which Mitchell had gone during his last days, was a contributor.

Had production gone smoothly both at Southampton and Castle Bromwich, a significantly larger force of Spitfires would have been available during the Battle of Britain in the summer and autumn of 1940 and there would most likely have been fewer deaths of British civilians and RAF personnel on the ground. However, in the context of the Mitchell legacy, there were enough of 'the few' to contribute significantly to Hitler's abandoning his invasion plans by the October, thus leading to the developing popular reputation of the Spitfire, even though over 60 per cent of the fighter force consisted of Hurricanes.

Although any immediate assessment of the relative merits of the Spitfire over the Hurricane could only be made by the Air Ministry and by the few pilots who had experience of both types, the shape of Mitchell's fighter embodied an aesthetic that contributed in no small way to the Mitchell legend. As Rendall has pointed out, the Spitfire was the aircraft which, par excellence, was a by-product of the new 'Streamline Moderne', a sleeker form of Art Deco that had swept the western world in the 1920s. (In passing, one notes that the Mitchells had frequented the luxurious Art Deco Burgh Island hotel in Devon, and that a suite is named after him.)

In architecture, as a reflection of the austere economic times of the thirties, the 'streamline moderne' represented a rejection of unnecessary ornament; it also favoured relatively uncluttered curving forms and long horizontal lines, reflected in the speed machines of the time—the Bentley and Bugatti racing cars now looked distinctly old-fashioned beside the sleek Mercedes and Auto Unions and, indeed, beside Sir Nigel Gresley's streamlined Class A4 locomotives, which culminated in the record-breaking Mallard, with its wind-tunnel-tested, aerodynamic body. Manufacturers of clocks, radios, telephones, furniture, and numerous other household appliances now embraced the new design concept (even though the theoretical disproportionate increase of drag with speed mentioned earlier was hardly relevant to such items). Twenty days after the first flight of K5054, a report in the *Southampton Evening Echo* showed an immediate reaction to the 'moderne' shape of the Spitfire: 'Even the uninitiated have realised when watching the streamlined monoplane flash across the sky at five miles a minute (300 mph) and more, that here is a plane out of the ordinary'.

The classic, and 'moderne' shape of the Supermarine fighter.

While Mitchell had professed not to be interested in the shape of his fighter's wing, as long as he could get the guns in, there is little doubt that its elliptical shape, echoed by the curved tail surfaces, was in keeping with the new shapes of speed; and the thinness of his wing further enhanced its appeal. The Air Ministry F.7/30 specification had called for a good 'fighting view' and, as a result, other prototypes had cockpit enclosures which were placed quite high on the fuselage but Mitchell, true to his Schneider experience, integrated his cockpit more completely into the streamlines of his fuselage, which was, like those of his Schneider trophy planes, especially slender.

In previous chapters, it has been shown how good fortune had, at times, favoured the career of our designer; this was also now apparent in the emergence of the Spitfire as a national icon, founded not in the theoretical calculations of contemporary aircraft design but in an aesthetic movement appealing to a much wider, popular audience. Following the onset of the daylight bombing of London, the British people were thankful for any response by the RAF and began to focus this gratitude on Mitchell's design which seemed so logically to combine power and speed with modern, curvaceous lines.

Illustrators of the time, responding to the aesthetically pleasing shape of his design, tended to single out his machine in their drawings of combat and, while pilots over Dunkirk and in the Battle of Britain had come to appreciate the fighting qualities of the Spitfire, the general public, 'knowing nothing of performance figures … have instinctively chosen one particular type as the paragon of protective types and they have guessed correctly' (*Flight*). It is noticeable how contemporary observers of aerial engagements and German pilots tended to report only Spitfires in action.

The more numerous Hurricane accounted for more successes than did the Spitfire and yet the Hawker machine, unfairly, has never been the popular image of the Battle of Britain, even though it was, if possible, employed not against the protecting fighters but against the enemy bombers, which obviously posed the real physical threat to the British populace. On 15 September 1945, on the fifth anniversary of the battle, the RAF staged a flypast over London of 300 aircraft; it was led by Douglas Bader in a Spitfire.

The reputation of Mitchell's fighter was further enhanced by the eventual lifting of the siege of Malta. In early 1941, the Luftwaffe took over the action from the Italians and reinforcements of Spitfires had had to be flown in. Eventually, by October 1942, sufficient numbers of Spitfires, the deployment of experienced pilots, and better organised ground support led to the lifting of the siege and even to a developing allied offensive strategy from the island.

The Spitfire was thus once again seen as the significant factor in another British 'backs-to-the-wall' campaign and featured prominently in *The Malta Story*. This film was followed by *Reach for the Sky* in 1956 and by *The Battle of Britain* in 1969. These films continued to keep the Spitfire legend alive, in no small part due to the availability of the Supermarine aircraft, thanks to its long production run—it was only on 20 February 1948 (almost twelve years from the prototype's first flight) that the last production Spitfire, an F. 24, left the production line (*see* 'Last Words'); just over 14,500 Hurricanes and Sea Hurricanes had been built, compared with nearly 23,000 Spitfires and Seafires.

The Continuation of the Spitfire Legend

When Mitchell first joined Supermarine, he saw the Channel conversions that he had worked on going to Scandinavia, South America, Japan, and New Zealand, but even with the unbounded optimism of youth, he could not have imagined the future worldwide employment of his Spitfire, in so many theatres of war—progressively, in the Mediterranean and the Middle East, Italy, Yugoslavia, France, the Low Countries, Burma, and the Pacific.

Nor could he have envisaged his fighter in the service of so many countries, particularly Russia in the early years of the war. Another request came from Australia, which received Mark Vs, which were faster than the Japanese Zero; unfortunately, they were not new aircraft and were not entirely reliable. Yet in November, 1943, it was agreed to send forty new Mark VIIIs, followed by a regular supply of the newest tropicalised versions which could also out-climb and out-dive the Zero. By the end of the year, the Japanese had abandoned their raids on the Australian mainland and the Spitfires then went into action over Borneo and elsewhere in the South Pacific. Mark V Spitfires had also arrived in Burma, followed by Mark VIIIs, and took part in the decisive battle of Kohima from April to June 1944.

America also had three separate 'Eagle' squadrons (Nos 71, 121, and 133) formed from the large number of American volunteers; these were eventually subsumed into the USAF. While the distinctive shape of the Spitfire/Seafire moved ever eastwards, Marks IX, VIII, and XII continued the Spitfire presence nearer to home and contributed significantly to allied air supremacy over Europe. In 1944, massed ranks of Mark V to Mark XIVs supported the Normandy landings on D-Day and then continued operations in Europe until the end of the war, including ground attack actions alongside the Hawker Tempest against V2 rocket installations in Holland.

A Spitfire F 22 awaiting delivery to the Royal Egyptian Air Force.

Despite the advent of the jet fighter at the very end of the war, the Spitfire continued post-war operational service in Malta, Cyprus, the Suez Canal Zone and the Persian Gulf. It was also deployed against communist activities in Malaya and Korea and PR19s, from Hong Kong, maintained discreet reconnaissance flights along the Chinese coast and even over mainland China. Sweden bought fifty of this mark to watch Soviet activities in the Baltic region while Soviet Union Spitfires reappeared in the Peoples' Republic of China. As jet aircraft began to equip air forces, other nations were keen to buy Spitfires as stopgaps: Belgium, Holland, Norway, Denmark, Yugoslavia, Greece, Italy, the Philippines, Thailand, Burma, Israel, Egypt, Syria, Turkey, Portugal, India, Czechoslovakia, South Africa, Southern Rhodesia, and Ireland.

Thus the Spitfire saw in the era of the all-metal, propeller-driven fighter and saw it out, but while these aircraft around the world were gradually replaced, the Spitfire icon still continued to have a physical presence, thanks to various preservation enterprises, led by the Battle of Britain Memorial Flight organisation. When the Spitfire was phased out of RAF service in 1957, three machines were being flown by the Temperature and Humidity Monitoring Flight at RAF Woodvale. These were PR19s and they were transferred to Biggin Hill on 11 July 1957 to form the Historic Aircraft Flight. Two were overhauled and, in April 1964, returned to what had now officially been renamed the Battle of Britain Flight. The Spitfire is also seen on occasions of national importance in Australia, New Zealand, India, and Israel.

Mitchell's fighter appears, therefore, destined to remain in the public eye for many years to come, not just because of the flight's activities but because of the industry that has grown up around the restoration of the type. The June 2010 edition of *Flypast* listed not only five Memorial Flight Spitfires but also another nineteen airworthy machines at various bases in the United Kingdom. Additionally, twenty other Spitfires and three Seafires were currently listed as under or awaiting restoration and one Seafire and fifteen Spitfires on display.

The Development of the Spitfire

In the preceding account of the widespread activities of the Supermarine fighter, various marks have been mentioned thanks to Joe Smith's elaboration of the type and the extent of these developments can be summarised by the following table:

	Spitfire Mark I	Seafire 47
Maximum speed	362 mph	452 mph
Engine power	1,050 hp	2,350 hp
Fuel capacity	85 gal.	287 gal. (incl. 90 gal. drop tank)
Normal loaded weight	5,820 lb	10,300 lb
Wing loading	24 lb/sq. ft	42.2 lb/sq. ft
Service ceiling	31,500 ft	43,100 ft
Maximum range	575 miles	1,475 miles
Climb to 20,000 ft	9.4 min.	4.8 min.
Rate of roll at 400 mph	14 degrees/sec.	68 degrees/sec.
Maximum diving speed	450 mph	500 mph

In the course of this development, the weight of ammunition carried had almost doubled and that of the protective armour now amounted to more than the weight of an average pilot. Indeed, Jeffrey Quill has pointed out that at its maximum gross take-off weight, the Seafire 47 was equivalent to a Mark I Spitfire with the additional load of thirty-two 'airline standard' passengers each with 40 lb of baggage. The following photograph of a 'svelte' Mark I and of a well-laden Seafire 47 makes the point.

While the extraordinary development of Mitchell's 'basic' fighter is incontrovertible, it would not be realistic to conclude with too triumphal an account of the Spitfire's development. Many modifications were rather desperate attempts, in wartime conditions, to avoid the production of a completely new type. Jeffrey Quill, who had by far the most extensive experience of testing the various Spitfire types, has made the following comment:

> Almost every design change introduced in the course of the extremely rapid development of the Spitfire was in some way basically detrimental to the flight handling, usually in terms of longitudinal or directional stability. My main preoccupation as chief test pilot was thus to ensure that the flight handling characteristics of the Spitfire remained within manageable limits, and it wasn't really possible in the prevailing circumstances to do more than this.
>
> To keep the flight handling situation under control, many expedients were forced upon us by the immense pressures of wartime production effort. The 'elegant' solutions were usually not available to us, simply because of the pressures of time; solutions had to be found at once and therefore we improvised—generally with good success. But our expedients were not always entirely successful and the flight handling of the Spitfire sometimes left a certain amount to be desired.

Some of the factors that most affected controllability were the progressive increase in speed and weight, in propeller blade area, and in moments of inertia due to the distribution of increasing weight. Quill reported:

The first production Mk I, Eastleigh, May 1938.

A well-laden Seafire 47, *c.* 1949.

The Spitfire was almost continually at the margins of longitudinal stability. The problem was to find ways of providing for greater ranges of centre-of-gravity movement. An aeroplane that gets on the negative side of longitudinal stability can sometimes be fun to fly but can become very, very dangerous at the high diving speeds. As time went on I became very conscious of the need to provide positive stability margins but everything militated against this. I knew, from George Pickering's accident, that Spitfires could suffer catastrophic structural failures. Unfortunately, his was not an isolated case; there were in fact something in the order of 25 catastrophic total structural failures with Spitfires in the air. There is no better way of risking overstressing an aeroplane than having negative stability margins longitudinally and then diving it up to somewhere near or beyond its maximum permissible diving speed. If you lose control of it then, that is when it breaks. Now I was only too acutely conscious of this and the problems involved in preserving positive margins as the aeroplane developed. It would not be any good ringing up and saying 'we want another 25% on the area of the tailplane as from next week please'. This would have been impossible. We had to make do with a whole series of expedients; mostly getting some returns on the stick-free stability by modifications of the elevator in order to keep this situation under control. Once or twice we had to go into all sorts of terrible things like putting inertia weights in the elevator circuit and so on, which pilots hated, but it had to be done.

There was also the major problem of converting the Spitfire into the Seafire for aircraft carrier operation, and an airman who flew Seafires throughout the war, Capt. George C. Baldwin, gave the following perspective of problems associated with aircraft-carrier landings with the early conversions:

> The Spitfire was designed to have excellent air to air combat qualities, it was a very light fragile aircraft and was really very unsuitable for the rugged flying … when not too experienced pilots were to throw it onto a flight deck and it was to be arrested in full flight by a hydraulic arrester gear …
>
> We had a curious little expression about the Spitfire which summed up our problems on the deck and we used to say it suffered from 'pecking, pintling and puckering'. Actually that was no joke, because 'pecking' was a phenomenon caused by the tail being thrown up as the aircraft caught the arrester-wire and the propeller touching the flight deck and, if it was a wooden propeller, pieces flew off in every direction. Believe it or not, that was cured by just taking a sharp knife and cutting three inches off the end of each blade with no noticeable loss of performance whatever. 'Pintling' was a phenomenon caused by the rather weak undercarriage. You could do a fairly reasonable, but slightly rough landing and thereafter you could either not get the undercarriage up when you took off or once you had retracted it you could not lower it again. It was because the pintle in the undercarriage had become misplaced. 'Puckering' was if you had made a successful landing, but had a little bump which might have caused pecking—you would also get puckering which meant that the tail would drop hard onto the flight deck and the fuselage would bend just in front of the empennage. Well, these were all difficult problems and they reduced serviceability somewhat considerably.

But, to end on a more positive note, many versions of the fighter were regarded as exceptional aircraft—in particular, perhaps the best fighter, from a handling point of view, was the Mark VIII; the most successful high-altitude fighter, the Mark XIV; the most outstanding PR variant, the PR19; and the most complete naval version, the Seafire 47.

A detailed account of the almost thirty main versions that went into quantity production is provided in Appendix II and indicates just how far Mitchell's basic design was capable of development, thanks to the dedicated wartime effort of Joe Smith and his design team. Meanwhile, drawings of their basic modifications will give an indication of these efforts.

The drawing opposite shows, first, Mitchell's original semi-elliptical planform, followed by the clipped wing version for higher manoeuvrability at low level. The next illustration gives Smith's most obvious departure from Mitchell's original concept, the pointed-wing version of the high-altitude Marks VI, VII, VIII, and 21; this was a particularly stopgap expedient and certainly lacked a great deal in elegance. Finally, the fourth drawing shows the revised wing and tail surfaces, as seen in Marks 22 and 24; whether they would have had a different outline if they had come from Mitchell's own drawing board can only be guessed at.

Perhaps a more graphic illustration of the continuous development of the wartime Spitfire can be seen in its changing side-views (*see* overleaf). Mitchell's original design concept remained most clearly evident in the Merlin-engined fighter Mark I–II–V–IX line of development, in the photoreconnaissance Mark I–VII sequence, and in the Seafire Mark I–II–III–XV series. The introduction of improved equipment brought some obvious changes; the Griffon engine and the extra oil requirement in the longer-range PR variants produced somewhat changed nose shapes and increases in power also necessitated redesigns of the tail surfaces. The more

Afterword: After Mitchell

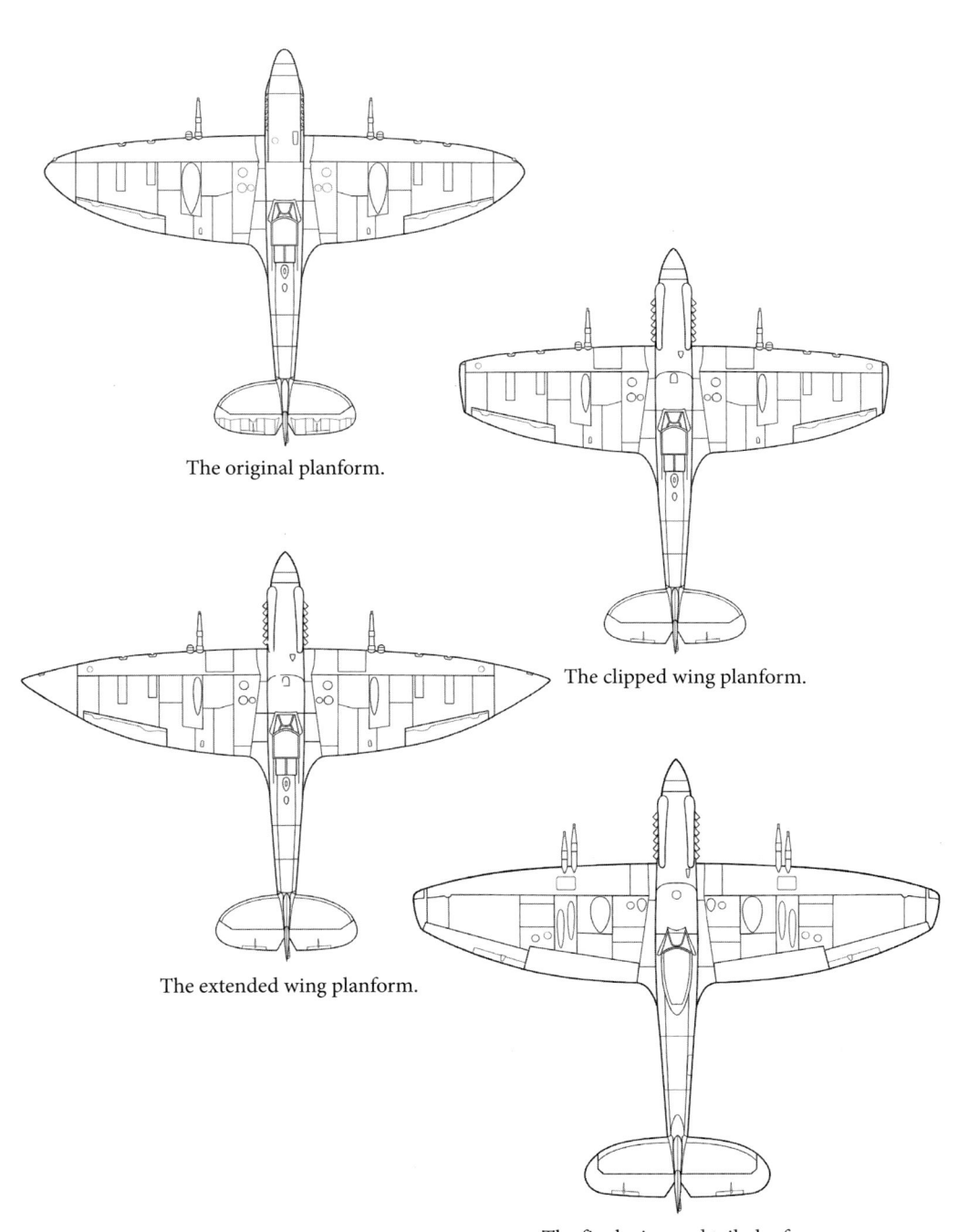

The original planform.

The clipped wing planform.

The extended wing planform.

The final wing and tail planform.

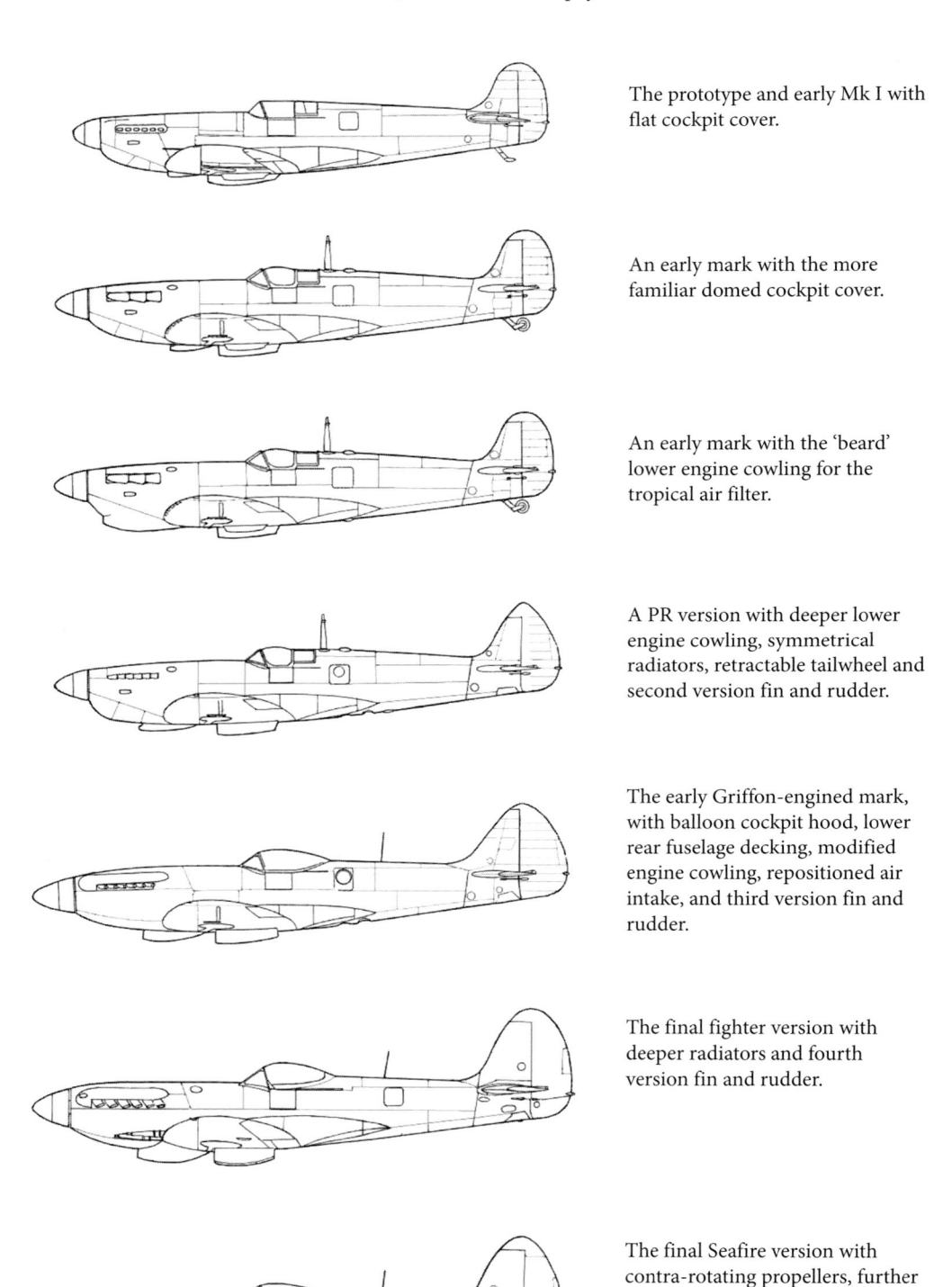

The prototype and early Mk I with flat cockpit cover.

An early mark with the more familiar domed cockpit cover.

An early mark with the 'beard' lower engine cowling for the tropical air filter.

A PR version with deeper lower engine cowling, symmetrical radiators, retractable tailwheel and second version fin and rudder.

The early Griffon-engined mark, with balloon cockpit hood, lower rear fuselage decking, modified engine cowling, repositioned air intake, and third version fin and rudder.

The final fighter version with deeper radiators and fourth version fin and rudder.

The final Seafire version with contra-rotating propellers, further revised air intake position and modified fourth rudder.

powerful later Merlins had given rise to the simple but makeshift change to a pointed and broader chord rudder, while the even more powerful Griffons necessitated a complete redesign of the unit (for example, in the Mark 18 and PR 19).

Another factor affecting a more fundamental redesign by other hands was the later availability of the tear-drop canopy, which resulted in a cut-down rear fuselage decking.

Retractable tailwheels, deeper engine cowlings or air filter coverings, and contra-rotating propellers also contributed to the gradual alteration of the Spitfire's appearance; however, the most significant change was the completely redesigned wing, as fitted to the Mark 21, 22, and 24 fighter and the Mark 45, 46, and 47 Seafire.

While many of the changing features were variously embodied during later stages of the production runs of other marks, it is with these last six types that the necessary movement away from Mitchell's original concept is at its most marked—the Seafire 47, the last version of the Spitfire, combined revised tail surfaces, rear-view canopy with cut-down rear top decking, and contra-rotating propellers, and the air intake filter was now more comprehensively faired into the lower engine cowling, with the duct opening positioned just behind the propellers.

The comparison between the Mark I and Seafire 47 quoted earlier gave further proof of how far Mitchell's original concept had been capable of development. However, setting aside the huge difference in load carrying between the two aircraft, it can be calculated that the latter's 125 per cent increase in engine power had only produced a 25 per cent increase in speed. Thus Mitchell's propeller design could be seen to be finally reaching the limits of its potential; nevertheless, one can surely agree with Rendall's assessment of the Spitfire:

> Few aircraft straddled the transition between the two ages of aviation so comprehensively, let alone so elegantly: the biplane and the monoplane ages, the piston age and the jet age, the subsonic and the supersonic.

A Selection of Photographs Showing Spitfire Development

One of the first Mk IIAs from Castle Bromwich.

The Mk V, two cannon version, with clipped wings.

An HF VII with extended wing and second version fin and rudder.

Mk XIIs of 41 Squadron. Redesigned cowling blisters for the Griffon engine are clearly evident on EB-B.

Mk XIV, showing the five-blade right-hand propeller and deeper radiators.

Mk 18, showing camera aperture, the redesigned fin and rudder, lower fuselage decking and 'tear-drop' cockpit canopy.

Mk F 22, showing the final revisions to flying surfaces and the fourth type fin.

Seafire F 46 with contra-rotating propellers and modified fin.

Schneider Trophy Full Circle

The earlier chapters describing the Schneider trophy events were felt to be essential to the story of the emergence of the Spitfire and so it is perhaps fitting to draw attention to the fact that among the very numerous Spitfire developments outlined in Appendix II, there was a Spitfire floatplane variant that, although it owed very little directly to its Schneider trophy predecessors, would seem to bring the Mitchell narrative to an appropriate conclusion. It was described, equally appropriately, by Jeffrey Quill:

> Yes, I flew the Spitfire floatplane. We developed this to meet a requirement for the Mediterranean operations … It was a very successful experiment altogether—the floats were very good; in fact, it would have been rather surprising if they were not; they were designed by Supermarine who did understand about making floats! It handled beautifully in water. The drag of the floats was surprisingly low; the Mark IX with floats was still faster than the standard Mark V without floats. Now [the Mark V floatplanes] did go out to the Mediterranean. There was a good deal of traffic across the Mediterranean with JU 52's and such like on supply lines to North Africa and the idea of these floatplanes was to lurk around some of the smaller islands and then suddenly pop up and surprise these chaps and shoot them down. However the outcome of events at the end of the Western Desert Campaign created a situation where the requirement was no longer there. But it was a very successful development, I think it is fair to say … they were great fun to fly.

Supermarine Spitfire F.IX Floatplane conversion, 1944.

Last Words

On the day of delivery to the RAF, VN496, the last Spitfire was pushed out from the hangar on to the apron and fuelled up. Just before the flight, for safety reasons, I installed the radio and batteries.

Sqd. Ldr Guy Morgan, our deputy Chief Test Pilot, climbed in and buckled up. He then went through his pre-flight checks, ran up his engine and gave the thumbs-up for chocks away. He taxied on to the grass runway, turned and took off, flying over South Stoneham Cemetery, about 200yds from the end of the runway.

This took place on April 4 1949. In South Stoneham Cemetery lie the remains of R. J. Mitchell, the designer of the Spitfire—so perhaps it was fitting that the last Spitfire to be built flew over the grave of the man who gave this country the greatest fighter plane in history. It also seems appropriate that the last Spitfire of more than 20,000 produced should have flown off the same airfield as the first, K5054, which had made its maiden flight there 13 years previously in March 1936.

I've always been proud to have been the last person to have completed the last job on the last Spitfire ever produced.

Brian Simpson

yesterdayremembered.co.uk/memory/1440/ (accessed on 23 October 2020)

Appendix I

Mitchell Family Letters

Copied below are previously unpublished letters kindly made available by Julian Mitchell, R. J. Mitchell's grand-nephew.

The first two letters are by Reginald Mitchell to his brother Eric, who was in the army in Egypt. They reflect the war effort that Reginald was part of at Supermarine during the last years of the First World War and also confirm the sense of humour that others have commented upon and which was to be seen in his speeches transcribed in previous chapters.

The first of the letters also reveals his frustrated wish to have been a pilot with the RFC and the second that, apparently, the younger brother disliked writing letters even more than has been reported of Reginald. He jokingly wonders if Eric, still in Egypt, could make it to his impending wedding, which, for reasons unknown, he dates one day earlier than actually occurred.

The third letter is from Reginald's wife to his brothers Eric and Billy. Compared with R.J.'s regular hand, his mother's rather cramped style would seem to betray the strain of coping during the last few months of her husband's life; he had been experiencing severe bouts of pain since late the previous year and died less than three months after this letter was written.

Gordon Mitchell's book has transcribed several letters from R.J. to his son, trying to shield him from what he knew was his terminal illness, discussing details of his will (including a concern that his now widowed mother should be provided for), and arranging with Vickers a settlement for his wife and son. This concern for his family and his fortitude are there clear to see, but the present letter gives a more poignant insight into the trauma for the family of his last days.

It was felt that a transcription following the copy of this last letter would be helpful.

Belgrave Villa,
Chapel St.,
Bitterne,
Southampton.
Sept. 9th '17

My Dear Eric,

How long ago did you give me up as a bad job? I was very surprised to hear from home that you had not received a letter from me thanking you for the photographs. I must thank you again very much. The Harding's were very pleased indeed with them as you can easily imagine under the circumstances.

I have changed my digs, twice since then. I rather like a change. I have been trying to get away from

Southampton, but have not succeeded. The restrictions on munition workers are rather exacting at present. We are turning out machines in large quantities now. I wonder if you see any of them over there. How should you like to go in for flying? You would stand a good chance of a commission if you thought anything of it, and set things going. I wish I could.

I suppose you are having the pleasant part of the year out there now, but I should think you get very tired of it. How long is it since you left England?

Reg. Paulger & Willis Dunn both called to see me recently — not together, in Southampton.

I was very pleased and surprised to see them.

There are very few signs of the war finishing yet, I suppose you get all the news.

Things are very dull here. We have to trust to an occasional air raid to liven things up a bit. They do it with aeroplanes now. The zepps. have 'done their bit'.

I haven't heard from home for quite a long time now – not since they returned from Blackpool.

Let me have just a line old chap when you can spare the time.

Cheers. Yours affectionately
Reg.

84 Avenue Rd,
Woolston,
Southampton,
16th June '18

My dear Eric,

You might have found time to answer one of my letters, but I suppose you are very busy and haven't much spare time. I always hear from home when they

get a letter from you.
You will no doubt have heard that I am getting married on July 21st. I wish you could have been here old son. I dont suppose it would be much use asking for leave would it? Still the war is sure to end sometime, at

least I should think so. I have very little news and have hardly any time for anything but aeroplanes, aeroplanes all the time. I occasionally have to work "an all night" during the week.

Do find time to drop me a line old Chap, I think it is running into years since

I heard from you, and have almost forgotten I have a brother who I always used to quarrel with – no – who always used to quarrel with me. What a time it does seem doesn't it?

Bye bye old chap I will write much oftener, even if you don't.

Affectionately yours

Reg

"HAZELDENE,"
RUSSELL PLACE,
SOUTHAMPTON.

Mch. 15/37

My dear Eric & Billy,

I am writing one letter as I haven't time for two. There are a few things I think I ought to tell you.

Gordon has been home again this week and Dad has now told him that he doesn't think that he is going to get better. Reg has talked a lot to me to Gordon & to both of us together, & we are gradually getting to know his wishes. I would like to tell you some of these now.

Reg told Gordon this morning that the more he thought of it, the less inclined

shall send this to the Works. Then you can use your discretion about reading it to your mother. You will know & I will upset her too much.

he was for Gordon to be an Engineer & he has asked him to consider it very carefully. He thinks it is highly probable that some other profession would be less strenuous & also he would like him to choose something that would enable him to spend considerable time out of doors.

Gordon is to remain at Clifton College another term & then Reg says if it takes 6 months or 12 months to make up his mind what he wants to do, it doesn't matter. He could, Reg says, go to University (Southampton) while he was thinking it out. Reg has almost made up his mind, he says, that he doesn't want him to go to Rolls at Derby. This morning also he said to me, "I think that I would like to be cremated". I have asked him to tell Dr Picken if he reaches a decision.

He has mentioned about people coming down & he told me that what he definitely didn't want was a lot of outside relations similar to people who came to his father's funeral. He said he well remembered looking after them

P.S. Reg has read this letter — we have no secrets. He says "You must tell Eric & Bill that if they are not well, they mustn't feel that they have to come. It says he knows that Eric isn't well & it would be the biggest mistake to come if not fit — that the running them to the station, — that the whole time that he was doing it the whole of his system revolted. He told me that he hoped that there would be nothing in the nature of a feast.

"HAZELDENE,"
RUSSELL PLACE,
SOUTHAMPTON.
TELEPHONE SOUTHAMPTON 4135.

Now this is a matter for you both to think about. For I am wondering what I shall be like later. He was naturally very definite. He said he thought it inadvisable for about both of you coming — whether there is anyone besides I, have at the moment, don't know. He says no one from long distances really wants to — he says it means losing business time & so on.

Sometimes I feel that I shall be unable to carry on — you can imagine how distressing it all is — then I have a great urge to know all that he would like, for I have never known anyone with such wonderful judgment & clear sightedness. I keep a little book when I am in the bedroom & I write down all his ideas which to me will be a sacred guidance.

4

This morning Reg had some very big pains. He asked sister to let him experiment & went longer without injections.

He was injected 5 hourly — now it is 4 hourly & an increased amount.

Reg has been downstairs twice — Sat in the Lounge & Sunday in the Dining Room.

Dr Picken suggested that if he felt like it to-day he should go in the garden but it is much too cold although the sun is shining.

And now about Reg as a patient. He is wonderful — so kind, thoughtful & very rarely depressed. everyone around him. I went in his room at 3 a.m. this morning — I couldn't sleep. Sister got me some hot milk & we all sat talking until 4 a.m. We are very fortunate now with our nurses (I have changed two) At the moment he has one of his men from the Works — he spoke himself over the 'phone & asked him to come.

Gordon is ringing at 7.5 p.m. to tell us of his safe arrival. Please excuse hasty scribble & forgive any badly expressed thoughts. I am Yours affectionately
Flo.

My dear Eric & Billy,

I am writing one letter as I haven't time for two. There are a few things I think I ought to tell you. Gordon has been home again this week end and Dad has now told him that he doesn't think that he is going to get better. Reg has talked a lot to me to Gordon and to both of us together, & we are gradually getting to know his wishes. I would like to tell you some of these now.

Reg told Gordon this morning that the more he thought of it, the less inclined [p. 2] he was for Gordon to be an Engineer & he has asked him to consider it very carefully. He thinks it is highly probable that some other profession would be less strenuous, & also he would like him to choose something that would enable him to spend considerable time out of doors.

Gordon is to remain at Clifton College another term & then Reg says if it takes 6 months or 12 months to make up his mind what he wants to do, it doesn't matter. He could, Reg says, go to University (Southampton) while he was thinking it out. Reg has almost made up his mind, he says, that he doesn't want him to go to Rolls at Derby.

This morning also, he said to me, 'I think that I would like to be cremated'. I have asked him to tell Dr Picken if he reaches a decision. He has mentioned about people coming down & he told me that what he definitely didn't want was a lot of outside relations such as similar to people who came to his father's funeral. He said he well remembered looking after them [p. 3] and running them to the station, & that the whole time that he was doing it the whole of his system revolted. He told me that he hoped that there would be nothing in the nature of a feast.

P.S. [top of page 3] Reg has read this letter—we have no secrets. He says 'You must tell Eric and Bill that if they are not well, they mustn't feel that they have to come. He says he knows that Eric isn't well and it would be the biggest mistake to come if not fit.

Now this is a matter for you both to think about [inserted] for I am wondering what I shall be like later. He was naturally very definite about both of you coming [inserted] he said he thought it inadvisable for his mother to come—whether there is anyone besides I, have at the moment, don't know. He says no one from long distances really wants to—he says it means losing business time & so on.

Sometimes I feel that I shall be unable to carry on—you can imagine how distressing it all is—then I have a great urge to know all that he would like, for I have never known anyone with such wonderful judgement and clear sightedness. I keep a little book when I am in the bedroom & I write down all his ideas which will to me be a sacred guidance.

[p. 4] This morning Reg had some very big pains. He asked sister to let him experiment & went longer without [morphine] injections. He was injected 5 hourly—now it is 4 hourly & an increasing amount.

Reg has been downstairs twice—Sat in the Lounge and Sunday in the Dining Room. Dr Picken suggested that if he felt like it today he should go in the garden but it is much too cold although the sun is shining.

And now about Reg as a patient. He is wonderful—so kind, thoughtful of everyone around him—& very rarely depressed. I went in his room at 3 a.m. this morning—I couldn't sleep. Sister got me some hot milk & we all sat talking until 4 a.m. We are very fortunate now with our nurses (I have changed two). At the moment he has one of his men from the works—he spoke himself over the 'phone & asked him to come.

Gordon is ringing at 7.5 p.m. to tell us of his safe arrival [at Clifton College]. Please excuse hasty scribble & forgive any badly expressed thoughts.

I am Yours affectionately,
Flo.

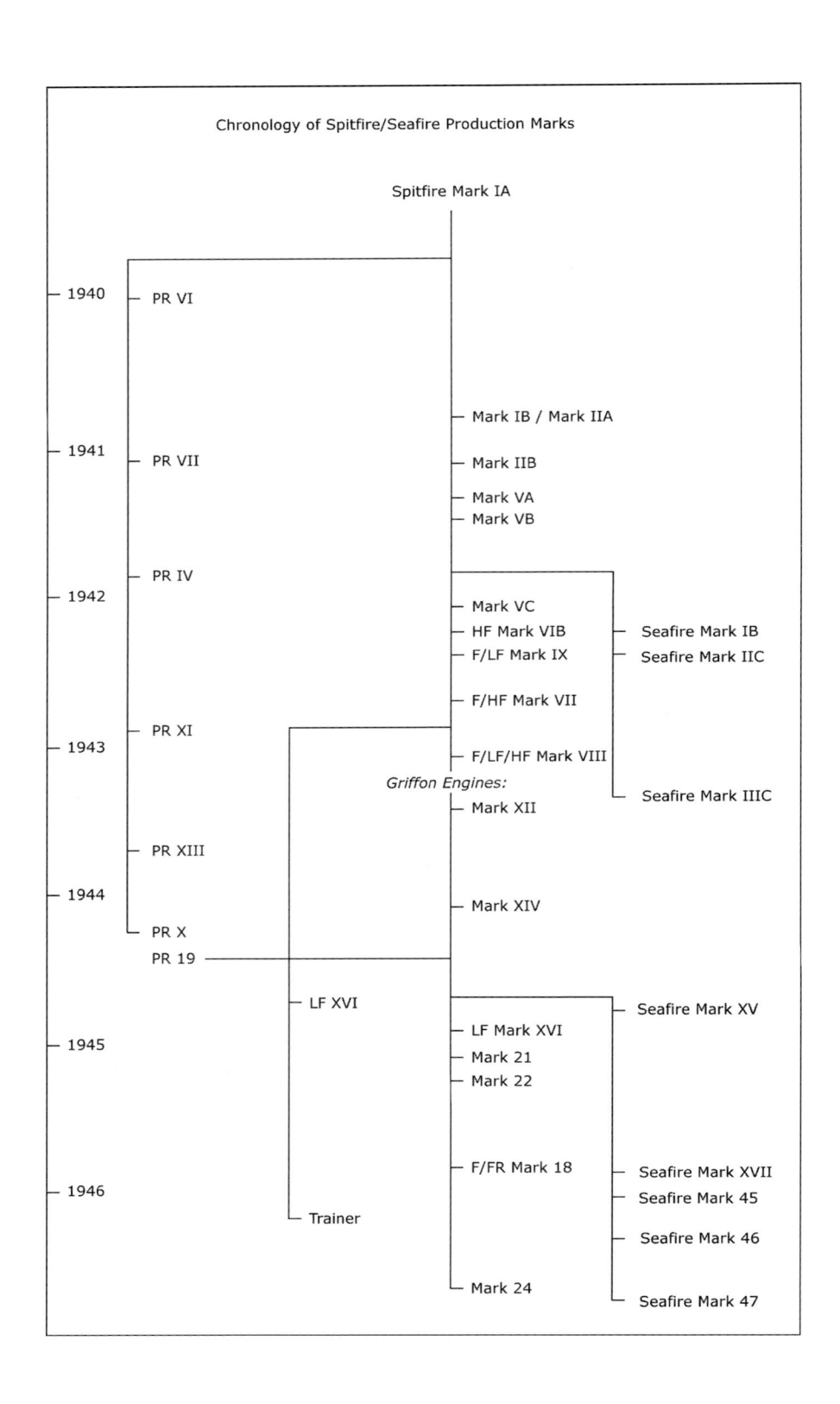

Chronology of Spitfire/Seafire Production Marks

```
                                    Spitfire Mark IA
                                         │
       ┌─────────────────────────────────┤
── 1940 │                                │
        ├─ PR VI                         │
        │                                │
        │                                ├─ Mark IB / Mark IIA
── 1941 │                                │
        ├─ PR VII                        ├─ Mark IIB
        │                                ├─ Mark VA
        │                                ├─ Mark VB
        │                                │
── 1942 │                                │
        ├─ PR IV                         ├─ Mark VC
        │                                ├─ HF Mark VIB     ─── Seafire Mark IB
        │                                ├─ F/LF Mark IX    ─── Seafire Mark IIC
        │                                │
        │                                ├─ F/HF Mark VII
── 1943 │                                │
        ├─ PR XI                         ├─ F/LF/HF Mark VIII
        │            ┌───────────────── Griffon Engines:
        │            │                   ├─ Mark XII        ─── Seafire Mark IIIC
        │            │                   │
        ├─ PR XIII   │                   │
── 1944 │            │                   ├─ Mark XIV
        ├─ PR X      │                   │
          PR 19 ─────┤                   │
                     │                   │                  ─── Seafire Mark XV
                     ├─ LF XVI           ├─ LF Mark XVI
── 1945              │                   ├─ Mark 21
                     │                   ├─ Mark 22
                     │                   │
                     │                   │
                     │                   ├─ F/FR Mark 18    ─── Seafire Mark XVII
── 1946              │                   │                  ─── Seafire Mark 45
                     └─ Trainer          │                  ─── Seafire Mark 46
                                         │
                                         └─ Mark 24         ─── Seafire Mark 47
```

Appendix II

Production Versions of the Spitfire

(i) General

Full accounts of the development of the Spitfire after Mitchell's death can be found in Robertson, Morgan and Shacklady, and in Price. There is a website that supplies the serial number and history of every Spitfire and Seafire built; there is also a very comprehensive pdf publication, by S. J. Lucas, illustrating all the different marks and main variants in 121 drawings (*see* Bibliography). It was felt, nevertheless, that a brief description ought to be included here for completeness' sake and to illustrate the remarkable development of the Spitfire that was possible after the death of R. J. Mitchell.

Mitchell's basic fighter was eventually developed, separately, for high altitude (HF) and low altitude (LF) operation, photoreconnaissance (PR) work, and ship- and carrier-based duties (the Seafires); there were also floatplanes and a two-seat trainer. The somewhat bewildering nomenclature of these different marks of Spitfire may be conveniently clarified via this appendix, as well as the non-consecutive dates of their appearance and the apparent inconsistency of the mark enumerations—for example, the Seafire 45 appeared before the Seafire XVII. In the course of the account, the exact reason for some of these apparently illogical mark numbers will become clear and such detailed nomenclature as 'ASR II' or 'LF XVIE' will also be explained, as well as the modifications of these sorts of letterings as Mitchell's aircraft underwent its progressive development.

The number of different marks of Spitfire is usually given as twenty-four, but this seems to be a simplistic conclusion based on the fact that the last Spitfire type was the Mark 24. This present survey shows that not all these marks were proceeded with (e.g. Marks III, IV and 23), and that the floatplane, trainer, and the PRIII versions of certain marks were, effectively, separate types; there were also five PR types produced without reference to the allocated twenty-four (e.g. Marks PR IV and VII and 45 to 47). It might therefore be more accurate to speak of at least twenty-eight different marks being produced: the present survey allows a judgement to be made.

Yet before describing the numerous production marks of Spitfire in some detail, it was thought useful to show a 'family tree' of these versions of the Spitfire, indicating the actual order of their appearance, which, for various technical reasons, is often very different from the numerical sequence of their mark numbers (*see* chart opposite).

(ii) The Spitfire Marks in Detail

Merlin-Engined Spitfires
The Mark I
The Mark I differed in outline very little from the prototype (*see* photo p. 365); there was, however, an increase in flap angle, and the substitution of a tailwheel for a skid. When the production model appeared, the wing plating was different and the wing leading-edge torsion box had been strengthened.

The prototype's Merlin 'E' was replaced by the Merlin II, with ejector exhausts, but the fixed pitch, two-bladed propeller was retained. On the seventy-fifth aircraft and subsequently, a three-bladed, two-position type was fitted, powered by a Merlin III of similar power (1,030 hp at 12,250 feet) but with a standardised shaft for three-blade airscrews; by the time of the Battle of Britain, a three-bladed, constant speed propeller was fitted as standard and all previous aircraft retrofitted accordingly. The speed of the Spitfire had now increased by 5 mph to 367 mph at 18,600 feet; the time taken to reach 20,000 feet was reduced by 3½ minutes.

One irritant was the damage to pilots' knuckles when operating the pump to raise the undercarriage, often producing an undulating flight while doing so; later Mark Is had an engine driven hydraulic system. A slab of bulletproof glass had also been attached to the outside of the front windscreen, 73 lb of armour plating fitted behind the pilot's seat and the straight-topped cockpit canopy given a domed cover—to the relief of taller pilots. During the Battle of Britain, combat considerations had reduced the Spitfire Is to a maximum speed of about 353 mph at 20,000 feet with a maximum rate of climb of 2,895 feet/min at 10,000 feet.

By now, the Spitfire in dives was exceeding the speed of the chief designer's specialist Schneider trophy racers and it had been found that the ailerons virtually locked solid in high-speed descents; also, the rate of roll was affected by them becoming heavy at speed. The problem was not, in fact, due to the proportions that had been decided on but rather to the conventional practice of keeping them light by using fabric covering. It was now discovered that this material tended to balloon out at speed and so the ailerons were returned to efficiency by being given a thin aluminium skinning. This cure involved a crash programme to modify all the Mark I aircraft that had been supplied to front-line units. This modification was undertaken by Air Service Training at Hamble; Quill wryly noted:

> The word swept round Fighter Command like wildfire and in no time the air around Hamble was thick with Spitfires of Wing Leaders and Squadron Commanders all trying to jump the queue to get their aircraft fitted with the new metal ailerons.

Quill also discovered shortly afterwards in a captured Messerschmitt Bf 109E that the problem had been just as bad on the other side.

One other concern with the skinning of the aircraft led to an investigation as to whether the extra complexity of flush riveting all the covering panels was justified. Split-peas were glued over the rivet heads to simulate the standard round-headed ones and discovering the effects of progressively removing them from different parts of the skinning. As a result, production Spitfires were built with dome-headed rivets to the fuselage while the wing surfaces continued to be flush riveted.

During the Battle of Britain, it was found that German bombers could often absorb hits from machine gun fire by virtue of their armour plating and so the attraction of the more penetrative but slower firing cannon led to the development of an alternative armament of two cannons and four machine guns. The Spitfires with the original eight-gun arrangement were therefore designated IA and the ones with the cannons IB. Joe Smith had to have the cannons mounted on their sides in the Spitfire's thin wing; this led to empty cartridge cases jamming in the breeches so frequently that the cannon version was withdrawn from front-line duties for reversion to the eight machine gun version until the problem of stoppages could be solved.

For photoreconnaissance versions of the Mark I, *see* the PR section that follows. It might also be mentioned here that one Spitfire, the forty-eighth in the Eastleigh production line, had been specially modified for an attempt on the world landplane speed record. This so-called Speed Spitfire is also described in the photoreconnaissance section.

There were 1,550 machines produced.

The Mark II (see photo p. 370)
In the summer of 1939, an early Mk I was fitted with a new version of the Merlin, the XII. With the success of the trial, it was decided to use this version of the Merlin in the Mk II, which, it was decided, would be the first version to be produced exclusively by the huge new Lord Nuffield shadow factory at Castle Bromwich. This mark represents the first of Joe Smith's variants and it had largely replaced the previous version in front-line service by the end of 1940, some in time to take part in the later stages of the Battle of Britain.

It was, basically, similar to the later production models of the Mark I, with its armour plating and bulletproof front windscreen; the IIA still had its eight machine guns and the IIB had the two cannons (now functioning properly) and four machine guns. The essential change from the Mark I was the more powerful Merlin XII (1,135 horsepower at 12,250 feet), which increased the top speed over the late Mk I by about 7 mph below 17,000 feet and produced a climb-rate of 2,995 feet per minute at 10,000 feet, although its top speed was 354 mph at 17,550 feet.

When the Mk II was taken out of front-line service, fifty of them were converted for air-sea rescue work, at first originally identified as Spitfire IIC, but with the advent of the 'C' wing (*see* below), it was re-designated ASR II. They were modified to operate by dropping dinghy and survival canisters to assist airmen until they were picked up by boat or seaplane; a small rack for smoke-marking bombs was fitted under the port wing, inboard of the oil cooler, and two flare chutes in the fuselage, just aft of the cockpit, housed a small dinghy and a metal food container.

There were 921 built.

The Mark III
The Mark III first flew in March 1940 and represented the first attempt to improve significantly on the Spitfire's performance, particularly by making the tailwheel retractable. Also, the wings were clipped—a modification which had been first tried out with the Speed Spitfire of 1939. In the present case, the concern was first and foremost with increasing the rate of roll, rather than speed, and looked forward to other later clipped wing versions—in particular, the low-level Mark VB, which was to appear a year later. The Mark III was powered by the Merlin XX, developing 1,240 hp at 10,000 feet, due to its two-speed supercharger, and the wingspan was reduced to 32 feet 7 inches, giving a maximum speed of 400 mph at 21,000 feet.

The strengthened main undercarriage was raked forward 2 inches, increasing ground stability, and had flaps to fully enclose the wheels when retracted. The windscreen was redesigned, with a built-in, internal laminated glass, bulletproof panel, and optically flat, laminated glass quarter panels. It also saw the introduction of the 'C' 'universal' wing, which allowed the fitting of either the 'A' or 'B' gun combinations or a four-cannon arrangement.

As Rolls-Royce could initially only produce a limited number of the XX engines, it was decided to give priority to re-engining the slower Hurricane and so the Mark III Spitfire never went beyond the prototype stage. However, as we shall see, a number of the experimental features of this machine were successfully adopted in other versions of the Spitfire; in particular, the test fittings of the new Merlin 60 series also made the Mark III virtually the prototype for the Mark IX.

There were two built.

The Mark IV
For the Mark IV, *see* the introduction to the Griffon-engined Spitfires section and the photoreconnaissance section below.

The Mark V
The Mark V (*see* photo p. 370) was intended as a stopgap type until a more comprehensively redesigned aircraft could be produced, but it ended up being the most numerous of all marks. The immediate concern was to be ready by 1941 for an anticipated second Battle of Britain, expected to be fought at a higher altitude and to counter the Messerschmitt Bf 109F when it appeared in early 1941, which had significantly greater speed and rate of climb than the Spitfire Mark II and could even out-turn it.

The Merlin 45 (1,470 hp at 11,500 feet) was to be fitted to the basic Mark II airframe, with the deepened oil cooler intake introduced with the Mark III. In the event, this proposed interim version was able to operate at the higher altitudes, despite the additional weight of extra armour plating around the ammunition boxes, under the pilot's seat, and in front of the coolant header tank. Later enemy comparison tests between a captured Mark V, fitted with a Daimler engine, and a Messerschmitt Bf 109G revealed that the Spitfire was slower at sea level but was superior in climb and altitude performance.

Fitted with external and jettisonable fuel tanks and progressively more powerful engines, this mark came out in three versions: the VA retained the original eight machine-gun layout and could reach a top speed of 369 mph at 20,000 feet; the VB had the wing with two 20-mm cannon and four machine-guns and became the main production version of the Mark V, especially as it now matched the Bf 109 in firepower; and the VC, which had the stronger wing of the Mark III, allowing four cannons to be installed, although a two-cannon arrangement was the most effective and favoured by pilots, the cannons being in the inner positions and each outer barrel position filled with a rubber plug. This arrangement had the advantage of doubling the number of rounds carried for each of the remaining cannons. There was also provision for carrying a 250- or 500-lb bomb under the fuselage; after the Battle of Malta, Spitfires had been fitted with improvised bomb racks in order to go on the offensive. The aircraft also had heating for the guns, which were now being subjected to more prolonged periods at higher altitudes, and provision for the carrying of a long-range, external, belly fuel tank.

Once the expected second Battle of Britain did not materialise, the Spitfire had been able to extend Fighter Command's largely defensive activities and take the fight to the enemy with sweeps over Northern France. For this new role as a low altitude fighter and fighter bomber, the LFV was introduced, having clipped wings and the lower-altitude-rated Merlin 45M (1,585 hp at 2,750 feet). Unfortunately, in the first half of 1942, partly to draw some of the Luftwaffe's fighters away from the Russian front, Fighter Command lost over 300 Mark Vs, largely as a result of operating at less advantageous altitudes, being more exposed to ground fire and meeting the new Focke-Wulf 190.

The Mark V could also be equipped with a bulky Vokes 'beard' air filter for tropical service and thus, with the various engines, the Mark V version was active in both temperate and tropical zones. In the latter regions, however, the filter cut down boost pressure at high levels and produced poor performance at low levels.

Earlier, the German invasion of Norway in 1940 had initiated an experiment to equip Spitfires with floats originally designed for a Blackburn Roc conversion, for use from sheltered waters, such as Norwegian fjords, but subsequent events led to an abandonment of this idea; however, the Japanese entry into the war gave rise to a later consideration of the floatplane fighter, to be based where the terrain was unsuitable for the construction of airfields or where there might be an important tactical advantage in the presence of fighters not being expected. At the time, it was thought that the floatplanes could operate from concealed bases in the Dodecanese Islands, disrupting supply lines to German outposts in the areas which relied on resupply by transport aircraft. This scheme came to naught when a large number of German troops, backed by the Luftwaffe, took over the British-held islands of Kos and Leros.

Now, three Mark VB machines were specially equipped with floats (fittingly designed by Arthur Shirvall who was responsible for those of the Supermarine Schneider trophy winners), and in view of its Schneider trophy predecessors, it is not surprising that the test pilot found that 'it was a most beautiful floatplane and all we had to do, predictably, was to increase the fin area to compensate for the float area ahead of the centre of gravity'. Underfins, unique to the floatplane Spitfire, were fitted, followed by the addition of a fillet added to the leading edge of the dorsal fin to achieve the extra area required and, with the floats and their well-faired vertical mountings, only reduced the speed by 30 mph. The floatplane had a maximum speed of 324 mph at 19,500 ft and maximum rate of climb of 2,450 feet/min at 15,500 feet. These aircraft were sent, in the end, not to the Far East but to Egypt, operating from the Great Bitter Lake, south of Port Said. However, they never saw operational service and no production series was ever initiated.

The Mark V was produced before America had joined the war and when Britain was heavily engaged in the Mediterranean and North African theatres of war. It was therefore produced in larger numbers than any other Spitfire mark; it remained the main RAF fighter until the summer of 1942 and the low-level LFV remained in use into 1946.

There were 6,475 built.

The Mark VI
The Mark VI was the first serious attempt to adapt the current Spitfire V, with a ceiling of about 30,000 ft, for higher altitudes. Desperate modifications to reduce weight had been made to some Mark VCs based at Aboukir to combat high-flying Junkers Ju 86P photoreconnaissance aircraft and resulted in great feats of endurance and determination on the part of the pilots at heights above 40,000 feet. As the lightening modifications involved stripping out the aircraft's

radio, the aircraft had to be accompanied by a second Spitfire, with radio, to follow ground control. Two Ju 86s were shot down and the patrols ceased.

However, any thought of standard operation at such heights or for any length of time was not possible owing to the strain on pilots and had to await the successful development of a pressurised cockpit and an increased wingspan. This increase, without all the additional production delays associated with a major redesign of the wing, was produced by the expedient of adding pointed tips which, although achieving a span of 40 feet 2 inches and a wing area increase 6.5 sq. feet, completely destroyed the appearance of Mitchell's original conception.

The pressurised cockpit, also, left much to be desired as the hood had to be locked on before take-off and could not be opened in flight; while it could be jettisoned in an emergency, the hood had to be completely removed for normal entrance and exit. The Mark VI had a Merlin 47 engine with a four-bladed propeller, producing 1,415 hp at 14,000 feet, a top speed of 356 mph at 21,800 feet, and a climb rate of 2,660 feet/min.

The German invasion of Russia in June 1941 caused fears of high altitude bombing to recede and so this Mark did not go into large scale production.

There were 100 built.

The Mark VII

The Mark VII (*see* photo p. 371) represented, along with the Mark VIII, a breakthrough in Spitfire development with the fitting of the Merlin 64 with its two-stage, two-speed supercharger. It did not appear straight away after the Mark V and VI as the substantial design changes decided on took longer to incorporate; these included wings re-designed to take internal fuel tanks, 11 gal. more tankage in the fuselage, and a retractable tailwheel. The airframe was now fully stressed to take the new Merlin (1,415 hp at 14,000 feet), and the pressurised cockpit (now with a sliding cabin hood but no hinged door in the side of the fuselage) was more satisfactorily sealed than that of the Mark VI.

It began appearing, rather slowly, in August, 1942, and later aircraft were fitted with an extended fin and broader chord rudder; the HF version, with the Merlin 71 (1,655 hp at 10,000 feet), had the expanded span wing tips. It now had a service ceiling of 45,100 feet and its top speed had risen to 416 mph, but as its performance proved to be no better than that of the lightened Mark IX, which was already being produced as a stopgap, no large production orders were placed for the Mark VII. Many of these variants found a role in meteorological work.

There were 140 built.

The Mark VIII

On the other hand, the Mark VIII was the third most numerous variant, employing clipped, standard, or extended wing planforms for its many roles, and eventually replacing the numerous Mark IX. The standard fighter 'F' version was powered by the Merlin 63 (1,710 hp at 8,500 feet) and had a top speed of 408 mph at 25,000 feet; the LF version was powered by the Merlin 66 (1,720 hp at 8,500 feet) and had a top speed of 404 mph at 21,000 feet; and the HF machine had the Merlin 70 (1,710 hp at 11,000 feet) and a top speed of 416 mph at 26,500 feet, with a service ceiling of 43,000 feet. This last was a non-pressurised version of the previous mark, with the revised fin and rudder but usually without the extended span wings, as action had now tended to take place below 25,000 feet with the ending of high-altitude attacks.

Fuel capacity was now increased to 124 gallons thanks to extra tanks in the wing roots and the tailwheel was again retractable. Provision was now made for a 250-lb bomb to be carried under each wing, thus enabling the fitting of an additional fuel tank under the fuselage. The Mark VIII was also fully tropicalised without the bulky 'beard'-type carburettor air filter housing that had been fitted to the Mark V and so it was used almost exclusively in the Middle East, India, Burma, and Australia.

As with the Mark VII, the aileron structure was stiffened by a reduction in the overhang outboard of the outer hinge and this modification, together with the Merlin 66 engine, produced an aircraft that was assessed by Jeffrey Quill as follows: 'I always thought the aeroplane which was the best from the pure text book handling point of view was the Mark VIII.... With the standard wing tip it was a really beautiful aeroplane'.

There were 1,658 built.

The Mark IX

The Mark IX was, like the Mark V, also planned as a short-term expedient until the Mark VIII could be put into production but, in the end, it became one of the most numerous of all Spitfire variants. While the Mark V had become the backbone of RAF Fighter Command, fresh responses were required to the better high-altitude performance of the Bf 109G and especially, to the Focke-Wulf 190.

This last had appeared over northern France in September 1941 and had been found to out-climb by 450 feet per minute, outrun by more than 20 mph, and outmanoeuvre the Mark V Spitfire, with or without clipped wings and with the assistance of 'Miss Shilling's orifice'; this latter was a stopgap device devised by Miss Beatrice 'Tilly' Shilling, whereby a hole was punched into a metal diaphragm placed across the float chamber of the Merlin carburettors to prevent fuel starvation in negative *g* manoeuvres—not a problem with the German fuel-injected motors. The year 1943 saw a permanent solution with the introduction of the Bendix-Stromburg carburettor which injected fuel at 5 psi through a nozzle direct into the supercharger.

The Mark IX, when it began to be produced in June 1942 was, essentially, the earlier Mark V, fitted initially with the vastly improved Merlin 60 series, giving outstandingly better performance than the Spitfire V, especially at heights above 20,000 feet, and finally proving an answer to the Fw 190. There were three versions: F Mark IX, LF Mark IX, and HF Mark IX, respectively. The early Spitfire FIXs were equipped with the Merlin 61, giving 1,565 hp at 11,250 feet and a maximum speed of 403 mph at 27,400 feet. The Merlin 61 was phased out early in 1943 in favour of the Merlin 63, giving 1,710 hp at 8,500 feet and a maximum speed of 408 mph at 25,000 feet. The LF version had the Merlin 66—1,720 hp at 5,750 feet, giving a maximum speed of 404 mph at 21,000 feet. The HF IX was powered by the specialised high-altitude Merlin 70 and entered service in the spring of 1944; it produced 1,710 hp at 11,000 feet, giving a maximum speed of 416 mph at 27,500 feet.

Lightened Mark IX versions were now able to go higher than the specially designed Mark VI and one Mark IX recorded the highest air battle of the Second World War, at 43,000 feet against one of the Junkers Ju 86 bombers; stripped of armour plate and equipped with only two cannons, it pursued the bomber and damaged it before the guns jammed. This action was, fittingly, over Southampton.

Some IXs were also pressed into service as photoreconnaissance machines—the FR IX was a standard, armed Mk IX modified with a single, port-facing, oblique camera. These aircraft

A Mark IX showing symmetrical radiator ducting and bomb attached.

were used for low-altitude 'Dicing' missions in tactical support of army operations and so carried the standard guns of the Mk IX fighter.

The new mark's top speeds marked the point where the dedicated record-breaking S.6B was overtaken in level flight by a fully equipped fighting machine. The extra power of the new Merlins now required a four-bladed propeller and increased radiation which resulted in symmetrical underwing ducting for the first time. Such changes were obviously not perceptible from any distance, especially as the standard Mark V elliptical wing was still the norm, and so enemy pilots, unsure whether or not they were approaching the new higher performance aircraft, were now more disposed to keep away from the older Mark V, which was still very active in the skies. Yet when the Mark IX was tested against a captured Fw 190 in July of the following year (*Oberleutnant* Arnim Faber had conveniently landed it, a little lost, at RAF Pembrey Sands on 23 June 1942), the differences in performance were too small for comfort and the German's rate of climb between 15,000 and 23,000 feet was superior.

The more powerful new Merlins also gave rise to experiments with increased fuel tankage and with a six-bladed contra-rotating propeller. Other subsequent modifications included clipped wings for low altitude operations and, subsequently, the pointed fin and broad-chord rudder; later, as with most aircraft after 1944, it was also produced with a 'teardrop' canopy and cut-down fuselage rear decking for better rearward visibility. Fuel capacity was also increasing so that, with the introduction of two 18 gal. fabric cells into the wings and a 72-gal. tank into the rear fuselage, the internal fuel capacity of the Spitfire had increased to nearly twice that of the prototype. With a further 45-gal. drop tank, Jeffrey Quill flew a Mark IX from Salisbury Plain to the Moray Firth and back at less than 1,000 feet—the equivalent of East Anglia to Berlin and back (and thereby proving that the Spitfire might be used if needs be as a bomber escort over Europe).

The 'C' wing with two cannons and four machine guns was still standard although an 'E' wing was introduced later, which offered the two cannons, together with two larger bore 0.50-inch Browning machine guns. To signify the change from the 'C' wing, a new designation was used: LF IXE and HF IXE.

There was also, in 1944, a floatplane conversion of the Mark IX with the modified fin of the Mark V conversion but without the 'beard' type tropical air filter; the carburettor air intake was also moved forward to avoid the entry of spray (for photo *see* p. ###). It was faster than the standard Hurricane and its handling on the water was extremely good. However, soon after testing started, the idea of using floatplane fighters was dropped and MJ982 was converted back to a landplane.

A Mk IX was converted for use as a trainer by the Soviets, but the two-seat Spitfire trainer was primarily a post-war programme. In 1946, a Mk VIII (MT818) was converted by moving the original cockpit 13½ inches further forward in order to allow for a separate instructor's cockpit that was behind and raised well above the other one.

Ten Spitfire T IXs were exported to India, and in 1951, a further six trainers were converted to train pilots for the Irish Air Corps Seafire fleet. In the end, twenty Mark IX aircraft were thus converted and sold to foreign air forces, giving rise to an unkind RAF speculation that 'johnny foreigner' needed two people to fly the Spitfire.

Two-seater trainer.

It must be admitted that Mitchell's concern to give the performance of his fighter 'paramount importance' did not allow enough fuselage volume for the creation of a very comfortable two-seater, although training accidents might have been reduced during the war if the RAF had had such a variant (a two-seat trainer version of the Hurricane had also been proposed as early as 1939).

There were 5,653 Mark IXs built.

Marks X and XI

For Marks X and XI, *see* the photoreconnaissance section.
By this time, the mark numbers were being allocated consecutively, whether the aircraft was a fighter, naval, or photo-reconnaissance type.

From September 1944, a version of the Mark IX, with the low altitude Merlin 266 (essentially, the low-rated Merlin 66 built under licence by the Packard Motor Co. of Detroit), was built exclusively at Castle Bromwich.

This version included many of the later modifications to the Mark IX, in particular the increased fuel tankage, the 'E' wing instead of the 'C' wing, and the modified 'rear-view' fuselage. Clipped wings were normal as the machine was intended mainly for ground attack roles. It was given the separate LF XVIE designation.

There were 1053 built.

Spitfire LF XVIE.

Griffon-Engined Spitfires

Rolls-Royce, soon after the outbreak of the war, were developing a new engine based on the Merlin but with a capacity of 36.7 litres instead of the 27 litres of its predecessor. Despite this increase, the firm was able to keep the frontal area of the new engine to no more than 6 per cent greater and its length to no more than 3 inches longer than its immediate Merlin predecessors. Its weight was also within 400 lb of the earlier type. Thus Rolls-Royce made it possible to adapt the Spitfire airframe to the enormously more powerful engine and Mitchell's design took on a completely new lease of life. The Griffon-engined Spitfires were never produced in the large numbers of the Merlin-engined variants, but later versions kept the Spitfire at the forefront of piston-engined fighter development.

The first Griffon-engined prototype was seen as combining the benefits of the new engine with the improvements built into the experimental Mark III—in particular, the retractable tailwheel; and the power of the new engine necessitated a change to a four-bladed propeller. The resultant machine first flew on 27 November 1941 and was originally designated Mark IV but, as other stopgap variants had had to be produced before it could be fully developed and to avoid confusion with the retitled Spitfire PR Mk IV (*see* later), it was re-designated the Mark XX.

Quill narrates how, in July 1942, he was asked to fly a Spitfire in a comparison test with the newly introduced Typhoon and a captured Fw 190. He took the new Griffon-engined machine, DP845, and caused quite a stir: in a race at 1,000 feet from Odiham to Farnborough, the Fw 190 had to drop back due to engine trouble but Quill was able to leave the new Typhoon well behind. The Air Ministry ordered the production of a Griffon-engined Spitfire and this led to the Mark XII.

The Mark XII (*see* photo p. 371) was thus the first production version of the Griffon-engined Spitfire, using the single-stage Griffon III (1,730 hp at 750 feet), and, because it was intended specifically for low level operation, was produced with clipped wings as standard.

DP845, the Mk IV/XX prototype with six cannon mock up.

The single-stage Griffon engine gave the aircraft superb low- and medium-level performance (397 mph at 17,800 feet), although its performance declined at higher altitudes: in comparative tests with a Mk IX, it was 14 mph faster at sea level, but above 20,000 feet, it was slower.

The first of 100 Supermarine-built production aircraft started appearing in October 1942 and were manufactured from Mk VC and Mk VIII airframes; the last forty-five or so were based on Mk VIIIs with two wing fuel tanks, each containing a maximum fuel load of 14 gal. It had a strengthened fuselage, the 'C' wing, and the pointed, broad-chord fin and rudder, made even more necessary by the increased power and length of the new engine and its four-bladed propeller. The top engine cowling was now modified with blisters over the cylinder banks of the new engine to assist the view of the pilot down the centre of the longer nose, which, with the new rudder, increased the overall length of the new mark to 31 feet 10 inches. Some of the earlier XIIs still had fixed tailwheels. Another important feature of the Griffon-engine Spitfires was the entirely flush-riveted finish, which was progressively introduced on all Spitfires.

Its improved performance was such that the enemy of 1943, when the new silhouette was identified, was none too anxious to be drawn into low altitude battles where the Mark XII was dominant—as proven near the end of its front-line service in summer 1944, when it shot down a respectable number of V-1 Flying Bombs (capable of 400+ mph at 5,000 feet).

Nevertheless, the Mark XII was an improvised machine with a poor rate of climb because of its single-stage supercharged engine. It was only built in limited numbers and was phased out in September, 1945. The Spitfire Mark IX was still the most useful all-round fighter.

There were 100 built.

(For the Mark XIII, *see* the photoreconnaissance section below.)

The Mark XIV (*see* photo p. 371) differed from the Mk XII in that it was provided with the much more powerful two-stage supercharged Griffon 65, producing 2,035 hp at 7,000 feet. A new five-bladed Rotol propeller of 10 feet 5 inches in diameter was used, and the increased cooling requirements of the Griffon engine meant that the radiators were much bigger and their underwing housings were deeper than previously. Due to its longer nose and the increased slipstream of the big five-bladed propeller, a new tail unit with a taller, broader fin and a rudder of increased area was adopted.

The fitting of an engine with two stage supercharging meant that no different high- or low- altitude versions were now necessary; however, pending the development of a 'super Spitfire', to be powered by this all-altitude Griffon engine (appearing eventually in 1946 as the Mark 18), the Mark XIV was another interim type, employing a strengthened Mark VIII airframe and the 'C' wing with two 31-gal. wing tanks—it now had a range of over 610 miles or 960 miles with a 90-gal. drop tank. There was still some directional instability, as in the previous Griffon mark, and so the fin and rudder area needed to be further enlarged. This was initially achieved by increasing the side area of the pointed fin version via a straightened leading edge; later the whole fin and rudder outline was redrawn to encompass the increased area and became the first thorough re-design of these components.

The Mark XIV called for vigilant flying—not only because, as part of a move towards standardisation, the Griffon engine rotated in the opposite direction from the Merlin: the swing during take-off was not only more powerful and now to the right; also the slightest throttle movement resulted in a dramatic surge of power. Nevertheless, Quill's first impression of the new machine was expressed in his phrase 'quantum jump', for the performance was spectacular: 445 mph at 25,000 feet and a from sea-level climb of over 5,000 feet per minute—the A & AEE later reported 447 mph at 25,600 feet and a climb to 40,000 feet in fifteen minutes; the absolute ceiling was no less than 44,600 feet. Although the next re-design of the tail surfaces, with the Mark 22, was the real solution to some control problems, the Mark XIV with the new two-stage engine was very successful at low level against the V-1s and was also the main high altitude superiority fighter until the end of the war.

Later versions were produced with lower fuselage decking and the improved rear view 'tear-drop' canopy. The normal 'C' wing armament later gave way to the 'E' type arrangement of the later Mark IXs and some machines had clipped wings. A few also were engined with the Griffon 85, geared for contra-rotating propellers.

This mark also represented the first appearance of the Spitfire in the FR category. A single camera was fitted, facing to port or starboard and was designated the FRXIV; it had the later cut-down rear fuselage with its tear drop canopy and an additional rear fuel tank of 34 gallons, which extended the Spitfire's range to over 600 miles. In total, over 430 FRXIVs were built.

The XIV could be equipped with four cannons and could carry bombs. Thus it could claim to have the best all-round performance of any current fighter apart from range. It formed the last substantial production run of any type of Spitfire and the last version to see significant action: the first Mark XIVs were produced in time for the invasion of Europe in June 1944 and one had the distinction of being the first aircraft to shoot down the formidable Messerschmitt Me 262 jet fighter; many hundreds were sent to India to assist with the Pacific War, but this ended before many of this latest variant saw active service.

There were 957 built.

(For the Mark XV, *see* the Seafire section below.)

(For the Mark XVI, *see* after the Mark IX above.)

(For the Mark XVII, *see* the Seafire section below.)

From 1943, it became the RAF convention to use Arabic numerals.

The Mark 18
The Mark 18 (*see* photo p. 372) was very similar to the Mark XIV, being also fitted with the Griffon 65 and incorporated the later features of the Mark XIV—the rear-view fuselage, retractable tailwheel, and the 'E' wing armament. Together with the PR 19, it represented the last F variant to embody the classic elliptical wing outline. The wings, however, were in fact, not the 'C' type of the Mark XIV, but a considerably re-designed unit with a strengthened wing centre section and undercarriage—with an 11-inch wider track width; fuel tankage was also increased, as was the depth of the radiators, and the FR version now carried two vertical cameras as well as the oblique type employed in the FRXIV.

It was produced two years after the Mark XIV and so too late for Second World War service; it did, nevertheless, see some action as late as 1951 against Communist forces in Malaya. Production ended in early 1946.

There were 300 built.

(For the Mark 19, *see* the photoreconnaissance section, below.)

(For the Mark XX—so designated because it was proposed before the adoption of Arabic mark numerals—*see* the introduction to the section on Griffon engined Spitfires, above.)

The Mark 21
The Mark 21 was similar, in many ways, to the Mark 18 and also had the Mark XIV fin and rudder, and five-bladed propeller. The wings were of the extended span type but it was soon supplied with the first completely revised wing in which the familiar Mitchell outline was altered and the area slightly increased.

The move to metal skinned ailerons had improved lateral control in the earlier Spitfires and metal skinning of the rudder and elevators had now been introduced. However, as speeds further increased, heaviness of the ailerons was again experienced and so a complete redesign with a 20 per cent increase in area was now incorporated into the new wings. Their structure had also to be further stiffened as the Griffon-engined Spitfires were now beginning to experience the problem of 'aileron reversal'; that is, the torsional load applied to the wing by the ailerons at the speeds now possible was causing the wings to twist and, in extreme cases, to reverse the expected effect of aileron movement. Apart from the internal modifications, the evident alteration to the wings was the move to half-rounded tips—a compromise between the clipped version and Mitchell's original elliptical configuration.

There were now two leading-edge fuel tanks in each wing and, for the first time, four 20-mm cannons were fitted and no machine guns. Small blisters in the top surface of each wing were required in order that the ammunition belt feed mechanisms were cleared; by way of compensation, however, doors were also provided to cover the lower half of the wheels

Mk 21 prototype with extended span wing and third type fin and rudder.

A typical Mk 21.

when retracted. As with the Mark XIV of the previous year, the larger diameter, five-bladed propeller was fitted to its Griffon 65 and this led, in turn, to a longer undercarriage, slightly repositioned. The take-off still needed care.

Some aircraft were fitted with the Griffon 85 (2,375 hp at 10,500 feet) designed to take a six-bladed contra-rotating propeller unit, which improved the machine's handling characteristics but the aircraft was still longitudinally unstable, with very sensitive elevators, and therefore in need of re-designed tail surfaces. RAF test pilots did not consider it an improvement on the Mark XIV as an all-round machine and that 'no further attempt should be made to perpetuate the Spitfire family'. On the other hand, Quill found the new mark to have 'a tremendous lightness of control' and 'revelled in aerobatics at speeds that would have been impossible before'. The major re-design work involved had been put in hand by 1942, but this mark was only operational at the end of 1944. It was particularly used against V-2 sites in northern Holland. It was not produced in large numbers as the war ended soon after its production began.

There were 121 built.

The Mark 22
The Mark 22 (*see* photo p. 373) was again powered by the Griffon 85 and being also completed very late—in 1945—did not proceed to large scale production. The development from the Mark 21 to the Mark 22 and to the Mark 24 was so seamless that no prototypes as such were necessary and the main difference between the last two variants was the increased fuel capacity of the later mark. They both had the new wing and the four-cannon arrangement of the Mark 21, but while the Mark 21 still retained the balloon type of cockpit hood and its associated rear fuselage decking, these latest machines were equipped from the outset with

a final rear-view fuselage and canopy configuration. A new fin was also fitted. During 1946, further development work resulted in the fitting of substantially revised and enlarged tail surfaces of the Spiteful type, further distancing the Mark 22 and the Mark 24 from Mitchell's original design. These tail surface increases, the new wing and fin, and the new rear-view cockpit arrangement, taken together, produced an even more marked departure from the original Spitfire shape than that of the Mark 21.

Very soon after the Mark 22 was produced, provision was made for carrying three 500-lb bombs, one under each wing and one under the fuselage. It equipped RAF auxiliary squadrons until 1951 and also two squadrons of the Southern Rhodesian Air Force until 1954.

There were 268 built.

The Mark 23
The Mark 23 was to be a Mk 22 incorporating a revised wing design, which featured an increase in incidence in order to improve the pilot's view over the nose in flight and increase the high-speed and dive performance of the aircraft. The modified wing was first fitted to a Mk VIII JG204 which was tested from July 1944. However, the tests were disappointing and it was decided to build a new prototype using the Mk 21 prototype PP139; in this form, the prototype was designated F Mk 23 and was to be renamed the Supermarine Valiant. However, the new wing gave less than perfect handling characteristics and so the Mk 23 never went into production.

The Mark 24
The Mark 24 was the final Spitfire variant; it was similar to the Mk 22 except that it had an increased fuel capacity, with two fuel tanks of 33 gal. each installed in the rear fuselage, and fittings for rocket projectiles under the wings.

Now that the stability problems associated with the increased power of the later Griffon engines had been overcome by the revised wing and tail planforms, it achieved a maximum speed of 446 mph at 27,000 feet and could reach an altitude of 30,000 feet in eight minutes, putting it on a par with the most advanced piston-engined fighters of the era. It could thus be regarded as the 'ultimate Spitfire' and showed how far it had been possible to develop Mitchell's prototype of 1936; in round terms, the engine power and the loaded weight had doubled, the fuel capacity had trebled and the maximum speed had increased by 100 mph—a similar advance as that achieved between the prototype Spitfire and the previous Gladiator. Introduced into service in 1946, the F24 was twice as heavy, more than twice as powerful and showed an increase in climb rate of 80 per cent over that of the prototype, K5054.

These impressive increases had all been, impressively, achieved by the progressive development of Mitchell's original formulation—as indicated by the fact that, in spite of all the increases just mentioned, the final wing area was less than 2 sq. ft more than that of the prototype. One does, however, tend to agree with Quill: 'the genius passed on by Mitchell had died. The beautiful symmetry had gone; in its place stood a powerful, almost ugly fighting machine'.

The final Spitfire came off the production line in February 1948. The mark equipped No. 80 Squadron which, after serving in Germany, went to Hong Kong; in January 1952, the aircraft were handed over to the Hong Kong Auxiliary Air Force.

There were seventy-four built.

Photoreconnaissance Spitfires
At the outbreak of war, the idea of photoreconnaissance by an unarmed fighter seemed like two contradictions in terms; however, the ability of such an aircraft to fly higher and faster than other standard designs was certainly worth considering for this very different role, especially after operational experience with Blenheims and Lysanders had shown the need for aircraft capable of avoiding, rather than trying to defend against, enemy machines in order to return safely with vital photographic information. Due to its high speed, the Spitfire was an obvious choice for the experiment, and the earliest mark was utilised even though there was severe competition for its services elsewhere.

As with the naval Seafire (*see* below), the photoreconnaissance version had never been envisaged by Mitchell although, interestingly enough, the first Supermarine machine considered for this sort of operation was the 'Speed Spitfire', which looked back to the earlier Mitchell days of record breaking. At an international aeroplane meeting at Zurich in July 1937, it was announced that a Messerschmitt Bf 109 had become the fastest fighter in the world, having attained a top speed of 379 mph. The Air Ministry ordered a competing model, and the forty-eighth Mark I was taken from the production line for modifications which included blunter wingtips, a reduced span of 33 feet 8 inches, and the fitting of a cockpit enclosure with a profile not unlike that of the de Havilland DH. 88 Comet, which won the MacPherson Robertson race from England to Australia in 1934. It had also reverted to a tailskid and increased radiator and oil cooler intakes to accommodate a greatly boosted Special Merlin engine, capable of 2,100 hp in short runs. A four-bladed fixed-pitch propeller was fitted to absorb the additional power and the royal blue upper surfaces, with silver undersides and fuselage flash, had filler applied to their joints and given a highly polished finish.

The Speed Spitfire.

At one stage, to cut down drag, the radiator was completely removed and the coolant allowed to boil away, but when, on 26 April 1939, a purpose-built Messerschmitt Me 209 put the speed record up to 469 mph (smashing the absolute speed record of 440 mph held by the Italian Macchi Mc 72 Schneider floatplane since 1934), the whole project was dropped as the Supermarine aircraft could not exceed 410 mph.

Nevertheless, it provided valuable information in respect of the PR machines described below. With the start of hostilities, it was fitted with an oblique camera and, as K9834 (its original production serial number), was tried out for photoreconnaissance work; not surprisingly, it had a very limited range and so it was not used for photographic work.

The most obvious influence of the Speed Spitfire project was that following PR aircraft were given a similar smooth and high gloss finish. In addition, these non-armed machines had their gun ports faired over. As a result, they were capable of up to 15 mph more than the corresponding standard fighter.

The first PR version appeared when two Spitfire Mark Is had their guns removed and coats of a special very pale blue-green paint called 'Camoutint' applied and polished. Two cameras, which could photograph a rectangular area below the aircraft, were installed in the wing space vacated by the inboard guns and their ammunition containers and heating equipment was installed (as on all PR Spitfires) to stop the cameras from freezing and the lenses from frosting over at altitude. These Spitfires later officially became the Spitfire PR IA, and on 18 November 1939, the first PR mission was flown to Aachen, a round trip of 564 miles.

Once this minimal modification had been proved successful, it was clear that the standard 84-gallon fuel capacity of the aircraft would have to be increased. Thus the PR IB, 'medium range' version was soon created by fitting a 29-gallon tank in the fuselage. A vertical camera was carried in a fairing beneath each wing. This version was first used on 10 February 1940, when it took photographs of the German naval bases at Wilhelmshaven and Emden.

By March 1940, a 'long-range' machine, designated the PR IC, was produced, carrying extra oxygen for maximum high-altitude flying, and a vertical camera was fitted in the fuselage for the first time. It also carried a total of 144 gallons of fuel and was the first photoreconnaissance aircraft to reach as far as Kiel. The extra fuel was carried in the tank behind the pilot and in a 30-gal. blister tank under the port wing, which was counterbalanced by a camera installation in a fairing under the starboard wing. The PR IC was the first PR version to be produced in significant numbers—in all, forty were produced by converting existing aircraft—and the PR Type 'A's and 'B's were brought up to Type 'C' standards. This type was later designated in 1941 as the PR III (*see* below).

The 'D' and 'F' versions required more extensive modifications and so came later. Meanwhile, it was also necessary to take low-altitude photographs, so at least one aircraft was fitted with oblique cameras, still mounted in and under the wings, and known as the PR IE. N3117, proved most useful as it was able to photograph targets under weather conditions that would make high-altitude photography impossible. Experience with this aircraft resulted in the development of the armed PR G (which became the PR VII (*see* below)). Some Spitfire IXs were also pressed into service as photoreconnaissance machines—the FR IX was a standard, armed Mk IX modified with a single, port-facing, oblique camera. These aircraft were used for low-altitude 'dicing' missions in tactical support of army operations and so carried the standard guns of the Mk IX fighter.

The PR IF, 'super long-range' machine was produced in March 1940. Redesignated as the PR VI, it was an interim long-distance version, awaiting the extensive conversion of the PRD/Mark IV version (*see* below). It contained the PR IC 29-gallon internal fuel tank behind the pilot and the 30-gallon fuel cell under the port wing; this latter was now doubled under the starboard wing and the engine was now the Merlin 45. It now had an endurance of four and a half hours, which allowed it to reach Berlin. The first flight to the German capital was made on 14 March 1941 and furnished final proof that the performance of Mitchell's fighter had also made possible the future development of an outstanding long-range reconnaissance type.

The cameras were mounted vertically in the rear of the fuselage, with the control cables to the rudder and elevators having to be re-routed. There was also provision for an oblique camera and for better heating around the equipment. Alternative camera combination mountings were also fitted, additional oxygen was carried, and, to improve downward vision, 'tear-drop' transparencies were fitted to each side of the cockpit hood. Nearly all the PRICs were modified to the PRIF/PRVI standard.

It was finished overall in a PRU blue, the standard colour for all future high-flying reconnaissance aircraft.

There were seventeen built.

The PR IV (PRD) version had had to wait for the adaptation of the wing leading edge sections to take fuel, as space was no longer needed for gun barrels. There was now no need for the drag-inducing blister tanks of the previous long-range Mark IF/PRVI as the gain was an extra 114 gallons in the wings, which, together with the original 84-gallon tankage and the extra 29 in the rear fuselage, now increased the aircraft's endurance from the Mk I Spitfire's original forty-five minutes to over five hours and the operational radius from about 130 miles to over 600—permitting a round trip to Stettin of over five hours in duration (with unheated cockpit).

A larger oil tank was now necessary, necessitating the reshaping of the nose to the distinctive PR Spitfire 'chin' (*see* sideview drawing, p. 368). When this version, known as 'the bowser', became the Mark IV, the wing tanks were further modified to take an extra 19 gallons, enabling the rear tank to be removed as the aircraft was not easy to take off and was incapable of flying straight and level for the first half hour afterwards.

It entered service in October 1940 (after the Mk VI) and was produced in much larger numbers than any other early PR Spitfire.

There were 241 built.

The PR VII was a more straightforward development of the PRG as it had normal Spitfire wings, in order to retain its armament (because of the low level at which it operated), and it was likewise equipped with bulletproof windscreen and armour plate. A 29-gallon fuel tank was fitted just behind the pilot. As with the PR IV, the oblique and vertical cameras were all installed in the fuselage, and 'tear-drop' transparencies were fitted to each side of the cockpit hood.

For this operational height, most of the PR IGs were camouflaged with a very pale pink in contrast to the high-flying variants. The first PRGs were converted from Mk I airframes and their Merlin II engines replaced with Merlin 45s. Late PRGs were converted from Mk V airframes.

These modifications signified the emergence of a coherent approach to photoreconnaissance operations and the development of a distinct type aircraft which, in the form of the PR IV and PRVII, was the backbone of this vital, if often unsung, RAF activity until the end of 1942.

There were forty-five built.

Hereafter, mark numbers were allocated consecutively, whether the aircraft was a fighter, naval, or photoreconnaissance type.

The PR X and XI represented the pressing into PR service of the new, more powerful Merlin 61. This was achieved in 1942 by, essentially, re-engining the Spitfire Mark IX and fitting a retractable tailwheel. Since no air combat was expected of these photoreconnaissance aircraft, the bulletproof windscreen was deleted in favour of a plain, curved one that, in combination with the retracted tailwheel and wing leading edges without gun ports, gave an increase of 5 mph in speed over a comparable Mark IX. The PRXI appeared before the allocated PRX as the latter had a pressurised cockpit and this involved the longer developmental period of the Mark VII that it was based on.

The PRX appeared in spring 1944, long after the PRXI. It was the PR version of the standard Mk VII fighter, produced by matching the fuselage from a Mk VII with the wings from the PR XI, with the guns replaced by two 66.5-gallon fuel tanks. It had the pressurised Mk VII cockpit, with a Lobelle sliding canopy, and retained the fighter style windscreen with the bulletproof glass panel. It was withdrawn in September 1945.

There were sixteen built.

The PR XI had begun to appear in November 1942 and was based on the Mark IX. It had the PR IV leading-edge fuel tanks, with a total capacity of 133 gallons, in addition to the normal fuselage tankage and a 90-gallon drop tank. No part of Germany was now immune from surveillance.

The fitting of the more powerful Merlins resulted in later machines having the pointed, broad-chord rudder which had appeared on the later Mark VIIs. The fuselage camera installations of the PR IV were later augmented by a camera fitted in a blister under each wing, just outboard of the wheel well. Some 260 Mk XIs were powered by Merlin 61, 63, or 63A engines, while the remaining 211 used the high-altitude Merlin 70. They were capable of a top speed of 417 mph at 24,000 feet and could cruise at 395 mph at 32,000 feet. Exceptionally, the aircraft could climb to 44,000 feet, although pilots could not withstand such altitudes for long in the non-pressurised cockpit.

It achieved the highest wartime speed of any Spitfire when being tested at Farnborough. On 27 April 1944, Sqn Ldr 'Marty' Martindale dived from 40,500 feet to a speed of 606 mph (Mach 0.89) before the engine blew up (he glided safely back to the airfield, despite almost no forward vision owing to a heavily oiled windscreen).

As this long-range Mark was also fully tropicalised, it not only served in European theatres but was also employed in the Middle East and the Pacific and, as such, could be regarded as the most effective photoreconnaissance aircraft of the Second World War. It was the main PR variant used by the RAF in Europe and the Far East in the second half of the war. In December 1944, it was phased out in favour of the PR 19 (*see* below).

There were 471 built.

The PR XIII signified an advance on the PR VII low level reconnaissance type in that it was fitted with a specially low-altitude-rated Merlin 32 (1,645 hp at 2,500 feet) and a 30-gallon drop tank. It had the same camera system but, instead of cockpit teardrops, a balloon hood was now fitted behind a bulletproof front windscreen but only four machine-guns were installed. It appeared in 1943, by which time, standard fighters were also being equipped, additionally, with cameras and operating as fighter-reconnaissance machines (e.g. the FR IX).

There were twenty-six built.

From 1943, it became the RAF convention to use Arabic numerals.

The PR 19 was powered by the Griffon 65 and represented the only Griffon-powered PR variant. Enemy improvements in location and interception of existing photoreconnaissance aircraft had created a need for the greater speed, range, and ceiling than the Griffon-engined fighters could achieve. A response was produced as quickly as possible by combining the Mk XIV fuselage, PR XI wings, and PR Mk X cabin along with camera arrangements of the PR XI. The first twenty-two aircraft were not pressurised.

The resulting aircraft was the last and most successful photographic reconnaissance variant of the Spitfire. Later machines were fitted with the Griffon 66 and had pressurised cockpits—now something of a necessity when flights of five to six hours and at an increased height were required. The leading-edge wing tanks were increased by 20 gallons on each side to give a total internal petrol capacity of 256 gallons, often supplemented by a 90- or 170-gallon drop-tank, producing the total equivalent weight of fifteen average-sized people on board.

Spitfire PR 19.

This airframe, which was produced in May 1944, was now able to take full advantage of the Griffon engine and resulted in one of the most outstanding of all the Spitfire variants. The PR pilots now had an aircraft that matched the performance of the FX IV, had a greater range than the PR XI, and the cockpit comfort of the PR X. With a top speed of 445 mph, it was one of the fastest piston-engined aircraft of all time; it could cruise at 370 mph and at 40,000 feet, beyond the effective reach even of the German jets at the end of the war—or, indeed, beyond the reach of any jet before the introduction of the swept-wing Sabres and the MiGs of the early 1950s. Indeed, on 5 February, 1952, Flight Lieutenant E. C. Powles claimed a climb to 51,550 feet and an emergency dive, when his cabin pressurisation failed, to a speed of Mach 0.96. This incident was incidentally in the last mark to embody the classic elliptical wing planform of Mitchell's original design, and one of the most functionally beautiful aircraft of the Second World War. As with the Spitfire 'F' Mark XIV, it was produced in time for the closing stages of the war in Europe and for limited active service in the Pacific and Far Eastern areas. A meteorological flight of Mark 19s was finally phased out in 1957.

There were 225 built

Naval Spitfires: The Seafires
At the beginning of the war, naval aviation was underdeveloped—attributed by C. G. Grey to the senior admirals being 'definitely anti-air-minded' and being 'solid ivory from the jaws up, except for a little hole from ear to ear to let useful knowledge go in and out'. He attributed the sinking of the *Prince of Wales* and the *Repulse* off the coast of Malaya and the prolonged hunting of the *Bismarck*, *Scharnhorst*, and *Prinz Eugen* to lack of effective naval aircraft.

The navy's first all-metal monoplane was the obsolescent and vulnerable Blackburn Skua dive bomber, whose bulk and lack of power resulted in too low a speed; the Roc, a turret fighter variant, was no match for the new enemy aircraft, and the weight and drag of the turret made it even slower than the Skua. The newer Fairey Fulmar, introduced in July 1940, was designed as an eight-gun fleet defence aircraft but was no great improvement; the navy had specified a two-seat machine, feeling that a second crew member was necessary for navigating over the open sea, but as a result, the Fulmar was far too large and unwieldy when it began to come up against single-seat opposition.

Thus the Admiralty had requested a navalised version of both the Spitfire and the Hurricane. A carrier deck was marked out on the Eastleigh runway and a Spitfire fitted with an arrester hook. The tests were satisfactory but other more pressing demands for these aircraft (e.g. photoreconnaissance) delayed the navy's acquisition of such sea-going fighters until the autumn of 1941. At this time, proper maritime tests were ordered, and in January 1942, a Mark V Spitfire with an arrester hook landed on HMS *Illustrious*. In view of shortages, some sixty Hurricanes had been put into service as a stopgap, but by mid-1942, mounting losses made it urgent that Spitfires should be finally employed.

In late 1941, a total of 166 Spitfire Mk VBs were converted, mostly from Mk VB machines coming in for repair; the main structural change was the incorporated an A-frame style arrestor hook and strengthened fuselage lower longerons.

The Seafire IIC was the next semi-naval variant and was based on the Spitfire VC. This version incorporated catapult spools and, because of the harsher nature of seaborne landings, was now given a strengthened undercarriage. The 'universal' wing fitted to this version resulted in the designation Seafire IIC, followed by the Seafire FR IIC, which signified the

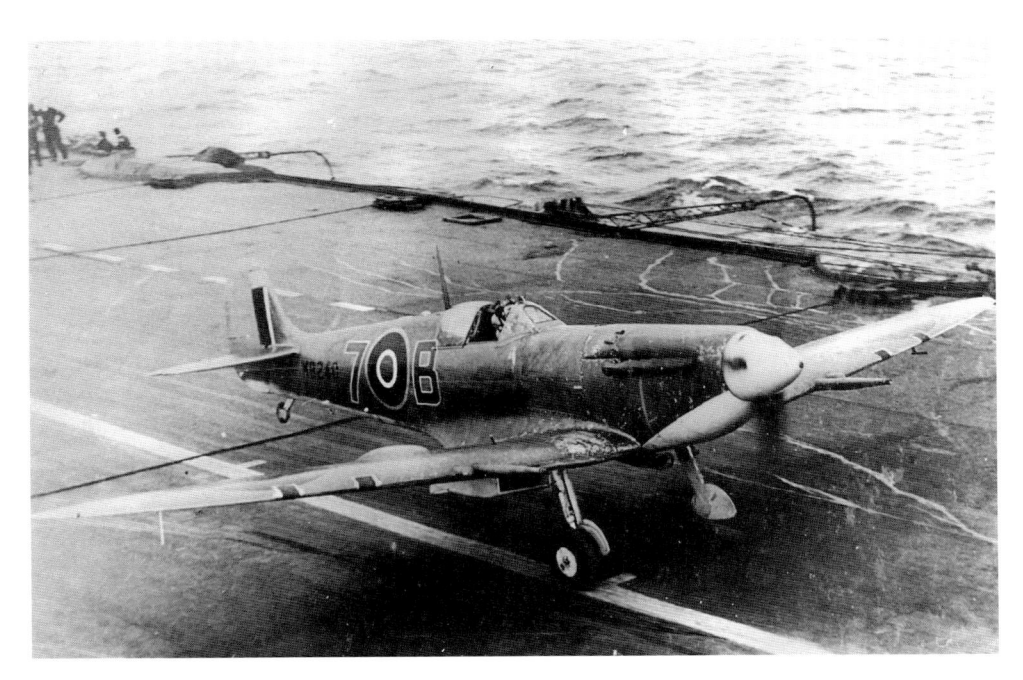

A well-weathered Seafire IIC taking off.

installation of cameras. This aircraft entered service in June, 1942, and its first action was in support of Albacore bombers during Operation Torch. A third subtype was the L IIC with clipped wings; powered by a low altitude Merlin 32, delivering 1,585 hp at 2,750 feet, it had a top speed of 340 mph at 5,500 feet.

There were 372 built.

The following extract from Adlam describes some of the problems associated with the early Seafire types; the detail of the Salerno operation (September 1943) makes chilling reading:

> The aircraft had a very limited range, no bomb load and, with the extra weight of the [arrester] hook was not all that much faster than the Wildcat and with lesser fire-power ... although a beautiful machine just to fly, it was very difficult to deck-land because of its tendency to 'float' over the wires when the engine was cut ...
>
> For the Seafire to land on the small deck of an Escort Carrier, even under ideal conditions, calls for considerable skill and experience on the part of the pilot. But at Salerno, the wind conditions were no better than a zephyr breeze and almost a dead calm, conditions entirely to have been expected at that time of the year. Thus the Seafires had to operate with a total wind speed over the deck of only sixteen knots, being the maximum speed of the Escort Carriers, whereas they needed a total wind speed over the deck of at least twenty-eight knots. These were desperately difficult landing conditions for the Seafire pilots; conditions which surely should have been anticipated at the outset when the whole Salerno operation was being planned by Rear Admiral Vian who, despite never having flown an aircraft or having served in an Aircraft Carrier, had been put in charge of this, the first multi Carrier Fleet of the Royal Navy ... After two days the four Escort Carriers had virtually run out of Seafires, no less than forty-eight of which had been written off as the pilots attempted to land in windless conditions.

The Seafire III (not to be confused with the Spitfire III prototype) was the first true carrier adaptation of the Spitfire design. It was developed from the Seafire IIC, with the introduction of specially designed folding wings that allowed its use on more compact carriers. It did not have to be stored and serviced on deck as previously. Another improvement on the FIIC was the more powerful Merlin 55M, driving a four-bladed propeller for maximum performance at low altitude; this was followed by the Seafire FR III with the installation of the Mark II camera provision. Due to the extensive modification to the wings, the Mark III did not become operational until late 1943; it was, however, the most numerous Seafire produced and was still in service at the end of the war with Japan.

There were 1,250 built.

By this time, the mark numbers were being allocated consecutively, whether the aircraft was a fighter, naval, or photoreconnaissance type.

The Seafire XV and XVII were the first Griffon-powered naval versions, with the Griffon VI rated at 1,850 hp at 2,000 feet. The first of these, the Seafire XV, basically, had a strengthened Seafire III airframe with folding wings, a Spitfire VIII tail, retractable tailwheel, and (on later aircraft) a newly designed spring-loaded 'sting' deck arrester hook that involved a slight modification to the broad chord rudder. It finally began to appear in September, 1944.

There were 390 built.

By now, the problems with the Seafire mentioned above had now been largely circumvented. Adlam again referenced a Seafire XV: 'a beautiful machine to fly. An absolute thoroughbred of an aircraft requiring only the most delicate pressures on the controls for it to respond immediately and perfectly ... On a runway with plenty of space, the simplest of aircraft to land'.

The Seafire XVII was the first naval version to be fitted with the later cut-down fuselage and rear-view canopy; it also had an extra 33-gallon fuel tank fitted in the rear fuselage. It continued the use of the Mark XV larger rudder and faired sting arrester hook but now had a curved windscreen and the comparative novelty of rocket-assisted take-off. The previous folding wing arrangement was retained but with a strengthened main spar and long-stroke undercarriage and, in view of the coming-together of all these improvements, this mark may therefore be regarded as the first dedicated carrier Spitfire. It was produced in September 1945—as much as four years after the first improvised naval versions—and phased out in November 1954. Thus, it was too late for the Second World War, but nevertheless, gave the navy its first 400-mph aircraft.

There were 233 built.

The Seafire Marks 45 and 46 were produced very soon after the Seafire XVII finally appeared despite their much higher mark numbers; these had been allocated to allow for future Spitfire developments, which, in the event, did not materialise beyond Mark 24.

The Seafire 45 was the first to use a Griffon 60 series engine with a two-stage, two-speed supercharger but, because this version was considered to be an interim type, the wing was unchanged from that of the Spitfire 21 and so was non-folding. The fuel capacity of this variant was 120 gallons distributed in two main forward fuselage tanks: the lower tank carried 48 gallons while the upper tank carried 36 gallons plus two fuel tanks built into the leading edges of the wings with capacities of 12.5 and 5.5 gallons respectively.

Although it was capable of another 45 mph above the top speed of the previous type, its more powerful engine produced a swing on take-off that did not render it popular for carrier operation, especially as the swing was towards the carrier superstructure. Some later aircraft were fitted with the Griffon 85 with contra-rotating airscrews which, together with increased rudder and elevator areas, made for a considerable improvement in directional stability.

There were fifty-one built.

The Seafire 46 (*see* photo p. 373) and FR 46 featured the cut-down rear fuselage and teardrop canopy but, again, the wing had not been modified to fold. The fuel system now incorporated an extra 32-gallon fuel tank in the rear fuselage, while the wings were plumbed to allow for a 22.5-gallon combat tank to be carried underneath each wing. In addition, a 50-gallon drop tank could be carried under the fuselage.

In April 1947, a decision was made to replace the Griffon 61s or 64s driving a five-bladed propeller unit with Griffon 85s or 87s driving two three-bladed contra-rotating propellers. All but the first few incorporated the Spiteful and Seafang tail units.

There were twenty-five built.

The Seafire 47 (*see* photo p. 365) was the last navy version of the Spitfire. There was no true prototype; instead, the first two production aircraft served as trials aircraft. It had the revised tail surfaces, rear-view canopy, and a Griffon 87 engine driving the contra-rotating six-bladed propellers of the later Marks 45 and 46; but it was also finally equipped with a wing-folding geometry without the folding wingtips of earlier marks and was now powered (the earlier manual arrangement of the Mark III required a five-man ground crew). The air intake filter was now more comprehensively faired into the lower engine cowling with the duct opening positioned just behind the propellers.

Like the final version of the photoreconnaissance types, it had a remarkable performance, including a top speed of 452 mph, and could outperform the standard American naval fighters, the Grumman F6F Hellcat or the Chance Vought F4U Corsair. Thus, the Seafire 47 can be seen as the most complete naval revision of the basic Spitfire landplane and a perfect illustration of how far it had been possible to develop Mitchell's original conception.

Although the Griffon-engined Seafires were not ready for use in the Second World War, the Mark 47 saw action in 1948 on board HMS *Triumph* during the Malayan Emergency of 1949 and during the Korean War in 1950. However, in 1951, all Seafires were withdrawn from front-line service. VR971, the last of the 22,000-plus aircraft built under the Spitfire/Seafire program, left the production line at Supermarine on 28 January 1949.

There were ninety built.

The website www.spitfires.ukf.net, which supplies the serial number and history of every machine, gives a grand total of 22,760 Spitfires and Seafires built. As machines were sometimes modified on the production line or afterwards, assigning numbers to marks when they entered service might easily account for discrepancies and so the above numbers of the various marks might not be entirely accurate. A study of the movement cards at the RAF Museum, comparison between the above web site details and those supplied by Andrews and Morgan and reference to the works by Bruce Robertson and Morgan and Shacklady should be pursued if one is so inclined.

Appendix III

Notes on R. J. Mitchell's Wooden Hulls

One of the fortuitous circumstances in R. J. Mitchell's career was joining a firm that had adopted a method of flying boat hull construction of considerable potential, while ever wooden hulls were in vogue. The Pemberton Billing PBI hull set the precedent for the firm's employment of sound boat-building techniques in the design of flying boat hulls, followed by the advice of Linton Hope and Admiralty staff (*see* Chapter 3).

The Air Ministry was concerned to see if the Linton-Hope type of hull could be adopted by aircraft of the large Felixstowe size. Thus, in 1917, Specification N.4 had been issued for this purpose. Capt. David Nicolson, in two articles for *Flight*, described and strongly advocated the Linton Hope approach:

> The P.5 and N.4 types patented by Major Linton Hope are entirely different in design and construction.... Being of circular cross-section, with fair and easy lines, they offer much less air resistance, consequently with the same horse-power are driven at higher speeds; they are much stronger weight for weight than the F [Felixstowe] type, more seaworthy, and generally show the impress of the trained naval architect's hand.

However, these types could not be built immediately by established aircraft manufacturers as these companies were fully committed to the wartime production of standard service machines. Supermarine and Mitchell's good fortune was that the building of two smaller prototype Linton Hope machines had meantime been contracted out to the then Pemberton Billing firm, and although Hope did not entirely get his own way, as he indicated in another *Flight* article, the less-than-perfect machine embodied this alternative and much more promising approach to flying-boat hull design:

> These boats were very difficult to get off the water … and with later experience it was obvious that the main step was too far aft and the rear step much too far forward. In spite of these faults in design, the [Pemberton Billing/Supermarine] AD boats showed the great strength of the flexible construction, and some bending and crushing tests carried out by the RAE works at Farnborough show what they were able to resist.

Structural strength was thus an inherited feature of Mitchell's hulls, and the eye of the yacht designer also imparted a relative sleekness to them which was far less the case in most contemporary land-based aircraft. Yet the immediate essential rightness of the Linton Hope approach was its flexibility, whereby a flying boat could absorb the shocks of sea landings and take-offs when there could be no recourse to the normal amelioration of aircraft undercarriages. Mitchell, as a young chief designer with a background in locomotive engineering and from the landlocked Potteries, was thus fortunate to inherit considerable sophisticated marine know-how and also a much more advantageous approach than that of the slab-sided Felixstowe flying boats of the First World War, particularly because of their shock absorption. As C. G. Grey said of these hulls, 'they were almost basket-like in their flexibility, and so got through the water without that jarring shock which was common to most high-speed motor boats.'

A small example of attention to the interface between rigidity and flexibility is mentioned in a *Flight* article about the Sea King: the pilot's 'controls are mounted on the triangular tubular frame so well known in all Supermarine boats, and whose function it is to allow the circular hull to flex and "give" in a seaway, without interfering with the smooth working of the controls.'

In a lecture to the Royal Aeronautical Society, Capt. D. Nicholson, who had been involved with the alternative flat-sided hulls of the Felixstowe flying boats, spoke approvingly of this approach and also of the economies of this constructional method:

> Construction is such that the structure is capable of resilient distortion, so that when alighting it can spring, reducing the shock. The hull cross-section is egg-shaped, very light, possesses great strength, and is built of longitudinal stringers with bent hoop timbers inside and light frames outside the stringers, skinned with double planking, through-fastened together. No web frames or cross-bracings are required, and the hull is a continuous structure with steps externally added.
>
> With a hull of the conventional [Felixstowe] F.5 type, such as the Cromarty, you start by criticising it as a commercial proposition, for you run into such items as turnbuckles, bolts and nuts, wires, cables, sheet metal, steel tubing … You must employ not one trade but a number, such as boatbuilders, carpenters, sheet metal workers, fitters, machine hands, riggers—and are immediately in the midst of demarcation troubles in arranging the working squads. With a Linton Hope hull, you need only one class of labour—boatbuilders; a small number of men and boys can be placed on the job, and if pieceworked under supervision, the chances of holdups are small; there is no complication, and they carry straight through and finish their job. A standard Supermarine [Channel] four-seat hull, 31 ft long, takes 3 men and 2 boys on an average 5.5 weeks to build, working a 47 hour week.

During his apprenticeship in the hull building section, Webb also noted how the brass nails and screws that held the final planking in place had to be fixed precisely in line and how the hull was then finally sanded down by hand and varnished until it had a surface 'akin to the best kept dining room table'. Cozens' description of the fate of the unsuccessful 1914 P.B.1 machine also indicates a similar concern with good workmanship and finish:

> A [Southampton] *Echo* "Letterbox" contributor wrote to say that his father, who was working at Supermarine was told to fetch an axe and Pemberton Billing, after looking at the beautiful machine for a long while, broke it up … All through the lifetime of the wooden flying boats the air of sturdy solidarity was due to the beautiful diagonal mahogany or Red Cedar planking of the hulls, covered by four coats of Copal varnish, which gave it a look of a piece of well-polished furniture.

As Webb had joined Supermarine in 1926, it would appear that he was speaking of work on the later Southampton flying boats and it is also possible that Cozen's account is influenced by the memories of the finish of the later machines. Earlier, Supermarine gave a variant description of the construction with reference to their Sea King II:

> The hull is of circular construction with built-on steps, which can be replaced in case of damage. The steps are divided into watertight compartments, the top side being of single-skin planking, covered with fabric treated with a tropical doping scheme.

Also a *Flight* description of the machine says:

> The boat hull is of the typical Supermarine type, boat built and through fastened, with copper or brass fixings throughout. The mahogany single-skin planking is riveted to rock elm timbers and frames, and covered externally with fabric suitably treated with pigmented dope.

Further, the Sea Lion III is described as having 'mahogany single-skin planking … covered externally with fabric suitably treated with pigmented dope.'

Where the planking was double, the top layer planking appears to have been usually laid longitudinally, fore-and-aft, and between the two layers was a layer of varnished fabric to aid waterproofing. Obviously, with single planking any fabric waterproofing would have to be on the outside of the wooden structure, and one is reminded of Cozens' report that when the Napier Lion engine of the Sea Lion was first started up, the vibration at the tail was so great that the pilot refused to fly it until the rear fuselage had been stiffened up by wrapping and gluing canvas around it, presumably onto an existing covering.

Specific centre of gravity considerations or design requirements might very well have led to Mitchell requiring variations in the planking and finishing in other of the firm's aircraft at about this time—for example, a Supermarine patent allows for planking to be omitted where external steps are to be added:

> If it is desired to reduce the weight of the hull to the greatest possible extent, the skin-planking on the hull proper may be omitted where side wings or other projections cover that portion of the hull. Where this planking is omitted it is preferred to use a fabric covering for the hull proper so that it is maintained watertight, even although the wing or other projection may be perforated. The close spacing of the bent timbers and stringers provide sufficient support for the fabric to be a satisfactory watertight skin in cases of emergency.

Thus, when we consider Mitchell's first complete designs—the Commercial Amphibian, Sea Eagle, Seagull II/III, Seal II, and Scarab/Sheldrake, which can be regarded as coming from a common stable—some or all may also have had canvas exteriors; indeed, *Flight* describes the Seal II as a 'boat built of planking over a light skeleton of timbers and stringers, and covered in fabric on the outside.' The machines in this group are, however, all about 11 feet longer than, for example, the Sea Kings and the Sea Lions, and would probably require the stiffening of double planking, especially bearing in mind the need here to design more staid, robust designs—with or without fabric doped on.

There is, however, an intriguing report in *Flight* of the visit of HRH the prince of Wales to Supermarine where it is said that 'the building of the Seagull flying boat hulls was greatly admired by His Royal Highness'. Perhaps the company saw an advantage in producing hulls that were, like the Southampton, fine examples of the boatbuilder's art, bearing in mind their British, Australian, and Spanish naval customers. However, it could be that the prince merely saw well-finished planking awaiting a protective layer of fabric to be doped on.

Incidentally, it is worth considering that wherever there was double planking, with the usual layer of canvas in between, fabric might also have been applied externally to protect the woodwork from splitting in the sun as well as to prevent the soaking up of water—one thinks particularly of the 'tropicalised' Seagull IIIs for Australia. The commonly held view that Supermarine hulls were a mahogany colour might be because of a varnished wood finish or because the doped fabric would allow the colour of the timber to show through; on the other hand, the 'pigmented dope' finish might be mahogany in hue and none too opaque, given that Supermarine might very well have been strongly attached to reminders of their boating heritage.

Thus, while the Supermarine general approach to wooden hull construction and finish is fairly well established, it is not possible to point to one single method being employed in all cases, especially as contemporary photographs do not usually supply the necessary information. Yet at least, readers today are now able to see the magnificent reconstruction of a Southampton hull at the RAF Museum and confirm for themselves the carefully aligned brass fixings and the 'luxury yacht' finish.

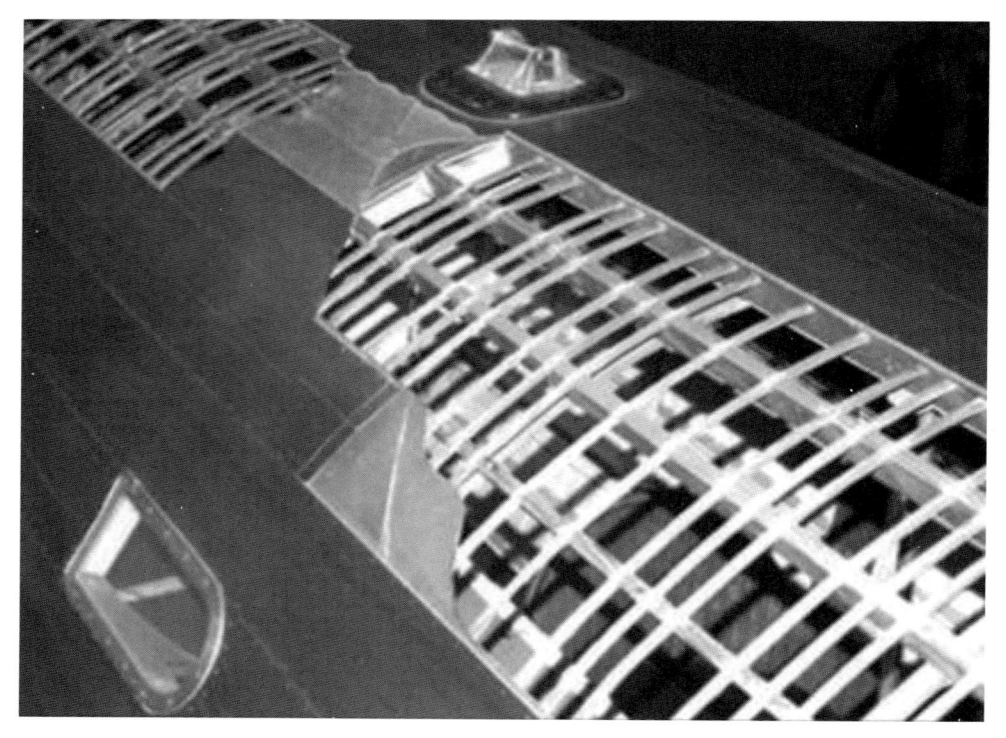

Detail of restored Southampton hull, showing the close-spaced hoops, the lengthwise stringers and the outer skin of thin mahogany strips.

Appendix IV

Jacques Schneider

Jacques Schneider was born near Paris on 25 January 1879. He was the son of the owner of the Schneider armaments factory at Le Creusôt and trained as a mining engineer, but his sights were soon set well above the ground. Ballooning had been a French passion ever since the 1780s, but there was an especial interest created in 1906 with the advent of the James Gordon Bennett balloon distance competitions. Schneider qualified as a free balloon pilot (licence no. 181), and in 1913, he gained and held for a long time the French altitude record of 10,081 metres and also made a cross country flight from France to the Black Sea in his balloon *Icare*. Charles Rolls was also a balloonist, with 170 ascents from 1901 until his death in 1910 when the tail of his Wright Flyer broke off.

Hydroplaning was another sport for the rich that had been developing at the beginning of the century, notably at Monaco, led by the Marquis Charles de Lambert, who made a breakthrough when he utilised an Antoinette aircraft internal combustion engine driving an aircraft propeller. He began to reach speeds approaching 50 km per hour; this attracted the attention of Jacques Schneider, who later drove one of these machines from Cairo to Khartoum with four passengers, including Lord Kitchener.

This event took place in 1914, four years after an accident in a hydroplane had caused multiple fractures of an arm and had prevented him from continuing with his third passion—flying. Schneider (who was at that time France's under minister for air) had met Wilbur Wright in 1908 when on a visit to Le Mans to demonstrate his aircraft. Schneider had also become a close friend of Louis Blériot; he joined the Aero Club of France in 1910 and was awarded his pilot's brevet (no. 409) in the March of the following year.

Due to his hydroplane crash, his name might have disappeared into the dusty annals of early aviation. However, his accident by no means diminished his passion for flight and, as race referee at a Monaco aviation meeting in 1912, he noticed that seaplane design was lagging far behind that of other types of aircraft. As aerodromes, obviously, did not exist,

Jacques Schneider in his hydroplane.

he foresaw that the best solution for long-range aerial passenger service between nations could be seaplanes—hybrid vehicles that had attributes of both hydroplanes and flying machines. Schneider thought that a seaplane competition would not only combine these two great loves of his but would also be the means by which such 'hydro-aeroplanes' might improve more quickly. By using his wealth to endow such a competition, he left his mark on the aeronautical world and his vision turned out to influence aircraft design for many years to come.

On 5 November 1912, at the banquet following the fourth Gordon Bennett Aviation Cup race for landplanes, he announced his trophy for a seaplane competition. The prize turned out to be a silver-plated Art Nouveau classic designed by E. Garbard, a work of art costing 25,000 francs (about £61,000 in 2000) and the proposed course was to be at least 150 nautical miles. This competition was known under various names: Schneider trophy, Schneider Cup, the Flying Flirt, and the Hat Rack; in Italy, it was the 'Coppa Schneider' while the official French name was 'Coupe d'Aviation Maritime Jacques Schneider'.

It required certain conditions to be fulfilled: (i) if a sponsoring aero club won three races in five years, it would retain the cup and the winning pilot would receive 75,000 francs; (ii) the annual race was to be hosted by the previous winning club and the races were to be supervised by the Fédération Aéronautique Internationale; and (iii) each club would be permitted to enter up to three competitors with an equal number of substitutes available.

In 1921, the course was increased from 150 to 212 nautical miles, preceded by a 2.5-nautical mile water navigation test. After 1921, an additional requirement was added: the competing aircraft had to remain afloat, moored to a buoy for six hours without crew aid.

There soon developed a keen public interest in this type of competition and crowds in excess of 250,000 began to gather to watch what were popularly known as the 'Schneider Cup races'. While the commercial flying boat did eventually develop into a very effective and 'civilised' form of intercontinental travel, the Schneider trophy is mainly remembered as a competition between nations for the prestige of merely flying faster than anyone else. However, as we have seen in previous chapters, the necessary concerns with streamlining and engine development in this endeavour had a far-reaching influence on the progress of aviation in general. Jacques Schneider did not live to see the full flowering of maritime aviation in the 1930s but, at least, he was able witness the modern streamlined competition monoplanes of 1925 and 1926. He was not able to attend the 1927 trophy event in Venice, due to ill health following an appendicitis operation; not long afterwards, on 1 May 1928, he died in reduced circumstance, aged forty-nine, at Beaulieu-sur-Mer, near Nice, not far from the Monaco course where the first Schneider competition had been held.

Appendix V

Kinkead's S.5 Crash

The account of the death of Flt Lt Samuel Kinkead in Chapter 6 was necessarily brief. The recently published book, *Racing Ace: the Fights and Flights of 'Kink' Kinkead* by Julian Lewis, to which we are indebted, has brought to light certain eyewitness accounts which suggest that the cause of the fatal accident might very well have been structural failure—contrary to earlier accounts and the findings of the internal RAF Court of Inquiry and the Southampton Coroner's Inquest, both of which gave the cause of death as 'stalling'. I would now like to consider various options.

(i) The possibility of a high-speed stall caused by violent manoeuvres can surely be ruled out as there is nothing in the accounts of Kinkead's flight pattern immediately prior to his accident to suggest that this highly experienced pilot and instructor, with the press watching, as well as foreign dignitaries, senior RAF personnel, Biard the Supermarine test pilot, and R. J. Mitchell, and with a world record for the taking, would be doing anything other than professionally descending steadily to the required height above the surface of the water, and doing nothing more than making minor corrections to his altitude or direction on the fatal approach run.

(ii) The possibility of a stall while having to make a landing approach because the visibility had deteriorated must take into account the fact that most of Kinkead's many decorations had been gained during the First World War and afterwards, while flying very low. Dr Lewis' book provides an invaluable service in describing these exploits and so one must pay due regard to Kinkead's airmanship in this respect even though he was now flying with the very reduced view from the cockpit that was an especial feature of the current batch of Schneider trophy machines. In particular, this necessitated the ability to feel one's way down to the water surface virtually blind—described by another Schneider pilot, Flt Lt H. M. Schofield, as 'a game of great patience'. Nothing Schofield wrote suggested that Kinkead would have adopted a different landing approach, particularly in misty conditions, and this contention is borne out by the *Times*' description of his skillful landing of the S.5 on the day before the record attempt:

> He chose an angle of glide which almost imperceptibly brought the floats nearer and nearer the water until the monoplane was just skimming the surface—a grey insect over a grey sea. Then a tiny feather of white foam broke behind the floats and rapidly grew bigger. The machine seemed

about to settle, but lifted just once in a long hop and then, touching again, threw up a spurt of spray, and gently floated on the water.

(iii) Even if Kinkead had made a rare landing misjudgement, there seems to have been no mention of a gradual decrease in engine sound before his crash, consistent with slowing down from high speed (expected to be over 300 mph) to the necessary landing approach speed (about 100 mph); on the contrary, spectators were impressed by the sound of an approaching high-revving engine which suddenly ceased and two commentators even described his impact with the water like that of a shell. Harold Perrin, the secretary of the Royal Aero Club, who had had a good view from the side, reported that the reappearance of fog, coupled with glare, prevented Kinkead from judging his height and that he flew straight in.

(iv) This last explanation of the crash would seem more plausible except for the fact that most witnesses reported an unexpected change of attitude; indeed, the coroner at the inquest is reported as 'trying to find out if there is a possible explanation of the sudden dive of the seaplane' and a Napier engineer's testimony was as follows:

> The machine soon appeared in sight, travelling towards me from Cowes at about 250 feet above the water, and going very fast.... The machine appeared to be intentionally descending and, after a few seconds, nose-dived very suddenly into the sea from about 50 feet up.

This account is echoed in the *Morning Post* headline, 'Vertical Nose-dive from 100 feet' or the *Times* report that Kinkead 'dived straight into the Solent from a height of between 100 feet and 50 feet' and that 'no man could have survived such a terrific impact with the water' as the machine had 'dived rather than flown into the sea'. Dr Lewis also records similar accounts of a sudden dive at high speed in the *Daily Sketch*, the *Daily Express* and in the local paper, the *Southern Daily Echo*.

It is, of course, well known how unreliable and interpretative are eyewitness accounts of unexpected events but, given the similarity of these particular reports and numerous testimonials to Kinkead's skill as a pilot, a mechanical failure rather than pilot error must thus be given particular attention—and it would foreshadow the alarming and near fatal oscillation of the S.6A rudder, three years later (*see* below).

Lewis cites newspaper reports from other observers with a view from the side of 'abnormal movement of the tail unit and fin' (the *Times*) and of the aircraft 'going at a very good speed' when its tail developed 'a pronounced flutter' (the *Daily Express*). Biard, who was standing next to Mitchell at the time of the accident, is also quoted as being quite certain that the crash was a result of structural failure and his likely reaction at the time might have contributed to Mitchell's reported distress for some time afterwards.

It should be acknowledged that the other two similar S.5 machines had successfully completed the Venice Schneider trophy course, which involved the taking of two extremely sharp corners on each of the required seven laps, while returning an average course speed of about 88 per cent of the top speed available to them. N221, the S.5 to be used for Kinkead's speed record, had not been extensively tested, having been held in reserve and consequently unused in the Schneider Contest a few months earlier, but the preliminary flight on the Sunday before the fatal crash had been without incident. The second mandatory flight, flown on the day of the accident, also went off without any problem (although heavy spray on the tail unit during porpoising prior to take-off was afterwards considered to have perhaps weakened the machine's structure), but its sprint-tuned engine and light fuel load might have allowed Kinkead to achieve a hitherto untested speed that brought with it unexpected structural problems.

(v) On the other hand, some reports of a sudden engine roar at the very end must be given due consideration. No evidence of a decoupling of engine and propeller was given at the inquest and so there thus remains the possibility that Kinkead had discovered a problem and had begun to try to get down, that he had throttled back but almost immediately poured on the power in an attempt to correct some worsening situation. As the speed of sound is slower than the speed of light, these last sounds would not be synchronous with what could be (imperfectly) seen by the observers in the misty conditions and so this consideration remains problematic.

(vi) But most problematic of the various discussions above, are the findings of the RAF Court of Inquiry that the accident was 'due to stalling of the machine' and the verdict of the Southampton Coroner's inquest that Kinkead's fatal injuries were caused by diving into the sea 'owing to lack of speed while attempting to alight'. In the latter case, it was also maintained that no evidence had been found in the wreckage to point to any physical causes for the accident although how this could be upheld in view of the extensive damage caused by impact and by the subsequent salvaging operation might perhaps only be explained by a wish to draw a discreet veil over the whole matter. One also reads in Lewis that a file concerning the private RAF Court of Inquiry, referred to in Kinkead's service record, has not survived.

Hugh Trenchard, chief of the air staff, had been a reluctant participant in the recent Schneider trophy preparations as he was still very protective of his new air force: he saw possibly fatal involvement in these competitions as peripheral at best to the main functions of his command and so not to be encouraged. From another perspective, certain senior Air Ministry officials were unlikely to be happy with findings of mechanical failure as, in their case, they were in favour of continuing RAF involvement in the Schneider contests for the sake of research and development and of the prestige accruing to the British aviation industry via this blue riband event.

It is thus interesting that at the inquest, the Inspector of Accidents, appointed by the Secretary of State for Air, felt able to assert that 'no part of the aircraft structure or controls broke, or failed to function normally during the flight' and that, while agreeing that 'the rudder or tail of the machine was seen to be fluttering', said that it was 'probably the reflection of the sunlight from the rudder that gave the impression' when the machine turned. Although we have only Southampton's *Southern Daily Echo* reports of the inquest to respond to (inquest transcripts are routinely destroyed after a period of time), this is the only mention here or in Lewis of the machine turning. Had a turn been necessary, it would surely have been made well before the crash site, in order to maximise the entry speed into the actual speed course, and one would in any case expect only slight movements of the rudder at the speed that Kinkead was going—producing equally slight, progressive, changes of colour tone to the rudder (but not with reference to the tail as a whole, as reported above by witnesses). And one wonders how bright was the sunlight if Kinkead had actually been attempting to land because of the worsening visibility.

While a stall due to 'pilot error' remains a possible reason for the death of Kinkead, there is, to say the least, no overwhelmingly supporting evidence and, indeed, R. W. Owen, a fitter who also looked after Kinkead's car, is reported as recording in his diary his incredulity at the inquest finding. He had also noted earlier that the aircraft had 'crashed from 50 ft full out ab[out] 340 mph (?) flying towards the sun'. It would seem that he might have been disposed to the Perrin view (iii above) but his queried note on Kinkead's possible speed is especially interesting.

This mention of a speed well above what had been possible with the Venice S.5s is borne out in more detail in an RAF press release:

> Kinkead had preserved complete reticence as to the exact speed at which he travelled in his trial flight on Sunday morning [March 11], and no one had realised that he had reached, on his airspeed indicator, a rate of no less than 330 miles per hour.... Kinkead was so enthusiastic after his trial flight that he said he believed he could attain probably 350 miles an hour. It should be realised that this type of monoplane had never before been flown, probably, at more than 300 miles an hour, and ... no one could be certain that stresses, which were within the capability of aircraft engine and propeller at 300 miles an hour, might not rise to an unexpected magnitude when the speed was increased to 350 miles an hour.... Kinkead had been urged to content himself with beating the existing record by the requisite 5 miles an hour, or at least to keep within a speed of 310 miles, but he, as a pilot, took a risk which designers and aircraft instructors would have rightly hesitated to permit in existing machines.

It is worth noting that this report only says that 'designers [unspecified] would have hesitated [not 'had hesitated'] to permit' a flat-out speed. The *New York Times* of 14 March, however, printed a more explicit version:

> The theory advanced as to the accident now is that in endeavoring to reach the higher speed the machine, despite all human skill and foresight could do to make it function perfectly, broke down under the strain.
>
> It was stated tonight that Lieutenant Kinkead had been urged to content himself with beating existing records and to keep within a speed of 310 miles per hour, as the designers of the machine thought it risky to exceed that limit.

This last version also asserts that advice to fly circumspectly came from 'the designers of the machine'. Mitchell (unnamed) was, of course, the chief designer of the S.5 and one wonders if Kinkead had mentioned to him anything unusual during his earlier test flight—as Biard had done, prior to the S.4 going to the 1925 Baltimore competition. If there had been a report of something not quite right, Mitchell would certainly have wished to avoid a repeat accident—given his well-known concern for the safety of his pilots, but it would not have been out of character for Kinkead to have taken upon himself the risk—in order to set a speed record that might not be broken by another country's machine for some considerable time. It is thus a great pity that it is not possible to assert unequivocally that Kinkead's death was the direct result of a desire to achieve the very best speed for the RAF and the empire (Kinkead was born in South Africa).

Three years later, Squadron Leader A. H. Orlebar's lucky escape during an early high-speed run with the first of the S.6As had been a result of an alarming oscillation of the rudder which caused the buckling of rear fuselage plates, stress cracks around some of the rivet holes and stretched control wires. Mitchell's improvised response, in the short time available before the Schneider competition was due to take place, was to stiffen up the rear fuselage and fit anti-flutter bob weights on the rudder and ailerons.

It is not to be expected that in 1928 Mitchell would have been aware that the suspected flutter of the control surfaces could very well have been the specific result of turbulence from the wing root/fuselage area. J. A. D. Ackroyd, writing about the Spitfire's wing fairings in 2013, summarised later knowledge:

> A wing root's pressure distribution does not match that around the fuselage. This mismatch can create local boundary-layer separation which results in increased drag and an irregular turbulent wake which can bombard the tailplane and elevator to detrimental effect.

It is noticeable that Mitchell's subsequent Schneider racing machines (1929 and 1931) did not have fairings at the intersection of the wing root and the fuselage, even though they had been evident as early as 1930 in America; yet, a further three years later, he closely inspected those of the Bellanca 'Irish Swoop' when it came to Eastleigh airfield in preparation for the 1934 MacRobertson Trophy England–Australia race and he discussed their effectiveness with its pilot. And it is worth noting that the company response to the later F.7/30 requirement for a new fighter drew attention to 'a rigid mounting for the tail unit and for the prevention of tail flutter.'

Perhaps one is here straying too far into the realms of speculation to assert that lack of wing-root fairings was the real reason for Kinkead's crash, but the findings of the RAF and of the inquest can be seen as the least worst outcome for all parties except the pilot. This is an especial pity as little mention is made of the Schneider trophy pilots when credits are given for winning the Battle of Britain and all that followed. If these pilots had not successfully flown their, frankly, dangerous aircraft, the Spitfire might not have been ready in time for the outbreak of the Second World War—one notes at least D'Arcy Greig's dedication in *My Golden Flying Years* 'to all those involved with the Schneider trophy races that helped so much in the development of the Spitfire in later years'.

It is surely worth a moment to consider, via Kinkead and his fellow pilots, what was involved in Schneider trophy flying. In 1927, the fastest RAF fighter they might have flown was the 155 mph Gloster Gamecock and the Fairey Flycatcher floatplane made available for practice by the High Speed Flight had a top speed of about 125 mph. The pilots then moved up to the previous Schneider trophy contender, the Gloster III, 100 mph faster and unstable when cornering. One has to bear in mind that many practice days were lost because of weather or sea conditions unsuitable for these sensitive machines and it was only a few months (in effect therefore, weeks) before the High Speed Flight received their much faster Gloster IV and Supermarine S.5 competition floatplanes—a total increase in top speed of about 170 mph since converting onto the Flycatcher floatplane.

In the ten years between the advent of the Gamecock and of the Gladiator, the top speeds of RAF fighters had risen by an average of about 10 mph per year and these landplanes were far more straightforward to fly than the Schneider floatplanes, which drenched and blinded their pilots on taking off, apart from their overall visibility problems in the air. Yet James (*Gloster Aircraft since 1917*) records that the Gloster IV machine (introduced to Schofield as 'the blind wonder') which Kinkead flew in 1927 was shipped to Venice after only fifty minutes of flying and that he flew it there, very low, after only 105 minutes on the type recorded in his logbook. And D'Arcy Greig states that suitable conditions resulted in his own total flying time in these specialist aircraft, between 25 July 1928 and 7 September 1929, as only eleven hours, twenty-three minutes. It should also be added that while parachutes were now becoming standard military equipment for the RAF, Kinkead and his fellow pilots would have had no chance of using them at the height they flew; nor would extricating themselves from their cramped cockpits have been easy whatever the circumstances. Blacking out from g forces was also a new phenomenon to contend with.

It is well recognised that Mitchell's Spitfire and its Rolls-Royce Merlin engine were ultimately a by-product of the Schneider trophy competitions, where manufacturers were free from inhibiting Air Ministry requirements, but not enough has been said in this context about the skills of the High Speed Flight pilots who took part in this early test flying. No doubt others would have come along and accepted the risks involved, but it was these particular pilots who led the way with their successive wins in 1927, 1929, and 1931. Of these, Kinkead's 1927 group can be seen as the one which took the primary and most dramatic leap into the unknown. Their flight leader, Sqn Ldr L. H. Slatter, spoke after the event of the skill of all his pilots but he singled out Kinkead for putting up the 'most extraordinary show'. Thereafter Kinkead was put in command of the nucleus of the High Speed Flight retained at Felixstowe and, had he not died, he would have been in charge of the full High Speed Flight for the next competition.

It is hoped that he will be remembered in this light rather than as a pilot who was said to have died because of an error of judgement.

Appendix VI

Lady Lucy Houston, DBE

The life story of Lady Houston presents a fascinating insight into the bygone late Victorian and Edwardian ages when wealth and privilege was confined to a far smaller few, when the gap between them and the poor was much more clearly defined, and when the British Empire was at its greatest extent and influence. She did not come from the privileged class but, nevertheless, rose to become the richest woman in Great Britain and a champion, however extreme and eccentric, of the status quo and, especially, of Britain and the British Empire; Winston Churchill described her as a 'modern Boadicea' and the historian A. J. P. Taylor wrote that 'the Battle of Britain was won by Chamberlain, or perhaps Lady Houston'. In a recent well-researched and well-written book, Miles Macnair has justly written:

> The mass production of allied fighters and bombers during the Second World War had been accepted by the public merely as a result of effective management, and this perception had swamped recognition of the key role played by a few pioneering visionaries, among whom Lucy deserves to have genuinely heroic status.

Born in 1857, Fanny Lucy Radmall claimed to be the seventh child of a seventh child (and always claimed to be at least seven years younger than she really was). Her father, Thomas Radmall, was described as a 'warehouseman' and, later, as a woollen draper. He then moved to live over his warehouse close to St Paul's Cathedral, and Lucy therefore considered herself to be pure Cockney as well as the descendant of Sussex yeoman stock—'before William the Conqueror came over to mess the place up'.

The family appears to have become reasonably prosperous but that Lucy was 'the wild one'; at the age of sixteen, she was described by the playwright Arthur Wing Pinero as 'a small-part actress', and in those days of 'mashers' at every stage door, she was almost immediately taken up by the thrity-four-year-old Frederick Gretton, of the well-known brewery Bass, Ratcliff &

Gretton of Burton-upon-Trent. His involvement with the firm was in the malting department but his main interest was in building up his own string of racehorses. Within six weeks of the start of her 'career', he met Lucy, and although he may have been already married, he eloped with her to Paris where they lived together as man and wife.

At the atelier of the artist Edouard Détaille she met Madame de Polés, whose friends included archdukes and princes as well as the future King Edward VII, which led to her becoming a royalist of the most romantic sort as well as learning the ways of the world, society manners, and the art of dressing. She also seemed to have copied Madame de Polés' habit of carrying a large, shabby handbag into which she randomly stuffed often large sums of money, expensive jewellery, and important documents.

After some nine years, Fred Gretton died, leaving her the then considerable sum of £7,000 per year for life. She leased a house in Portland Place and surrounded herself with all the necessary servants: butler, lady's maid, footmen, maids, and coachman for her two carriages. Half a century later, she told a friend: 'Today is a very sad day to me. Someone I loved dearly died on this day 50 years ago. He worshipped me and said I was the apple of his eye'. It would appear that her time with Gretton was her happiest but one year later, in September 1883, she met Sir Theodore Brinckman.

Brinckman was twenty-one and, when he married her, thought that she was nineteen (but add seven). Marriage to him conferred respectability, however she divorced him in 1894 on the grounds of his adultery. Lucy was, of course, financially independent but she received a hunting lodge in Scotland as a parting present and they remained friends throughout her lifetime. Then, in 1901, giving her age as thirty-six, she married the ninth Lord Byron of Rochdale, aged forty-five (in fact only one year older than Lucy). George Byron was bankrupt but his title enabled Lucy, as Lady Byron, to wear robes, ermine, and a tiara at the resplendent coronation of the man she had met in Paris—Edward VII.

She bought a house adjoining Hampstead Heath and named it Byron Cottage, although her husband was confined to the rear of the house. Meanwhile, she enjoying the charmed life of a well-to-do socialite, and was notable for her contribution to the 1914–18 war effort—in particular by setting up a much-needed rest home for overworked and traumatised nurses, and organising fund-raising for Polish people suffering from pillaging by the Kaiser's troops. As a result, she became the fifth lady to be created a 'Dame of the British Empire'. Among later donations was £30,000 to the Miners' Relief Fund, £30,000 to the Lord Mayor's Distress Fund, £10,000 to the Navy League Fighting Fund, £40,000 to King George's Jubilee Fund, £10,000 to the Liverpool Cathedral Fund, and £10,000 to the Maternity and Child Welfare Fund. Much of her charitable work, however, was completely unsung, such as seeking out and giving money to tramps on Hampstead Heath. Later in life, her donations amounted to well over £400,000, as itemised by her recent biographer, Macnair—as were her many acts of kindness, which have been overshadowed by her more public affairs.

The £100,000 given to subsidise the final British Schneider trophy entry is, of course, the reason for her being the subject of this appendix, and there was also a similar sum donated later to enable the first flight over Everest. Such vast sums (for the 1930s) were possible, thanks to her subsequent marriage to Lord Houston. Lord Byron had died in 1917, and in 1922, on the yacht of Sir Thomas Lipton (the 'boating grocer'), she met Sir Robert Paterson Houston, the owner of the Houston line of steamships. He also owned a yacht, the 1,600-ton steam yacht *Liberty*, on which she met members of the Russian royal family and learned at first hand of the brutalities of the Bolsheviks, which further increased her developing dread of the spread of their influence in world affairs. They were married in December 1924 and so she thus became Lady Houston, although not before she had refused to choose from a selection of jewellery as a birthday gift: on being asked what she considered was appropriate, she indicated a string of black pearls but informed her future husband she thought he would consider them too expensive at £50,000—they arrived the next day.

Sir Robert's gesture was not in vain as Lucy later persuaded him that an economic slump was coming and to sell his entire shipping fleet. As it turned out, he did so at the peak of the market and, as a result, doubled his cash fortune. Later, on being shown his will, which left her £1 million, she tore it up, declaring that if that was all she was worth, she wanted nothing. The will was remade, and when Lord Houston died in 1926, he not only left her six million pounds but also the yacht. A very bad attack of jaundice and her extreme reaction to Lord Houston's death led to questions as to her ability to prove the will or manage her affairs and the Jersey Royal Court appointed a curator to administer her estate.

Almost two months later, Lucy sent for four eminent brain specialists who declared her perfectly capable of conducting her own affairs; however, they had to return ten days later and, together with three other specialists, finally succeeded in removing the restraints of the curator. The will was finally proved in 1928 and she took up residence again at Byron Cottage.

The Houstons had been domiciled in Jersey and his estate was not subject to British taxation, but his widow was now contacted by the Treasury with reference to death duties. Having ascertained that it might very well cost her £20,000 in legal fees to settle the matter, she went herself to see Winston Churchill, who was then chancellor of the exchequer. At a second visit, she presented Churchill with a cheque for £1.5 million by way of a final settlement. Thereafter, she was still the richest woman in England but was spending much of the time in her bedroom, suffering from very low blood pressure. The house began to take on a distinct air of neglect; a contributory factor was the high turnover of servants, due to her demanding nature and irascibility.

Lucy was now in her seventies, and partly in an attempt to avoid the avalanche of begging letters that now began to pour in, she started to spend much of her time on *Liberty*, cruising off the coast of the Riviera, at anchor in the harbour at Cannes or on the Seine, between Paris and the coast. The main deck of *Liberty* was off-limits to her crew at certain hours as she took daily exercise, whatever the weather, with no clothes on. More publicly, her tirades against Russia and her championship of the British Empire had by now become extreme, for she saw the Labour governments of Ramsay MacDonald in 1922 and 1929 as threatening to erode the domination of the British Empire and of the social order, in which she had led such a charmed life. She published *Potted Biographies, a Dictionary of anti-National Biography*, in which she gave chapter and verse of alleged anti-war activities or speeches by Labour MPs which appeared to belittle Britain, and she intervened in numerous by-elections with poster campaigns that she financed herself.

The vehemence of her published views thus made good copy in the press, and it was by no means ill-founded as the premierships of Ramsay MacDonald and Stanley Baldwin now attract most blame for British unpreparedness for war in 1939. Seen particularly from a modern standpoint, her imperialist outlook was becoming increasingly unfashionable and unrealistic, but she also had an uncanny sense of the way that international events were moving. Notably, seven years before the beginning of the Second World War, her ire had been especially raised by the reception of the offer she had made to MacDonald's National Government to pay for about seventy aircraft to defend London. She had sent her secretary-companion to the private residence of the Chancellor of the Exchequer, at the time Neville Chamberlain, with a £200,000 cheque to finance the purchase of these fighters. No reply was received and so, three weeks later, she wrote a stinging letter to the chancellor. It then became front page news when the government refused the offer on the grounds that it could not accept money when accompanied with conditions as to how it would be spent. (It may be that the prime minister, smarting from her many attacks upon himself, did not want to provide reasons why she might be given any higher honours than her DBE.)

A few days later, she anchored off various ports on the south coast of England with *Liberty* decked out with 6-foot lettering, lit up at night, as *Time* reported: 'this week irrepressible Dame ("Fanny") Lucy was at it again on her yacht, the *Liberty*, on which Lady Houston lives with steam constantly up, blazes at her whim an electric sign DOWN WITH MACDONALD, THE TRAITOR'. Unfortunately, from her point of view, the top-hamper of her yacht prevented her reaching moorings off the Houses of Parliament with her message.

There followed a spate of pamphleteering in favour of parliamentary candidates opposed to the left-wing tendencies and Russian leanings of members of the government. In the following year, 1933, she bought the *Saturday Review*—as she informed the editor she appointed, 'it must carry my message into every home in Britain. We must warn people of the dangers this Government is leading us into.' She was thereafter wont to draw up outside her offices and dictate her copy: *Time* gives an instance of the problems that her interventions caused her editor:

> Cringingly he told her that the leading wholesale newsdealers of Great Britain, on advice of their solicitors, had refused to distribute the next copy of the Saturday Review if it should contain, as planned, Lady Houston's personally penned opinion of the Prime Minister ... that he was 'squandering millions on peace conferences' while he let the Empire's defence forces go to ruin. This was only to be expected, she slashed, from a man who, like Scot MacDonald, urged British munitions workers to strike during the War at a time when British soldiers at the front were short of shells. 'How can you be secure?' Dame Lucy planned to query the readers of the Saturday Review. 'How can you be sure your dear ones will not be sacrificed through the treachery of this traitor?'

It is thus possible to see how Lady Houston's funding of the 1931 Schneider trophy entry was in some measure influenced by a wish to embarrass Ramsay MacDonald and his government, which had refused to put public money into the project. Her opposition to their moves to give India a measure of self-government was also behind her financing (again, to the tune of £100,000) the successful British attempt to fly over Everest for the first time in 1933; but, while it can be seen as an imperialist gesture in support of the British Raj, Lady Houston was also concerned with the wider view that any withdrawal from India would leave a vacuum that Russia would seek to fill. She sent a telegram to the Viceroy of India asking him to give the expedition 'every assistance required' and received a gracious reply and viceregal support when it arrived in India.

Later, at the Everest Flight celebratory luncheon, the extreme jingoism of her 'message' from her yacht was not read out, despite her financial backing of the project. The following extract, in characteristic 'syntax', explains why she had supported the flight over Everest:

Some great deed of heroism might rouse India and make them remember that though they are a different Race—they are British Subjects—under the King of England—who is Emperor of India—and what more can they want? … this is surely a proof to them that pluck and courage are not dead in our Race and perhaps—who can tell?—this may make them remember all the advantages and privileges they have enjoyed under English Rule

A recompense for being snubbed at the Everest Flight luncheon came when a lake that had been discovered on the southern slopes of Mount Everest in the course of the flight was named Parvati Tal, the Lady of the Mountains.

For the next four years, despite approaching her eightieth birthday, she bombarded her editor with expensive last-minute alterations to layout as well as text, to the extent of expending perhaps £60,000 on the magazine. She also renewed her offer of £20,000 to purchase aircraft to defend London; when this was rejected again, she distributed the money to numerous causes. Yet despite, or because of, her many stunts, despite her munificent gestures, her pamphlets and the wide circulation that the *Saturday Review* had achieved, her influence with the political establishment was not commensurate with her wealth or her acquaintance with the great and the good; while many at the time shared her initial admiration for such 'strong men' as Hitler and Mussolini, they shrank from being associated with her unrestrained attacks upon the British government.

A final example of her inability to influence events was her public concerns over the issue of the abdication of Edward VIII. One might have expected that Lady Houston would have been violently opposed to the idea of an American becoming the queen of England; however, she had met Edward VII in her Paris days and his grandson had even visited Byron Cottage, so her personal feelings for him took pride of place, especially as Baldwin (who had succeeded Ramsay Macdonald but who was no better in Lady Houston's eyes) was opposed to the king's proposed marriage. She had hopes that Edward VIII would lead the country back its former prosperity and provide the strong leadership of the British Empire for which she had campaigned for so many years and whom she exhorted 'to get rid of the political hacks who would destroy you and your Kingdom'. She exchanged letters with royalty, but the abdication took place on 10 December 1936 nevertheless.

Now almost eighty years old, Lady Houston printed in her *Review* a letter she had sent to his successor, King George VI, which repeated some of her views about the present government but expressed an expectation (forlorn hope?) that he would maintain the scepticism of its policies that his departed brother had sometimes appeared to voice.

There had thus been much to convince her that her fears for the demise of the world she believed in were well founded and that there was little to show that she had been able to halt the work of those in power whom she considered, with some justification, to be, at best, inept. Food now had no interest for her and she died on the night of 29 December 1936.

Mitchell being introduced to Lady Houston, on the occasion of the 1931 Schneider Trophy competition.

Bibliography

Supermarine Aviation Works

The Aeroplane/The Aeroplane Monthly

Andrews, C. F. and Morgan, E. B., *Supermarine Aircraft since 1914* (Putnam, 1981)

Cozens, G. A., 'Concerning the Aircraft Industry in South Hampshire', Unpublished MS, Solent Sky Museum

Flight/Flight International

Griffiths, H., *Testing Times; Memoirs of a Spitfire Boffin* (United Writers, Cornwall, 1992)

Hillier-Graves, Tim, *LMS Locomotive Design and Development: the Life and Work of Tom Coleman* (Pen & Sword, 2018)

Holt, L. T. C., *Landscape with Machines* (The History Press, 2017)

Jane's All the World's Aircraft (Sampson Low, 1921–1937)

King, H. F., 'Sires of the Swift: A Forty Year Record of Supermarine Achievement' in *Flight*, October, 2006

Key, D., *The Supermariners: The Men and Women who Created a Legend*, supermariners.wordpress.com/company-history/ (accessed 15 April 2021)

Roussell, Mike, *Spitfire's Forgotten Designer: the Career of Supermarine's Joe Smith* (The History Press, 2013)

Russell, C. R., *Spitfire Odyssey* (Kingfisher Railway Productions, 1985)

Scott, J. D. *Vickers: a History* (Weidenfeld and Nicholson, 1962)

Shelton, J. K., *From Nighthawk to Spitfire; the Aircraft of R. J. Mitchell* (The History Press, 2015); *Schneider Trophy to Spitfire: the Design Career of R. J. Mitchell* (Haynes, 2008)

Smithies, E., *Aces, Erks and Backroom Boys* (Orion Books, 1990)

Webb, Denis Le P., *Never a Dull Moment at Supermarine: a personal history* (J. and K. H. Publishing, 2001)

The Schneider Trophy

Air Ministry Aeronautical Research Committee, 'Reports on the Schneider Trophy Contests for the years 1927 and 1931' HMSO

Banks, F. R., 'Memories of the Last Schneider Trophy Contests' in *Journal of the Royal Aeronautical Society*, January 1966

Barker, R., *The Schneider Trophy Races* (Chatto and Windus, 1971)

Bazzocchi, Dr E. 'Technical Aspects of the Schneider Trophy and the World Speed Record for Seaplanes' in *Journal of the Royal Aeronautical Society*, February 1972

Buchanan, Maj. J. S., 'The Schneider Cup Race, 1925' in Proceedings of the Tenth Meeting, 61st Session of the Royal Aeronautical Society

Design Staff of Supermarine under R. J. Mitchell, 'The Schneider Trophy Seaplane—Some Notes on the Special Features of the S.6B, in *Aircraft Engineering*, October 1932

Eves, E., *The Schneider Trophy Story* (Airlife Publishing, 2001)

Gouge, M., 'Doolittle wins in Baltimore' in *Airpower*, November 2005

Hawkes, E., *British Seaplanes Triumph in the International Schneider Trophy Contest, 1913–1932* (Real Photographs, 1945)

Hirsch, R., *Schneider Trophy Racers* (Motorbooks International, 1993)

James, D. N., *Schneider Trophy Aircraft, 1913–1931* (Putnam, 1981)

Mitchell, R. J., 'Racing Seaplanes and their Influence on Design', in Aeronautical Engineering Supplement to *The Aeroplane*, 25 December 1929; 'Schneider Trophy Machine Design, 1927', in Proceedings of the Third Meeting, 63rd Session of the Royal Aeronautical Society

Waghorn, Flg Off. R. D. H., 'The Schneider Trophy, 1929', Royal Aeronautical Society, May, 1930, Yeovil Branch

Mondey, D., *The Schneider Trophy* (R. Hale, 1975)

The Supermarine S.4–S.6B, Profile Publications No. 39

Orlebar, Wing Commander A. H., *The Schneider Trophy* (A. F. C. Seeley Service and Co., 1933)

The Spitfire and Other Supermarine Aircraft

Ackroyd, J. A. D., 'The Aerodynamics of the Spitfire' in *Journal of Aeronautical History*, Paper No. 2016/03; 'The Spitfire Wing Planform: a Suggestion' in *Journal of Aeronautical History*, Paper, No. 2013/02

Alcorn, J. 'Battle of Britain Top Guns', in *The Aeroplane Monthly*, September 1996; 'Battle of Britain Top Guns Update' in *The Aeroplane Monthly*, July 2000

Caygill, P., *The Darlington Spitfire* (Airlife, 1999). See also the Roger Darlington World [blog] rogerdarlington.me.uk/Spitfire.html (accessed 30 October 2016)

Doyle, N., *From Sea-Eagle to Flamingo* (The Self Publishing Association Ltd, Upton-upon-Severn, 1991)

Lucas, S. J., *Spitfire Mark by Mark, including the Seafire* pdf 2nd Edition spitfiremarkbymark.co.uk (accessed 3 June 2021)

McKinstry, L., *Spitfire: Portrait of a Legend* (Murray, 2007)

Morgan, E. B. and Shacklady, E., *Spitfire: the History* (Kay Publishing, 1987)

Neil, Wing Commander Tom, DFC & bar, AFC and AE, *The Silver Spitfire* (Weidenfeld and Nicolson, 2013)

Nicholl, G. W. R., *The Supermarine Walrus; the Story of a Unique Aircraft* (G.T. Foulis and Co., 1966)

Price, A., *The Spitfire Story* (Jane's, 1982); *Supermarine Spitfire* (Chevron Publishing Ltd, 2010)

Robertson, B., *Spitfire; the Story of a Famous Fighter* (Harleyford, 1960)

Royal Aeronautical Society, Southampton Branch, 'Forty Years of the Spitfire', Proceedings of the R. J. Mitchell Memorial Symposium, 6 March, 1976

Sarkar, D., *How the Spitfire Won the Battle of Britain* (Amberely, 2010)

'Spitfire 70', a *FlyPast Special* (Key Publishing, 2006)

The Supermarine Spitfire I and II, Profile Publications, No. 41

The Supermarine Walrus and Seagull Variants, Profile Publications, No. 244

Twenty-first Profile, Vol. 1 No. 6 'the B.12/36 Bomber' and Vol. 1 No. 9 'the Air Yacht' (21st Profile Ltd, ISSN 0961-8120)

R. J. Mitchell

Black, A., 'R. J. Mitchell: Designer of Aircraft' in The Reginald Mitchell County Primary School Commemorative Brochure, 1959.

Dommett, Roy, Page 35 C1379/14 Track 2 The British Library Board <http://sounds.bl.uk> (accessed 12.6.21)

Mitchell, Dr Gordon, 'R. J. Mitchell: My Father' in *Aeroplane Monthly*, March 1986; *Reginald Mitchell, 1895–1937* (RAF Souvenir Book, 1966); [editor and in part author of] *R. J. Mitchell: Schooldays to Spitfire* (Nelson and Saunders, 1986; reprinted by Tempus Publishing, 2006).

Smith, Joe, 'R. J. Mitchell, Aircraft Designer' in *The Aeroplane*, 29 January 1954; 'The First Mitchell Memorial Lecture' in *Journal of the Royal Aeronautical Society*, 58, 1954

Pilots' Accounts

Adlam, Hank, *On and Off the Flight Deck* (Pen and Sword, 2007)
Battle, H. F. V., OBE, DFC, *Line!* (Newbury, 1984)
Biard, H. C., *Wings* (Hurst and Blackett, 1935)
Greig, Air Commodore D'Arcy A., *My Golden Flying Years* (Grub St., 2010)
Henshaw, A., *Sigh for a Merlin* (Blackett, 1977; reprinted by Crecy Publishing, Ltd, 2007)
Lewis, Julian, *Racing Ace: the Fights and Flights of 'Kink' Kinkead* (Pen and Sword, 2011)
Livock, G. E., *To the Ends of the Air* (HMSO, 1973)
Pudney, J., *A Pride of Unicorns: Richard and David Atcherley of the RAF* (Oldbourne Book Co. Ltd, 1960)
Quill, J., *Spitfire: a Test Pilot's Story* (Murray,1983; reprinted by Crecy Publishing Ltd, 1998)
Schofield, Flt Lt H. M., *The High Speed and Other Flights* (John Hamilton Ltd, 1932)
Snaith, Grp Capt. L. C., 'Schneider Trophy Flying', 1968 Lecture to the Royal Aeronautical Society Historical Group
Wellum, G., *First Light* (Penguin Books, 2003)

Aviation in General

Anderson, J. D., *A History of Aerodynamics and its Impact on Flying Machines* (Cambridge University Press, 1997)
Baker, A., *From Biplane to Spitfire: The Life of Air Chief Marshal Sir Geoffrey Salmond* (Pen and Sword, 2003)
Boyle, A., *Trenchard* (Collins, 1962)
Broughton, T. and Parnell, N. *Flypast: A Record of Aviation in Australia* (Australian Govt Pub. Service, 1995)
Duval, G. R., *British Flying Boats and Amphibians, 1909–1952* (Putnam, 1966)
Foxworth, T., *The Speed Seekers* (Doubleday, 1974)
Godwin, J., *Early Aeronautics in Staffordshire* (Staffordshire Libraries, Arts and Archives, 1986).
Goodall, M. H., *The Norman Thompson File* (Air-Britain, 1995)
Grey, C. G., *Sea Flyers* (Faber and Faber, 1942)
Hendrie, Andrew, *The Cinderella Service: RAF Coastal Command, 1939–1945* (Pen and Sword, 2006)
Jarrett, P., ed., *Biplane to Monoplane Aircraft Development, 1919–1933* (Putnam, 1997)
Killen, J., *A History of Marine Aviation* (Muller, 1969)
King, Allan J., *Wings on Windermere: The History of the Lake District's Forgotten Flying Boat Factory* (Mushroom Model Publications, 2009)
King, H. F., *Aeromarine Origins* (Putnam,1966)

Lewis, P., *British Racing and Record-Breaking Aircraft* (Putnam, 1970)
London, P., *British Flying Boats* (Sutton Publishing Co., 2003)
Mason, T., *British Flight Testing: Martlesham Heath, 1920–1939* (Putney, 1993)
Mason, Tim, *The Seaplane Years, A History of the Marine & Armament Experimental Establishment, 1920–1924, and the Marine Aircraft Experimental Establishment, 1924–1956* (Hikoki Publications, 2010)
Master of Semphill, Colonel, *Air and the Plain Man* (Elkin, Matthews and Marrot, 1931)
Meekoms, K. J. and Morgan, E. B., *The British Aircraft Specifications File, 1920-1949* (Air Britain, 1994)
Munson, K., *Flying Boats and Seaplanes since 1910* (MacMillan, 1971)
Nayler, J. L. and Ower, E., *Aviation: Its Technical Development* (Owen, 1965)
Penny, R. E., 'Seaplane Development' in *Journal of the Royal Aeronautical Society*, September 1927 [Contribution by R. J. Mitchell]
Penrose, H., *British Aviation: the Adventuring Years: 1920–1929* (Putnam. 1973); *British Aviation: the Great War and Armistice: 1915–1919* (Putnam, 1969); British Aviation: Widening Horizons: 1930–1934 (Putnam,1979).
Shenstone, B. S., 'Transport Flying Boats: Life and Death' in. *Journal of the Royal Aeronautical Society*, December 1969
Sinnot, C., *The Royal Air Force and Aircraft Design, 1923–1939* (Frank Cass, 2001)
Smith, C. B., *Testing Time* (Cassell, 1961)
Stroud, J., *Annals of British and Commonwealth Air Transport 1919–1960* (Putnam, 1962)
Templewood, Viscount [Sir Samuel Hoare] *Empire of the Air: the Advent of the Air Age, 1922–1929* (Collins, 1957)
The Centenary Journal of the Royal Aeronautical Society, 1866–1966

Aero Engines
Banks, Air Commodore F. R., 'Fifty Years of Engineering Learning' in *Journal of the Royal Aeronautical Society*, March 1968; *I Kept No Diary* (Airlife publications, 1978)
Harker, R. R., *Rolls Royce from the Wings* (Oxford Illustrated Press, 1976)
Lovesay, A. C., 'Milestones and Memories from Fifty Years of Aero Engine Development', 11th Sir Henry Royce Memorial Lecture, Royal Aeronautical Society, 7 November 1966

Lady Houston
Allen, W., *Lady Houston DBE One of the Few* (Constable, 1947)
Macnaie, M., *Lady Lucy Houston DBE Aviation Champion and Mother of the Spitfire* (Pen & Sword, Aviation, 2016)
Wentworth Day, J., *Lady Houston DBE The Richest Woman in England* (Allan Wingate, 1958)

Other Aircraft
Andrews, C. F. and Morgan, E. B., *Vickers Aircraft since 1908* (Putnam, 1974)
Barnes, C. H., *Bristol Aircraft since 1910* (Putnam, 1964); *Shorts Aircraft since 1900* (Putnam, 1967)
Jackson, A. J., *Blackburn Aircraft since 1909* (Putnam, 1968)
James, D. N., *Gloster Aircraft since 1917* (Putnam, 1971)
London, P., *Hawker and Saro Aircraft since 1917* (Putnam, 1974)
Mason, F. K., *Saunders Aircraft since 1920* (Putnam, 1961)
Taylor, H. A., *Fairey Aircraft since 1915* (Putnam, 1974)
'Hurricane Special' edition of *The Aeroplane*, October 2007

Profile Publications:
No. 3 *The Focke-Wulf Fw 190A*
No. 11 *The Handley Page Halifax BIII, VI, VII*
No. 40 *The Messerschmitt Bf 109E*
No. 44 *The Fairey IIIA*
No. 57 *The Hawker Fury*
No. 65 *The Aero Lancaster I*
No. 76 *The Junkers Ju 87A and B*
No. 81 *The Hawker Typhoon*
No. 84 *The Short Empire Boats*
No. 98 *The Gloster Gladiator*
No. 111 *The Hawker Hurricane I*
No. 142 *The Short Stirling*
No. 183 *The Consolidated PBY Catalina*
No. 197 *The Hawker Tempest*

Index

(Page references in *italic* indicate photographs or illustrations)

Admiralty design team 46
AD Boats 56, *56*, 58, ***58***, 60
Air Ministry
   Specifications:
      4/27: 238
      7/20: 61
      14/21: 82
      20/27: 303
      21/22: 114
      29/24: 172
      B.12/36: 349
      F.10/35: 314–5, 325
      F.5/34: 314–5, 325
      F.7/30: ***298***, 299–302
      F.37/34: 316, 320, 325
      N.4: 113, 118, 131
      R.18/24: 132
      R.20/28: 246
      R.24/31: 287, 288
Armstrong Siddley Engines 65, 183, 240–3, 279
Atcherley, Fg Off. F. R. L. 29, 160, 215, 218, 224, 225, 228, 259

Baltic Flight, *see* Royal Air Force, Baltic Flight
Banks, F. R. (later Air Commodore) 199, 209, 215

Bazzocchi, E. 142
Beardmore engine 65, 84
Bellanca 'Irish Swoop' 310
Bernard V-2: 23, ***142***, 143
Bernardi, Maj. M. de, *see* de Bernardi
Biard, Capt. Henri C. 9, 30, ***30***, 59–60, 71–2, 76, 88–91, ***95***, ***99***, 101–3, ***104***, 116–7, 119, ***130***, 144–8, 150, ***161***, ***164***, 204, 240, 242–5, 347
Bird, Cdr James 93, 105, 134, ***164***, 209
Billing, *see* Pemberton-Billing
Black, A. 28, ***29***, 33, 155, 157, 177, 205, 345
Blackburn Aircraft Co.
   Iris 236
   Pellet 97
   Perth 276
   Sydney 251
Blackburne Thrush 127
Boothman, Flt Lt J. N. 17, 215, 259, 266
Brancker, W. S. (later Sir Sefton) 108–9
Brinton, Lt G. L. 263–4, ***264***
Bristol Aircraft Co.
   Bulldog 302

Jupiter engine 248, 304
   Pegasus engine 288, 291
   Type 123: ***298***, 303
   Type 133: ***298***, 304, 314
Buchanan, Maj. J. S. 9, 148, 314
Bulman, Maj. G. P. 22, 169, 208–9, 215, 266, 314

Camm, Sidney (later Sir) ***36***, 127
CAMS flying boats 99–101, ***101***
Catalina, *see* Consolidated Catalina
Cave-Brown-Cave, Grp Capt. H. M. 181–2, 314
Churchill, Winston 208, 314, 359
Clifton, Alan 21–3, 28, 32, 105, 112, 141, 143, 156, 284, 300, 323, 328, 332
Consolidated Catalina 246
Cozens, G. A. 9, 30, 47, 54, 59, 67, 88, 91, 119–20, 134, 144, 177, 267
Cross, V. 20, 31–2, 162, 329, 345, 347
Crusader, *see* Bristol Aircraft Co., Crusader

Curtiss Aeroplane and Motor Co.:
CR-1: 99
CR-3/R3C 100, **100**, **101**, 102, 145, 148, 150–1, 325
D-12 engine 99, 141, 151, 304
Hawk 151, 152
V.1400 engine 150

Davis, J. 30, 33, 157, 162, 326
de Bernardi, Maj. M. 151, 198, 203
De Havilland Aircraft Co.:
DH.9: 178
DH.60 Moth 21, **21**, 170
Dornier Flugzeugwerke:
Do X 246–7, 251
Wal 240, **240**
Dowding, A. V. M. H. (later lord) 313, 359

Edward VIII, *see* prince of Wales

Far East Flight, *see* Royal Air Force, Far East Flight
Fairey Aviation Co.:
Fawn 93
III 175, 180, 276
Titania 131
Felixstowe flying boats 69, 75, 93, 113, 131, 287
Fiat Aviatzione:
AS.2 engine 151, 190
AS.5 engine 210
C.29: 220
First of the Few (film) 19–20, 43, 225

Gloster Aircraft Co.:
Gladiator 304, 336
Gloster II 141
Gloster III 145, 148, **149**
Gloster IV 190, **200**
Gloster VI 212, 214, 221

Greig, Flt Lt D'Arcy D. 113, 205, 214, 218, 222, 225, 259, 263, 269
Grey, C. G. 45, 66, 75, 97, 251, 254, 302, 325
Griffiths, H. 9, 28, 32, 157, 160, 162, 177, 243, 345–6
Grigorovich flying boat 136
Guazzetti, Capt. F. 198–9
Guinness, the Hon. A. E. 185, 242–3, 246

Hargreaves, F. J. 45, 62, 64, 357
Hawker Aircraft Ltd:
Cygnet 127
Fury/Super Fury 253, 315
Hornet 303
Hurricane 127, 324, 329, 335
P.V.3: 303
Tempest Typhoon 232, 266, 286
Henshaw, A. 159, 295
Heinkel Flugzeugwerke:
He 70: 328
He 112: 112, **327**
High Speed Flight, *see* Royal Air Force, High Speed Flight
Hispano-Suiza engine 65, 84, 88
Hoare, Sir Samuel (later Viscount Templewood) 9, 92, 132, 208, 236, 254
Hope, Linton, *see* under Linton
Houston, Lady Lucy 255, 266–7, **266**, **267**, 429–33, **429**, **434**

Imperial Airways Ltd 111–2
Isotta-Franschini engine 210, 212

James, Mrs J. J. 111–2
Junkers Ju 87: 309, **309**

Kalinin K-7: 247, **248**
Kawasaki Ki-5: 309, **309**
Kerr Stuart and Co. **34**, 37–40, 47, 49
Kinkead, Flt Lt S. M. 198–200, 203–5, 423–8

Lathan flying boats 97, 114
Linton Hope, Flt Lt E. J. L. 259, 263, **264**
Linton Hope, H. 56
hull construction method 75, 85–6, 93, 120, 417–20
Lion engines, *see* Napier Lion engines
Livock, Sqn Ldr G. E. 181–2
Long, Flt Lt F. W. 259, **260**
Loewenstein Capt. A. 72
Lowell-Cooper, E. 18, 20, 33, 48, 66, 155, 158–9, 162, 235

McLean, Sir Robert 32, 155, 158, 165, 235, 319, 337, 358
Macchi Aeronautica:
M.7: 66
M.33: 89, **149**, **151**
M.39: 145, 148, **149**
M.52: 190, 205, 210, 255
M.67: 210, 220, 225, 265
M.72: 265–6
Mansbridge, E. H. 33, 157, 308
Messerscmitt Bf 109: 22
Mitchell, Billy, *see* Mitchell, W.
Mitchell, Eric **41**, 55, **211**, 347
Mitchell, Florence (née Dayson) 17, 22, 31, 57, 75, 112, 197, 201, **233**, 268, **287–9**, **348**, 385–9
Mitchell, Gordon 7, 13, 17, 19, 75, 162–3, 202, **342**, 343, **344**
Mitchell, Herbert 37, 39, 41, 42, 57, 161, **233**
Mitchell, Jim 31

Mitchell, Julian 9, 11, 15, 273
Mitchell, R. J. *7*, *16*, *21*, *29*, *37*, *48*, *49*, *52*, *54*, *62*, *72*, *73*, *76*, *88*, *95*, *104*, *120*, *123*, *130*, *146*, *154*, *161*, *174*, *186*, *189*, *206*, *211*, *213*, *216*, *228*, *229*, *233*, *264*, *267*, *268*, *342*, *378–84*, *434*
  aesthetics 23–4, 31, 288, 326
  appearance 13, 19, 57
  cars/motorcycle 18, 75, 210, *210*, 340, **340**
  CBE 118, 195
  concern for safety of pilots 203–5, 264
  design team 27, 30, 105, 160
  designs in general 14–5, 21, 23–4, 27–8, 30, 152, 251
  estimations 219, 260–1, 351
  good fortune 92–3, 187, 208–9, 226, 256, 313
  greatest Midlander 13
  hopes for air transport 14, 42, 48, 51, 60–1, 185
  life:
    apprenticeship 33–40
    assistant works manager 56
    attempts to join RFC 40, 273
    birth 35
    cancer/reaction to 20–2, 287, 314, 318, 344–5, 389
    chief designer 61, 66
    chief engineer 75
    death/funeral 346–8
    director 112
    early years at Supermarine 54–8, 61, 61
    early years/education 35–7, 42–4
    houses 36, 57–8, 75, 160, 211
    marriage 57
  personal assistant 45
  personality 13–15, 17–20, 22, 29, 31–2, 155–165, 189, 202, 208, 210, 218, 220, 228–9, 261, 308, 319, 329, 340, 343, 348
  pilot's licence 21–2
  production statistics 21
  responsibilities 18, 220, 222, 334–5
  salary negotiation 112
  speeches/writings etc. 18, 41, 55, 193, 202, 220–3, 240, 254, 267–9, 302, 328–9, 378–84
  status 18, 187, 202–3, 223, 228–9, 256, 268, 349
  work methods/ management style 13, 28–30, 32, 112, 160, 346
Mitchell, William (Billy) 31, 211
Molin, D. 222, 225, 265
Monti, Lt G. 224, 265
Mussolini, B. 150, 152, 201, 208

N.1 Baby, see Pemberton-Billing
Napier Lion engines 69, 88–9, 88, 93, 97, 99, 109, 118, 126, 129, 137, 144, 150, 178, 190, 205, 208, 212
Navy-Wright NW-2: 100
Nighthawk, see Pemberton-Billing
Norman Thompson N.T.2B 48, 54, 74
Northrop Alpha/Gamma 310

Orlebar, Sqn Ldr A. H. 9, 206, 215–9, 228, 260, 266

Payn, Maj. H. 329, 351, 357
Pemberton-Billing, N. 41, 45, 46, 47–9, 54–5

N.1 Baby 62–3
P.B.7: 113
P.B.25: 48
P.B.29E 48
P.B.31E Nighthawk 48, 49
Penrose, H. J. 9, 56, 143, 148, 242, 246, 264, 336
Piaggio P.7: 212, 220, 321–2, 322
Pickering, Flt Lt G. 276, 287, 295
Porte-Felixstowe, see Felixstowe flying boats
prince of Wales, HRH Edward/King Edward VIII 104, 111, 117, 123, 164, 229, 229, 338

Quill, J. 9, 19, 27, 308, 328, 332–5, 340, 364

Roe, A. V. 35
Rolls-Royce engines 19, 208–9, 256
  Buzzard 208–9, 256
  Condor 118
  Eagle 73, 106, 109, 113, 118, 120, 126
  Goshawk 303–4, 318
  Griffon 400–6
  Kestrel 208, 272, 274
  Merlin/PV-12: 19, 320–1
  'R' engine 212, 215, 216, 222, 256
Rose, T. 243–4, 246
Rowledge, A. J. 208–9
Royal Air Force:
  Baltic Flight 181–2, 182
  Far East Flight 166, 180–1
  High Speed Flight 215, 220–1, 229, 262–3, 264, 267, 269, 347
Royce, H. (later Sir Henry) 157, **213**, 267

Saunders/Saro/Saunders Roe Ltd:
  A.3 Valkyrie 236
  A.7 Severn 236
  A.14: 236
  A.17 Cutty Sark 246
  A.19 and A.29 Cloud 246, 276
  A.27 London 236, 276, 288, 292
  A.33: 245
Savoia-Marchetti:
  S.51: *90*, 90–2, 139, 141, *141*
  S.65: 212
Schneider, J. 43, 198, 421–2, *421*, *422*
Schneider Trophy 44
  contests 45, 86, 188, 207, 252, 269
  1919: 64–5
  1920/21: 86
  1922: 89–91, *90*
  1923: 100–103
  1925: 139–152
  1927: 199–201
  1929: 221–9, *223*, *224*, *266*
  1931: *224*, 265–7
Schofield, Flt Lt H. M. 9, 189, 201, 204, 262–3
Scott-Paine, H. 45, 66, *76*, 88, *88*, *89*, 90, 92, 102, 105, *111*, 117, 134
Seafire, *see* Supermarine, Seafire
Shenstone, B. 9, 32, 159, 248, 252, 319, 324, 327–8, 334
Shirvall, A. 32, 105, 158
Short Bros 143, 195, 235, 357
  Cromarty 69, 235
  Crusader 189, 197–8, *322*
  S.2: 235
  S.5 Singapore 236, 260, 276, 288, 292
  S.8 Calcutta 236, 242
  S.8/8 Rangoon 236
  S.14 Sarafand 247, 288
  S.15: 237
  S.17 Kent 236, 247
  S.18 Knuckleduster 276
  S.38: 48
  Sunderland 245, 357
  Type 184: 48, 55
Sikorsky Aircraft:
  S-40: *136*, 249
  S-42: *249*
Smith, Joe 24, 30, 32, 105, 155–6, 158, 161, 250, 324, 327, 357–8, *357*
Snaith, Fg Off. L. S. 9, 29, 259, *264*
Sopwith, Aviation Co.:
  Bat Boat 70
  Schneider 97
  Snipe 302
Sorley, Sqn Ldr R. 339
Spitfire, *see* below under 'Supermarine, Spitfire' *and also* Appendix II
Stainforth, Flt Lt G. H. 215, 257, 259, *264*, 266, 268
Summers, J. ('Mutt') 29, 275, 300, 307, 333–4
Supermarine *46*, *50*, *58*, 59, *61*, *73*, 101, *109*, *112*, *166*, *345*
  Air Yacht 238–46, *238*, *239*, *241*, *242*; *see also* Supermarine, Solent
  B.12/36 Bomber 349–53, *350*, *351*, *352*
  Channel flying boats 59–61, *59*, *61*
  Commercial Amphibian 67–75, *68*, *70*, *71*, *72*, *73*
  Giant 246–50, *247*, *249*, *250*, *260*
  Nanok/Solent 182–5, *184*, *185*
  S.4: 23, 28, 130, 139–49, *140*, *143*, *145*, *147*
  S.5: *186*, 190–7, *191*, *192*, *196*, *200*, 203–5, 423–8
  S.6: *7*, 212–4, *217*, 221, *223*
  S.6A 265–6
  S.6B 24, *24*, *252*, 256–62, *258*, *259*, *260*, *263*, 266
  Scapa 272–7, *273*, *275*, *276*, *277*
  Scarab 123–6, *123*, *124*, *125*
  Scylla 113–4, *113*
  Sea Eagle 106–12, *107*, *108*, *109*, *110*, *112*
  Sea King I 65–6, 89
  Sea King II *63*, 82–6, *83*, *84*
  Sea Lion I *63*, 64, *64*
  Sea Lion II 24, *25*, *63*, *76*, 86–91, *87*, *91*
  Sea Lion III 97–103, *98*, *99*, *101*, *102*
  Sea Otter 353, *353*
  Sea Urchin 134, 141
  Seafire *365*, *373*, 412–5
  Seagull II 93, *94*, *95*, *96*, 278
  Seagull III 170, *171*, *172*, 278–80
  Seagull IV 171
  Seagull V 278–87, *282*, *283*, *285*, *287*
  Seagull ASR I 354, *354*
  Seal II 77–82, *78*, *79*, *82*
  Seamew 172–5, *173*, *174*, *175*, 279
  Sheldrake 121–3, *121*, *122*
  Solent, *see* Supermarine, Nanok
  Southampton I 26, 50, 132–9, *133*, *134*, *135*, *179*, *420*
  Southampton II 178–80, *179*, *180*, 236
  Southampton IV 272
  Southampton X *234*, 236–7
  Southampton development 175–80
  Sparrow I 126–9, *127*, *128*

Sparrow II 168–70, **169**, **170**
Spitfire:
    acceptance 388–9
    changing planforms/
       sideviews **367–8**
    comparisons with
       Hurricane 335, 339, 362
    development 358, 364–9
    elliptical/thin wing
       320–9
    floatplane Spitfires 374,
       374
    last Spitfire, the 375
    legend 360–3
    Griffon engine marks
       371, **372**, **373**, 400–6,
       401, **404**, **405**, **411**
    Merlin engine marks
       363, **365**, 370–99, **370**,
       371, **398**, **399**, **400**, **413**
    name 336–7
    photoreconnaissance
       Spitfires 407–12, **411**
    production numbers
       358, 416

production chart 390
production problems 339
prototype/K5054: **31**,
    312, **327**, **330**, 331–41,
    332, **333**, **335**, **341**, **344**
Speed Spitfire 357, **407**
Stranraer 270, 288–92,
    289, **290**, **292**, 355–6,
    365
Swan 104, 114–20, **115**,
    116, **118**, **119**, **120**
Type 179, *see*
    Supermarine, Giant
Type 224: 304–10, **305**,
    306, **308**, **310**, 315
Type 300: 315–29
Walrus **26**, 82, 126, 172,
    175, **281**, 293–7, **294**,
    296, 354–5, **355**; *see also*
    Supermarine, Seagull V

Templewood, Viscount *see*
    Hoare, Sir Samuel
Trenchard, Sir H. 22, 313

Verdon-Roe, A., *see* Roe, A. V.
Vickers (Aviation) 69, 72
    Jockey 303
    Venom 319
    Viking 69–70, 93

Waghorn, Fg Off. H. R. D.
    (later Acting Air Vice
    Marshal) 215, 217–9,
    221–2, 225–8, 259, 262
Wallace, B. (later Sir) 159
Webb, Denis Le P. 9, 162, 243,
    293, 331
Webster, Flt Lt S. N. 198, 201,
    215
Welch, Ann 296
Westbrook, T. 178
Westland Aircraft:
    F.7/30: **298**
    Woodpigeon 127
Worsley, Flt Lt O. E. 198,
    200–1